W9-ALW-020

ANTIQUE TRADER BOOKS

American Pressed Glass & Bottles

Price Guide

Edited by
Kyle Husfloen

Consulting Editors
Neila and Tom Bredehoft

An illustrated comprehensive price guide to all types of
pressed glass & bottles.

Antique Trader Books
P.O. Box 1050
Dubuque, IA 52004

STAFF

Assistant Editor . . . . .Marilyn Dragowick

Production Coordinator/Editorial Assistant . . . .Louise Paradis

Production Assistant/Editorial Assistant . . . . .Ruth Willis

Production Assistant . . . . .Kristen Bushman

Cover Design . . . . .Jaro Sebek

Subscription Manager . . . . .Bonnie Rojemann

Copyright © 1994 by The Antique Trader. All rights
reserved. No part of this publication may be reproduced, stored in a retrieval system, or transmitted in
any form or by any means, electronic, mechanical,
photocopying, recording or otherwise, without prior
permission in writing from the publisher.

ISBN: 0-930625-50-1
Library of Congress Catalog Card No. 94-79664

Other books and magazines published by Antique Trader Publications:

Antiques & Collectibles Annual Price Guide	The Antique Trader Weekly
Ceramics Price Guide	Collector Magazine & Price Guide
Toy Trader	Big Reel
Discoveries	Baby Boomer Collectibles
Postcard Collector	Military Trader

To order additional copies of this book or
other publications listed above, contact:

**Antique Trader Publications
P.O. Box 1050
Dubuque, Iowa 52004
1-800-334-7165**

Introduction

For twenty-five years The Antique Trader has been publishing a periodical price guide covering the whole realm of antiques and collectibles, first as a semi-annual and then a quarterly publication and then, from 1984 to 1993, a bi-monthly magazine. In 1985 we introduced a single annual edition to compliment the periodical issues and this yearly edition remains a mainstay of our publishing efforts today.

Earlier this year, we broadened our coverage of specialized collecting interests with the release of our new ANTIQUE TRADER BOOKS POTTERY AND PORCELAIN - CERAMICS PRICE GUIDE. This reference focuses on only pieces made from clay including fine porcelain and earthenware, stoneware pottery, Art pottery and 20th century collectible ceramics. We are now pleased to introduce our latest title - ANTIQUE TRADER BOOKS AMERICAN PRESSED GLASS AND BOTTLES PRICE GUIDE. In this volume we offer an in depth guide to all sorts of popular American-made glasswares of the 19th and 20th centuries.

For over sixty years Victorian pressed glass has been a passion for hundreds of collectors and in recent decades, a more diverse range of wares has joined the ranks of collectibility including Carnival glass and Depression glass, and the products of such well known 20th century American manufacturers as Heisey, Cambridge and Imperial.

In this volume we are covering all the most popular categories of glassware produced with the use of molds and machines. In general this includes all types of glasswares, both decorative and useful, which were originally marketed to attract the broadest spectrum of middle class consumers possible. Attractive and relatively inexpensive, such glasswares have been widely available to American housewives since the mid-19th century and have served to brighten the tables and sideboards of this country for generations. Today few of the great old glass-producing firms are still operating in the U.S. and the wares they marketed to our mothers, grandmothers and great-grandmothers are increasingly collectible.

Over 150 years of American glass manufacture are covered in this volume and I hope it will serve today's glass lover well. If, per chance, your favorite line of glass isn't included here, take heart as we are planning a sequel to this work which will cover in depth American and European Art and Decorative Glasswares of the 19th and 20th centuries, everything from

Bohemian to Tiffany and Custard glass to Venini. In the meantime, don't miss the chance to learn about mass-produced bottles and glasswares we're covering here.

My staff and I have worked diligently to gather a wide spectrum of accurate and in-depth descriptions for this expanded volume on American glass and we have also added a large selection of photographs to highlight our listings. To start you off we provide a chapter on "Collecting Guidelines" and a series of sketches of typical forms you may encounter in glass. Our price listings themselves are arranged alphabetically by the name of the type of glass or the producing company and each section begins with a brief introduction to that glassware. Although not many American companies permanently marked their pieces, a few did. So, where applicable, we include a sketch of the company marking or label. To round out our text we provide a "Glossary of Terms" relating to pressed and mold-blown glass and bottles as well as Appendices covering various collector clubs, associations and museums. Finally, we have carefully indexed and cross-referenced all of the listings included in this price guide.

We think you'll find this book a useful and informative guide to one of America's most popular collecting fields. It's hoped that our hard work will pay off in your greater understanding and appreciation of America's glassmaking heritage. In closing I wish to express sincere appreciation to my staff for their hard work and perseverance in producing this book and to Cecil Munsey, Poway, California, for his help in the Bottles section and Ruth Schinestuhl, Marmora, New Jersey, for her work on the Carnival Glass listings. A special thank you goes to Consulting Editors Neila and Tom Bredehoft who have reviewed a number of our categories and offered invaluable insights into how to make this the most comprehensive yet easy-to-use guide available. The Bredehofts are well known in glass collecting circles for their wide ranging knowledge and glass scholarship and it was a real pleasure to work with them on this project.

I hope you'll find this a useful guide to a fascinating and diverse collecting realm. We're always interested in comments from our readers, especially those of constructive critique, and we'll do our best to respond to your requests or suggestions. Sit back now and take an armchair tour of over 200 years of American glassmaking history.

Kyle Husfloen, Editor

Please note: Though listings have been double-checked and every effort has been made to insure accuracy, neither the compilers, editors nor publisher can assume responsibility for any losses that might be incurred as a result of consulting this guide, or of errors, typographical or otherwise.

Photography Credits

Photographers who have contributed to this issue include: E. A. Babka, East Dubuque, Illinois; Stanley L. Baker, Minneapolis, Minnesota; Donna Bruun, Galena, Illinois; Herman C. Carter, Tulsa, Oklahoma; J.D. Dalessandro, Cincinnati, Ohio; Jeff Grunewald, Chicago, Illinois; Kevin McConnell, Pilot Point, Texas; the late Don Moore, Alameda, California; Louise Paradis, Galena, Illinois; and Ruth Schinestuhl, Marmora, New Jersey.

For other photographs, artwork, data or permission to photograph in their shops, we sincerely express appreciation to the following auctioneers, galleries, museums, individuals and shops: The Burmese Cruet, Montgomeryville, Pennsylvania; Burns Auction Service, Bath, New York; Collector's Auction Services, Oil City, Pennsylvania; Collector's Sales and Service, Middletown, Rhode Island; DeFina Auctions, Austinburg, Ohio; T. Ermert, Cincinnati, Ohio; Garth's Auctions, Inc., Delaware, Ohio; Glass-Works Auctions, East Greenville, Pennsylvania; Glick's Antiques, Galena, Illinois; and Grunewald Antiques, Hillsborough, North Carolina.
Also to the Gene Harris Antique Auction Center, Marshalltown, Iowa; the late William Heacock, Marietta, Ohio; The House in the Woods Auction Gallery, Eagle, Wisconsin; International Carnival Glass Assoc., Mentone, Indiana; Jewel Johnson, Tulsa, Oklahoma; Sherry Klabo, Seattle, Washington; Peter Kroll, Sun Prairie, Wisconsin; James Lehnhardt, Galena, Illinois; J. Martin, Mt. Orab, Ohio; Randall McKee, Kenosha, Wisconsin; Jim Ludescher, Dubuque, Iowa; Joy Luke Gallery, Bloomington, Illinois; Dr. James Measell, Berkley, Michigan; Jane Rosenow, Galva, Illinois; Tammy Roth, East Dubuque, Illinois; Robert W. Skinner, Inc., Bolton, Massachusetts; Sotheby's, New York, New York; Temples Antiques, Minneapolis, Minnesota; Lee Vines, Hewlett, New York; Woody Auctions, Douglass, Kansas; The Yankee Peddler Antiques, Denton, Texas; and Yesterday's Treasures, Galena, Illinois.

ON THE COVER: Upper left: Amber Imperial 'Loganberry' pattern 10" h. vase. Lower left: Consolidated 'Dogwood' pattern 10½" h. vase. Lower right: Daisy & Button pattern 7¾" l. canoe in sapphire blue.

Cover design by Jaro Sebek.

Collecting Guidelines

It has been over 25 years since I first became enamored with early American glass and I still remember the piece that set my pulse racing - a tall clear pressed whale oil lamp with a large band of hearts encircling the font. "It's Sandwich," my dealer friend informed me, "and quite rare." I thought it was one of the loveliest antiques I'd seen in my budding collecting career and, if my meager allowance had allowed I would have certainly added it to my collection. However, it was priced out of my range so, as an alternative I soon discovered later 19th century pressed glass and began a collection of this much more affordable and available glassware. Today my love of American glass continues unabated and, although I still have to watch my budget, I've been able to add quite a few nice pieces to my collection.

I will admit that when I first got interested in American glass I found it a very daunting prospect...there are so many types available in so many styles and colors. I wasn't sure I'd ever understand all the intricacies of this diverse field. However, year by year and book by book my understanding and knowledge grew. About the time I first discovered pattern glass the interest in Depression era glassware developed, spurred on by Hazel Marie Weatherman's first book. That reference became one of the first in my library. Soon after I discovered the pioneering works on American pressed glass by Ruth Webb Lee who, in the early 1930s, became the moving force behind the collecting mania for 19th century American pressed glass. Other books on glass and other antiques topics have gradually found their way into my library but it's still a long way from complete.

Anyone who collects anything should know that building a good reference library is vital to the success of your collecting forays and an investment which will pay big dividends over the years. Today there are dozens of fine books available on all types of American glass and there's still glass available in a style and price range to fit nearly every pocketbook. If you are fortunate, like I was, to have a knowledgeable antiques dealer who is also a good friend, you're well ahead of the game. Learning firsthand from a dealer or fellow collector can give you many valuable insights into collecting which books alone may not.

Today there are also any number of national glass collecting clubs which anyone is free to join. These groups have become vital links between collectors and serve as a major source of important research information through their newsletters, books and conventions. The National Early American Glass Club was the first such organization, founded over 60 years ago. It has been joined in the last twenty years by many other groups formed to focus on such popular glasswares as Depression era glass, Heisey, Fostoria, Milk Glass, Cambridge and many others. In a special Appendix at the back of this book we list these clubs for easy reference.

Although each glass collecting topic has its own specialized vocabulary and methodology for collecting, certain guidelines apply to most glass specialties. First and foremost, as I mentioned above, is to begin building your reference library. Second, make contact with others who share your passion and become an avid student of the field. Finally, start out conservatively and try to specialize in one company, pattern, piece or even color of glass. Focusing your collecting is helpful to the novice collector, no matter what your interest, and this is especially true in a field as broad as American glass.

I have found, over the years, that certain factors will affect the collectibility and value of American glass, and they hold true for all types of glass, from Lacy glass to Depression or Lalique to Venini. The first factor is the *condition* of a piece. Glass, unlike ceramic wares, can not be easily and invisibly repaired or restored. Once a piece is chipped or cracked it will stay that way and such damages will greatly affect its market value unless it is exceedingly rare or unique. Buy only perfect pieces, especially if you are just starting out, since they will undoubtedly maintain their value and appreciate over time.

A second factor which determines overall value is *rarity of form*. In glassware very large or very small pieces are often the scarcest, and unusual forms can bring premium prices. For example, in early Lacy glass from the 1820-1850 era, some common clear cup plates can sell for a few dollars since they were produced in such abundance, whereas a rare set of green Cherry Blossom salt and pepper shakers in Depression Glass (ca. 1930s) may bring over $1,000.

It's a matter of the rarity of the piece as well as a third factor of value: *color*. Over the past two hundred years a vast majority of the glass produced for everyday use was made in clear glass and, in fact, early manufacturers strove to make the clearest and brightest glass possible. It wasn't until around the 1880s that it became possible to more inexpensively produce pressed glass in various bright hues. Since then glass tablewares in shades of blue, purple, green, yellow and amber have become more common although clear wares still lead production.

Since it required certain chemicals in the glass batch to produce certain colors, these additives added to the cost of production and some colors, such as a true red, were very difficult to produce. This is still true today and that is why red remains one of the scarcer and most expensive colors to collect in most glass patterns. The popularity of the color blue with the general public has meant that more of it was produced than red, but it is always a choice color for collectors today. The varied hues of purple, green, yellow and amber also have their following, but blue generally leads in collector appeal, no matter what type of glass it is.

Keep in mind, of course, that certain colors or pieces may be rare in one pattern of glass but common in another pattern of the same vintage. Sorting out what makes one piece or pattern unique and desirable is the challenge of glass collecting. This hunt for hidden treasure is one of the great pleasures in any collecting field and the broad realm of American-made glass means the likelihood of making such a discovery is even greater.

The collecting of American glass, no matter the type or age, is an exciting and fascinating pastime but, unfortunately there are some pitfalls which need to be touched upon. The biggest frustration today for collectors and dealers in glass is dealing with reproductions. This is not a new problem but one that continues to haunt us. Luckily for today's collector it is much easier to share information on troublesome pieces using the numerous trade publications, newsletters and magazines which serve the collecting market When author Ruth Webb Lee released her book, *Antique Fakes and Reproductions,* over fifty years ago

it was one of the few publications to address the problem, especially as it pertains to American 19th century pressed glass. Although no longer in print, Mrs. Lee's pioneering volume is still an invaluable source of information.

In more recent years many other books have been published which deal with this problem. In my 1992 book, *Collector's Guide to American Pattern Pressed Glass, 1825-1915,* I provided as much detail as possible on what patterns and pieces have been reproduced in pressed glass made before World War I. Other books which have added greatly to this field of knowledge include *Early American Pattern Glass, 1850-1910 - Major Collectibles Table Settings* by Bill Jenks and Jerry Luna (Wallace-Homestead, 1990) and a more recent release, *Identifying Pattern Glass Reproductions, by* Bill Jenks, Jerry Luna and Darryl Reilly (Wallace-Homestead, 1993). Many other glass categories have been covered in reference books which offer some coverage of reproductions to avoid. For the many collectors interested in Depression era glass, *The Collector's Encyclopedia of Depression Glass,* by Gene Florence (Collector Books) is especially helpful in guiding collectors through the repro maze.

Although the thought of being stung by reproductions may at first discourage some new collectors, they should know that it really isn't as big an obstacle to building a fine collection as they may think. Armed with some key reference books and the support and enthusiasm of fellow collectors you can quite easily maneuver your way through that mine field. With the enormous volume of American pressed and mold-blown glass produced in the past 150 years, everyone should be able to find a line of glass that fits their budget and taste. We hope this new book will help prepare you for an exciting and fulfilling collecting career, an adventure sure to bring you hours of satisfaction and enjoyment.

Kyle Husfloen

TYPICAL FORMS
Bowls in Pressed Glass

Candy Dish, 6" - 8" d.

A. Deeply ruffled openwork (latticework) sides with a lightly scalloped rim

B. Footring

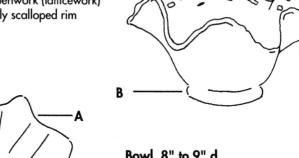

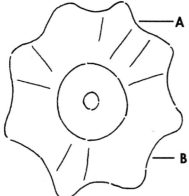

Bowl, 8" to 9" d.

A. Gently ruffled sides with (B.) Smooth rim.

Bowl, 8" to 9" d.

A. Gently ruffled rim

B. Tiny scallops at the edge. A rim with evenly spaced small crimps is sometimes called a "piecrust" rim, while one with multiple rounded looping crimps is sometimes called a "ribbon candy" rim.

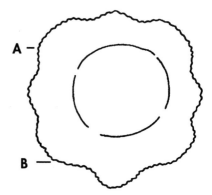

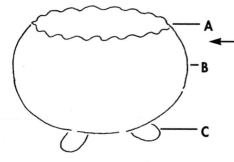

Rose Bowl, 4" d.

A. Incurved (or "closed") rim with small ruffles

B. Spherical, bulbous body

C. Knob feet

TYPICAL FORMS
Creamers & Pitchers
Blown & Pressed Glass

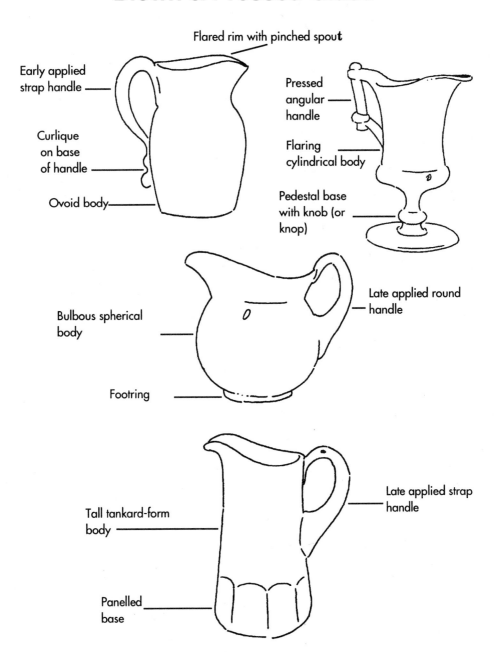

Flared rim with pinched spout

Early applied
strap handle

Pressed
angular
handle

Curlique
on base
of handle

Flaring
cylindrical body

Ovoid body

Pedestal base
with knob (or
knop)

Bulbous spherical
body

Late applied round
handle

Footring

Tall tankard-form
body

Late applied strap
handle

Panelled
base

TYPICAL FORMS
Celery Vases, Spillholders & Spooners in Pattern Glass

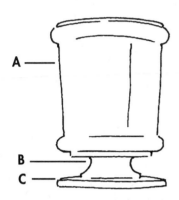

Flint Spillholder (Spooner)
ca. 1850-60, 5" - 5½" h.

A. Heavy, thick nearly cylindrical body
B. Short, thick applied pedestal
C. Thick, round applied foot

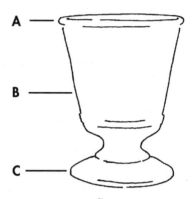

Non-flint Spooner
ca. 1880, 4½" - 6" h.

A. Flaring, flat rim
B. Tapering cylindrical body
C. Short pressed pedestal and round foot

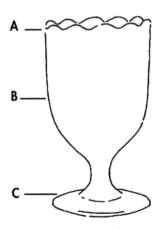

Non-flint Spooner
ca. 1880, 4½" - 6" h.

A. Scalloped rim
B. Bell-form rounded body
C. Slender pressed pedestal on round foot

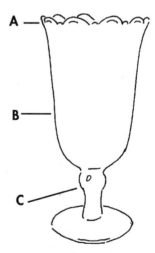

Non-flint Celery Vase
ca. 1885, 8" - 10" h.

A. Flaring and scalloped rim
B. Tall bell-form body
C. Slender pressed pedestal with knob (or knop), on round foot

AKRO AGATE

This glass was made by the Akro Agate Company in Clarksburg, West Virginia between 1932 and 1951. The company was famous for their marble production but also produced many novelty items in various colors of marbleized glass and offered a popular line of glass children's dishes in plain colors and marbleized glass. Most articles bear the company mark of a crow flying through a capital letter A.

Akro Agate Trademark

GENERAL LINE

Mexicali Powder Jar

Cup & saucer, demitasse, marbleized orange & white $15.00
Flowerpot, miniature, ribbed rim, green opaque, 2¾" h. 9.00
Flowerpot, miniature, ribbed rim, orange opaque, 2¾" h. 14.00
Flowerpot, scalloped rim, black amethyst, 3" h. 35.00
Flowerpot, scalloped rim, embossed graduated dart decoration, white, No. 297, 3" h. 15.00
Flowerpot, royal blue w/floral decoration, No. 1310 ....75.00
Flowerpot, scalloped rim, cobalt blue, large................................18.00
Flowerpot, white w/floral decoration, No. 1311 ....75.00
Jardiniere, ribbed & fluted rim, pumpkin opaque, No. 306CF, 5" h.. 30.00
Lamp, marbleized orange & white, 9" h. 65.00
Planter, rectangular, blue w/decoration, No. 653, 8" l. 20.00

Powder jar, Colonial Lady cover, pink opaque, 6¼" h. 75.00
Powder jar, Colonial Lady cover, powder blue opaque base, white cover, 6¼" h. 65.00
Powder jar, Colonial Lady cover, turquoise opaque, 6¼" h. 95.00
Powder jar, cov., Concentric Ring patt., marbleized blue & yellow 22.00
Powder jar, Mexicali w/sombrero cover, marbleized orange & white (ILLUS.) 42.50
Powder jar, Mexicali w/sombrero cover, milk white opaque 40.00
Powder jar, Scottie Dog cover, white opaque 75.00
Smoking set: four ashtrays & cov. box; marbleized green & white, 5 pcs. 35.00
Vase, 6¼" h., scalloped rim, embossed graduated dart decoration, pumpkin opaque, No. 316 .... 40.00
Vase, 6¼" h., tab handles, marbleized orange & white 30.00

CHILDREN'S DISHES

Bowl, cereal, Interior Panel patt., marbleized green & white 23.50
Bowl, cereal, Interior Panel patt., marbleized oxblood & lemon 35.00
Bowl, cereal, Stacked Disc & Panel patt., transparent cobalt blue 50.00
Creamer, Chiquita patt., transparent cobalt blue 24.50
Creamer, Interior Panel patt., azure blue 30.00
Creamer, large, Octagonal patt., transparent green 6.00
Creamer, small, Raised Daisy patt., yellow opaque 45.00
Cup, small, Interior Panel patt., marbleized blue & white................... 31.00
Cup, Octagonal patt., pumpkin 18.00
Cup, Raised Daisy patt., green opaque.. 35.00
Cup & saucer, Chiquita patt., transparent cobalt blue 14.50
Cup & saucer, Stippled Band patt., blue opaque 39.00
Plate, dinner, 3¼" d., Interior Panel patt., marbleized blue & white 16.00
Plate, dinner, 3¼" d., Raised Daisy patt., blue opaque 14.50
Plate, dinner, 4¼" d., Concentric Rings patt., transparent cobalt blue 12.00
Plate, dinner, 4¼" d., Interior Panel patt., marbleized green & white 13.00
Plate, dinner, 4¼" d., Interior Panel patt., marbleized oxblood & white......14.00
Plate, dinner, 4¼" d., Octagonal patt., marbleized green & white 10.00

Saucer, Interior Panel patt.,
marbleized oxblood & white 9.00
Sugar bowl, cov., Interior Panel patt.,
marbleized green & white 42.00
Sugar bowl, cov., Raised Daisy patt.,
yellow opaque 85.00
Sugar bowl, cov., Stacked Disc &
Panel patt., transparent cobalt
blue 85.00
Teapot, cov., Interior Panel patt.,
marbleized green & white 40.00
Teapot, cov., Octagonal-O patt.,
marbleized blue & white 23.00
Teapot, cov., Raised Daisy patt.,
medium blue opaque 52.50
Teapot, cov., Stippled Band patt., blue
opaque 75.00
Tumbler, small, Octagonal patt.,
yellow opaque 10.00
Tumbler, Raised Daisy patt., yellow
opaque 26.00
Tumbler, Stacked Disc & Panel patt.,
transparent cobalt blue, 2" h. 20.00

ANIMALS

Americans evidently like to collect glass animals and, for the past fifty years, American glass manufacturers have turned out a wide variety of animals to please the buying public. Some were produced for long periods and some were later reproduced by other companies, while others were made for only a short period of time and are rare. We have not included late productions in our listings and have attempted to date the productions where possible. Evelyn Zemel's book, American Glass Animals A to Z *will be helpful to the novice collector.*

Giraffe by Heisey

Airedale Dog, clear frosted, un-
marked, 6½" l., 5¾" h.................... $250.00

Angelfish book end, clear, A.H.
Heisey & Co., 2¼ x 3½" wave
base, 7" h. 115.00
Bear, Mama, clear, New Martins-
ville Glass Mfg. Co., 6" l.,
4½" h. ....165.00 to 180.00
Chinese Pheasant, blue, Paden City
Glass Mfg. Co., ca. 1940, 13¾" l.,
5¾" h. ....125.00 to 150.00
Deer sitting, clear, Fostoria Glass Co.,
1940-43, 1 x 2" base, 2¼" h. 45.00
Deer standing, clear, Fostoria Glass
Co., 1 x 2" base, 4½" h. 42.00
Elephant book end, clear, New
Martinsville Mfg. Co., 3¼ x 5¼"
base, 6¼" l., 5¼" h. 80.00
Elephant figure w/trunk up, clear, A.H.
Heisey & Co., 1944-53, large,
6½" l., 4¼" h................................... 425.00
Giraffe w/head turned, clear,
A.H. Heisey & Co., 1942-52,
11" h.(ILLUS.) ....175.00 to 200.00
Goose, wings up, clear, A.H.
Heisey & Co., 1942-53, 7½" l.,
6½" h................................ 90.00 to 125.00
Hen, clear, A.H. Heisey & Co.,1948-
49, 2¾ x 2½" base, 4½" h. 425.00
Horses, Clydesdale, clear, A.H.
Heisey & Co., 1942-48, 8" l., 8" h.,
pr. ....400.00 to 450.00
Horse, Pony ashtray, clear, K.R.
Haley, 5½" d. tray, pony 2½" h.
at ears 23.00
Horse, Plug (Sparky), clear, A.H.
Heisey & Co., 1941-46, 3½" l.,
4¼" h...95.00
Horse, Pony, standing, clear, A.H.
Heisey & Co., 1940-52, 1½ x 2¼"
base, 3" l., 5" h. ....75.00 to 100.00
Horse rearing book ends, clear, A.H.
Heisey & Co., 3¼ x 6½ " base,
7¾" h., pr. 235.00
Horse rearing book ends, black, L.E.
Smith, 1940s, 3 x 5¼" base, 5¾" l.,
8" h., pr. 120.00
Horse Head (double heads) ashtray,
clear, A.H. Heisey & Co. 45.00
Horse Head book ends, clear, A.H.
Heisey & Co., 1937-55, 2¾ x 4¾"
base, 7¼" h., pr...............250.00 to 300.00
Pelican, clear, New Martinsville Glass
Mfg. Co., 8¼" h. 85.00
Pouter Pigeon book ends, clear,
Cambridge Glass Co., 4 x 5" base,
6" h., pr. 160.00
Pouter Pigeon book ends, clear,
Paden City Glass Mfg. Co., 3 x 3¾"
base, 6½" h., pr................................140.00
Rabbit, Bunnies, clear, ears up, ears
back or ears lying down, New
Martinsville Glass Mfg. Co., 1",
each ....55.00 to 65.00

Seal w/ball candleholders, clear, New
Martinsville Glass Mfg. Co., 7¼" h.,
pr.....................................100.00 to 125.00
Starfish book end, clear, New
Martinsville Glass Mfg. Co.,
2¾ x 6¼" base, 7¾" h.......................50.00
Swan dish, green opalescent, Imperial
Swan, Imperial Glass Co., 1930s,
4½" h..28.00
Swan dish, clear w/cobalt blue neck &
head, New Martinsville Glass Co.,
11" l...85.00
Swan figure, wings up, clear,
A.H. Heisey & Co., 1947-53,
7" h..................................475.00 to 525.00
Swan figure, Pall Mall patt., clear,
Duncan & Miller Glass Co.,10½" h. ...60.00
Swordfish, blue opalescent frosted,
Duncan & Miller Glass Co., 3¼" l.,
5" h...395.00
Tiger book end, head up, clear, New
Martinsville Glass Mfg.Co.,
3¼" x 5¾" base, 6½" h. 165.00
Tiger paperweight, black opaque,
Imperial Glass Co. (Heisey mold),
1982-83, 8" l., 2⅔" h. 75.00

BLOWN THREE MOLD

*This type of glass was entirely or
partially blown in a mold from about 1820
to 1840 in the United States. The object
was formed and the decoration impressed
upon it by blowing the glass into a metal
mold, usually of three but sometimes more
sections, hinged together. Mold-blown
glass actually dates back to ancient times.
Recent research reveals that certain
geometric patterns were reproduced in the
1920s and collectors are urged to read all
recent information available. Reference
numbers are from George L. and Helen
McKearin's book,* American Glass.

Blown Three Mold Bottle

Bottle, miniature, geometric, chestnut
flask-shaped w/flattened sides,
sheared & fire-polished lip, clear,
4¼" h., probably GII-2 (slight
interior residue) $2,805.00
Bottle, geometric, spherical body
tapering to a slender cylindrical neck
w/applied collared rim, pale green,
7¾" h., minor interior stain, minor
open blisters inside neck, similar
to GII-7 (ILLUS.) 3,740.00
Bottle, geometric, barrel-shaped body
w/ribbed medial band, slender tall
neck w/applied sloping lip, grass
green, 8¼" h., GII-7 (slight
roughness on bottom)...................2,750.00
Bowl, 4⅛" d., 1½" h., geometric,
folded rim, sixteen diamond base
w/pontil, clear (GII-19) 121.00
Bowl, 4⅛" d., geometric, shallow
sides w/folded rim, rayed base, clear
(GIII-24) 88.00
Bowl, 4⅞" d., 2½" h., geometric, deep
conical sides w/flared & folded rim,
sixteen diamond base w/pontil, clear
(GII-21) 302.50
Bowl, 5" d., 2" h., overall diamond
point design w/folded rim & rayed
base, clear (GII-18) 148.50
Bowl, 5¹⁄₁₆" d., 1⅝" h., geometric,
folded rim, rayed base, clear (GIII-
21)..88.00
Bowl, 5¼" d., 1¾" h., geometric,
shallow rounded sides w/folded rim,
rayed base, clear (GIII-21) 143.00
Bowl, 5½" d., 1⅜" h., shallow upright
sides w/a folded rim, ringed base
w/pontil, clear (GIII-25) 99.00
Bowl, 5½" d., 2" h., geometric, folded
rim, rayed base, clear (GIII-20)..........99.00
Bowl, 5⅞" d., 1½" h., shallow flaring
sides w/folded rim, rayed base
w/pontil, clear, shape D-6 (GIII-19)..121.00
Bowl, 8½" d., 1¼" h., geometric, low
sides w/folded rim, clear, probably
Boston & Sandwich (GIII-6) 297.00
Bowl, 9" d., 5½" h., geometric, deep
rounded sides w/folded rim, on
applied round foot, clear, GII-18
(minor wear, small broken blister
on bottom interior).........................3,630.00
Bowl, 10⅝" d., 1½" h., wide shallow
sides w/folded rim, geometric, clear
(GIII-5) 990.00
Celery vase, geometric, tall bell-form
bowl on an applied foot, clear,
7¼" h. (GII-18) 1,430.00
Celery vase, geometric, cylindrical
bowl w/deeply rolled rim, on applied
knopped stem & round disc foot,
clear, probably Pittsburgh, 7½" h.
(GII-27) 1,320.00

Celery vase, tall flaring cylindrical
bowl w/molded swirled scrolls,
applied knopped stem & round foot,
clear, 8¼" h., GV-21 (wear) 1,375.00

Celery vase, geometric, flaring
cylindrical shape w/diamond point
band design, on applied solid base,
clear (GIII-34)...............................1,200.00

Cologne bottle w/original Tam
O'Shanter stopper, swirled ribs,
sapphire blue, 5¾" h. (GI-3,
type 2)...522.50

Cologne bottle w/old blue Tam
O'Shanter stopper, ribbed, deep
amethyst (GI-7, type III) 330.00

Cordial, geometric, small tapering
conical bowl on an applied round
foot, plain rim, clear, 2⅝" h.
(GI-6) 302.50

Creamer, toy-size, geometric, applied
strap handle, clear, 2⅝" h. 368.50

Creamer, geometric, applied strap
handle, brilliant sapphire blue,
3⅞" h. (GIII-24) 2,750.00

Creamer, ovoid body tapering to a
flared rim, applied strap handle,
geometric, probably Boston &
Sandwich, clear, 4" h. (GII-18).........313.50

Blown Three Mold Creamer

Creamer, geometric, ovoid body
w/widely flaring rim w/pinched spout,
applied strap handle, cobalt blue,
4¼" h., tool mark on tip of spout,
GIII-6 (ILLUS.) 1,980.00

Creamer, wide center band of bold
ribs flanked by narrow bands,
applied strap handle, sapphire blue,
4½" h., GI-29 (roughness at stone in
tip of spout) 2,310.00

Cruet stand bottle w/pressed wheel
stopper, geometric, bulbous body
above a cylindrical base, clear, pint
(GII-18) 324.50

Cup plate, geometric, folded rim,
rayed base w/pontil, clear, 4¼" d.
(GII-16) 142.00

Decanter w/original pressed wheel
stopper, miniature, geometric, clear,

3⅞" h., ¼ pint (GIII-21) 418.00

Decanter w/original bulbous ribbed
stopper, ribbed sides flank center
band w/embossed "BRANd/y,"
clear (GI-8).....................................522.50

Decanter w/original Tam O'Shanter
stopper, ribbed, purplish blue,
6¼" h. (GI-29) 715.00

Decanter w/Tam O'Shanter stopper,
wide ribs on sides & paneled
shoulder, Boston & Sandwich,
medium greyish blue, half pint
(GI-29) 935.00

Decanter w/pressed wheel stopper,
geometric, three-ringed neck, clear,
8⅜" h. (GII-18) 192.50

Square Blown Three Mold Decanter

Decanter w/original flattened bulbous
stopper, geometric, square sides &
paneled shoulders, emerald green,
probably Keene, New Hampshire,
pinpoint flake on lip, GII-28
(ILLUS.) 4,455.00

Decanter w/original bulbous patterned
stopper, swirled ribs w/a body band
molded "R U M," clear, quart (GIII-2,
type 2)...302.50

Decanter w/original bulbous swirled
rib stopper, swirled ribs above a
wide body band embossed
"BRANDY," flanged lip, clear, quart,
GIII-2 (slight interior haze) 385.00

Decanter w/original bulbous patterned
stopper, geometric, sixteen molded
vertical ribs, three applied neck
rings, clear, quart (GIII-5).................990.00

Decanter w/pressed wheel stopper,
rounded arch design, flanged &
folded rim, clear, 7⅜" h. (GIV-5) 247.50

Decanter w/original bulbous ribbed
stopper, baroque, clear, half-pint,
GV-8 (slight interior haze)................302.50

Decanter w/original patterned stopper,
Gothic arch w/oval panel embossed
"G I N," clear, pint (GIV-7)...............357.50

Decanter, no stopper, geometric,
cylindrical body w/paneling around

bottom edge, diamond quilted w/a wide ringed shoulder tapering to a cylindrical neck w/flared mouth, clear w/distinct brownish amethyst tint, probably New England Glass Company, quart (GII-10) 192.50

Decanter, no stopper, geometric, wide starburst in diamond band between ribbed base & long twisted ribs up the shoulder, Mt. Vernon Glass Works, Vernon, New York, ca. 1830, olive green, quart (GIII-2, type 1) ..2,200.00

Decanter, no stopper, geometric, wide diamond band below swirling ribbing on the shoulder & neck, flattened flared rim, grass green, 8" h. (GIII-2, type 2) 5,720.00

Decanter, no stopper, narrow sloping lip, geometric, olive amber, Keene, New Hampshire, quart (GIII-20)....2,200.00

Dish, footed, geometric, made from a tumbler, flattened sides w/upturned folded rim, clear, 5/8" h. (GII-18)........143.00

Dish, geometric, round w/shallow sides & folded rim, clear, 5¾" d., 1" h. (GII) 93.50

Dish, geometric, round w/shallow sides & folded rim, clear, 6" d., 1⅛" h. (GIII) 66.00

Dish, geometric, round w/low sides & folded rim, clear, 6½" d., 1⅜" h. (GII)..82.50

Dish, geometric, round w/low sides & folded rim, clear, 7¼" d., 2⅛" h. (GIII)..137.50

Dish, round w/low sides & folded rim, ringed base, clear, 5½" d. (GI-6)......132.00

Flip glass, geometric, tapering cylindrical form, clear, 3¾" d., 4½" h. (GII-21) 170.50

Flip glass, geometric, slightly tapering cylindrical form, diamond point band, rayed base, 4¾" d., 5¾" h. (GIII-22) 198.00

Flip glass, geometric, tall slightly flaring cylindrical body, clear, 6" h., GIII-22 (flakes on pontil) 192.50

Flip glass, slightly tapering cylindrical form, geometric, tooled rim, plain base, clear, 4½" d., 6" h. (GIII-22) ...225.50

Inkwell, geometric, low cylindrical form w/rounded edges, clear (GIII-25) ..1,800.00

Inkwell, cylindrical drum shape, geometric, olive amber, 2¼" d., 1½" h. (GIII-29) 176.00

Lamp, whale oil, table-type, a ribbed 'light bulb' shaped font above a ringed knop & an applied pressed lacy octagonal base w/an acanthus leaf design, original tin drop burner, clear, 8" h., GI-7 (unseen chip on underside of base, usual mold roughness) 1,650.00

Pitcher, miniature, 2⅛" h., geometric, applied handle, clear (GIII-12) 550.00

Pitcher, miniature, 3" h., geometric, applied handle, clear (GIII-21) 412.50

Pitcher, 6" h., geometric, wide ovoid body tapering to a flared rim w/pinched spout, applied strap handle, clear, quart (GIII-5)..............990.00

Blown Three Mold Pitcher

Pitcher, 6½" h., geometric, ovoid body tapering to a flaring neck w/pinched spout, applied strap handle, clear, GIII-5 (ILLUS.) 1,457.50

Pitcher, 6¾" h., 5" d., Gothic arch, applied strap handle, tooled rings around the mouth, rayed & ringed base w/pontil, clear, GIV-7 (slight residue in bottom) 2,090.00

Pitcher, 7" h., Arch & Fern patt., applied solid handle w/a medial rib & curled end, clear (GIV-6) 950.00

Salt dip, geometric, round bowl w/incurved sides raised on a short applied pedestal foot, cobalt blue, probably Boston & Sandwich, 3⅛" d., 1⅞" h. (GIII-25) 522.50

Salt dip, geometric, round bowl on low pedestal foot, clear, 2" h. (GIII-3).....275.00

Salt dip, miniature, geometric, wide flat-rimmed & flat-sided bowl tapering to an applied foot, clear, 2½" h. (GII-18) 247.50

Salt dip, geometric, cylindrical bowl w/tapering base to applied round foot, cobalt blue, 2⅝" h. (GIII-24) ..1,072.50

Salt dip, miniature, geometric, bell-form bowl w/galleried rim, applied foot, clear, 2¾" h. (GII-18) 302.50

Salt dip, geometric, ovoid bowl tapering to a low pedestal w/applied round foot, a widely flaring galleried rim, clear, 2¾" h. (GIII-13)................412.50

Sugar bowl, cov., geometric, cylindrical bowl w/galleried rim raised on a trumpet foot, the tapering domed cover w/a button finial, clear, 5" d., 7¾" h. (GII-21) ..3,850.00

Toddy glass, geometric, tapering conical bowl on an applied crimped foot, clear, 4¼" h., GIV-2 (rim lightly ground) 550.00

Tumbler, barrel-shaped, geometric,
probably Boston & Sandwich, very
pale blue, 3" d., 3⅛" h. (GII-18) 280.50
Tumbler, cylindrical, geometric, clear,
3¼" d., 3¼" h. (GII-18) 143.00
Tumbler, geometric, cylindrical, clear,
3¼" h. (GII-22) 225.50
Tumbler, barrel-shaped, geometric,
clear, 3½" h. (GII-21) 209.00
Tumbler, geometric, tapering
cylindrical body, clear, 4¾" h.
(GIII-16) 99.00
Whimsey, model of a top hat,
geometric, wide cylindrical bowl,
rolled & folded rim, clear, 2⅞" d.,
2" h. (GIII-8) 143.00
Whimsey, model of a top hat, folded
rim, geometric, clear, 2¼" h. (GIII) ...137.50
Whimsey, model of a top hat, geometric, folded rim, rayed base,
clear, 2¼" h. (GIII-3) 495.00
Whimsey, model of a top hat,
geometric, tall conical crown, rolled
& folded rim, clear, 2⅛" d., 2¼" h.
(GIII-4) 176.00
Whimsey, model of a top hat,
unrecorded geometric variation,
clear, 2⅜" h. (GII-44) 522.50
Whiskey taster, geometric, tapering
cylindrical body, tooled rim, clear,
2⅛" h. (GII-16) 110.00
Whiskey taster, geometric, conical
body, tooled rim, clear, 2¼" h.,
GII-19 (two small rim flakes) 88.00
Wine glass, geometric, conical bowl
w/ribbed band, applied ringed stem
& round foot, clear, 3⅞" h., GI-6
(small ground spot on foot) 253.00
Wine glass, geometric, tapering
conical bowl on applied ringed stem
& round foot, 3⅞," h. (GII-19)...........440.00

BOTTLES & FLASKS

BITTERS

*(Numbers with some listings below
refer to those used in Carlyn Ring's* For
Bitters Only.)

African Stomach Bitters, Spruance,
Stanley & Co., round, light amber,
9⅝" h...$125.00
Angostura Bark Bitters, Eagle Liqueur
Distiller, globe-shaped, amber,
7" h..75.00
Atwood (Moses F.) in script - None
Genuine Without My Signature,
round, aqua, 6¼" h. 25.00
Atwood's - Vegetable Dyspeptic -
Bitters, rectangular, aqua, 6¾" h. 85.00

Baker's Orange Grove - Bitters,
square w/roped corners, reddish
amber, 3 x 9½"................................335.00
Beggs' Dandelion Bitters, rectangular
w/beveled edges, smooth base,
tooled lip, yellow w/olive tone,
7¾" h..231.00
Berliner Magen Bitters Co., square,
amber, 9" h. 260.00
Big Bill Best Bitters, tapering square,
golden amber, ca. 1870-90,
12⅛" h..110.00
Boyce's (Dr.) Tonic Bitters, 12-sided,
deep aqua, 7¾" h...............................45.00
Brady's (Dr.) Mandrake Bitters,
Honesdale, Pennsylvania, paper
label only, rectangular, smooth
base, tooled lip, clear, 8⅛" h.............77.00
Brown's Celebrated Indian Herb
Bitters - Patented 1867, figural
Indian Queen, golden amber,
12¼" h..605.00

Brown's Celebrated Herb Bitters

Brown's Celebrated Indian Herb
Bitters - Patented Feb. 11, 1868,
figural Indian Queen, medium
amber, 12¼" h. (ILLUS.) 550.00
Caldwells Herb Bitters (below) The
Great Tonic, triangular, amber,
12⅜" h..187.00
Caldwell's (Dr.) Herb Bitters (below)
The Great Tonic, triangular, golden
amber, ca. 1860-80, 12¾" h. 263.00
California Fig Bitters - California
Extract of Fig Co., San Francisco,
Cal., square, amber, 10" h. 88.00
California Fig & Herb Bitters -
California Fig Products Co., San
Francisco, Cal., square, amber,
4½" h..195.00
California Herb Bitters, Pittsburgh,
Pa., G.W. Frazier, square, amber,
9½" h..200.00
Capuziner Stomach Bitters, Spellman
Distilling Co., Peoria, Illinois, square,
amber, w/paper label, qt., 8¼" h. 500.00
Celebrated Crown Bitters - F.

Chevalier & Co., Sole Agents, square, light honey amber, 2¾ x 8⅞"..265.00

Clotworthy's - Oriental Tonic Bitters, square, amber, 2⅞ x 9½"................345.00

Clotworthy's - Oriental Tonic Bitters, square, honey amber, 2⅞ x 9¾"......285.00

Cole Bros. - Vegetable Bitters - Binghamton N.Y. - G.L. Cole Prop'r, rectangular, aqua, 7⅞" h....................95.00

Demuth's Stomach Bitters, Philada, square, light golden amber, 9⅜" h...165.00

Doyle's - Hop - Bitters - 1872 (on shoulders), square, amber, 9⅝" h......52.00

Drakes Plantation Bitters - Patented 1862, cabin-shaped, five-log, chocolate amber w/a hint of puce, 10" h. (D-109) 275.00

Drakes Plantation Bitters - Patented 1862, cabin-shaped, five-log, golden yellowish amber, 10" h. (D-106)......357.50

Drakes Plantation Bitters - Patented 1862, cabin-shaped, five-log, lemon amber, 10" h. (D-109) 175.00

Drakes Plantation Bitters - Patented 1862, cabin-shaped, five-log, strawberry puce, 10" h. (D-109).......325.00

Drakes Plantation Bitters - Patented 1862, arabesque variant, square w/six embossed logs above label panels, medium puce, 10" h. (D-102)..325.00

Drake's (S T) 1860 Plantation Bitters - Patented 1862, no "X," cabin-shaped, four-log, light honey amber (D-110)..100.00

Drake's (S T) 1860 Plantation Bitters - Patented 1862, no "X," cabin-shaped, four-log, orange amber (D-110)..60.00

Drake's (S T) 1860 Plantation Bitters - Patented 1862, no "X," cabin shaped, four-log, yellow (D-110)......475.00

Drake's (S T) 1860 Plantation Bitters - Patented 1862, no "X," cabin-shaped, six-log, deep puce, 10" h. (D-103)..160.00

Drake's (S T) 1860 Plantation X Bitters - Patented 1862, cabin-shaped, six-log, deep cherry puce, 10" h. (D-105) 93.50

Drake's (S T) 1860 Plantation X Bitters - Patented 1862, cabin-shaped, six-log, deep puce, 10" h., D-105..................................110.00

Drake's (S T) 1860 Plantation X Bitters - Patented 1862, cabin-shaped, six-log, medium amber, 10" h. (D-105) 66.00

Drake's (S T) 1860 Plantation X Bitters - Patented 1862, cabin-shaped, six-log, bright yellow w/hint of olive, 10" h. (D-108) 495.00

Drake's (S T) 1860 Plantation X

Bitters - Patented 1862, cabin-shaped, six-log, dark burgundy puce, 10" h. (D-108)........................165.00

Drake's (S T) 1860 Plantation X Bitters - Patented 1862, cabin-shaped, six-log, light pinkish puce, 10" h. (D-108) 395.00

Drake's (S T) 1860 Plantation X Bitters - Patented 1862, cabin-shaped, six-log, medium pinkish puce, 10" h. (D-108)........................231.00

Eagle Angostura Bark Bitters, globe-shaped, amber, 4" h..........................62.50

Electric Bitters - H.E. Bucklen & Co., Chicago, Ill., square, amber, 9⅞" h....30.00

"Electric" Brand Bitters - H.E. Bucklen & Co., Chicago, Ill., square, original label, amber, 8⅞" h............................25.00

Ferro Quina Bitters, D.P. Rossi, Dogliani, Italia, square, light amber, 1 x 2½"..125.00

Fischs (Doctor) Bitters - W.H. Ware, Patent 1866, figural fish, golden amber, ca. 1860-80, 11¾" h. 308.00

Fischs (Doctor) Bitters - W.H. Ware, Patent 1866, figural fish, light amber, 11¾" h. 225.00

Fischs (Doctor) Bitters - W.H. Ware, Patented 1866, figural fish, medium amber, 11¾" h. 195.00

Fish (The) Bitters - W.H. Ware, Patented 1866, figural fish, medium root beer amber, 11½" h. 165.00

Fisher's N.E. Cough Bitters, Atlanta, GA., rectangular, aqua, 5¾" h. 125.00

Genuine Bull Wild Cherry Bitters, rectangular, clear, 8¾" h. 150.00

Globe (The) Tonic - Bitters, square, golden amber, 9⅝" h........................132.00

Grand Prize Bitters, square, amber, 9¼" h..325.00

Greeley's Bourbon Bitters, barrel-shaped, ten rings above & below center band, copper puce, 9⅜" h.....264.00

Greeley's Bourbon Bitters, barrel-shaped, ten rings above & below center band, deep wine, 9⅜" h. 412.50

Greeley's Bourbon Bitters, barrel-shaped, ten rings above & below center band, medium smoky puce, 9⅛" h..357.50

Greeley's Bourbon Bitters, barrel-shaped, ten rings above & below center band, smoky greyish green, 9⅜" h..1,045.00

Hall's Bitters – E.E. Hall New Haven, Established 1842, barrel-shaped, ten-rib, yellow, 9⅛" h. 210.00

Herb (H.P.) Wild Cherry Bitters, Reading, Pa., square, cabin-shaped w/cherry tree motif & roped corners, golden amber, ca. 1860-80, 10" h...286.00

Highland Bitters and Scotch Tonic,
barrel-shaped, ten-rib, light reddish
amber, 9⅝" h. 1,900.00
Holtzermann's - Patent Stomach
Bitters, cabin-shaped, stylized logs
like hoops on barrels, golden
orangish amber, 9¼" h................ 1,800.00

Holtzermans Patent Stomach Bitters

Holtzermans Patent Stomach Bitters
(on shoulder), cabin-shaped w/four
roofs, golden amber, w/paper label,
ca. 1870-90, 9⅝" h. (ILLUS.) 330.00
Home Bitters - St. Louis, Mo. -
Prepared Black - Berry Brandy,
round, amber, 3¼" d., 11½" h. 250.00
Hostetter's (Dr. J.) Stomach Bitters,
square, bright green, 9" h. (H-195) ..475.00
Hostetter's (Dr. J.) Stomach Bitters,
square, smooth base, applied
mouth, yellow, 9" h. (H-195) 165.00
Iron & Quinine Bitters - Burlington,
Vt. - N.K. Brown, rectangular, aqua,
7⅛" h..190.00
Johnson's Calisaya Bitters -
Burlington, Vt., square, collared
mouth w/ring, amber, 10" h...............90.00
Kelly's Old Cabin Bitters - Patd March
1870, cabin-shaped, dark root beer
amber, 9¼" h. 2,420.00
Kelly's Old Cabin Bitters - Patd March
1870, cabin-shaped, medium
amber, 9¼" h. 1,155.00
Kimball's Jaundice - Bitters - Troy,
N.H., rectangular, yellowish amber,
7" h..................................450.00 to 550.00
King's 25 Cent Bitters, oval, aqua,
6¾" h..110.00
King Solomon's Bitters, Seattle,
Wash., rectangular, 8⅜" h. 75.00
Lacour's Bitters - Sarsapariphere,
round, lettering in sunken side
panels, lime green, 9" h. 5,060.00
Lacour's Bitters - Sarsapariphere,
round, lettering in sunken side
panels, yellowish root beer amber,
9" h...1,650.00
Landsberg (M.G.) Chicago (bitters),
square, amber, 11" h. 742.50

Landsberg (M.G.) Chicago (bitters),
square, light golden amber, 11" h. ...687.50
Langley's (Dr.) Root & Herb Bitters -
76 Union St., Boston, round aqua......55.00
Leipziger Burgunder Wein Bitter,
The Hockstadter Co., round, green,
11¾" h..200.00

Litthauer Stomach Bitters

Litthauer Stomach Bitters (paper
label), Hartwig Kantorowicz, Posen,
Berlin, Hamburg, Germany, square
case gin shape, milk white, 9½" h.
(ILLUS.) 135.00
Litthauer Stomach Bitters Invented
1864 by Josef Loewenthal, Berlin,
square case gin shape, milk white,
9½" h..176.00
Loew's (Dr.) Celebrated Stomach
Bitters & Nerve Tonic - The Loew &
Sons Co., Cleveland, O., square,
emerald green, 9¼" h. 325.00
Mack's Sarsaparilla Bitters - Mack &
Co. Prop'rs. San Francisco,
rectangular w/concave corners,
medium amber, 9¼" h.....................242.00
Mills' Bitters - A.M. Gilman - Sole
Proprietor, lady's leg shape,
yellowish amber, 11¼" h...............1,540.00
Moffat (John) - Phoenix Bitters - Price
$1.00 - New York, rectangular
w/wide beveled corners, olive green,
½ pt., 5½" h.....................................412.50
Moffat (Jno.) - Price $1 - Phoenix
Bitters - New York, rectangular
w/wide beveled corners, pontil
scarred base, applied mouth, olive
green, 5½" h. 385.00
National Bitters, embossed "Pat.
Applied For" on base, figural ear of
corn, amber, 12½" h. 275.00
National Bitters - Patent 1867, figural
ear of corn, aqua, 12⅝" h. 3,400.00
National Bitters - Patent 1867, figural
ear of corn, deep golden amber,
12⅝" h..262.00

National Bitters - Patent 1867, figural
ear of corn, light shading to medium
pinkish puce, 12⅝" h.....................3,300.00

National Bitters

National Bitters - Patent 1867, figural
ear of corn, yellowish amber,
12⅝" h. (ILLUS.) 1,265.00
Niagara Star (John W. Steele's),
square w/roofed shoulders, three
stars on roof & 1864, collared mouth
w/ring, golden amber, 10" h. 715.00
Niagara Star (John W. Steele's),
square w/roofed shoulders, three
stars on roof & 1864, collared
mouth w/ring, deep golden amber,
10¼" h...385.00
Nibol Kidney and Liver Bitters, The
Best Tonic Laxative & Blood Purifier,
square, amber, 9½" h. 165.00
Old Homestead Wild Cherry Bitters -
Patent (on shoulders), cabin-
shaped, deep strawberry puce,
9⅞" h...3,080.00
Old Homestead Wild Cherry Bitters -
Patent (on shoulders), cabin-shaped
w/shingles, yellowish amber,
9⅞" h...412.50
Old Sachem Bitters and Wigwam
Tonic, barrel-shaped, ten-rib,
bright golden amber, ca. 1860-80,
9½" h...550.00
Old Sachem Bitters and Wigwam
Tonic, barrel-shaped, ten-rib,
ginger ale yellow, ca. 1860-80,
9½" h...770.00
Old Sachem Bitters and Wigwam
Tonic, barrel-shaped, ten-rib,
golden amber, ca. 1860-80,
9½" h. (ILLUS. top next column) 175.00
Old Sachem Bitters and Wigwam
Tonic, barrel-shaped, ten-rib, light
yellowish amber, 9½" h. 450.00
Old Sachem Bitters and Wigwam
Tonic, barrel-shaped, ten-rib,
medium copper color, 9½" h. 467.50

Old Sachem Bitters

Old Sachem Bitters and Wigwam
Tonic, barrel-shaped, ten-rib,
medium orangish amber, 9½" h. 742.50
Old Sachem Bitters and Wigwam
Tonic, barrel-shaped, ten-rib,
medium pinkish strawberry puce,
9½" h...715.00
Old Sachem Bitters and Wigwam
Tonic, barrel-shaped, ten-rib,
orangish amber, 9½" h.....................325.00
Old Sachem Bitters and Wigwam
Tonic, barrel-shaped, ten-rib,
yellowish amber, 9½" h. 154.00
Old Sachem Bitters and Wigwam
Tonic, barrel-shaped, ten-rib,
aqua, 10⅛" h.................................4,620.00
Original Pocahontas Bitters, Y.
Ferguson, barrel-shaped w/ten
horizontal ribs above & below
embossing, narrow square collar,
aqua, 2¼" d., 9⁵⁄₁₆" h. 2,695.00
Orruro - Bitters (on shoulders),
cylindrical, green, ¾ qt., 10⅝" h.........25.00
Oxygenated for Dyspepsia, Asthma &
General Debility, rectangular, aqua,
½ pt., 7⅝" h.....................................140.00
Pepsin Bitters - R.W. Davis Drug Co.,
Chicago, U.S.A., rectangular, apple
green, 1⅜ x 2¼", 4⅛" h. 200.00
Pepsin Calisaya Bitters, Dr. Russell
Med. Co., rectangular, green, pt.,
7⅞" h...105.00
Peruvian Bitters. w/"P.B.Co."
monogram in shield, square, amber,
9¼" h..................................50.00 to 70.00
Peychaud's American Aromatic
Cocktail Bitters (paper label),
cylindrical, amber, 6" h.......................40.00
Pierce's (Dr. Geo.) - Indian
Restorative Bitters - Lowell, Mass,
greenish aqua, 7⅞" h. 135.00
(Pineapple), W. & Co., N.Y.,
pineapple-shaped, bright yellowish
green, 8⅞" h. 4,510.00

(Pineapple), W. & Co., N.Y.,
pineapple-shaped, medium orangish
amber, 8⅞" h. 125.00

Reed's Bitters (repeated on shoulder),
cylindrical, lady's leg neck, light
orange amber, 12½" h. ....250.00 to 300.00

Richardson's (S.O.) - Bitters - South
Reading - Mass., rectangular
w/wide beveled corners, aqua, pt.,
6⅞" h..................................65.00 to 85.00

Richardson's (W.L.) - Bitters - South
Reading - Mass., rectangular, aqua,
7" h..98.00

Roback's (Dr. C.W.) Stomach Bitters,
Cincinnati, O, barrel-shaped, golden
amber, 9⅜" h. 231.00

Root's (John) Bitters - Buffalo, N.Y. -
1867 (on two sides), rectangular,
amber, 9¾" h. 1,595.00

Royal Italian Bitters, Registered,
Trade Mark, A.M.F. Gianella,
Genova, round, brilliant medium
amethyst, 2¾" d., 13½" h. (some
minor interior wear) 484.00

Royal Italian Bitters, Registered,
Trade Mark, A.M.F. Gianella,
Genova, round, light to medium
pinkish amethyst, 2¾" d.,
13½" h...2,640.00

Royal Italian Bitters, Registered,
Trade Mark, A.M.F. Gianella,
Genova, round, pinkish amethyst,
2¾" d., 13½" h. 990.00

Royce's Sherry Wine Bitters,
rectangular, smooth base, aqua,
8" h...90.00

Rush's - Bitters - A.H. Flanders M.D.,
New York, square, amber, 8⅞" h. 40.00

Russ' St. Domingo Bitters - New York,
rectangular, light yellowish amber,
9⅞" h...275.00

Sanborn's Kidney and Liver
Vegetable Laxative Bitters,
rectangular, amber, 10" h. 150.00

Sazarac Aromatic Bitters, lady's leg
neck, milk white, 10⅛" h. 522.50

Sazarac Aromatic Bitters, w/"PHD &
Co." monogram, lady's leg neck,
milk white, 12½" h. ....225.00 to 250.00

Schroeder's Bitters, Louisville, KY - S.
B. & G. Co., lady's leg neck, tooled
lip, smooth base, orangish amber,
9" h...467.50

Severa (W.F.) - Stomach Bitters,
square, amber, 9⅝" h. 70.00

Simon's Centennial Bitters - Trade
Mark, figural bust of Washington on
pedestal, aqua, ¾ qt., 9¾" h. 650.00

Solomons' Strengthening &
Invigorating Bitters - Savannah,
Georgia, square, cobalt blue,
³⁄₁₆" stress crack, 9⅝" h.
(S-140) 1,072.00

Specialitat Richter's Rossbacher
Magen Bitter, Patentamtlich Christof
Richter & Bruder, Hof in Baiern,
applied mouth, smooth base, olive
green, 11" h., ca. 1870-80 (tiny flake
on one corner) 231.00

Swiss - Stomach Bitters - WM. F.
Zoeller - Pittsburgh, PA., w/paper
label, rectangular, applied mouth,
smooth base, yellowish amber,
9¼" h...220.00

Tippecanoe Bitters

Tippecanoe (birch bark & canoe
motif), H.H. Warner & Co.,
cylindrical, amber, 9" h.
(ILLUS.) ....80.00 to 100.00

Tonic Bitters, J.T. Higby, Milford, Ct.,
square, amber, 9½" h. 55.00

Von Hopfs (Dr.) - Curacoa Bitters -
Chamberlain & Co., Des Moines
Iowa, rectangular, amber, w/labels,
½ pt., 7½" h.........................60.00 to 80.00

Wakefield's Strengthening Bitters,
rectangular w/beveled corners,
aqua, 8" h..70.00

Wear & Upham & Ostrom - Julien's
Imperial - Aromatic Bitters, N.Y.,
lady's leg-shaped, yellowish amber,
12½" h..3,035.00

Wheeler's - Berlin - Bitters - Baltimore,
hexagonal, lettering reading reversed & base to shoulder, iron
pontil, yellowish olive green,
9½" h..7,150.00

Wonser's (Dr.) U.S.A., Indian Root
Bitters, round w/fluted shoulder,
dark aqua, ¾ qt., 11" h..................3,080.00

Wonser's (Dr.) U.S.A., Indian Root
Bitters, round w/fluted shoulder,
root beer amber, ¾ qt., 11" h. 4,730.00

Yerba Buena - Bitters, S.F. Cal., flask-
shaped, amber, 8½" h........................80.00

Zu Zu Bitters, square, amber,
8⅜" h...310.00

FIGURALS

Cherub & Medallion Bottle

Bust of George Washington, applied sloping collared mouth, pontil scar, aqua, 10½" h.....................................27.50

Busts of three people, two men & one woman, atop of waisted paneled column, probably Europe, ca. 1880-1900, milk white cased in clear, 13½" h...220.00

Cherub holding a medallion on his shoulder w/pressed wheel stopper in the short cylindrical neck, tooled lip, American-made, ca. 1890-1910, emerald green, 11" h. (ILLUS.) 192.50

Cherub holding a medallion on his shoulder w/pressed wheel stopper in the short cylindrical neck, tooled lip, American-made, ca. 1890-1910, medium purplish amethyst, 11" h. ...198.00

Cigar, amber glass, 5¼" l. ......25.00 to 35.00

Cigar, ground top w/screw cap, amber glass 82.50

Dutchman Bottle

Cucumber, horizontal ribbing, pontil scar on one end, applied knob on other, American-made, ca. 1880-1900, medium sapphire blue, 7¾" l...77.00

Dutchman standing wearing baggy pants, jacket w/kerchief & hat, holding a long pipe, probably from Germany, ca. 1890-1910, amber, 11½" h. (ILLUS. previous column) ...825.00

Ham, amber glass 60.00

Klondyke gold nugget flask, milk white glass, 6" h. 62.50

Potato, sponge-daubed earthenware pottery, blue sponging on white, 8" l..165.00

FLASKS

GI-2 - Washington bust below "General Washington" - American Eagle w/shield w/seven bars on breast, head turned to right, edges w/horizontal beading w/vertical medial rib, plain lip, pontil, aqua, pt..245.00

GI-19 - "Washington" above bust - "Baltimore Glass Works." in semicircle around Battle Monument, Baltimore, smooth edges, plain lip, pontil, copper w/puce tones, ca. 1830-50, pt....................................1,980.00

GI-22 - Washington bust (facing right) below "Baltimore X Glass Works" (all S's reversed) - classical bust facing right, three vertical ribs w/heavy medial rib, plain lip, pontil, clear, ca. 1820-40, pt. 1,210.00

GI-25 - Washington bust (facing right) below "Bridgetown New Jersey," - Classical bust below "Bridgetown New Jersey," plain lip, aqua, qt., 8¼" h., light inside haze...................220.00

GI-28 -Washington bust below "Albany Glass Works," "Albany N Y" below bust - full-rigged ship sailing to right, plain lip, vertically ribbed edges, pontil, medium amber, pt. 660.00

GI-34 - "Washington" above bust (facing right) - "Jackson" above bust, plain lip, vertically ribbed edges w/heavy medial rib, pontil, light yellow olive green, ½ pt. 230.00

GI-37 - Washington bust below "The Father of His Country" - Taylor bust, "Gen. Taylor Never Surrenders, Dyottville Glass Works, Philad.a," smooth edges, plain lip, pontil, citron, qt. 375.00

GI-37 - Washington bust below "The Father of His Country" - Taylor bust, "Gen. Taylor Never Surrenders, Dyottville Glass Works, Philad.a," plain lip, smooth edge, pontil, topaz, qt. 1,450.00

GI-40 - Washington bust below "The Father of His Country" - Taylor bust, "Gen. Taylor Never Surrenders," smooth edges, sheared lip, pontil, aqua, pt. 70.00

GI-40 - Washington bust below "The Father of His Country" - Taylor bust, "Gen. Taylor Never Surrenders," smooth edges, sheared lip, pontil, bright medium green, pt. 253.00

GI-42 - Washington bust below "The Father of His Country" - Taylor bust, "A little More Grape Captain Bragg, Dyottville Glass Works, Philad.a," smooth edges, plain lip, pontil, aqua, qt. 85.00

GI-42 - Washington bust below "The Father of His Country" - Taylor bust, "A little More Grape Captain Bragg, Dyottville Glass Works, Philad.a," smooth edges, plain lip, pontil, cobalt blue, ca.1840-60, qt. 3,740.00

GI-42 - Washington bust below "The Father of His Country" - Taylor bust, "A little More Grape Captain Bragg, Dyottville Glass Works, Philad.a," smooth edges, plain lip, pontil, peacock blue, qt................................325.00

GI-43 - Washington bust below "The Father of His Country" - Taylor bust below "I Have Endeavour,d To Do My Duty," plain lip, smooth edges, pontil, dark golden amber, ca. 1840-60, qt.....................................1,210.00

GI-43 - Washington bust below "The Father of His Country" - Taylor bust below "I Have Endeavour,d To Do My Duty," plain lip, smooth edges, pontil, yellow w/slight olive tone, ca. 1840-60, qt. 495.00

GI-65 - "General Jackson" surrounding bust - American Eagle w/shield on oval frame, "J.T. & Co." below oval frame, thirteen small five-pointed stars above eagle, horizontal beading w/vertical medial rib, plain lip, pontil mark, aqua, 1829-32, pt......................................363.00

GI-77 - Taylor bust below "Rough & Ready" - American Eagle w/shield w/eight vertical & three horizontal bars on breast, head turned left, "Masterson" above 13 five-pointed stars above eagle, plain lip, open pontil, aqua, ca. 1830-40, qt. 1,045.00

GI-80 - "Lafayette" above & "T.S." & bar below - "DeWitt Clinton" above bust & "Coventry C-T" below, plain lip, horizontally corrugated edges, pontil, light yellowish olive, ca. 1824-25, pt. 630.00

GI-80 - "Lafayette" above bust & "T.S." & bar below - "DeWitt Clinton" above bust & "Coventry C-T" below, plain lip, horizontally corrugated edges, pontil, yellowish olive, ca. 1824-25, pt. 550.00

GI-85 - "Lafayette" above bust & "Covetry (sic) - C-T" below - French liberty cap on pole & semicircle of eleven five-pointed stars above, "S & S" below, fine vertical ribbing, two horizontal ribs at base, plain lip, pontil mark, yellowish olive, ca. 1824-25, pt. 242.00

GI-86 - "Lafayette" above bust & "Coventry - C-T" below - French liberty cap on pole & semicircle of eleven five-pointed stars above, "S & S" below, fine vertical ribbing, two horizontal ribs at base, plain lip, pontil mark, yellowish olive green, ca. 1824-25, ½ pt. 440.00

GI-92 - Lafayette bust facing right below Masonic Arch & a fleur-de-lis, "Genl Lafayette" along sides - American Eagle w/shield on breast below seven stars all in an oval & "Wheeling" in semicircle above upper part of panel & "Knox & McKee" in semicircle around lower panel, smooth edges, plain lip, pontil mark, brilliant pale green, ca. 1820-40, pt. 4,070.00

GI-95 - Franklin bust below "Benjamin Franklin" - Dyott bust below "T.W. Dyott, M.D.," three vertical ribs w/heavy medial rib, plain lip, pontil mark, aqua, ca. 1820-40, pt. 242.00

GI-96 - Franklin bust below "Benjamin Franklin" - Dyott bust below "T.W. Dyott, M.D.," edges embossed "Eripuit Coelo Fulmen. Sceptrumque Tyrannis" and "Kensington Glass Works, Philadelphia," plain lip, pontil, aqua, qt. 200.00

Benjamin Franklin Flask

GI-98 - Franklin bust below "Benjamin Franklin" - "Wheeling Glassworks" in semi-circle above bust of Thomas Dyott, vertically ribbed edges, plain neck, aqua, pt. (ILLUS.) 2,750.00

GI-104 - "Jeny (sic) Lind" above bust - View of Glasshouse, calabash, vertically ribbed edges, rounded collar, pontil, brilliant light powder blue, ca. 1845-60, qt. 396.00

GI-113 - "Kossuth" above bust - tall tree in foliage, calabash, smooth edges, iron pontil, light greyish blue, ca. 1840-60, qt. 495.00

American Eagle Flask

GII-1a - American Eagle on oval, head turned to right & 10 stars in semi-circle above eagle (eight 5-pointed stars & two 6-pointed stars) obverse & reverse, beaded edges w/narrow vertical medial rib, plain sheared lip, open pontil, amber, pt. (ILLUS.) 23,650.00

GII-6 - American Eagle w/head turned right on oval w/inner band of tiny pearls, nine pearls above eagle - large Cornucopia with Produce, horizontally ribbed edges, plain lip, greenish aqua, pt. 250.00

GII-18 - American Eagle w/head turned to right above oval frame enclosing "Zanes - Ville" - Cornucopia with Produce, vertically ribbed edges, plain lip, pontil mark, aqua, ½ pt. 30.50

GII-23 - American Eagle above oval, ribbon & two semi-circular rows of stars above, oval w/elongated eight-point star - large floral medallion above oval containing an elongated eight-pointed star, edges corrugated horizontally w/vertical medial rib, plain lip, pontil, aqua, ca. 1850-55, pt. 495.00

GII-26 - American Eagle above stellar motif obverse & reverse, horizontally corrugated edges, plain lip, aqua, qt. 115.00

GII-30 - American Eagle in a small circular medallion obverse & reverse, overall heavy vertical ribbing except for medallions, plain lip, pontil, brilliant aqua, ca. 1855-60, ½ pt. 374.00

GII-31 - American Eagle in large oval medallion obverse & reverse, overall heavy vertical ribbing except for medallions, pontil, aqua, qt. 180.00

GII-48 - American Eagle on oval - American flag w/"Coffin & Hay." above & "Hammonton" below, vertically ribbed edges, plain lip, pontil, aqua, qt. 190.00

GII-61 - American Eagle below "Liberty" - inscribed in four lines, "Willington - Glass, Co - West Willington - Conn," smooth edges, deep olive green, qt. 187.00

GII-61 - American Eagle below "Liberty" - inscribed in four lines, "Willington - Glass, Co - West Willington - Conn," smooth edges, orange amber, ca. 1860-72, qt. 209.00

GII-62 - American Eagle below "Liberty" - "Willington Glass, Co West, Willington Conn," smooth edges, plain lip, emerald green, ca. 1860-72, pt. 330.00

GII-62 - American Eagle below "Liberty" - "Willington Glass, Co West, Willington Conn," smooth edges, plain lip, reddish amber, pt. ...308.00

GII-63 - American Eagle below "Liberty" - inscription in five lines, "Willington - Glass - Co - West Willington - Conn.," smooth edges, plain lip, deep reddish amber, ½ pt. 198.00

GII-64 - American Eagle below "Liberty" - inscription in four lines, "Willington - Glass, Co - West Willington - Conn," smooth edges, plain lip, pontil, golden amber, pt. 187.00

GII-65 - American Eagle below "Liberty" - inscribed in five lines "Westford - Glass - Co - Westford - Conn.," smooth edges, plain lip, deep yellowish olive, ca. 1860-73, ½ pt. 253.00

GII-67 - American Eagle below nine five-pointed stars standing on large laurel wreath - large anchor w/"New London" in a banner above & "Glass Works" in a banner below, smooth edges, plain lip, pontil, aqua, ca. 1860-66, ½ pt. 286.00

GII-67 - American Eagle below nine five-pointed stars standing on large laurel wreath - large anchor w/"New London" in a banner above & "Glass Works" in a banner below, smooth edges, plain lip, pontil, medium orangish amber, ½ pt. 467.50

GII-68 - American Eagle in flight below seven five-pointed stars - large anchor w/"New London" in a banner above & "Glass Works" in a banner below, smooth edges, plain lip, pontil, bright orangish amber, ca. 1860-66, pt. 467.50

GII-70 - American Eagle lengthwise obverse & reverse, vertically ribbed edges, plain lip, pontil, yellowish olive, ca. 1830-48, pt. 165.00

GII-71 - American Eagle lengthwise obverse & reverse, vertically ribbed edges, plain lip, pontil, bright yellowish olive, ½ pt. 176.00

GII-73 - American Eagle w/head turned to the right & standing on rocks - Cornucopia with Produce & "X" on left, vertically ribbed edges, plain lip, pontil, deep golden yellow, pt. 220.00

GII-105 - American Eagle above oval obverse & reverse, w/"Pittsburgh, Pa." in oval obverse & reverse, narrow vertical ribbing on edges, sheared lip w/applied flat collar, smooth base, deep green, pt. 250.00

GII-106 - American Eagle above oval obverse & reverse, w/"Pittsburgh, PA" in oval on obverse, narrow vertical rib on edges, honey amber, pt...185.00

GII-115 - American Eagle above oval obverse & reverse, w/"Louisville KY." in oval obverse & "Glass Works" in oval on reverse, narrow vertical ribbing on edges, applied rounded collar & seamed base w/depression, aqua, pt......................195.00

GIII-1 - Cornucopia with Produce surrounded by an oval beaded panel - large circular beaded medallion enclosing a star-shaped design w/six ribbed points & a small eight-petaled rosette center, above a symmetrical palm motif, edges w/horizontal beading, plain lip, pontil mark, pale yellowish green, ca. 1820-40, ½ pt. 412.50

GIII-2 - Cornucopia with Produce obverse & reverse, vertically ribbed edges, sheared, tooled lip, pontil, aqua, ½ pt. 105.00

GIII-4 - Cornucopia with Produce - Urn with Produce, vertically ribbed edges, plain lip, pontil, bright medium green, pt. (some exterior high point wear, inner mouth flake)..319.00

GIII-7 - Cornucopia with Produce - Urn with Produce, vertically ribbed edges, sheared lip, pontil, aqua, ½ pt...126.50

GIII-12 - Cornucopia with Produce & curled to right - Urn with Produce, plain lip, vertically ribbed edges, pontil, yellowish olive, ½ pt. 88.00

GIII-16 - Cornucopia with Produce & curled to right - Urn with Produce & w/"Lancaster.Glass.Works N.Y" above, sheared mouth, vertically ribbed edges, iron pontil, yellowish olive amber, pt. 770.00

GIV-1 - Masonic Emblems - American Eagle w/ribbon reading "E Pluribus Unum" above & "IP" (old-fashioned J) below in oval frame, tooled mouth, five vertical ribs, bright bluish green, pt. ....275.00 to 300.00

GIV-1 - Masonic Emblems - American Eagle w/ribbon reading "E Pluribus Unum" above & "IP" (old-fashioned J) below in oval frame, tooled mouth, five vertical ribs, medium bluish green, pt. 192.50

GIV-3 - Masonic Emblems - American Eagle w/heavily crimped ribbon above & "J.K. - B." below in oval frame, tooled lip, five vertical ribs, light bluish green, pt. 412.50

GIV-7 - Masonic Arch - American Eagle holding shield w/twelve dots (representing stars), open pennant ribbon above, oval frame w/eight-pointed star below, vertically ribbed sides, pontil, aqua, pt. 220.00

GIV-14 - Masonic Arch, pillars & pavement w/Masonic emblems inside the arch - American Eagle above oval frame w/elongated eight-pointed star, plain rim, vertically ribbed sides, light green, ½ pt..........440.00

GIV-17 - Masonic Arch, pillars & pavement w/Masonic emblems - American Eagle w/oval frame enclosing "KEENE" below, edges smooth w/single vertical rib, plain lip, pontil, olive green, pt........................187.50

GIV-20 - Masonic Arch, pillars & pavement w/Masonic emblems - American Eagle w/"KCCNC" in oval frame below, edges w/single vertical rib, plain lip, pontil, yellowish olive, pt. 165.00

GIV-24 - Masonic Arch, pillars & pavement w/Masonic emblems - American Eagle grasping large balls in talons & without shield on breast, plain oval frame below, smooth edges w/single medial rib, plain lip, pontil, bright light yellow amber, ½ pt. 132.00

GIV-24 - Masonic Arch, pillars & pavement w/Masonic emblems - American Eagle grasping large balls in talons & without shield on breast, plain oval frame below, smooth edges w/single medial rib, plain lip, pontil, light yellowish olive green, ½ pt. 187.00

GIV-27 - Masonic Arch, pillars & pavement w/Masonic emblems & radiating triangle enclosing the letter "G" - American Eagle w/"NEG Co" in oval frame below, vertically ribbed edges, tooled lip, pontil mark, light green, pt. 325.00

GIV-32 - Masonic Arch w/"Farmer's Arms," sheaf of rye & farm implements within arch - American Eagle, w/shield w/seven bars on breast, head turned to right, "Zanesville" above, eagle stands on oval frame w/"Ohio" inside & "J. Shepard & Co." beneath, vertically ribbed edges, open pontil, amber, pt. 330.00

GIV-32 - Masonic Arch w/"Farmer's Arms," sheaf of rye & farm implements within arch - American Eagle, w/shield w/seven bars on breast, head turned to right, "Zanesville" above, eagle stands on oval frame w/"Ohio" inside & "J. Shepard & Co." beneath, vertically ribbed edge, open pontil, aqua, pt. ....225.00 to 250.00

GIV-32 - Masonic Arch w/"Farmer's Arms," sheaf of rye & farm implements within arch - American Eagle w/shield w/seven bars on breast, head turned to right, "Zanesville" above, eagle stands on oval frame w/"Ohio" inside & "J. Shepard & Co." beneath, vertically ribbed edge, open pontil, golden yellow w/olive tone, ca. 1820-30, pt. 1,980.00

GIV-34 - Masonic Arch w/"Farmer's Arms," sheaf of rye & farm imple- ments within arch & "Kensington Glass Works Philadelphia" around edge - Sailing frigate above "Franklin" w/"Free Trade and Sailors Rights" around edge, aqua, pt. 192.50

GIV-36 - Masonic Arch w/"Farmer's Arms," sheaf of rye & farm imple- ments within arch - full rigged frigate sailing to right, "Franklin" below, edges horizontally beaded w/medial rib, plain lip, pontil, aqua, pt. 550.00

GV-3 - "Success to the Railroad" around embossed horse pulling cart - similar reverse, sheared lip, pontil, yellowish olive amber, pt. 132.00

GV-3 - "Success to the Railroad" around embossed horse pulling cart - similar reverse, sheared lip, pontil, yellowish olive green, pt. 627.00

GV-5 - "Success to the Railroad" around embossed horse pulling cart - similar reverse, plain lip, pontil, vertically ribbed edges, aqua, ca. 1840-60, pt. 374.00

GV-5 - "Success to the Railroad" around embossed horse pulling cart - similar reverse, plain lip, pontil, vertically ribbed edges, forest green, ca. 1840-60, pt. 247.50

GV-6 - "Success to the Railroad" around embossed horse pulling cart obverse & reverse, w/"Success" above scene, plain lip, pontil, vertically ribbed edges, golden amber, ca. 1840-60, pt. 198.00

GV-6 - "Success to the Railroad" around embossed horse pulling cart obverse & reverse, w/"Success" above scene, plain lip, pontil, vertically ribbed edges, olive amber, pt. 192.50

GV-6 - "Success to the Railroad" around embossed horse pulling cart obverse & reverse, w/"Success" above scene, plain lip, pontil, vertically ribbed edges, yellowish olive ca. 1830-48, pt. 253.00

GV-8 - "Success to the Railroad" around embossed horse pulling cart - large American Eagle w/head turned left & holding a shield w/seven vertical & two horizontal bars on breast, seventeen large five- pointed stars surround eagle, three vertically ribbed edges w/heavy medial rib, plain lip, pontil mark, yellowish olive amber, pt. 165.00

GV-9 - "Success to the Railroad" around embossed horse pulling cart - large eagle & seventeen five- pointed stars, vertically ribbed edges w/heavy medial rib, plain lip, pontil mark, bright yellowish olive, pt. 264.00

GV-9 - "Success to the Railroad" around embossed horse pulling cart - large eagle & seventeen five- pointed stars, vertically ribbed, heavy medial rib, plain lip, pontil mark, deep olive green, pt. 192.50

GV-9 - "Success to the Railroad" around embossed horse pulling cart - large eagle & seventeen five- pointed stars, vertically ribbed, heavy medial rib, plain lip, pontil mark, medium olive amber, pt. 176.00

GV-10 - "Railroad" above horse- drawn cart on rail & "Lowell" below - American Eagle lengthwise & 13

five-point stars, vertically ribbed
edges , sheared lip, pontil ,
yellowish olive, ½ pt. 253.00

GVI-2 - "Balto" below monument -
"Fells" above & "Point" below a
small sloop w/pennant flying &
sailing to the right, vertically ribbed
edges w/three heavy medial ribs,
plain lip, pontil mark, pale aqua,
½ pt. 247.50

GVI-4a - Washington Monument in
large oval panel - "Corn For The
World" in semicircle above ear of
corn, plain lip, smooth edges, aqua,
qt. (flake on mouth) 275.00

GVIII-2 - Sunburst w/twenty-four
triangular sectioned rays obverse &
reverse, plain lip, pontil, clear, ca.
1826-30, pt. 687.50

GVIII-2 - Sunburst w/twenty-four
triangular sectioned rays obverse &
reverse, plain lip, pontil, light green,
ca. 1815-30, pt. 440.00

Scarce Sunburst Flask

GVIII-3 - Sunburst w/twenty-four
rounded rays obverse & reverse,
horizontal corrugated edges, plain
lip, pontil mark, olive amber, pt.
(ILLUS.) 605.00

GVIII-5 - Sunburst w/twenty-four
rounded rays obverse & reverse,
horizontal corrugated edges, plain
lip, pontil mark, bright yellowish
olive, ca. 1815-30, pt 880.00

GVIII-8 - Sunburst w/twenty-eight
triangular sectioned rays obverse &
reverse, center raised oval
w/"KEEN" on obverse & w/"P & W"
on reverse, pontil, yellowish olive,
pt. 247.50

GVIII-9 - Sunburst w/twenty-nine
triangular sectioned rays obverse &
reverse, center raised oval

w/"KEEN" reading from top to
bottom on obverse & w/"P & W" on
reverse, sheared lip, pontil, olive
green, ½ pt. ....250.00 to 300.00

GVIII-9 - Sunburst w/twenty-nine
triangular sectioned rays obverse &
reverse, center raised oval
w/"KEEN" reading from top to
bottom on obverse & w/"P & W" on
reverse, sheared lip, pontil,
yellowish olive, ca. 1815-30, ½ pt. 258.50

GVIII-16 - Sunburst w/twenty-one
triangular sectioned rays obverse &
reverse, plain lip, open pontil, bright
yellowish olive green, ca. 1815-30,
½ pt. 286.00

GVIII-18 - Sunburst w/twenty-four
rounded rays obverse & reverse,
horizontal corrugated edges, plain
lip, pontil mark, olive green, ½ pt. 275.00

GVIII-18 - Sunburst w/twenty-four
rounded rays obverse & reverse,
horizontal corrugated edges, plain
lip, pontil mark, yellowish olive
amber, ca. 1815-30, ½ pt. 577.50

GVIII-18 - Sunburst w/twenty-four
rounded rays obverse & reverse,
horizontal corrugated edges, plain
lip, pontil mark, yellowish olive
green, ½ pt. 302.50

GVIII-22 - Sunburst w/thirty-six
slender rays forming a scalloped
ellipse w/five small oval ornaments
in center obverse & reverse, smooth
sides, pontil, pale green, pt. 159.50

GVIII-25 - Sunburst w/twenty-four
slender rays tapering to rounded
ends obverse & reverse, five oval-
shaped ornaments forming five-
petaled flower in middle of sunburst,
plain lip, pontil, aqua, ½ pt. 192.50

GVIII-25 - Sunburst w/twenty-four
slender rays tapering to rounded
ends obverse & reverse, five oval-
shaped ornaments forming five-
petaled flower in middle of sunburst, plain lip, pontil, medium to
deep burgundy, ½ pt. 3,960.00

GVIII-28 - Sunburst w/sixteen rays
obverse & reverse, rays converging
to a definite point at center &
covering entire side of flask,
horizontally corrugated edges, plain
lip, open pontil, light aqua, ½ pt. 220.00

GVIII-29 - Sunburst in small sunken
oval w/twelve rays obverse &
reverse, panel w/band of tiny
ornaments around inner edge, entire
flask except panels covered
w/heavy, narrow widely spaced
vertical ribbing, pontil, deep aqua,
¾ pt. ....300.00 to 315.00

GVIII-29 - Sunburst in small sunken

oval w/twelve rays obverse &
reverse, panel w/band of tiny
ornaments around inner edge, entire
flask except panels covered
w/heavy, narrow widely spaced
vertical ribbing, pontil, greenish
aqua, ¾ pt. 140.00

GVIII-29 - Sunburst in small sunken
oval w/twelve rays obverse &
reverse, panel w/band of tiny
ornaments around inner edge, entire
flask except panels covered
w/heavy, narrow, widely spaced
vertical ribbing, pontil, medium
bluish green, ¾ pt. ....165.00 to 185.00

GIX-2 - Scroll w/two six-point stars
obverse & reverse, vertical
rib, long neck w/plain lip, deep
sapphire blue, qt., 9" h. (small
mouth flake) 2,310.00

GIX-6 - Scroll w/two six-point stars
obverse & reverse, one side
w/"Louisville KY," the other
w/"Glassworks," vertical medial rib,
plain lip, pontil mark, light yellowish
green, qt..269.50

GIX-10 - Scroll w/two eight-point stars
obverse & reverse, golden amber,
ca. 1840-60, pt. 352.00

GIX-10 - Scroll w/two eight-point stars
obverse & reverse, golden amber
w/olive tones, ca. 1840-60, pt. 385.00

GIX-10c - Scroll w/two eight-point
stars, a small one in upper space &
medium sized one in midspace
obverse - seven-point upper star
reverse, vertical medial rib, plain
neck, bluish green, ½ pt....................352.00

GIX-11 - Scroll w/two eight-point stars
obverse & reverse, emerald green,
pt. (minor interior stain) 935.00

GIX-11 - Scroll w/two eight-point stars
obverse & reverse, golden amber,
pt...319.00

GIX-11 - Scroll w/two eight-point stars
obverse & reverse, sapphire blue,
pt. (pinpoint flakes) 1,760.00

GIX-12 - Scroll w/two seven-point
stars above "Louisville" in straight
line near base obverse & reverse,
vertical medial rib, plain neck, bright
medium olive green, ca. 1840-60,
pt...605.00

GIX-14 - Scroll w/two six-pointed stars
above seven-pointed star obverse &
reverse, vertical medial on edge,
plain lip, pontil, aqua, pt. 82.50

GIX-20 - Scroll w/large oval ornament
above large eight-point star above
large six-petaled flower obverse &
reverse, vertical medial rib,
plain lip, pontil, medium green, pt. ...192.50

GIX-27 - Scroll w/two eight-point large

stars in upper & mid-space w/slightly
sunken rectangular panel near base
obverse - a large nine-point star
above large eight-point star reverse,
vertical medial rib, plain neck, aqua,
pt. 660.00

Early Scroll Flasks

GIX-34 - Scroll w/large eight-point star
above a large pearl over a large
fleur-de-lis obverse & reverse,
vertical medial rib on edge, tooled
broad rounded collar w/lower bevel,
iron pontil, aqua, ½ pt., rough lip,
5⅝" h. ((ILLUS. left) 55.00

GIX-34a - Scroll w/large eight-point
star above a medium-sized pearl
over a large fleur-de-lis similar to
obverse w/very small pearl, vertical
medial rib, plain lip, aqua, ½ pt. 104.50

GIX-36 - Scroll w/medium-sized eight-
point star above a large fleur-de-lis
& a medium-sized pearl below
obverse & reverse, vertical medial
rib on edge, tooled broad collar
w/lower bevel, iron pontil, aqua,
½ pt., 5⅞" h. (ILLUS. right) 93.50

GIX-39 - Scroll w/knobbed shoulder &
nine-petaled flower at top & embossed initials "BP & B" near bottom
obverse & reverse, vertical medial
rib, plain lip, clear, ca. 1845-60,
½ pt. 495.00

GIX-43 - Scrolls w/large pearl below
each curved line at base of inner
frame, above a long oval finial
containing a large pearl above "JR &
SON" & two large pearls below
scrolls at top of outer frame - fleur-
de-lis w/two large pearls below top
scroll left & right, vertical medial
rib, plain lip; pontil mark, aqua, pt. ...495.00

GIX-45 - Scroll w/elaborate scroll
decoration forming acanthus leaves
w/four-petal flower at the top &
diamond at center obverse &
reverse, vertical medial ribs, bluish
aqua, pt. 330.00

GIX-47 - Scroll w/four graduated

finger-like ribs following the pear-shaped contour, large eight-point star in upper center & "R. Knowles & Co." (follow left rib), "Union Factory" (follow right rib) & "South Wheeling" in circle around "VA" - similar scroll w/large fleur-de-lis between inner ribs, plain lip, pontil mark, aqua, pt. 852.50

GX-2 - Stag standing above "Good" & "Game" at right of stag - Weeping willow tree, vertically ribbed edges, plain lip, aqua, ½ pt. 332.50

Sheaf of Rye Flask

GX-3 - Sheaf of Rye - Bunch of Grapes w/stem & three large leaves, vertically ribbed edges, sheared lip, pontil, aqua, ½ pt. (ILLUS.) 140.00

GX-4 - Cannon, "Genl Taylor Never Surrenders" inscribed in semicircle around cannon - vine & grape form a semicircular frame containing the inscription "A Little More Grape Capt Bragg," vertically ribbed w/heavy medial ribbing, plain lip, pontil, aqua, pt. 302.50

GX-4 - Cannon, "Genl Taylor Never Surrenders" inscribed in semicircle around cannon - vine & grape form a semicircular frame containing the inscription "A Little More Grape Capt Bragg," vertically ribbed w/heavy medial ribbing, plain lip, pontil, olive green, pt. 2,805.00

GX-8A - Sailboat (sloop) w/pennant on waves surrounded w/large oval frame - eight-point star w/three-pointed ornaments surrounded w/large oval frame, smooth edges, plain lip, pontil, aqua, ½ pt. 220.00

GX-14 - "Murdock" in semi-circle - "&·-Cassel" in two straight lines, beneath rectangular band of heavy diagonal ribbing & below that a wider band of heavy vertical ribs extend to the base - "Zanesville" in semi-circle & "Ohio" in straight line, below ribbing similar to obverse, vertically ribbed edges w/narrow

medial rib, plain lip, pontil, light bluish green, ca. 1830-37, pt. 1,760.00

GX-15 - "Summer" Tree - "Winter" Tree, plain lip, smooth edges, pontil, light olive green, pt. 324.50

GX-19 - Summer Tree - Winter Tree, plain lip, smooth edges, pontil, golden olive amber, qt. 770.00

GX-21 - Early American steamboat w/paddle wheel & "The American" above & "System" below in the water - "Use Me But Do Not Abuse Me" in semicircle above sheaf of grain, herringbone ribbing on edges, plain lip, pontil mark, pale yellowish green, pt. 4,180.00

GXI-11 - Prospector w/tools & cane standing on oblong frame - American Eagle w/pennant above oval frame, aqua, pt. 70.00

GXI-22 - "For Pike's Peak" above prospector w/short staff & pack standing on oblong frame - American Eagle w/long pennant above oblong frame, aqua, pt. 82.50

GXI-50 - "For Pike's Peak" above prospector w/tools & cane - Hunter shooting stag, molded collar, plain edges, olive green, pt. 550.00

GXII-2 - Clasped hands, all inside shield, w/ "Waterford" above - American Eagle above oval frame, light yellow w/an olive tone, qt. 852.50

GXII-6 - Clasped hands above oval, all inside shield - American Eagle above oval frame, yellowish green, qt. 137.50

GXII-15 - Clasped hands above oval, all inside shield, w"Union" above - American Eagle above frame w/"E. Wormser C ("o" of Co just outside frame), flat collar, narrow beveled edge, aqua, qt. 110.00

GXII-31 - Clasped hands above oval, all inside shield - American Eagle above oval, golden amber, ½ pt. 154.00

GXII-37 - Clasped hands above oval all inside shield w/ "Union" above shield obverse & reverse, aqua, qt. ...55.00

GXII-38 - Clasped hands above oval, all inside shield w/ "Union" above - large cannon & American flag, smooth base, collared lip, aqua, qt. 52.50

GXII-40 - Clasped hands above oval w/ "FA & Co.," all inside shield w/"Union" above - Small cannon & large American flag, smooth base, aqua, pt. 90.00

GXII-43 - Clasped hands above square & compass above oval

w/"Union" all inside shield -
American Eagle, calabash, round
collar, deep golden amber, qt. 242.00
GXIII-3 - Girl wearing a full-length skirt
& hat & riding a bicycle - American
Eagle w/head turned right above
oval frame embossed w/"A & DH.C,"
smooth edges, collared lip,
aqua, qt. 137.50
GXIII-8 - Sailor dancing a hornpipe on
an eight-board hatch cover, above a
long rectangular bar - banjo player
sitting on a long bench, smooth
edges, plain lip, pontil mark, aqua,
½ pt. 115.00
GXIII-13 - Soldier wearing a spiked
helmet - rectangular frame enclosing
"Balt. MD." below, smooth edges,
plain lip, pontil mark, yellowish olive
green, ca. 1860-80, pt......................825.00
GXIII-22 - Flora Temple obverse,
plain reverse, smooth edges, small
handle, ginger ale w/olive tone, ca.
1860-80, pt.......................................467.50
GXIII-35 - Sheaf of Grain w/rake &
pitchfork crossed behind sheaf -
"Westford Glass Co., Westford
Conn," smooth sides, reddish
amber, pt...110.00
GXIII-35 - Sheaf of Grain w/rake &
pitchfork crossed behind sheaf -
"Westford Glass Co., Westford
Conn," plain lip, smooth edges,
yellowish amber, ca. 1860-72,
pt...132.00
GXIII-36 - Sheaf of Grain w/rake &
pitchfork crossed behind sheaf &
five-pointed star centered between
rake & pitchfork handles - "Westford
Glass Co., Westford Conn," plain lip,
smooth edges, reddish amber, pt. ...143.00
GXIII-37 - Sheaf of Grain w/rake &
pitchfork crossed behind sheaf -
"Westford Glass Co., Westford
Conn," smooth sides, deep yellow-
ish olive, ca. 1857-60, ½ pt. 907.50
GXIII-37 - Sheaf of Grain w/rake &
pitchfork crossed behind sheaf -
"Westford Glass Co., Westford
Conn," smooth sides, deep golden
amber, ca. 1860-73, ½ pt.................121.00
GXIII-55 - Anchor w/fork-ended
pennants inscribed "Isabella" &
"Glass Works" on obverse - three-
quarter view of glasshouse, plain lip,
smooth edges, aqua, qt. 121.00
GXIII-64 - Anchor w/cable - plain
reverse, smooth edges, round collar
w/lower bevel, amber, qt...................55.00
GXIII-75 - Key at center, plain
reverse, wide bevel each side to
mold seam, narrow round collar,
aqua, pt..65.00

GXIV-1 - "Traveler's Companion"
arched above & below star formed
by a circle of eight small triangles -
Sheaf of Grain w/rake & pitchfork
crossed behind, applied flat collar,
seamed base, deep golden amber,
ca. 1860-72, qt. 132.00
GXIV-1 - "Traveler's Companion"
arched above & below star formed
by a circle of eight small triangles -
Sheaf of Grain w/rake & pitchfork
crossed behind, crude sloping
collared mouth, smooth base, olive
amber, qt...104.50
GXIV-1 - "Traveler's Companion"
arched above & below star formed
by a circle of eight small triangles -
Sheaf of Grain w/rake & pitchfork
crossed behind, applied flat collar,
seamed base, yellowish olive,
ca. 1860-73, qt. 143.00
GXIV-2 - "Traveler's Companion"
arched above & below star formed
by a circle of eight small triangles -
Star like obverse & "Ravenna"
above & "Glass Co" below, applied
flat collar, brilliant golden amber,
qt. 852.00
GXIV-3 - "Traveler's Companion"
arched above & below star formed
by a circle of eight small triangles -
Sheaf of Grain w/rake & pitchfork
crossed behind, deep aqua,
pt. ....110.00 to 160.00
GXIV-8 - "Traveler's" arched above &
"Companion" arched below - plain
reverse, plain lip, aqua, ½ pt............165.00
GXV-7 - "Granite - Glass - Co."
inscribed in three lines - "Stoddard -
NH" inscribed in two lines, smooth
edges, plain lip w/applied double
collar, smooth base, golden amber,
ca. 1860-70, pt. 176.00
GXV-7 - "Granite - Glass - Co."
inscribed in three lines - "Stoddard -
NH" inscribed in two lines, smooth
edges, plain lip w/applied double
collar, smooth base, golden olive
amber, pt...90.00
GXV-23 - "Union Glass Works" in an
arc & - "New London - Ct" in straight
lines below, plain reverse, round
collar w/lower bevel, smooth base,
light bluish green, ca. 1815-30, pt....473.00
Chestnut, forest green, free-blown,
applied mouth, pontil, New England,
ca. 1780-1830, 8⅝" h.......................187.00
Chestnut, yellowish olive, collared
mouth, pontil, New England, ca.
1780-1830, 5¾" h. 132.00
Chestnut, yellowish olive, collared
mouth, pontil, New England, ca.
1780-1830, 9⅝" h. 154.00

Chestnut, ten-diamond, amber, short
cylindrical neck w/flat flared rim,
Zanesville, Ohio, 4¾" h. 3,410.00
Chestnut, ten-diamond, amber, short
flaring cylindrical neck, fire polished
pontil, 4⅝" h. 1,210.00

Ten-Diamond Chestnut Flask

Chestnut, ten-diamond, light green,
short flaring cylindrical neck,
sheared lip, fire polished pontil,
4⅝" h. (ILLUS.) 3,410.00

Chestnut, 16 swirled ribs, aqua,
Mantua, Ohio, 6" h. 165.00
Chestnut, 16 vertical ribs, aqua,
5⅝" h..137.50
Chestnut, 18 swirled ribs, pale green,
Midwestern, 6½" h. 192.50

Ribbed Chestnut Flask

Chestnut, 18 vertical ribs, pale green,
sheared lip, Midwestern, minor
stains, wear & scratches, 7" h.
(ILLUS.) 126.50
Chestnut, 24 broken swirled ribs,
amber, applied lip, pontil, 7¼" h.......660.00
Chestnut, 24 swirled ribs, red amber,
sheared lip, 4⅞" h. 130.00
Chestnut, 24 swirled ribs, aqua,
Zanesville, Ohio, 7½" h. 550.00

Chestnut, 24 swirled ribs, golden
honey amber, applied lip, pontil,
8" h..1,760.00
Chestnut, 24 vertical ribs, deep
amber, sheared lip, Zanesville,
Ohio, 4⅞" h. 247.50
Chestnut, 24 vertical ribs, dark amber
brown, sheared & fire polished lip,
pontil, 6½" h. 275.00
Chestnut, 24 vertical ribs, golden
amber, Zanesville, Ohio, 4¾" h........275.00
Chestnut, checkered diamond design,
clear, sheared lip, 6⅞" h. 1,100.00
Pitkin, 16 slightly swirled ribs, amber,
half post neck w/sheared lip, pontil,
5½" h...275.00
Pitkin, 24 vertical ribs, golden amber,
sheared mouth, pontil, Midwestern,
1820-40, 5" h. 209.00
Pitkin, 24 vertical ribs, light olive
brown, sheared mouth, pontil scar,
Zanesville, 7⅞" h. 385.00
Pitkin, 30 broken ribs swirled to the
left, yellowish olive green, slightly
flared sheared mouth, pontil,
7¼" h...357.50
Pitkin, 30 broken ribs swirled to the
right, light bluish green, sheared
neck, pontil, New England, ca.
1780-1830, 5⅛" h. (some light
interior base stain, tiny mouth
flake) 286.00
Pitkin, 32 broken ribs swirled to the
right, bright medium green, sheared
neck, pontil, ca. 1800-30, 6⅝" h. 467.50
Pitkin, 35 broken ribs swirled, pale
green, sheared lip, pontil, Midwestern, ca. 1800-30, 7⅛" h. 330.00

Ribbed Pitkin Flask

Pitkin, 36 broken swirled ribs, amber,
half post neck w/sheared & fire
polished lip, tubular pontil, 6" h.
(ILLUS.) 770.00
Pitkin, 36 broken swirled ribs, golden
olive amber, half post neck
w/sheared & fire polished lip, pontil,
5¾" h...880.00

Pitkin, 36 broken ribs swirled to the left, yellowish olive, sheared lip, pontil, New England, ca. 1780-1830, 5⅛" h..506.00

Pitkin, 36 broken ribs swirled to the left, yellowish olive green, sheared lip, 5¼" h. 440.00

Pitkin, 36 broken ribs swirled to the right, bright olive green, sheared lip, pontil, New England, ca. 1780-1830, 5¹⁄₁₆" h. 357.50

Pitkin, 36 broken ribs swirled to the right, yellow olive, sheared lip, pontil, New England, ca. 1780-1830, 5⅛" h..385.00

Pitkin, 36 broken ribs swirled to the right, bright yellowish olive, sheared lip, pontil, New England, ca. 1780-1830, 6⅜" h. 341.00

Pitkin, 36 broken ribs swirled to the right, olive green, sheared lip, pontil, New England, ca. 1780-1830, 6⅝" h...330.00

Pitkin, 36 broken swirled ribs, olive, half-post neck, ½ pt., 4⅞" h. 313.50

INKS

Bulbous Master Ink Bottle

Bulbous, master ink, clear glass nearly spherical body w/raised rings flanking the paper label w/"Paul's Safety Ink...," tall stick neck w/tooled rim & original pour spout, ca. 1880-1900, 8¼" h. (ILLUS.) 110.00

Cathedral, six Gothic arch panels, cobalt blue glass, embossed "Carter" around bottom edge, smooth base, qt., 9¾" h. 110.00

Cylindrical, medium sapphire blue, embossed "Harrison's Columbian Ink," applied flared mouth, 1¹³⁄₁₆" d., 4⅛" h..577.50

Cylindrical, medium green glass,

embossed "S. Fine, Blk Ink," inward rolled mouth & pontil scar, ca. 1830-50, 2⅞" h...........................467.50

Cylindrical, master size, light to medium bluish green glass, rounded shoulder embossed "Hover - Phila.," cylindrical neck w/flared lip, 6" h. (professionally cleaned) 176.00

Domed octagonal w/offset neck, aqua glass, "Harrisons - Columbian - Ink," sheared & tooled lip, dug, ca. 1860-75, 1½" h. (light outside & inside content stain) 176.00

Domed w/central neck, medium amber glass, sheared & ground lip, ca. 1870-80, 1⅞" h. (tiny iridescent bruise on inside of lip) 132.00

Domed w/central neck, olive amber, mold blown glass, embossed "Bertinguiot," 2½" d., 2" h. 154.00

House-shaped, aqua glass, embossed "NE - Plus - Ultra - Fluid" on the roof, crudely sheared mouth, pontil, ca. 1860-80, 2⅝" h. 385.00

Octagonal, yellowish olive glass, tooled collared mouth, pontil scar, New England, ca. 1780-1830, 2⅜" d., 2¼" h. 242.00

Square w/central neck, clear glass, "Tinta - American," tooled & rolled lip, ca. 1840-55, 1¾" h. 253.00

Teakettle-type fountain inkwell w/neck extending up at angle from base, cobalt blue glass, ground mouth w/original lid, smooth base, 2" h. 550.00

Teakettle-type fountain inkwell w/neck extending up at angle from base, lime sherbet clambroth opaque glass, ground mouth, smooth base, 3½" d., 2¼" h. 715.00

Teakettle-type fountain inkwell w/neck extending up at angle from base of the tapering hexagonal body, ground lip, deep amethyst glass, ca. 1870-90, 2" h. (two flat chips on lip) 412.50

Teakettle-type fountain inkwell w/neck extending at angle from base of the tapering domical mushroom-form body w/six panels w/bull's-eyes divided by thin ribs, medium yellowish green glass, ground lip w/original metal neck ring, ca. 1870-90, 2¾" h. 935.00

Teakettle-type fountain inkwell w/angled neck extending from base of double-stepped domical octagonal body, attributed to Boston & Sandwich Glass Co., ca. 1870, opaque lime green glass, 2" h. 715.00

Teakettle-type fountain inkwell w/neck extending up at angle from base of tapering hexagonal body, each

Rare Cut Teakettle-form Inkwell

panel cut & polished w/a diamond
design, ground lip w/original brass
lid, turquoise blue glass, ca.
1875-90, 2⅜" h. (ILLUS.) 715.00
Umbrella-type (8-panel cone shape),
amber glass, sheared lip, open
pontil, ca. 1830-50, 2½" h. 175.00
Umbrella-type (8-panel cone shape),
medium amber glass, rolled lip,
open pontil, ca. 1840-55, 2⅜" h.
(few spots of haze) 132.00

Eight-Sided Umbrella Ink

Umbrella-type (8-panel cone shape),
yellow w/amber tone glass, rolled
lip, pontil-scarred base, ca. 1840-55,
minor spotty stain inside, partially
open discolored bubble on base
edge, 2⅜" h. (ILLUS.) 825.00
Umbrella-type (8-panel cone shape),
yellowish olive glass, rolled lip, open
pontil, ca. 1830-50, 2⅜" h. 357.50

Twelve-Sided Umbrella Ink

Umbrella-type (12-panel cone shape),
light green glass, rolled lip, open
pontil, ca. 1840-55, few minor spots
of inside haze, 2⅝" h. (ILLUS.) 242.00

MEDICINES
American (embossed bottle)
Compound - Phila, rectangular
w/paneled sides, aqua, applied
mouth, open pontil, ca. 1845-55,
5⅛" h. (lightly cleaned) 93.50
Angell's (Dr. N.) Rheumatic Gun,
rectangular, deep aqua, applied
mouth, pontiled base, ca. 1850-60,
7⅜" h. (light spotty interior haze) 302.50
Baker's (Dr.) - Pain Panacea,
rectangular, pontil, aqua, 5" h. 100.00
Balsam of Honey, rounded, aqua,
3⅛" h. 55.00
Barnett (E.I.) Magic Cure Liniment,
Easton, PA, rectangular, aqua,
6⅜" h. 26.00
Barrell's Indian Liniment - H.G.O.
Cary, rectangular, aqua,
1 x 1⁹⁄₁₆ x 4¾" 70.00
Bears Oil, pictures walking bear
above "Oil," flared lip, open pontil,
rectangular, aqua, 2¾" h. 450.00
Bennett's (Dr.) Quick Cure - A.L.
Scovill & Co, rectangular, rolled lip,
aqua, 4⅝" h. 31.00

Dr. Blendigo's Celery Tonic

Blendigo's (Dr.) Celery Tonic -
Peptonized - John Schweyer & Co.,
Sole Distributors, Chicago, Ill.,
rectangular w/paneled sides, amber,
tooled lip, ca. 1880-1900, 9½" h.
(ILLUS.) 255.00
Brinkerhoff's Health Restorative, New
York, rectangular, pontil, emerald
green, 7" h. 650.00
Brown's (F.) Ess of Jamaica Ginger
Philada., oval, aqua, 5½" h. 25.00

Brown's Blood Cure - Philadelphia -
M.B.W., U.S.A., yellowish green,
6⅛" h. 130.00

Brunet's Universal Remedy

Brunet's Universal Remedy - Philada,
cylindrical, aqua, applied mouth,
open pontil, overall interior stain, ca.
1845-60, 8" h. (ILLUS.) 264.00
Brunet's (Dr.) Worm Syrup,
rectangular w/beveled corners,
aqua, applied mouth, open pontil,
ca. 1840-55, 6¾" h. (some faint
inside haze) 275.00

Burton's (Dr. W.) Syrup - Philada,
cylindrical, pale green, applied
mouth, pontiled base, ca. 1845-60,
6¼" h. (light inside haze spots) 440.00
Callan's (Prof.) World Renowned
Brazillian (sic) Gum," rectangular,
orangish amber, 4¼" h. 35.00
Cann's Kidney Cure, 1876, clear,
8½" h. 24.00
Celery Compound - Compound (over
a stack of celery), square w/paneled
sides, yellowish amber, tooled lip,
ca. 1880-90, 10" h. 88.00
Clarke's World Famed Blood Mixture,
blue 65.00
Davis' (Perry) Pain Killer, rectangular,
pontil, aqua, 8¼" h. 25.00
Davis Vegetable Pain Killer,
rectangular, aqua, 4⅝" h. 35.00
Dewitts Colic & Cholera Cure - E. C.
Dewitt & Co., Chicago, U.S.A.,
aqua, paper label, 4⅞" h. 30.00
Dewitts (Dr.) Eclectic Cure, W J
Parker & Co, Baltimore, MD,
rectangular, 5⅝" h. 26.00
Fahrney's (Dr.) Health Restorer,
Hagerstown, MD., amber, 7⅛" h. 17.50
Fenner's (Dr. M.M.) Kidney &
Backache Cure, oval, amber, 90%
label, 10⅜" h. 68.00
Fenner's (Dr. M.M.) Peoples

Remedies - Fredonia, N.Y. - U.S.A.
1872-1891, rectangular, blown in
mold, aqua, 1¼ x 2¼ x 7¾" 32.00
Foley's Kidney & Bladder Cure - Foley
& Co. - Chicago, U.S.A., rectan-
gular, amber, paper label, 9½" h. 38.00
Folger's Olosaonian - (Dr Robt. B. -
New-York, rectangular w/deeply
beveled corners, pontil, aqua,
1½ x 2½ x 7¾" 55.00
Freeman's (Dr. Clarkson) Indian
Specific, square, aqua, 5" h. 125.00
Gesteria (Dr. J.), Regulator Gesteria,
amber, 5" h. 20.00
Gould (L.A.), Portland, ME., paper
label w/"White Clover Cream for
Chapped Hands, Sunburn, etc...,"
rectangular, clear, 4½" h. 16.00
Grove's (Dr.) Anodyne for Infants,
Philada., rectangular, aqua, 5½" h.
(w/paper label) 22.00
Hagan's Magnolia Balm, rectangular,
milk white, 5" h. 9.00
Hall's Balsam for the Lungs, John F.
Henry & Co., New York, rectangular,
aqua, 7¾" h. 25.00
Hall's Catarrh Cure, round, aqua,
1⅝" d., 4⅝" h. 15.00
Hanford's (Dr.) Celery Cure or Nerve
Food Cures Rheumatism -
Neuralgia - Insomnia - & C & C,
rectangular w/beveled corners,
rolled lip, pontil, aqua, 1¾ x 2½",
7⅝" h. 45.00
Healy & Bigelow's Kickapoo Cough
Syrup, cylindrical, aqua, 1¼" d.,
6¼" h. 20.00
Hills (embossed H w/arrow) Trade
Mark Dys Pep Cu, Cures Chronic
Dyspepsia, Indiana Drug Specialty
Co., St. Louis & Indianapolis,
rectangular w/fluted corners, amber,
8⅛" h. 110.00
Hobensack's Medicated Worm Syrup,
Philada., rectangular w/indented
panels, aqua, 4½" h. 39.00
Hollis' (Thomas) Balm of America,
round, aqua, 5" h. 18.00
Hooker's (Dr.) Cough and Croup
Syrup, round, aqua, 5⅝" h. 89.00
Hough's (Dr.) Anti Scrofula Syrup,
rectangular, aqua, applied mouth,
open pontil, ca. 1845-60, 9½" h.
(light inside stain, small stress
fissure in neck) 176.00
Hunter's (H.C:) Palm Lotion, Marlboro,
Mass., paper label reading
"Chapped Hands, Sunburn, Chafing
& ...," rectangular, amber, 5¼" h. 38.00
Hyatt's - Infallible - Life Balsam, N.Y.,
rectangular w/beveled corners,
smooth base, deep aqua, 9½" h.
(minor lip bruise) 140.00

James' (Dr.) Cherry Tar Syrup, Pittsburgh, Penna, U.S.A., aqua, 5¾" h.................................12.50

James (Dr. H.) Cannabis Indica, Crabbock & Co., Proprietors, No. 1032 Pace St. Phila. Pa., cylindrical, aqua, applied lip, 7¾" h..................................302.50

Kauffman's (Dr. J.) Angeline Internal Rheumatism Cure, Hamilton, Ohio, deep amethyst, 7⅝" h. 25.00

Kilmer's (Dr.) Female Remedy, Bing- hamton, N.Y., rectangular, aqua, w/paper label & contents, 8⅜" h. 300.00

Kilmer's (Dr.) Indian Cough Remedy Consumption Oil, Binghamton, N.Y. U.S.A., rectangular, aqua, 5½" h. 25.00

Kilmer's (Dr.) Ocean Weed Heart Remedy, The Blood Specific, rectangular, embossed heart, aqua, 8½" h.....................175.00

Kilmer's (Dr.) Swamp-Root Kidney Cure, Binghamton, N.Y., Sample Bottle, cylindrical, aqua, 3⅛" h...........20.00

Kilmer's (Dr.) Swamp-Root Kidney, Liver & Bladder Cure, Binghamton, N.Y., Sample Bottle, round, 3¼" h. 12.00

Kilmer's (Dr.) Swamp-Root Kidney, Liver & Bladder Cure, London, E.C., rectangular w/beveled corners, aqua, 7" h...........................25.00

Kilmer's (Dr.) Swamp-Root Kidney, Liver & Bladder Cure, rectangular, amethyst, 7" h. 45.00

K.K. Cures Bright's Disease and Cystitis, rectangular, aqua, 7½" h. 25.00

Lindsey's - Blood + Searcher - Hollidaysburg (Pennsylvania), rectangular, aqua, qt. 89.00

Lorman's (Prof.) Indian Oil Philada., PA., rectangular, aqua, 5¼" h...........21.00

Low's (Prof.) Magnetic Liniment, Philada, Pa., rectangular, aqua, 6⅛" h................................18.00

McLean's (Dr. J.H.) Strengthening Cordial & Blood Purifier, oval, aqua, 8" h....................................45.00

Miles' (Dr.) Restorative Nervine, aqua, 8½" h....................................15.00

Myers (Dr.) Bilious King - Smith Myers & Co., square w/beveled corners, amber, applied mouth, ca. 1870-80, 9" h. (ILLUS. top next column) 93.50

National Remedy Company, New York, rectangular, amber, w/paper label, 7⅝" h. 25.00

Pierce's (Dr.) Anuric Tablets for Kidneys and Backache, cylindrical, aqua, 3½" h.....................15.00

Pierce's (Dr.) Golden Medical Discovery - R.V. Pierce, M.D. - Buffalo, N.Y., rectangular, amber, 8⅜" h................................40.00

Dr. Myers Bilious King

Polar Star Cough Cure, embossed star, aqua...........................25.00

Ransom's Hive Syrup & Tolu, square, aqua, 3½" h.......................15.00

Rheumatic Syrup

Rheumatic (embossed tree) Trade Mark Syrup 1882 - R.S. Co., Rochester, N.Y., rectangular w/paneled sides, medium amber, slightly tilted applied mouth, ca. 1870-80, 9¾" h. (ILLUS.) 176.00

Richter (F.A.) & Co., New York (embossed anchor) Pain-Expeller, Reg. U.S. Patt. Off. For Rheu- matism, Gout, Neuralgia, Colds, etc., rectangular w/beveled corners, aqua, 4⅞" h..........................12.50

Rowand's - Tonic Mixture - Vegetable - Febrifuge - Philad, six-sided, open pontil, aqua, 5¾" h. ....140.00 to 180.00

Schrage's Rheumatic Cure, Swanson Rheumatic Cure Company, Chicago, aqua....................................39.00

Seabury's Cough Balsam, open
pontil, aqua, 1¼" d., 4¾" h...40.00 to 50.00
Simonds Pain Cure, rectangular,
aqua, 4¾" h..15.00
Sparks Perfect Health (embossed
man) for Kidney & Liver Diseases,
amber, 9⅜" h. 50.00
Swaim's Vermifuge - Fever -
Dysentery - Cholera Morbus -
Dyspepsia, paneled sides, aqua,
thin flared lip, open pontil, ca.
1835-45, 4¼" h. 247.50
Sykes' (Dr.) Sure Cure For Catarrh,
medium apple green, 6⅝" h. 65.00
Thatcher's (Dr.) Liver & Blood Syrup,
Chattanooga, Tenn., amber, sample
size, 3" h. 28.00
Thatcher's (Dr.) Liver & Blood Syrup,
Chattanooga, Tenn., amber, 8⅜" h....45.00
Thomson's - Compound - Syrup of
Tar for Consumption - Philada,
rectangular w/paneled sides, aqua,
applied mouth, open pontil, ca.
1840-55, 5¾" h. 60.50
Turlington's (Robt.) Balsam of Life,
paneled pear-shape, flared lip, open
pontil, aqua, England, 2⅝" h. 93.50
(Warner's) Log Cabin - Extract,
Rochester, NY., three indented
panels on front, flat back, dark
yellow amber, 8⅛" h. 95.00
Warner's Safe Cure, London, emerald
green, ½ pt., 7½" h. 80.00
Warner's Safe Cure, Melbourne,
w/safe, oval tooled blob lip, smooth
base, amber, 1880-90, 7" h. 85.00
Warner's Safe Cure, Melbourne,
w/safe, reddish amber, 9½" h. 45.00
Warner's Safe Cure (safe) Pressburg,
oval, olive green, 9½" h. 1,925.00

Warner's Safe Diabetes Cure

Warner's Safe Diabetes Cure - Pressburg, w/safe, amber, applied mouth,
tiny lip ding, 9½" h. (ILLUS.) 2,640.00

Warner's Safe Kidney & Liver Cure,
Rochester, N.Y., w/reversed (or
"left-handed") picture of safe, oval,
amber, 9¾" h. 80.00
Warner's Safe Nervine, Frankfurt A/M,
w/safe, oval, amber, applied mouth,
9¼" h..1,375.00
Warner's Safe Rheumatic Cure
Rochester, NY., U.S.A., w/safe,
oval, light yellow, 9½" h. (spotty
haze) 40.00
Wishart's (L.Q.C.) - Pine Tree Tar
Cordial Phila. - (embossed pine
tree) Patent 1859, square w/beveled
corners, emerald green, 8" h. 242.00

Wishart's Pine Tree Tar Cordial

Wishart's (L.Q.C.) - Pine Tree Tar
Cordial Phila. - (embossed pine
tree) Patent 1859, square w/beveled
corners, medium bluish green, 8" h.
(ILLUS.) 100.00
Wishart's (L.Q.C.) - Pine Tree Tar
Cordial Phila. - (embossed pine
tree) Patent 1859, square w/beveled
corners, yellowish green, 8" h.........121.00
Wishart's (L.Q.C.) Pine Tree Tar
Cordial Phila. - Trade (embossed
pine tree) Mark, square w/beveled
corners, sapphire blue, tooled lip,
9¾" h. (some light scratching on
back panel) 797.50
Wistar's (Dr.) - Balsam of - Wild
Cherry - John D. Park - Cincinnati,
Ohio, octagonal, deep aqua,
6½" h...30.00
Wynkoop's Katharismic Sarsaparilla -
New York, rectangular, medium
sapphire blue, applied mouth, iron
pontil, lightly cleaned, ca. 1845-60,
10" h. (ILLUS. top next page) 7,150.00
Zollickoffer's Anti Rheumatic Cordial -
Philada, rectangular w/paneled
sides, yellowish olive amber, applied

Wynkoop's Katharismic Sarsaparilla

mouth, open pontil, ca. 1840-50,
6⅜" h...1,595.00

MILK

Individual Cream-Size Bottles

Amber, embossed "Golden Royal,"
½" gal..8.50
Brilliant grass green, embossed
"Return to - H.B. Day," tapering
cylindrical-form w/tooled square
collared mouth, smooth base,
10¼" h..198.00
Clear, individual cream-size,
enameled "Blanding's - Greenville,
Mich. (ILLUS. left) 21.00
Clear, individual cream-size,
enameled "Country Club Dairy"
(ILLUS. right) 24.00
Clear, individual cream-size, enam-
eled "McDonald's White House
Dairy" (ILLUS. left, top next column)..21.00
Clear, individual cream-size,
enameled "Suncrest Farms and
Mowrer's, Inc." (ILLUS. right, top
next column) 26.00
Clear, "Maui - Haleakala Dairy," qt. 30.00
Clear, "Oahu - Moanaloa Dairy,"
12 oz. 12.00

McDonald's & Suncrest Bottles

Clear, embossed "Registered Strictly
Pure Milk - Bottled by the Empire
State Dairy Company (state seal) -
502 & 506 Broadway, Brooklyn -
Trade Mark," tooled lip, smooth
base, ca. 1900-20, qt., 9" h. 66.00

Robinson & Woolworth Bottle

Clear, embossed "Robinson &
Woolworth - 1667 B'way, N.Y. - This
Bottle to be Washed and Returned
Not to be Bought or Sold," base
w/"Whiteman Maker - 144 Chamber
St., New York," tooled lip w/original
metal lid stamped "Jan. 5.1875,
Patd. April 3.1889," wire closure,
smooth base, qt., 8½" h. (ILLUS.)......99.00
Clear, embossed "F.K. Wards - Milk
Preserving Jar - Sealed Stopper -
Patents 1890 & 1892 - When Empty
Return to - Ward's Alderney Milk
P & C Association - Washington,
D.C. - Wash Clean When Empty,"
embossed on smooth base "This Jar
Has Been Stolen If Offered For
Sale" & on lip "Refuse A Broken
Seal" & cow's head, w/original glass
lid & wire bail, ca. 1890-95, pt.......1,155.00

Clear, embossed "Woodrow Wilson
Dairy, Palmyria, WI.," pt. 10.00
Clear, "Your Dairy New London, WI,"
red paint, qt. 10.00

MINERAL WATERS

Congress & Empire Spring Co.

Caladonia (sic) Spring, Wheelock, Vt.,
Saratoga-type, yellowish amber, qt.,
9½" h..660.00
Congress & Empire Spring Co.,
Hotchkiss' Sons, "C," New York,
Saratoga, N.Y., Congress Water,
smooth base, applied mouth,
emerald green, ca. 1865-75, pt.,
7¾" h. (ILLUS.) 170.00

Congress & Empire Spring Co., "C,"
Saratoga, N.Y., Congress Water,
smooth base, applied mouth, deep
emerald green, ca. 1865-75, pt.
7⅝" h. (dug, fair amount of
scratching & scuffing on the
outside) 121.00
Geyser Spring. Saratoga Springs.
State of New York. - "The Saratoga"
Spouting Spring, smooth base,
applied mouth, bluish aqua, ca.
1865-75, qt., 9⅜" h. 99.00
Highrock Congress Spring - motif of
rock - C & W, Saratoga, N.Y.,
smooth base, applied mouth, teal
blue, ca. 1850-70, pt., 7⅝" h. 253.00
Hutchinson & Co., Celebrated Mineral
Water, Chicago, iron pontil, applied
mouth, medium cobalt blue w/tiny
seed bubbles, ca. 1845-55,
7¼" h..253.00
Knowlton (D.A.), Saratoga, N.Y.,
smooth base, applied mouth, deep
olive amber, ca. 1860-70, qt. 110.00
Meincke & Ebberwein, 1882,
Savannah, Geo., Mineral "M&E,"
Water, smooth base, applied mouth,
electric cobalt blue, ca. 1865-75,
7⅞" h. (lightly cleaned) 66.00

John Ryan Excelsior Mineral Water

Ryan (John) Excelsior Mineral Water,
Savannah, Ga., 1859, Union Glass
Works, Phila. This bottle is never
sold, smooth base, applied mouth,
cobalt blue, lightly cleaned, ca.
1865-75, 7⅛" h. (ILLUS.) 121.00
Weston (G.W.) & Co., Saratoga, N.Y.,
pontil mark, applied mouth, olive
green, ca. 1855-65, qt., 9⅝" h. 187.00

NURSING

Blown Nursing Bottle

Aqua, mold-blown glass w/eighteen
swirled ribs, Midwestern, 6½" l...........66.00
Aqua, mold-blown glass w/twelve
vertical ribs, flattened ovoid shape
tapering at base, slightly flared lip,
Midwestern, 8¼" l. 60.50
Aqua, pressed glass, "Burr - Boston,"
embossed medallion.........................82.50
Clear, mold-blown glass, thick &
heavy flask-form, pontil mark,
sheared lip, 6¾" h. 55.00
Clear, pressed glass, "Corning -
Pyrex," 4 oz., w/original wrapper 10.00

Clear, pressed glass, tilted neck,
    embossed "Empire," ca. 1910............12.00
Clear, pressed glass, embosssed
    "Rexall" & w/a stork............................15.00
Deep cobalt blue, mold-blown glass,
    flask-form, pontil mark, sheared lip,
    America, ca. 1830-50, 7¼" h.
    (ILLUS.) 231.00
Greenish aqua, mold-blown glass,
    flask-form, diamond pattern, pontil
    mark, sheared lip, America, ca.
    1830-50, 6½" h. 88.00
Pale green, mold-blown glass
    w/expanded ogival pattern, flattened
    ovoid shape tapering at base,
    slightly flared lip, Midwestern,
    6¼" l..27.50
Pale green, mold-blown glass
    w/twenty vertical ribs, flattened
    ovoid shape tapering at base,
    slightly flared lip, Midwestern,
    7" l...192.50
Yellowish green w/black amber neck
    & shoulder, mold-blown glass,
    flattened ovoid shape tapering at
    base, slightly flared lip, sheared &
    fire polished lip, 7⅛" l.......................225.50

PICKLE BOTTLES & JARS

Cathedral Pickle with Lattice Windows

Aqua, four-sided, cathedral-type
    w/Gothic arch windows, rolled lip,
    smooth base, Willington Glass
    Works, West Willington, Connecti-
    cut, ca. 1860-72, 11⅞" h. (light
    interior haze)....................................247.50
Aqua, four-sided, cathedral-type
    w/Gothic arch windows w/diamond
    lattice, smooth base, rolled lip,
    America, ca. 1865-75, small open
    bubble on one corner at base,
    13¾" h. (ILLUS.) 203.50
Bright yellow green, barrel-shaped
    w/embossed rows of rings at top &

Barrel-Shaped Pickle Jar

base, pontil mark, tooled lip,
    America, ca. 1860-70, 9½" h.
    (ILLUS.) 148.50
Clear, cathedral-type, 13" h. 165.00
Deep aqua, four-sided, cathedral-type
    w/Gothic arch windows w/diamond
    lattice, smooth base, rolled lip,
    America, ca. 1865-75, 11" h. (overall
    milky stain inside) 198.00
Deep aqua, four-sided, cathedral-type
    w/Gothic arch windows w/diamond
    lattice, smooth base, rolled lip,
    America, ca. 1865-75, 13¾" h. 275.00

Large Cathedral Pickle Jar

Greenish aqua, four-sided, cathedral-
    type w/Gothic arch windows, smooth
    base, rolled lip, America, ca.
    1865-75, 8¾" h. (ILLUS.) 143.00
Light green, four-sided, cathedral-type
    w/Gothic arch windows, iron pontil,
    rolled lip, America, ca. 1855-65,
    11½" h..297.00
Medium green, four-sided, cathedral-
    type w/Gothic arch windows, rolled
    collared mouth, pontil scar, Willing-

ton Glass Works, West Willington,
Connecticut, ca. 1840-60,
13⅝" h..2,310.00

POISONS

Poison Bottle with Hobnails

Clear, blown half post w/hobnails,
applied flared lip, 4¾" h. (ILLUS.) 27.50
Clear, flattened flask shape w/overall
small square raised knobs, sheared
mouth, pontil, pint, ca. 1850.............231.00
Cobalt blue, six-sided, embossed
"POISON" & ribbed design,
3½" h..28.00
Cobalt blue, six-sided, embossed
"POISON" & ribbed design,
5½" h..29.00
Cobalt blue, rectangular, embossed
"POISON" & ribbed design, 6" h. 29.00
Green, six-sided, embossed
"POISON" & ribbed design, 3¼" h. 21.00
Green, six-sided, embossed
"POISON" & ribbed design, 6" h. 24.00

WHISKEY & OTHER SPIRITS

Black Label Beer

Beer, "American Brewing Co.,
Bennett, PA," embossed w/eagle &
flags, blob top, light amber, pt...........25.00
Beer, "Black Label Beer," slightly
rounded cylindrical form w/tapering
neck, paper label, w/screw cap,
amber, 18" h. (ILLUS.) 5.50
Beer, "Bunker Hill Lager, Charles-
town, Mass.," w/lightning stopper,
golden amber, pt...............................20.00
Beer, "Golden Gate Bottling Works,
San Francisco," embossed bear
holding a glass, blob top, reddish
amber, ½ pt.....................................240.00
Beer, "Gold Medal, C. Maurer,"
applied lip, golden amber, ½ pt.........85.00

Heineken Lager Beer

Beer, "Heineken Lager Beer," green
w/paper labels, 18" h. (ILLUS.) 5.50
Beer, "Hinckel Brewing, Albany,
Manchester, Boston" embossed in
script, smoky golden amber, pt..........25.00
Beer, "Kerns (E.L.)," w/embossed
moose head, greenish aqua, pt. 25.00
Beer, D. Lagrange, Moravia, NY.,"
whittled neck, lightning stopper, honey
amber, pt. 20.00
Beer, "Norfolk Brewing Co., Boston,"
amber, pt. 25.00
Beer, "Rainier Beer, Seattle," blob top,
light amber, miniature bottle 80.00
Beer, "Seitz Bros., Easton PA,"
embossed w/large "S" on back, blob
top, light amber, pt............................20.00
Bourbon, "Old Crow Bourbon Rawlins
Wyoming Robt. Freedman," flask-
shape, amber, pt. 300.00
Bourbon, "Phoenix Old Bourbon, Naber,
Alfs and Brune, San Francisco, Sole
Proprts," & an embossed eagle,
orangish amber, ½ pt. 200.00
Case gin, "Wistar's Club House," iron
pontil, single collared lip, red puce,
qt. 750.00

Case gin, blown half post, polychrome floral enameling, light olive green, pewter lip & cap, 6⅝" h. (minor stain)..495.00

Case gin, dip-molded, square tapered-form, mushroom mouth, pontil scar, yellowish olive, ca. 1780-1830, 9½" h. 104.50

Case gin, dip-molded, tapering square-form, w/rolled & flared mouth, pontil, deep yellow olive, 5¼" d., 16⅞" h.........770.00

Gin, "London Jockey Club House Gin," embossed horse & jockey, square w/beveled corners, sloping collared mouth, smooth base, bright green, 9" h. 275.00

Gin, "Olive Tree," tapered square-form, crude sloping collared mouth, smooth base, Netherlands, olive green, ca. 1860-80, 9¾" h. 242.00

Schnapps, "Udolpho Wolfe's," yellowish amber 35.00

Schnapps, "Udolpho Wolfe's - Aromatic - Schnapps - Schiedam," Stoddard-type, open pontil, crude, sandy amber, qt. 65.00

Spirits, applied seal w/"David Provost 1723," squat onion-form, free blown, applied collar, olive green, 7⅜" h. 1,925.00

Spirits, demijohn,"Saml Bowne 1759" on applied seal, pontil, applied lip, olive green, 8¾" h. (rough lip, minor wear & scratches) 880.00

Spirits, free-blown, bladder-shaped, "Thomas Morley 1730" on applied seal, green..1,500.00

Globular Spirits Bottles

Spirits, globular, tall neck, twenty-four swirled ribs, pontil mark, applied lip, Zanesville, Ohio, amber, 7¼" h. (ILLUS. left)......................................660.00

Spirits, globular, tall neck, twenty-four swirled ribs, pontil mark, applied lip, Zanesville, Ohio, golden honey amber, 8" h. (ILLUS. right) 1,760.00

Spirits, pumpkin seed, marked "Union Pacific Tea Company 1873" & embossed w/two men on an elephant, clear, ½ pt. 135.00

Spirits, rectangular w/beveled corners, ground mouth w/pewter collar & cap, pontil scar, clear ground decorated w/red, blue, yellow & white enameled bird & florals, 5½" h. 313.50

Spirits, squat, cylindrical-form w/sheared mouth w/string rim, free-blown, pontil scar, olive green, Netherlands, 1700-30, 4½" d., 5⅝" h..385.00

Spirits, squat onion-form, free-blown, sheared mouth w/string rim, pontil scar, dark yellowish olive, England, ca. 1700-30, 6" d., 6" h. 418.00

Spirits, squat onion-form, free-blown, tooled mouth w/an applied wide neck ring, pontil scar, yellowish olive, Netherlands, 1700-30, 5½" d., 7⅛" h..2,530.00

Whiskey, "Ambrosial" on applied seal, flattened chestnut-form w/applied mouth w/ring, pontil scar, golden amber, 9" h. (interior stain spots throughout) 132.00

Whiskey, "E.G. Booz's Old Cabin Whiskey," cabin-shaped, golden amber, 7⅞" h. 440.00

Whiskey, "Chapin & Gore Chicago Sour Mash 1867," barrel-shaped, inside threaded neck, amber (no stopper)..125.00

Whiskey, "Chestnut Grove," chestnut flask-shaped w/applied handle, open pontil, dark amber 170.00

Whiskey, "Chestnut Grove Whiskey," flattened globular-form, pontil, applied mouth ring & handle, golden amber, 8⅞" h. 143.00

Whiskey, "Cyrus Eaton Denver - One Quart You Bet," blob top, light amber, qt...750.00

Whiskey, Goodman (Geo.) Wholesale, Paducah, KY, embossed w/sign of the Red Rock, clear, ½ gal. 90.00

Whiskey, Pierce (S.S.) Co., Est., 1831, Inc. 1891, Boston, embossed shield w/lion & eagle logo, clear, ½ gal. 45.00

Whiskey, mold-blown, globular form, 14 swirled ribs, light blue, Zanesville, Ohio, 8¼" h. 605.00

Whiskey, mold-blown, globular form, 16 swirled ribs, aqua, Midwestern, 7⅛" h...148.50

Whiskey, mold-blown, globular form, 24 melon ribs, aqua, Zanesville, Ohio, 7½" h. 192.50

Whiskey, mold-blown, globular form, 24 swirled ribs, amber, Zanesville, Ohio, 7¼" h. 660.00

Whiskey, mold-blown, globular form,
24 swirled ribs, cornflower blue,
Zanesville, Ohio, 8¼" h. 5,170.00
Whiskey, mold-blown, globular form,
24 swirled ribs, golden honey
amber, Zanesville, Ohio, 8" h. 1,760.00

(End of Bottles Section)

CAMBRIDGE

Statuesque Line Compote

*The Cambridge Glass Company was
founded in Ohio in 1901. Numerous pieces
are now sought, especially those designed
by Arthur J. Bennett, including Crown
Tuscan. Other productions included
crystal animals, "Black Amethyst," "blanc
opaque," and other types of colored glass.
The firm was finally closed in 1954. It
should not be confused with the New
England Glass Co., Cambridge, Massachusetts.*

NEAR
CUT

TUSCAN

Various Cambridge Marks

Ashtray, shell-shaped, pressed
Caprice patt., Moonlight
(pale blue) $9.00
Ashtray, Statuesque line, Royal Blue
(dark blue) bowl, clear Nude Lady
stem 135.00
Banana bowl, pressed Caprice patt.,
Crystal...195.00
Basket, etched Rose Point patt.,
Crystal, 7" h. 750.00
Bonbon, upright handles, pressed
Caprice patt., Crystal, 5" sq. 12.00

Bonbon, handled, Inverted Strawberry
patt., clear, 5½" 40.00
Bowl, 5 x 12½", Decagon line, etched
Vintage patt., Crystal 65.00
Bowl, 5¾" d., Strawberry (No. 2780)
line, clear 38.00
Bowl, 6" d., Inverted Strawberry patt.,
clear 15.00
Bowl, 10½" d., pressed Caprice patt.,
clear & frosted....................................35.00
Bowl, 11", etched Chantilly patt.,
No. 400, Crystal 85.00
Bowl, 11" d., rolled rim, etched Rose
Point patt., No. 3400/2, Crystal........125.00
Bowl, 12" d., footed, etched Apple
Blossom patt., Amber 70.00
Bowl, 12" d., crimped rim, footed,
Caprice patt., Cobalt Blue..................85.00
Bowl, 12" oval, pressed Caprice patt.,
Mandarin Gold (medium yellow) 125.00
Bowl, 12" d., etched Rose Point patt.,
Crystal...85.00
Bowl, 12½" d., bell-shaped, four-
footed, pressed Caprice patt.,
No. 62, Moonlight...............................85.00
Bowl, 13½" d., crimped rim, footed,
pressed Caprice patt., Mandarin
Gold 75.00
Bowl, salad, 13½" d., pressed Caprice
patt., Cobalt Blue 110.00
Bowl w/underplate: 9½" d. bowl
w/ruffled rim, 10½" d. underplate;
Strawberry (No. 2780) line, clear,
2 pcs. 98.00
Brandy, Tally-Ho line, Carmen (ruby
red) bowl, clear stem 38.00
Bridge set: four tumblers & tray
w/center handle; etched Rose Point
patt., Crystal, 5 pcs. 250.00
Butter dish, cov., pressed Caprice
patt., Crystal.....................................359.00
Butter dish, cov., Gadroon (No. 3500)
line, Crystal 40.00
Butter dish, cov., Thistle (No. 2766)
line, green 90.00
Cake plate, handled, etched Rose
Point patt., Crystal, 12" d. 85.00
Candleholders, two-light, etched
Apple Blossom patt., Mandarin
Gold, pr. 50.00
Candleholders, two-light, pressed
Caprice patt., w/prisms, Crystal,
6" h., pr. 140.00
Candlesticks, Pristine line, No. 499
Calla Lily design, Amber, 6" h., pr......75.00
Candlesticks, Pristine line, No. 499,
Calla Lily design, Crystal, 6" h.,
pr...54.00
Candlesticks, etched Diane patt.,
Crystal, 2½" h., pr. 35.00
Candlesticks, three-light, etched Rose
Point patt., Crystal, pr. .....150.00 to 200.00

Candlesticks w/rams' heads, etched
Rose Point patt., No. 3500/74,
Crystal, 4" h., pr. 180.00
Candlesticks, two-light, keyhole stem,
etched Wildflower patt., Crystal, pr. ...75.00
Candy box, cover w/sterling silver
finial, etched Chantilly patt., Crystal,
three-part, 7" l. 90.00
Candy box, cov., footed, Sea Shell
line, Charleton decoration, milk
white, 6" h. 85.00
Candy dish, heart-shaped, pressed
Caprice patt., Moonlight, 5"................35.00
Candy dish, cov., Honeycomb line,
Rubina 245.00
Champagne, etched Portia patt.,
Crystal..21.00
Champagne, etched Rose Point patt.,
Crystal..24.50
Champagne, Statuesque line, Car-
men bowl, clear Nude lady stem......125.00
Champagne, etched Wildflower patt.,
Crystal, 6 oz.....................................24.50
Champagnes, hollow stem, etched
Laurel Wreath patt., Crystal, set
of 6...90.00
Cigarette holder, Mt. Vernon line,
No. 66 on No. 1066 stem,
Carmen 88.00
Cigarette set: cov. box & two
ashtrays; Statuesque line, Cobalt
Blue box & ashtrays, clear Nude
Lady stem, 3 pcs...............................825.00
Claret, etched Rose Point patt.,
Crystal..55.00
Claret, etched Wildflower patt.,
Crystal..40.00
Cocktail, etched Chantilly patt.,
Crystal..9.50
Cocktail, Mt. Vernon line, Crystal,
3½ oz..9.00
Cocktail, Statuesque line, Carmen
bowl, clear Nude Lady stem 120.00
Cocktail, Statuesque line, Dianthus
(light pink) bowl, clear Nude Lady
stem, 3 oz. 150.00
Cocktail, Statuesque line, Royal Blue
bowl, clear Nude Lady stem 110.00
Cocktail, etched Wildflower patt.,
Crystal..20.00
Cocktail shaker w/original glass top,
etched Blossom Time patt.,
Crystal..85.00
Cocktail shaker w/original glass top,
etched Rose Point patt., Crystal,
32 oz..185.00
Cocktail shaker w/original top, Tally-
Ho line, Cobalt Blue 175.00
Compote, open, 5½" d., etched
Chantilly patt., Crystal......................30.00
Compote, open, 6½" d., 5" h., Tally-
Ho line, Amber 30.00

Compote, open, 7" d., 9½" h.,
Statuesque line, Carmen bowl, clear
Nude Lady stem (ILLUS.) 150.00
Compote, open, 8" d., Statuesque
line, Cobalt Blue bowl, clear Nude
Lady stem 295.00
Console bowl, pressed Caprice patt.,
Mandarin Gold w/silver overlay..........32.00
Console bowl, etched Diane patt.,
Crystal..65.00
Console set: bowl & pair of candle-
holders; Everglade line, Crystal,
3 pcs. 250.00
Console set: 9" d., ram's head-
handled bowl & pair 9½" h. Doric
Column candlesticks; Jade (blue-
green opaque), 3 pcs. ......300.00 to 350.00
Cordial, etched Apple Blossom patt.,
Topaz (vaseline) bowl w/amber
stem 95.00
Cordial, etched Rose Point patt.,
No. 3121, Crystal, 1 oz. 70.00
Cordial, etched Rose Point patt.,
Carmen bowl w/clear embossed
base 150.00
Cordial, Statuesque line, Topaz bowl,
clear Nude Lady stem 140.00
Cordials, pressed Caprice patt.,
Moonlight, 1 oz., set of 12...............149.00
Cordials, etched Wildflower patt.,
No. 3121, Crystal, 1 oz., set of 6 .....325.00
Creamer, individual size, etched
Chantilly patt., Crystal.......................12.00

Child's Colonial Creamer

Creamer, child's, Colonial patt.,
Emerald (ILLUS.) 25.00
Creamer & open sugar bowl,
individual size, pressed Caprice
patt., No. 40, Crystal, pr. 27.00
Creamer & open sugar bowl,
individual size, pressed Caprice
patt., Moonlight, pr. 40.00
Creamer & open sugar bowl,
Decagon line, Crystal, 2 pcs. 34.00
Creamer & open sugar bowl,
individual size, Gadroon (No. 3500)
line, Crystal, 2 pcs. 16.00

Creamer & open sugar bowl, etched
Wildflower patt., No. 3900/41,
Crystal, pr. 30.00
Creamer, sugar bowl & underplate,
Decagon line, Ebony, 3 pcs. 65.00
Crown Tuscan cake plate w/open
handles, Gadroon (No. 3500) line,
13" d...98.00
Crown Tuscan candy dish, cov.,
three-part, Gadroon (No. 3500/57)
line 50.00

Crown Tuscan Center Bowl

Crown Tuscan center bowl, footed,
Seashell line ("Flying Lady"), shell-
shaped bowl w/nude lady at one
end, gold & floral trim, 10" d.
(ILLUS.) 265.00
Crown Tuscan cocktail, Statuesque
line, Nude Lady stem, Mandarin
Gold 110.00
Crown Tuscan compote, open, 7" w.,
Sea Shell line....................................25.00
Crown Tuscan compote, open, 8" d.,
Statuesque line, Nude Lady stem,
"Charleton" (roses) decoration.........200.00
Crown Tuscan vase, 7" h., Sea Shell
line 110.00
Cruet w/original stopper, pressed
Caprice patt., Crystal, 5 oz. 85.00
Cruet w/original stopper, Strawberry
(No. 2780) line, clear 38.00
Cruet w/original stopper & undertray,
pressed Caprice patt., Moonlight,
2 pcs. 95.00
Cruet set: two cruets w/original
stoppers & underplate; pressed
Caprice patt., Crystal, 3 pcs..............60.00
Cup & saucer, etched Cleo patt.,
Emerald (light green) 18.00
Cup & saucer, Mt. Vernon line, Crystal ..8.00
Decanter w/original stopper, etched
Rose Point patt., No. 1321,
Crystal...275.00
Decanter w/original stopper, footed,
No. 1321, Crystal, 28 oz. 30.00
Decanter w/original stopper, Mt.
Vernon line, Crystal, 40 oz.................65.00
Decanter w/original stopper, Nautilus
line, Cobalt Blue, 80 oz.....................120.00

Figure flower holder, "Bashful
Charlotte," Emerald, 13" h. 275.00
Figure flower holder, "Draped Lady,"
Amber, 8½" h. 165.00
Figure flower holder, "Draped Lady,"
yellow, 8½" h...................250.00 to 275.00
Figure flower holder, "Draped Lady,"
Crystal, 13" h. 140.00
Figure flower holder, "Draped Lady,"
frosted Amber, 13" h. 265.00
Figure flower holder, "Draped Lady,"
pink, 13" h. ....250.00 to 275.00
Figure flower holder, "Mandolin Lady,"
Forest Green (dark green), 9" h.......350.00
Figure flower holder, "Two-Kid," La
Rosa (light to medium pink),
8¾" h..210.00
Figure flower holder, "Two-Kid,"
Emerald (light green), 8¾" h. 240.00
Finger bowl, Martha Washington line,
No. 4, Royal Blue..............................18.00
Flower holder, Sea Gull, Crystal,
9½" h..50.00
Flower holder, Sea Gull, Dianthus
(pink), 10½" h...................................350.00
Goblet, pressed Caprice patt., Crystal,
7½" h..14.00
Goblet, pressed Caprice patt.,
No. 300, Moonlight, 9 oz. 38.50
Goblet, Martha Washington line,
Crystal..8.00
Goblet, Mt. Vernon line, Crystal,
12 oz. 14.00
Goblet, No. 1401, Mandarin Gold.........12.00
Goblet, etched Rose Point patt.,
No. 3121, Crystal, 10 oz. 25.00
Goblet, Statuesque line, Amber bowl,
clear Nude Lady stem 155.00
Goblet, water, etched Wildflower patt.,
Crystal w/gold trim 28.00
Honey dish, cov., Gadroon (No. 3500)
line, Crystal, Farberware cover
w/embossed peony design,
5½" sq...16.50
Ice bucket w/tongs, etched Apple
Blossom patt., Topaz (vaseline) 140.00
Ice bucket, etched Cleo patt., blue 135.00
Ice bucket, etched Cleo patt., pink 80.00
Ice bucket w/bail handle, etched
Diana patt., Crystal 70.00
Ice bucket w/chrome handle & tongs,
etched Rose Point patt., Crystal,
2 pcs. 150.00
Ice bucket, etched Wildflower patt.,
Crystal..75.00
Ice bucket & six tumblers, Decagon
line, Royal Blue, 7 pcs. 175.00
Ivy ball w/keyhole stem, Carmen..........60.00
Ivy ball, Statuesque line, Royal Blue
bowl, clear Nude Lady stem 150.00
Lemon plate, handled, pressed
Caprice patt., Crystal, 6½" d. 10.00

Marmalade jar, cov., etched Chantilly
patt., Crystal, silver plate cover &
base 80.00
Mayonnaise dish & ladle, etched
Rose Point patt., Crystal, 2 pcs. 55.00
Mayonnaise dish & underplate,
etched Cleo patt., Crystal, 2 pcs........45.00
Model of a swan, Dianthus, 6½" l. 85.00
Model of a swan, Ebony, 6½" l. 75.00
Mug, beer, Everglade line, milk
white 45.00
Mustard jar, cov., etched Rosepoint
patt., Crystal.....................................135.00
Oyster cocktail, etched Rose Point
patt., Crystal.....................................38.00
Perfume bottle w/original stopper,
Nautilus line, Cobalt Blue, 1½ oz. 85.00
Pitcher, Gadroon (No. 3500) line,
Amber, Farber chrome holder,
76 oz. 55.00
Pitcher, ball-shaped, etched Rose
Point patt., Amber, 80 oz. 45.00
Pitcher w/ice lip, etched Rose Point
patt., Crystal, 80 oz. 180.00
Plate, bread & butter, 6½" d., etched
Rose Point patt., Crystal 15.00
Plate, 7½" d., Decagon line,
Moonlight 10.00
Plates, 7½" d., etched Wildflower
patt., Crystal.....................................11.00
Plate, 7¾" d., etched Cleo patt., blue ...20.00
Plate, 7¾" d., etched Cleo patt.,
Crystal..20.00
Plate, 7¾" w., Decagon line, Moonlight..7.00
Plate, 8" d., etched Elaine patt.,
Crystal..12.50
Plate, 8½" d., etched Apple Blossom
patt., yellow......................................18.00
Plate, 8½" d., Mt. Vernon line, Crystal....7.00
Plate, 8½" d., etched Rose Point patt.,
Crystal..40.00
Plate, sandwich, 11½" d., tab handles,
etched Rose Point patt., Amber.........16.00
Plate, torte, 13" d., three-footed,
etched Chantilly patt., Crystal 42.00
Plate, 14" d., Mt. Vernon line, Crystal...19.00
Plates, salad, 7½" d., Caprice patt.,
Crystal, set of 7 ....62.50
Platter, 11½" oval, three-footed,
pressed Caprice patt., Crystal 25.00
Relish dish, etched Apple Blossom
patt., Crystal, 9" l..............................13.00
Relish, pressed Caprice patt., Crystal,
12" l. 40.00
Relish dish, five-part, etched Chantilly
patt., Crystal.....................................35.00
Relish, three-part, etched Diane patt.,
No. 3400/91, Crystal, 8" l. 22.00
Relish, two-part, etched Elaine patt.,
Crystal, 9" l.......................................32.00
Relish dish, five-part, etched Portia
patt., Crystal, 12" 80.00
Relish dish, five-part, Pristine line,
Crystal, 10" l.....................................20.00

Relish, three-part, etched Rose Point
patt., Crystal, 12" l.............................85.00
Salt & pepper shakers w/original tops,
etched Chantilly patt., Crystal,
pr...25.00
Salt & pepper shakers w/original tops,
tilt-type, Nautilus line, Cobalt Blue,
pr...55.00
Salt & pepper shakers, footed,
No. 3400/77 line, etched Rose Point
patt., Crystal, pr. 60.00
Sherbet, pressed Caprice patt.,
Crystal..18.00
Sherbet, pressed Caprice patt.,
Moonlight, 5¾" h. 20.00
Sherbet, tall, etched Cleo patt.,
Crystal..22.00
Sherbet, high stem, Mt. Vernon line,
Crystal, 6½ oz. 9.00
Sherbet, low, etched Rose Point patt.,
Crystal..16.00
Sherbet, sq., No. 3797, Crystal
"crackle" 55.00

Child's Colonial Pattern Spooner

Spooner, child's, Colonial patt.,
Emerald (ILLUS.) 30.00
Tumbler, Apple Blossom etching,
Emerald, 12 oz..................................45.00
Tumbler, footed, pressed Caprice
patt., Moonlight, 12 oz. 40.00
Tumbler, whiskey, pressed Caprice
patt., Crystal.....................................20.00
Tumbler, footed, etched Cleo patt.,
Crystal, 5½" h., 12 oz........................45.00
Tumbler, iced tea, etched Grape patt.,
Crystal, 10 oz. 20.00
Tumbler, Mt. Vernon line, Crystal.........10.00
Tumbler, footed, etched Rose Point
patt., Crystal, 12 oz. 30.00
Tumbler, iced tea, etched Rose Point
patt., Crystal.....................................40.00
Urn, cov., Mt. Vernon line, Carmen 105.00
Vase, 3½" h., pressed Caprice patt.,
Amber 80.00
Vase, bud, 5" h., etched Rose Point
patt., Crystal w/gold trim 70.00

Vase, 10" h., keyhole base, etched
  Rose Point patt., Crystal 65.00
Vase, 10½" h., pressed Block Optic
  patt., Rubina 155.00
Vase, 12" h., etched Wildflower patt.,
  Crystal...85.00
Water set: 32 oz. pitcher & six 5 oz.
  tumblers; pressed Caprice patt.,
  Moonlight, 7 pcs...............................575.00
Wine, etched Rose Point patt.,
  Crystal...43.00
Wine, Statuesque line, Carmen bowl,
  clear Nude Lady stem, 7¾" h..........125.00
Wine set: decanter & six wines; Mt.
  Vernon line, Crystal w/gold trim,
  7 pcs. 150.00

CARNIVAL GLASS

*Earlier called Taffeta glass, the
Carnival glass now being collected was
introduced early in this century. Its
producers gave it an iridescence that
attempted to imitate that of some Tiffany
glass. Collectors will find available books
by leading authorities Donald E. Moore,
Sherman Hand, Marion T. Hartung and
Rose M. Presznick.*

ACANTHUS (Imperial)

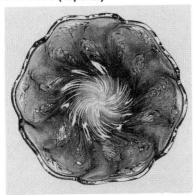

Acanthus Bowl

Bowl, 7" d., green $20.00
Bowl, 7" d., marigold...........................46.50
Bowl, 7½" d., purple............................80.00
Bowl, 7¾" d., smoky 45.00
Bowl, 8" to 9" d., green 88.00
Bowl, 8" to 9" d., marigold
  (ILLUS.) 62.00
Bowl, 8" to 9" d., purple 95.00
Bowl, 8" to 9" d., smoky 85.00
Plate, 9" to 10" d., marigold 193.00
Plate, 9" to 10" d., smoky...................250.00

ACORN (Fenton)
Bowl, 3½" d., marigold..........................50.00

Bowl, 5" d., milk white w/marigold
  overlay 322.00
Bowl, 6" d., aqua.................................128.00
Bowl, 6" d., blue....................................45.00
Bowl, 6" d., ruffled, sapphire blue.........90.00
Bowl, 6" d., vaseline 40.00
Bowl, 7" d., ruffled, amber 98.00
Bowl, 7" d., aqua..................................82.50
Bowl, 7" d., blue....................................44.00
Bowl, 7" d., green 68.00
Bowl, 7" d., ice blue 150.00
Bowl, 7" d., lime green 55.00
Bowl, 7" d., marigold.............................35.00
Bowl, 7" d., peach opalescent 185.00
Bowl, 7" d., ruffled, peach opales-
  cent 300.00
Bowl, 7" d., purple.................................45.00
Bowl, 7" d., red ....550.00 to 600.00
Bowl, 7" d., vaseline 170.00
Bowl, 7" d., ruffled, vase-
  line ....100.00 to 125.00
Bowl, 8" to 9" d., blue...........................55.00
Bowl, 8" to 9" d., ice blue 350.00
Bowl, 8" to 9" d., marigold....................35.00
Bowl, 8" to 9" d., ribbon candy rim,
  purple 115.00
Bowl, 8" to 9" d., ruffled,
  red...................................700.00 to 750.00
Bowl, ice cream shape, aqua 125.00
Bowl, ice cream shape, blue.................35.00
Bowl, ice cream shape, green 65.00
Bowl, ice cream shape, ice blue
  w/marigold overlay..............................75.00
Bowl, ice cream shape, moon-
  stone 185.00
Bowl, ice cream shape, red slag.........650.00
Bowl, ice cream shape, teal blue..........75.00
Bowl, ruffled, aqua opalescent 125.00
Bowl, ruffled, green...............................70.00
Bowl, ruffled, marigold 30.00
Bowl, ruffled, moonstone 450.00
Bowl, ruffled, peach opalescent..........362.00
Bowl, white 180.00

ACORN BURRS (Northwood)
Berry set: master bowl & 5 sauce
  dishes; purple, 6 pcs........350.00 to 400.00
Berry set: master bowl & 6 sauce
  dishes; green, 7 pcs...........................350.00
Bowl, master berry, 10" d., green 80.00
Bowl, master berry, 10" d., mari-
  gold 78.00
Bowl, master berry, 10" d., purple 175.00
Butter dish, cov., green.......300.00 to 375.00
Butter dish, cov., marigold 178.00
Butter dish, cov., purple......175.00 to 200.00
Creamer, green 90.00
Creamer, marigold...............................100.00
Creamer, purple...................................100.00
Creamer & sugar bowl, purple, pr.......250.00
Pitcher, water, marigold.......................325.00
Pitcher, water, purple..........350.00 to 400.00
Punch bowl & base, purple, 2 pcs. 795.00

Punch cup, aqua opalescent 1,800.00
Punch cup, blue.....................................85.00
Punch cup, green 40.00
Punch cup, ice blue 100.00
Punch cup, ice green...........................97.00
Punch cup, marigold.............................21.00
Punch cup, purple.................................30.00
Punch cup, white 55.00
Punch set: bowl, case & 5 cups;
   green, 7 pcs. ....1,200.00 to 1,600.00
Punch set: bowl, base & 6 cups; ice
   blue, 8 pcs. 7,000.00
Punch set: bowl, base & 6 cups;
   marigold, 8 pcs. 1,000.00
Punch set: bowl, base & 6 cups;
   purple, 8 pcs. 1,500.00
Punch set: bowl, base & 6 cups;
   white, 8 pcs....................................4,000.00
Sauce dish, green................................37.50
Sauce dish, marigold 30.00
Sauce dish, purple................................45.00
Spooner, green....................................150.00
Spooner, marigold 88.00
Spooner, purple ....100.00 to 125.00
Table set: cov. sugar bowl, creamer,
   spooner & cov. butter dish;
   marigold, 4 pcs. 900.00
Table set, purple, 4 pcs 1,000.00
Tumbler, green 78.00
Tumbler, marigold...................................50.00
Tumbler, purple.......................................58.00
Water set: pitcher & 4 tumblers;
   marigold, 5 pcs. ....600.00 to 650.00
Water set: pitcher & 6 tumblers;
   green, 7 pcs. 1,200.00
Water set: pitcher & 6 tumblers;
   purple, 7 pcs. ....750.00 to 800.00

ADVERTISING & SOUVENIR ITEMS

BPOE Elks Plate

Basket, "Feldman Bros. Furniture,
   Salisbury, Md.," open edge,
   marigold ....50.00 to 75.00
Basket, "John H. Brand Furniture Co.,
   Wilmington, Del.," marigold................60.00
Bell, souvenir, BPOE Elks, "Atlantic
   City, 1911," blue............................2,250.00

Bell, souvenir, BPOE Elks, "Parkers-
   burg, 1914," blue............................1,250.00
Bowl, "Isaac Benesch," 6¼" d.,
   purple (Millersburg) ....300.00 to 325.00
Bowl, "Bernheimer Brothers,"
   blue 1,000.00
Bowl, "Dreibus Parfait Sweet," ruffled,
   smoky lavender...................................400.00
Bowl, "Horlacher," Peacock Tail patt.,
   green...100.00
Bowl, "Horlacher," Thistle patt.,
   green...100.00
Bowl, "Ogden Furniture Co.,"
   purple...225.00
Bowl, "Sterling Furniture," purple........600.00
Bowl, souvenir, BPOE Elks, "Atlantic
   City, 1911," blue, one-eyed Elk........675.00
Bowl, souvenir, BPOE Elks, "Detroit,
   1910," blue, one-eyed Elk................550.00
Bowl, souvenir, BPOE Elks, "Detroit,
   1910," green, one-eyed Elk 1,000.00
Bowl, souvenir, BPOE Elks, "Detroit,
   1910," ruffled, green 250.00
Bowl, souvenir, BPOE Elks, "Detroit,
   1910," marigold 845.00
Bowl, souvenir, BPOE Elks, "Detroit,
   1910," purple, one-eyed Elk.............385.00
Bowl, souvenir, BPOE Elks, "Detroit,
   1910," purple, two-eyed Elk
   (Millersburg) ....775.00 to 825.00
Bowl, souvenir, "Brooklyn Bridge,"
   marigold ....300.00 to 325.00
Bowl, souvenir, Brooklyn Bridge,
   unlettered, marigold ....475.00 to 550.00
Bowl, souvenir, "Millersburg
   Courthouse," purple 550.00
Bowl, souvenir, Millersburg
   Courthouse, unlettered, purple 965.00
Card tray, "Fern Brand Chocolates,"
   turned-up sides, 6¼" d., purple........175.00
Card tray, "Isaac Benesch," Holly
   Whirl patt., marigold.............50.00 to 70.00
Dish, "Compliments of Pacific Coast
   Mail Order House, Los Angeles,
   California" 700.00
Hat, "Arthur O'Dell," green...................75.00
Hat, "General Furniture Co." 1910,
   Peacock Tail patt., green 75.00
Hat, "Horlacher," Peacock Tail patt.,
   green...70.00
Hat, "John Brand Furniture,"
   green...42.00
Hat, "John Brand Furniture," open
   edge, marigold 45.00
Hat, "Miller's Furniture - Harrisburg,"
   basketweave, marigold 75.00
Paperweight, souvenir, BPOE Elks,
   green...625.00
Paperweight, souvenir, BPOE Elks,
   purple (Millersburg) ....600.00 to 700.00
Plate, "Ballard, California," purple
   (Northwood) 900.00
Plate, "Bird of Paradise," purple 220.00

Plate, "Brazier Candies," w/handgrip,
6" d., purple.......................500.00 to 600.00
Plate, "Davidson Chocolate Society,"
6¼" d., purple....................................230.00
Plate, "Dreibus Parfait Sweets,"
6¼" d., purple....................................400.00
Plate, "Eagle Furniture Co.,"
purple...750.00
Plate, "Fern Brand Chocolates,"
6" d., purple.......................................700.00
Plate, "Gervitz Bros., Furniture &
Clothing," w/handgrip, 6" d.,
purple...1,350.00
Plate, "Greengard Furniture Co.,"
purple...625.00
Plate, "F.A. Hudson Furniture Co.,"
7" d., purple (Northwood).................225.00
Plate, "Jockey Club," w/handgrip,
6" d., purple.......................................500.00
Plate, "Old Rose Distillery," Grape &
Cable patt., stippled, 9" d., green.....370.00
Plate, "Roods Chocolate, Pueblo,"
purple...750.00
Plate, "Season's Greetings - Eat
Paradise Soda Candies," 6" d.,
purple...178.00
Plate, "Spector's Department Store,"
Heart & Vine patt., 9" d., mari-
gold...450.00
Plate, "Utah Liquor Co.," w/handgrip,
6" d., purple.......................................950.00
Plate, "We Use Brocker's," 7" d.,
purple...495.00
Plate, souvenir, BPOE Elks,
"Atlantic City, 1911," blue
(ILLUS.)..........................800.00 to 900.00
Plate, souvenir, BPOE Elks, "Par-
kersburg, 1914," 7½" d.,
blue..1,050.00
Vase, "Howard Furniture," Four Pillars
patt., green...80.00

AMARYLLIS (Dugan)
Compote, tri-corner, miniature,
marigold...........................225.00 to 275.00
Compote, marigold.............................143.00
Compote, purple.................................112.00

APPLE BLOSSOMS
Bowl, 5½" d., purple.............................42.50
Bowl, 6" d., marigold.............................22.00
Bowl, 6" d., deep, purple......................30.00
Bowl, 7" d., collared base, mari-
gold...32.00
Bowl, 7" d., collared base, purple.........70.00
Bowl, 7" d., ribbon candy rim,
marigold..25.00
Bowl, 7" d., ribbon candy rim, white....135.00
Lamp, kerosene-type, small,
green..1,200.00
Lamp, kerosene-type, large w/pat-
tern on interior of lamp base,
green..3,100.00

Rose bowl, marigold.............................65.00
Tumbler, enameled, blue....................120.00

APPLE BLOSSOM TWIGS
Banana boat, ruffled, peach
opalescent..175.00
Bowl, 8" to 9" d., blue...........................80.00
Bowl, 8" to 9" d., marigold.......55.00 to 75.00
Bowl, 8" to 9" d., peach opales-
cent..143.00
Bowl, 8" to 9" d., purple......................115.00
Bowl, 8" to 9" d., white..........................90.00
Bowl, 9" d., ice cream shape,
white...............................150.00 to 175.00
Plate, 9" d., blue.................................265.00
Plate, 9" d., ruffled, blue.....................210.00
Plate, 9" d., marigold..........................100.00
Plate, 9" d., ruffled, marigold..............130.00
Plate, 9" d., peach opalescent............400.00
Plate, 9" d., purple.............200.00 to 300.00
Plate, 9" d., flat, smooth edge,
purple...900.00
Plate, 9" d., white................200.00 to 250.00
Plate, 9" d., ruffled, white....................165.00
Plate, chop, peach opales-
cent................................375.00 to 400.00

APPLE TREE
Pitcher, water, marigold......................115.00
Pitcher, water, white............................350.00
Tumbler, blue..70.00
Tumbler, marigold.................................42.00
Tumbler, white....................................250.00
Water set: pitcher & 6 tumblers;
blue, 7 pcs..820.00

APRIL SHOWERS (Fenton)
Vase, 8" h., green..................................40.00
Vase, 8½" h., Peacock Tail interior,
purple...85.00
Vase, 11" h., blue..................................47.00
Vase, 11½" h., marigold........................35.00
Vase, 12" h., Peacock Tail interior,
marigold..35.00
Vase, 12" h., Peacock Tail interior,
purple...50.00
Vase, 12" h., vaseline.........................110.00
Vase, green...45.00
Vase, purple opalescent.....700.00 to 750.00

AUSTRALIAN
Berry set: master bowl & 6 sauce
dishes; Magpie, marigold,
7 pcs...325.00
Bowl, 5½" d., Swan, marigold...............45.00
Bowl, 9" to 10" d., Emu, aqua.............550.00
Bowl, 9" to 10" d., Emu, marigold.......145.00
Bowl, 9" to 10" d., Kangaroo,
marigold..100.00
Bowl, 9" to 10" d., Kangaroo,
purple...............................150.00 to 170.00
Bowl, 9" to 10" d., Kingfisher,
purple...150.00

Bowl, 9" to 10" d., Kiwi, ruffled,
marigold 250.00
Bowl, 9" to 10" d., Kiwi, purple 250.00
Bowl, 9" to 10" d., Kookaburra,
marigold 98.00
Bowl, 9" to 10" d., Magpie, mari-
gold 115.00
Bowl, 9" to 10" d., Magpie, purple.......110.00
Bowl, 9" to 10" d., Swan, purple 175.00
Bowl, 9" to 10" d., Thunderbird,
marigold 200.00
Bowl, 9" to 10" d., Thunderbird,
purple 165.00
Bowl, 11" d., ice cream shape,
Kookaburra, marigold 135.00
Bowl, 11" d., ice cream shape,
Kookaburra variant, marigold...........135.00
Bowl, 11" d., ice cream shape,
Kookaburra variant, purple 300.00
Bowl, pin-up, purple 65.00
Cake plate, Butterfly & Bells,
marigold 78.00
Compote, Butterflies & Waratah,
aqua.....................................135.00
Compote, Butterflies & Waratah,
marigold ....175.00 to 200.00
Compote, Butterflies & Waratah,
purple 210.00
Compote, Butterfly & Bush, mari-
gold 86.00
Sauce dish, Kangaroo, marigold 70.00
Sauce dish, Kangaroo, purple 64.00
Sauce dish, Kingfisher, marigold 60.00
Sauce dish, Kookaburra, marigold 65.00
Sauce dish, Kookaburra, purple 45.00
Sauce dish, Swan, marigold 65.00
Sauce dish, Thunderbird, marigold.......65.00
Sauce dish, Thunderbird, purple 85.00

BANDED DRAPE
Mug, marigold.......................................25.00
Pitcher, water, green 450.00
Pitcher, water, marigold w/enameled
iris 600.00
Water set: tankard pitcher & 6 tum-
blers; h.p. decoration, marigold,
7 pcs. 395.00

BASKET (Fenton's Open Edge)
Amber......................200.00 to 250.00
Amberina, w/two rows, two sides
turned up.............................125.00
Aqua 74.00
Aqua, w/two rows, jack-in-the-pulpit
shape ....100.00 to 125.00
Aqua, w/two rows, two sides turned
up 110.00
Aqua opalescent...............................145.00
Black amethyst 365.00
Blue 50.00
Celeste blue.......................................92.00
Green...53.00
Green, hat shape................................85.00

Green, low sides.................125.00 to 175.00
Ice blue 195.00
Ice blue, w/two rows, open edge, six
ruffled ....225.00 to 295.00
Ice blue, w/three rows.........................600.00
Ice green...240.00
Ice green, w/three rows 450.00
Marigold, 5" h., w/applied crystal
handle 75.00
Marigold...40.00
Purple 110.00
Red..340.00
Red, hat shape ....400.00 to 450.00
Red, jack-in-the-pulpit
shape ....425.00 to 450.00
Red, w/two rows, small.....................325.00
Reverse Amberina..............................650.00
Vaseline.......................75.00 to 100.00
Vaseline, plain interior 275.00
Vaseline, w/two rows, large 75.00
White, w/two rows..............................150.00
White, 6" ....200.00 to 250.00

BASKET (Northwood) or BUSHEL BASKET
Aqua, 4½" d., 4¾" h. 425.00
Aqua opalescent, 4½" d.,
4¾" h...............................450.00 to 500.00
Blue 147.00
Blue w/electric iridescence 160.00
Celeste blue....................................1,900.00
Clambroth...400.00
Cobalt blue ....150.00 to 200.00
Green..540.00
Honey amber ....400.00 to 500.00
Horehound, variant..........................1,250.00
Ice blue ....600.00 to 800.00
Ice green.............................275.00 to 300.00
Lavender...190.00
Lime green..350.00
Lime green opalescent 1,500.00
Marigold..108.00
Olive green 550.00
Purple ....100.00 to 125.00
Sapphire blue 1,750.00
Smoky..750.00
Teal blue...450.00
Vaseline...2,600.00
White ....125.00 to 150.00

BEADED BULL'S EYE (Imperial)
Vase, 8" h., marigold 38.00
Vase, 10½" h., marigold 50.00
Vase, 10½" h., purple 195.00
Vase, green 35.00
Vase, marigold.....................................35.00
Vase, purple 38.00

BEADED CABLE (Northwood)
Bowl, 7" d., three-footed, green 50.00
Bowl, 7" d., three-footed, ruffled,
marigold 35.00
Candy dish, green 50.00

Candy dish, marigold...........................30.00
Candy dish, purple...............................55.00
Rose bowl, aqua.................................350.00
Rose bowl, aqua opalescent 305.00
Rose bowl, blue ....100.00 to 125.00
Rose bowl, blue w/electric
  iridescence.....................................300.00
Rose bowl, green...............................108.00
Rose bowl, ice blue ....850.00 to 1,000.00
Rose bowl, ice green ....950.00 to 1,300.00
Rose bowl, lime green opalescent...1,200.00
Rose bowl, marigold.............................75.00

Beaded Cable Rose Bowl

Rose bowl, purple (ILLUS.) 97.00
Rose bowl, white ....450.00 to 550.00

BEADED SHELL (Dugan or Diamond Glass Co.)
Bowl, 8½" d., footed, purple...............165.00
Creamer, marigold................................65.00
Mug, blue...........................150.00 to 200.00
Mug, marigold....................................120.00
Mug, purple...91.00
Mug, purple, souvenir........................150.00
Mug, white 1,000.00
Sauce dish, marigold...........................30.00
Spooner, footed, marigold 60.00
Sugar bowl, cov., marigold 55.00
Table set, marigold, 4 pcs. 275.00
Tumbler, blue....................................118.00
Tumbler, lavender................................80.00
Tumbler, marigold................................55.00
Tumbler, purple 62.00

BEAUTY BUD VASE
Purple, 6½" h ....75.00 to 100.00
Marigold, 8" h.......................................30.00
Purple, 8" h. 40.00
Marigold, 9½" h....................................35.00

BIG FISH BOWL (Millersburg)
Green...595.00
Green, square.................900.00 to 1,000.00
Marigold...507.00
Marigold, ice cream shape 550.00
Marigold, square................................850.00
Purple, ice cream shape....................660.00

Big Fish Bowl
Purple, ruffled (ILLUS.).......................704.00
Purple, square 700.00

BIRD WITH GRAPES

Bird with Grapes Wall Vase
Wall vase, marigold, 7½" w., 8" h.
  (ILLUS.) 60.00

BLACKBERRY (Fenton)
Basket, aqua......................................150.00
Basket, blue...42.00
Basket, clambroth................................45.00
Basket, green 95.00
Basket, marigold..................................65.00
Basket, purple......................................72.00
Basket, red 250.00
Basket, smoky w/marigold over-
  lay 75.00
Bowl, 5" d., purple................................30.00
Bowl, 7" d., purple................................80.00
Bowl, 8" to 9" d., ruffled, green 90.00
Bowl, 8" to 9" d., ruffled, marigold.........50.00
Bowl, 8" to 9" d., ruffled, purple 58.00
Bowl, 10" d., ruffled, blue...................650.00
Bowl, nut, open edge, Basketweave
  exterior, purple...................................60.00
Plate, openwork rim, marigold............550.00
Vase, whimsey, open edge, blue
  opalescent 900.00

Vase, whimsey, open edge, mari-
gold 650.00

BLACKBERRY BRAMBLE
Compote, ruffled, green.......................54.00
Compote, ruffled, lavender 50.00
Compote, ruffled, marigold 45.00
Compote, ruffled, purple 46.00

BLACKBERRY MINIATURE COMPOTE
Blue 113.00
Blue, flat top.......................................325.00
Blue, w/red stem 350.00
Green...200.00
Marigold...87.00
Purple 85.00
White 448.00

BLACKBERRY SPRAY
Bonbon, marigold 30.00
Bowl, 7" d., marigold............................20.00
Compote, 5½" d., purple......................95.00
Hat shape, amber ....100.00 to 150.00
Hat shape, Amberina..........280.00 to 300.00
Hat shape, aqua 75.00
Hat shape, jack-in-the-pulpit,
crimped rim, aqua 85.00
Hat shape, aqua opalescent...............475.00
Hat shape, jack-in-the-pulpit, aqua
opalescent 300.00
Hat shape, blue 40.00
Hat shape, blue opalescent................585.00
Hat shape, jack-in-the-pulpit, crimped
rim, blue 50.00
Hat shape, jack-in-the-pulpit, crimped
rim, clambroth 27.00
Hat shape, green 75.00
Hat shape, ice green opalescent........350.00
Hat shape, jack-in-the-pulpit,
lime green w/marigold overlay 35.00
Hat shape, lime green opalescent......325.00
Hat shape, marigold 32.50
Hat shape, purple 50.00
Hat shape, red.....................................388.00
Hat shape, red slag 475.00
Hat shape, Reverse Amberina 450.00
Hat shape, vaseline 70.00
Hat shape, jack-in-the-pulpit, crimped
rim, vaseline.......................................65.00
Hat shape, vaseline w/marigold
overlay 54.00

BLACKBERRY WREATH (Millersburg)
Bowl, 5" d., green 52.00
Bowl, 5" d., marigold............................35.00
Bowl, 5" d., ruffled, mari-
gold 100.00 to125.00
Bowl, 5" d., purple................................55.00
Bowl, 5" d., candy ribbon edge,
purple................................75.00 to 100.00
Bowl, 7" d., green 68.00
Bowl, 7" d., marigold............................50.00

Bowl, 7" d., purple................................70.00
Bowl, 7½" d., three-in-one edge,
clambroth 75.00
Bowl, 8" to 9" d., green 93.00
Bowl, 8" to 9" d., marigold....................55.00
Bowl, 8" to 9" d., purple 85.00
Bowl, 10" d., blue...............850.00 to 950.00
Bowl, 10" d., green 82.00
Bowl, 10" d., marigold...........................90.00
Bowl, 10" d., purple.............................165.00
Bowl, ice cream, large, marigold 68.00
Bowl, ice cream, large,
purple...............................200.00 to 225.00

BOUQUET
Pitcher, water, blue.............................550.00
Tumbler, blue...57.00
Tumbler, marigold..................................32.00
Water set: pitcher & 1 tumbler; blue,
2 pcs. 400.00
Water set: pitcher & 4 tumblers;
marigold, 5 pcs. 375.00

BROKEN ARCHES (Imperial)

Broken Arches Punch Cup

Punch bowl, purple, 12" d..................500.00
Punch bowl & base, marigold,
12" d., 2 pcs.....................................300.00
Punch bowl & base, purple, 12" d.,
2 pcs. 450.00
Punch cup, marigold.............................25.00
Punch cup, purple (ILLUS.) 38.00
Punch set: bowl, base & 6 cups;
purple, 8 pcs. 915.00

BUSHEL BASKET - See Basket
(Northwood) Pattern

BUTTERFLY (Northwood)
Bonbon, threaded exterior,
blue ....250.00 to 270.00
Bonbon, handled, threaded exterior,
blue w/electric iridescence 450.00
Bonbon, threaded exterior, ice
blue 2,200.00
Bonbon, green.......................................88.00
Bonbon, marigold 50.00
Bonbon, purple 74.00
Bonbon, threaded exterior,
purple................................225.00 to 250.00
Bonbon, smoky....................................350.00

BUTTERFLY & BERRY (Fenton)

Butterfly & Berry Pitcher

Berry set: master bowl & 5 sauce
  dishes; marigold, 6 pcs. 240.00
Bowl, 7" d., three-footed, mari-
  gold..65.00
Bowl, 8" to 9" d., footed, blue................55.00
Bowl, 8" to 9" d., footed, mari-
  gold..72.00
Bowl, 8" to 9" d., footed, purple 175.00
Bowl, master berry or fruit, four-
  footed, blue 95.00
Bowl, master berry or fruit, four-
  footed, green.....................................150.00
Bowl, master berry or fruit, four-
  footed, marigold..................................82.00
Bowl, master berry or fruit, four-
  footed, purple....................................120.00
Bowl, master berry or fruit, four-
  footed, white ....250.00 to 275.00
Butter dish, cov., blue..........................250.00
Butter dish, cov., green.......................280.00
Butter dish, cov., marigold..................126.00
Centerpiece bowl, purple.....................500.00
Creamer, blue...85.00
Creamer, marigold..................................70.00
Creamer, purple....................................145.00
Creamer & cov. sugar bowl, mari-
  gold, pr..190.00
Hatpin holder, blue 1,900.00
Hatpin holder, marigold 1,550.00
Nut bowl, purple...................................437.00
Pitcher, water, blue..............................425.00
Pitcher, water, marigold
  (ILLUS.) ....225.00 to 275.00
Sauce dish, blue.....................................42.00
Sauce dish, green...................................45.00
Sauce dish, marigold..............................30.00
Sauce dish, purple.................50.00 to 75.00
Spooner, blue 120.00
Spooner, marigold...................................62.00
Spooner, purple....................................140.00
Sugar bowl, cov., blue 120.00
Sugar bowl, cov., marigold 82.00
Tumbler, blue...60.50

Tumbler, green 85.00
Tumbler, marigold...................................39.50
Tumbler, purple 325.00
Vase, 6" h., marigold 35.00
Vase, 7" h., blue 65.00
Vase, 7" h., green..................................145.00
Vase, 7" h., marigold 30.00
Vase, 8" h., blue 65.00
Vase, 8" h., marigold 35.00
Vase, 9" h., blue 80.00
Vase, 9" h., marigold 50.00
Vase, 9" h., purple 50.00
Vase, 10" h., blue 50.00
Vase, amber 130.00
Vase, green 170.00

BUTTERFLY & FERN (Fenton)

Pitcher, water, blue..............................425.00
Pitcher, water, green 425.00
Pitcher, water, marigold......275.00 to 325.00
Tumbler, blue...45.00
Tumbler, green 59.00
Tumbler, marigold...................................32.00
Tumbler, pastel marigold.......................35.00
Tumbler, purple 45.00
Water set: pitcher & 6 tumblers;
  blue, 7 pcs. 775.00
Water set: pitcher & 6 tumblers;
  green, 7 pcs. 850.00
Water set: pitcher & 6 tumblers;
  marigold, 7 pcs. 515.00

BUZZ SAW - See Double Star Pattern

CAPTIVE ROSE

Bonbon, two-handled, blue,
  7½" d...125.00
Bowl, 6" d., blue.....................................35.00
Bowl, 8" to 9" d., blue.............................77.00
Bowl, 8" to 9" d., green...........................60.00
Bowl, 8" to 9" d., marigold......................68.00
Bowl, 8" to 9" d., purple 46.00
Bowl, 8" to 9" d., ribbon candy rim,
  green..70.00
Bowl, 8" to 9" d., ribbon candy rim,
  marigold..67.00
Bowl, 8" to 9" d., ribbon candy rim,
  purple...68.00
Bowl, 8" to 9" d., ruffled rim, blue..........80.00
Bowl, 8" to 9" d., ruffled rim,
  green..125.00
Bowl, 8" to 9" d., ruffled rim, mari-
  gold...35.00
Compote, blue 75.00
Compote, marigold 55.00
Compote, white......................................125.00
Compote, ribbon candy rim,
  purple...100.00
Plate, 6" d., marigold 65.00
Plate, 9" d., blue ....425.00 to 525.00
Plate, 9" d., green 975.00
Plate, 9" d., marigold 321.00
Plate, 9" d., purple 485.00

CARNIVAL HOLLY - See Holly Pattern

CAROLINE
Banana bowl, peach opalescent...........65.00
Basket w/applied handle, peach
   opalescent ....375.00 to 400.00
Bowl, 8" d., handgrip, ruffled, peach
   opalescent 140.00
Bowl, 8" to 9" d., peach opales-
   cent 65.00
Bowl, 8" to 9" d., tricornered, peach
   opalescent ....125.00 to 150.00
Bowl, 9" d., ruffled, peach
   opalescent 160.00
Bowl, 9" sq., peach opalescent.............65.00
Plate, w/handgrip, peach opales-
   cent 125.00

CATTAILS & WATER LILY - See Water Lily & Cattails Pattern

CHATELAINE

Chatelaine Pitcher

Pitcher, purple (ILLUS.) 2,500.00
Tumbler, purple 255.00

CHERRY (Dugan)
Bowl, 6" d., clambroth opalescent 30.00
Bowl, 6" d., Jeweled Heart exterior,
   purple 45.00
Bowl, 6" d., purple...............................60.00
Bowl, 7" d., three-footed, crimped rim,
   peach opalescent..............................95.00
Bowl, 8" d., ruffled, purple...................125.00
Bowl, 8" to 9" d., three-footed,
   marigold..135.00
Bowl, 8" to 9" d., three-footed, peach
   opalescent ....250.00 to 300.00
Bowl, 8" to 9" d., three-footed,
   purple...116.00
Bowl, 10" d., Jeweled Heart exterior,
   purple...260.00
Bowl, large, peach opalescent............240.00
Bowl, large, Jeweled Heart exterior,
   purple...275.00

Dish, ruffled, marigold, 6" d. 80.00
Dish, ruffled, purple, 6" d. 50.00
Plate, 6" d., ruffled, purple 150.00
Plate, 6½" d., candy ribbon rim,
   purple..............................225.00 to 250.00
Plate, 6½" d., ruffled, Jeweled Heart
   exterior, purple..................................95.00
Sauce dish, peach opalescent.............65.00
Sauce dish, Jeweled Heart exterior,
   ruffled, peach opalescent...................75.00
Sauce dish, purple...............................45.00

CHERRY or CHERRY CIRCLES (Fenton)

Red Cherry Bonbon

Bonbon, two-handled, aqua...............280.00
Bonbon, two-handled, blue...................50.00
Bonbon, two-handled, marigold............38.00
Bonbon, two-handled, red
   (ILLUS.) 7,250.00
Bowl, 5" d., fluted, blue 30.00
Bowl, 5" d., marigold...........................32.00
Bowl, 5" d., purple...............................40.00
Bowl, 7" d., three-footed, marigold 42.50
Bowl, 7" d., three-footed, peach
   opalescent w/plain interior 90.00
Bowl, 10" d., vaseline w/ marigold
   overlay 75.00
Bowl, 10" d., ruffled, white 100.00
Card tray, aqua..................................125.00
Plate, 6" d., blue 100.00
Plate, 6" d., Orange tree exterior,
   marigold 80.00
Plate, 6" d., purple 275.00

CHERRY or HANGING CHERRIES (Millersburg)
Banana compote (whimsey), blue 625.00
Banana compote (whimsey),
   green...1,500.00
Bowl, 4" d., green 75.00
Bowl, 5" d., blue.................825.00 to 875.00
Bowl, 5" d., green 62.00
Bowl, 5" d., ruffled, marigold.................50.00
Bowl, 5" d., piecrust rim, purple 49.00
Bowl, 6" d., ruffled, green 95.00
Bowl, 7" d., marigold............................80.00
Bowl, 7" d., purple................................88.00

Bowl, 7" d., ice cream shape,
    marigold 112.00
Bowl, 8" to 9" d., ruffled, green 264.00
Bowl, 8" to 9" d., ice cream shape,
    green................................175.00 to 200.00
Bowl, 8" to 9" d., dome-footed,
    marigold 70.00
Bowl, 8" to 9" d., purple 60.00
Bowl, 9" d., Hobnail exterior, mari-
    gold 795.00
Bowl, 10" d., ice cream shape,
    green................................194.00
Bowl, 10" d., ice cream shape,
    marigold 125.00
Bowl, 10" d., ice cream shape,
    purple ....175.00 to 200.00
Bowl, 10" d., three-in-one rim,
    marigold 245.00
Bowl, 10" d., purple..........................310.00
Bowl, 10½" d., ruffled, white 125.00
Bowl, ruffled, Hobnail exterior,
    marigold, large 468.00
Butter dish, cov., green......................227.00
Butter dish, cov., marigold.................190.00
Compote, green..............................1,400.00
Creamer, green 77.00
Creamer, marigold...............................70.00
Creamer, purple....................................75.00
Pitcher, milk, marigold 600.00
Pitcher, milk, purple 418.00
Pitcher, water, marigold......................200.00
Pitcher, water, purple..........................600.00
Plate, 7" d., purple 225.00
Spooner, green......................................68.00
Spooner, marigold 75.00
Sugar bowl, cov., marigold 85.00
Tumbler, green 290.00
Tumbler, marigold...............................200.00

CHERRY CIRCLES - SEE CHERRY (Fenton) Pattern

CHRISTMAS COMPOTE

Christmas Compote

Marigold (ILLUS.) 4,000.00
Purple 3,500.00

CHRYSANTHEMUM or WINDMILL & MUMS
Bowl, 8" to 9" d., three-footed,
    blue 125.00

Bowl, 8" to 9" d., three-footed,
    green..78.00
Bowl, 8" to 9" d., three-footed,
    marigold 46.00
Bowl, 9" d., ruffled, blue......................115.00
Bowl, 9" d., ruffled, green ...175.00 to 200.00
Bowl, 9" d., marigold............................52.00
Bowl, 9" d., ruffled, marigold...............120.00
Bowl, 9" d., ruffled, purple....................150.00
Bowl, 9" d., red w/amber center.......4,100.00
Bowl, 10" d., three-footed, marigold 82.00
Bowl, 10" d., three-footed, purple 75.00
Bowl, 10" d., collared base, red 5,000.00
Bowl, 11" d., three-footed, blue 200.00
Bowl, 11" d., three-footed, green 250.00
Bowl, 11" d., three-footed, marigold 52.00
Bowl, 12" d., three-footed, ruffled,
    black amethyst................................575.00
Bowl, 12" d., three-footed, vaseline 275.00
Bowl, collared base, green 238.00
Bowl, collared base,
    purple ....300.00 to 350.00
Bowl, orange, footed, vaseline 350.00

COBBLESTONES BOWL (Imperial)
Marigold, 7" d..67.00
Green, 9" d. 100.00
Purple, 9" d. 112.00

COIN DOT

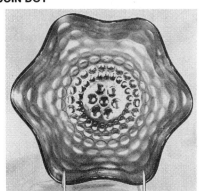

Coin Dot Bowl

Bowl, 6" d., green 25.00
Bowl, 6" d., ice cream shape red 1,500.00
Bowl, 6½" d., lavender.........................30.00
Bowl, 6½" d., stippled, purple 32.00
Bowl, 7" d., blue....................................30.00
Bowl, 7" d., green 30.00
Bowl, 7" d., marigold............................38.00
Bowl, 7" d., red 1,500.00
Bowl, 7" d., ribbon candy rim, green.....50.00
Bowl, 7" d., ribbon candy rim, mari-
    gold 40.00
Bowl, 7" d., ribbon candy rim, purple 40.00
Bowl, 8" to 9" d., amber 65.00
Bowl, 8" to 9" d., stippled, aqua............46.00
Bowl, 8" to 9" d., blue............................32.00
Bowl, 8" to 9" d., blue opalescent 300.00

Bowl, 8" to 9" d., green 42.50
Bowl, 8" to 9" d., stippled, green...........25.00
Bowl, 8" to 9" d., lavender.....................75.00
Bowl, 8" to 9" d., marigold.....................35.00
Bowl, 8" to 9" d., stippled, mari-
    gold 75.00
Bowl, 8" to 9" d., peach opalescent 173.00
Bowl, 8" to 9" d., purple (ILLUS.) 43.00
Bowl, 8" to 9" d., ruffled, vaseline 55.00
Bowl, 9½" d., ruffled, purple 68.00
Bowl, 9½" d., stippled, purple 35.00
Bowl, 10" d., green 35.00
Bowl, 10" d., stippled, marigold 28.00
Bowl, 10" d., ruffled, peach opales
    cent 165.00
Bowl, aqua...65.00
Bowl, red..1,700.00
Pitcher, water, marigold......................150.00
Plate, 9" d., aqua 80.00
Plate, 9" d., purple 90.00
Rose bowl, green....................................80.00
Rose bowl, stippled, green 75.00
Rose bowl, marigold 50.00
Rose bowl, large, marigold 78.00
Rose bowl, purple..................................52.00
Rose bowl, stippled, purple 80.00
Tumbler, marigold................................50.00

COIN SPOT (Dugan)

Compote, 7" d., marigold.....................35.00
Compote, 7" d., peach opalescent........60.00
Compote, 7" d., fluted, peach
    opalescent ....85.00 to 100.00
Compote, 7" d., fluted, purple 65.00
Vase, 10" h., purple 25.00
Water set: lemonade pitcher &
    4 tumblers; marigold, 5 pcs..............365.00

COMET or RIBBON TIE (Fenton)

Comet Bowl

Bowl, 8" to 9" d., blue (ILLUS) 70.00
Bowl, 8" to 9" d., green 45.00
Bowl, 8" to 9" d., ribbon candy rim,
    lavender 90.00
Bowl, 8" to 9" d., marigold.....................45.00
Bowl, 8" to 9" d., purple 55.00

Plate, 9" d., ruffled, blue 173.00
Plate, 9" d., ruffled, purple 180.00

CONCAVE DIAMOND - See Diamond Concave Pattern

CONSTELLATION (DUGAN)

Compote, green....................................95.00
Compote, marigold 100.00
Compote, purple 275.00
Compote, white....................................113.00

CORAL (Fenton)

Bowl, 8" to 9" d., collared base, blue ..250.00
Bowl, 8" to 9" d., collared base,
    green.................................125.00 to 150.00
Bowl, 8" to 9" d., collared base,
    marigold 125.00
Plate, 9" d., marigold 700.00

CORN BOTTLE

Green..230.00
Ice green...............................250.00 to 275.00
Marigold................................250.00 to 275.00
Smoky..210.00

CORN VASE (Northwood)

Aqua opalescent...............................1,500.00
Aqua w/light marigold overlay..........1,975.00
Green...800.00
Ice blue...1,400.00
Ice green...375.00
Marigold..............................800.00 to 900.00
Pastel marigold......................................475.00
Purple 625.00
White 308.00

CORNUCOPIA

Candlestick, ice blue.............................75.00
Vase, 5" h., marigold 25.00

COSMOS

Bowl, 5" d., green 50.00
Bowl, 5" d., ice cream shape, green.....40.00
Bowl, 6" d., clambroth...........................35.00
Bowl, 6" d., green 45.00
Bowl, 9" d., blue....................85.00 to 110.00
Bowl, 9" d., green 50.00
Bowl, 9" d., marigold.............................30.00
Bowl, 10" d., marigold...........................45.00
Bowl, 10" d., purple...............................48.00
Bowl, 10½"d., ice cream shape,
    blue ....75.00 to 100.00
Plate, 6" d., green 75.00
Plate, chop, 10½" d., marigold............245.00

CRAB CLAW (Imperial)

Bowl, 8" to 9" d., clambroth.................100.00
Bowl, 8" to 9" d., fluted, smoky 40.00
Bowl, 10" d., ruffled, marigold...............70.00
Bowl, fruit, w/base, marigold.................90.00
Pitcher, marigold (ILLUS.) 255.00

Crab Claw Pitcher

Sauce dish, marigold 29.00
Tumbler, marigold.................................52.00

CRACKLE
Automobile vase w/bracket, marigold...25.00
Automobile vases, marigold, pr. (no
  brackets) 20.00
Bowl, 7½" d., marigold.........................15.00
Plate, 6" d., marigold 40.00
Plate, 8" d., marigold 20.00
Rose bowl, low, marigold......................25.00
Salt & pepper shakers, w/original
  tops, light blue, pr. 25.00
Tumbler, green 37.00
Tumbler, dome-footed, marigold 12.00
Vase, fan-shaped, marogold 20.00
Wall pocket, marigold 30.00
Water set: pitcher & 6 footed
  tumblers; marigold, 7 pcs.................150.00
Water set: pitcher & 8 footed
  tumblers; marigold, 9 pcs.................195.00

CRUCIFIX
Candlesticks, marigold, pr. 1,000.00

CUT COSMOS
Tumbler, marigold...............................258.00

DAISY & PLUME

Daisy & Plume Rose Bowl

Bowl, 8" to 9" d., three footed, green ..150.00
Bowl, 8" to 9" d., three footed,
  marigold 90.00
Candy dish, footed, blue.....................185.00
Candy dish, footed, marigold................50.00
Candy dish, footed, peach opalescent
  (Dugan) 100.00
Candy dish, footed, purple...................75.00
Candy dish, footed, white 125.00
Compote, green.....................................50.00
Compote, marigold 38.00
Compote, purple 55.00
Rose bowl, three-footed, blue.............250.00
Rose bowl, three-footed, green
  (ILLUS.) 92.00
Rose bowl, three-footed, ice blue 900.00
Rose bowl, three-footed, ice green.....900.00
Rose bowl, three-footed, marigold........56.00
Rose bowl, three-footed, purple 85.00
Rose bowl, three-footed, white 850.00

DAISY CUT BELL

Daisy Cut Bell

Marigold (ILLUS.) ....425.00 to 450.00

DAISY SQUARES
Compote, green..................575.00 to 675.00
Compote, marigold 400.00
Goblet, purple 800.00
Rose bowl, stemmed,
  green................................550.00 to 650.00
Rose bowl, jack-in-the-pulpit type,
  light green w/marigold overlay 725.00
Rose bowl, marigold 550.00

DAISY WREATH (Westmoreland)
Bowl, 8" to 9" d., blue opales-
  cent..................................400.00 to 500.00
Bowl, 8" to 9" d., moon-
  stone ....200.00 to 220.00
Bowl, 8" to 9" d., peach opalescent 95.00

DANDELION (Northwood)
Mug, aqua opalescent ....475.00 to 500.00
Mug, blue............................440.00 to 480.00
Mug, green ....500.00 to 600.00
Mug, ice blue opalescent....................895.00
Mug, marigold.....................375.00 to 400.00

Mug, pastel marigold ....275.00 to 300.00
Mug, purple.........................200.00 to 275.00
Mug, Knights Templar, ice blue 1,000.00
Mug, Knights Templar, ice green.....1,100.00
Mug, Knights Templar, marigold.........500.00
Mug, Knights Templar, purple 295.00
Pitcher, water, tankard, blue...............260.00
Pitcher, water, tankard,
    green.........................1,000.00 to 1,200.00

Dandelion Pitcher

Pitcher, water, tankard, marigold
    (ILLUS.) ....400.00 to 450.00
Pitcher, water, tankard,
    purple..............................650.00 to 750.00
Tumbler, blue..60.00
Tumbler, green ....75.00 to 100.00
Tumbler, ice blue 200.00
Tumbler, ice green..............................900.00
Tumbler, lavender................................225.00
Tumbler, marigold.................................45.00
Tumbler, purple 60.00
Tumbler, smoky 250.00
Tumbler, white 195.00
Water set: pitcher & 1 tumbler; white,
    2 pcs. 2,500.00
Water set: pitcher & 2 tumblers;
    pastel marigold, 3 pcs. 875.00
Water set: pitcher & 5 tumblers;
    green, 6 pcs. 1,400.00
Water set: pitcher & 6 tumblers; blue,
    7 pcs. 695.00
Water set: pitcher & 6 tumblers;
    purple, 7 pcs. ....925.00 to 975.00

DANDELION, PANELED (Fenton)
Pitcher, water, blue.............................450.00
Pitcher, water, green 475.00
Pitcher, water, marigold......................350.00
Pitcher, water, purple..........400.00 to 500.00
Tumbler, blue..65.00
Tumbler, green 40.00
Tumbler, marigold.................................40.00
Tumbler, purple 50.00
Water set: pitcher & 1 tumbler; blue,
    2 pcs. 130.00

Water set: pitcher & 6 tumblers; blue,
    7 pcs. ....800.00 to 850.00

DIAMOND & RIB VASE (FENTON)
Vase, 6" h., green 40.00
Vase, 7" h., marigodl 25.00
Vase, 7" h., purple 34.00
Vase, 8" h., white.................................75.00
Vase, 10" h., green 40.00
Vase, 10" h., marigold 35.00
Vase, 10" h., purple 35.00
Vase, 10" h., white...............................85.00
Vase, 11" h., aqua 40.00
Vase, 11" h., green 38.00
Vase, 11" h., ice green 80.00
Vase, 11" h., marigold 70.00
Vase, 12" h., purple 32.50
Vase, 13" h., blue 35.00
Vase, 15" h., marigold 55.00
Vase, 16" h., purple ....50.00 to 75.00
Vase, 19" h., purple 95.00
Vase, 19" h., funeral, purple 1,150.00

DIAMOND CONCAVE or CONCAVE
DIAMOND (Dugan)
Pitcher w/cover, blue 100.00
Tumbler, celeste blue 35.00
Tumbler, olive green...........................165.00
Tumbler, vaseline ....130.00 to 160.00

DIAMOND LACE (Imperial)

Diamond Lace Tumbler

Bowl, 8" to 9" d., clambroth..................65.00
Bowl, 8" to 9" d., marigold.....................40.00
Bowl, 8" to 9" d., purple 50.00
Bowl, 10" d., purple..............................76.00
Pitcher, water, purple.........................250.00
Sauce dish, marigold, 5" d...................25.00
Sauce dish, purple, 5" d.......................35.00
Tumbler, marigold...............................425.00
Tumbler, purple (ILLUS.) 50.00
Water set: pitcher & 4 tumblers;
    purple, 5 pcs. 450.00

DIAMOND POINT COLUMNS
Bowl, 5" d., 2½" h., marigold................20.00
Butter dish, cov., marigold...................40.00
Vase, 6" h., green 42.00
Vase, 6" h., marigold 30.00
Vase, 7" h., green 125.00
Vase, 7" h., purple 40.00

Vase, 7½" h., white.............150.00 to 200.00

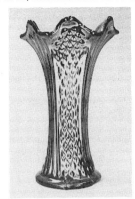

Diamond Point Columns Vase

Vase, 8" h., green (ILLUS.)..................40.00
Vase, 9" h., purple 75.00
Vase, 10" h., green..............................80.00
Vase, 10" h., purple 62.00
Vase, 10" h., white...............................65.00
Vase, 11" h., green 30.00
Vase, 11" h., ice blue.........................240.00
Vase, 12" h., marigold 28.00
Vase, 12" h., purple 35.00
Vase, 16" h., blue ....250.00 to 300.00

DIAMOND RING (Imperial)

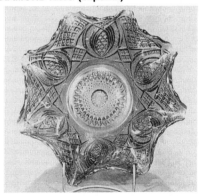

Diamond Ring Bowl

Bowl, 8" to 9" d., marigold.....................60.00
Bowl, 8" to 9" d., purple 75.00
Bowl, 8" to 9" d., smoky (ILLUS.)..........40.00
Rose bowl, marigold 300.00
Sauce dish, marigold 22.50
Sauce dish, smoky 28.00

DIAMONDS (Millersburg)

Pitcher, water, aqua.............................225.00
Pitcher, water, green 225.00
Pitcher, water, marigold......125.00 to 150.00
Pitcher, water, purple..........................160.00
Punch bowl & base, green, 2 pcs....2,000.00
Tumbler, aqua 85.00

Tumbler, green 55.00
Tumbler, lavender..................................70.00
Tumbler, marigold..................................40.00
Tumbler, purple 55.00
Water set: pitcher & 1 tumbler;
  marigold, 2 pcs. 250.00
Water set: pitcher & 4 tumblers;
  purple, 5 pcs. 475.00
Water set: pitcher & 6 tumblers;
  green, 7 pcs. 600.00

DIVING DOLPHINS FOOTED BOWL (Sowerby)

Diving Dolphins Bowl

Aqua blue, embossed scroll interior ...325.00
Marigold...150.00
Purple (ILLUS.)....................................500.00

DOGWOOD SPRAYS

Bowl, 7" d., collared base, peach
  opalescent 60.00
Bowl, 8" to 9" d., dome-footed,
  marigold 36.00
Bowl, 8" to 9" d., dome-footed, peach
  opalescent 80.00
Bowl, 8" to 9" d., dome-footed,
  purple 65.00
Bowl, blue opalescent.........................300.00

DOUBLE DUTCH BOWL

Marigold, 5" d..20.00
Marigold, 8" to 9" d., footed 40.00
Purple, 8" to 9" d., footed...................135.00
Clambroth, 10" d., ruffled......................69.00

DOUBLE STAR or BUZZ SAW (Cambridge)

Cruet w/stopper, green, small, 4" 500.00
Cruet w/stopper, green, large,
  6".....................................400.00 to 425.00
Cuspidor whimsey (made from
  tumbler mold), green....................2,500.00
Pitcher, water, green ....300.00 to 325.00
Pitcher, water, marigold..................1,500.00
Tumbler, green 65.00
Tumbler, purple 130.00
Water set: pitcher & 6 tumblers,
  green, 7 pcs. 775.00

DOUBLE STEM ROSE
Bowl, 7" d., dome-footed, marigold.......35.00
Bowl, 8" to 9" d., dome-footed,
  aqua..450.00
Bowl, 8" to 9" d., dome-footed, celeste
  blue 600.00
Bowl, 8" to 9" d., dome-footed,
  lavender 250.00
Bowl, 8" to 9" d., dome-footed,
  marigold 45.00
Bowl, 8" to 9" d., dome-footed, peach
  opalescent ....125.00 to 150.00
Bowl, 8" to 9" d., dome-footed, purple ..60.00
Bowl, 8" to 9" d., dome-footed,
  white ....100.00 to 125.00
Bowl, 10" d., peach opalescent 175.00
Plate, dome-footed, purple 145.00
Plate, dome-footed, white...................150.00

DRAGON & LOTUS (Fenton)

Dragon & Lotus Bowl

Bowl, 7" to 9" d., three-footed, blue 68.00
Bowl, 7" to 9" d., three-footed, green....75.00
Bowl, 7" to 9" d., three-footed, laven-
  der...125.00
Bowl, 7" to 9" d., three-footed, lime
  green opalescent 300.00
Bowl, 7" to 9" d., three-footed,
  marigold 45.00
Bowl, 7" to 9" d., three-footed, peach
  opalescent 500.00
Bowl, 7" to 9" d., three-footed, purple ...70.00
Bowl, 8" to 9" d., collared base,
  amber...............................200.00 to 225.00
Bowl, 8" to 9" d., collared base, blue ..117.00
Bowl, 8" to 9" d., collared base,
  green..108.00
Bowl, 8" to 9" d., collared base, lime
  green..325.00
Bowl, 8" to 9" d., collared base, lime
  green opalescent ....550.00 to 650.00
Bowl, 8" to 9" d., collared base,
  marigold 60.00
Bowl, 8" to 9" d., collared base,
  moonstone 1,100.00
Bowl, 8" to 9" d., collared base, peach
  opalescent 550.00

Bowl, 8" to 9" d., collared base,
  purple 150.00
Bowl, 8" to 9" d., red 1,750.00
Bowl, 9" d., ice cream shape, collared
  base, amber.....................150.00 to 200.00
Bowl, 9" d., ice cream shape, collared
  base, aqua opalescent.................3,400.00
Bowl, 9" d., ice cream shape, collared
  base, blue 103.00
Bowl, 9" d., ice cream shape, collared
  base, marigold 50.00
Bowl, 9" d., ice cream shape, collared
  base, moonstone w/peach marigold
  overlay 1,250.00
Bowl, 9" d., ice cream shape, collared
  base, red (ILLUS.) 4,500.00
Bowl, 9" d., ice cream shape, col-
  lared base, Reverse Amber-
  ina ....675.00 to 725.00
Bowl, 9" d., marigold.............................82.00
Bowl, 9" d., three-in-one edge,
  green..135.00
Bowl, ice cream shape, spade-footed,
  purple 100.00
Bowl, ruffled, blue 86.00
Bowl, ruffled, lavender 195.00
Bowl, ruffled, marigold 55.00
Bowl, ruffled, marigold opalescent......675.00
Bowl, ruffled, purple.............................75.00
Bowl, vaseline...................................200.00
Plate, 9" d., marigold 2,600.00
Plate, collared base,
  blue ....1,500.00 to 2,000.00
Plate, collared base, ruffled, mari-
  gold 2,200.00
Plate, edge turned up, blue 250.00
Plate, spatula-footed, marigold..........638.00

DRAGON & STRAWBERRY BOWL or
DRAGON & BERRY (Fenton)
Bowl, 9" d., blue................................600.00
Bowl, 9" d., green 682.00
Bowl, 9" d., marigold...........350.00 to 375.00
Bowl, 9" d., purple.............................625.00

DRAPERY (Northwood)
Candy dish, tricornered, ice
  blue ....175.00 to 195.00
Candy dish, tricornered, ice
  green................................150.00 to 200.00
Candy dish, tricornered, marigold........62.50
Candy dish, tricornered, purple 400.00
Candy dish, tricornered, white...........135.00
Rose bowl, aqua opalescent 325.00
Rose bowl, blue ....250.00 to 300.00
Rose bowl, blue w/electric
  iridescence......................................600.00
Rose bowl, ice blue ....800.00 to 1,000.00
Rose bowl, lavender 110.00
Rose bowl, marigold...........325.00 to 375.00
Rose bowl, pastel marigold 385.00
Rose bowl, purple..............200.00 to 250.00
Rose bowl, white ....225.00 to 275.00

Vase, 4" h., ice blue..............................170.00
Vase, 7" h., blue 67.50
Vase, 7" h., ice green 95.00
Vase, 7" h., marigold 50.00
Vase, 8" h., blue...................................50.00
Vase, 8" h., ice blue..............................60.00
Vase, 8" h., ice green 150.00
Vase, 8" h., marigold 42.50
Vase, 8" h., white................................100.00
Vase, 9" h., blue 95.00
Vase, 9" h., purple 150.00
Vase, 10" h., ice blue...........................425.00
Vase, 10" h., ice green 185.00
Vase, 10" h., marigold ....75.00 to 100.00
Vase, squatty, purple.............................85.00

EMBROIDERED MUMS (Northwood)
Bonbon, stemmed, white 1,150.00
Bowl, 8" to 9" d., amber 1,000.00
Bowl, 8" to 9" d., ruffled, aqua
  opalescent 3,400.00
Bowl, 8" to 9" d., blue..........350.00 to 400.00
Bowl, 8" to 9" d., ruffled, blue...........1,350.00
Bowl, 8" to 9" d., blue w/electric
  iridescence.......................................500.00
Bowl, 8" to 9" d., ice blue 900.00
Bowl, 8" to 9" d., ice
  green............................900.00 to 1,000.00
Bowl, 8" to 9" d., marigold...................500.00
Bowl, 8" to 9" d., ruffled, marigold.......230.00
Bowl, 8" to 9" d., pastel marigold.........500.00
Bowl, 8" to 9" d., purple ......350.00 to 400.00
Bowl, aqua......................................1,400.00
Bowl, lavender 1,600.00
Bowl, lime green opalescent............1,800.00
Bowl, piecrust rim, sapphire blue.....2,700.00
Plate, ice green.............2,000.00 to 2,500.00

ESTATE (Westmoreland)
Creamer, peach opalescent 60.00
Creamer & sugar bowl, peach
  opalescent, pr. 250.00
Mug, marigold, souvenir 150.00
Mug, marigold......................................88.00
Mug, peach opalescent 125.00
Perfume bottle & stopper, smoky 1,100.00
Sugar bowl, marigold, souvenir 50.00
Sugar bowl, peach opalescent 75.00
Sugar bowl, peach opalescent,
  souvenir 40.00

FAN (Dugan)
Sauceboat, peach opalescent 137.00
Sauceboat, purple 60.00

FANCIFUL (Dugan)
Bowl, 8" to 9" d., blue...........................85.00
Bowl, 8" to 9" d., marigold....................24.00
Bowl, 8" to 9" d., piecrust rim,
  marigold ....100.00 to 125.00
Bowl, 8" to 9" d., peach opalescent 192.00
Bowl, 8" to 9" d., ruffled, purple 135.00
Bowl, 8" to 9" d., ruffled,
  white ....160.00 to 190.00

Bowl, 10" d., ruffled, white ..150.00 to 175.00
Bowl, ice cream shape, marigold..........60.00
Bowl, ice cream shape, peach
  opalescent 144.00
Bowl, ice cream shape, purple 325.00
Bowl, ice cream shape, white..............95.00
Plate, 9" d., blue ....250.00 to 275.00
Plate, 9" d., marigold ....100.00 to 150.00
Plate, 9" d., peach opales-
  cent ....275.00 to 325.00
Plate, 9" d., purple ....250.00 to 275.00
Plate, 9" d., white...............................245.00
Plate, 9½" d., ruffled, white................200.00

FANTAIL
Bowl, 9" d., footed, blue.....................185.00
Bowl, 9" d., shallow, footed, w/Butter-
  fly & Berry exterior, blue 175.00
Bowl, 9" d., ice cream shape,
  w/Butterfly & Berry exterior,
  marigold...200.00
Bowl, 9" d., footed, marigold................70.00

FARMYARD (Dugan)

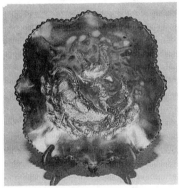

Farmyard Square Bowl

Bowl, purple.....................................2,600.00
Bowl, fluted, purple 3,500.00
Bowl, ribbon candy rim, purple 3,500.00
Bowl, square, purple (ILLUS.) 2,900.00
Plate, 10" d., purple 6,000.00

FASHION (Imperial)
Bowl, 9" d., marigold............................25.00
Bowl, 9" d., ruffled, smoky 40.00
Creamer, marigold...............................25.00
Creamer, smoky 130.00
Creamer & sugar bowl, marigold, pr.....60.00
Creamer & sugar bowl, purple, pr.......325.00
Pitcher, water, marigold, (ILLUS.
  top next page)................100.00 to 125.00
Pitcher, water, purple..........................950.00
Punch bowl & base, marigold, 12" d.,
  2 pcs. 104.00
Punch cup, marigold............................15.00
Punch cup, red 325.00
Punch cups, marigold, set of 6 ....105.00
Punch set: bowl, base & 8 cups;
  marigold, 10 pcs. 325.00

Fashion Pitcher

Rose bowl, green...............................425.00
Rose bowl, marigold, 7" d....................90.00
Tumbler, marigold................................20.00
Tumbler, purple 175.00
Tumbler, smoky...................................90.00
Water set: pitcher & 3 tumblers;
    smoky, 4 pcs.................................700.00
Water set: pitcher & 6 tumblers;
    marigold, 7 pcs. ....300.00 to 350.00

FEATHER & HEART

Feather & Heart Pitcher

Pitcher, water, green (ILLUS.) 450.00
Pitcher, water, marigold......300.00 to 350.00
Tumbler, green 200.00
Tumbler, marigold................................70.00
Water set: pitcher & 1 tumbler; purple,
    2 pcs. 975.00

FEATHER STITCH BOWL

Aqua 225.00
Blue 236.00
Green...100.00
Marigold...55.00
Vaseline, three-in-one edge 995.00

FEATHERED SERPENT

Bowl, 8" to 9" d., green 60.00

Bowl, 8" to 9" d., marigold....................40.00
Bowl, 8" to 9" d., purple 70.00
Bowl, 10" d., ruffled, blue....................65.00
Bowl, 10" d., fluted, green....................55.00
Bowl, 10" d., marigold..........................60.00
Bowl, 10" d., flared, purple..................55.00
Bowl, 12½" d., ruffled, blue.................95.00
Sauce dish, blue 27.50
Sauce dish, green.................................28.00
Sauce dish, marigold 15.00
Sauce dish, purple...............................35.00
Whimsey, tricornered, marigold...........45.00

FENTONIA

Berry set: master bowl & 4 sauce
    dishes; marigold, 5 pcs. 175.00
Bowl, master berry, blue....................275.00
Bowl, master berry, marigold...............55.00
Butter dish, cov., footed, marigold......137.50
Creamer, blue.....................................100.00
Creamer, marigold................................60.00
Sugar bowl, cov., blue 115.00
Table set: creamer, cov. sugar bowl &
    spooner; blue, 3 pcs. 350.00
Tumbler, blue..65.00
Tumbler, marigold.................................44.00

FENTON'S FLOWERS ROSE BOWL -
See Orange Tree Pattern

FERN

Compote, w/Daisy & Plume
    exterior, green (Northwood) 95.00
Compote, w/Daisy & Plume
    exterior, marigold (Northwood) 78.00
Compote, w/Daisy & Plume
    exterior, purple (Northwood) 75.00
Dish, hat-shaped, marigold
    (Fenton) 27.00

FIELD FLOWER (Imperial)

Pitcher, water, amber 350.00
Pitcher, water, green 325.00
Pitcher, water, marigold......................165.00
Pitcher, water, purple..........400.00 to 425.00
Tumbler, amber 39.00
Tumbler, blue......................................100.00
Tumbler, green 70.00
Tumbler, marigold................................32.00
Tumbler, purple 55.00

FIELD THISTLE (English)

Bowl, 5" d., berry, marigold..................40.00
Compote, marigold 275.00
Plate, 6" d., marigold 190.00
Plate, 9" d., marigold 435.00
Tumbler, marigold.................................46.00

FILE (Imperial)

Bowl, 8" d., marigold.............................40.00
Pitcher, water, marigold......................650.00
Spooner, marigold 70.00
Tumbler, marigold..............175.00 to 200.00

Vase, marigold.................................250.00

FILE & FAN
Compote, blue opalescent..250.00 to 300.00
Compote, marigold 45.00
Compote, milk white w/marigold
   overlay 225.00
Compote, peach opalescent................80.00

FINECUT & ROSES (Northwood)
Candy dish, three-footed, aqua
   opalescent ....400.00 to 450.00
Candy dish, three-footed, blue
   w/electric iridescence.........................67.50
Candy dish, three-footed, green 65.00
Candy dish, three-footed, ice
   blue ....300.00 to 350.00
Candy dish, three-footed, ice green ...175.00
Candy dish, three-footed, marigold 40.00
Candy dish, three-footed, purple 50.00
Candy dish, three-footed,
   white ....125.00 to 150.00
Rose bowl, amber.............................550.00
Rose bowl, aqua opales-
   cent ....1,000.00 to 1,300.00
Rose bowl, green...............................250.00
Rose bowl, ice blue 315.00
Rose bowl, ice green 200.00
Rose bowl, marigold............................88.00
Rose bowl, purple................................75.00
Rose bowl, white ....425.00 to 450.00
Rose bowl/whimsey, straight top,
   lavender 650.00
Rose bowl/whimsey, purple...............195.00

FINECUT FLOWERS
Compote, marigold 35.00
Compote, marigold, clear stem,
   5 x 6½"...20.00

FINE RIB (Northwood & Fenton)

Fine Rib Vase

Bowl, master berry, 9" d., marigold.......35.00
Bowl, 10½" d., green 50.00

Bowl, purple...35.00
Compote, ruffled, green.......................45.00
Plate, 9" d., eight-sided, marigold.........85.00
Sauce dish, vaseline...........................25.00
Vase, 6½ h., 5" d., blue 25.00
Vase, 6½ h., 5" d., green......................30.00
Vase, 6½ h., 5" d., marigold 25.00
Vase, 7" h., green...............................42.50
Vase, 7" h., marigold 35.00
Vase, 7½" h., white..............................80.00
Vase, 8" h., aqua 62.50
Vase, 8½" h., blue 38.00
Vase, 8½" h., red...............................195.00
Vase, 9" h., green 65.00
Vase, 9" h., purple 55.00
Vase, 9" h., red (Fenton) 275.00
Vase, 9½" h., blue 45.00
Vase, 9½" h., vaseline (Fenton) 50.00
Vase, 10" h., amber (Fenton) 40.00
Vase, 10" h., aqua (Northwood) 70.00
Vase, 10" h., blue (ILLUS.) 40.00
Vase, 10" h., purple 45.00
Vase, 10" h., red (Fenton) 500.00
Vase, 12" h., red (Fenton) 650.00
Vase, 12" h., vaseline
   (Fenton) ....50.00 to 75.00
Vase, 14" h., marigold 36.00
Vase, 15" h., blue 60.00
Vase, 16" h., marigold 45.00
Vase, 17" h., marigold 85.00

FISHERMAN'S MUG
Marigold............................190.00 to 210.00
Marigold opalescent 1,200.00
Pastel marigold...................200.00 to 250.00
Peach opalescent.........1,100.00 to 1,250.00
Purple 125.00

FISHSCALE & BEADS
Banana boat, peach opalescent, 7" l. ...73.00
Bonbon, marigold, 6" 45.00
Bonbon, peach opalescent, 6"..............55.00
Bowl, 7" d., marigold.............................21.00
Bowl, 7" d., ribbon candy rim, purple....40.00
Card tray, peach opalescent, 4 x 7"......70.00
Plate, 7" d., marigold 79.00
Plate, 7" d., pastel marigold..................75.00
Plate, 7" d., ruffled rim, peach
   opalescent ....125.00 to 150.00
Plate, 7" d., purple 375.00
Plate, 7" d., white...............................115.00
Plate, 7½" d., marigold 95.00
Plate, 7½" d., purple 130.00
Plate, 8" d., purple 1,000.00

FLEUR DE LIS (Millersburg)
Bowl, 8" to 9" d., dome-footed,
   marigold..200.00
Bowl, 8" to 9" d., dome-footed,
   purple...............................225.00 to 250.00
Bowl, 10" d., green ....175.00 to 200.00

Fleur-de-Lis Bowl

Bowl, 10" d., marigold (ILLUS.) 180.00
Bowl, 10" d., purple.............300.00 to 400.00
Bowl, dome-footed, ruffled, marigold..150.00
Bowl, dome-footed, purple..................350.00
Bowl, tricornered, footed, marigold.....300.00
Bowl, tricornered, footed, purple.........245.00
Rose bowl, dome-footed, purple......3,300.00

FLORAL & GRAPE (Dugan or Diamond Glass Co.)
Pitcher, water, blue.............................395.00
Pitcher, water, green 275.00
Pitcher, water, marigold........................90.00
Pitcher, water,
    purple................................150.00 to 200.00
Pitcher, water, white 350.00
Pitcher, water, variant, white 750.00
Tumbler, black amethyst 80.00
Tumbler, blue.......................................35.00
Tumbler, green 175.00
Tumbler, marigold................................25.00
Tumbler, purple 40.00
Tumbler, white.....................................70.00
Water set: pitcher & 4 tumblers; white,
    5 pcs. 695.00
Water set: pitcher & 6 tumblers;
    marigold, 7 pcs. ....225.00 to 250.00
Whimsey, hat-shaped (from tumbler
    mold), marigold 80.00

FLORAL & WHEAT COMPOTE (Dugan)
Marigold..45.00
Peach opalescent..................50.00 to 75.00
Purple 40.00
White 135.00

FLOWERS & BEADS
Card tray, tricornered, purple, 7" w.......62.00
Plate, 7½" w., six-sided, peach
    opalescent 65.00
Plate, flat, purple.................................55.00
Plate, six-sided, purple 80.00

FLOWERS & FRAMES
Bowl, 7" d., single handle, peach
    opalescent 33.00
Bowl, 7" d., dome-footed, purple 100.00
Bowl, 9" d., dome-footed, green 275.00
Bowl, 9" d., dome-footed, peach
    opalescent 145.00
Bowl, 9" d., dome-footed, fluted,
    purple...............................150.00 to 200.00
Bowl, tricornered, peach opales-
    cent...................................100.00 to 125.00
Bowl, tricornered, dome-footed,
    purple..125.00

FLUTE (Imperial)
Berry set: master bowl & 6 sauce
    dishes; marigold, 7 pcs. 135.00
Bowl, 8" to 9" d., marigold....................28.00
Bowl, 8" to 9" d., purple 65.00
Butter dish, cov., marigold 60.00
Compote, green....................................25.00
Creamer, breakfast size, marigold........50.00
Creamer, breakfast size, purple 60.00
Creamer & open sugar bowl,
    breakfast size, purple, pr. 130.00
Match holder, purple.............................900.00
Pitcher, water, clambroth......................175.00
Pitcher, water, marigold.......................275.00
Pitcher, water, purple...........................293.00
Punch cup, green 25.00
Punch cup, marigold.............................35.00
Punch cup, purple.................................25.00

Flute Punch Set

Punch set: bowl, base & 6 cups;
    purple, 8 pcs. (ILLUS.) .....750.00 to 850.00
Rose bowl, marigold 24.00
Sauce dish, green.................................34.00
Sauce dish, marigold 15.00
Sauce dish, purple................................50.00
Sugar bowl, open, breakfast size,
    amber..65.00
Sugar bowl, open, breakfast size,
    green..60.00
Sugar bowl, open, breakfast size,
    purple...60.00
Toothpick holder, green.........................48.00
Toothpick holder, lavender ...75.00 to 100.00

Toothpick holder, marigold 65.00
Toothpick holder, purple 80.00
Tumbler, aqua 175.00
Tumbler, cobalt blue 400.00
Tumbler, marigold.................................40.00
Tumbler, purple 82.00
Tumbler, red 275.00
Tumbler, smoky 425.00
Vase, 9" h., aqua 70.00
Vase, 9" h., purple 82.00
Vase, 12" h., funeral, green 32.00
Vase, 17" h., green 65.00
Water set: pitcher & 6 tumblers;
    marigold, 7 pcs. 650.00

FLUTE (Northwood)
Pitcher, milk, marigold 20.00
Pitcher, water, clambroth....................175.00
Salt dip, master size, blue 45.00
Salt dip, master size, vaseline 95.00
Tumbler, dark marigold.........................95.00
Tumbler, marigold.................................55.00
Tumbler, marigold, variant....................85.00
Vase, 13" h., funeral, marigold 35.00
Vase, funeral, green 175.00

FLUTE & CANE
Compote, marigold, 6½" d., 6" h.........125.00
Goblet, marigold 55.00
Pitcher, marigold.................................200.00
Pitcher, milk, marigold 140.00

FLUTED SCROLL
Cuspidor, purple 2,500.00
Tumbler, blue opalescent 75.00

FORMAL
Vase, marigold.....................................125.00
Vase, rolled top, purple.......................425.00
Vase, jack-in-the-pulpit, marigold 350.00
Vase, jack-in-the-pulpit, purple 500.00

FOUR FLOWERS - See Pods & Posies Pattern

FOUR SEVENTY FOUR (Imperial)
Compote, green.....................................95.00
Goblet, water, marigold 75.00
Pitcher, milk, green..............................400.00
Pitcher, milk, marigold 162.00
Pitcher, water, marigold.......................150.00
Pitcher, water, purple..........................725.00
Punch cup, green 60.00
Punch cup, marigold.............................22.00
Punch cup, purple.................................50.00
Punch cup, teal blue 40.00
Punch set: bowl, base & 6 cups;
    marigold, 8 pcs. 425.00
Tumbler, blue......................................200.00
Tumbler, marigold.................................35.00
Tumbler, purple 75.00
Water set: pitcher & 6 tumblers;
    marigold, 7 pcs. 385.00

FROLICKING BEARS (U.S. Glass)
Pitcher, green ....5,000.00 to 7,000.00
Tumbler, green 9,500.00

FROSTED BLOCK
Bowl, 6" d., marigold............................19.00
Bowl, 8" to 9" d., scalloped & fluted,
    clambroth 35.00
Bowl, square, clambroth.......................30.00
Bowl, square, marigold 40.00
Bowl, square, "USA," white...................45.00
Compote, clambroth 100.00
Compote, white....................................150.00
Nut dish, clambroth...............................55.00
Pitcher, milk, marigold 50.00
Plate, 7¾" sq., marigold.......................30.00
Plate, 7¾" sq., smoky.........................100.00
Plate, 9" d., clambroth 70.00
Plate, 9" d., marigold 50.00
Plate, 9" d., smoky 50.00
Relish, marigold....................................35.00
Rose bowl, clambroth.........................280.00
Rose bowl, marigold 50.00
Rose bowl, white 55.00
Vase, smoky 35.00

FRUIT SALAD
Punch bowl (no base), marigold...........95.00
Punch cup, marigold..............................28.00
Punch set: bowl, base & 6 cups;
    marigold, 8 pcs. 350.00

FRUITS & FLOWERS (Northwood)

Fruits & Flowers Bonbon

Berry set: master bowl & 4 sauce
    dishes; purple, 5 pcs......................395.00
Bonbon, stemmed, two-handled,
    amber..375.00
Bonbon, stemmed, two-handled, aqua
    opalescent ....475.00 to 500.00
Bonbon, stemmed, two-handled,
    blue 163.00
Bonbon, stemmed, two-handled,
    electric blue.....................................250.00
Bonbon, stemmed, two-handled,
    green..125.00
Bonbon, stemmed, two-handled, ice
    blue ....700.00 to 750.00

Bonbon, stemmed, two-handled, ice
green...450.00
Bonbon, stemmed, two-handled,
lavender 650.00
Bonbon, stemmed, two-handled,
marigold (ILLUS.)...............................90.00
Bonbon, stemmed, two-handled, olive
green...135.00
Bonbon, stemmed, two-handled,
pastel marigold 115.00
Bonbon, stemmed, two-handled,
purple...95.00
Bonbon, stemmed, two-handled,
white ....375.00 to 400.00
Bowl, 6" d., ruffled, green 48.00
Bowl, 6" d., ruffled, marigold.................60.00
Bowl, 6" d., ruffled, purple....................48.00
Bowl, 7" d., blue...................................85.00
Bowl, 7" d., blue w/electric
iridescence.......................300.00 to 350.00
Bowl, 7" d., green 53.00
Bowl, 7" d., purple.................................60.00
Bowl, 7" d., ruffled, blue......200.00 to 275.00
Bowl, 7" d., ruffled, ice green..............350.00
Bowl, 7" d., ruffled, marigold.................15.00
Bowl, 9½" d., ruffled, Basketweave
exterior, purple 61.00
Bowl, master berry, 10" d., green 82.00
Bowl, master berry, 10" d., marigold.....45.00
Bowl, master berry, 10" d., purple 66.00
Bowl, 10" d., ruffled, ice green...........475.00
Bowl, 10" d., ruffled, purple.................150.00
Bowl, piecrust rim, purple 225.00
Card tray, green...................................125.00
Plate, 7" d., green 170.00
Plate, 7" d., marigold 125.00
Plate, 7" d., purple 175.00
Plate, 7½" d., handgrip, green 165.00
Plate, 7½" d., handgrip,
purple..............................150.00 to 175.00
Sauce dish, marigold 31.00
Sauce dish, purple.................................45.00

Bowl, 6" d., peach opalescent,
variant 60.00
Bowl, 6" d., ruffled, purple....................45.00
Bowl, 6" d., ruffled, white 45.00
Bowl, 9" d., ice cream shape, mari-
gold 60.00
Bowl, 9" d., ice cream shape, purple ..700.00
Bowl, 10" d., ruffled, marigold..............80.00
Bowl, 10" d., ruffled, peach
opalescent 282.00
Bowl, 10" d., ruffled, white ..300.00 to 325.00
Bowl, fruit, peach opalescent,
variant 550.00
Bowl, white, variant............................120.00
Plate, 6" d., peach opalescent............625.00
Plate, 6½" d., white.............................400.00
Plate, chop, 11" d., peach
opalescent 4,200.00
Plate, chop, 11" d., purple
(ILLUS.) 7,500.00
Plate, peach opalescent, variant 500.00
Sauce dish, peach opalescent..............80.00

GARLAND ROSE BOWL (Fenton)

Garland Rose Bowl

Blue (ILLUS.) 60.00
Marigold..................................50.00 to 75.00

GOD & HOME

God & Home Tumbler

Pitcher, blue.....................................1,130.00

GARDEN PATH

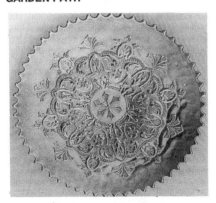

Garden Path Chop Plate

Tumbler, blue (ILLUS.) 275.00
Water set: pitcher & 6 tumblers; blue,
   7 pcs. 2,500.00

GODDESS OF HARVEST (FENTON)
Bowl, 8" d., piecrust rim, purple 6,750.00

GOLDEN HARVEST or HARVEST TIME
(U.S. Glass)
Decanter w/stopper, marigold.............146.00
Wine, marigold....................................25.00
Wine, purple 40.00

GOOD LUCK (Northwood)

Good Luck Ruffled Bowl

Bowl, 8" d., ruffled, blue......................285.00
Bowl, 8" d., ruffled, stippled, blue 374.00
Bowl, 8" d., ruffled, blue w/electric
   iridescence......................................285.00
Bowl, 8" d., ruffled, stippled, blue
   w/electric iridescence.......375.00 to 400.00
Bowl, 8" d., ruffled, green 263.00
Bowl, 8" d., ruffled, Basketweave
   exterior, green.................250.00 to 300.00
Bowl, 8" d., ruffled, marigold...............125.00
Bowl, 8" d., ruffled, Basketweave
   exterior, marigold ....150.00 to 200.00
Bowl, 8" d., ruffled, stippled, mari-
   gold 169.00
Bowl, 8" d., ruffled, purple...200.00 to 225.00
Bowl, 8" d., ruffled, Basketweave
   exterior, purple.................................225.00
Bowl, 8" to 9" d., piecrust rim, aqua
   opalescent 1,800.00
Bowl, 8" to 9" d., piecrust rim, blue 403.00
Bowl, 8" to 9" d., piecrust rim,
   stippled, blue....................................321.00
Bowl, 8" to 9" d., piecrust rim,
   clambroth 450.00
Bowl, 8" to 9" d., piecrust rim,
   green...............................375.00 to 425.00
Bowl, 8" to 9" d., piecrust rim,
   marigold 170.00

Bowl, 8" to 9" d., piecrust rim,
   stippled, marigold.............................190.00
Bowl, 8" to 9" d., piecrust rim, purple..322.00
Bowl, 8" to 9" d., piecrust rim, teal
   blue ....2,500.00 to 3,000.00
Bowl, 8" to 9" d., ruffled, aqua opales-
   cent 1,300.00
Bowl, 8" to 9" d., ruffled, green 800.00
Bowl, 8" to 9" d., ruffled, ice blue 4,200.00
Bowl, 8" to 9" d., ruffled, lav-
   ender................................200.00 to 250.00
Bowl, 8" to 9" d., ruffled, marigold
   (ILLUS.) 125.00
Bowl, 8" to 9" d., ruffled, purple 297.00
Bowl, 8" to 9" d., ruffled, teal
   blue ....1,200.00 to 1,500.00
Bowl, aqua..1,200.00
Bowl, piecrust rim, stippled, ribbed
   exterior, blue w/electric irides-
   cence 775.00
Bowl, ruffled, sapphire blue 1,300.00
Plate, 9" d., blue 425.00
Plate, 9" d., blue w/electric
   iridescence.................1,250.00 to 1,275.00
Plate, 9" d., green 700.00
Plate, 9" d., marigold 500.00
Plate, 9" d., purple 475.00
Plate, 9" d., stippled, purple................600.00
Plate, 9" d., Basketweave exterior,
   purple 525.00

GRAPE & CABLE

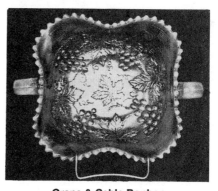

Grape & Cable Bonbon

Banana boat, banded rim, stippled,
   blue ....1,000.00 to 1,200.00
Banana boat, green 525.00
Banana boat, ice blue.........550.00 to 600.00
Banana boat, ice green 750.00
Banana boat, marigold 140.00
Banana boat, stippled, marigold.........225.00
Banana boat, purple 225.00
Banana boat, white.............650.00 to 685.00
Berry set: master bowl & 6 sauce
   dishes; green, 7 pcs. 300.00
Berry set: master bowl & 6 sauce
   dishes; marigold, 7 pcs. 275.00

Berry set: master bowl & 6 sauce
dishes; purple, 7 pcs. ....375.00 to 400.00
Bonbon, two-handled, stippled, aqua
opalescent (ILLUS.) 3,900.00
Bonbon, two-handled, blue..................95.00
Bonbon, two-handled, stippled,
blue ....200.00 to 225.00
Bonbon, two-handled, green 58.00
Bonbon, two-handled, stippled,
green...............................100.00 to 125.00
Bonbon, two-handled, marigold............75.00
Bonbon, two-handled, stippled,
marigold 45.00
Bonbon, two-handled, purple...............68.00
Bonbon, two-handled,
white ....650.00 to 750.00
Bowl, 5" d., blue (Fenton) 50.00
Bowl, 5" d., green 40.00
Bowl, 5" d., marigold............................38.00
Bowl, 5" d., purple................................32.00
Bowl, 6" d., ruffled, purple....................40.00
Bowl, 6½" d., marigold..........................38.00
Bowl, 7" d., ice cream shape, aqua
(Fenton) 300.00
Bowl, 7" d., ice cream shape, ice
green...315.00
Bowl, 7" d., ice cream shape,
marigold (Fenton) 125.00
Bowl, 7" d., ice cream shape, milk
white w/marigold overlay
(Fenton) ....150.00 to 250.00
Bowl, 7" d., ice cream shape,
red (Fenton) 750.00
Bowl, 7" d., blue (Fenton) 40.00
Bowl, 7" d., ice blue 750.00
Bowl, 7" d., red (Fenton).....................500.00
Bowl, 7" d., ruffled, purple....................42.50
Bowl, 7" d., ruffled, teal blue 250.00
Bowl, 7" d., ruffled, vaseline (Fenton)...47.50
Bowl, 8" to 9" d., piecrust rim, aqua
opalescent (Northwood)...............3,200.00
Bowl, 8" to 9" d., piecrust rim, blue
w/electric iridescence......................350.00
Bowl, 8" to 9" d., piecrust rim,
stippled, blue...................................340.00
Bowl, 8" to 9" d., piecrust rim,
green...147.00
Bowl, 8" to 9" d., piecrust rim, Basket-
weave exterior, green 60.00
Bowl, 8" to 9" d., piecrust rim, ice
blue 1,000.00
Bowl, 8" to 9" d., piecrust rim,
marigold 100.00
Bowl, 8" to 9" d., piecrust rim,
purple...............................250.00 to 275.00
Bowl, 8" to 9" d., piecrust rim,
Basketweave exterior, purple 160.00
Bowl, 8" to 9" d., ball-footed, blue
(Fenton) 85.00
Bowl, 8" to 9" d., ball-footed, green
(Fenton) 76.00
Bowl, 8" to 9" d., ball-footed, pastel
marigold (Fenton) 50.00

Bowl, 8" to 9" d., ball-footed, purple
(Fenton) 50.00
Bowl, 8" to 9" d., ball-footed, smoky
(Fenton) 275.00
Bowl, 8" to 9" d., ball-footed, teal
blue 275.00
Bowl, orange, 10½" d., footed,
Persian Medallion interior, blue
(Fenton) ....225.00 to 250.00
Bowl, orange, 10½" d., footed,
Persian Medallion interior, green
(Fenton) ....225.00 to 250.00
Bowl, orange, 10½" d., footed,
Persian Medallion interior, marigold
(Fenton) 140.00
Bowl, orange, 10½" d., footed,
Persian Medallion interior, purple
(Fenton) 267.00
Bowl, orange, 10½" d., footed,
blue ....350.00 to 450.00
Bowl, orange, 10½" d., footed,
stippled, blue w/electric iridescence
(Northwood) 895.00
Bowl, orange, 10½" d., footed,
clambroth 350.00
Bowl, orange, 10½" d., footed,
green...............................300.00 to 350.00
Bowl, orange, 10½" d., footed, ice
blue 1,250.00
Bowl, orange, 10½" d., footed, ice
green............................950.00 to 1,150.00
Bowl, orange, 10½" d., footed,
marigold 202.00
Bowl, orange, 10½" d., footed,
stippled, marigold............................300.00
Bowl, orange, 10½" d., footed,
purple...325.00
Bowl, orange, 10½" d., footed,
white 1,250.00
Bowl, orange, 10½" d., lavender.........395.00
Bowl, 10½" d., ruffled, Basketweave
exterior, green..................................100.00
Breakfast set: individual size creamer
& sugar bowl; green, pr....................123.00
Breakfast set: individual size
creamer & sugar bowl; purple,
pr.....................................200.00 to 250.00
Bride's basket, purple 2,975.00
Butter dish, cov., amber......................155.00
Butter dish, cov., green........................180.00
Butter dish, cov., ice green 250.00
Butter dish, cov., marigold 165.00
Butter dish, cov., purple.......................190.00
Candle lamp, green ....650.00 to 700.00
Candle lamp, marigold........500.00 to 550.00
Candle lamp, purple ....500.00 to 600.00
Candle lamp shade, green 750.00
Candlestick, green...............................135.00
Candlestick, marigold 72.00
Candlestick, purple ....100.00 to 125.00
Candlesticks, blue, pr. 275.00
Candlesticks, marigold, pr. 235.00

Card tray, green......,.........................350.00
Card tray, horehound...........................80.00
Card tray, marigold 50.00
Card tray, purple...................................80.00
Centerpiece bowl, green....................775.00
Centerpiece bowl, ice blue 825.00
Centerpiece bowl, ice green..............910.00
Centerpiece bowl, marigold...............260.00
Centerpiece bowl, purple...................425.00
Centerpiece bowl, white 632.00
Cologne bottle w/stopper,
  green.........................225.00 to 250.00
Cologne bottle w/stopper, ice blue 950.00
Cologne bottle w/stopper, marigold 165.00
Cologne bottle w/stopper, purple........259.00
Cologne bottle w/stopper, sapphire
  blue 795.00
Cologne bottle w/stopper,
  white ....625.00 to 650.00
Compote, cov., large, green 425.00
Compote, cov., large, marigold........1,450.00
Compote, cov., small,
  purple...............................325.00 to 350.00
Compote, cov., large, purple 450.00
Compote, open, large, green..............795.00
Compote, open, large, mari-
  gold ....300.00 to 350.00
Compote, open, small, purple.............225.00
Compote, open, large,
  purple...............................425.00 to 525.00
Cracker jar, cov., ice green................800.00
Cracker jar, cov., marigold..................300.00
Cracker jar, cov., purple 400.00
Cracker jar, cov., white 875.00
Creamer, green 125.00
Creamer, marigold................................90.00
Creamer, purple....................................88.00
Creamer, individual size, green...........65.00
Creamer, individual size, marigold 68.00
Creamer, individual size, purple 65.00
Creamer & cov. sugar bowl, purple,
  pr..278.00
Cup & saucer, blue.............................275.00
Cup & saucer, marigold 250.00
Cup & saucer, purple..........................450.00
Cuspidor, purple 3,000.00
Decanter w/stopper, whiskey,
  marigold ....600.00 to 625.00
Dresser set, purple, 7 pcs................2,500.00
Dresser tray, blue 250.00
Dresser tray, green.............250.00 to 275.00
Dresser tray, ice blue......................1,500.00
Dresser tray, marigold 150.00
Dresser tray, purple 195.00
Fernery, ice blue..............................1,300.00
Fernery, purple ....650.00 to 700.00
Hatpin holder, blue 1,300.00
Hatpin holder, green 285.00
Hatpin holder, ice blue....................2,500.00
Hatpin holder, ice green 1,700.00
Hatpin holder, lavender ......400.00 to 450.00
Hatpin holder, marigold 256.00
Hatpin holder, purple ....250.00 to 275.00

Grape & Cable Hatpin Holder

Hatpin holder, white (ILLUS.) 1,800.00
Hat shape, green................225.00 to 250.00
Hat shape, marigold 50.00
Hat shape, purple ....50.00 to 60.00
Humidor (or tobacco jar), cov.,
  blue 1,000.00
Humidor, cov., stippled, blue 1,500.00
Humidor, cov., marigold......275.00 to 300.00
Humidor, cov., stippled, marigold 160.00
Humidor, cov., purple ....700.00 to 900.00
Ice cream set: master bowl & 1
  individual dish; marigold, 2 pcs........425.00
Ice cream set: master bowl & 6
  individual dishes; white, 7 pcs. 1,500.00
Nappy, single handle, green................75.00
Nappy, single handle, ice blue...........600.00
Nappy, single handle, marigold 47.00
Nappy, single handle, purple 130.00
Nappy, cup whimsey, hairpin, purple....50.00
Perfume bottle w/stopper, marigold....417.00
Perfume bottle w/stopper,
  purple...............................650.00 to 675.00
Pin tray, green 225.00
Pin tray, ice blue.................................900.00
Pin tray, marigold...............140.00 to 150.00
Pin tray, purple ....250.00 to 275.00
Pitcher, water, 8¼" h., green 400.00
Pitcher, water, 8¼" h., marigold..........205.00
Pitcher, water, 8¼" h., purple 319.00
Pitcher, tankard, 9¾" h., marigold 540.00
Pitcher, tankard, 9¾" h., purple 600.00
Plate, 5" to 6" d., purple (North-
  wood) ....130.00 to 140.00
Plate, 7½" d., turned-up handgrip,
  green...95.00
Plate, 7½" d., turned-up handgrip,
  marigold ....100.00 to 125.00
Plate, 7½" d., turned-up handgrip,
  purple...114.00
Plate, 8" d., clambroth 850.00
Plate, 8" d., footed, green (Fenton) 185.00
Plate, 8" d., green (Northwood) 140.00
Plate, 8" d., footed, marigold 92.00

Plate, 8" d., footed, purple 84.00
Plate, 8" d., purple ....225.00 to 275.00
Plate, 9" d., spatula-footed, blue.........150.00
Plate, 9" d., stippled, blue 600.00
Plate, 9" d., green ....300.00 to 400.00
Plate, 9" d., marigold 250.00

Grape & Cable Plate

Plate, 9" d., spatula-footed, green
  (ILLUS.) 165.00
Plate, 9" d., spatula-footed, ice
  green ....850.00 to 875.00
Plate, 9" d., marigold 109.00
Plate, 9" d., spatula-footed, marigold....85.00
Plate, 9" d., purple 128.00
Plate, 9" d., spatula-footed, purple 125.00
Plate, 9" d., Basketweave exterior,
  green...150.00
Plate, 9" d., Basketweave exterior,
  marigold ....100.00 to 125.00
Plate, 9" d., Basketweave exterior,
  purple...179.00
Plate, 9" d., stippled, green.................302.00
Plate, 9" d., stippled, green, variant....900.00
Plate, 9" d., stippled, marigold 150.00
Plate, 9" d., stippled, marigold,
  variant...750.00
Plate, 9" d., stippled, purple................525.00
Plate, 9" d., stippled, sapphire
  blue ....3,500.00 to 3,800.00
Plate, 9" d., stippled, teal 2,700.00
Plate, chop, 12" d., white 5,000.00
Plate, olive green................................900.00
Plate, pastel marigold 300.00
Powder jar, cov., blue 600.00
Powder jar, cov., green........................160.00
Powder jar, cov., marigold...................125.00
Powder jar, cov., purple.......................129.00
Punch bowl & base, green, 11" d.,
  2 pcs. 1,100.00
Punch bowl & base, marigold, 11" d.,
  2 pcs. 250.00
Punch bowl & base, purple, 11" d.,
  2 pcs. 450.00
Punch bowl & base, purple, 14" d.,
  2 pcs. ....500.00 to 525.00

Punch bowl & base, marigold, 17" d.,
  2 pcs. 1,100.00
Punch cup, aqua opalescent 895.00
Punch cup, blue....................................50.00
Punch cup, stippled, blue ....50.00 to 75.00
Punch cup, green 38.00
Punch cup, stippled, green 45.00
Punch cup, ice blue 90.00
Punch cup, ice green.............................80.00
Punch cup, lavender..............................25.00
Punch cup, marigold..............................30.00
Punch cup, purple..................................25.00
Punch cup, white ....60.00 to 75.00
Punch set: 11" bowl & 6 cups; blue,
  7 pcs. 1,550.00
Punch set: 11" bowl & 6 cups; white,
  7 pcs. 1,750.00
Punch set: 11" bowl, base & 8 cups;
  green, 10 pcs. 600.00
Punch set: 14" bowl & 10 cups; ice
  green, 11 pcs. 2,300.00
Punch set: 14" bowl, base & 5 cups;
  purple, 7 pcs. 895.00
Punch set: 14" bowl, base & 6 cups;
  marigold, 8 pcs. 585.00
Punch set: 14" bowl, base & 6 cups;
  white, 8 pcs.................................3,500.00
Punch set: 14" bowl, base & 8 cups;
  blue, 10 pcs. 2,300.00
Punch set, master: 17" bowl, base &
  6 cups; purple, 8 pcs.....................2,000.00
Punch set, master: 17" bowl, base &
  8 cups; green, 10 pcs. 3,800.00
Punch set, master: 17" bowl, base &
  10 cups; white, 12 pcs. 6,000.00
Punch set, master: 17" bowl, base &
  12 cups; marigold, 14 pcs. 2,500.00
Spooner, green................................125.00
Spooner, marigold 42.00
Spooner, purple..................................100.00
Sugar bowl, cov., green........................85.00
Sugar bowl, cov., marigold 85.00
Sugar bowl, cov., purple 104.00
Sugar bowl, individual size, green........60.00
Sugar bowl, individual size, marigold ...35.00
Sugar bowl, individual size, purple 68.00
Sweetmeat jar, cov., marigold 1,800.00
Sweetmeat jar, cov.,
  purple..............................225.00 to 275.00
Table set, green, 4 pcs. 525.00
Tumbler, green ....45.00 to 65.00
Tumbler, ice green..............700.00 to 800.00
Tumbler, marigold.................................36.00
Tumbler, stippled, marigold 60.00
Tumbler, purple 45.00
Tumbler, stippled, purple 50.00
Tumbler, tankard, blue..........................72.00
Tumbler, tankard, green .....200.00 to 225.00
Tumbler, tankard, marigold...................48.00
Tumbler, tankard, stippled, marigold 65.00
Tumbler, tankard, purple ....45.00 to 55.00
Tumbler, tankard, stippled, purple 89.00

Water set: pitcher & 2 tumblers; blue,
  3 pcs. 450.00
Water set: pitcher & 4 tumblers;
  purple, 5 pcs. 625.00
Water set: pitcher & 6 tumblers;
  green, 7 pcs. 1,150.00
Water set: pitcher & 6 tumblers;
  marigold, 7 pcs. ....500.00 to 550.00
Water set: tankard pitcher
  & 6 tumblers; marigold,
  7 pcs. ....700.00 to 800.00
Whimsey compote (sweetmeat
  base), purple 135.00
Whimsey punch cup, green 100.00
Whimsey punch cup, marigold 125.00
Whimsey teacup, purple .....100.00 to 125.00
Whiskey shot glass, marigold 165.00
Whiskey shot glass, purple.................173.00

GRAPE & GOTHIC ARCHES (Northwood)

Grape & Gothic Arches Pitcher

Berry set: master bowl & 6 sauce
  dishes; marigold, 7 pcs. 140.00
Bowl, master berry, blue......................70.00
Bowl, master berry, marigold................43.00
Butter dish, cov., blue 300.00
Creamer, blue.......................................85.00
Creamer, green 200.00
Creamer, marigold................................45.00
Creamer & cov. sugar bowl,
  marigold, pr. 100.00
Pitcher, water, blue.............350.00 to 375.00
Pitcher, water, marigold (ILLUS.) 190.00
Sauce dish, blue 30.00
Sauce dish, green..................................35.00
Sauce dish, marigold 15.00
Sauce dish, pearl pastel milk white 45.00
Spooner, blue 65.00
Spooner, green 200.00
Spooner, marigold 45.00
Sugar bowl, cov., blue 100.00
Sugar bowl, cov., marigold 55.00
Sugar bowl, cov., purple 90.00
Table set, blue, 4 pcs. ....350.00 to 450.00
Table set, marigold, 4 pcs. 300.00
Tumbler, amber 50.00
Tumbler, blue 49.00
Tumbler, clambroth..............................150.00

Tumbler, green 75.00
Tumbler, marigold..................................35.00
Tumbler, pearl pastel milk
  white ....125.00 to 150.00
Tumbler, purple 50.00
Water set: pitcher & 4 tumblers; blue,
  5 pcs. 600.00
Water set: pitcher & 6 tumblers;
  green, 7 pcs. 700.00
Water set: pitcher & 6 tumblers;
  marigold, 7 pcs. 375.00
Water set: pitcher & 6 tumblers;
  purple, 7 pcs. 600.00

GRAPE ARBOR (Northwood)
Bowl, 10" d., footed, marigold
  (Dugan) 90.00
Bowl, 10" d., footed, purple
  (Dugan) ....350.00 to 375.00
Hat shape, blue 75.00
Hat shape, marigold ....75.00 to 100.00
Hat shape, white...................................110.00
Pitcher, tankard, marigold...250.00 to 275.00
Pitcher, tankard, purple 600.00
Pitcher, tankard, white ....550.00 to 650.00
Tumbler, blue ....200.00 to 250.00
Tumbler, ice blue ....125.00 to 175.00
Tumbler, ice green.............400.00 to 500.00
Tumbler, lavender................................175.00
Tumbler, marigold..................................30.00
Tumbler, pastel marigold 40.00
Tumbler, purple 62.50
Tumbler, teal blue................................175.00
Tumbler, white ....125.00 to 150.00
Water set: tankard pitcher & 4
  tumblers; white, 5 pcs. 1,250.00
Water set: tankard pitcher & 6 tum-
  blers; marigold, 7 pcs.......500.00 to 575.00

GRAPE DELIGHT

Grape Delight Rose Bowl

Nut bowl, six-footed, blue 85.00
Nut bowl, six-footed, ice blue...............60.00
Nut bowl, six-footed, marigold 45.00
Nut bowl, six-footed, purple.................80.00
Nut bowl, six-footed, white....80.00 to 100.00
Rose bowl, six-footed, amber 70.00
Rose bowl, six-footed, blue ....60.00 to 90.00

Rose bowl, six-footed, lavender 225.00
Rose bowl, six-footed, marigold
 (ILLUS.) 75.00
Rose bowl, six-footed, purple 90.00
Rose bowl, six-footed,
 white ....75.00 to 100.00

GRAPE LEAVES (Northwood)
Bonbon, handled, purple 26.00
Bowl, 8" d., green 90.00
Bowl, 8" d., ribbon candy rim, green...295.00
Bowl, ice blue 1,200.00
Bowl, 9" d., marigold...............50.00 to 75.00
Bowl, 9" d., purple..............................120.00
Bowl, marigold (Millersburg) 500.00
Bowl, purple...75.00

GRAPEVINE LATTICE
Bowl, 7" d., ruffled, ice white..............185.00
Bowl, 7" d., ruffled, white ....50.00 to 60.00
Bowl, fluted, white.................................85.00
Hat shape, white..................................150.00
Pitcher, water, blue.............................287.00
Pitcher, water, purple..........450.00 to 475.00
Pitcher, water, white ....600.00 to 800.00
Plate, 6" to 7" d., marigold....................58.00
Plate, 6" to 7" d., purple......150.00 to 175.00
Plate, 6" to 7" d., white........................94.00
Plate, 8" d., ruffled, marigold 110.00
Tumbler, marigold.................................40.00
Tumbler, purple ....50.00 to 70.00
Tumbler, smoky 40.00
Tumbler, white.....................................165.00
Water set: pitcher & 1 tumbler; blue,
 2 pcs..800.00
Water set: pitcher & 1 tumbler; white,
 2 pcs. 1,500.00
Water set: pitcher & 6 tumblers;
 marigold, 7 pcs. ....475.00 to 525.00

GREEK KEY (Northwood)

Greek Key Plate

Bowl, 8" to 9" d., blue..........................500.00
Bowl, 8" to 9" d., fluted, green 185.00

Bowl, 8" to 9" d., ruffled, marigold.........85.00
Bowl, 8" to 9" d., purple 118.00
Bowl, 8" to 9" d., ruffled,
 purple.............................150.00 to 200.00
Bowl, eight-sided, 6½" w., 4" h.,
 purple...75.00
Bowl, dome-footed, green 55.00
Bowl, piecrust rim, blue w/electric
 iridescence....................................1,950.00
Bowl, piecrust rim, green....................400.00
Pitcher, water, green ....1,300.00 to 1,400.00
Pitcher, water, purple..........500.00 to 700.00
Plate, 9" d., blue 2,800.00
Plate, 9" d., green (ILLUS.)...............1,100.00
Plate, 9" d., marigold 800.00
Plate, 9" d., purple ....300.00 to 400.00
Tumbler, green ....75.00 to 100.00
Tumbler, marigold.................................60.00
Tumbler, purple ....75.00 to 100.00
Water set: pitcher & 4 tumblers;
 purple, 5 pcs. 1,250.00

HAMMERED BELL
Chandelier shade, white 40.00

HANGING CHERRIES - See Cherry (Millersburg) Pattern

HARVEST FLOWER (Dugan or Diamond Glass)
Pitcher, tankard,
 marigold ....1,200.00 to 1,500.00
Tumbler, amber 125.00
Tumbler, lime green............................395.00
Tumbler, marigold.................................85.00
Tumbler, purple 900.00

HARVEST TIME See Golden Harvest Pattern

HATTIE (Imperial)

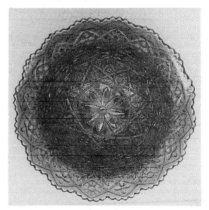

Hattie Bowl

Bowl, 8" to 9" d., green 69.00
Bowl, 8" to 9" d., marigold....................35.00

Bowl, 8" to 9" d., purple 70.00
Bowl, 8" to 9" d., smoky (ILLUS.)..........63.00
Plate, chop, green ....650.00 to 750.00
Plate, chop, purple...........................2,500.00
Rose bowl, amber..............................325.00

HEART & HORSESHOE (Fenton's Good Luck)
Bowl, marigold 1,000.00

HEART & VINE (Fenton)

Heart & Vine Plate

Bowl, 8" to 9" d., blue............75.00 to 100.00
Bowl, 8" to 9" d., ribbon candy rim,
  blue 55.00
Bowl, 8" to 9" d., green 85.00
Bowl, 8" to 9" d., ribbon candy rim,
  green...75.00
Bowl, 8" to 9" d., marigold.....................45.00
Bowl, 8" to 9" d., ribbon candy rim,
  marigold..67.50
Bowl, 8" to 9" d., purple 81.00
Bowl, 8½" d., ribbon candy rim,
  purple..95.00
Plate, 9" d., blue (ILLUS.)...350.00 to 450.00
Plate, 9" d., purple 450.00

HEARTS & FLOWERS (Northwood)
Bowl, 8" to 9" d., aqua opales-
  cent............................1,000.00 to 1,500.00
Bowl, 8" to 9" d., blue...........................600.00
Bowl, 8" to 9" d., piecrust rim, blue 500.00
Bowl, 8" to 9" d., piecrust rim, blue
  w/electric iridescence....................1,175.00
Bowl, 8" to 9" d., piecrust rim, ice
  blue ....550.00 to 650.00
Bowl, 8" to 9" d., piecrust rim, ice
  green...2,600.00
Bowl, 8" to 9" d., piecrust rim,
  marigold ....450.00 to 550.00
Bowl, 8" to 9" d., piecrust rim,
  purple...............................350.00 to 375.00
Bowl, 8" to 9" d., ruffled, blue..............454.00
Bowl, 8" to 9" d., ruffled, green 700.00
Bowl, 8" to 9" d., ruffled, ice
  blue ....450.00 to 475.00

Bowl, 8" to 9" d., ruffled, ice
  green.............................800.00 to 1,000.00
Bowl, 8" to 9" d., ruffled, marigold.......350.00
Bowl, 8" to 9" d., ruffled,
  purple.............................400.00 to 425.00
Bowl, 8" to 9" d., ruffled, white............275.00
Compote, 6¾" h., aqua opales-
  cent................................500.00 to 600.00
Compote, 6¾" h., blue ....475.00 to 500.00
Compote, 6¾" h., blue opales-
  cent...1,500.00
Compote, 6¾" h., blue w/electric
  iridescence......................................270.00
Compote, 6¾" h.,
  green..........................2,250.00 to 2,700.00
Compote, 6¾" h., ice blue 950.00
Compote, 6¾" h., ice green...............933.00
Compote, 6¾" h., lime green 2,000.00
Compote, 6¾" h., marigold 204.00
Compote, 6¾" h., moonstone 5,000.00
Compote, 6¾" h., purple.....450.00 to 500.00
Compote, 6¾" h., sapphire blue 895.00
Compote, 6¾" h., white ......150.00 to 175.00
Plate, green ....1,500.00 to 1,700.00
Plate, ice blue 4,000.00
Plate, ice green..............................3,900.00
Plate, marigold................700.00 to 1,000.00
Plate, purple ....900.00 to 1,000.00
Plate, white 2,500.00

HEAVY GRAPE (Dugan, Diamond Glass or Millersburg)
Bowl, 6" d., purple.................................40.00
Bowl, 7" d., ruffled, green 35.00
Bowl, 7" d., ruffled, vaseline 40.00
Bowl, 8" sq., ruffled, blue w/electric
  iridescence......................................325.00
Bowl, 8" d., marigold.............................65.00
Bowl, 9" d., purple.................................60.00
Bowl, 10" d., marigold...........................45.00
Bowl, master berry, 10" d.,
  purple...............................350.00 to 400.00
Nappy, marigold 28.00
Nappy, purple 50.00
Sauce dish, blue w/electric
  iridescence, 5" sq..............................95.00

HEAVY GRAPE (Imperial)
Bowl, 4" d., lavender.............................25.00
Bowl, 5" d., purple...............................150.00
Bowl, 6" d., green 32.50
Bowl, 6" d., marigold.............................45.00
Bowl, 6" d., purple.................................38.00
Bowl, 7" d., fluted, green.......................30.00
Bowl, 7" d., marigold.............................20.00
Bowl, 7" d., purple.................................42.50
Bowl, 8" to 9" d., green 58.00
Bowl, 8" to 9" d., marigold....................55.00
Bowl, 8" to 9" d., purple 85.00
Bowl, 8" to 9" d., smoky 75.00
Bowl, 10" d., marigold...........................80.00
Bowl, 10" d., purple.............................335.00
Bowl, square, purple...........................550.00

Nappy, handled, green 38.00
Nappy, handled, marigold....................28.00
Nut bowl, six-footed, purple 75.00
Plate, 7" to 8" d., amber......150.00 to 200.00
Plate, 7" to 8" d., blue-green...............195.00
Plate, 7" to 8" d., green.......................55.00
Plate, 7" to 8" d., lavender 140.00
Plate, 7" to 8" d., marigold 56.00
Plate, 7" to 8" d., purple 120.00
Plate, 7" to 8" d., smoky.....................125.00
Plate, chop, 11" d., amber 462.00
Plate, chop, 11" d., blue.....................400.00
Plate, chop, 11" d., green 235.00
Plate, chop, 11" d., marigold...............140.00
Plate, chop, 11" d.,
    purple...............................300.00 to 325.00
Plate, chop, 11" d., smoky 2,500.00

Heavy Grape Punch Bowl

Punch bowl & base, green, 2 pcs.
    (ILLUS.) ....250.00 to 300.00
Punch cup, amber 50.00
Punch cup, green 45.00
Punch cup, marigold.............................20.00
Punch cup, purple................................38.00
Punch set: bowl, base & 4 cups;
    purple, 6 pcs. 800.00

HEAVY IRIS (Dugan or Diamond Glass)
Pitcher, water, marigold .....300.00 to 350.00
Pitcher, water, tankard,
    marigold ....300.00 to 350.00
Tumbler, clambroth.............................65.00
Tumbler, marigold...............................68.00
Tumbler, pastel lavender 350.00
Tumbler, purple 70.00
Tumbler, white ....200.00 to 250.00
Water set: pitcher & 5 tumblers;
    marigold, 6 pcs. ....650.00 to 685.00
Water set: pitcher & 6 tumblers;
    purple, 7 pcs. 2,000.00

HOBNAIL (Millersburg)
Butter dish, cov., marigold (ILLUS. top
    next column) 895.00
Creamer, blue.....................................650.00

Hobnail Butter Dish

Cuspidor, marigold 700.00
Cuspidor, purple ....600.00 to 700.00
Rose bowl, green............................1,500.00
Rose bowl, marigold...........300.00 to 400.00
Rose bowl, purple...............300.00 to 400.00
Tumbler, blue ....700.00 to 900.00
Tumbler, purple 600.00

**HOBNAIL, SWIRL - See Swirl Hobnail
Pattern**

HOBSTAR (Imperial)
Butter dish, cov., green.......................245.00
Butter dish, cov., marigold 110.00
Celery vase, two-handled, marigold 75.00
Compote, green....................................60.00
Compote, purple.................................110.00
Cracker jar, cov., marigold....................70.00
Creamer, marigold................................40.00
Creamer, purple....................................75.00
Humidor, cov., marigold.....................100.00
Punch set: bowl, base & 12 cups,
    marigold, 14 pcs. 300.00
Spooner, marigold 35.00
Spooner, purple 90.00
Sugar bowl, cov., green.......................70.00
Sugar bowl, cov., marigold 60.00

HOBSTAR & FEATHER (Millersburg)
Punch bowl & base, purple 3,300.00
Punch cup, blue....................................65.00
Punch cup, marigold.............................35.00
Punch cup, purple...............................100.00
Punch set: bowl, base & 6 cups;
    marigold, 8 pcs. 1,250.00
Whimsey, cuspidor-shaped,
    purple...5,000.00

HOBSTAR BAND
Pitcher, marigold ....150.00 to 200.00
Tumbler, marigold (ILLUS. top next
    column) 40.00

Hobstar Band Tumbler

HOLLY, HOLLY BERRIES & CARNIVAL HOLLY (Fenton)

Holly Bowl

Bonbon, two-handled, green 55.00
Bonbon, two-handled, marigold..........110.00
Bonbon, two-handled, purple................65.00
Bowl, 5" d., marigold............................25.00
Bowl, 5" d., scalloped, red 450.00
Bowl, 8" to 9" d., amber.......................125.00
Bowl, 8" to 9" d., aqua 550.00
Bowl, 8" to 9" d., blue............................65.00
Bowl, 8" to 9" d., celeste blue 500.00
Bowl, 8" to 9" d., green 70.00
Bowl, 8" to 9" d., lavender...175.00 to 200.00
Bowl, 8" to 9" d., light blue w/marigold
    overlay 200.00
Bowl, 8" to 9" d., marigold.......40.00 to 50.00
Bowl, 8" to 9" d., milk white
    w/marigold overlay........................1,050.00
Bowl, 8" to 9" d., purple 55.00
Bowl, 8" to 9" d., red,
    (Fenton) ....1,000.00 to 1,125.00
Bowl, 8" to 9" d., vaseline 85.00
Bowl, 8" to 9" d., white ....100.00 to 125.00
Bowl, 8" to 9" d., ice cream shape,
    blue...66.00

Bowl, 8" to 9" d., ice cream shape,
    celeste blue..................................4,000.00
Bowl, 8" to 9" d., ice cream shape,
    clambroth 85.00
Bowl, 8" to 9" d., ice cream shape,
    cobalt blue 275.00
Bowl, 8" to 9" d., ice cream shape,
    green (ILLUS.) 103.00
Bowl, 8" to 9" d., ice cream shape,
    ice green 3,200.00
Bowl, 8" to 9" d., ice cream shape,
    marigold 80.00
Bowl, 8" to 9" d., ice cream shape,
    moonstone ....850.00 to 900.00
Bowl, 8" to 9" d., ice cream shape,
    purple 75.00
Bowl, 8" to 9" d., ice cream shape,
    red...1,300.00
Bowl, 8" to 9" d., ice cream shape,
    vaseline...130.00
Bowl, 8" to 9" d., ice cream shape,
    white 135.00
Bowl, 8" to 9" d., ribbon candy rim,
    amethyst ....100.00 to 125.00
Bowl, 8" to 9" d., ribbon candy rim,
    blue 55.00
Bowl, 8" to 9" d., ribbon candy rim,
    green..135.00
Bowl, 8" to 9" d., ribbon candy rim,
    marigold 65.00
Bowl, 8" to 9" d., ribbon candy rim,
    pastel green 65.00
Bowl, 8" to 9" d., ribbon candy rim,
    purple ....100.00 to 125.00
Bowl, 8" to 9" d., ruffled, blue
    opalescent 1,400.00
Bowl, 8" to 9" d., ruffled, emerald
    green...300.00
Bowl, 8" to 9" d., ruffled,
    green..................................100.00 to 125.00
Bowl, 8" to 9" d., ruffled, marigold.........45.00
Bowl, 8" to 9" d., ruffled, pastel
    blue ....50.00 to 75.00
Bowl, 8" to 9" d., ruffled, peach
    opalescent 35.00
Bowl, 8" to 9" d., ruffled, purple 130.00
Bowl, 8" to 9" d., ruffled,
    red...............................900.00 to 1,000.00
Bowl, 8" to 9" d., ruffled, vaseline 225.00
Compote, small, aqua w/marigold
    overlay ....100.00 to 125.00
Compote, small, blue.............................40.00
Compote, small, green ....50.00 to 75.00
Compote, small, lavender.......50.00 to 75.00
Compote, small, lime green
    opalescent 735.00
Compote, small, marigold....................28.00
Compote, small, marigold w/vaseline
    stem 65.00
Compote, small, purple.......100.00 to 125.00
Compote, small, red ....450.00 to 550.00
Compote, small, vaseline 70.00
Compote, ice green opalescent..........625.00

Compote, red.....................................1,000.00
Dish, hat-shaped, amber, 5¾"..............75.00
Dish, hat-shaped, Amberina..............450.00
Dish, hat-shaped, amethyst opales-
cent..425.00
Dish, hat-shaped, aqua, 5¾"...............75.00
Dish, hat-shaped, aqua opalescent....275.00
Dish, hat-shaped, aqua w/marigold
overlay...55.00
Dish, hat-shaped, blue, 5¾"................50.00
Dish, hat-shaped, green, 5¾".............36.00
Dish, hat-shaped, green w/marigold
overlay...29.00
Dish, hat-shaped, ice blue w/marigold
overlay, 5¾".....................................75.00
Dish, hat-shaped, lavender..................85.00
Dish, hat-shaped, lime green,
5¾"......................................50.00 to 75.00
Dish, hat-shaped, marigold, 5¾".........30.00
Dish, hat-shaped, milk white
w/marigold overlay.........................118.00
Dish, hat-shaped, moonstone............200.00
Dish, hat-shaped, purple, 5¾".............35.00
Dish, hat-shaped, purple opalescent,
5¾"...300.00
Dish, hat-shaped, red,
5¾"..................................430.00 to 450.00
Dish, hat-shaped, vaseline, 5¾"..........72.00
Goblet, blue..35.00
Goblet, green..70.00
Goblet, marigold...................................27.00
Goblet, red (Fenton)...........................429.00
Plate, 9" to 10" d., amethyst............1,050.00
Plate, 9" to 10" d., blue.......350.00 to 450.00
Plate, 9" to 10" d., celeste blue
(Fenton).......................................9,500.00
Plate, 9" to 10" d., clambroth.............125.00
Plate, 9" to 10" d.,
green.............................800.00 to 1,000.00
Plate, 9" to 10" d., mari-
gold.................................125.00 to 175.00
Plate, 9" to 10" d., pastel marigold......200.00
Plate, 9" to 10" d., purple....400.00 to 600.00
Plate, 9" to 10" d., white......200.00 to 225.00
Sauceboat, handled, peach opales-
cent..102.00
Sauceboat, handled, purple................110.00
Sherbet, blue..40.00
Sherbet, green......................................25.00
Sherbet, lime green..............................75.00
Sherbet, lime green opalescent..........675.00
Sherbet, marigold.................................35.00
Sherbet, red..425.00

HOLLY SPRIG - See Holly Whirl Pattern

**HOLLY WHIRL or HOLLY SPRIG
(Millersburg & Dugan)**
Bowl, 6" w., tricornered, amethyst......125.00
Bowl, 6" w., tricornered, green.............85.00
Bowl, 6" w., tricornered, purple...........125.00
Bowl, 6" d., ruffled, marigold................95.00
Bowl, 6" d., ruffled, purple....................92.50
Bowl, 7" d., green.................................60.00

Bowl, 7" d., marigold............................55.00
Bowl, 7" d., ruffled, purple....................60.00
Bowl, 8" d., ice cream shape,
marigold, variant..............................68.00
Bowl, 8" d., ice cream shape,
white...110.00
Bowl, 8" to 9" d., ruffled, blue...............50.00
Bowl, 8" to 9" d., green.........75.00 to 100.00
Bowl, 8" to 9" d., marigold....................55.00
Bowl, 8" to 9" d., peach opalescent......75.00
Bowl, 8" to 9" d., purple........75.00 to 100.00
Bowl, 10" d., ruffled, marigold..............50.00
Bowl, 10" d., ruffled,
purple.............................100.00 to 125.00
Hat shape, green, 6"............................38.00
Nappy, single handle, marigold...........45.00
Nappy, single handle, peach
opalescent (Dugan).........................62.00
Nappy, single handle, purple
(Dugan)............................75.00 to 100.00
Nappy, tricornered, green (Dugan).....110.00
Nappy, tricornered, marigold
(Millersburg)...................................110.00
Nappy, tricornered, purple (Dugan)....100.00
Nappy, tricornered, purple
(Millersburg)....................175.00 to 200.00

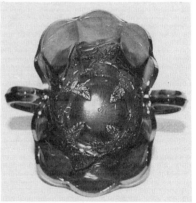

Holly Whirl Nappy

Nappy, two-handled, amethyst,Millers-
burg (ILLUS.).....................................68.00
Nappy, two-handled, green
(Dugan)............................75.00 to 100.00
Nappy, two-handled, green
(Millersburg).....................................80.00
Nut dish, two-handled, green...............75.00
Nut dish, two-handled, marigold..........68.00
Nut dish, two-handled, purple..............72.50
Rose bowl, blue..................................300.00
Rose bowl, small, marigold.................325.00
Sauceboat, peach opalescent
(Dugan)...135.00
Sauce dish, green, 6½" d.
(Millersburg)....................100.00 to 125.00
Sauce dish, deep, purple....................350.00

**HOMESTEAD - See NU-ART HOMESTEAD
PLATE**

HONEYCOMB

Honeycomb Rose Bowl

Bonbon, marigold 28.00
Bonbon, green.....................................53.00
Rose bowl, peach opalescent
 (ILLUS.)........................200.00 to 250.00
Vase, 7" h., green...............................52.50

HORSE HEADS OR HORSE MEDALLION (Fenton)

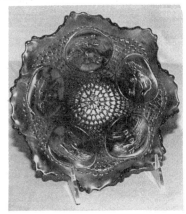

Horse Heads Bowl

Bowl, 5" d., footed, marigold.................57.00
Bowl, 6" d., blue.....................................60.00
Bowl, 6" d., collared base, marigold 85.00
Bowl, 7" to 8" d., amber 395.00
Bowl, 7" to 8" d., blue...........................115.00
Bowl, 7" to 8" d., green (ILLUS.).........135.00
Bowl, 7" to 8" d., marigold.....75.00 to 100.00
Bowl, 7" to 8" d., purple 118.00
Bowl, 7" to 8" d., red .....1,250.00 to 1,500.00
Bowl, ice cream shape, amber 280.00
Bowl, ice cream shape, blue..............235.00
Bowl, 7" d., ice cream shape, mari-
 gold 85.00
Bowl, 7" d., ice cream shape, purple ..425.00
Bowl, ruffled, collared base,
 Amberina 450.00

Bowl, jack-in-the-pulpit shaped,
 amber...495.00
Bowl, jack-in-the-pulpit shaped,
 blue ....150.00 to 175.00
Bowl, jack-in-the-pulpit shaped,
 green..............................250.00 to 300.00
Bowl, jack-in-the-pulpit shaped,
 marigold 130.00
Bowl, jack-in-the-pulpit shaped,
 purple...265.00
Bowl, jack-in-the-pulpit shaped,
 teal green 675.00
Bowl, jack-in-the-pulpit shaped,
 vaseline...........................400.00 to 425.00
Bowl, 7" to 8" d., blue.........................750.00
Bowl, 7" to 8" d., marigold...200.00 to 225.00
Nut bowl, three-footed, amethyst........225.00
Nut bowl, three-footed, blue 150.00
Nut bowl, three-footed, green.............195.00
Nut bowl, three-footed, marigold 85.00
Nut bowl, three-footed,
 red..............................1,500.00 to 1,700.00
Nut bowl, three-footed, vase-
 line ....250.00 to 300.00
Rose bowl, blue 225.00
Rose bowl, marigold 136.00
Rose bowl, smoky blue........................400.00
Rose bowl, vaseline.............................750.00

HORSESHOE CURVE - See Twins Pattern

ILLINOIS SOLDIER'S & SAILOR'S PLATE
Blue 1,000.00

ILLUSION (Fenton)

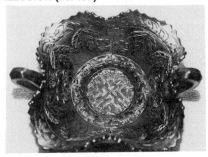

Illusion Bonbon

Bonbon, two-handled, blue (ILLUS.) 68.00
Bonbon, two-handled, marigold............65.00
Bonbon, two-handled, purple..............150.00

IMPERIAL GRAPE (Imperial)
Basket, marigold....................................80.00
Basket, smoky 118.00
Berry set: master bowl & 2 sauce
 dishes; purple, 3 pcs.......................225.00
Berry set: master bowl & 4 sauce
 dishes; green, 5 pcs.........125.00 to 150.00
Bowl, 6" d., marigold.............................35.00
Bowl, 6" d., ruffled, purple....................70.00
Bowl, 7" d., 2½" h., green 42.00

Bowl, 7" d., 2½" h., marigold................20.00
Bowl, 7" d., 2½" h., ruffled, purple 70.00
Bowl, 8" to 9" d., aqua 75.00
Bowl, 8" to 9" d., green 48.00
Bowl, 8" to 9" d., marigold......................43.00
Bowl, 8" to 9" d., purple 120.00
Bowl, 10" d., green 40.00
Bowl, 10" d., marigold..............................45.00
Bowl, 10" d., purple................................117.00
Bowl, 10" d., smoky 33.00
Bowl, 11" d., ruffled, purple..................100.00
Compote, amber 60.00
Compote, clambroth 35.00
Compote, green...45.00
Compote, lavender swirled w/amber ..140.00
Compote, purple 500.00
Compote, smoky..35.00
Cup, purple 20.00
Cup & saucer, amber................................65.00
Cup & saucer, green..................................85.00

Imperial Grape Cup & Saucer

Cup & saucer, marigold (ILLUS.)..........80.00
Decanter w/stopper,
   green...................................125.00 to 150.00
Decanter w/stopper, marigold................94.00
Decanter w/stopper,
   purple.................................225.00 to 250.00
Goblet, aqua teal 90.00
Goblet, clambroth 75.00
Goblet, green...35.00
Goblet, marigold 35.00
Goblet, purple 55.00
Goblet, smoky.......................75.00 to 100.00
Pitcher, water, amber 650.00
Pitcher, water, marigold........75.00 to 100.00
Pitcher, water, smoky ....300.00 to 400.00
Plate, 6" d., amber ....125.00 to 150.00
Plate, 6" d., green....................................60.00
Plate, 6" d., marigold 48.00
Plate, 6" d., purple ....100.00 to 150.00
Plate, 7" d., green....................................85.00
Plate, 7" d., marigold 30.00
Plate, 8" d., green....................................50.00
Plate, 8" d., marigold 50.00
Plate, 8" d., purple ....75.00 to 100.00
Plate, 9" d., ruffled, clambroth 75.00
Plate, 9" d., flat, green 75.00
Plate, 9" d., ruffled, green 137.00
Plate, 9" d., flat, marigold......75.00 to 100.00
Plate, 9" d., ruffled, mari-
   gold....................................50.00 to 100.00

Plate, 9" d., ruffled, purple 100.00
Plate, 9" d., ruffled, smoky....................95.00
Rose bowl, amber.................................675.00
Rose bowl, green.....................................65.00
Rose bowl, purple....................................60.00
Rose bowl, white 70.00
Sauce dish, amber...................................17.00
Sauce dish, green....................................25.00
Sauce dish, ruffled, marigold.................20.00
Tray, center handle, amber 30.00
Tray, center handle, clambroth...............45.00
Tray, center handle, marigold.................75.00
Tray, center handle, smoky 35.00
Tumbler, amber 98.00
Tumbler, aqua 130.00
Tumbler, green 28.00
Tumbler, lilac 59.00
Tumbler, marigold....................................25.00
Tumbler, purple 50.00
Water bottle, green.............100.00 to 125.00
Water bottle, marigold ....75.00 to 100.00
Water bottle, purple ....150.00 to 175.00
Water bottle, smoky..............................450.00
Water set: pitcher & 6 tumblers;
   marigold, 7 pcs. 225.00
Water set: pitcher & 6 tumblers;
   purple, 7 pcs. 700.00
Wine, clambroth..18.00
Wine, green 33.00
Wine, marigold...28.00
Wine, purple 35.00
Wine, smoky 75.00
Wine set: decanter w/stopper & 6
   wines; marigold, 7 pcs. 260.00
Wine set: decanter w/stopper & 6
   wines; purple, 7 pcs. ....475.00 to 500.00

INVERTED COIN DOT
Pitcher, marigold ....75.00 to 100.00
Tumbler, marigold....................................60.00
Water set: pitcher & 1 tumbler;
   marigold, 2 pcs. ....250.00 to 300.00

INVERTED FEATHER (Cambridge)
Compote, jelly, marigold.......................75.00
Cracker jar, cov., green ......200.00 to 250.00
Parfait, marigold 90.00
Pitcher, milk, pastel marigold 475.00
Tumbler, green 750.00
Vase, 6" h., marigold (Cambridge) 75.00
Vase, 6" h., marigold (Northwood)........45.00

INVERTED STRAWBERRY (Cambridge)
Bowl, 6½" d., green, marked Near-
   Cut 52.00
Bowl, 7" d., green 125.00
Candlestick, marigold 128.00
Candlesticks, green, 7" h., pr.............225.00
Compote, open, 5" d., 6" h.,
   marigold...225.00
Compote, open, giant,
   marigold ....225.00 to 250.00
Creamer, blue.......................................300.00

Cuspidor, green 1,000.00
Cuspidor, marigold ....800.00 to 850.00
Pitcher, tankard, marigold...................950.00
Powder jar, cov., green.......150.00 to 200.00
Powder jar, cov., marigold 100.00
Sherbet w/flared sides, blue 625.00
Spooner, green....................................225.00
Sugar bowl, cov., green.....................250.00
Table set, marigold, 4 pcs. 1,000.00
Table set, purple, 4 pcs. 1,500.00
Tumbler, green 275.00
Tumbler, marigold..............125.00 to 150.00
Tumbler, purple ....175.00 to 200.00
Water set: pitcher & 1 tumbler;
    green, 2 pcs. 1,500.00
Water set: pitcher & 6 tumblers;
    marigold, 7 pcs. 1,700.00

Inverted Strawberry Water Set

Water set: pitcher & 6 tumblers;
    purple, 7 pcs. (ILLUS.) 3,750.00
Whimsey, made from two-handled
    nappy, marked "Near-Cut,"
    green..1,400.00

INVERTED THISTLE (Cambridge)
Bowl, purple..65.00
Pitcher, milk, purple 2,500.00
Tumbler, purple 225.00
Water set: pitcher & 6 tumblers;
    purple, 7 pcs. ....3,500.00 to 4,300.00

IRIS
Compote, 6¾" d., blue 285.00
Compote, 6¾" d., green........................68.00
Compote, 6¾" d., marigold 40.00
Compote, 6¾" d., etched "Mother,
    1909," marigold.................................30.00
Compote, 6¾" d., purple.......................55.00
Compote, 7½" d., wide top, marigold....55.00
Goblet, buttermilk, green 65.00
Goblet, buttermilk, marigold.................85.00
Goblet, buttermilk, marigold, souvenir ..80.00
Goblet, buttermilk, purple 80.00

IRIS, HEAVY - See Heavy Iris Pattern

JEWELED HEART (Dugan or Diamond Glass)
Basket, peach opalescent,
    6" h...................................525.00 to 625.00

Bowl, master berry, 10½" d., fluted,
    peach opalescent............................135.00
Bowl, 10" d., purple............................100.00
Bowl, white 165.00

Jeweled Heart Pitcher
Pitcher, marigold (ILLUS.) ..650.00 to 850.00
Sauce dish, peach opalescent.............38.00
Sauce dish, peach opalescent
    w/rayed interior 32.00
Tumbler, amber 115.00
Tumbler, green 35.00
Tumbler, marigold.................................65.00

KITTENS (Fenton)
Bowl, cereal, blue ....450.00 to 500.00
Bowl, cereal, marigold 193.00
Bowl, ruffled, blue 775.00
Bowl, ruffled, marigold ....100.00 to 125.00
Bowl, four-sided, blue 350.00
Bowl, four-sided, ruffled, marigold 159.00
Bowl, six-sided, ruffled, mari-
    gold ....175.00 to 200.00
Cup, blue 675.00
Cup, marigold 129.00
Cup & saucer, blue 2,600.00
Cup & saucer, marigold ......200.00 to 275.00
Dish, turned-up sides, blue.................550.00
Dish, turned-up sides, mari-
    gold ....125.00 to 150.00
Dish, turned-up sides, purple..............525.00
Plate, 4½" d., marigold ....125.00 to 150.00
Spooner, blue 280.00
Spooner, marigold 150.00
Toothpick holder, blue ....400.00 to 475.00
Toothpick holder, marigold 185.00
Vase, marigold.....................................250.00
Vase, child's, ruffled, marigold............145.00

LATTICE & GRAPE (Fenton)
Pitcher, tankard, mari-
    gold ....200.00 to 250.00
Tumbler, blue...46.00
Tumbler, marigold (ILLUS. top next
    page)...35.00
Tumbler, white 135.00

Lattice & Grape Tumbler

Water set: tankard pitcher &
1 tumbler; white, 2 pcs. 900.00
Water set: tankard pitcher &
6 tumblers; blue, 7 pcs. 685.00
Water set: tankard pitcher &
6 tumblers; marigold, 7 pcs. 685.00

LATTICE & POINSETTIA (Northwood)

Lattice & Poinsettia Bowl

Bowl, cobalt blue (ILLUS.) ..500.00 to 550.00
Bowl, ice blue 3,000.00
Bowl, marigold 425.00
Bowl, purple ....500.00 to 550.00

LATTICE & POINTS

Hat shape, clambroth 42.00
Hat shape, marigold 28.00
Vase, 3½" h., marigold 30.00
Vase, 8" h., purple 65.00
Vase, 15½" h., marigold 45.00
Vase, purple 85.00
Vase, white...55.00

LEAF & BEADS (Northwood)

Candy bowl, footed, green....................48.00
Candy bowl, footed, marigold...............45.00
Candy bowl, footed, purple...................55.00
Nut bowl, aqua opalescent 575.00
Nut bowl, handled, green......................60.00
Nut bowl, handled, mari-
gold.....................................75.00 to 100.00

Nut bowl, handled, purple....................95.00
Nut bowl, handled, white 275.00
Rose bowl, aqua..................................300.00
Rose bowl, aqua opales-
cent ....325.00 to 350.00
Rose bowl, blue ....200.00 to 250.00
Rose bowl, blue w/electric irides-
cence ....200.00 to 250.00
Rose bowl, green.................................114.00
Rose bowl, interior pattern,
green...................................75.00 to 85.00
Rose bowl, ice blue 1,400.00
Rose bowl, lime green 450.00
Rose bowl, marigold.............................96.00
Rose bowl, interior pattern,
marigold ....75.00 to 100.00
Rose bowl, olive green ....225.00 to 275.00
Rose bowl, pastel marigold 50.00
Rose bowl, purple.................................96.00
Rose bowl, purple w/smooth
rim ....350.00 to 375.00
Rose bowl, interior pattern, purple......150.00
Rose bowl, interior pattern, teal
blue 1,000.00
Rose bowl, white 900.00

LEAF & FLOWERS or LEAF & LITTLE FLOWERS (Millersburg)

Compote, miniature, green.................300.00
Compote, miniature, marigold 285.00
Compote, miniature,
purple...............................375.00 to 400.00

LEAF CHAIN (Fenton)

Leaf Chain Bowl

Bowl, 5" d., ruffled, marigold................45.00
Bowl, 6" d., ruffled, red 600.00
Bowl, 7" d., ruffled, Amberina 450.00
Bowl, 7" d., ruffled, green 75.00
Bowl, 7" d., aqua................125.00 to 150.00
Bowl, 7" d., blue...................................52.00
Bowl, 7" d., lavender..........................150.00
Bowl, 7" d., marigold............................48.00
Bowl, 7" d., red ....1,000.00 to 1,200.00

Bowl, 7" d., vaseline 100.00
Bowl, 7" d., white 62.00
Bowl, 8" to 9" d., blue (ILLUS.) 75.00
Bowl, 8" to 9" d., clambroth...................48.00
Bowl, 8" to 9" d., green 65.00
Bowl, 8" to 9" d., marigold....................50.00
Bowl, 8" to 9" d., vaseline 95.00
Bowl, 8" to 9" d., white 88.00
Plate, 7" to 8" d., blue 80.00
Plate, 7" to 8" d., marigold 75.00
Plate, 9" d., blue 180.00
Plate, 9" d., clambroth ....115.00 to 130.00
Plate, 9" d., green 135.00
Plate, 9" d., marigold ....125.00 to 175.00
Plate, 9" d., pastel marigold................370.00
Plate, 9" d., white...............200.00 to 225.00

LEAF RAYS NAPPY
Marigold..25.00
Peach opalescent 38.00
Purple 40.00
Purple, "Souvenir of Cedar City,
   Michigan" 60.00
White 50.00

LEAF SWIRL COMPOTE
Amber 45.00
Marigold..45.00
Purple 75.00
Teal blue...100.00
Vaseline...95.00

LEAF TIERS
Butter dish, cov., marigold 150.00
Sauce dish, footed, marigold 40.00
Shade, milk white w/marigold
   overlay 60.00
Tumbler, marigold.................................62.00
Vase, purple 65.00

LILY OF THE VALLEY (Fenton)

Lily of the Valley Pitcher

Pitcher, water, blue (ILLUS.) 5,000.00

Tumbler, blue.....................250.00 to 300.00
Tumbler, marigold..............................400.00

LINED LATTICE VASE
Blue 68.00
Lavender, pastel ....100.00 to 150.00
Marigold..45.00
Peach opalescent, 6" h. 95.00
Purple 47.00
White 76.00
White, 10" h., pr. 225.00

LION (Fenton)

Lion Plate

Bowl, 5" d., marigold...........................105.00
Bowl, 6" d., marigold...........100.00 to 140.00
Bowl, 7" d., blue..................250.00 to 300.00
Bowl, 7" d., marigold.............................40.00
Bowl, 7" d., ice cream shape, blue 315.00
Bowl, 7" d., ice cream shape, mari-
   gold 104.00
Bowl, ruffled, red.................................675.00
Plate, 7" d., marigold (ILLUS.) 700.00

LITTLE BARREL PERFUME

Little Barrel Perfume

Green (ILLUS.) 200.00
Marigold..............................100.00 to 125.00
Smoky...97.00

LITTLE DAISIES (Fenton)
Bowl, 9" to 10" d., marigold................950.00

LITTLE FISHES (Fenton)
Bowl, 6" d., three-footed, marigold 62.50
Bowl, 8" to 9" d., three-footed, blue 245.00
Bowl, 8" to 9" d., three-footed, mari-
   gold................145.00
Bowl, 10" d., three-footed,
   blue................175.00 to 225.00
Bowl, 10" d., three-footed,
   marigold................125.00
Bowl, 10" d., three-footed,
   white................1,000.00
Sauce dish, three-footed, aqua,
   5" d................210.00
Sauce dish, three-footed, blue,
   5" d................90.00
Sauce dish, three-footed, marigold,
   5" d................48.00
Sauce dish, three-footed, purple,
   5" d................100.00
Sauce dish, three-footed, vaseline,
   5" d................95.00

LITTLE FLOWERS (Fenton)

Little Flowers Chop Plate

Berry set: master bowl & 4 sauce
   dishes; purple, 5 pcs................240.00
Berry set: master bowl & 6 sauce
   dishes; green, 7 pcs................250.00
Bowl, 6" d., ice cream shape,
   blue................30.00 to 40.00
Bowl, 6" d., ruffled, vaseline................35.00
Bowl, 6½" d., marigold................20.00
Bowl, 6½" d., purple................65.00
Bowl, 8" to 9" d., blue................110.00
Bowl, 8" to 9" d., green................45.00
Bowl, 8" to 9" d., marigold................58.00
Bowl, 8" to 9" d., purple................65.00
Bowl, 10" d., blue................110.00
Bowl, 10" d., green................75.00
Bowl, 10" d., ruffled, green................110.00
Bowl, 10" d., ruffled, lavender................116.00
Bowl, 10" d., ruffled, marigold................75.00
Bowl, 10" d., purple................95.00

Bowl, 10" d., spatula-footed,
   red................750.00 to 800.00
Plate, 6" d., marigold................450.00
Plate, chop, footed, marigold
   (ILLUS.)................400.00
Sauce dish, 5" d., blue................40.00
Sauce dish, 5" d., green................25.00
Sauce dish, 5" d., marigold................32.00
Sauce dish, 5" d., purple................40.00

LITTLE STARS BOWL (Millersburg)
Bowl, 7" d., green................97.00
Bowl, 7" d., marigold................95.00
Bowl, 7" d., fluted, marigold................95.00
Bowl, 7" d., purple................140.00
Bowl, 7½" d., three-in-one edge,
   marigold................100.00
Bowl, 8" d., ruffled, green................181.00
Bowl, 8" d., ruffled, marigold................90.00
Bowl, 8" d., ruffled, pastel marigold 135.00
Bowl, 8" d., ruffled, purple................125.00
Bowl, ice cream, 8" d., marigold..........95.00
Bowl, ice cream, 10" d., blue..............300.00
Plate, 9" d., marigold................475.00

LOGANBERRY VASE (Imperial)
Amber................500.00
Green................325.00
Marigold................180.00
Purple................550.00 to 600.00

LONG HOBSTAR
Bowl, fruit, marigold................60.00

LONG THUMBPRINTS
Creamer, marigold................22.00
Creamer & sugar bowl, marigold, pr.....50.00
Sugar bowl, marigold................37.00
Vase, 9½" h., purple................64.00

LOTUS & GRAPE (Fenton)

Lotus & Grape Plate

Bonbon, two-handled, green................90.00
Bonbon, two-handled, marigold............45.00
Bonbon, two-handled, purple..............225.00

Bonbon, two-handled, red 1,800.00
Bonbon, two-handled, vaseline 90.00
Bowl, 5" d., footed, green 67.00
Bowl, 5" d., footed, marigold................45.00
Bowl, 7" d., footed, marigold................45.00
Bowl, 7½" d., ice cream shape,
    blue...65.00
Bowl, 8" d., collared base, ruffled,
    marigold on vaseline.........................75.00
Bowl, 8" to 9" d., blue.......................105.00
Bowl, 8" to 9" d., green 95.00
Bowl, 8" to 9" d., marigold...................125.00
Bowl, 8" to 9" d., purple 95.00
Plate, 9" d., blue (ILLUS.) 1,400.00
Plate, 9" d., green............................1,200.00

LOUISA (Westmoreland)

Louisa Rose Bowl

Bowl, 5" oval, footed, teal blue 20.00
Bowl, 7" d., footed, green 45.00
Bowl, 8" to 9" d., three-footed, amber...50.00
Bowl, 8" to 9" d., three-footed, peach
    opalescent 375.00
Bowl, 8" to 9" d., three-footed, purple ...55.00
Bowl, 8" to 9" d., three-footed, teal
    blue...65.00
Nut bowl, footed, green 60.00
Nut bowl, footed, purple.......................60.00
Plate, 9½" d., footed, amber...............137.50
Plate, 9½" d., footed, marigold 100.00
Plate, 9½" d., footed, purple 140.00
Rose bowl, footed, amber.....................95.00
Rose bowl, footed, aqua.......................90.00
Rose bowl, footed, blue 80.00
Rose bowl, footed, green (ILLUS.) 65.00
Rose bowl, footed, lavendar 70.00
Rose bowl, footed, marigold.................40.00
Rose bowl, footed, purple.....................78.00

LUSTRE FLUTE (Northwood)

Bowl, berry, green 45.00
Creamer, green 32.00
Creamer, purple...................................50.00
Cup, green...12.00
Hat shape, fluted, green, 5" d. 35.00
Hat shape, fluted, marigold, 5" d. 22.00
Hat shape, fluted, purple, 5" d. 55.00
Nappy, green...........................45.00 to 50.00

Nappy, marigold 32.00
Punch cup, green ....25.00 to 30.00
Sugar bowl, green 45.00
Sugar bowl, marigold............................27.50
Tumbler, marigold.................................25.00

LUSTRE ROSE (Imperial)

Lustre Rose Bowl

Bowl, 7" d., three-footed, clambroth 75.00
Bowl, 7" d., three-footed, green............35.00
Bowl, 7" d., three-footed, marigold 42.00
Bowl, 7" d., three-footed, vaseline......100.00
Bowl, 8" to 9" d., three-footed,
    clambroth ....50.00 to 75.00
Bowl, 8" to 9" d., three-footed,
    marigold (ILLUS.)................................40.00
Bowl, 8" to 9" d., three-footed,
    purple..117.00
Bowl, 8" to 9" d., three-footed,
    smoky 35.00
Bowl, 8" to 9" d., three-footed,
    vaseline...125.00
Bowl, 10½" d., three-footed,
    clambroth 50.00
Bowl, 10½" d., three-footed, mari-
    gold 35.00
Bowl, 10½" d., three-footed, smoky......74.00
Bowl, 11" d., ruffled, collared base,
    green...85.00
Bowl, 11" d., ruffled, footed, mari-
    gold 50.00
Bowl, 11" d., ruffled, footed,
    purple..650.00
Bowl, fruit, red...................................2,400.00
Bowl, whimsey, centerpiece, amber ...250.00
Bowl, whimsey, centerpiece, purple ...550.00
Butter dish, cov., marigold 65.00
Butter dish, cov., purple.....................110.00
Creamer, marigold...............................37.00
Creamer, purple...................................125.00
Fernery, amber 80.00
Fernery, blue 75.00
Fernery, green, 7½" d., 4" h.................60.00
Fernery, green w/marigold overlay 125.00
Fernery, marigold 45.00
Fernery, olive.......................................70.00
Fernery, red 1,000.00

Pitcher, water, clambroth......................65.00
Pitcher, water, green 90.00
Pitcher, water, marigold......................85.00
Plate, 9" d., green...............................75.00
Plate, 9" d., marigold 60.00
Plate, 9" d., purple 600.00
Plate, 10½" d., marigold 85.00
Rose bowl, amber.................................70.00
Rose bowl, green..................................40.00
Rose bowl, marigold 45.00
Rose bowl, purple.................................30.00
Sauce dish, clambroth..........................30.00
Sauce dish, marigold 12.00
Spooner, purple 125.00
Sugar bowl, cov., green........................50.00
Tumbler, amber 17.00
Tumbler, aqua 395.00
Tumbler, green 25.00
Tumbler, honey amber 45.00
Tumbler, marigold.................................25.00
Tumbler, purple 50.00
Tumbler, white.....................................39.00
Water set: pitcher & 4 tumblers;
    purple, 5 pcs. 700.00
Water set: pitcher & 6 tumblers;
    marigold, 7 pcs. 250.00
Whimsey, flattened fernery, green......110.00

MANY FRUITS (Dugan)
Punch bowl & base, marigold,
    2 pcs. 400.00
Punch bowl & base, purple, 2 pcs. 715.00
Punch cup, green 35.00
Punch cup, purple................................28.00

MANY STARS (Millersburg)
Bowl, 8" to 9" d., ruffled, green 425.00
Bowl, 8" to 9" d., ruffled, marigold.......410.00
Bowl, 10" d., ruffled, blue.................2,800.00
Bowl, 10" d., ruffled, purple................450.00
Bowl, ice cream, 10" d., green............700.00
Bowl, ice cream, 10" d., purple...........800.00

MAPLE LEAF (Dugan)

Maple Leaf Creamer

Berry set: master bowl & 6 small berry
    bowls; pedestaled, purple, 7 pcs. 300.00
Bowl, 6" d., small berry, marigold 25.00
Bowl, 6" d., small berry, purple.............30.00

Bowl, master berry or fruit, purple 100.00
Bowl, ice cream, footed, marigold 35.00
Butter dish, cov., blue 82.50
Butter dish, cov., marigold 175.00
Butter dish, cov., purple.....................195.00
Creamer, marigold................................42.00
Creamer, purple (ILLUS.) 58.00
Pitcher, water, blue.............................275.00
Spooner, blue 70.00
Spooner, marigold 43.00
Spooner, purple 60.00
Table set, blue, 4 pcs. 295.00
Tumbler, amber 75.00
Tumbler, blue.......................................65.00
Tumbler, lavender...............................150.00
Tumbler, marigold.................................24.00
Tumbler, pastel marigold 75.00
Tumbler, purple 38.00
Water set: pitcher & 6 tumblers;
    purple, 7 pcs. 725.00

MARILYN (Millersburg)
Pitcher, water, marigold......................575.00
Tumbler, green 200.00
Tumbler, purple 92.00
Water set: 8½" h. pitcher & 3 tumblers;
    marigold, 4 pcs. 675.00
Water set: pitcher & 6 tumblers;
    purple, 7 pcs. 1,200.00

MARY ANN VASE (Dugan)
Marigold...................................50.00 to 70.00
Purple 165.00

MAYAN (Millersburg)
Bowl, 8" to 9" d., green 116.00
Bowl, 8" to 9" d., purple 125.00

MEMPHIS (Northwood)

Memphis Punch Bowl

Bowl, master berry, marigold................75.00
Fruit bowl & base, ice blue, 2 pcs....4,500.00
Fruit bowl & base, marigold,
    2 pcs. ....150.00 to 200.00

Fruit bowl & base, purple,
  2 pcs. ....425.00 to 475.00
Fruit bowl & base, white, 2 pcs. 700.00
Punch bowl & base, marigold,
  2 pcs. 175.00
Punch bowl & base, purple, 2 pcs.
  (ILLUS.) 600.00
Punch cup, green 46.00
Punch cup, ice blue 65.00
Punch cup, ice green...........................70.00
Punch cup, marigold............................25.00
Punch cup, purple................................38.00
Punch cup, white 40.00
Punch set: bowl, base & 4 cups; white,
  6 pcs. 900.00
Punch set: bowl, base & 6 cups;
  green, 8 pcs. 1,250.00
Punch set: bowl, base & 6 cups;
  marigold, 8 pcs. 415.00
Punch set: bowl, base & 6 cups;
  purple, 8 pcs. 1,300.00

MIKADO (Fenton)
Compote, 10" d., blue 412.00
Compote, 10" d., marigold 154.00

MILADY (Fenton)
Pitcher, water, blue.........................1,000.00
Pitcher, water, marigold.....................675.00
Tumbler, blue.......................................89.00
Tumbler, green 675.00
Tumbler, marigold................................84.00
Tumbler, purple 116.00
Water set: pitcher & 6 tumblers;
  blue, 7 pcs. 800.00

MILLERSBURG PIPE HUMIDOR - See Pipe Humidor Pattern

MILLERSBURG TROUT & FLY - See Trout & Fly Pattern

MIRRORED LOTUS
Bowl, 7" d., blue...................................55.00
Bowl, 7" d., ice green..........................400.00
Bowl, 7" d., marigold............................55.00
Rose bowl, white 500.00

MORNING GLORY (Millersburg)
Pitcher, tankard, purple (ILLUS. top
  next column) ....6,350.00 to 7,500.00
Tumbler, green 1,000.00
Tumbler, marigold............................1,400.00
Tumbler, purple 1,300.00
Vase, 4¼" h., marigold 30.00
Vase, 5" h., marigold 48.00
Vase, 5½" h., marigold 72.00
Vase, 6" h., green 79.00
Vase, 6" h., purple 73.00
Vase, 7" h., smoky...............................95.00
Vase, 8" h., purple 75.00
Vase, purple 125.00
Vase, funeral, 10 x 12", marigold.......280.00

Morning Glory Pitcher

Vase, funeral, 9½ x 13", purple 300.00

MULTIFRUITS & FLOWERS (Millersburg)

Multifruits & Flowers Pitcher

Pitcher, water, marigold (ILLUS.) 3,300.00
Pitcher, water, purple.......................4,500.00
Punch bowl & base, marigold,
  2 pcs. 600.00
Punch bowl & base, purple, 2 pcs. 850.00
Punch cup, green 60.00
Punch cup, marigold............................70.00
Punch cup, purple................................40.00
Punch set: bowl, base & 5 cups; green,
  7 pcs. 1,675.00
Tumbler, green 1,000.00
Tumbler, marigold............................1,000.00

MY LADY
Powder jar, cov., marigold...................89.00

NAUTILUS (Dugan)
Bowl, peach opalescent......200.00 to 250.00
Bowl, footed, purple............................175.00
Creamer, peach opalescent 295.00
Creamer, purple.................225.00 to 250.00

Dish, flattened boat shape, peach
   opalescent, 6 x 7½", 3" h. 295.00
Sugar bowl, open, peach
   opalescent 250.00
Sugar bowl, open, purple...................225.00

NESTING SWAN (Millersburg)
Bowl, 10" d., amber 325.00
Bowl, 10" d., green ....300.00 to 325.00
Bowl, 10" d., marigold........................220.00
Bowl, 10" d., purple.............300.00 to 350.00

NIGHT STARS (Millersburg)
Bonbon, green...................450.00 to 475.00
Bonbon, marigold 950.00
Bonbon, purple 450.00

NIPPON (Northwood)

Nippon Bowl

Bowl, 8" to 9" d., blue..........................275.00
Bowl, 8" to 9" d., 3" h., green 164.00
Bowl, 8" to 9" d., 2¼" h., ice blue
   (ILLUS) 286.00
Bowl, 8" to 9" d., ice green..............1,000.00
Bowl, 8" to 9" d., marigold...................100.00
Bowl, 8" to 9" d., purple 174.00
Bowl, 8" to 9" d., fluted, white 225.00
Bowl, 8" d., piecrust rim, ice blue........325.00
Bowl, 8" d., piecrust rim, ice green 900.00
Bowl, 8" d., piecrust rim,
   marigold ....200.00 to 250.00
Bowl, 8" d., piecrust rim, pastel lime
   green w/opal tips............................3,000.00
Bowl, 8" d., piecrust rim, purple 225.00
Bowl, 8" d., piecrust rim, white............225.00
Plate, 9" d., ice blue........................5,000.00
Plate, 9" d., marigold 392.00
Plate, 9" d., purple 640.00

NU-ART CHRYSANTHEMUM PLATE (Imperial)
Amber 600.00
Marigold..495.00
Purple (ILLUS. top next column) 1,200.00

Nu-Art Chrysanthemum Plate

White 700.00

NU-ART HOMESTEAD PLATE (Imperial)
Amber ....1,200.00 to 1,500.00
Blue 5,250.00
Emerald green.................................3,000.00
Green.................................750.00 to 850.00
Helios..395.00
Lavender...900.00
Marigold..400.00
Purple ....875.00 to 975.00
White 758.00

OCTAGON (Imperial)

Octagon Goblet

Bowl, 8" to 9" d., marigold....................38.00
Butter dish, cov., marigold..................100.00
Creamer, marigold................................60.00
Creamer, purple..................................165.00
Decanter w/stopper, green 700.00
Decanter w/stopper, marigold..............68.00
Decanter w/stopper, purple 230.00
Goblet, water, light blue w/marigold
   overlay..70.00
Goblet, water, marigold (ILLUS.) 40.00
Pitcher, milk, marigold 88.00
Pitcher, milk, purple ....250.00 to 275.00
Pitcher, water, 8" h., marigold...............89.00
Pitcher, water, 8" h., purple 525.00
Pitcher, water, tankard, 9¾" h.,
   marigold 100.00

Pitcher, water, tankard, 9¾" h.,
  purple 400.00
Punch set: bowl, ladle & 12 cups;
  marigold, 14 pcs. 2,400.00
Salt shaker, purple................................95.00
Spooner, marigold 45.00
Spooner, purple 165.00
Sugar bowl, cov., marigold 50.00
Toothpick holder, marigold 135.00
Tumbler, green 150.00
Tumbler, marigold................................25.00
Tumbler, purple ....125.00 to 175.00
Vase, 8" h., marigold 100.00
Water set: pitcher & 6 tumblers;
  purple, 7 pcs. 950.00
Wine, marigold.....................................27.00
Wine set: decanter & 1 wine; purple,
  2 pcs. 450.00
Wine set: decanter & 6 wines; mari-
  gold, 7 pcs. 275.00

OHIO STAR (Millersburg)
Vase, green 1,100.00
Vase, marigold...................................750.00
Vase, purple 1,150.00
Vase, white 550.00

ORANGE PEEL
Punch bowl, marigold 55.00
Punch cup, marigold.............................16.50
Punch cup, teal....................................40.00
Punch set: bowl & 12 cups; marigold,
  13 pcs. 500.00

ORANGE TREE (Fenton)

Orange Tree Mug

Bowl, 8" to 9" d., blue...........................105.00
Bowl, 8" to 9" d., clambroth...................83.00
Bowl, 8" to 9" d., green 155.00
Bowl, 8" to 9" d., marigold.....................57.00
Bowl, 8" to 9" d., pastel marigold 60.00
Bowl, 8" to 9" d., purple ....75.00 to 100.00
Bowl, 8" to 9" d., red 2,100.00
Bowl, 8" to 9" d., white 156.00
Bowl, 10" d., three-footed, blue 233.00
Bowl, 10" d., three-footed, green 235.00

Bowl, 10" d., three-footed, marigold ...100.00
Bowl, 10" d., three-footed, purple 325.00
Bowl, 10" d., three-footed, white.........200.00
Bowl, 10" d., Rose Tree interior,
  blue 1,100.00
Bowl, ice cream shape, blue 100.00
Bowl, ice cream shape, green 185.00
Bowl, ice cream shape, marigold..........45.00
Bowl, ice cream shape, red 1,400.00
Bowl, ice cream shape, white 125.00
Bowl, moonstone 2,000.00
Bowl, peach opalescent...................1,900.00
Breakfast set: individual size creamer
  & cov. sugar bowl; blue, pr. 130.00
Breakfast set: individual size creamer
  & cov. sugar bowl; marigold, pr. 195.00
Breakfast set: individual size creamer
  & cov. sugar bowl; purple, pr. 130.00
Breakfast set: individual size creamer
  & cov. sugar bowl; white, pr. 150.00
Butter dish, cov., blue 400.00
Butter dish, cov., blue w/electric
  iridescence......................................350.00
Butter dish, cov., marigold 250.00
Centerpiece bowl, footed, marigold,
  12" d., 4" h. 80.00
Compote, 5" d., blue 62.50
Compote, 5" d., marigold 35.00
Creamer, footed, blue...........................80.00
Creamer, footed, purple........................50.00
Creamer, individual size, blue 45.00
Creamer, individual size, purple 75.00
Creamer, individual size, white.............85.00
Creamer & sugar bowl, footed, blue,
  pr..100.00
Dish, ice cream, footed, blue 38.00
Dish, ice cream, footed, marigold 50.00
Goblet, amber.......................................62.50
Goblet, blue 75.00
Goblet, green.......................................190.00
Goblet, marigold 48.00
Hatpin holder, blue ....300.00 to 325.00
Hatpin holder, green 800.00
Hatpin holder, marigold 239.00
Loving cup, blue ....225.00 to 250.00
Loving cup, green 350.00
Loving cup, marigold ....175.00 to 200.00
Loving cup, purple 400.00
Mug, amber 114.00
Mug, Amberina 395.00
Mug, aqua..163.00
Mug, blue (ILLUS.) 57.00
Mug, lavender......................................135.00
Mug, lime green...................................500.00
Mug, lime green w/vaseline base 150.00
Mug, marigold.......................................30.00
Mug, marigold, souvenir 75.00
Mug, marigold w/aqua base 75.00
Mug, marigold w/vaseline base 150.00
Mug, purple...80.00
Mug, red ....350.00 to 400.00
Mug, sapphire blue ....300.00 to 350.00
Mug, smoky blue 155.00
Mug, vaseline 100.00

Mug, white 1,000.00
Plate, 9" d., flat, blue...........350.00 to 400.00
Plate, 9" d., flat, clambroth..................215.00
Plate, 9" d., flat, green 2,000.00
Plate, 9" d., flat, marigold....225.00 to 250.00
Plate, 9" d., flat, pastel marigold 140.00
Plate, 9" d., flat, teal blue....................375.00
Plate, 9" d., flat, white 210.00
Plate, 9" d., flat, Beaded Berry
   exterior, blue 550.00
Plate, 9" d., trunk center, flat, Beaded
   Berry exterior, marigold 185.00
Plate, 9" d., trunk center,
   white ....250.00 to 275.00
Plate, 9" d., Blackberry exterior,
   "Souvenir of Hershey," blue 245.00
Powder jar, cov., blue 105.00
Powder jar, cov., green........................412.00
Powder jar, cov., marigold......65.00 to 70.00
Powder jar, cov., purple.......................160.00
Punch bowl & base, blue, 2 pcs. 255.00
Punch bowl & base, marigold,
   2 pcs. 153.00
Punch bowl & base, white,
   2 pcs. ....700.00 to 800.00
Punch cup, blue.....................................25.00
Punch cup, green 90.00
Punch cup, marigold..............................12.00
Punch cup, white 35.00
Punch set: bowl, base & 4 cups;
   marigold, 6 pcs. ....300.00 to 350.00
Punch set: bowl, base & 6 cups;
   blue, 8 pcs. ....500.00 to 525.00
Rose bowl, blue.....................................85.00
Rose bowl, green..................................160.00
Rose bowl, marigold 58.00
Rose bowl, purple...................................95.00
Rose bowl, red.................900.00 to 1,200.00
Rose bowl, white 275.00
Sauce dish, footed, blue 30.00
Sauce dish, footed, marigold 21.00
Sauce dish, footed, white 65.00
Shaving mug, Amberina 450.00
Shaving mug, blue..................................50.00
Shaving mug, clambroth.........................35.00
Shaving mug, marigold...........................32.00
Shaving mug, marigold, large.............125.00
Shaving mug, purple.............................265.00
Shaving mug, red 650.00
Shaving mug, vaseline 110.00
Spooner, marigold 50.00
Sugar bowl, cov., blue 60.00
Sugar bowl, cov., marigold 110.00
Sugar bowl, cov., white........................100.00
Sugar bowl, open, individual size,
   marigold 40.00
Sugar bowl, open, individual size,
   purple...52.00
Sugar bowl, open, individual size,
   white 75.00
Tumbler, blue..55.00
Tumbler, clambroth.................................55.00
Tumbler, marigold...................................45.00
Tumbler, pastel marigold 49.00

Tumbler, purple 42.00
Tumbler, white 100.00
Water set: pitcher & 6 tumblers; blue,
   7 pcs. 700.00
Wine, aqua 300.00
Wine, blue..52.00
Wine, clambroth.......................................65.00
Wine, marigold...25.00

ORANGE TREE ORCHARD (Fenton)

Pitcher, blue..500.00
Pitcher, marigold...................................250.00
Pitcher, white 515.00
Tumbler, blue...50.00
Tumbler, marigold....................................79.00

ORANGE TREE SCROLL

Pitcher, blue......................................1,000.00
Tumbler, blue...100.00
Tumbler, marigold....................................65.00

ORIENTAL POPPY (Northwood)

Oriental Poppy Pitcher

Pitcher, water, green 1,250.00
Pitcher, water, marigold.....................325.00
Pitcher, water, purple (ILLUS.) 950.00
Tumbler, blue...200.00
Tumbler, green 60.00
Tumbler, ice blue 155.00
Tumbler, ice green..................................475.00
Tumbler, lilac...39.00
Tumbler, marigold....................................40.00
Tumbler, pastel marigold 45.00
Tumbler, purple 45.00
Tumbler, white 135.00
Water set: pitcher & 1 tumbler;
   white, 2 pcs. 1,900.00
Water set: pitcher & 6 tumblers;
   ice blue, 7 pcs. 5,000.00
Water set: pitcher & 6 tumblers;
   marigold, 7 pcs. 850.00
Water set: pitcher & 6 tumblers;
   purple, 7 pcs. 1,600.00

PALM BEACH (U.S. Glass Co.)
Bowl, 8½" d., marigold..........................50.00

Butter dish, cov., white 250.00
Creamer, marigold..................................68.00
Pitcher, water, white 700.00

Palm Beach Rose Bowl

Rose bowl, amber (ILLUS.) 125.00
Rose bowl, w/Gooseberry interior,
   white 225.00
Sauce dish, marigold............................30.00
Sauce dish, white 48.00
Spooner, marigold 80.00
Spooner, white......................................125.00
Sugar bowl, cov., marigold 75.00
Table set, white, 4 pcs.........................975.00
Tumbler, amber 175.00
Tumbler, white......................................125.00
Whimsey banana boat, marigold,
   6"...75.00 to 90.00
Whimsey banana boat, purple, 6".......120.00

**PANELED DANDELION - See Dandelion,
Paneled Pattern**

PANELED HOLLY (Northwood)
Bonbon, green 45.00
Bonbon, marigold 35.00
Candy, handled, green 80.00

PANTHER (Fenton)

Panther Centerpiece Bowl

Berry set: master bowl & 4 sauce
   dishes; marigold, 5 pcs. 325.00
Bowl, 5" d., footed, aqua.....................425.00
Bowl, 5" d., footed, blue......................100.00
Bowl, 5" d., footed, clambroth..............35.00
Bowl, 5" d., footed, green 90.00
Bowl, 5" d., footed, marigold................52.00

Bowl, 5" d., footed,
   red..............................1,000.00 to 1,300.00
Bowl, 9" d., claw-footed, blue 390.00
Bowl, 9" d., claw-footed,
   green.................................625.00 to 675.00
Bowl, 9" d., claw-footed, mari-
   gold...................................200.00 to 250.00
Bowl, 9" d., claw-footed, white...........750.00
Bowl, berry, Butterfly & Berry exterior,
   marigold 35.00
Bowl, low, marigold.............................300.00
Centerpiece bowl, marigold
   (ILLUS.) ....575.00 to 600.00

PEACH (Northwood)
Berry set: master bowl & 4 sauce
   dishes; white, 5 pcs. 395.00
Bowl, 7" d., w/hand enameling 60.00
Butter dish, cov., white 225.00

Peach Pitcher

Pitcher, water, blue (ILLUS.) 1,250.00
Pitcher, water, white 800.00
Sauce dish, white 45.00
Spooner, white.....................................150.00
Sugar bowl, cov., white........................175.00
Table set, white, 4 pcs........................450.00
Tumbler, blue..85.00
Tumbler, white 95.00

PEACH & PEAR OVAL FRUIT BOWL
Marigold...77.00
Purple 125.00

PEACOCK & DAHLIA (Fenton)
Bowl, 6" d., ice cream shape, mari-
   gold...45.00
Bowl, 6" d., ice cream shape,
   vaseline...100.00
Bowl, 6¼" d., ice cream shape,
   green..120.00
Bowl, 6½" d., 2" h., scalloped edge,
   green..125.00
Bowl, 7" d., ice cream shape,
   vaseline...110.00
Bowl, 7" d., ruffled, aqua opalescent ..125.00

Bowl, 7" d., ruffled, blue........................85.00
Bowl, 7" d., marigold..............................50.00
Bowl, 7" d., ruffled, purple....................75.00
Bowl, 7" d., vaseline 150.00
Bowl, 7½" d., purple w/blue base 100.00
Plate, 7½" d., marigold 550.00
Sauce dish, marigold 25.00

PEACOCK & GRAPE (Fenton)

Bowl, 8" d., collared base, amber 120.00
Bowl, 8" d., collared base, blue 53.00
Bowl, 8" d., collared base, ruffled,
    green..75.00
Bowl, 8" d., collared base, ruffled,
    ice green 225.00
Bowl, 8" d., collared base, marigold 40.00
Bowl, 8" d., collared base, peach
    opalescent 580.00
Bowl, 8" d., collared base, purple 76.00
Bowl, 8" d., collared base, ruffled,
    red...1,200.00
Bowl, 8" d., collared base, smoky.......585.00
Bowl, 8" d., collared base, vaseline 275.00
Bowl, 8" d., collared base, ribbon
    candy rim, blue 80.00
Bowl, 8" d., collared base, ribbon
    candy rim, lavendar 75.00
Bowl, 8" d., spatula-footed, blue...........50.00
Bowl, 8" d., spatula-footed, green.........72.00
Bowl, 8" d., spatula-footed, ice green
    opalescent 418.00
Bowl, 8" d., spatula-footed,
    lavender ....150.00 to 200.00
Bowl, 8" d., spatula-footed, marigold 60.00
Bowl, 8" d., spatula-footed, milk
    white w/marigold overlay 360.00
Bowl, 8" d., spatula-footed, peach
    opalescent ....325.00 to 350.00
Bowl, 8" d., spatula-footed, purple........68.00
Bowl, 8" d., spatula-footed, red..........934.00
Bowl, 8" d., spatula-footed, smoky 90.00
Bowl, 8" d., spatula-footed, vaseline
    opalescent ....450.00 to 550.00
Bowl, ice cream shape, Amberina......650.00
Bowl, 8" d., ice cream shape, green.....85.00
Bowl, 8" d., ice cream shape, mari-
    gold...85.00
Bowl, 8" d., ice cream shape, red....1,650.00
Bowl, 9" d., ice cream shape, red 695.00
Bowl, ice cream shape, collared
    base, vaseline...................................185.00
Bowl, 9" d., ruffled, collared base,
    blue ....100.00 to 150.00
Bowl, 9" d., ruffled, ice blue w/mari-
    gold overlay 195.00
Bowl, 9" d., ruffled, ice blue w/smoky
    overlay 395.00
Bowl, 9" d., ruffled, purple....................75.00
Bowl, 9" d., ruffled, red 300.00
Bowl, ruffled, iridized moonstone........325.00
Plate, 9" d., collared base, blue 325.00
Plate, 9" d., collared base, marigold ...275.00
Plate, 9" d., flat base, marigold..........525.00

Plate, 9" d., collared base, berry
    exterior, smoky ice blue 800.00
Plate, 9" d., spatula-footed,
    green..............................150.00 to 175.00
Plate, 9" d., spatula-footed, marigold..350.00

PEACOCK & URN (Millersburg, Fenton & Northwood)

Berry set: master bowl & 5 sauce
    dishes; purple, 6 pcs........750.00 to 850.00
Bowl, 5½" d., ruffled, blue
    (Millersburg) 1,240.00
Bowl, 6" d., ice cream shape, blue,
    stippled 175.00
Bowl, 6" d., ice cream shape, green
    (Millersburg) 325.00
Bowl, 6" d., ice cream shape, ice
    green...315.00
Bowl, 6" d., ice cream shape, mari-
    gold (Millersburg) 75.00
Bowl, 6" d., ice cream shape, mari-
    gold (Northwood) 50.00
Bowl, 6" d., ice cream shape, purple 75.00
Bowl, 6" d., ice cream shape, purple
    (Millersburg) 162.00
Bowl, 6" d., ice cream shape, purple
    satin 195.00
Bowl, 6" d., ice cream shape, white....150.00
Bowl, 7" d., ruffled, blue (Millers-
    burg) 400.00
Bowl, 7" d., ruffled, green (Millers-
    burg) 250.00
Bowl, 7" d., ruffled, marigold
    (Millersburg) 395.00
Bowl, 7" d., ruffled, purple (Millers-
    burg) 350.00
Bowl, 8" d., collared base, moon-
    stone (Fenton) 1,825.00
Bowl, 8" d., ice cream shape, blue
    (Fenton) 195.00
Bowl, 8" d., ice cream shape, green
    (Fenton) 200.00
Bowl, 8" d., ice cream shape,
    marigold (Fenton) 108.00
Bowl, 8" d., ice cream shape, Beaded
    Berry exterior, purple 275.00
Bowl, 8" d., ice cream shape,
    white 350.00
Bowl, 8" to 9" d., blue (Fenton) 226.00
Bowl, 8" to 9" d., green (Fenton).........300.00
Bowl, 8" to 9" d., green (Millers-
    burg) ....400.00 to 425.00
Bowl, 8" to 9" d., marigold (Fenton) 122.00
Bowl, 8" to 9" d., marigold (Millers-
    burg) ....200.00 to 250.00
Bowl, 8" to 9" d., purple (Fenton)........180.00
Bowl, 8" to 9" d., purple (Millers-
    burg) 275.00
Bowl, 8" to 9" d., white (Fenton) 349.00
Bowl, 10" d., ice cream shape, aqua
    opalescent 950.00
Bowl, 10" d., ice cream shape, blue
    (Northwood) 625.00

Bowl, 10" d., ice cream shape, blue,
   stippled 1,250.00
Bowl, 10" d., ice cream shape, blue
   w/electric iridescence (North-
   wood) 1,450.00
Bowl, 10" d., ice cream shape, green
   (Northwood) 2,500.00
Bowl, 10" d., ice cream shape, green,
   w/bee (Millersburg) ....825.00 to 850.00
Bowl, 10" d., ice cream shape, ice
   blue (Northwood) ....900.00 to 1,000.00
Bowl, 10" d., ice cream shape, ice
   green (Northwood) .....1,200.00 to 1,300.00
Bowl, 10" d., ice cream shape, mari-
   gold (Millersburg) 375.00
Bowl, 10" d., ice cream shape,
   marigold (Northwood) 443.00
Bowl, 10" d., ice cream shape, pastel
   marigold (Northwood) ......650.00 to 700.00
Bowl, 10" d., ice cream shape,
   stippled, pastel marigold
   (Northwood) 485.00
Bowl, 10" d., ice cream shape,
   periwinkle blue (Northwood) 4.000.00
Bowl, 10" d., ice cream shape, purple
   (Millersburg) 465.00
Bowl, 10" d., ice cream shape, purple
   (Northwood) 700.00
Bowl, 10" d., ice cream shape, smoky
   (Northwood) 900.00
Bowl, 10" d., ice cream shape, white
   (Northwood) ....575.00 to 600.00
Compote, green (Millersburg
   Giant) ....1,350.00 to 1,400.00
Compote, marigold (Millersburg
   Giant) 1,900.00
Compote, purple (Millersburg
   Giant) 3,000.00
Goblet, Marigold (Fenton).....................50.00
Ice cream dish, purple, 5¾" d.
   (Millersburg) ....350.00 to 400.00
Ice cream dish, aqua opalescent,
   small (Northwood).........................1,500.00
Ice cream dish, stippled, blue, small
   (Northwood) 145.00
Ice cream dish, blue, small (North-
   wood) 82.50
Ice cream dish, blue w/electric
   iridescence, small 175.00
Ice cream dish, ice blue, small 600.00
Ice cream dish, ice green, small 425.00
Ice cream dish, lavender, small
   (Northwood) 225.00
Ice cream dish, marigold, small 85.00
Ice cream dish, purple, small 86.00
Ice cream dish, white, small 200.00
Ice cream set: large bowl & 6 small
   dishes; purple, 7 pcs. (Millers-
   burg) ....800.00 to 1,000.00
Plate, 6½" d., green (Millersburg) 3,600.00
Plate, 6½" d., marigold (Millers-
   burg) 275.00
Plate, 6½" d., purple (Millersburg) 500.00

Plate, 9" d., blue (Fenton)...................550.00
Plate, 9" d., marigold (Fenton)............408.00
Plate, 9" d., white
   (Fenton) ....450.00 to 500.00
Plate, chop, 11" d., marigold (Millers-
   burg) 2,200.00
Plate, chop, 11" d., marigold (North-
   wood) 995.00
Plate, chop, 11" d., purple (Millers-
   burg) 3,500.00
Plate, chop, 11" d., purple (North-
   wood) ....1,200.00 to 1,400.00
Sauce dish, blue (Millersburg) 250.00
Sauce dish, blue (Northwood) 120.00
Sauce dish, green (Millersburg)............75.00
Sauce dish, ice blue (Northwood).......200.00
Sauce dish, ice blue, 6" d. 70.00
Sauce dish, ice green, 6" d. (North-
   wood) 415.00
Sauce dish, lavender (Millersburg) 45.00
Sauce dish, marigold (Northwood) 50.00
Sauce dish, purple (Millersburg).........125.00
Sauce dish, purple (Northwood) 100.00
Sauce dish, white (Northwood)...........185.00
Whimsey sauce dish, marigold, 5¼"
   (Millersburg) 175.00
Whimsey sauce dish, purple,
   5¼" d. ....275.00 to 300.00

PEACOCK AT FOUNTAIN (Northwood)

Peacock at Fountain Water Set

Berry set: master bowl & 2 sauce
   dishes; ice blue, 3 pcs. 640.00
Berry set: master bowl & 4 sauce
   dishes; purple, 5 pcs.......................450.00
Berry set: master bowl & 6 sauce
   dishes; blue, 7 pcs. 600.00
Bowl, master berry, blue.....................325.00
Bowl, master berry, green 600.00
Bowl, master berry, ice blue 380.00
Bowl, master berry, marigold..............150.00
Bowl, master berry, purple..................200.00
Bowl, master berry, white 250.00
Bowl, orange, three-footed, aqua
   opalescent 1,100.00
Bowl, orange, three-footed, lav-
   ender..525.00
Bowl, orange, three-footed, mari-
   gold 320.00

Bowl, orange, three-footed, purple 488.00
Butter dish, cov., green.....................500.00
Butter dish, cov., marigold.................210.00
Butter dish, cov., purple....................275.00
Compote, aqua opalescent.............3,100.00
Compote, blue 587.00
Compote, ice blue...........................1,200.00
Compote, ice green 1,400.00
Compote, marigold 400.00
Compote, purple 800.00
Compote, white..................550.00 to 650.00
Creamer, marigold.............................65.00
Creamer, purple...................75.00 to 100.00
Pitcher, water, blue............................450.00
Pitcher, water, marigold.....................250.00
Pitcher, water, white ....950.00 to 1,000.00
Punch bowl & base, blue,
  2 pcs. 2,300.00
Punch bowl & base, ice blue,
  2 pcs. 8,000.00
Punch bowl & base, ice green,
  2 pcs. 9,500.00
Punch bowl & base, marigold,
  2 pcs. 900.00
Punch bowl & base, purple,
  2 pcs. 1,500.00
Punch cup, aqua opalescent 1,400.00
Punch cup, blue.................................50.00
Punch cup, blue w/electric irides-
  cence 95.00
Punch cup, ice blue 125.00
Punch cup, ice green..........................525.00
Punch cup, lavender............................88.00
Punch cup, marigold............................45.00
Punch cup, purple................................38.00
Punch cup, white 75.00
Punch set: bowl, base & 2 cups;
  marigold, 4 pcs. 675.00
Punch set: bowl, base & 5 cups;
  ice green, 7 pcs. 10,750.00
Punch set: bowl, base & 6 cups;
  purple, 7 pcs. 1,750.00
Punch set: bowl, base & 6 cups;
  ice blue, 8 pcs. 7,000.00
Punch set: bowl, base & 6 cups;
  white, 8 pcs. 6,000.00
Sauce dish, blue 40.00
Sauce dish, ice blue ....100.00 to 150.00
Sauce dish, marigold 21.00
Sauce dish, purple...............................31.00
Sauce dish, white 50.00
Spooner, blue 150.00
Spooner, ice blue...............................260.00
Spooner, marigold 76.00
Spooner, purple ....100.00 to 150.00
Spooner, white...................................175.00
Sugar bowl, cov., ice blue..................265.00
Sugar bowl, cov., marigold 85.00
Table set, ice blue, 4 pcs.................2,600.00
Table set, marigold, 4 pcs. 475.00
Table set, purple, 4 pcs. .....450.00 to 500.00
Tumbler, amber 89.00
Tumbler, blue......................................50.00

Tumbler, green ....300.00 to 350.00
Tumbler, ice blue..............400.00 to 425.00
Tumbler, lavender...............................125.00
Tumbler, marigold................................45.00
Tumbler, purple 55.00
Tumbler, teal blue..............................139.00
Tumbler, white 225.00
Water set: pitcher & 5 tumblers;
  marigold, 6 pcs. 500.00
Water set: pitcher & 6 tumblers; blue,
  7 pcs. 775.00
Water set: pitcher & 6 tumblers;
  purple, 7 pcs. (ILLUS.).....................900.00

PEACOCK, FLUFFY (Fenton)
Pitcher, water, green 750.00
Pitcher, water, marigold......................425.00
Pitcher, water, purple..........575.00 to 600.00
Tumbler, blue......................................85.00
Tumbler, marigold................................63.00
Tumbler, purple 75.00

PEACOCK TAIL (Fenton)

Peacock Tail Plate
Berry set: 9" d. bowl & four 5" d. bowls;
  green, 5 pcs. 140.00
Bonbon, two-handled, green 80.00
Bonbon, two-handled, marigold...........28.00
Bonbon, two-handled, purple...............65.00
Bonbon, tricornered, green..................55.00
Bonbon, tricornered, marigold 22.50
Bonbon, tricornered, purple.................40.00
Bowl, 5" d., ruffled, marigold...............27.00
Bowl, 5" d., ruffled, purple...................28.00
Bowl, 6" d., blue.................................45.00
Bowl, 6" d., ruffled, peach
  opalescent 700.00
Bowl, 6" d., ruffled, red 1,850.00
Bowl, 7" d., green 35.00
Bowl, 7" d., purple...............................37.00
Bowl, 8" d., green 75.00
Bowl, 8" d., purple................................40.00
Bowl, 9" d., crimped, green..................55.00
Bowl, 9" d., ribbon candy rim, green
  w/electric iridescence......................175.00
Bowl, 9" d., ribbon candy rim, green...125.00

Bowl, 10" d., ribbon candy rim,
green...225.00
Bowl, 10" d., green 75.00
Bowl, ice cream, green........................35.00
Bowl, ice cream, purple 25.00
Compote, 6" d., 5" h., blue...................38.00
Compote, 6" d., 5" h., green 69.00
Compote, 6" d., 5" h., marigold.............68.00
Compote, 6" d., 5" h., purple................70.00
Plate, 6" d., blue 245.00
Plate, 6" d., green 100.00
Plate, 6" d., marigold (ILLUS.) 275.00
Whimsey, hat-shaped, green................75.00
Whimsey, hat-shaped, w/advertising,
green...75.00
Whimsey, hat-shaped, purple..............25.00

PEACOCKS ON FENCE (Northwood Peacocks)

Bowl, 8" to 9" d., piecrust rim, aqua
opalescent 3,000.00
Bowl, 8" to 9" d., piecrust rim, blue 485.00
Bowl, 8" to 9" d., piecrust rim, blue,
stippled w/ribbed back 795.00
Bowl, 8" to 9" d., piecrust rim, blue
w/electric iridescence......................995.00
Bowl, 8" to 9" d., piecrust rim,
green.........................1,800.00 to 1,875.00
Bowl, 8" to 9" d., piecrust rim, ice
blue 1,675.00
Bowl, 8" to 9" d., piecrust rim, ice
green..1,850.00
Bowl, 8" to 9" d., piecrust rim,
lavender 550.00

Peacocks on Fence Bowl

Bowl, 8" to 9" d., piecrust rim,
marigold (ILLUS.)............................288.00
Bowl, 8" to 9" d., piecrust rim,
stippled, marigold.............400.00 to 425.00
Bowl, 8" to 9" d., piecrust rim, pastel
marigold ....325.00 to 350.00
Bowl, 8" to 9" d., piecrust rim,
purple...500.00
Bowl, 8" to 9" d., piecrust rim,
white 850.00

Bowl, 8" to 9" d., ruffled rim, aqua
opalescent 1,000.00
Bowl, 8" to 9" d., ruffled rim, blue........525.00
Bowl, 8" to 9" d., ruffled rim,
green.........................1,100.00 to 1,200.00
Bowl, 8" to 9" d., ruffled rim, ice
blue 1,750.00
Bowl, 8" to 9" d., ruffled rim, ice
green..1,400.00
Bowl, 8" to 9" d., ruffled rim, mari-
gold..243.00
Bowl, 8" to 9" d., ruffled rim, purple 395.00
Bowl, 8" to 9" d., ruffled rim,
smoky 2,500.00
Bowl, 8" to 9" d., ruffled rim, white......650.00
Bowl, 9" d., stippled, green.............1,100.00
Bowl, ruffled, lime green opales-
cent 4,000.00
Bowl, ruffled, ribbed back, white.........875.00
Plate, 8" d., blue ....700.00 to 750.00
Plate, 9" d., blue w/electric
iridescence...................................1,050.00
Plate, 9" d., stippled, cobalt
blue ....650.00 to 700.00
Plate, 9" d., green ....1,550.00 to 1,650.00
Plate, 9" d., ice blue......1,650.00 to 1,750.00
Plate, 9" d., ice green 450.00
Plate, 9" d., lavender ....1,100.00 to 1,200.00
Plate, 9" d., marigold 456.00
Plate, 9" d., stippled, mari-
gold ....450.00 to 500.00
Plate, 9" d., purple ....625.00 to 650.00
Plate, 9" d., white...............450.00 to 470.00
Plate, 9" d., white, decorated..........1,100.00

PERFECTION (Millersburg)

Pitcher, water, green 2,630.00
Pitcher, water, purple.......................3,100.00
Tumbler, green 400.00
Tumbler, purple 326.00

PERSIAN GARDEN (Dugan)

Bowl, 5" d., peach opalescent 45.00
Bowl, 5" d., white 83.00
Bowl, 6" d., ice cream shape, white......55.00
Bowl, 9" d., ruffled, marigold...............150.00
Bowl, 11" d., ice cream shape,
lavender tint 345.00
Bowl, 11" d., ice cream shape, peach
opalescent ....850.00 to 900.00
Bowl, 11" d., ice cream shape,
purple...800.00
Bowl, 11" d., ice cream shape,
white ....300.00 to 325.00
Fruit bowl (no base), marigold,
11½" d..160.00
Fruit bowl (no base), peach
opalescent, 11½" d. 350.00
Fruit bowl (no base), white, 11½" d. ...250.00
Fruit bowl & base, marigold,
2 pcs. 275.00
Fruit bowl & base, peach opalescent,
2 pcs. 650.00

Fruit bowl & base, purple, 2 pcs. 800.00
Fruit bowl & base, white, 2 pcs. 500.00
Hair receiver, blue 115.00
Hair receiver, marigold 75.00
Plate, 6" to 7" d., marigold 92.00
Plate, 6" to 7" d., pastel marigold..........50.00
Plate, 6" to 7" d., purple 250.00
Plate, 6" to 7" d., white........................188.00
Plate, 9" d., marigold 125.00
Plate, chop, 11" d., purple 5,500.00

PERSIAN MEDALLION (Fenton)

Persian Medallion Chop Plate

Bonbon, two-handled, aqua...............215.00
Bonbon, two-handled, blue....................58.00
Bonbon, two-handled, celeste blue 500.00
Bonbon, two-handled, green 75.00
Bonbon, two-handled, lavender...........60.00
Bonbon, two-handled, marigold............37.00
Bonbon, two-handled, purple..50.00 to 60.00
Bonbon, two-handled, red 1,000.00
Bonbon, two-handled, vaseline 230.00
Bowl, 5" d., aqua.................125.00 to 150.00
Bowl, 5" d., blue....................................34.00
Bowl, 5" d., green 30.00
Bowl, 5" d., marigold............................35.00
Bowl, 5" d., purple................................58.00
Bowl, 6" d., ruffled, aqua......................95.00
Bowl, 6" d., ruffled, green 120.00
Bowl, 6" d., ruffled, marigold................30.00
Bowl, 7" d., green 75.00
Bowl, 7" d., marigold............................45.00
Bowl, 7" d., ice cream shape, purple 32.50
Bowl, 7" d., ribbon candy rim,
  marigold...40.00
Bowl, 8" to 9" d., fluted, blue 75.00
Bowl, 8" to 9" d., ice cream shape,
  green...135.00
Bowl, 8" to 9" d., ribbon candy rim,
  blue 80.00
Bowl, 8" to 9" d., ribbon candy rim,
  green..55.00
Bowl, 8" to 9" d., marigold....................50.00

Bowl, 8" to 9" d., purple 65.00
Bowl, 8" to 9" d., ribbon candy rim,
  purple...95.00
Bowl, 9½" d., purple...........................100.00
Bowl, 10½" d., fluted, blue 85.00
Bowl, 10½" d., ruffled, green 100.00
Bowl, orange, marigold.......................100.00
Compote, 6½" d., 6½" h., blue...........110.00
Compote, 6½" d., 6½" h., clambroth.....90.00
Compote, 6½" d., 6½" h., green 274.00
Compote, 6½" d., 6½" h., marigold.......66.00
Compote, 6½" d., 6½" h.,
  purple..................................75.00 to 100.00
Compote, 6½" d., 6½" h., white 500.00
Compote, ribbon candy rim, cobalt
  blue 275.00
Compote, ribbon candy rim, purple 350.00
Compote, three-in-one rim, purple......575.00
Hair receiver, blue 100.00
Hair receiver, marigold 68.00
Hair receiver, white.............................125.00
Plate, 6½" d., blue ....100.00 to 125.00
Plate, 6½" d., marigold 59.00
Plate, 6½" d., purple 175.00
Plate, 6½" d., white..............................130.00
Plate, 7" d., blue 125.00
Plate, 7½" d., blue 100.00
Plate, 8" d., marigold 55.00
Plate, 9" d., blue 225.00
Plate, 9" d., clambroth 195.00
Plate, 9" d., marigold 275.00
Plate, 9" d., white 2,800.00
Plate, chop, 10½" d., blue
  (ILLUS.) ....475.00 to 495.00
Rose bowl, blue 150.00
Rose bowl, clambroth 300.00
Rose bowl, marigold 80.00
Rose bowl, white 125.00

PETAL & FAN (Dugan)

Bowl, 5" d., peach opalescent 55.00
Bowl, 5" d., purple.................................50.00
Bowl, 5⅜" d., black amethyst...............40.00
Bowl, 6" d., ruffled, peach
  opalescent 145.00
Bowl, 9" d., ruffled, dome base,
  peach opalescent.............................145.00
Bowl, 10" d., ruffled, peach
  opalescent 150.00
Bowl, 11" d., marigold...........................65.00
Bowl, 11" d., peach opalescent 250.00
Bowl, 11" d., ruffled,
  purple.............................250.00 to 300.00
Bowl, 11" d., star-shaped, stippled,
  Jeweled Heart exterior, purple.........325.00
Bowl, 11" d., fluted, white ...500.00 to 600.00
Bowl, 12" d., Jeweled Heart exterior,
  white 125.00
Plate, 6" d., ribbon candy rim,
  Jeweled Heart exterior, peach
  opalescent 275.00
Plate, 6" d., ribbon candy rim, purple..700.00

PETALS (Northwood)

Petals Compote

Compote, green (ILLUS.) 60.00
Compote, marigold 37.00
Compote, purple 60.00

PETER RABBIT (Fenton)
Bowl, 8" d., blue...............700.00 to 1,000.00
Bowl, 8" d., green ....850.00 to 900.00
Bowl, 8" d., marigold.......................1,500.00
Plate, blue......................................1,900.00

PILLOW & SUNBURST (Westmoreland)
Bowl, purple...41.00
Bowl, teal blue 60.00

PINEAPPLE (Sowerby, England)
Bowl, 8" d., marigold............................25.00
Compote, aqua 100.00
Compote, purple 72.00
Creamer, marigold, 4½" h......................35.00
Pitcher, miniature, purple......................60.00
Plate, 8" d., stemmed, marigold............65.00
Rose bowl, marigold.............................75.00
Sugar bowl, marigold............................38.00

PINE CONE (Fenton)

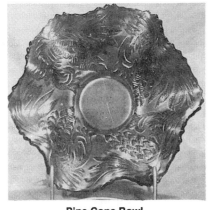

Pine Cone Bowl
Bowl, 5" d., blue (ILLUS.) 40.00

Bowl, 5" d., marigold..............................40.00
Bowl, 5" d., purple.................................35.00
Bowl, 6" d., ruffled, blue 45.00
Bowl, 6" d., marigold 25.00
Bowl, 7" d., ruffled, blue 50.00
Bowl, 7" d., marigold..............................28.00
Bowl, 7" d., ruffled, purple....................65.00
Plate, 6½" d., blue 122.00
Plate, 6½" d., green 200.00
Plate, 6½" d., marigold 50.00
Plate, 6½" d., purple 110.00
Plate, 7½" d., amber 425.00
Plate, 7½" d., blue 125.00
Plate, 7½" d., marigold 100.00
Plate, 7½" d., purple 65.00
Plate, 7¾" d., blue 225.00

PIPE HUMIDOR (Millersburg)
Green...6,500.00
Marigold..5,000.00

PLAID (Fenton)
Bowl, 9" d., ruffled, blue......300.00 to 325.00
Bowl, 9" d., ruffled, green ...325.00 to 425.00
Bowl, 9" d., ruffled,
    marigold ....100.00 to 125.00
Bowl, 9" d., ruffled, purple................1,500.00
Bowl, 9" d., ruffled,
    red....................3,250.00 to 3,750.00
Bowl, ice cream, 10" d., blue 300.00
Bowl, ice cream, 10" d.,
    green..............................800.00 to 900.00
Bowl, ice cream, 10" d.,
    purple ....400.00 to 450.00
Bowl, ice cream, 10" d.,
    purple w/gold overlay......................800.00

PLUME PANELS VASE (Fenton)
Blue 65.00
Green...48.00
Marigold...44.00
Purple (amethyst) 35.00
Red....................................750.00 to 950.00

PODS & POSIES or FOUR FLOWERS (Dugan)
Bowl, 6" d., peach opalescent 68.00
Bowl, 6" d., purple.................................55.00
Bowl, 8" to 9" d., marigold.....................45.00
Bowl, 8" to 9" d., purple 95.00
Bowl, 10" d., peach opales-
    cent ....150.00 to 175.00
Bowl, 10" d., purple.............................145.00
Plate, 6" d., peach opalescent............150.00
Plate, 6" d., purple 295.00
Plate, 9" d., green 790.00
Plate, 9" d., purple 500.00
Plate, chop, 11" d., peach opales-
    cent ....450.00 to 500.00

POINSETTIA (Imperial)
Pitcher, milk, green.............................245.00
Pitcher, milk, marigold 121.00
Pitcher, milk, smoky............................135.00

POINSETTIA & LATTICE
Bowl, amethyst 400.00
Bowl, aqua opalescent 3,600.00
Bowl, blue w/electric iridescence........850.00
Bowl, cobalt blue ....525.00 to 575.00
Bowl, ice blue 3,200.00
Bowl, marigold.....................................575.00
Bowl, purple..500.00
Bowl, white 4,000.00

POLO
Ashtray, marigold..................................35.00

POND LILY
Bonbon, blue 75.00
Bonbon, green..66.00
Bonbon, marigold 35.00
Bonbon, white..90.00

PONY
Bowl, 8" to 9" d., aqua ....450.00 to 500.00
Bowl, 8" to 9" d., ice green.................932.00
Bowl, 8" to 9" d., marigold....................70.00
Bowl, 8" to 9" d., purple ......200.00 to 250.00
Plate, marigold....................................275.00

POPPY (Millersburg)

Millersburg Poppy Compote

Compote, green...................................500.00
Compote, marigold 375.00
Compote, purple (ILLUS.)...............1,200.00

POPPY (Northwood)

Northwood Poppy Pickle Dish

Pickle dish, amber 225.00
Pickle dish, aqua opalescent...........1,200.00
Pickle dish, blue (ILLUS.) 146.00
Pickle dish, green 325.00
Pickle dish, ice blue 700.00
Pickle dish, marigold.............................80.00
Pickle dish, pastel marigold 50.00
Pickle dish, purple ....200.00 to 250.00
Pickle dish, white ....500.00 to 600.00

POPPY SHOW (Northwood)

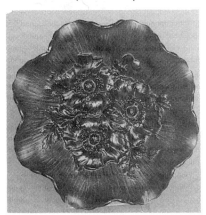

Poppy Show Bowl

Bowl, 8" to 9" d., aqua opales-
   cent 18,500.00
Bowl, 8" to 9" d., blue (ILLUS.) 600.00
Bowl, 8" to 9" d., blue w/electric
   iridescence...................500.00 to 1,000.00
Bowl, 8" to 9" d., green 1,300.00
Bowl, 8" to 9" d., ice blue 1,800.00
Bowl, 8" to 9" d., ice green..............2,300.00
Bowl, 8" to 9" d., marigold...525.00 to 600.00
Bowl, 8" to 9" d., purple 650.00
Bowl, 8" to 9" d., white 375.00
Plate, blue..3,000.00
Plate, blue w/electric iridescence 1,750.00
Plate, green 5,800.00
Plate, ice blue ....1,600.00 to 2,000.00
Plate, ice green.............3,800.00 to 4,200.00
Plate, marigold................................1,250.00
Plate, pastel marigold 1,000.00
Plate, purple ....1,200.00 to 1,400.00
Plate, white ....600.00 to 650.00

POPPY SHOW VASE (Imperial)
Green (ILLUS. top next column).........460.00
Marigold..............................700.00 to 750.00
Pastel marigold...................................325.00
Purple ....2,150.00 to 2,500.00
Smoky..........................2,600.00 to 3,000.00

PRAYER RUG (Fenton)
Bonbon, milk white w/marigold
   overlay 425.00

Poppy Show Vase

PRIMROSE BOWL (Millersburg)
Blue 2,400.00
Green..112.00
Marigold..77.00
Purple 125.00

PRINCESS LAMP
Purple, complete.............................1,700.00
Purple, base only................................550.00

PRISMS
Bonbon, marigold ....40.00 to 60.00
Bonbon, purple 54.00
Bonbon, two-handled, purple..............125.00
Bonbon, two-handled, white 40.00
Compote, 4½" d., two-handled,
    purple..95.00
Compote, 7¼" d., 2½" h., two-
    handled, marigold 48.00
Compote, 7¼" d., 2½" h., two-
    handled, purple 70.00

PULLED LOOP
Vase, 9½" h., peach opalescent...........53.00
Vase, 10" h., marigold 20.00
Vase, 10" h., purple 37.00
Vase 10½" h., cobalt blue....................90.00
Vase, 11" h., marigold ....30.00 to 35.00
Vase, 11" h., peach opalescent............30.00
Vase, 11½" h., celeste blue 500.00
Vase, 12" h., purple 42.50

PUZZLE
Bonbon, marigold ....30.00 to 50.00
Bonbon, stemmed, peach
    opalescent 55.00
Bonbon, two-handled, purple................80.00
Bonbon, white...65.00
Compote, marigold 25.00
Compote, peach opalescent.................65.00
Compote, purple 58.00

QUESTION MARKS
Bonbon, footed, marigold, 6" d.,
    3¾" h...38.00

Bonbon, footed, peach opalescent,
    6" d., 3¾" h. 80.00
Bonbon, footed, purple, 6" d.,
    3¾" h...45.00
Bonbon, footed, white, 6" d.,
    3¾" h...130.00
Bonbon, stemmed, marigold................35.00
Bonbon, stemmed, peach
    opalescent 45.00
Bonbon, stemmed, purple 60.00
Bonbon, stemmed, white......................48.00
Compote, crimped edge, marigold 45.00
Compote, crimped edge, peach
    opalescent 83.00
Plate, dome-footed, Georgia Peach
    exterior, purple.................................250.00
Plate, stemmed, marigold....................80.00
Plate, stemmed, white 325.00

QUILL (Dugan or Diamond Glass Co.)
Pitcher, water, marigold..................2,500.00
Pitcher, water, purple.........................950.00
Tumbler, blue...40.00
Tumbler, marigold................................250.00
Tumbler, pastel marigold 195.00
Tumbler, purple 300.00
Water set: pitcher & 6 tumblers;
    purple, 7 pcs. 4,000.00

RAINDROPS (Dugan)

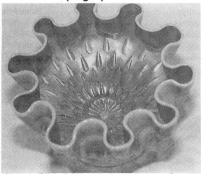

Raindrops Bowl

Bowl, 7" d., turned-up, fluted, peach
    opalescent 85.00
Bowl, 9" d., dome-footed, peach
    opalescent 126.00
Bowl, 9" d., dome-footed, ribbon
    candy rim, peach opalescent
    (ILLUS.) 85.00
Bowl, 9" d., dome-footed, ribbon
    candy rim, purple 225.00
Bowl, 9" d., dome-footed,
    purple..........................100.00 to 125.00

RAMBLER ROSE (Dugan)
Pitcher, water, blue.............................150.00
Tumbler, amber 29.00
Tumbler, blue...45.00
Tumbler, marigold.................................25.00
Tumbler, purple 36.00

Water set: pitcher & 6 tumblers;
marigold, 7 pcs. 295.00

RANGER

Butter dish, marigold............................80.00
Pitcher, milk, marigold ....100.00 to 125.00
Pitcher, marigold.................................60.00
Sherbet, marigold 20.00
Sugar bowl, marigold..........................100.00
Whiskey shot glass, marigold 400.00

RASPBERRY (Northwood)

Raspberry Sauceboat

Pitcher, milk, green.............................250.00
Pitcher, milk, ice blue....1,900.00 to 2,100.00
Pitcher, milk, marigold.........................136.00
Pitcher, milk, purple 290.00
Pitcher, milk, white........1,000.00 to 1,200.00
Pitcher, water, green ....275.00 to 295.00
Pitcher, water, ice blue 2,100.00
Pitcher, water, marigold......................125.00
Pitcher, water, purple..........225.00 to 250.00
Sauceboat, green (ILLUS.)..................225.00
Sauceboat, marigold.............................70.00
Sauceboat, purple 80.00
Tumbler, green 48.00
Tumbler, ice blue ....275.00 to 300.00
Tumbler, ice green..............550.00 to 650.00
Tumbler, marigold.................................35.00
Tumbler, purple 42.00
Tumbler, white....................................675.00
Water set: pitcher & 4 tumblers;
green, 5 pcs. 495.00
Water set: pitcher & 4 tumblers;
marigold, 5 pcs. 350.00
Water set: pitcher & 5 tumblers;
purple, 6 pcs. 490.00

RAYS & RIBBONS (Millersburg)

Bowl, 8" to 9" d., green ....50.00 to 70.00
Bowl, 8" to 9" d., marigold....................80.00
Bowl, 8" to 9" d., purple 75.00
Bowl, 9" d., ruffled, three-in-one edge,
marigold..150.00
Bowl, 10" d., green 85.00
Bowl, 10", ice cream shape, turned-
down rim, green 125.00
Bowl, 10" d., marigold..........................75.00
Bowl, 10" d., purple..............................65.00
Bowl, 10" d., ice cream shape,
purple..70.00
Bowl, ice cream shape, marigold........135.00

RIBBED FUNERAL VASE

Aqua opalescent, 11" h.......175.00 to 200.00
Marigold, 6" h.......................................30.00
Olive green 125.00
Peach opalescent..................................40.00
Purple, 13" h. 85.00

RIBBON TIE - See Comet Pattern .

RIPPLE VASE

Amber, 7½" h. 58.00
Amber, 10" h. 60.00
Amber, 11½" h. 75.00
Amber, 15¼" h. 81.00
Aqua, 12" h. 78.00
Green, 6" h. 95.00
Green, 13" h. 45.00
Green, 14½" h. 75.00
Ice green, 14½" h. 245.00
Marigold, 5" h. 70.00
Marigold, 6" h..................100.00 to 150.00
Marigold, 6½" h.....................................55.00
Marigold, 8" h. 35.00
Marigold, 9½" h.....................................30.00
Marigold, 10½" h...................................40.00
Marigold, 12" h......................................50.00
Marigold, 15" h......................................45.00
Marigold, 16½" h., funeral.....................50.00
Marigold, 20" h..................150.00 to 200.00
Purple, 8" h. 40.00
Purple, 10" h. 45.00
Purple, 11" h. 55.00
Smoky, 12" h. 95.00
Teal blue, 6¾" h. 50.00
Teal blue, 10½" h. 100.00
White, 8" h. 155.00

RISING SUN

Pitcher, water, pedestal base,
marigold 825.00
Tumbler, marigold...............................442.00

ROBIN (Imperial)

Mug, green w/marigold overlay, green
base 50.00
Mug, marigold.......................................42.00
Mug, smoky 275.00
Mug, smoky w/marigold overlay 158.00
Mug, unstippled, marigold 125.00
Pitcher, water, marigold......250.00 to 300.00
Tumbler, marigold.................................80.00

ROCOCO

Bowl, 8¼" d., dome-footed, ice cream
shape, marigold 160.00
Candy dish, smoky 45.00
Vase, marigold.....................................119.00
Vase, smoky ....150.00 to 175.00
Vase, teal...70.00

ROSALIND (Millersburg)

Bowl, 5½" d., purple............................800.00

Bowl, 9" d., ruffled, green 350.00
Bowl, 9" d., ruffled, purple...200.00 to 225.00
Bowl, 10" d., ruffled, green 200.00
Bowl, 10" d., marigold.........125.00 to 175.00
Bowl, 10" d., purple.............................185.00
Bowl, 10½" d., ruffled, aqua teal.........450.00
Compote, 6" d., small, ruffled,
    purple...795.00

ROSE SHOW
Bowl, 9" d., aqua.................650.00 to 750.00
Bowl, 9" d., aqua opalescent 1,400.00
Bowl, 9" d., blue.................................566.00
Bowl, 9" d., blue opales-
    cent............................1,500.00 to 1,950.00
Bowl, 9" d., blue w/electric irides-
    cence 1,250.00
Bowl, 9" d., green ....3,000.00 to 4,000.00
Bowl, 9" d., ice blue 1,600.00
Bowl, 9" d., ice green....1,500.00 to 2,000.00
Bowl, 9" d., ice green opalescent 2,150.00
Bowl, 9" d., lavender.......................3,500.00
Bowl, 9" d., marigold..........................552.00
Bowl, 9" d., purple...........................1,275.00
Bowl, 9" d., sapphire blue 3,200.00
Bowl, 9" d., smoky 1,100.00
Bowl, 9" d., white ....350.00 to 400.00
Plate, 9" d., aqua opalescent...........8,000.00
Plate, 9" d., blue ....1,200.00 to 1,400.00
Plate, 9" d., clambroth 1,350.00
Plate, 9" d., custard 4,500.00
Plate, 9" d., green w/electric irides-
    cence 7,500.00
Plate, 9" d., green 3,600.00
Plate, 9" d., ice blue......1,800.00 to 2,000.00
Plate, 9" d., marigold ....600.00 to 650.00
Plate, 9" d., moonstone 7,000.00
Plate, 9" d., pastel mari-
    gold ....1,000.00 to 1,500.00
Plate, 9" d., purple 1,500.00
Plate, 9" d., vaseline 3,400.00
Plate, 9" d., white...............................500.00

ROSES & FRUIT (Millersburg)
Bonbon, blue 2,600.00
Bonbon, green 900.00
Bonbon, marigold 375.00
Bonbon, pedestal, light marigold 850.00
Bonbon, purple 525.00
Compote, purple 1,450.00

ROSETTE
Bowl, 7" d., purple.................................35.00
Bowl, footed, green.............................110.00
Bowl, footed, purple (Northwood) 85.00

ROUND UP (Dugan)
Bowl, 9" d., low, fluted, blue................110.00
Bowl, 9" d., white 225.00
Bowl, ice cream shape, marigold..........68.00
Bowl, ice cream shape, peach
    opalescent ....200.00 to 225.00
Bowl, ice cream shape, purple 225.00

Bowl, ice cream shape, white.............250.00

Round Up Plate

Plate, 9" d., blue (ILLUS.)...................325.00
Plate, 9" d., ruffled, marigold 148.00
Plate, 9" d., flat, peach opalescent 425.00
Plate, 9" d., ruffled, peach opales-
    cent 350.00
Plate, 9" d., flat, purple 250.00
Plate, 9" d., ruffled, purple ..250.00 to 350.00
Plate, 9" d., white...............................350.00

RUSTIC VASE

Rustic Vase

Blue, 9" h. 45.00
Blue, 10" h. 30.00
Blue, 10½" h. 35.00
Blue, 11" h. 45.00
Blue, 16" h. ....100.00 to 150.00
Blue, funeral, 18" h. ....475.00 to 500.00
Blue, funeral, 19½" h. 795.00
Green, 10½" h. 35.00
Green, 16" h. 95.00
Lime green opalescent, 11" h. 600.00
Marigold, 9½" h. (ILLUS.) 75.00
Marigold, 11" h.......................................30.00

Marigold, 15" h.....................................80.00
Marigold, 16" to 20" h. 250.00
Marigold, funeral, 21½" h.....................300.00
Purple, 11" h.......................................50.00
Purple, 14" h.......................................90.00
Purple, 16" h.....................................195.00
Purple, 18½" h...................................325.00
Purple, funeral 1,050.00
Red, 10" h., crimped top 3,700.00
White, 6" h...46.00
White, 8" h...80.00
White, 10" h.......................................85.00
White, 12½" h.....................................60.00
White, 14" h.......................................160.00
White, 16" h.......................................200.00

SAILBOATS (Fenton)

Sailboats Bowl

Bowl, 5" d., amber 250.00
Bowl, 5" d., aqua................................110.00
Bowl, 5" d., ruffled, blue........................55.00
Bowl, 5" d., green 125.00
Bowl, 5" d., marigold.............................28.00
Bowl, 5" d., ice cream shape, mari-
  gold 40.00
Bowl, 5" d., purple...............................120.00
Bowl, 5" d., ruffled, red ....500.00 to 550.00
Bowl, 5" d., vaseline 175.00
Bowl, 6" d., blue..................................60.00
Bowl, 6" d., ruffled, green (ILLUS.) 105.00
Bowl, 6" d., ruffled, marigold.................32.00
Bowl, 6" d., Orange Tree exterior,
  marigold...60.00
Bowl, 6" d., ruffled, purple...................150.00
Bowl, ruffled, vaseline.........................250.00
Compote, marigold 55.00
Dish, square, marigold.........................115.00
Goblet, water, green ....250.00 to 350.00
Goblet, water, marigold 125.00
Goblet, water, purple 300.00
Plate, 6" d., blue 195.00
Plate, 6" d., marigold 400.00
Wine, blue...120.00
Wine, marigold.....................................35.00

SAILING SHIP PLATE
Amber, 8" d..75.00

Marigold, 8" d.......................................25.00

SCALE BAND
Pitcher, marigold....................................85.00
Plate, 6" d., flat, marigold.....................22.00
Plate, 6½" d., flat, vaseline 65.00
Plate, 7" d., flat, marigold.....................38.00
Tumbler, blue......................................325.00
Tumbler, marigold..................................30.00
Tumbler, pastel marigold 19.00

SCALES
Bowl, 5" d., purple.................................30.00
Bowl, 6" d., peach opalescent 62.00
Bowl, 7" d., marigold.............................24.00
Bowl, 7" d., peach opalescent 43.00
Bowl, 7" w., tricornered, peach
  opalescent ....130.00 to 135.00
Bowl, 7" d., purple.................................57.50
Bowl, 8" to 9" d., aqua opalescent......308.00
Bowl, 8" to 9" d., marigold w/opales-
  cent edge 40.00
Bowl, 8" to 9" d., milk white w/marigold
  overlay 225.00
Bowl, 8" to 9" d., peach
  opalescent ....80.00 to 100.00
Plate, 6½" d., amber 40.00
Plate, 6½" d., marigold 38.00
Plate, 6½" d., peach opalescent...........60.00
Plate, 6½" d., purple 57.00
Plate, 9" d., turned-up sides (two),
  peach opalescent...............................125.00

SCOTCH THISTLE COMPOTE
Blue 55.00
Green..................................50.00 to 70.00
Marigold...38.00
Purple ....55.00 to 60.00

SCROLL EMBOSSED
Bowl, 5½" d., File exterior, purple.........25.00
Bowl, 7" d., aqua..................................85.00
Bowl, 7" d., purple.................................45.00
Bowl, 8" d., clambroth...........................35.00
Bowl, 8" to 9" d., green 39.00
Bowl, 8" to 9" d., marigold....................40.00
Bowl, 8" to 9" d., pastel marigold..........43.00
Bowl, 8" to 9" d., purple 55.00
Bowl, 8" to 9" d., File exterior, purple....68.00
Compote, green....................................75.00
Compote, marigold 49.00
Compote, File exterior, marigold 50.00
Compote, purple 76.00
Compote, miniature, purple 250.00
Plate, 9" d., green ....90.00 to 100.00
Plate, 9" d., marigold 125.00
Plate, 9" d., pastel marigold...............125.00
Plate, 9" d., purple ....225.00 to 250.00
Sauce dish, purple, 5½" d....................35.00
Sauce dish, ruffled, purple, 5¾" d.........75.00

SEACOAST PIN TRAY (Millersburg)
Green..400.00

Marigold..............................450.00 to 500.00
Purple 575.00

SEAWEED (Millersburg)
Bowl, 6" d., purple................................450.00
Bowl, 8½" d., ice cream shape,
    marigold...350.00
Bowl, 8¾" d., low, mari-
    gold...................................450.00 to 525.00
Bowl, 10" d., ruffled, green.................275.00
Bowl, 10" d., ruffled, mari-
    gold...................................175.00 to 200.00
Bowl, ice cream shape, green.........1,650.00
Lamp, marigold....................................300.00

SHELL (Imperial)
Bowl, 5" d., footed, green.....................35.00
Bowl, 5" d., purple................................25.00
Bowl, 7¾" d., stippled, green...............60.00
Bowl, 8" d., purple..............................100.00
Bowl, 8" d., ruffled, green.....................50.00
Bowl, footed, marigold..........................20.00
Bowl, footed, purple..............................45.00
Bowl, ruffled, green...............................35.00
Plate, smoky.......................................300.00

SHELL & JEWEL
Creamer, cov., green.............................40.00
Creamer & cov., sugar bowl, green,
    pr..90.00
Sugar bowl, cov., marigold....................35.00
Sugar bowl, open, green.......................11.00

SHELL & SAND
Bowl, 8" to 9" d., marigold.....................50.00
Bowl, 8" to 9" d., ruffled, purple............69.00
Plate, purple....................725.00 to 1,025.00
Plate, smoky.......................................450.00
Tumbler, purple.....................................50.00

SHELL & WILD ROSE
Bowl, 8½" d., marigold..........................13.50
Bowl, small, purple...............................25.00
Dish, open heart-shaped rim, footed,
    green...32.50
Dish, open heart-shaped rim, footed,
    purple...41.00
Rose bowl, in-curved points, green......54.00

SHIP & STARS PLATE
Marigold..31.00

SINGING BIRDS (Northwood)
Berry set: master bowl & 3 sauce
    dishes; green, 4 pcs........................132.00
Berry set: master bowl & 6 sauce
    dishes; purple, 7 pcs.......................325.00
Bowl, ice cream shape, green..............48.00
Bowl, ice cream shape, marigold..........48.00
Bowl, master berry, blue.....................225.00
Butter dish, cov., purple......................350.00
Creamer, green...................................150.00
Creamer, marigold.................................52.00

Creamer, purple..................125.00 to 150.00
Mug, aqua opalescent ..1,000.00 to 1,550.00
Mug, blue...175.00
Mug, stippled, blue..............................575.00
Mug, blue w/electric irides-
    cence...............................200.00 to 250.00
Mug, green...250.00
Mug, stippled, green............................424.00
Mug, ice blue.....................750.00 to 800.00
Mug, lavender......................................400.00
Mug, marigold......................................134.00
Mug, stippled, marigold.......................129.00
Mug, purple..105.00
Mug, purple, w/advertising, "Amazon
    Hotel"..125.00
Mug, white..585.00
Pitcher, green.....................275.00 to 325.00
Pitcher, marigold................250.00 to 275.00
Pitcher, purple....................350.00 to 400.00
Sauce dish, blue....................................65.00
Sauce dish, blue w/electric irides-
    cence...90.00
Sauce dish, green..................................28.00
Sauce dish, marigold.............................32.00
Spooner, green....................................150.00
Spooner, marigold.................................62.00
Sugar bowl, cov., marigold...90.00 to 100.00
Table set, purple, 4 pcs......................750.00
Tumbler, amber.....................................60.00
Tumbler, green......................................45.00
Tumbler, green w/marigold overlay......60.00
Tumbler, marigold..................40.00 to 45.00
Tumbler, purple.....................................55.00
Water set: pitcher & 6 tumblers;
    green, 7 pcs.....................................790.00
Water set: pitcher & 6 tumblers;
    purple, 7 pcs....................................795.00

SINGLE FLOWER
Basket, handled, ruffled, peach
    opalescent.......................................750.00
Bowl, 7½" d., ribbon candy rim,
    peach opalescent..............................70.00
Bowl, 8¾" d., ruffled, peach
    opalescent...55.00
Bowl, 9", framed, tricornered, peach
    opalescent...65.00
Bowl, 9" d., peach opalescent..............55.00
Bowl, 9" d., three-in-one edge, peach
    opalescent.......................................110.00
Bowl, 9" d., purple................................50.00
Bowl, ribbon candy rim, peach
    opalescent.......................................125.00
Bowl, framed, ribbon candy rim,
    peach opalescent............................110.00
Plate, crimped rim, peach
    opalescent...75.00
Plate, framed, w/hand grip, peach
    opalescent...85.00

SIX PETALS (Dugan)
Bowl, 7" d., crimped, peach
    opalescent...45.00

Bowl, 7" w., tricornered, peach
 opalescent 85.00
Bowl, 7" d., purple...............................190.00
Bowl, 7" d., white 50.00
Bowl, 8" d., peach opalescent 80.00
Bowl, 8" d., purple................................75.00
Bowl, 8" d., white 85.00
Bowl, 9" d., dome-footed, peach
 opalescent 70.00

SKI STAR (Dugan)
Banana bowl, peach opalescent.........190.00
Basket, peach opalescent 520.00
Berry set: master bowl & 6 sauce
 dishes; peach opalescent, 7 pcs......600.00
Bowl, 5" d., peach opalescent 40.00
Bowl, 5" d., fluted, peach opalescent....35.00
Bowl, 5" d., ruffled, peach opales-
 cent..45.00
Bowl, 5" d., ruffled, purple....................55.00
Bowl, 6" d., ruffled, peach opales-
 cent..50.00
Bowl, 8" d., ruffled, purple...425.00 to 450.00
Bowl, 8" to 9" d., dome-footed, peach
 opalescent 100.00
Bowl, 8" to 9" d., dome-footed,
 purple...130.00
Bowl, 10" d., marigold...........................62.00
Bowl, 10" d., peach opalescent 75.00
Bowl, 10" d., purple.............................175.00
Bowl, 11" d., peach opales-
 cent.............................125.00 to 175.00
Bowl, 11" d., purple.............................185.00
Bowl, tricornered, dome-footed, peach
 opalescent 100.00
Plate, 6" d., crimped rim, peach
 opalescent ....150.00 to 200.00
Plate, 8½" d., dome-footed, w/hand-
 grip, peach opalescent.....165.00 to 185.00
Plate, 8½" d., dome-footed, w/hand-
 grip, purple 295.00

SOUTACHE (Dugan)
Bowl, 8" d., dome-footed, ruffled,
 peach opalescent...............................95.00
Bowl, 8" to 9" d., dome-footed, pie-
 crust rim, peach opalescent............145.00
Plate, 9½" d., dome-footed, peach
 opalescent ....250.00 to 300.00

SPRINGTIME (Northwood)
Butter dish, cov., green.......................343.00
Butter dish, cov., marigold..................250.00
Butter dish, cov., purple......................300.00
Creamer, purple.................100.00 to 150.00
Pitcher, green ....950.00 to 1,000.00
Pitcher, marigold.................300.00 to 400.00
Pitcher, purple 750.00
Sauce dish, 5" d., green 55.00
Sauce dish, 5" d., purple.......................50.00
Spooner, green....................................145.00
Spooner, pastel marigold....................140.00
Spooner, purple 425.00

Sugar bowl, cov., purple.....................200.00
Table set, green,
 4 pcs. ....1,000.00 to 1,500.00
Table set, marigold,
 4 pcs. ....500.00 to 800.00

Springtime Tumbler
Tumbler, green (ILLUS.)......................175.00
Tumbler, marigold.................................80.00
Tumbler, purple 115.00

"S" REPEAT (Dugan)
Punch cup, purple...............................100.00
Punch set: bowl, base & 8 cups;
 purple, 10 pcs. 2,850.00
Toothpick holder, blue 100.00
Toothpick holder, marigold 28.00
Tumbler, marigold.............450.00 to 500.00
Tumbler, w/advertising, dated 1910,
 marigold 350.00

STAG & HOLLY (Fenton)

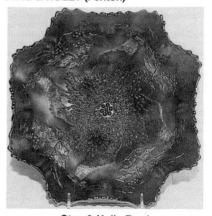

Stag & Holly Bowl
Bowl, 7" d., spatula-footed,
 blue ....125.00 to 175.00
Bowl, 7" d., spatula-footed,
 marigold 55.00
Bowl, 7" d., spatula-footed,
 purple...78.00
Bowl, 7" d., spatula-footed,
 red...2,500.00

Bowl, 8" d., footed, ice cream shape,
  blue 185.00
Bowl, 8" d., footed, ice cream shape,
  green...255.00
Bowl, 8" to 9" d., spatula-footed,
  blue ....225.00 to 250.00
Bowl, 8" to 9" d., spatula-footed,
  green..228.00
Bowl, 8" to 9" d., spatula-footed,
  lavender ....175.00 to 200.00
Bowl, 8" to 9" d., spatula-footed,
  marigold 90.00
Bowl, 8" to 9" d., spatula-footed,
  peach opalescent.........................1,900.00
Bowl, 8" to 9" d., spatula-footed,
  purple 167.00
Bowl, 10" to 11" d., three-footed,
  amber.............................450.00 to 500.00
Bowl, 10" to 11" d., three-footed,
  aqua..800.00
Bowl, 10" to 11" d., three-footed,
  blue 300.00
Bowl, 10" to 11" d., three-footed,
  cobalt blue 125.00
Bowl, 10" to 11" d., three-footed,
  marigold ....100.00 to 125.00
Bowl, 10" to 11" d., three-footed,
  purple (ILLUS.) 435.00
Bowl, 10" to 11" d., three-footed,
  vaseline...........................175.00 to 275.00
Bowl, 11" d., flat, amber......................750.00
Bowl, 11" d., flat, blue w/electric irides-
  cence 450.00
Bowl, 11" d., flat, green...................1,250.00
Bowl, 11" d., flat, marigold..100.00 to 125.00
Bowl, 11" d., ruffled, blue...................232.00
Bowl, 11" d., ruffled, green w/marigold
  overlay 250.00
Bowl, 12" d., ice cream shape, blue ...325.00
Bowl, 12" d., ice cream shape,
  green...170.00
Bowl, 12" d., ice cream shape,
  marigold ....100.00 to 125.00
Bowl, spatula-footed, green................100.00
Plate, 9" d., marigold ....300.00 to 350.00
Plate, chop, 12" d., three-footed,
  marigold ....750.00 to 850.00
Rose bowl, blue, large 995.00
Rose bowl, marigold, large 275.00

STAR & FILE (Imperial)
Bowl, 5" d., marigold............................22.00
Bowl, 7" d., marigold............................22.00
Bowl, 8" d., ice cream shape,
  marigold 15.00
Bowl, 8" sq., marigold...........................50.00
Bowl, two-handled, marigold 35.00
Card tray, two turned-up sides,
  marigold, 6¼" d.................................32.00
Celery vase, two-handled, clambroth ...35.00
Celery vase, two-handled, marigold 65.00
Compote, jelly, marigold 50.00
Compote, large, marigold 30.00
Creamer, marigold................................30.00

Pitcher, milk, marigold 70.00
Pitcher, water, marigold......100.00 to 120.00
Plate, 6" d., marigold 95.00
Relish tray, two-handled, marigold 34.00
Rose bowl, marigold 50.00
Sherbet, marigold 25.00
Sugar bowl, marigold............................12.00
Tumbler, marigold...............................106.00
Water set: pitcher & 6 tumblers;
  marigold, 7 pcs. 750.00
Wine, marigold......................................70.00
Wine decanter w/stoper, marigold 275.00

STARFISH

Starfish Compote
Bonbon, peach opalescent.................120.00
Bonbon, purple 58.00
Compote, peach opalescent
  (ILLUS.) 65.00
Compote, purple 45.00

STAR FLOWER
Pitcher, blue.................1,250.00 to 1,275.00
Pitcher, marigold............................2,400.00

STAR MEDALLION
Bowl, 5" sq., marigold...........................25.00
Bowl, 8" d., marigold.............................22.50
Bowl, 8" d., smoky 40.00
Compote, marigold ....35.00 to 40.00
Goblet, marigold 35.00
Goblet, smoky.......................................50.00
Pitcher, milk, clambroth ....50.00 to 75.00
Pitcher, milk, marigold 86.00
Pitcher, milk, smoky...............75.00 to 100.00
Plate, 9" to 10" d., clambroth 50.00
Plate, 9" to 10" d., marigold 35.00
Punch cup, marigold.............................20.00
Sherbet, stemmed, marigold 35.00
Tumbler, marigold.................................25.00
Tumbler, tall, tankard form, marigold....28.00
Vase, 6" h., marigold 40.00

STAR OF DAVID (Imperial)
Bowl, 7" d., ruffled, purple...................140.00
Bowl, 8" to 9" d., collared base, blue 75.00

Bowl, 8" to 9" d., collared base,
green...85.00
Bowl, 8" to 9" d., collared base,
marigold...48.00
Bowl, 8" to 9" d., collared base,
purple..85.00
Bowl, 9" d., flat, ruffled,
purple...............................80.00 to 100.00

STAR OF DAVID & BOWS (Northwood)

Star of David & Bows Bowl

Bowl, 7" d., dome-footed, green...........60.00
Bowl, 7" d., dome-footed, marigold
(ILLUS.)..38.00
Bowl, 7" d., dome-footed, purple..........65.00
Bowl, 8" to 9" d., dome-footed, fluted,
green...110.00
Bowl, 8" to 9" d., ome-footed, fluted,
purple..72.00
Bowl, Embossed Scroll exterior,
purple...105.00

STIPPLED FLOWER (Dugan)

Bowl, 8" d., peach opalescent..............43.00
Bowl, 8½" w., tricornered, peach
opalescent..65.00
Bowl, 8½" d., stippled, fluted, peach
opalescent..60.00

STIPPLED PETALS

Bowl, peach opalescent.........................72.00
Bowl, purple..80.00

STIPPLED RAYS

Bonbon, two-handled, green.................48.00
Bonbon, two-handled, lime green.......200.00
Bonbon, two-handled, marigold............30.00
Bonbon, two-handled, purple................28.00
Bonbon, two-handled, red..................350.00
Bowl, 5" d., Amberina........................175.00
Bowl, 5" d., blue...................................50.00
Bowl, 5" d., green................................33.00
Bowl, 5" d., marigold............................20.00
Bowl, 5" d., purple................................30.00
Bowl, 5" d., red...................350.00 to 400.00
Bowl, 6" d., Amberina........................225.00
Bowl, 6½" d., ruffled, red....300.00 to 350.00

Bowl, 7" d., dome-footed, green..........32.00
Bowl, 7" d., red..................................250.00
Bowl, 7" d., ruffled rim, red................450.00
Bowl, 8" to 9" d., blue........................225.00
Bowl, 8" to 9" d., green........................55.00
Bowl, 8" to 9" d., ribbon candy rim,
green...75.00
Bowl, 8" to 9" d., marigold...................32.00
Bowl, 8" to 9" d., purple.......................46.00
Bowl, 8" to 9" d., ribbon candy rim,
purple...70.00
Bowl, 8" to 9" d., red..........................605.00
Bowl, 10" d., green...............................65.00
Bowl, 10" d., ruffled, green.................110.00
Bowl, 10" d., ruffled, lavender..............75.00
Bowl, 10" d., white..............150.00 to 200.00
Bowl, 10" w., tricornered, crimped rim,
green...85.00
Bowl, 11" d., Basketweave exterior,
ruffled, marigold..............................60.00
Bowl, 11" sq., dome-footed, ribbon
candy rim, green.............................115.00
Bowl, dome-footed, Greek Key &
Scales exterior, purple......................90.00
Bowl, Wild Rose exterior, green...........75.00
Bowl, Wild Rose exterior, purple........110.00
Creamer, blue.......................................25.00
Creamer & sugar bowl, marigold, pr.....45.00
Plate, 6" to 7" d., green........................95.00
Plate, 6" to 7" d., marigold...................32.00
Plate, 6" to 7" d., red.......................1,250.00
Rose bowl, green...................................80.00
Rose bowl, purple..................................65.00
Sherbet, Amberina...............................275.00
Sugar bowl, individual size, marigold...10.00
Sugar bowl, open, blue..........................25.00
Sugar bowl, open, marigold...................18.00

STORK (Imperial)
Vase, marigold......................................45.00

STORK & RUSHES (Dugan or Diamond Glass Works)
Basket, handled, marigold...................175.00
Berry set: master bowl & 6 sauce
dishes, marigold, 7 pcs....................245.00
Bowl, master berry or fruit, marigold.....55.00
Butter dish, cov., marigold...................135.00
Creamer, marigold.................................72.00
Hat shape, blue.....................................40.00
Mug, amethyst.......................................40.00
Mug, lavender......................................175.00
Mug, marigold..25.00
Mug, purple..125.00
Pitcher, water, blue..............................375.00
Pitcher, water, marigold.......................375.00
Pitcher, water, purple...........................575.00
Punch bowl & base, marigold,
2 pcs...225.00
Punch bowl & base, purple, 2 pcs......185.00
Punch cup, marigold..............................17.50
Punch cup, purple..................................35.00
Punch set: bowl, base & 6 cups;
marigold, 8 pcs..............300.00 to 325.00

Sauce dish, marigold 50.00
Sauce dish, purple 75.00
Spooner, marigold 80.00
Tumbler, blue..54.00
Tumbler w/lattice band, blue................55.00
Tumbler, marigold.................................28.00
Tumbler w/lattice band, marigold..........30.00
Tumbler, purple 35.00
Tumbler w/lattice band, purple 69.00
Water set: pitcher & 1 tumbler; blue,
   2 pcs. ....450.00 to 500.00

STRAWBERRY (FENTON)
Bonbon, Amberina.............................200.00
Bonbon, reverse Amber-
   ina....................................325.00 to 400.00
Bonbon, one-handled, marigold 135.00
Bonbon, two-handled, amber 75.00
Bonbon, two-handled, blue...................65.00
Bonbon, two-handled, ice green
   opalescent 450.00
Bonbon, two-handled, marigold............32.00
Bonbon, two-handled, vaseline
   w/marigold iridescence 155.00
Bonbon, two-handled, vaseline
   opalescent ....600.00 to 650.00

STRAWBERRY (Millersburg)
Bowl, 6" d., ruffled, purple...................135.00
Bowl, 7" d., green 95.00
Bowl, 7" d., purple..............................115.00
Bowl, 8" to 9" d., marigold...................260.00
Bowl, 8" to 9" d., purple ......225.00 to 250.00
Bowl, 8" to 9" d., vaseline 1,250.00
Bowl, 9" w., tricornered, marigold.......200.00
Bowl, 9½" w., square, green...............600.00
Bowl, 9½" w., square, ribbon candy
   rim, purple 400.00
Bowl, 9½" d., Basketweave exterior,
   marigold...55.00
Bowl, 9½" d., Basketweave exterior,
   purple..................................75.00 to 100.00
Bowl, 10" w., tricornered, ribbon
   candy rim, purple 450.00
Compote, marigold 275.00
Compote, purple 225.00

STRAWBERRY (Northwood)
Bowl, 8" to 9" d., stippled, blue 900.00
Bowl, 8" to 9" d., stippled, ice
   green..1,100.00
Bowl, 8" to 9" d., stippled,
   purple..............................200.00 to 250.00
Bowl, 8" to 9" d., ruffled, Basketweave
   exterior, green....................................95.00
Bowl, 8" to 9" d., ruffled, Basketweave
   exterior, marigold 60.00
Bowl, 8" to 9" d., ruffled, Basketweave
   exterior, purple ....100.00 to 125.00
Bowl, 8" to 9" d., ruffled, white 1,350.00
Bowl, 8" to 9" d., blue...........................80.00

Bowl, 8" to 9" d., piecrust rim,
   green................................100.00 to 150.00
Bowl, 8" to 9" d., marigold....................40.00
Bowl, 8" to 9" d., purple 108.00
Bowl, 9" d., ruffled, stippled, ribbed
   exterior, purple..............................1,000.00
Bowl, 9" d., stippled, ribbed exterior,
   marigold 150.00
Plate, 9" d., green 135.00
Plate, 9" d., marigold...........................115.00
Plate, 9" d., pastel marigold................125.00
Plate, 9" d., purple 228.00
Plate, 9" d., Basketweave exterior,
   green................................200.00 to 275.00
Plate, 9" d., Basketweave exterior,
   marigold ....125.00 to 150.00
Plate, 9" d., Basketweave exterior,
   purple...213.00
Plate, 9" d., stippled, Basketweave
   exterior, green..................................400.00
Plate, 9" d., stippled, green.................600.00
Plate, 9" d., stippled, mari-
   gold ....800.00 to 1,000.00
Plate, 9" d., stippled, purple.............1,500.00

STRAWBERRY SCROLL (Fenton)

Strawberry Scroll Pitcher

Pitcher, water, blue (ILLUS.) 1,990.00
Pitcher, water, marigold..................1,225.00
Tumbler. blue......................................200.00
Tumbler. marigold...............................175.00

STREAM OF HEARTS (Fenton)
Compote, marigold 100.00

SUNFLOWER BOWL (Northwood)
Bowl, 8" d., footed, blue (ILLUS. top
   next page)..650.00
Bowl, 8" d., footed, blue w/electric
   iridescence.......................................650.00
Bowl, 8" d., footed, clambroth............350.00
Bowl, 8" d., footed, green ....75.00 to 95.00
Bowl, 8" d., footed, ice blue 200.00
Bowl, 8" d., footed, marigold................60.00
Bowl, 8" d., footed, purple....................68.00

Sunflower Bowl

Bowl, 8" d., footed, Meander
exterior, purple.................100.00 to 150.00

SUNFLOWER PIN TRAY (Millersburg)
Green..................................175.00 to 200.00
Marigold..450.00
Purple ....450.00 to 475.00

SWAN PASTEL NOVELTIES (Dugan)
Salt dip, amber 125.00
Salt dip, celeste blue 38.00
Salt dip, ice blue 40.00
Salt dip, ice green..................................35.00
Salt dip, marigold................100.00 to 125.00
Salt dip, peach opales-
cent...................................300.00 to 325.00
Salt dip, pink 35.00
Salt dip, purple....................................272.00

SWIRL HOBNAIL (Millersburg)
Cuspidor, marigold 725.00
Cuspidor, purple 475.00
Rose bowl, marigold 300.00
Rose bowl, purple...............275.00 to 325.00
Vase, green 700.00
Vase, marigold....................................200.00
Vase, purple 225.00

SWIRL RIB
Tumbler, marigold.................................28.00
Vase, 8" h., 6" d., smoky......................20.00
Vase, 10½" h., peach opalescent.........60.00

TARGET VASE (Dugan)
7" h., white..75.00
10" h., peach opalescent 75.00
11" h., white...100.00
11½" h., marigold..................................15.00
11½" h., peach opalescent 60.00
12" h., white ....100.00 to 125.00

TEN MUMS (Fenton)
Bowl, 8" to 9" d., ribbon candy rim,
blue...140.00
Bowl, 8" to 9" d., ribbon candy rim,
green...125.00

Bowl, 8" to 9" d., ribbon candy rim,
purple..180.00
Bowl, 10" d., ruffled, blue....................130.00
Bowl, 10" d., footed, green 80.00
Bowl, 10" d., ribbon candy rim,
green..175.00
Bowl, 10" d., footed, marigold............225.00
Bowl, 10" d., ribbon candy rim,
marigold...300.00
Bowl, 10" d., ruffled, marigold............105.00
Bowl, 10" d., ribbon candy rim,
purple..110.00
Bowl, 10" d., ruffled, purple................155.00

Ten Mums Pitcher

Pitcher, water, blue (ILLUS.) 1,650.00
Pitcher, water, marigold......................475.00
Tumbler. amber 65.00
Tumbler. blue...75.00
Tumbler. marigold..................................50.00
Tumbler. white 153.00
Water set: pitcher & 1 tumbler;
marigold, 2 pcs. 575.00

THIN RIB VASE
7" h., ice blue (Northwood) 500.00
8" h., green 30.00
9" h., aqua opalescent..........................85.00
9" h., blue..35.00
9" h., green 40.00
9" h., teal blue.....................................105.00
9½" h., green (Northwood) 45.00
10" h., blue..35.00
10" h., green (Northwood) 40.00
10" h., marigold.....................................48.00
10" h., purple (Northwood)....................32.50
10" h., white 70.00
10½" h., peach opalescent 40.00
11" h., aqua opalescent......................125.00
11" h., green 75.00
12" h., aqua 75.00
12" h., blue..40.00
12" h., green 85.00
12" h., purple 45.00
13" h., aqua opalescent (North-
wood) 1,100.00

13" h., green ....100.00 to 125.00
13" h., purple 100.00
13" h., funeral, white 200.00
13" h., funeral, green (Northwood) 100.00
14" h., funeral, purple 135.00
16½" h., green 135.00

THISTLE (Fenton)
Banana boat, blue 400.00
Banana boat, celeste blue 350.00
Banana boat, green 285.00
Banana boat, marigold 224.00
Banana boat, purple ....350.00 to 400.00
Bowl, 7" d., purple..................................45.00
Bowl, 7½" d., ice cream shape,
   purple 85.00
Bowl, 8" to 9" d., ribbon candy rim,
   blue 80.00
Bowl, 8" to 9" d., ruffled, blue...............90.00
Bowl, 8" to 9" d., flared, green 42.00
Bowl, 8" to 9" d., ribbon candy rim,
   green..112.00
Bowl, 8" to 9" d., ruffled, green 106.00
Bowl, 8" to 9" d., ruffled, lavender.........45.00
Bowl, 8" to 9" d., ribbon candy rim,
   marigold.............................50.00 to 75.00
Bowl, 8" to 9" d., ruffled, marigold.........35.00
Bowl, 8" to 9" d., ribbon candy rim,
   purple...66.00
Bowl, 8" to 9" d., ruffled, purple 58.00
Bowl, ruffled, aqua...............................600.00
Centerpiece bowl, blue 380.00
Plate, 9" d., blue ....2,500.00 to 3,000.00
Plate, 9" d., green............................3,000.00
Plate, marigold...................................3,500.00
Vase, 6" h., green 75.00

THISTLE & THORN (Sowerby's, England)
Bowl, 5" to 6" d., footed, marigold.........60.00
Bowl, 9" d., footed, marigold.................40.00
Creamer, marigold.................................30.00

THREE FRUITS (Northwood)
Bowl, 5" d., marigold.............................30.00
Bowl, 5" d., purple.................................30.00
Bowl, 6" d., green 40.00
Bowl, 6" d., marigold.............................30.00
Bowl, 8" d., ruffled, green 75.00
Bowl, 8" d., ruffled, mari-
   gold ....75.00 to 100.00
Bowl, 8" d., ruffled, purple...................100.00
Bowl, 8" d., dome-footed, Basket-
   weave & Grapevine exterior, white ..350.00
Bowl, 8½" d., ruffled, blue.....................95.00
Bowl, 8½" d., collared base, Basket-
   weave & Grapevine exterior, green ...65.00
Bowl, 8½" d., dome-footed,
   green...............................150.00 to 175.00
Bowl, 8½" d., piecrust rim, green..........98.00
Bowl, 8½" d., piecrust rim, stippled,
   green..400.00
Bowl, 8½" d., piecrust rim, marigold 60.00
Bowl, 8½" d., purple............................100.00

Bowl, 8½" d., piecrust rim, purple 70.00
Bowl, 9" d., footed, Meander reverse,
   black amethyst...................................750.00
Bowl, 9" d., piecrust rim, collared
   base, blue w/electric iridescence 700.00
Bowl, 9" d., ruffled, stippled, aqua
   opalescent 875.00
Bowl, 9" d., ruffled, blue.....................210.00
Bowl, 9" d., green 66.00
Bowl, 9" d., ruffled, green 100.00
Bowl, 9" d., stippled, mari-
   gold...75.00 to125.00
Bowl, 9" d., ruffled, pastel marigold 90.00
Bowl, 9" d., ruffled, collared base,
   marigold...60.00
Bowl, 9" d., purple.................................88.00
Bowl, 9" d., stippled, purple 200.00
Bowl, 9" d., stippled, white..................762.50
Bowl, 9" d., dome-footed, Basket-
   weave & Grapevine exterior, green ...70.00
Bowl, 9" d., dome-footed, Basketweave & Grapevine exterior, ice
   green...675.00
Bowl, 9" d., dome-footed, Basket-
   weave & Grapevine exterior,
   marigold...85.00
Bowl, 9" d., dome-footed, Basket-
   weave & Grapevine exterior,
   purple...60.00
Bowl, 9" d., dome-footed, Basket-
   weave & Grapevine exterior,
   white ....350.00 to 380.00
Bowl, 9" d., piecrust rim, stippled,
   ribbed exterior, green.......................795.00
Bowl, 9" d., spatula-footed, aqua
   opalescent ....500.00 to 550.00
Bowl, 9" d., spatula-footed, emerald
   green...425.00
Bowl, 9" d., spatula-footed, ruffled,
   green...60.00
Bowl, 9" d., spatula-footed, ice
   green..1,100.00
Bowl, 9" d., spatula-footed, marigold 95.00
Bowl, 9" d., spatula-footed, pastel
   honey amber (smoke tint) 350.00
Bowl, 9" d., spatula-footed, purple......152.00
Bowl, 9" d., spatula-footed, white 360.00
Bowl, 10" d., ruffled, ice green............375.00
Bowl, collared base, aqua opales-
   cent ....1,100.00 to 1,200.00
Bowl, piecrust rim, stippled, green...1,425.00
Bowl, spatula-footed, stippled,
   purple...175.00
Bowl, stippled, ruffled, blue.................700.00
Bowl, collared base, stippled, mari-
   gold...78.00
Bowl, collared base, stippled,
   white ....750.00 to 775.00
Bowl, piecrust rim, stippled,
   green.........................1,000.00 to 1,200.00
Bowl, ruffled, stippled, footed, ice
   blue ....800.00 to 1,000.00
Bowl, ruffled, footed, Meander
   exterior, ice blue 450.00

Bowl, stippled, blue w/electric irides-
cence 475.00
Plate, 7½" d., Basketweave &
Grapevine exterior, green 175.00
Plate, 8" d., w/handgrip, ribbed
exterior, purple 150.00
Plate, 9" d., stippled, aqua opales-
cent ....1,850.00 to 2,000.00
Plate, 9" d., stippled, blue w/electric
iridescence......................800.00 to 900.00
Plate, 9" d., green 168.00
Plate, 9" d., Basketweave exterior,
green...100.00
Plate, 9" d., horehound 295.00
Plate, 9" d., lavender 325.00
Plate, 9" d., stippled, lav-
ender.........................1,250.00 to 1,400.00
Plate, 9" d., marigold 113.00
Plate, 9" d., stippled, marigold 230.00
Plate, 9" d., purple 173.00
Plate, 9" d., stippled,
purple ....300.00 to 325.00
Plate, 9" d., stippled, ribbed exterior,
purple..1,000.00
Plate, 9" d., stippled, teal blue 3,500.00
Plate, 9½" w., 12-sided, blue
(Fenton) 100.00
Plate, 9½" w., 12-sided, green
(Fenton) 150.00
Plate, 9½" w., 12-sided, marigold
(Fenton) 150.00
Plate, 9½" w., 12-sided, purple
(Fenton) 110.00
Plate, plain back, stretch "electric"
finish, purple 275.00
Plate, two sides up, green 150.00
Plate, Basketweave exterior, green....195.00
Plate, Basketweave exterior, mari-
gold 125.00
Plate, Basketweave exterior, purple ...275.00

TIGER LILY (Imperial)

Pitcher, water, green ....150.00 to 200.00
Pitcher, water, purple..........................365.00
Tumbler, blue.....................................250.00
Tumbler, clambroth..............................65.00
Tumbler, green 45.00
Tumbler, marigold................................30.00
Tumbler, olive green...........................115.00
Tumbler, purple 80.00
Water set: pitcher & 4 tumblers;
marigold, 5 pcs. 310.00
Water set: pitcher & 6 tumblers;
aqua, 7 pcs. 2,205.00

TORNADO VASE (Northwood)

Blue 1,700.00
Green (ILLUS. top next column).........255.00
Marigold...425.00
Marigold, small, ribbed 600.00
Purple, ribbed 400.00

Tornado Vase

TOWN PUMP NOVELTY (Northwood)

Town Pump Novelty

Green (ILLUS.) 2,600.00
Marigold........................1,275.00 to 1,300.00
Purple 750.00

TRACERY (Millersburg)

Tracery Bonbon

Bonbon, handled, square, green
(ILLUS.) 675.00
Bonbon, handled, oval, purple............550.00

TREE TRUNK VASE (Northwood)

Tree Trunk Vase

6" h., purple, squatty...........150.00 to 175.00
6¼" h., squatty, marigold........55.00 to 60.00
6¾" h., marigold....................................75.00
7" h., green 45.00
7" h., ice blue 400.00
7½" h., squatty, green.........................150.00
7" to 11" h., ice green ....134.00 to 220.00
8" to 10" h., blue 92.00
8" to 10" h., ice blue...........................250.00
8" to 11" h., green.................35.00 to 45.00
9" h., aqua 95.00
9" h., white 100.00
9" to 12" h., aqua opalescent..............475.00
9" to 10" h., marigold 35.00
9" to 10" h., purple (ILLUS.)..................52.50
10½" h., blue w/electric iridescence ...115.00
11" h., ice blue 350.00
11" h., purple 85.00
11" h., white 70.00
12" h., blue...........................150.00 to 175.00
12" h., ice blue 275.00
12" h., ice green..................................440.00
12" h., marigold...................130.00 to 150.00
12" h., purple 185.00
12" h., white 175.00
13" h., green ....200.00 to 225.00
13" h., purple 300.00
13½" h., blue ....375.00 to 400.00
14" h., purple 125.00
15" h., purple, w/elephant foot.........1,300.00
17" h., white, funeral 1,000.00
18" h., green 550.00
18" h., purple 975.00
19" h., purple, funeral 1,800.00
20" h., cobalt blue, funeral 1,300.00

TROUT & FLY (Millersburg)

Bowl, ice cream shape, green 850.00
Bowl, ice cream shape, lavender.....1,350.00
Bowl, ice cream shape, mari-
    gold ....475.00 to 525.00
Bowl, ice cream shape,
    purple ....595.00 to 650.00

Bowl, ribbon candy rim, green 712.00
Bowl, ribbon candy rim, lavender 1,400.00
Bowl, ribbon candy rim, marigold 350.00
Bowl, ribbon candy rim, purple 575.00
Bowl, ruffled, green.............450.00 to 500.00
Bowl, ruffled, lavender 1,800.00
Bowl, ruffled, marigold........400.00 to 475.00
Bowl, ruffled, marigold, satin finish.....385.00
Bowl, ruffled, pastel marigold, satin
    finish 500.00
Bowl, ruffled, purple............550.00 to 600.00
Bowl, ruffled, purple, satin finish.........675.00
Bowl, square, green......1,400.00 to 1,500.00
Bowl, square, marigold 700.00
Bowl, square, purple...........................825.00

TULIP & CANE

Bowl, small, berry, marigold 25.00
Compote, marigold 50.00
Goblet, marigold, 4 oz. 60.00

TWIG VASE

3½" h., purple ....550.00 to 600.00
3½" h., pleated jack-in-the-pulpit rim,
    purple 195.00
4" h., ruffled, purple 425.00
9½" h., purple 50.00
Bud, marigold 29.00

TWINS or HORSESHOE CURVE (Imperial)

Bowl, 5" d., green 42.00
Bowl, 6" d., green 45.00
Bowl, 6" d., marigold............................22.50
Bowl, 10" d., marigold...........................35.00
Fruit bowl & base, clambroth, 2 pcs. 80.00
Fruit bowl & base, marigold, 2 pcs. 80.00
Fruit bowl & base, white, 2 pcs...........650.00

TWO FLOWERS (Fenton)

Bonbon, stemmed. blue........................85.00
Bowl, 6" d., footed, blue........................75.00
Bowl, 6" d., footed, lime green..............45.00
Bowl, 6" d., footed, marigold 26.00
Bowl, 6" d., footed, purple....................75.00
Bowl, 6" d., footed, vase-
    line ....100.00 to 125.00
Bowl, 7" to 8" d., footed, blue...............60.00
Bowl, 7" to 8" d., footed, clambroth.......90.00
Bowl, 7" to 8" d., footed,
    green................................80.00 to 100.00
Bowl, 7" to 8" d., footed, marigold.........60.00
Bowl, 7" to 8" d., footed, fluted,
    purple...47.00
Bowl, 7" to 8" d., footed, red 2,247.00
Bowl, 8" d., footed,
    Amberina ....1,500.00 to 1,900.00
Bowl, 8" d., collared base, mari-
    gold ....100.00 to 125.00
Bowl, 8" d., collared base, ice cream
    shape, marigold 175.00
Bowl, 8½" d., footed, blue....................99.00
Bowl, 9" d., footed, marigold................75.00
Bowl, 9" d., footed, ice cream shape,
    marigold 125.00

Bowl, 9½" d., ruffled, purple................150.00
Bowl, 10" d., footed, scalloped rim,
    blue 85.00
Bowl, 10" d., footed, scalloped rim,
    green 75.00
Bowl, 10" d., footed, scalloped rim,
    marigold 60.00
Bowl, 10" d., footed, scalloped rim,
    purple 135.00
Bowl, 10" d., footed, blue....100.00 to 125.00
Bowl, 10" d., footed, mari-
    gold ....80.00 to 100.00
Bowl, 10" d., ruffled, footed, red 2,000.00
Bowl, 10" d., footed, vaseline 350.00
Bowl, 10" d., footed, white 750.00
Bowl, 10½" d., ruffled, blue.................162.00
Bowl, 11" d., aqua..............................650.00
Bowl, 11" d., green 1,050.00
Bowl, 11" d., footed, ruffled, purple.....750.00
Bowl, 11" d., ice cream shape, blue ...125.00
Bowl, 11" d., ice cream shape, mari-
    gold 40.00
Bowl, 11½" d., footed, blue.................125.00
Bowl, 11½" d., ball-footed, marigold 55.00
Plate, 6½" d., marigold 125.00
Plate, 9" d., footed, marigold 425.00
Plate, chop, 11½" d., three-footed,
    marigold 350.00
Plate, chop, 13" d., three-footed,
    marigold 575.00
Rose bowl, three-footed,
    blue ....175.00 to 225.00
Rose bowl, three-footed, mari-
    gold ....50.00 to 75.00
Rose bowl, three-footed, purple 257.00

TWO FRUITS
Banana boat, marigold 60.00
Bonbon, divided, blue.........................100.00
Bonbon, divided, green.......................130.00
Bonbon, divided, marigold......60.00 to 65.00
Bowl, large, in metal holder,
    marigold 165.00

VENETIAN GIANT ROSE BOWL
(Cambridge)
Green..1,200.00
Marigold...1,700.00

VICTORIAN
Bowl, 11" d., purple.............................325.00
Bowl, 11½" d., eight-ruffle, purple.......525.00

VINEYARD
Pitcher, water, marigold.......................100.00
Pitcher, water, peach opalescent 1,200.00
Pitcher, water, purple..........................315.00
Tumbler, amber 29.00
Tumbler, green 39.00
Tumbler, lavender.................................79.00
Tumbler, marigold.................................26.00
Tumbler, purple 55.00

VINTAGE or VINTAGE GRAPE

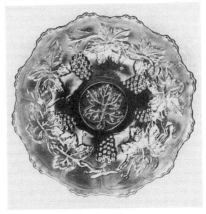

Vintage Plate

Bonbon, two-handled, blue (Fenton) 50.00
Bonbon, two-handled, green (Fenton)..50.00
Bonbon, two-handled, marigold
    (Fenton) 30.00
Bonbon, two-handled, purple
    (Fenton) 35.00
Bowl, 6" d., blue (Fenton) 35.00
Bowl, 6" d., green (Fenton)...................45.00
Bowl, 6" d., purple (Fenton) 32.50
Bowl, 6½" d., ice cream shape,
    green 35.00
Bowl, 7" d., fluted, aqua opales-
    cent (Fenton) 925.00
Bowl, 7" d., fluted, green (Fenton)........32.50
Bowl, 7" d., fluted, purple (Fenton) 28.00
Bowl, 7" d., purple (Millers-
    burg) ....50.00 to 75.00
Bowl, 7" d., ruffled, vaseline 110.00
Bowl, 7½" d., ice cream shape,
    blue 36.00
Bowl, 7½" d., ice cream shape,
    green 32.00
Bowl, 7½" d., ice cream shape,
    purple 35.00
Bowl, 8" d., ribbon candy rim, aqua
    opalescent ....1,600.00 to 1,900.00
Bowl, 8" d., ribbon candy rim, Wide
    Panel exterior, blue...........................55.00
Bowl, 8" to 9" d., aqua opales-
    cent ....1,000.00 to 1,200.00
Bowl, 8" to 9" d., ruffled, aqua
    opalescent ....850.00 to 1,000.00
Bowl, 8" to 9" d., footed, blue
    (Fenton) 42.50
Bowl, 8" to 9" d., ruffled, blue 50.00
Bowl, 8" to 9" d., green (Fenton)...........50.00
Bowl, 8" to 9" d., green (Millersburg) 30.00
Bowl, 8" to 9" d., marigold (Fenton) 35.00
Bowl, 8" to 9" d., fluted, Persian
    blue 630.00
Bowl, 8" to 9" d., footed, purple
    (Fenton) 38.00

Bowl, 8" to 9" d., ruffled,
  red ....1,700.00 to 1,800.00
Bowl, 8" to 9" d., fluted, teal blue 75.00
Bowl, 8" to 9" d., vaseline 225.00
Bowl, 9½" d., ruffled, dome-footed,
  marigold 68.00
Bowl, 10" d., blue ....75.00 to 100.00
Bowl, 10" d., green, Hobnail exterior
  (Millersburg) 950.00
Bowl, 10" d., marigold, Hobnail
  exterior (Millersburg) 575.00
Bowl, 10" d., ruffled, green 85.00
Bowl, 10" d., ruffled, purple...................55.00
Bowl, 10" d., ruffled, red 3,250.00
Bowl, 10" d., ice cream shape, blue ...200.00
Bowl, 10" d., ice cream shape, red
  (Fenton) ....1,300.00 to 1,900.00
Bowl, 10" d., ice cream shape,
  vaseline (Fenton) 225.00
Bowl, 11" d., ice cream shape,
  marigold 600.00
Bowl, ruffled, domed base, celeste
  blue 825.00
Compote, 7" d., fluted, aqua
  opalescent 925.00
Compote, 7" d., blue (Fenton) 75.00
Compote, 7" d., fluted, green
  (Fenton) 46.00
Compote, 7" d., marigold (Fenton) 40.00
Compote, 7" d., purple (Fenton) 45.00
Cuspidor, marigold 2,300.00
Epergne, blue (Fenton).......................110.00
Epergne, green, large.........................235.00
Epergne, green (Fenton) 150.00
Epergne, marigold (Fenton)................110.00
Epergne, purple, small........................150.00
Epergne, purple, large 365.00
Epergne, purple (Fenton) 130.00
Fernery, footed, blue (Fenton)..............85.00
Fernery, footed, green (Fenton) 75.00
Fernery, footed, marigold (Fenton).......42.50
Fernery, footed, purple (Fenton)...........63.00
Fernery, footed, red
  (Fenton) ....1,400.00 to 1,600.00
Ice cream set: master ice cream
  bowl & four 6" d. bowls; cobalt blue,
  5 pcs. 450.00
Nut dish, footed, blue, 6" d. (Fenton)....70.00
Nut dish, footed, green, 6" d.
  (Fenton) 110.00
Nut dish, footed, purple, 6" d.
  (Fenton) 62.00
Plate, 5" d., blue 75.00
Plate, 6" d., blue 140.00
Plate, 6" d., purple 65.00
Plate, 6½" d., stippled, marigold 50.00
Plate, 7" d., blue (Fenton)
  (ILLUS.) ....65.00 to 75.00
Plate, 7" d., green
  (Fenton) ....175.00 to 185.00
Plate, 7" d., marigold (Fenton) 125.00
Plate, 7" d., purple
  (Fenton) ....125.00 to 150.00

Plate, 7" d., purple 70.00
Plate, 8" d., blue 125.00
Plate, 8" d., green...............................165.00
Powder jar, cov., marigold (Fenton) 80.00
Powder jar, cov., marigold 75.00
Powder jar, cov., purple (Fenton) 100.00
Sandwich tray, handled, clambroth 28.00
Sandwich tray, handled, marigold 30.00
Sauce dish, blue 30.00
Sauce dish, blue, Hobnail exterior
  (Millersburg) 450.00
Sauce dish, green.................................25.00
Sauce dish, marigold (Fenton) 25.00
Sauce dish, ice cream shape, Hobnail
  exterior, marigold (Millersburg) 700.00
Tumbler, marigold (Fenton) 25.00
Wine, marigold (Fenton) 25.00
Wine, purple (Fenton)..........................32.00

VINTAGE BAND
Mug, marigold.......................................28.00
Pitcher, water, marigold......................175.00
Tumbler, marigold...............................695.00

VINTAGE GRAPE - See Vintage Pattern

WAFFLE BLOCK
Basket w/tall handle, clambroth,
  10" h...55.00
Basket w/tall handle, marigold,
  10" h...45.00
Basket w/tall handle, pastel marigold,
  10" h...145.00
Basket w/tall handle, teal, 10" h...........95.00
Basket w/tall handle, turquoise,
  10" h...100.00
Bowl, 7½" sq., marigold 36.00
Bowl, 8½" d., clambroth........................55.00
Compote, clambroth 135.00
Creamer, clambroth...............................35.00
Punch cup, marigold.............................12.00
Sugar bowl, clambroth..........................30.00
Tumbler, marigold...............................215.00
Water set: pitcher & 2 tumblers;
  pastel marigold 350.00

WATER LILY (Fenton)
Banana boat, blue 160.00
Banana boat, marigold 70.00
Bonbon, blue, 7½" d. 65.00
Bonbon, white..60.00
Bowl, 5" d., aqua...................................95.00
Bowl, 5" d., marigold.............................28.00
Bowl, 6" d., aqua.................................140.00
Bowl, 6" d., ruffled, aqua.....................185.00
Bowl, 6" d., blue....................................37.00
Bowl, 6" d., footed, blue........................58.00
Bowl, 6" d., green 160.00
Bowl, 6" d., footed, green 245.00
Bowl, 6" d., footed, lime green..............45.00
Bowl, 6" d., footed, marigold.................35.00
Bowl, 6" d., footed, purple...................150.00
Bowl, 6" d., footed, red ....550.00 to 600.00

Bowl, 6" d., footed, red opales-
cent ....900.00 to 950.00
Bowl, 6" d., footed, vaseline 125.00
Bowl, 6" d., vaseline w/marigold
overlay 85.00
Bowl, 8½" d., marigold.........................50.00
Bowl, 9" d., footed, black amethyst.......75.00
Bowl, 9" d., footed, marigold.................50.00
Bowl, 10" d., footed, fluted, blue 120.00
Bowl, 10" d., footed, green 115.00
Bowl, 10" d., footed, marigold.............100.00
Bowl, 10" d., footed, purple...................75.00

WATER LILY & CATTAILS
Bonbon, two-handled, marigold, large..50.00
Bowl, 5" d., marigold.............................32.00
Bowl, 9" d., marigold.............................80.00
Bowl, 9" d., purple................................60.00
Butter dish, cov., marigold..................156.00
Dish, three turned up sides, marigold,
6" d...29.00
Pitcher, water, marigold......................548.00
Plate, 6" d., marigold 55.00
Rose bowl, marigold 20.00
Sauce dish, marigold 12.00
Sugar bowl, cov., marigold 75.00
Table set, marigold, 4 pcs. 675.00
Toothpick holder, marigold 65.00
Tumbler, blue.................................2,700.00
Tumbler, marigold.................................45.00
Tumbler, purple 22.50
Whimsey, marigold 32.50
Whimsey, purple 55.00

WHIRLING LEAVES BOWL (Millersburg)
9" d., green 70.00
9" d., marigold......................80.00 to 100.00
9" d., purple 75.00
9½" w., tricornered, green 345.00
9½" w., tricornered, marigold..............140.00
9½" w., tricornered, vaseline 635.00
10" d., green ....50.00 to 75.00
10" d., marigold.....................................75.00
10" d., purple ....100.00 to 150.00

WHITE OAK TUMBLER
Marigold...242.00

WIDE PANEL
Banana bowl, amber.............................40.00
Basket, green 80.00
Bowl, 8" to 9" d., marigold....................19.00
Bowl, 8" to 9" d., purple 60.00
Bowl, 8½" d., Ragged Robin, 3 in l
rim, blue 135.00
Bowl, 10" d., console, blue 40.00
Bowl, 10" d., console, vaseline 40.00
Bowl, 12" d., marigold...........................45.00
Candy dish, cov., marigold 30.00
Candy dish, cov., red...........................350.00
Candy dish, cov., white.........................55.00
Compote, miniature, marigold 25.00
Compote, vaseline................................65.00

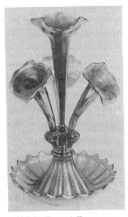

Wide Panel Epergne

Epergne, four-lily, green (ILLUS.)....1,250.00
Epergne, four-lily, ice blue 225.00
Epergne, four-lily, marigold.................525.00
Epergne, four-lily, purple 950.00
Epergne, four-lily, white 2,600.00
Goblet, marigold 15.00
Goblet, red...175.00
Plate, 8" d., marigold 45.00
Plate, 8" d., red.....................................57.00
Plate, chop, 12" d., vaseline 50.00
Plate, chop, 14" d., marigold................40.00
Plate, chop, 14" d., red 195.00
Plate, chop, 14" d., smoky 53.00
Plate, chop, 14" d., white......................28.00
Rose bowl, clambroth 20.00
Rose bowl, marigold..............................25.00
Rose bowl, purple..................................29.00
Salt dip, marigold..................................50.00
Salt set: master pedestal salt dip &
6 individual size salt dips; marigold
(Northwood), 7 pcs. 150.00
Vase, 6" h., marigold 55.00
Vase, 8½" h., 7½" d., smoke over milk
white glass 185.00
Vase, 15" h., marigold 110.00

WILD ROSE
Bowl, 5½" d., three-footed, open
heart rim, green 47.00
Bowl, 7" d., three-footed, open heart
rim, green (Northwood) 48.00
Bowl, 7" d., three-footed, open heart
rim, marigold (Northwood) 52.00
Bowl, 7" d., three-footed, open heart
rim, purple (Northwood) ....50.00 to 70.00
Bowl, 8" to 9" d., marigold
(Northwood) 32.50
Bowl, 8" to 9" d., green (Northwood) 38.00
Candy dish, open edge, blue,
5¾" d...150.00
Candy dish, open edge, green 75.00
Candy dish, open edge, purple.............90.00
Lamp, three portrait medallions,
w/original burner & etched chimney
shade, green, small (Millersburg) 850.00

Lamp, w/original burner & etched
chimney shade, green, medium
(Millersburg) ....1,250.00 to 1,450.00
Lamp, w/original burner & etched
chimney shade, marigold, medium
(Millersburg) ....1,100.00 to 1,300.00
Lamp, w/original burner & etched
chimney shade, purple
(Millersburg) 1,400.00
Syrup pitcher, marigold.......750.00 to 950.00

WILD STRAWBERRY (Northwood)
Bowl, 6" d., green 55.00
Bowl, 6" d., purple...................................48.00
Bowl, 6" d., ruffled, purple..................100.00
Bowl, 7" d., marigold.............................85.00
Bowl, 10" d., green ....175.00 to 225.00
Bowl, 10" d., ice green.....................1,750.00
Bowl, 10" d., marigold...........................85.00
Bowl, 10" d., purple.............................185.00
Plate, 6" to 7" d., w/handgrip,
green...............................200.00 to 225.00
Plate, 6" to 7" d., w/handgrip,
marigold...........................125.00 to 150.00
Plate, 6" to 7" d., w/handgrip,
purple..125.00
Plate, 8" d., w/handgrip, green 100.00
Plate, 8" d., w/handgrip, purple...........150.00

WINDFLOWER
Bowl, 8" to 9" d., blue.............................60.00
Bowl, 8" to 9" d., ice green.................350.00
Bowl, 8" to 9" d., marigold.....................32.00
Bowl, 8" to 9" d., pastel marigold..........75.00
Bowl, 8" to 9" d., purple 60.00
Bowl, 8" to 9" d., smoky 125.00
Plate, 8" d., marigold 130.00
Plate, 9" d., blue 175.00
Plate, 9" d., marigold ....75.00 to 100.00
Plate, 9" d., pastel marigold................125.00
Sauceboat, ice green...........................425.00
Sauceboat, marigold.............................40.00
Sauceboat, purple 35.00
Tumbler, marigold.................................200.00
Tumbler, purple 50.00

WINDMILL or WINDMILL MEDALLION (Imperial)
Bowl, 7" d., marigold.............................40.00
Bowl, 7" d., purple.................................56.00
Bowl, 8" to 9" d., green 35.00
Bowl, 8" to 9" d., ruffled, marigold.........75.00
Bowl, 8" to 9" d., ruffled, purple 145.00
Bowl, 8" to 9" d., ruffled, vaseline 65.00
Bowl, 8" to 9" d., ruffled, smoky 52.00
Bowl, 9" d., footed, marigold.................30.00
Bowl, 9" d., footed, purple...................115.00
Dresser tray, oval, marigold..................48.00
Pickle dish, aqua teal...........................275.00
Pickle dish, green 50.00
Pickle dish, lavender.............................70.00
Pickle dish, marigold.............................28.00
Pickle dish, purple 50.00

Pitcher, milk, clambroth 45.00
Pitcher, milk, ice green 110.00
Pitcher, milk, marigold 60.00
Pitcher, milk, purple ....500.00 to 700.00
Pitcher, milk, smoky.............................225.00
Pitcher, water, marigold.........................78.00
Pitcher, water, purple..........450.00 to 500.00
Plate, 8" d., marigold 18.00
Sauce dish, clambroth..........................35.00
Sauce dish, green..................................32.00
Sauce dish, marigold.............................20.00
Sauce dish, purple.................................35.00
Tumbler, green 39.00

Windmill Tumbler

Tumbler, marigold (ILLUS.) 35.00
Tumbler, purple 100.00
Water set: pitcher & 1 tumbler;
marigold, 2 pcs. 130.00
Water set: pitcher & 2 tumblers;
purple, 3 pcs. 1,200.00

WINDMILL & MUMS - See Chrysanthemum Pattern

WINDMILL MEDALLION - See Windmill Pattern

WINE & ROSES

Wine & Roses Pitcher

Goblet, blue 75.00
Goblet, marigold 38.00
Goblet, vaseline..................................75.00
Pitcher, water, marigold (ILLUS.) 350.00
Wine, blue...60.00
Wine, marigold....................................25.00

WISHBONE (Northwood)

Wishbone Bowl

Bowl, 7" d., three-footed, ruffled rim,
    marigold 50.00
Bowl, 8" to 9" d., footed, blue..............300.00
Bowl, 8" to 9" d., footed, clambroth......90.00
Bowl, 8" to 9" d., footed, green 103.00
Bowl, 8" to 9" d., footed, ice blue
    (ILLUS.) 2,200.00
Bowl, 8" to 9" d., footed, ice green...1,850.00
Bowl, 8" to 9" d., footed, lavender.......200.00
Bowl, 8" to 9" d., footed,
    marigold ....50.00 to 75.00
Bowl, 8" to 9" d., footed, pastel
    marigold 85.00
Bowl, 8" to 9" d., footed, purple 111.00
Bowl, 8" to 9" d., footed, white 550.00
Bowl, 10" d., footed, blue....500.00 to 600.00
Bowl, 10" d., piecrust rim, blue
    w/electric iridescence....................2,300.00
Bowl, 10" d., piecrust rim,
    green.............................225.00 to 250.00
Bowl, 10" d., piecrust rim, Basket-
    weave exterior, green 1,175.00
Bowl, 10" d., piecrust rim, marigold 92.00
Bowl, 10" d., piecrust rim, Basket-
    weave exterior, marigold..................140.00
Bowl, 10" d., ruffled, green 145.00
Bowl, 10" d., ruffled, marigold.............150.00
Bowl, 10" d., ruffled, Basketweave
    exterior, purple...................................125.00
Bowl, 10" d., piecrust rim,
    purple ....125.00 to 150.00
Bowl, 10" d., footed, ruffled, purple.....135.00
Bowl, 10" d., footed, piecrust rim,
    smoky 1,300.00
Bowl, 10" d., footed, piecrust rim,
    white 750.00

Bowl, footed, clambroth......................115.00
Epergne, green...................................675.00
Epergne, ice blue..............................2,500.00
Epergne, marigold ....400.00 to 450.00
Epergne, purple ....400.00 to 450.00
Epergne, white...............................1,950.00
Pitcher, water, green 1,800.00
Pitcher, water, marigold..................1,500.00
Pitcher, water, purple....1,150.00 to 1,250.00
Plate, 8½" d., footed, marigold 475.00
Plate, 8½" d., footed, purple 300.00
Plate, 8½" w., footed, tricornered,
    green..675.00
Plate, 8½" w., footed, tricornered,
    purple ....350.00 to 400.00
Plate, chop, 11" d., marigold...............500.00
Plate, chop, 11" d., purple 645.00
Tumbler, green 180.00
Tumbler, marigold...............................130.00
Tumbler, purple 135.00

WISHBONE & SPADES
Berry set: master bowl & 4 sauce
    dishes; purple, 5 pcs. 500.00
Bowl, 5" d., peach opalescent 80.00
Bowl, 5" d., purple................................40.00
Bowl, 6" d., ruffled, peach opalescent ..55.00
Bowl, 10" d., peach opalescent 375.00
Bowl, 10" d., purple............................270.00
Bowl, footed, green...............................85.00
Bowl, ruffled, purple 100.00
Plate, 6" d., purple 350.00
Plate, 6½" d., peach opalescent.........325.00
Plate, chop, 11" d.,
    purple...............................775.00 to 800.00
Sauce dish, peach opalescent..............70.00
Sauce dish, purple................................45.00
Whimsey from 10½" ruffled chop
    plate, sides folded-up like a napkin
    holder, peach opalescent.............1,400.00

WREATHED CHERRY (Dugan)
Berry set: master bowl & 4 sauce
    dishes; marigold, 5 pcs. 140.00
Berry set: master bowl & 4 sauce
    dishes; white, 5 pcs. 675.00
Bonbon, two-handled, green, 8" 45.00
Bonbon, two-handled, marigold, 8"......40.00
Bowl, berry, 9 x 12" oval, lavender 65.00
Bowl, berry, 9 x 12" oval, marigold 90.00
Bowl, berry, 9 x 12" oval, pastel
    marigold 150.00
Bowl, berry, 9 x 12" oval, peach
    opalescent ....200.00 to 250.00
Bowl, berry, 9 x 12" oval, purple 153.00
Bowl, berry, 9 x 12" oval, white...........245.00
Butter dish, cov., marigold....................70.00
Butter dish, cov., purple......175.00 to 225.00
Compote, three-footed, peach
    opalescent 75.00
Creamer, blue.......................................55.00
Pitcher, water, marigold......................225.00
Pitcher, water, white w/gold
    cherries ....700.00 to 750.00

Sauce dish, 5" to 6" l., oval, marigold ...30.00
Sauce dish, 5" to 6" l., oval, peach
 opalescent 140.00
Sauce dish, 5" to 6" l., oval, purple 40.00
Sauce dish, 5" to 6" l., oval, white........42.50
Spooner, marigold 65.00
Spooner, purple 60.00
Spooner, white.....................................95.00
Toothpick holder, marigold 100.00
Tumbler, marigold 32.50
Tumbler, purple 65.00
Tumbler, white 100.00
Tumbler, white w/red-stained
 cherries 115.00
Water set: pitcher & 4 tumblers;
 marigold, 5 pcs. 600.00

WREATH OF ROSES

Bonbon, two-handled, blue, 8" d...........75.00
Bonbon, two-handled, green, 8" d. 55.00
Bonbon, two-handled, marigold, 8" d....50.00
Bonbon, two-handled, purple,
 8" d...................................100.00 to 125.00
Bonbon, two-handled, white, 8" d. 150.00
Compote, 6" d., blue 65.00
Compote, 6" d., fluted, green 50.00
Compote, 6" d., honey amber
 (variant)..35.00
Compote, 6" d., marigold 40.00
Compote, 6" d., fluted, purple 45.00
Punch bowl, Persian Medallion
 interior, blue 300.00
Punch bowl & base, Persian
 Medallion interior, marigold,
 2 pcs. 225.00
Punch cup, blue....................................22.00
Punch cup, Persian Medallion interior,
 blue 28.00
Punch cup, Vintage interior, blue..........25.00
Punch cup, green 25.00
Punch cup, Persian Medallion interior,
 green...35.00
Punch cup, Vintage interior, green 37.00
Punch cup, marigold.............................14.00
Punch cup, Persian Medallion interior,
 marigold 25.00
Punch cup, Vintage interior, marigold...30.00
Punch cup, purple.................................25.00
Punch cup, Persian Medallion interior,
 purple..27.00
Punch cup, Vintage interior, purple 32.50
Punch set: bowl, base & 2 cups;
 green, 4 pcs. 425.00
Punch set: bowl, base & 4 cups;
 Persian Medallion interior, marigold,
 6 pcs. 395.00
Punch set: bowl, base & 5 cups;
 Vintage interior, purple, 7 pcs. 800.00
Rose bowl, marigold (Dugan) 50.00
Rose bowl, purple (Dugan)...................55.00
Whimsey, tricornered, marigold
 (Dugan) 45.00

ZIG ZAG (Millersburg)

Bowl, 9½" d., marigold........................195.00
Bowl, 9½" d., green 420.00
Bowl, 10" d., green ....250.00 to 275.00
Bowl, 10" d., marigold.........................185.00
Bowl, 10" d., purple.............................240.00
Bowl, 10" w., tricornered, piecrust
 rim, green...200.00
Bowl, 10" w., tricornered, purple.........430.00
Bowl, ribbon candy rim, marigold 225.00
Bowl, ribbon candy rim,
 purple...............................250.00 to 300.00

ZIPPERED HEART

Zippered Heart Rose Bowl

Bowl, berry, 10" d., purple 130.00
Rose bowl, green (ILLUS.) 3,600.00
Sauce dish, purple, 5" d........................22.50
Vase, 9" h., green 2,100.00
Vase, marigold....................................550.00

ZIPPERED LOOP LAMP (Imperial)

Zippered Loop Lamp

Hand, marigold, 4½" h. 1,200.00
Hand, marigold, medium 675.00
Sewing, marigold, small.....................325.00
Sewing, marigold,
    medium ....600.00 to 675.00
Sewing, smoky,
    medium ....950.00 to 1,000.00
Sewing, marigold,
    large (ILLUS.) ....550.00 to 575.00

(End of Carnival Glass Section)

CONSOLIDATED

The Consolidated Lamp and Glass Company of Coraopolis, Pennsylvania was founded in 1894 and for a number of years was noted for its lighting wares but also produced popular lines of pressed and blown tablewares. Highly collectible glass patterns of this early era include the Cone, Florette and Guttate lines.

Lamps and shades continued to be good sellers but in 1926 a new "art" line of molded decorative wares was introduced. This "Martelé" line was developed as a direct imitation of the fine glasswares being produced by René Lalique of France and many Consolidated patterns resembled their French counterparts. Other popular lines produced during the 1920s and 1930s were "Dancing Nymph," the delightfully Art Deco "Ruba Rombic," introduced in 1928, and the "Catalonian" line, imitating 17th century Spanish glass, which debuted in 1927.

Although the factory closed in 1933, it was reopened under new management in 1936 and prospered through the 1940s. It finally closed in 1967. Collectors should note that many later Consolidated patterns closely resemble wares of other competing firms, especially the Phoenix Glass Company. Careful study is needed to determine the maker of pieces from the 1920-40 era.

A recent book which will be of help to collectors is Phoenix & Consolidated Art Glass, 1926-1980, *by Jack D. Wilson (Antique Publications, 1989).*

Consolidated Martelé Label

Bulging Loops
Pitcher, water, cased pink $360.00

Sugar shaker w/original top, blue
    opaque...450.00
Tumbler, cased yellow.........................45.00

Cone
Butter dish, cov., cased yellow 135.00
Pickle castor, cased pink, ornate
    silver plate frame, elaborate side &
    top trim, w/tongs 450.00
Pickle castor, cased yellow, silver
    plate frame.......................275.00 to 325.00
Sugar shaker w/original top, cased
    blue satin ....125.00 to 150.00
Sugar shaker w/original top, green
    opaque...165.00
Sugar shaker w/original top, cased
    pink, glossy finish.............................145.00
Syrup pitcher w/original top, tall, blue
    opaque...295.00
Syrup pitcher w/original top, squatty,
    cased blue 210.00
Syrup pitcher w/original top, squatty,
    cased pink........................250.00 to 275.00
Toothpick holder, cased pink...............75.00
Water set: pitcher & four tumblers;
    blue opaque, 5 pcs. 285.00

Florette

Florette Cracker Jar

Butter dish, cov., cased pink
    satin ....250.00 to 275.00
Cracker (or biscuit) jar w/original silver
    plate rim, lid & bail handle, cased
    pink (ILLUS.) 295.00
Cruet w/original stopper, pink 185.00
Cruet w/original frosted stopper,
    frosted handle, cased pink satin 145.00
Lamp, kerosene-type, wall bracket-
    type, green opaque, 6" d.................175.00
Mustard pot w/hinged metal lid, cased
    yellow satin 75.00
Pitcher, water, pink satin 275.00
Salt shaker w/original top, cased
    pink ....75.00 to 100.00
Spooner, cased pink, metal rim &
    handles 50.00
Sugar bowl, cov., cased pink..............125.00

Sugar bowl, cov., cased pink satin.....115.00
Syrup pitcher w/original ornate silver plate hinged lid & handle, cased pink satin..........................250.00 to 290.00
Toothpick holder, cased blue................65.00
Toothpick holder, cased green..................................75.00 to 100.00
Toothpick holder, cased pink ....100.00 to 125.00

Guttate

Celery vase, cased pink .....150.00 to 175.00
Pitcher, water, 9½" h., applied clear handle, cased pink satin 395.00
Salt shaker w/brass top, cased blue.....52.00
Salt & pepper shakers, cased pink, pr...75.00
Salt & pepper shakers w/original tops, cased pink satin, pr. 55.00
Spooner, cased pink.............75.00 to 100.00
Sugar shaker w/original top, cased pink satin..........................200.00 to 300.00
Syrup pitcher w/original top, cranberry..450.00

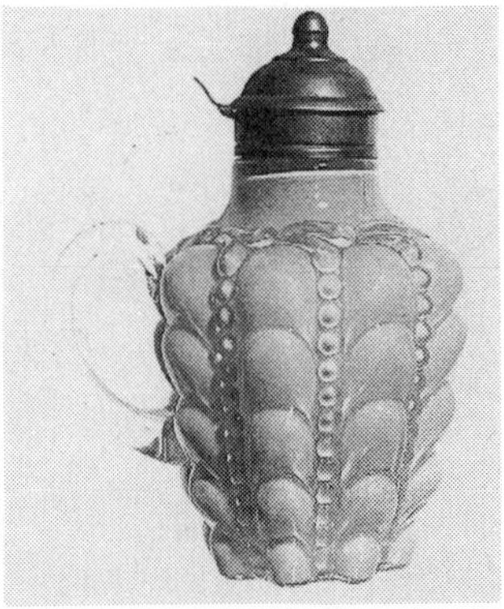

Guttate Syrup Pitcher

Syrup pitcher w/original top, cased pink (ILLUS.)....................350.00 to 400.00
Table set: cov. butter dish, sugar bowl, creamer & spooner; white w/gold trim, 4 pcs.............................225.00
Water set: pitcher & four tumblers; cased pink satin, 5 pcs. 595.00

Later Lines

Ruba Rombic Dresser Jar

Ashtray, oblong, Santa Maria line, amber...45.00
Banana boat, oblong, Love Birds patt., Martelé line, three-color decoration on custard ground 500.00
Bowl, 9" d., 4" h., Catalonian line, yellow 55.00
Bowl, 13" d., Cockatoo patt., Martelé line, gold wash 125.00
Bowl, 13" d., Cockatoo patt., Martelé line, green wash..............................145.00
Bowl, 15" d., Fish patt., Martelé line, green wash 375.00
Candlesticks, Catalonian line, emerald green, pr. ....40.00 to 60.00
Cookie jar, cov., Con-Cora line, roses decoration on a milk white ground, 6½" h...95.00
Cookie jar, cov., Con-Cora line, violets decoration on a milk white ground, 9" h. 145.00
Creamer & open sugar bowl, Catalonian line, pink, pr. 38.00
Dresser jar, cov., oblong, Ruba Rombic line, frosted amber, some staining, 5½" w., 4" h. (ILLUS.) 546.00
Lamp, table model, brass base & shade cap, Bittersweet patt., Martelé line, straw opal................................165.00
Lamp, table model, brass base & shade cap, Cockatoo patt., Martelé line, blue & brown on a custard ground, 9½" d., 8½" h. 295.00
Lamp, table model, brass base & shade cap, Foxglove patt., Martelé line, green wash..............................145.00
Lamp, table model, brass base & shade cap, Foxglove patt., Martelé line, two-color decoration on a custard ground 175.00
Lamp base, table model, brass fittings, baluster-form, Dogwood patt., Martelé line, salmon decoration on a milk white ground, 10½" h. glass insert, overall 15" h..135.00
Lamp, table model, brass fittings, Thistle patt., Martelé line, umbrella vase-type, blue & irridescent white, overall 25" h. 550.00
Lamp base, table model, Cockatoo patt., Martelé line, matte blue on cream 175.00
Lamp base, table model, Peony patt., peach w/green leaves, brown stems, factory drilled, 6¼" h. 65.00
Plate, 8½" d., Dancing Nymph line, clear frosted 77.00
Plate, 10" d., Dancing Nymph line, green frosted..................................150.00
Plate, 12" d., Five Fruits patt., Martelé line, milk white ground 95.00

Puff box, cov., Hummingbird patt.,
Martelé line, green wash,
4" d...250.00

Snack plate, pear-shaped, Five Fruits
patt., Catalonian line, jade green
wash, 9¼" d. 18.00

Ruba Rombic Tumbler

Tumblers, conical, Ruba Rombic line,
opal green, one w/polished-down
rim, 7¼" h., pr. (ILLUS. of one) 690.00

Vase, 6" h., ovoid, Dragonfly &
Cattails patt., Martelé line, brown &
coral decoration on a milk white
ground...............................95.00 to 110.00

Vase, 6" h., ovoid, Dragonfly &
Cattails patt., Martelé line, milk white
w/gold trim 70.00

Vase, 6" h., Hummingbird & Orchids
patt., Martelé line, yellow cased........80.00

Vase, 6½" h., Chickadee patt.,
Martelé line, satin milk
white ....95.00 to 110.00

Vase, 6½" h., Chickadee patt.,
Martelé line, tri-color highlighting
on satin custard 195.00

Vase, 6½" h., Chickadee patt.,
Martelé line, yellow wash.................125.00

Vase, 6½" h., flattened fan shape,
shape No. 2201, Florentine line,
green..185.00

Vase, 6½" h., 7" d., Pine Cone patt.,
Martelé line, ruby stain on crystal 195.00

Vases, 6¾" h., Ruba Rombic line, tall
conical body on a flaring foot,
green, pr. 770.00

Vase, 8" h., 9" d., Catalonian line,
amethyst wash...................................65.00

Vase, 8½" h., 9" d., Cockatoo patt.,
Martelé line, three-color decoration
on a white ground 225.00

Vase, 9" h., Tropical Fish patt.,
Martelé line, brown highlighting on
satin milk white ground 175.00

Vase, 9½" h., Bittersweet patt.,
Martelé line, purple berries & brown
leaves on a creamy white ground 125.00

Vase, 9½" h., baluster-form, Bittersweet patt., Martelé line, two-color
decoration on a white ground 75.00

Vase, 9½" h., Bittersweet patt.,
Martelé line, three-color decoration
on a custard ground.........................125.00

Vase, 10" h., triangular, Catalonian
line, red wash...................100.00 to 115.00

Vase, 10" h., bulbous ovoid body,
Line 700, French Crystal..................260.00

Vase, 10½" h., Dogwood patt.,
Martelé line, tan decoration
on a custard ground.........................150.00

Vase, 10½" h., Dogwood patt.,
Martelé line, three-color decoration
on a white ground 135.00

Dancing Girls Vase

Vase, 11½" h., Dancing Girls patt.,
Martelé line, blue figures on a
custard ground (ILLUS.) ..495.00 to 525.00

Vase, 11½" h., Dancing Girls patt.,
Martelé line, clear figures on a
frosted background ....400.00 to 425.00

Water set: pitcher & six tumblers; Five
Fruits patt., Martelé line, yellow
wash, 7 pcs. 375.00

CRUETS

Amber, blown, bulbous body, applied
blue handle, blue stopper, ca.
1880s $140.00

Amber, pressed, I.O.U. patt., original
faceted stopper 110.00

Amber lustre w/raised rounded
swirled ribs, applied clear handle &
original faceted stopper, polished
pontil 150.00

Blue, blown, squared bulbous body,
decorated w/enameled red, white &
blue flowers & green leaves, all

outlined in gold, applied amber spun
rope handle, original amber facet-
cut stopper, 7¼" h., 3¼" d...............165.00
Blue opalescent, blown, Christmas
Bead & Panel patt., applied blue
handle, original stopper 225.00
Champagne, mold-blown, Inverted
Thumbprint patt., bulbous body
tapering to a cylindrical neck
w/pinched lip, applied sapphire blue
handle, sapphire blue facet-cut
stopper, 3" d., 5¾" h. 75.00
Clear, blown, Swirl patt., applied clear
closed round handle, original ball
stopper, 4½" h...................................22.50
Clear, pressed, Peacock Feather
patt., original stopper, 10" h. 125.00
Cobalt blue, blown, ovoid body taper-
ing to a cylindrical neck & pinched
spout, upper body decorated w/pink
flowers & green leaves on a enameled gold ground, the lower body
decorated w/white lacy dotting,
applied cobalt blue handle, cobalt
blue teardrop-shaped stopper,
2⅝" d., 6¼" h. 85.00
Cobalt blue, blown, ovoid body
tapering to a cylindrical neck
w/pinched lip, enameled w/bands of
sanded gold leaves & white dot
decoration, applied cobalt blue
handle, original cobalt blue ball
stopper, 3½" d., 8" h. 165.00
Cobalt blue, pattern-molded, bulbous
body tapering to a slender neck
w/high arched spout, applied strap
handle, hollow ball stopper,
Midwest, early 19th c., 7½" h. plus
stopper (minor residue, slight check
at handle) 1,210.00
Cranberry, blown, Moire satin finish,
applied clear frosted handle, clear
bubble stopper 295.00
Cranberry, blown, baluster-form body,
cylindrical neck w/tricorner rim,
enameled w/blue & white flowers &
yellow leaves, applied clear handle,
original clear bubble stopper, 3⅛" d.,
8¼" h...195.00
Cranberry, blown, ovoid body tapering
to long slender neck & applied clear
handle, decorated w/overall gold
enameled scrolling & dainty gold
flowers, gold trim on original clear
bubble stopper, 10½" h., 3⅜" d........195.00
Emerald green, pressed, The Prize
patt., w/original stopper....................225.00
Green, pressed, Geneva patt., original
stopper..290.00
Green, pressed, Georgia Gem patt.,
gold trim, original stopper 350.00
Light blue, mold-blown, square body,

cylindrical neck w/flared spout,
enameled w/rust, blue, white &
yellow flowers & leaves, applied
amber handle, original amber facet-
cut stopper, 3½" d., 7½" h................165.00
Lime green, blown, ovoid body
tapering to a cylindrical neck
w/pinched spout, decorated w/dainty
enameled dot flowers & gold trim,
applied clear handle, clear facet-cut
stopper, 3⅛" d., 7¼" h. 100.00
Lime green, blown, bulbous body
w/applied lime green handle,
decorated w/small white daisies &
gold foliage, original lime green
bulbous stopper, 3¼" d., 8" h...........110.00
Orange, blown, Optic patt., tapering
cylindrical body w/slender ringed
neck w/petal-form spout, decorated
w/dainty white enameled daisies,
applied clear handle, original squatty
bulbous stopper, 3" d., 8½" h...........165.00
Pink-stained, Blazing Cornucopia
patt., original stopper 89.00

Enamel-Decorated Cruet

Sapphire blue, blown, ovoid body
w/slender cylindrical neck w/pinched
lip, decorated w/multicolored
enameled Queen Anne's lace
decoration, applied sapphire blue
handle & original teardrop-shaped
stopper, 7½" h. (ILLUS.) 375.00
Sapphire blue, blown, ovoid body
tapering to a short rim & amber
applied handle, decorated
w/enameled white foliage, white
w/yellow flowers & gold trim, original
amber ball stopper, 3" d., 7½" h.......165.00
Sapphire blue, blown, bulbous body
w/a slender cylindrical neck,
decorated w/pink foliage w/deeper
pink & white flowers, applied
sapphire blue handle, original blue
bubble stopper, 3½" d., 8" h.............165.00

Sapphire blue, blown, ovoid body
w/slender neck & applied clear
handle, decorated w/lavender
flowers & green leaves, gold
decoration & gold trim, original clear
bubble stopper, 3¾" d., 9" h.............165.00
Sapphire blue, blown, ovoid shape
tapering to a cylindrical neck,
enameled w/rose pink florals
w/green & gold foliage, applied light
blue handle, original bubble-shaped
stopper, 4" d., 9" h. 165.00
Sapphire blue, blown, white enameled
decoration & matching enameled
stopper, applied amber handle 55.00

Mold Blown Cruet

Sapphire blue, mold-blown, 16-rib
globular body tapering to a narrow
neck w/high arched spout, applied
hollow handle, original stopper,
Midwestern, 7" h. plus stopper
(ILLUS.) 2,310.00
Sapphire blue, mold-blown, bulbous
body tapering to a cylindrical neck
w/pinched spout, decorated w/pink
blossoms, orange flowers & pink
branches, applied sapphire blue
handle, original sapphire blue
bubble stopper, 4" d., 8¼" h.............165.00

CUP PLATES

*Produced in numerous patterns
beginning some 160 years ago, these little
plates were designed to hold a cup while
the tea or coffee was allowed to cool in a
saucer. Cup plates were also made of
ceramics. Where numbers are listed below,
they refer to numbers assigned these plates
in the book,* American Glass Cup Plates, *by
Ruth Webb Lee and James H. Rose. Plates
are of clear glass unless otherwise noted. A
number of cup plates have been
reproduced.*

L & R 87, plain round, 4⁷⁄₁₆" d. $16.00

L & R 95, octagonal, shields &
tree-like devices in border, opal
opaque..143.00
L & R 109, Thistle patt., octagonal
w/incurved edges (some mold
roughness on rim) 55.00
L & R 174, round w/petaled rim, eight-
petaled design in center, opal
opaque..385.00
L & R 243, round w/small rim
scallops, quatrefoil in center
surrounded by small blossomheads,
scrolls in border, opalescent
(underfill on one scallop, mold
roughness).......................................148.50
L & R 388, diamond point border,
eight-petal center flower (minor rim
nip) 30.00
L & R 465F, Heart patt., round, violet
blue (several scallops missing or
tipped) 302.50
L & R 563, Henry Clay, no name
variant, opalescent (three tipped
scallops, mold roughness) 467.50
L & R 572, round w/small rim
scallops, Queen Victoria bust design
(mold roughness) 132.00
L & R 610B, Ship Cadmus patt.............30.00
L & R 655, Eagle patt., round,
Pittsburgh (fin & mold roughness) ...126.50
L & R 691, round w/beaded rim, Lyre
patt. (several beads tipped, overall
mold roughness) 33.00

DEPRESSION GLASS

*The phrase "Depression Glass" is used
by collectors to denote a specific kind of
transparent glass produced primarily as
tablewares, in crystal, amber, blue, green,
pink, milky-white, etc., during the late
1920s and 1930s when this country was in
the midst of a financial depression. Made
to sell inexpensively, it was turned out by
such producers as Jeannette, Hocking,
Westmoreland, Indiana and other glass
companies. We compile prices on all the
major Depression Glass patterns.
Collectors should consult Depression Glass
references for information on those
patterns and pieces which have been
reproduced.*

ADAM (Process-etched)

Ashtray, clear, 4½" sq...........................$8.50
Ashtray, green, 4½" sq. 16.50
Ashtray, pink, 4½" sq............................24.50
Bowl, dessert, 4¾" sq., green...............15.50
Bowl, dessert, 4¾" sq., pink 13.00
Bowl, cereal, 5¾" sq., green.................37.00

Bowl, cereal, 5¾" sq., pink 41.00
Bowl, nappy, 7¾" sq., green................21.50
Bowl, nappy, 7¾" sq., pink 18.50
Bowl, cov., 9" sq., green 75.00
Bowl, cov., 9" sq., pink........................53.00
Bowl, 9" sq., pink 18.00
Bowl, 10" oval vegetable, green 22.50
Bowl, 10" oval vegetable, pink.............27.50
Butter dish, cov., green......................265.00
Butter dish, cov., pink 76.00
Cake plate, footed, green or pink,
    10" sq. 22.00
Candlesticks, green, 4" h., pr...............84.00
Candlesticks, pink, 4" h., pr 75.00
Candy jar, cov., green 96.50
Candy jar, cov., pink.............................82.00
Coaster, green, 3¼" sq.........................17.00
Coaster, pink, 3¼" sq. 21.00
Creamer, green 17.50
Creamer, pink 16.00
Cup, green..16.00
Cup, pink 20.00
Pitcher, 8" h., 32 oz., cone-shaped,
    green..37.00
Pitcher, 8" h., 32 oz., cone-shaped,
    pink 30.00
Pitcher, 32 oz., round base, pink 44.50
Plate, sherbet, 6" sq., green 7.00
Plate, sherbet, 6" sq., pink.....................6.00
Plate, salad, 7¾" sq., green or pink......10.50
Plate, salad, round, pink 60.00
Plate, salad, round, yellow.................110.00
Plate, dinner, 9" sq., green 19.00
Plate, dinner, 9" sq., pink.....................26.00
Plate, grill, 9" sq., green or pink............17.00
Platter, 11¾" l., green 18.00
Platter, 11¾" l., pink..............................23.00
Relish dish, two-part, green or pink,
    8" sq..16.50
Salt & pepper shakers, footed, green,
    4" h., pr. 75.00

Adam Salt & Pepper Shakers

Salt & pepper shakers, footed, pink,
    4" h., pr. (ILLUS.) 60.00
Saucer, pink, 6" sq..................................6.50
Saucer, round, green.............................5.50

Saucer, round, pink 6.00
Sherbet, green, 3" h..............................31.50
Sherbet, pink, 3" h. 25.00
Sugar bowl, cov., green...................... 41.00
Sugar bowl, cov., pink 34.00
Tumbler, cone-shaped, green, 4½" h.,
    7 oz...22.50
Tumbler, cone-shaped, pink,4½" h.,
    7 oz...23.50
Tumbler, iced tea, green, 5½" h.,
    9 oz...41.50
Tumbler, iced tea, pink, 5½" h.,
    9 oz...55.00
Vase, 7½" h., green...............................53.00
Vase, 7½" h., pink................................185.00
Water set: pitcher & 6 tumblers;
    pink, 7 pcs..162.50

AMERICAN SWEETHEART
(Process-etched)

American Sweetheart Plate

Bowl, berry, 3¾" d., pink.......................38.00
Bowl, cream soup, 4½" d., Monax......106.00
Bowl, cream soup, 4½" d., pink 70.00
Bowl, cereal, 6" d., Cremax 8.00
Bowl, cereal, 6" d., Monax...................11.50
Bowl, cereal, 6" d., pink 12.50
Bowl, berry, 9" d., Cremax.................. 28.50
Bowl, berry, 9" d., Monax.....................55.00
Bowl, berry, 9" d., pink.........................35.00
Bowl, soup w/flange rim, 9½" d.,
    Monax 70.00
Bowl, soup w/flange rim, 9½" d., pink...58.00
Bowl, 11" oval vegetable, Monax..........67.00
Bowl, 11" oval vegetable, pink............ 55.00
Console bowl, Monax, 18" d. 425.00
Creamer, footed, blue...........................95.00
Creamer, footed, Monax........................8.50
Creamer, footed, pink...........................13.00
Creamer, footed, ruby red 93.00
Cup, Monax 9.00
Cup, pink 13.50
Cup & saucer, ruby red.......................118.00
Lamp shade, Monax...........................545.00
Pitcher, 7½" h., 60 oz., jug-type,
    pink 530.00
Pitcher, 8" h., 80 oz., pink..................440.00

Plate, bread & butter, 6" d., Monax
or pink 4.50
Plate, salad, 8" d., blue.........................84.00
Plate, salad, 8" d., Monax......................8.00
Plate, salad, 8" d., pink 11.00
Plate, salad, 8" d., ruby red 64.00
Plate, luncheon, 9" d., Monax..............10.00
Plate, dinner, 9¾" d., Monax 22.00
Plate, dinner, 9¾" d., pink 30.00
Plate, dinner, 10¼" d., Monax 21.00
Plate, dinner, 10¼" d., pink..................30.00
Plate, chop, 11" d., Monax.................. 13.50
Plate, salver, 12" d., Monax.................16.00
Plate, salver, 12" d., pink (ILLUS.)........15.00
Plate, salver, 12" d., ruby red 170.00
Plate, 15½" d., w/center handle,
Monax 205.00
Platter, 13" oval, Monax.......................55.00
Platter, 13" oval, pink.......................... 40.00
Salt & pepper shakers, footed,
Monax, pr...270.00
Salt & pepper shakers, footed, pink,
pr..330.00
Saucer, Monax or pink............................3.00
Sherbet, footed, pink, 3¾" h. 18.50
Sherbet, footed, Monax, 4¼" h. 19.00
Sherbet, footed, pink, 4¼" h. 13.50
Sherbet, metal holder, clear 6.00
Sugar bowl, cov., Monax (only) 265.00
Sugar bowl, open, Monax.......................7.50
Sugar bowl, open, pink 10.00
Sugar bowl, open, ruby red 100.00
Tidbit server, two-tier, Monax 70.00
Tidbit server, two-tier, pink 56.00
Tidbit server, two-tier, ruby red..........220.00
Tumbler, pink, 3½" h., 5 oz..................67.00
Tumbler, pink, 4½" h., 9 oz...................68.00
Tumbler, pink, 4¾" h., 10 oz................73.50

**BLOCK or Block Optic
(Press-mold)**

Block Butter Dish

Bowl, berry, 4¼" d., green 6.50
Bowl, 4½" d., green 27.00
Bowl, cereal, 5¼" d., green....................11.50
Bowl, cereal, 5¼" d., pink 19.50
Bowl, salad, 7" d., green.......................25.00
Bowl, large berry, 8½" d., green 22.00
Bowl, large berry, 8½" d., pink..............19.00
Butter dish, cov., rectangular, green,
3 x 5" (ILLUS.) 42.00
Candlesticks, amber, 1¾" h., pr............92.00
Candlesticks, green, 1¾" h., pr...........105.00

Candlesticks, pink, 1¾" h., pr. 67.00
Candy jar, cov., green, 2¼" h. 41.00
Candy jar, cov., pink, 2¼" h..................36.50
Candy jar, cov., yellow, 2¼" h. 48.00
Candy jar, cov., clear, 6¼" h.................24.50
Candy jar, cov., green, 6¼" h. 48.00
Candy jar, cov., pink, 6¼" h..................110.00
Compote, 4" d., cone-shaped,
green..23.50
Creamer, various styles, green.............14.00
Creamer, various styles, pink 9.00
Creamer, various styles, yellow............11.50
Cup, various styles, green 6.00
Cup, various styles, pink or yellow 7.00
Goblet, cocktail, pink, 4" h. 26.00
Goblet, wine, clear, 4½" h.....................14.00
Goblet, wine, green or pink, 4½" h. 38.50
Goblet, clear, 5¾" h., 9 oz. 13.00
Goblet, green, 5¾" h., 9 oz...................19.50
Goblet, pink, 5¾" h., 9 oz. 26.00
Goblet, yellow, 5¾" h., 9 oz. 30.00
Goblet, clear, 7¼" h., 9 oz. 9.00
Goblet, green, 7¼" h., 9 oz....................21.00
Goblet, pink, 7¼" h., 9 oz. 18.00
Goblet, yellow, 7¼" h., 9 oz..................29.00
Ice bucket, w/metal bail handle, clear...17.50
Ice bucket, w/metal bail handle,
green..35.00
Ice bucket, w/metal bail handle, pink....61.00
Ice tub, tab handles, green 40.00
Ice tub, tab handles, pink......................76.00
Mug, green 32.00
Pitcher, 8" h., 80 oz., clear....................25.00
Pitcher, 8" h., 80 oz., green....................67.00
Pitcher, 8½" h., 54 oz., clear................16.00
Pitcher, 8½" h., 54 oz., green 42.00
Pitcher, 8½" h., 54 oz., pink..................36.00
Plate, sherbet, 6" d., clear, green
or pink 2.50
Plate, sherbet, 6" d., yellow 3.00
Plate, luncheon, 8" d., clear...................3.50
Plate, luncheon, 8" d., green 4.50
Plate, luncheon, 8" d., pink or yellow......5.50
Plate, dinner, 9" d., green.....................16.00
Plate, dinner, 9" d., pink........................21.00
Plate, dinner, 9" d., yellow 24.50
Plate, grill, 9" d., green 15.50
Plate, sandwich, 10¼" d., clear 15.50
Plate, sandwich, 10¼" d., green...........21.00
Salt & pepper shakers, squat, green,
pr..71.00
Salt & pepper shakers, footed, clear,
pr..22.00
Salt & pepper shakers, footed, green,
pr..31.00
Salt & pepper shakers, footed, pink,
pr..73.00
Salt & pepper shakers, footed, yellow,
pr..65.00
Sandwich server w/center handle,
green..42.00
Sandwich server w/center handle,
pink 48.00

Saucer, green, 5¾" d. 10.50
Saucer, pink, 5¾" d. 6.00
Saucer, green, 6⅛" d. 8.50
Saucer, pink, 6⅛" d. 5.00
Saucer, yellow, 6⅛" d. 7.00
Sherbet, cone-shaped, footed, green 4.50
Sherbet, stemmed, clear, 3¼" h.,
  5½ oz. 3.00
Sherbet, stemmed, green, 3¼" h.,
  5½ oz. 5.00
Sherbet, stemmed, pink or yellow,
  3¼" h., 5½ oz. 6.50
Sherbet, stemmed, clear, 4¾" h.,
  6 oz. 6.00
Sherbet, stemmed, green, pink or
  yellow, 4¾" h., 6 oz. 12.50
Sugar bowl, open, various styles, clear ..7.00
Sugar bowl, open, various styles,
  green, pink or yellow 10.50
Tumbler, whiskey, pink, 1⅝" h., 1 oz. ...32.00
Tumbler, whiskey, clear, 2¼" h., 2 oz. 8.00
Tumbler, whiskey, green, 2¼" h.,
  2 oz. 26.00
Tumbler, whiskey, pink, 2¼" h., 2 oz. ...32.00
Tumbler, footed, green, 2⅝" h., 3 oz. ...20.00
Tumbler, footed, pink, 2⅝" h., 3 oz. 30.00
Tumbler, juice, green, 3½" h., 5 oz. 17.50
Tumbler, juice, pink, 3½" h., 5 oz. 20.00
Tumbler, footed, clear, 9 oz. 5.00
Tumbler, footed, green, 9 oz. 16.50
Tumbler, footed, pink or yellow, 9 oz. ...15.00
Tumbler, green, 3⅞" h., 9½ oz. 18.00
Tumbler, pink, 3⅞" h., 9½ oz. 11.00
Tumbler, iced tea, footed, green,
  6" h., 10 oz. 26.00
Tumbler, iced tea, footed, pink, 6" h.,
  10 oz. 19.50
Tumbler, green, 5" h., 10 to 11 oz. 15.50
Tumbler, pink, 5" h., 10 to 11 oz. 14.50
Tumbler, green, 4⅞" h., 12 oz. 22.50
Tumbler, pink, 4⅞" h., 12 oz. 19.00
Tumbler, green, 5¼" h., 15 oz. 33.00
Tumbler, pink, 5¼" h., 15 oz. 30.00
Tumble-up bottle, green 14.50
Tumble-up set: bottle & 3" h. tumbler;
  green, 2 pcs. 52.00
Vase, 5¾" h., green 275.00

BUBBLE, Bullseye or Provincial
(Press-mold)
Bowl, berry, 4" d., blue..........................15.00
Bowl, berry, 4" d., clear or milk white......3.00
Bowl, berry, 4" d., green 9.50
Bowl, fruit, 4½" d., blue 9.50
Bowl, fruit, 4½" d., clear or milk white.....3.50
Bowl, fruit, 4½" d., green or ruby red 7.50
Bowl, cereal, 5¼" d., blue 10.50
Bowl, cereal, 5¼" d., clear 8.00
Bowl, cereal, 5¼" d., green...................12.00
Bowl, soup, 7¾" d., blue 13.00
Bowl, soup, 7¾" d., clear 7.00
Bowl, soup, 7¾" d., pink 10.00
Bowl, 8⅜" d., blue................................13.50

Bowl, 8⅜" d., clear or milk white............7.50
Bowl, 8⅜" d., green 14.00
Bowl, 8⅜" d., ruby red 24.00
Candlesticks, clear, pr. 12.00
Creamer, blue.......................................29.00
Creamer, clear..6.00
Creamer, green 11.50
Creamer, milk white................................4.00
Cup, blue 3.50
Cup, green 7.00
Cup, ruby red..6.50
Cup & saucer, clear 3.50
Cup & saucer, milk white 3.00
Lamps, clear (electric), pr. 56.00
Pitcher w/ice lip, 64 oz., clear 65.00
Pitcher w/ice lip, 64 oz., ruby red..........48.00
Plate, bread & butter, 6¾" d., blue..........3.50
Plate, bread & butter, 6¾" d., clear..........2.00
Plate, bread & butter, 6¾" d., green 4.50
Plate, dinner, 9⅜" d., blue 6.00
Plate, dinner, 9⅜" d., clear 4.50
Plate, dinner, 9⅜" d., green 15.00
Plate, dinner, 9⅜" d., ruby red 12.50
Plate, grill, 9⅜" d., blue........................16.50
Plate, grill, 9⅜" d., clear 7.50
Platter, 12" oval, blue............................13.00
Platter, 12" oval, clear...........................11.50
Saucer, blue, green or ruby red..............3.50
Sugar bowl, open, blue.........................17.50
Sugar bowl, open, clear..........................6.00
Sugar bowl, open, green 10.50
Sugar bowl, open, milk white.................4.50
Tidbit server, two-tier, blue 44.00
Tumbler, juice, green, 6 oz. 10.50
Tumbler, juice, ruby red, 6 oz. 7.00
Tumbler, old fashioned, clear, 3¼" h.,
  8 oz. 6.00
Tumbler, old fashioned, ruby red,
  3¼" h., 8 oz. 13.00
Tumbler, water, clear, 9 oz. 8.00
Tumbler, water, ruby red, 9 oz. 9.50
Tumbler, iced tea, clear, 4½" h.,12 oz. ..10.50

Bubble Iced Tea Tumbler

Tumbler, iced tea, ruby red, 4½" h.,
  12 oz. (ILLUS.).................................9.00
Tumbler, lemonade, clear, 5⅞" h.,
  16 oz. 13.00

Tumbler, lemonade, ruby red, 5⅞" h.,
  16 oz. 16.00
Water set: pitcher & 8 tumblers; ruby
  red, 9 pcs. 130.00

CAMEO or Ballerina or Dancing Girl (Process-etched)

Bowl, sauce, 4¼" d., clear 6.50
Bowl, cream soup, 4¾" d., green..........98.00
Bowl, cereal, 5½" d., clear 6.50
Bowl, cereal, 5½" d., green...................27.00
Bowl, cereal, 5½" d., yellow...................29.00
Bowl, salad, 7¼" d., green....................54.00
Bowl, large berry, 8¼" d., green 35.00
Bowl, soup w/flange rim, 9" d., green ...47.00
Bowl, 10" oval vegetable, green 22.50
Bowl, 10" oval vegetable, yellow 37.00
Butter dish, cov., green.......................175.00

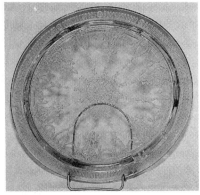

Cameo Footed Cake Plate

Cake plate, three-footed, green,10" d.
  (ILLUS.) 19.00
Candlesticks, green, 4" h., pr..............100.00
Candy jar, cov., green, 4" h. 58.00
Candy jar, cov., yellow, 4" h. 64.00
Candy jar, cov., green, 6½" h. 160.00
Compote, mayonnaise, 5" d., 4" h.,
  cone-shaped, green.........................28.00
Console bowl, three-footed, green,
  11" d..63.00
Console bowl, three-footed, pink,
  11" d..46.00
Console bowl, three-footed, yellow,
  11" d..75.00
Cookie jar, cov., green..........................44.00
Creamer, green, 3¼" h. 20.00
Creamer, yellow, 3¼" h. 16.00
Creamer, green, 4¼" h. 21.00
Creamer, pink, 4¼" h. 65.00
Cup, clear 5.50
Cup, green...13.50
Cup, yellow..7.50
Decanter w/stopper, green, 10" h. 135.00
Decanter w/stopper, green frosted,
  10" h..35.00
Domino tray, clear, 7" d. 85.00
Domino tray, green, 7" d.......................145.00

Goblet, wine, green, 4" h. 59.00
Goblet, water, green, 6" h......................51.00
Goblet, water, pink, 6" h. 167.00
Ice bowl, tab handles, green, 5½" d.,
  3½" h...165.00
Jam jar, cov., closed handles, green,
  2"...155.00
Pitcher, syrup or milk, 5¾" h., 20 oz.,
  green..200.00
Pitcher, juice, 6" h., 36 oz., green........48.00
Pitcher, water, 8½" h., 56 oz., jug-
  type, green..50.00
Plate, sherbet (or ringless saucer),
  6" d., clear...2.00
Plate, sherbet (or ringless saucer),
  6" d., green or yellow 3.50
Plate, salad, 7" d., clear........................4.00
Plate, luncheon, 8" d., green or
  yellow...10.50
Plate, 8½" sq., green 37.00
Plate, dinner, 9½" d., green 15.50
Plate, dinner, 9½" d., yellow 7.50
Plate, sandwich, 10" d., green..............14.00
Plate, sandwich, 10" d., pink.................57.00
Plate, dinner, 10½" d., trimmed,
  green..12.50
Plate, 10½" d., closed handles,
  green..14.50
Plate, 10½" d., closed handles,
  yellow...24.00
Plate, grill, 10½" d., green 9.00
Plate, grill, 10½" d., yellow.....................6.50
Plate, grill, 10½" d., closed handles,
  green..78.00
Plate, grill, 10½" d., closed handles,
  yellow...6.50
Platter, 10½" oval, green 18.00
Platter, 10½" oval, yellow 36.00
Platter, 12", closed handles, green.......21.00
Platter, 12", closed handles,yellow 36.00
Relish, footed, three-part, green, 7½"...25.00
Salt & pepper shakers, green, pr..........64.00
Salt & pepper shakers, pink, pr. 950.00
Saucer w/cup ring, green....................155.00
Sherbet, green, 3⅛" h..........................13.00
Sherbet, pink, 3⅛" h.............................83.00
Sherbet, yellow, 3⅛" h 35.00
Sherbet, thin, high stem, green,
  4⅞" h..26.00
Sherbet, thin, high stem, yellow,
  4 ⅞" h...30.00
Sugar bowl, open, green, 3¼" h. 15.50
Sugar bowl, open, yellow, 3¼" h. 13.00
Sugar bowl, open, green, 4¼" h. 20.00
Sugar bowl, open, pink, 4¼" h..............67.50
Tumbler, juice, footed, green, 3 oz. 61.00
Tumbler, juice, green, 3¾" h.,5 oz........25.00
Tumbler, juice, pink, 3¾" h., 5 oz. 185.00
Tumbler, water, clear, 4" h., 9 oz.........10.00
Tumbler, water, green, 4" h., 9 oz. 25.00
Tumbler, water, pink, 4" h., 9 oz. 95.00
Tumbler, footed, green, 5" h., 9 oz. 25.00
Tumbler, footed, yellow, 5" h., 9 oz. 14.50

Tumbler, green, 4¾" h., 10 oz. 21.50
Tumbler, yellow, 4¾" h., 10 oz. 83.00
Tumbler, green, 5" h., 11 oz. 27.50
Tumbler, yellow, 5" h., 11 oz. 58.00
Tumbler, footed, green, 5¾" h.,
    11 oz. 56.00
Tumbler, green, 5¼" h., 15 oz. 46.00
Vase, 5¾" h., green...........................160.00
Vase, 8" h., green 27.50
Water bottle, dark green "White
    House Vinegar" base, 8½" h. 18.50

CHERRY BLOSSOM (Process-etched)

Cherry Blossom Pattern

Bowl, berry, 4¾" d., Delphite or pink 13.50
Bowl, berry, 4¾" d., green 15.50
Bowl, cereal, 5¾"d., green 30.00
Bowl, cereal, 5¾" d., pink 31.00
Bowl, soup, 7¾" d., green 54.00
Bowl, soup, 7¾" d., pink 57.00
Bowl, berry, 8½" d., Delphite 35.50
Bowl, berry, 8½" d., green 40.00
Bowl, berry, 8½" d., pink 41.00
Bowl, 9" d., two-handled, Delphite........30.00
Bowl, 9" d., two-handled, green 27.50
Bowl, 9" d., two-handled, pink 26.00
Bowl, 9" oval vegetable, Delphite 38.00
Bowl, 9" oval vegetable, green 35.00
Bowl, 9" oval vegetable, pink 30.00
Bowl, fruit, 10½" d., three-footed,
    green or pink 72.00
Butter dish, cov., green 79.00
Butter dish, cov., pink 67.00
Cake plate, three-footed, green,
    10¼" d. 22.50
Cake plate, three-footed, pink,
    10¼" d. 25.00
Coaster, green 11.50
Coaster, pink 17.50
Creamer, Delphite or pink 17.50
Creamer, green 16.50
Cup, Delphite 18.00
Cup, green 17.00
Cup, pink 15.00
Mug, green, 7 oz. 195.00
Mug, pink, 7 oz. 180.00

Pitcher, 6¾" h., 36 oz., overall patt.,
    Delphite 77.00
Pitcher, 6¾" h., 36 oz., overall patt.,
    green 56.00
Pitcher, 6¾" h., 36 oz., overall patt.,
    pink 54.00
Pitcher, 8" h., 36 oz., footed, cone-
    shaped, patt. top, Delphite 66.00
Pitcher, 8" h., 36 oz., footed, cone-
    shaped, patt. top, green 52.00
Pitcher, 8" h., 36 oz., footed, cone-
    shaped, patt. top, pink 48.50
Pitcher, 8" h., 42 oz., patt. top, green
    (ILLUS.) 51.00
Pitcher, 8" h., 42 oz., patt. top,pink 51.00
Plate, sherbet, 6" d., Delphite 8.50
Plate, sherbet, 6" d., green 6.00
Plate, sherbet, 6" d., pink 7.00
Plate, salad, 7" d., green or pink 18.00
Plate, dinner, 9" d., Delphite 17.50
Plate, dinner, 9" d., green or pink 20.00
Plate, grill, 9" d., green 21.00
Plate, grill, 9" d., pink...........................22.00
Platter, 11" oval, green or pink 31.00
Platter, 13" oval, green 51.00
Platter, 13" oval, pink 49.00
Platter, 13" oval, divided, green 52.00
Platter, 13" oval, divided, pink 58.00
Salt & pepper shakers, green, pr. ...1,085.00
Sandwich tray, handled, Delphite or
    green, 10½" d. 21.00
Sandwich tray, handled, pink,10½"d. ..19.50
Saucer, Delphite or green 4.00
Saucer, pink 5.50
Sherbet, Delphite 12.00
Sherbet, green or pink 15.00
Sugar bowl, cov., clear 15.00
Sugar bowl, cov., Delphite 35.00
Sugar bowl, cov., green 32.00
Sugar bowl, cov., pink 27.50
Sugar bowl, open, Delphite 17.50
Sugar bowl, open, green or pink 13.00
Tumbler, patt. top, green, 3½" h.,4 oz.
    (ILLUS. right) 21.50
Tumbler, patt. top, pink, 3½" h.,
    4 oz. 16.50
Tumbler, juice, footed, overall patt.,
    Delphite, 3¾" h., 4 oz. 18.00
Tumbler, juice, footed, overall patt.,
    green or pink, 3¾" h., 4 oz. 16.00
Tumbler, footed, overall patt.,
    Delphite, 4½" h., 8 oz. 20.00
Tumbler, footed, overall patt., green,
    4½" h., 8 oz. 28.50
Tumbler, footed, overall patt., pink,
    4½" h., 8 oz. 26.00
Tumbler, patt. top, green, 4¼" h.,
    9 oz. (ILLUS. left)............................20.00
Tumbler, patt. top, pink, 4¼" h., 9 oz....17.50
Tumbler, footed, overall patt., Delphite,
    4½" h., 9 oz......................................19.00
Tumbler, footed, overall patt., green,
    4½" h., 9 oz.......................................29.00

Tumbler, footed, overall patt., pink,
4½" h., 9 oz. 28.00
Tumbler, patt. top, green, 5'" h.,
12 oz. 65.00
Tumbler, patt. top, pink, 5" h., 12 oz......55.00
Water set: pitcher & 6 tumblers;
green, 7 pcs. 165.00

JUNIOR SET:
Creamer, Delphite 36.00
Creamer, pink 38.00
Cup, pink 30.00
Cup & saucer, Delphite.......................37.00
Plate, 6" d., Delphite 10.50
Plate, 6" d., pink....................................7.50
Saucer, pink..4.00
Sugar bowl, Delphite or pink................35.00
14 pc. set, Delphite............................260.00
14 pc. set, pink 270.00

CLOVERLEAF (Process-etched)

Cloverleaf Sugar Bowl

Ashtray w/match holder in center,
black, 4" d. 64.00
Ashtray w/match holder in center,
black, 5¾" d. 68.00
Bowl, dessert, 4" d., green....................17.50
Bowl, dessert, 4" d., pink 12.50
Bowl, cereal, 5" d., green.....................23.00
Bowl, cereal, 5" d., yellow.....................25.00
Bowl, salad, 7" d., deep, green............36.50
Bowl, salad, 7" d., deep, yellow 47.00
Bowl, 8" d., green 47.00
Candy dish, cov., green.......................45.00
Creamer, footed, black, 3⅝" h. 16.00
Creamer, footed, green, 3⅝" h. 8.50
Creamer, footed, yellow, 3⅝" h. 14.50
Cup, black..13.00
Cup, green or pink 7.00
Cup, yellow...9.00
Plate, sherbet, 6" d., black...................30.00
Plate, sherbet, 6" d., green or yellow......5.50
Plate, luncheon, 8" d., black 16.50
Plate, luncheon, 8" d., clear 4.00
Plate, luncheon, 8" d., green or pink.......6.50
Plate, luncheon, 8" d., yellow...............11.50
Plate, grill, 10¼" d., green 21.50
Salt & pepper shakers, black, pr...........75.00
Salt & pepper shakers, green, pr..........29.00
Salt & pepper shakers, yellow, pr. 86.00
Saucer, black, pink or yellow.................4.50
Saucer, green...3.00

Sherbet, footed, black, 3" h. 16.50
Sherbet, footed, clear, 3" h. 3.00
Sherbet, footed, green or pink, 3" h........5.50
Sherbet, footed, yellow, 3" h.................10.00
Sugar bowl, open, footed, black or
yellow, 3⅝" h....................................14.50
Sugar bowl, open, footed, green,
3⅝" h. (ILLUS.) 8.00
Tumbler, green, 4" h., 9 oz. 37.50
Tumbler, flared, green, 3¾" h., 10 oz. ..32.50
Tumbler, flared, pink, 3¾" h., 10 oz......20.50
Tumbler, footed, green, 5¾" h., 10 oz. .21.00
Tumbler, footed, yellow, 5¾" h.,
10 oz. 27.00

COLONIAL or Knife & Fork, Hocking Glass Co., 1934-36 (Press-mold)

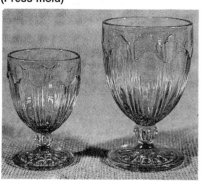

Colonial Cordial & Wine Goblets

Bowl, berry, 3¾" d., pink......................40.00
Bowl, berry, 4½" d., clear......................5.00
Bowl, berry, 4½" d., green 13.50
Bowl, berry, 4½" d., pink......................11.50
Bowl, cream soup, 4½" d., clear 35.00
Bowl, cream soup, 4½" d., green..........54.00
Bowl, cream soup, 4½" d., pink 48.00
Bowl, cereal, 5½" d., green...................66.00
Bowl, soup, 7" d., green.......................48.50
Bowl, soup, 7" d., pink 51.50
Bowl, 9" d., clear...................................13.50
Bowl, 9" d., green or pink......................25.00
Bowl, 10" oval vegetable, clear............17.00
Bowl, 10" oval vegetable, green 31.50
Bowl, 10" oval vegetable, pink.............26.00
Butter dish, cov., clear 34.00
Butter dish, cov., green........................52.50
Celery or spooner, clear 61.00
Celery or spooner, green.....................115.00
Celery or spooner, pink 104.50
Creamer or milk pitcher, clear, 5" h.,
16 oz. 14.00
Creamer or milk pitcher, green, 5" h.,
16 oz. 20.50
Cup, clear 7.00
Cup green...10.00
Cup, pink 10.50
Cup & saucer, clear................................9.00
Cup & saucer, milk white 9.50
Goblet, cordial, clear, 3¾" h., 1 oz........15.00

Goblet, cordial, green, 3¾" h., 1 oz.
(ILLUS. left)...26.50
Goblet, wine, clear, 4½" h., 2½ oz........15.50
Goblet, wine, green, 4½" h., 2½ oz.
(ILLUS. right)......................................23.50
Goblet, cocktail, clear, 4" h., 3 oz. 12.00
Goblet, cocktail, green, 4" h., 3 oz........22.50
Goblet, claret, clear, 5¼" h., 4 oz. 14.50
Goblet, claret, green, 5¼" h., 4 oz........24.00
Goblet, clear, 5¾" h., 8½ oz. 14.50
Goblet, green, 5¾" h., 8½ oz...............25.50
Mug, green, 4½" h., 12 oz. 750.00
Pitcher, ice lip or plain, 7" h., 54 oz.,
clear 23.50
Pitcher, ice lip or plain, 7" h., 54 oz.,
green..44.00
Pitcher, ice lip or plain, 7" h., 54 oz.,
pink 49.50
Pitcher, ice lip or plain, 7¾" h., 68 oz.,
clear 122.50

Colonial Pitcher

Pitcher, ice lip or plain, 7¾" h., 68 oz.,
green (ILLUS. w/ice lip) 57.50
Pitcher, ice lip or plain, 7¾" h., 68 oz.,
pink 53.00
Plate, sherbet, 6" d., clear 3.50
Plate, sherbet, 6" d., green or pink 5.00
Plate, luncheon, 8½" d., clear.................4.00
Plate, luncheon, 8½" d., green 8.00
Plate, luncheon, 8½" d., pink 9.00
Plate, dinner, 10" d., clear 21.50
Plate, dinner, 10" d., green...................50.50
Plate, dinner, 10" d., pink......................45.00
Plate, grill, 10" d., clear.........................12.00
Plate, grill, 10" d., green 24.50
Plate, grill, 10" d., pink..........................23.00
Platter, 12" oval, clear............................16.50
Platter, 12" oval, green 22.50
Platter, 12" oval, pink.............................27.00
Salt & pepper shakers, clear, pr. 46.00
Salt & pepper shakers, pink, pr. 112.00
Saucer, green..5.50
Saucer, pink...6.00
Sherbet, pink, 3" h. 18.50
Sherbet, clear, 3⅜" h.............................5.50
Sherbet, green, 3⅜" h............................12.50
Sherbet, pink, 3⅜" h. 10.00

Sugar bowl, cov., clear 19.00
Sugar bowl, cov., green.........................30.50
Sugar bowl, cov., pink............................46.00
Tumbler, whiskey, clear, 2½" h.,
1½ oz..7.00
Tumbler, whiskey, green, 2½" h.,
1½ oz..12.00
Tumbler, whiskey, pink, 2½" h.,
1½ oz..10.50
Tumbler, cordial, footed, clear, 3¼" h.,
3 oz...11.00
Tumbler, cordial, footed, green,
3¼" h., 3 oz......................................22.50
Tumbler, cordial, footed, pink, 3¼" h.,
3 oz...15.00
Tumbler, juice, green, 3" h., 5 oz..........22.00
Tumbler, juice, pink, 3" h., 5 oz. 15.50
Tumbler, footed, clear, 4" h., 5 oz. 14.00
Tumbler, footed, green, 4" h., 5 oz. 34.50
Tumbler, footed, pink, 4" h., 5 oz. 23.50
Tumbler, water, clear, 4" h., 9 oz..........12.00
Tumbler, water, green, 4" h., 9 oz. 21.00
Tumbler, water, pink, 4" h., 9 oz. 18.50
Tumbler, footed, clear, 5¼" h.,
10 oz...22.50
Tumbler, footed, green, 5¼" h.,
10 oz...41.00
Tumbler, footed, pink, 5¼" h.,
10 oz...38.00
Tumbler, pink, 5⅛" h., 11 oz.................31.50
Tumbler, iced tea, green, 12 oz............32.00
Tumbler, iced tea, pink, 12 oz. 45.00
Tumbler, lemonade, green, 15 oz........72.50
Tumbler, lemonade, pink, 15 oz. 60.00

**COLUMBIA, Federal Glass Co.,
1938-42 (Press-mold)**
Bowl, cereal, 5" d., clear.......................13.00
Bowl, soup, 8" d., clear.........................16.00
Bowl, salad, 8½" d., clear.....................17.00
Bowl, 10½" d., ruffled rim, clear............18.00
Butter dish, cov., clear 16.50
Cup & saucer, clear...............................10.00
Plate, bread & butter, 6" d., clear............3.00
Plate, bread & butter, 6" d., pink...........14.50
Plate, luncheon, 9½" d., clear.................8.00
Plate, luncheon, 9½" d., pink 33.00
Plate, chop, 11" d., clear.......................10.50
Saucer, pink...12.50
Snack plate, handled, clear 29.00
Snack plate, handled, w/cup, clear.......38.50
Tumbler, juice, 2⅞" h., 4 oz., clear 10.00
Tumbler, water, clear, 9 oz. 25.00

**CUBE or Cubist, Jeannette Glass Co.,
1929-33 (Press-mold)**
Bowl, dessert, 4½" d., clear.....................3.50
Bowl, dessert, 4½" d., green....................6.50
Bowl, dessert, 4½" d., pink 5.00
Bowl, 4½" d., deep, clear.........................3.50
Bowl, 4½" d., deep, green 4.50
Bowl, 4½" d., deep, pink..........................6.50
Bowl, salad, 6½" d., clear........................5.00

Bowl, salad, 6½" d., green....................11.50
Bowl, salad, 6½" d., pink 9.50
Bowl, salad, 6½" d., ultramarine...........55.00
Butter dish, cov., green.........................50.00
Butter dish, cov., pink 51.50
Candy jar, cov., green, 6½" h. 25.50
Candy jar, cov., pink, 6½" h..................23.50
Coaster, green, 3¼" d.............................6.50
Coaster, pink, 3¼" d. 5.50
Creamer, clear, 2⅝" h...........................1.00

Cube Creamer

Creamer, pink, 2⅝" h. (ILLUS.) 3.50
Creamer, green, 3½" h. 8.00
Creamer, pink, 3½" h..............................5.50
Cup & saucer, green.............................17.00
Cup & saucer, pink 9.50
Pitcher, 8¾" h., 45 oz., green 211.00
Pitcher, 8¾" h., 45 oz., pink.:..............139.00
Plate, sherbet, 6" d., clear 1.00
Plate, sherbet, 6" d., green or pink 3.00
Plate, luncheon, 8" d., green or pink 5.50
Powder jar, cov., three-footed, green ...18.50
Powder jar, cov., three-footed, pink......21.50
Salt & pepper shakers, green or pink,
  pr..31.00
Sherbet, footed, green............................7.00
Sherbet, footed, pink 5.50
Sugar bowl, cov., green, 3" h................18.50
Sugar bowl, cov., pink, 3" h...................16.00
Sugar bowl, open, clear, 2⅜" h..............1.00
Sugar bowl, open, green, 2⅜" h 4.00

Cube Sugar Bowl

Sugar bowl, open, pink, 2⅜" h.
  (ILLUS.) 3.00
Tray for 3½" h. creamer & open sugar
  bowl, clear, 7½" 4.00
Tumbler, green, 4" h., 9 oz. 59.50
Tumbler, pink, 4" h., 9 oz......................45.00

**DAISY or Number 620, Indiana Glass
Co., amber, 1940; clear, 1933 & red, late
1930s (Press-mold)**

Daisy Vegetable Bowl

Bowl, berry, 4½" d., amber 7.50
Bowl, berry, 4½" d., clear........................5.00
Bowl, cream soup, 4½" d., amber..........9.50
Bowl, cream soup, 4½" d., clear 6.50
Bowl, cereal, 6" d., amber....................25.00
Bowl, cereal, 6" d., clear........................9.00
Bowl, berry, 7⅜" d., amber 15.00
Bowl, berry, 7⅜" d., clear......................6.00
Bowl, berry, 9⅜" d., amber 25.00
Bowl, 10" oval vegetable, amber
  (ILLUS.) 14.00
Creamer, footed, amber 6.50
Creamer, footed, clear............................4.50
Cup, amber...5.50
Cup & saucer, clear 3.50
Plate, sherbet, 6" d., amber 2.50
Plate, salad, 7⅜" d., amber 7.50
Plate, salad, 7⅜" d., clear......................4.50
Plate, luncheon, 8⅜" d., amber 5.50
Plate, luncheon, 8⅜" d., clear................3.50
Plate, dinner, 9⅜" d., amber 7.50
Plate, dinner, 9⅜" d., clear 5.00
Plate, grill, 10⅜" d., amber 11.00
Plate, grill, 10⅜" d., clear.......................6.50
Plate, 11½" d., amber (cake or
  sandwich)...12.50
Plate, 11½" d., clear (cake or
  sandwich)...11.00
Platter, 10¾" l., amber 13.00
Relish dish, three-part, amber, 8⅜"......25.00
Relish dish, three-part, clear, 8⅜" 8.00
Saucer, amber 2.00
Sherbet, footed, amber...........................7.00
Sherbet, footed, clear 4.00
Sugar bowl, open, footed, amber 7.00
Sugar bowl, open, footed, clear..............4.00
Tumbler, footed, amber, 9 oz. 17.50
Tumbler, footed, clear, 9 oz...................8.00
Tumbler, footed, amber, 12 oz. 35.50
Tumbler, footed, clear, 12 oz...............19.00

**DIAMOND QUILTED or Flat Diamond,
Imperial Glass Co., late 1920s -
early 1930s (Press-mold)**

Bowl, cream soup, 4¾" d., black 17.50

Bowl, cream soup, 4¾" d., blue 15.00
Bowl, cream soup, 4¾" d., green or
    pink 8.50
Bowl, 5½" d., single handle, black........15.00
Bowl, 5½" d., single handle, pink............7.00
Bowl, 7" d., crimped rim, black 21.50
Bowl, 7" d., crimped rim, blue...............15.50
Bowl, 7" d., crimped rim, green...............9.50
Bowl, 7" d., crimped rim, pink 8.00
Bowl, 7" d., crimped rim, red.................18.00
Candlesticks, flat or domed base,
    black, pr. 35.00
Candlesticks, flat or domed base,
    green, pr. 23.50
Candlesticks, flat or domed base,
    pink, pr. 19.00
Candy jar, cov., footed, pink 85.00
Compote, open, 6" h., 7¼" d., green 40.00
Console bowl, rolled edge, pink...........33.00
Creamer, black 16.50
Creamer, blue.......................................13.50
Creamer, green 7.50
Creamer, pink 8.50
Cup & saucer, amber..............................7.50
Cup & saucer, green.............................10.00
Cup & saucer, pink 12.00
Ice bucket, black..................................72.50
Mayonnaise dish, three-footed
    w/plate, green, 2 pcs..........................27.00
Pitcher, 64 oz., green 42.00
Plate, sherbet, 6" d., blue 4.50
Plate, sherbet, 6" d., green or pink 3.50
Plate, salad, 7" d., green 5.00
Plate, luncheon, 8" d., black 12.00
Plate, luncheon, 8" d., blue...................13.50
Plate, luncheon, 8" d., green or pink 5.50
Plate, sandwich, 14" d., pink.................18.00
Sherbet, black or blue...........................10.50
Sherbet, green..5.00
Sherbet, pink 6.50
Sugar bowl, open, amber 8.00
Sugar bowl, open, black or blue 14.50
Sugar bowl, open, green 7.50
Sugar bowl, open, pink 8.50
Tumbler, whiskey, green, 1½ oz..............6.50
Tumbler, iced tea, green, 12 oz..............9.00

DIANA, Federal Glass Co., 1937-41 (Press-mold)

Bowl, cereal, 5" d., amber.....................11.00
Bowl, cereal, 5" d., clear 3.50
Bowl, cereal, 5" d., pink..........................7.50
Bowl, cream soup, 5½" d., amber.........14.00
Bowl, cream soup, 5½" d., clear or
    pink 4.00
Bowl, salad, 9" d., amber.....................11.00
Bowl, salad, 9" d., clear 5.00
Bowl, salad, 9" d., pink 19.00
Bowl, 12" d., scalloped rim, clear...........7.50
Bowl, 12" d., scalloped rim, pink...........15.00
Candy jar, cov., round, amber or pink ..31.00
Candy jar, cov., round, clear.................13.00
Coaster, amber, 3½" d..........................13.00

Coaster, clear, 3½" d.............................4.50
Coaster, pink, 3½" d. 6.50
Console bowl, amber, 11" d....................12.00
Console bowl, clear, 11" d. 6.00
Console bowl, pink, 11" d. 8.00
Creamer, oval, amber.............................8.00
Creamer, oval, clear 3.00

Diana Demitasse Cup & Saucer

Cup & saucer, demitasse, clear
    (ILLUS.) 10.00
Cup & saucer, demitasse, pink.............40.00
Cup & saucer, amber..............................8.00
Cup & saucer, clear 4.50
Cup & saucer, pink 15.00
Plate, bread & butter, 6" d., amber
    or clear...1.50
Plate, bread & butter, 6" d., pink............3.00
Plate, dinner, 9½" d., amber 7.50
Plate, dinner, 9½" d., clear 5.00
Plate, dinner, 9½" d., pink....................13.00
Plate, sandwich, 11¾" d., amber..........10.50
Plate, sandwich, 11¾" d., clear 5.00
Plate, sandwich, 11¾" d., pink..............18.00
Platter, 12" oval, amber 11.00
Platter, 12" oval, clear............................4.50
Salt & pepper shakers, amber, pr.........89.00
Salt & pepper shakers, clear, pr. 22.00
Salt & pepper shakers, pink, pr. 73.00
Sherbet, amber or pink.........................10.00
Sugar bowl, open, oval, amber or
    pink 7.50
Sugar bowl, open, oval, clear 2.00
Tumbler, amber, 4⅛" h., 9 oz. 22.00
Tumbler, clear, 4⅛" h., 9 oz..................25.00
Junior set: 6 cups, saucers & plates
    w/round rack; clear, set.....................76.50
Child's cup, clear 4.50
Child's cup & saucer, clear 11.00

DOGWOOD or Apple Blossom or Wild Rose, MacBeth-Evans, 1929-32 (Process-etched)

Bowl, cereal, 5½" d., green or pink.......23.50
Bowl, berry, 8½" d., Cremax.................31.00
Bowl, berry, 8½" d., green 85.00
Bowl, berry, 8½" d., Monax...................44.00
Bowl, berry, 8½" d., pink......................53.50
Bowl, fruit, 10½" d., green 133.00

Bowl, fruit, 10½" d., pink 370.00
Cake plate, heavy solid foot, green,
   13" d..77.50
Creamer, thin, green, 2½" h. 37.00
Creamer, thin, footed, pink, 2¼" h. 17.50
Creamer, thick, footed, pink, 3¼" h. ..18.00
Cup & saucer, green............................30.50
Cup & saucer, Monax 39.00

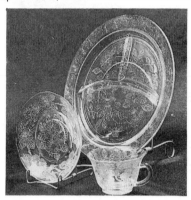

Dogwood Pattern

Cup & saucer, pink (ILLUS.) 19.00
Pitcher, 8" h., 80 oz., American
   Sweetheart style, pink......................565.00
Pitcher, 8" h., 80 oz., decorated,
   green...415.00
Pitcher, 8" h., 80 oz., decorated,
   pink 165.00
Plate, bread & butter, 6" d., green 4.50
Plate, bread & butter, 6" d., pink.............7.00
Plate, luncheon, 8" d., clear....................4.00
Plate, luncheon, 8" d., green 6.50
Plate, luncheon, 8" d., pink 7.50
Plate, dinner, 9¼" d., pink.....................28.50
Plate, grill, 10½" d., overall patt. or
   border design only, green 15.00
Plate, grill, 10½" d., border design,
   pink 16.00
Plate, grill, 10½" d., overall patt., pink
   (ILLUS.) 17.50
Plate, salver, 12" d., Monax..................20.50
Plate, salver, 12" d., pink......................31.00
Platter, 12" oval, pink...........................400.00
Sherbet, low foot, green 40.00
Sherbet, low foot, pink 27.00
Sugar bowl, open, thin, green,
   2½" h..40.00
Sugar bowl, open, thin, pink, 2½" h. 15.00
Sugar bowl, open, thick, footed, pink,
   3¼" h...15.00
Tumbler, decorated, green, 4" h.,
   10 oz. 75.00
Tumbler, decorated, pink, 4" h.,
   10 oz. 32.50
Tumbler, decorated, green, 4¾" h.,
   11 oz. 147.50
Tumbler, decorated, pink, 4¾" h.,
   11 oz. 46.00

Tumbler, decorated, pink, 5" h.,
   12 oz. 54.50
Tumbler, molded band, pink 15.00
Water set: decorated pitcher & 6
   decorated tumblers; pink, 7 pcs.......298.00

**DORIC, Jeannette Glass Co.,
1935-38 (Press-mold)**

Doric Salt & Pepper Shakers

Bowl, berry, 4½" d., green or pink 7.00
Bowl, cereal, 5½" d., green....................55.00
Bowl, cereal, 5½" d., pink 44.00
Bowl, large berry, 8¼" d., green 17.50
Bowl, large berry, 8¼" d., pink..............16.50
Bowl, 9" d., two-handled, green or
   pink 13.50
Bowl, 9" oval vegetable, green 27.00
Bowl, 9" oval vegetable, pink................24.50
Butter dish, cov., green..........................75.00
Butter dish, cov., pink 58.00
Cake plate, three-footed, green,
   10" d...25.50
Cake plate, three-footed, pink, 10" d. ...20.50
Candy dish, three-section, Delphite or
   green, 6" 10.50
Candy dish, three-section, pink, 6".........9.00
Candy jar, cov., green, 8" h. 37.50
Candy jar, cov., pink, 8" h....................29.00
Coaster, green or pink, 3" d.................20.00
Creamer, green, 4" h. 16.50
Creamer, pink, 4" h...............................11.50
Cup, green..8.50
Cup, pink 10.00
Pitcher, 6" h., 36 oz., green or pink 32.00
Pitcher, 7½" h., 48 oz., footed, pink....425.00
Plate, sherbet, 6" d., green or pink 3.50
Plate, salad, 7" d., green 14.00
Plate, salad, 7" d., pink.........................17.50
Plate, dinner, 9" d., green.....................14.50
Plate, dinner, 9" d., pink.......................13.00
Plate, grill, 9" d., green 15.00
Plate, grill, 9" d., pink 17.00
Platter, 12" oval, green 21.50
Platter, 12" oval, pink............................20.00
Relish tray, green, 4 x 4" 11.50
Relish tray, pink, 4 x 4"..........................12.50
Relish tray, green, 4 x 8" 14.00
Relish tray, pink, 4 x 8"..........................11.50

Relish or serving tray, green, 8 x 8"......15.00
Relish or serving tray, pink, 8 x 8" 19.00
Relish, square inserts in metal holder,
  pink 48.00
Salt & pepper shakers, green, pr.
  (ILLUS.) 35.50
Salt & pepper shakers, pink, pr. 32.00
Sandwich tray, handled, green or
  pink, 10" d. 13.00
Saucer, green 4.00
Saucer, pink 3.50
Sherbet, footed, Delphite 5.00
Sherbet, footed, green 12.50
Sherbet, footed, pink 11.00
Sugar bowl, cov., green 28.50

Doric Sugar Bowl

Sugar bowl, cov., pink (ILLUS.) 23.00
Tumbler, green, 4½" h., 9 oz. 85.50
Tumbler, pink, 4½" h., 9 oz. 59.50
Tumbler, footed, green, 4" h., 10 oz. 52.50
Tumbler, footed, pink, 4" h., 10 oz. 48.00
Tumbler, footed, green, 5" h., 12 oz. 94.00
Tumbler, footed, pink, 5" h., 12 oz. 69.00

**DORIC & PANSY, Jeannette Glass Co.,
1937-38 (Press-mold)**

Doric & Pansy Cup & Saucer

Bowl, berry, 4½" d., clear or pink 8.00
Bowl, berry, 4½" d., ultramarine 17.00
Bowl, large berry, 8" d., clear 25.00
Bowl, large berry, 8" d., pink 18.00

Bowl, large berry, 8" d., ultramarine 68.00
Bowl, 9" d., handled, ultramarine 35.00
Butter dish, cov., ultramarine 470.00
Creamer, pink 32.00
Creamer, ultramarine 160.00
Cup & saucer, clear 14.00
Cup & saucer, ultramarine (ILLUS.) 24.50
Plate, sherbet, 6" d., clear 8.00
Plate, sherbet, 6" d., pink......................6.50
Plate, sherbet, 6" d., ultramarine 10.00
Plate, salad, 7" d., ultramarine.............30.50
Plate, dinner, 9" d., ultramarine 27.50
Salt & pepper shakers, ultramarine,
  pr...385.00
Sugar bowl, open, pink 32.00
Sugar bowl, open, ultramarine...........138.00
Tray, handled, ultramarine, 10" 24.00
Tumbler, ultramarine, 4½" h., 9 oz. 74.00

PRETTY POLLY PARTY DISHES
Creamer, pink 28.50
Creamer, ultramarine...........................33.50
Cup, ultramarine 29.50
Cup & saucer, pink 33.50
Cup & saucer, ultramarine....................46.00
Plate, pink..6.50
Plate, ultramarine 12.00
Saucer, pink...5.50
Saucer, ultramarine 6.50
Sugar bowl, pink 27.50
Sugar bowl, ultramarine.......................37.00
14 piece set, pink...............................200.00
14 piece set, ultramarine 280.00

**ENGLISH HOBNAIL, Westmoreland
Glass Co., 1920s - '40s (Handmade -
not true Depression)**

English Hobnail Salt Dip

Ashtray, clear, various shapes 12.00
Basket, handled, clear, 5" h.................25.00
Bowl, nappy, 4½" d., clear 7.00
Bowl, nappy, 4½" d., green....................9.50
Bowl, nappy, 4½" d., ice blue 43.00
Bowl, nappy, 4½" sq., clear 5.00
Bowl, nappy, 4½" sq., green...................8.00
Bowl, cream soup, 4¾" d., clear............6.50
Bowl, cream soup, 4¾" d., green........20.00
Bowl, 6" d., amber or clear 9.00
Bowl, grapefruit, 6½" d., clear..............14.50
Bowl, fruit, 8" d., two-handled, footed,
  cobalt blue 120.00

Bowl, fruit, 8" d., two-handled, footed,
  green...40.00
Bowl, nappy, 8" d., amber.....................17.00
Bowl, nappy, 8" d., clear.....................11.50
Bowl, nappy, 11" d., blue.....................38.00
Bowl, 12" d., flared, green...................40.00
Candlesticks, amber, 3½" h., pr............19.00
Candlesticks, blue, 3½" h., pr..............33.50
Candlesticks, clear, 3½" h., pr.............14.50
Candlesticks, pink, 3½" h., pr..............21.00
Candlesticks, clear, 8½" h., pr.............58.00
Candlesticks, green, 8½" h., pr............67.50
Candlesticks, pink, 8½" h., pr. 40.00
Candlesticks, turquoise, 8½" h., pr.......61.00
Candy dish, cov., cone-shaped,
  amber, ½ lb.....................................40.00
Candy dish, cov., cone-shaped,
  clear, ½ lb. 26.00
Candy dish, cov., cone-shaped,
  green, ½ lb.......................................61.00
Candy dish, cov., urn-shaped, green,
  15" h...300.00
Celery tray, clear, 12" l. 17.00
Cigarette box, cov., clear.....................35.50
Cologne bottle, clear or green 28.00
Cologne bottle, turquoise.....................36.00
Cologne bottles w/stoppers, blue, pr. ...55.00
Cologne bottles w/stoppers, cobalt
  blue, pr..91.50
Creamer, flat or footed, clear...............11.00
Cup & saucer, demitasse, clear...........25.50
Cup & saucer, clear..............................8.00
Cup & saucer, turquoise.....................23.00
Dish, cov., three-footed, amber 60.00
Dish, cov., three-footed, clear..............33.00
Dish, cov., three-footed, green 57.00
Egg cup, clear......................................17.00
Goblet, cordial, clear, 1 oz...................16.50
Goblet, wine, clear, 2 oz......................17.00
Goblet, cocktail, amber or pink, 3 oz. ...15.00
Goblet, cocktail, clear, 3 oz. 10.00
Goblet, cocktail, green, 3 oz. 16.00
Goblet, claret, clear, 5 oz......................7.00
Goblet, clear, 6¼ oz. 16.00
Goblet, green, 6¼ oz. 21.50
Goblet, pink, 6¼ oz..............................18.00
Goblet, turquoise, 6¼ oz. 44.00
Goblet, water, green, 8 oz. 22.00
Goblet, water, ice blue, 8 oz. 50.00
Hat, high, clear 15.00
Ice tub, clear.......................................65.00
Lamp, electric, clear, 6¼" h. 30.50
Lamp, electric, amber, 9¼" h...............71.00
Lamp, electric, blue, 9¼" h. 85.00
Lamp, electric, clear, 9¼" h. 27.00
Lamp, electric, pink, 9¼" h. 89.00
Marmalade jar, cov., clear 29.50
Marmalade jar, cov., green..................35.00
Marmalade jar, cov., pink 31.50
Oil bottle, clear, 2 oz............................17.50
Parfait, footed, round, clear 19.00
Pitcher, 23 oz., clear............................75.00
Pitcher, ½ gal., straight sides, clear....169.00

Pitcher, ½ gal., straight sides, green ..235.00
Plate, sherbet, 5½" or 6½" d., clear.......5.50
Plate, sherbet, 5½" or 6½" d., green 3.50
Plate, sherbet, 5½" or 6½" d., pink 2.50
Plate, luncheon, 8" round or
  square, amber...................................10.00
Plate, luncheon, 8" round or square,
  clear 6.50
Plate, luncheon, 8" round or square,
  green...9.00
Plate, luncheon, 8" round or square,
  ice blue 25.00
Plate, luncheon, 8" round or square,
  pink 8.00
Plate, luncheon, 8" round or square,
  turquoise...15.00
Plate, dinner, 10" d., clear 7.50
Puff box, cov., clear.............................27.50
Puff box, cov., green............................34.50
Relish dish, three-part, clear, 8" oval....29.00
Rose bowl, clear, 6"..............................21.00
Salt & pepper shakers, amber, pr.........72.50
Salt & pepper shakers, clear, pr. 47.00
Salt & pepper shakers, green, pr..........74.50
Salt & pepper shakers, turquoise,
  pr..110.00
Salt dip, footed, amber, 2" 13.00
Salt dip, footed, blue, 2" 10.50
Salt dip, footed, clear, 2".....................10.00
Salt dip, footed, cobalt blue, 2"............31.00
Salt dip, footed, green, 2" 14.50
Salt dip, footed, pink, 2" (ILLUS.) 15.00
Salt dip, footed, turquoise, 2" 16.50
Sherbet, footed, amber.........................12.50
Sherbet, footed, clear 9.00
Sherbet, footed, green..........................13.00
Sherbet, footed, ice blue......................23.00
Sugar bowl, open, footed or flat,
  clear 12.00
Sugar bowl, open, footed or flat,
  pink 19.50
Tumbler, whiskey, clear, 1½ oz..............8.00
Tumbler, whiskey, clear, 3 oz. 15.50
Tumbler, clear, 3¾" h., 5 oz.................10.00
Tumbler, footed, clear, 7 oz.................11.00
Tumbler, clear, 3¾" h., 9 oz.................13.50
Tumbler, footed, clear, 9 oz.................12.00
Tumbler, iced tea, clear, 4" h., 10 oz......8.50
Tumbler, iced tea, ice blue, 4" h.,
  10 oz. 48.00
Tumbler, iced tea, clear, 5" h.,
  12 oz. 13.50
Tumbler, footed, clear, 12½ oz.............15.00
Vase, 7¼" h., amber.............................85.00
Vase, 7¼" h., clear 42.50
Vase, 7¼" h., pink................................101.00

**FLORAL or Poinsettia, Jeannette
Glass Co., 1931-35 (Process etched)**
Bowl, berry, 4" d., green or pink 16.00
Bowl, salad, 7½" d., green....................20.00
Bowl, salad, 7½" d., pink 18.00

Butter dish, cov., green.........................84.50
Butter dish, cov., pink 86.50
Coaster, green, 3¼" d...........................9.00
Coaster, pink, 3¼" d. 14.00
Creamer, green 12.50
Creamer, pink 14.50
Cup, pink 10.50
Cup & saucer, green............................21.50
Flower frog for vase, green.............1,200.00
Pitcher, 5½" h., 24 oz., green 630.00

Floral Pitcher & Tumblers

Pitcher, 8" h., 32 oz., cone-shaped,
    green (ILLUS.) 33.50
Pitcher, 8" h., 32 oz., cone-shaped,
    pink 32.00
Pitcher, lemonade, 10¼" h., 48 oz.,
    green..230.00
Pitcher, lemonade, 10¼" h., 48 oz.,
    pink 285.00
Plate, sherbet, 6" d., green or pink 6.00
Plate, salad, 8" d., green or pink...........10.00
Plate, dinner, 9" d., green 16.50
Plate, dinner, 9" d., pink 15.50
Platter, 10¾" oval, green or pink 16.00
Platter, 11" oval, scalloped edge, pink..60.00
Salt & pepper shakers, footed, green,
    4" h., pr 50.00
Salt & pepper shakers, footed, pink,
    4" h., pr 44.00
Sherbet, green or pink 15.00
Sugar bowl, cov., green.........................26.50
Sugar bowl, cov., pink 20.00
Sugar bowl, open, green 10.00
Sugar bowl, open, pink..........................9.50
Tray, closed handles, green, 6" sq. 21.00
Tray, closed handles, pink, 6" sq..........17.50
Tumbler, juice, footed, green or pink,
    4" h., 5 oz. 18.50
Tumbler, water, footed, green, 4¾" h.,
    7 oz. (ILLUS.)....................................18.50
Tumbler, water, footed, pink, 4¾" h.,
    7 oz. 17.50
Tumbler, green, 4½" h., 9 oz. 170.00
Tumbler, lemonade, footed, green or
    pink, 5¼" h., 9 oz. 45.00
Vase, 6⅞" h., octagonal, clear............300.00

Vase, 6⅞" h., octagonal, green 505.00

(OLD) FLORENTINE or Poppy No. 1
Hazel Atlas Glass Co., 1932-35
(Process-etched)

Ashtray, clear, 5½" 18.00
Ashtray, green, 5½" 20.00
Ashtray, pink or yellow, 5½" 27.50
Bowl, berry, 5" d., clear or pink.............10.00
Bowl, berry, 5" d., cobalt blue or
    yellow...12.00
Bowl, berry, 5" d., green 11.00
Bowl, cereal, 6" d., clear or pink 20.00
Bowl, cereal, 6" d., yellow.....................35.00
Bowl, 8½" d., clear................................15.00
Bowl, 8½" d., green 25.00
Bowl, 8½" d., pink 31.00
Bowl, 8½" d., yellow...............................27.50
Bowl, cov. vegetable, 9½" oval, clear ...45.00
Bowl, cov. vegetable, 9½" oval, green..40.00
Bowl, cov. vegetable, 9½" oval, pink 60.00
Bowl, 9½" oval vegetable, green 22.50
Bowl, 9½" oval vegetable, pink.............26.00
Bowl, 9½" oval vegetable, yellow 27.50
Butter dish, cov., clear or green..........106.00
Butter dish, cov., pink 156.00
Butter dish, cov., yellow.......................146.00
Coaster-ashtray, yellow, 3¾" d.............26.00
Creamer, plain rim, clear 8.00
Creamer, plain rim, green 9.00
Creamer, plain rim, pink 15.50
Creamer, plain rim, yellow 11.50
Creamer, ruffled rim, clear....................30.00
Creamer, ruffled rim, cobalt blue 60.00
Creamer, ruffled rim, green 23.00
Creamer, ruffled rim, pink 26.00
Cup, clear 6.50
Cup, green...8.00
Cup & saucer, pink or yellow................13.50
Nut dish, handled, ruffled rim, clear or
    pink 15.00
Nut dish, handled, ruffled rim, cobalt
    blue 44.50
Nut dish, handled, ruffled rim, green 21.00
Pitcher, 6½" h., 36 oz., footed, clear.....37.50
Pitcher, 6½" h., 36 oz., footed, green ...39.00
Pitcher, 6½" h., 36 oz., footed, pink or
    yellow...43.00
Pitcher, 7½" h., 48 oz., clear.................59.00
Pitcher, 7½" h., 48 oz., green 75.00
Pitcher, 7½" h., 48 oz., pink...............100.00
Plate, sherbet, 6" d., clear 3.00
Plate, sherbet, 6" d., green 6.00
Plate, sherbet, 6" d., pink.......................5.00
Plate, salad, 8½" d., clear 6.50
Plate, salad, 8½" d., green 7.50
Plate, salad, 8½" d., pink 11.00
Plate, salad, 8½" d., yellow...................10.00
Plate, dinner, 10" d., clear 11.00
Plate, dinner, 10" d., green or yellow....15.00
Plate, dinner, 10" d., pink......................26.50
Plate, grill, 10" d., clear.........................9.50

Plate, grill, 10" d., green 10.50
Plate, grill, 10" d., pink...........................15.50
Plate, grill, 10" d., yellow.......................13.00
Platter, 11½" oval, green 15.50
Platter, 11½" oval, pink.........................19.50
Platter, 11½" oval, yellow 21.00
Saucer, clear or green...........................3.50
Salt & pepper shakers, footed, clear,
  pr..33.00
Salt & pepper shakers, footed, green,
  pr..34.50
Salt & pepper shakers, footed, pink,
  pr..46.00
Salt & pepper shakers, footed, yellow,
  pr..52.00
Sherbet, footed, clear or green, 3 oz. 8.50
Sherbet, footed, pink, 3 oz.....................9.00
Sherbet, footed, yellow, 3 oz. 10.00
Sugar bowl, cov., clear..........................19.50
Sugar bowl, cov., green or pink 25.50
Sugar bowl, cov., yellow 28.00
Sugar bowl, open, clear..........................8.00
Sugar bowl, open, green 9.00
Sugar bowl, open, pink..........................12.00
Sugar bowl, open, yellow.......................10.50
Sugar bowl, open, ruffled rim, clear 27.50
Sugar bowl, open, ruffled rim, cobalt
  blue 45.00
Sugar bowl, open, ruffled rim, green 30.00
Sugar bowl, open, ruffled rim, pink 28.00
Tumbler, footed, green, 3¼" h., 4 oz. 8.00
Tumbler, juice, footed, clear, 3¾" h.,
  5 oz. 11.50
Tumbler, juice, footed, green, 3¾" h.,
  5 oz. 13.50
Tumbler, juice, footed, pink or yellow,
  3¾" h., 5 oz.......................................19.00
Tumbler, ribbed, clear, 4" h., 9 oz.........12.00
Tumbler, ribbed, pink, 4" h., 9 oz..........15.00
Tumbler, water, footed, green, 4¾" h.,
  10 oz. 20.00
Tumbler, water, footed, pink, 4¾" h.,
  10 oz. 29.50
Tumbler, water, footed, yellow, 4¾" h.,
  10 oz. 19.00
Tumbler, iced tea, footed, green, 5¼" h.,
  12 oz. 16.00
Tumbler, iced tea, footed, pink, 5¼" h.,
  12 oz. 17.50
Tumbler, iced tea, footed, yellow, 5¼" h.,
  12 oz. 21.50

**FLORENTINE or Poppy No. 2, Hazel Atlas
Glass Co., 1932-35 (Process-etched)**
Bowl, berry, 4½" d., clear.......................9.00
Bowl, berry, 4½" d., green 11.00
Bowl, berry, 4½" d., pink.......................13.00
Bowl, berry, 4½" d., yellow 17.50
Bowl, cream soup, plain rim, 4¾" d.,
  clear 9.50
Bowl, cream soup, plain rim, 4¾" d.,
  green...11.50
Bowl, cream soup, plain rim, 4¾" d.,

pink 15.00
Bowl, cream soup, plain rim, 4¾" d.,
  yellow...19.00
Bowl, 5½" d., clear................................20.50
Bowl, 5½" d., green 45.00
Bowl, 5½" d., yellow..............................41.00
Bowl, cereal, 6" d., yellow....................35.00
Bowl, 8" d., clear...................................22.00
Bowl, cov. vegetable, 9" oval, green.....35.00
Bowl, cov. vegetable, 9" oval, yellow.....60.00
Bowl, 9" oval vegetable, green 22.50
Bowl, 9" oval vegetable, yellow 26.00
Butter dish, cov., green...........................96.00
Butter dish, cov., yellow......................137.00
Candlesticks, green, 2¾" h., pr............47.00
Candlesticks, yellow, 2¾" h., pr..........56.50
Candy dish, cov., clear 67.50
Candy dish, cov., green.........................95.00
Candy dish, cov., pink 114.00
Candy dish, cov., yellow 145.00
Coaster-ashtray, clear, 3¾" d. 16.00
Coaster-ashtray, green, 3¾" d..............18.00
Coaster-ashtray, yellow, 3¾" d............21.00
Coaster-ashtray, green, 5½" d.............19.00
Coaster-ashtray, yellow, 5½" d.............31.50
Compote, 3½", ruffled, clear 23.00
Compote, 3½", ruffled, cobalt blue 50.00
Compote, 3½", ruffled, pink 13.00
Condiment set: creamer, cov. sugar
  bowl, salt & pepper shakers & 8½" d.
  tray; yellow, 5 pcs. 161.00
Creamer, clear 6.50
Creamer, green 8.00

Florentine Creamer

Creamer, yellow (ILLUS.) 9.00
Cup, clear 6.00
Cup, green...7.50
Cup & saucer, pink 11.50
Cup & saucer, yellow............................12.50
Custard cup, green 70.00
Custard cup, yellow 79.00
Gravy boat, yellow 50.00
Gravy boat w/platter, yellow, 11½"
  oval 81.00
Pitcher, 6¼" h., 24 oz., cone-shaped,
  yellow...142.00
Pitcher, 7½" h., 28 oz., cone-shaped,
  green...36.00
Pitcher, 7½" h., 48 oz., straight sides,
  green...48.00
Pitcher, 7½" h., 48 oz., straight sides,
  pink 121.00
Pitcher, 7½" h., 48 oz., straight sides,
  yellow...144.00
Pitcher, 8¼" h., 76 oz., clear................61.00

Pitcher, 8¼" h., 76 oz., clear 80.00
Pitcher, 8¼" h., 76 oz., pink 219.00
Pitcher, 8¼" h., 76 oz., yellow 400.00
Plate, sherbet, 6" d., clear 3.00
Plate, sherbet, 6" d., green 4.00
Plate, sherbet, 6" d., yellow 5.50
Plate, 6¼" d., w/indentation, yellow 24.50
Plate, salad, 8½" d., clear or pink 6.50
Plate, salad, 8½" d., green or yellow 8.00
Plate, dinner, 10" d., clear 10.50
Plate, dinner, 10" d., green 13.50
Plate, dinner, 10" d., yellow 12.50
Plate, grill, 10¼" d., clear.....................11.00
Platter, 11" oval, yellow 16.50
Platter, 11½", for gravy boat, yellow 38.00
Relish dish, three-part or plain,
  clear, 10" 13.00
Relish dish, three-part or plain,
  yellow, 10" 26.00
Salt & pepper shakers, clear, pr. 27.50
Salt & pepper shakers, green, pr..........40.00
Salt & pepper shakers, yellow, pr. 44.00
Saucer, clear 3.00
Saucer, green..4.00
Sherbet, clear, green or yellow...............9.50
Sugar bowl, cov., clear 22.00
Sugar bowl, cov., green.........................19.00
Sugar bowl, cov., yellow 29.00
Sugar bowl, open, clear..........................6.50
Sugar bowl, open, green 7.50
Sugar bowl, open, yellow........................9.50
Tray, yellow, 8½" d. 83.00
Tumbler, footed, green, 3¼" h., 5 oz. ...11.50
Tumbler, footed, yellow, 3¼" h., 5 oz. ..13.00
Tumbler, juice, clear, 3½" h., 5 oz. 9.00
Tumbler, juice, green, 3½" h., 5 oz........12.00
Tumbler, footed, green, 4" h., 5 oz. 11.50
Tumbler, footed, yellow, 4" h., 5 oz. 15.00
Tumbler, blown, clear, 3½" h., 6 oz. 16.00
Tumbler, blown, green, 3½" h., 6 oz.....12.50
Tumbler, water, clear, 4" h., 9 oz..........10.00
Tumbler, water, green, 4" h., 9 oz. 11.50
Tumbler, water, pink, 4" h., 9 oz. 13.50
Tumbler, water, yellow, 4" h., 9 oz.........19.00
Tumbler, footed, clear, 4½" h., 9 oz.......11.50
Tumbler, footed, green, 4½" h., 9 oz. ...21.00
Tumbler, footed, yellow, 4½" h., 9 oz. ..30.00
Tumbler, blown, clear, 5" h., 12 oz. 19.50
Tumbler, blown, green, 5" h., 12 oz.....16.00
Tumbler, iced tea, clear, 5" h., 12 oz. ...19.50
Tumbler, iced tea, green, 5" h., 12 oz...26.00
Tumbler, iced tea, yellow, 5" h.,
  12 oz. 41.00
Vase (or parfait), 6" h., clear.................26.00
Vase (or parfait), 6" h., green 36.50
Vase (or parfait), 6" h., yellow...............54.50

GEORGIAN or Lovebirds, Federal Glass Co., 1931-36 (Process-etched)
(All items in green only)
Bowl, berry, 4½" d. 7.50
Bowl, cereal, 5¾" d..............................20.00

Bowl, 6½" d., deep.................................64.00
Bowl, berry, 7½" d. 57.00
Bowl, 9" oval vegetable 61.00
Butter dish, cov. 70.00

Georgian Pattern
Creamer, footed, 3" h. (ILLUS.) 10.50
Creamer, footed, 4" h. 14.50
Cup (ILLUS.)...8.50
Hot plate, center design, 5" d. 44.50
Plate, sherbet, 6" d. 4.50
Plate, luncheon, 8" d..............................8.00
Plate, dinner, 9¼" d. 26.50
Plate, 9¼" d., center design only 18.50
Platter, 11½" oval, closed handles 58.50
Saucer (ILLUS.).....................................3.50
Sherbet..11.50
Sugar bowl, cov., footed, 3" h..............42.00
Sugar bowl, cov., footed, 4" h...............76.00
Sugar bowl, open, footed, 3" h.
  (ILLUS.) 8.50
Sugar bowl, open, footed, 4" h. 10.00
Tumbler, 4" h., 9 oz. 52.00
Tumbler, 5¼" h., 12 oz. 103.00

HOBNAIL, Hocking Glass Co., 1934-36 (Press-mold)
Cup & saucer, clear 5.00
Cup & saucer, pink 7.00
Decanter w/stopper, clear, 32 oz..........24.00
Decanter w/stopper, clear w/red trim,
  32 oz. 22.00
Goblet, iced tea, clear, 13 oz.................7.50
Pitcher, milk, 18 oz., clear 17.50
Pitcher, 67 oz., clear.............................24.00
Plate, sherbet, 6" d., clear 2.00
Plate, sherbet, 6" d., pink.......................4.00
Plate, luncheon, 8½" d., clear................3.00
Plate, luncheon, 8½" d., clear w/red
  trim 4.50
Plate, luncheon, 8½" d., pink 5.50
Sherbet, clear 3.00
Sherbet, pink 6.00
Sugar bowl, open, footed, clear..............2.50
Tumbler, whiskey, clear, 1½ oz. 4.50
Tumbler, wine, footed, clear, 3 oz. 5.50
Tumbler, cordial, footed, clear, 5 oz. 4.00
Tumbler, water, clear, 9 oz. 5.00
Tumbler, water, clear, 10 oz. 5.50
Tumbler, iced tea, clear, 15 oz. 6.00
Wine set: decanter & 6 footed wines;
  clear, 7 pcs. 32.00

HOLIDAY or Buttons and Bows, Jeannette Glass Co., 1947-mid 50s (Press-mold)
(All items in pink unless otherwise indicated)

Holiday Berry Bowl

Bowl, berry, 5⅛" d. (ILLUS.) 11.00
Bowl, flat soup, 7¾" d. 43.00
Bowl, berry, 8½" d. 20.00
Bowl, 9½" oval vegetable 23.00
Butter dish, cov.....................................37.50
Cake plate, three-footed, 10½" d..........96.50
Candlesticks, 3" h., pr...........................93.00
Console bowl, 10¾" d.........................106.00
Creamer, footed.....................................8.50
Cup...7.00
Pitcher, milk, 4¾" h., 16 oz.,
    iridescent 23.50
Pitcher, milk, 4¾" h., 16 oz., pink 52.50
Pitcher, 6¾" h., 52 oz. 34.00
Plate, sherbet, 6" d. 5.00
Plate, dinner, 9" d. 15.00
Plate, chop, 13¾" d. 92.50
Platter, 8 x 11⅜" oval, iridescent 17.50
Platter, 8 x 11⅜" oval, pink...................18.50
Sandwich tray, 10½" d..........................16.00
Saucer..5.50
Sherbet...6.50
Sugar bowl, cov. 23.00
Sugar bowl, open....................................7.00
Tumbler, footed, iridescent, 4" h., 5 oz. ...8.50
Tumbler, footed, pink, 4" h., 5 oz.........35.00
Tumbler, footed, 6" h., 9 oz. 122.00
Tumbler, 4" h., 10 oz. 18.50

HOMESPUN or Fine Rib, Jeannette Glass Co., 1939-49 (Press-mold)
(All items in pink only, except child's tea set)
Bowl, 4½" d., closed handles.................9.50
Bowl, cereal, 5" d..................................17.00
Bowl, berry, 8¼" d. 11.50
Butter dish, cov.....................................48.00
Coaster-ashtray.......................................9.50
Creamer, footed......................................7.50
Cup...7.00
Plate, sherbet, 6" d. 5.00
Plate, dinner, 9¼" d. 15.50
Platter, 13", closed handles 15.00
Saucer..3.50
Sherbet...15.50
Sugar bowl, open, footed........................8.00
Tumbler, footed, 4" h., 5 oz. 7.00

Tumbler, water, 4" h., 9 oz....................17.00
Tumbler, footed, 6¼" h., 9 oz. 7.50
Tumbler, iced tea, 5¼" h., 13 oz..........35.00
Tumbler, footed, 6½" h., 15 oz. 23.00

CHILD'S TEA SET
Cup, clear 18.50
Cup & saucer, pink 20.50
Plate, clear...6.50
Plate, pink...12.50
Saucer, pink..8.00
14 piece set, pink................................285.00

IRIS or Iris & Herringbone, Jeannette Glass Co., 1928-32, 1950s and 1970s (Press-mold)
Berry set: 11" d. ruffled fruit bowl & 6
    sauce dishes; clear, 7 pcs. 68.00
Bowl, berry, 4½" d., beaded rim,
    amber iridescent 9.00
Bowl, berry, 4½" d., beaded rim,
    clear 37.00
Bowl, cereal, 5" d., clear 116.00
Bowl, sauce, 5" d., ruffled rim, amber
    iridescent 23.00
Bowl, sauce, 5" d., ruffled rim, clear 9.00
Bowl, soup, 7½" d., amber iridescent ...64.00
Bowl, soup, 7½" d., clear....................150.00
Bowl, berry, 8" d., beaded rim, amber
    iridescent 23.50
Bowl, berry, 8" d., beaded rim, clear.....85.00
Bowl, salad, 9½" d., amber iridescent ..12.50
Bowl, salad, 9½" d., clear 13.50
Bowl, fruit, 11" d., straight rim, clear 56.00
Bowl, fruit, 11½" d., ruffled rim, amber
    iridescent 14.00
Bowl, fruit, 11½" d., ruffled rim, clear....13.00
Butter dish, cov., amber iridescent 42.00
Butter dish, cov., clear 45.00
Candlesticks, two-branch, amber
    iridescent, pr.....................................41.00
Candlesticks, two-branch, clear, pr. 36.00
Candy jar, cov., clear...........................137.00
Coaster, clear 102.00
Creamer, footed, amber iridescent.......12.00
Creamer, footed, clear..........................10.00
Cup, demitasse, clear...........................34.50
Cup & saucer, demitasse, clear..........176.00
Cup & saucer, demitasse, ruby 250.00
Cup, amber iridescent 13.00
Cup, clear 15.50
Goblet, wine, amber iridescent, 4¼" h.,
    3 oz. 29.00
Goblet, wine, clear, 4¼" h., 3 oz..........15.50
Goblet, cocktail, clear, 4¼" h., 4 oz. 23.00
Goblet, clear, 5¾" h., 4 oz. 22.50
Goblet, amber iridescent, 5¾" h.,
    8 oz. 12.00
Goblet, clear, 5¾" h., 8 oz. 23.00
Lamp shade, blue 59.00
Lamp shade, clear 57.00
Lamp shade, clear frosted 83.50
Lamp shade, pink 62.00

Lamp shade, pink frosted 65.00
Nut set: 11½" d. ruffled bowl in metal
  holder, w/nutcracker & picks; amber
  iridescent, the set............................100.00
Nut set: 11½" d. ruffled bowl in metal
  holder, w/nutcracker & picks; clear,
  the set..64.00
Pitcher, 9½" h., footed, amber
  iridescent 38.00
Pitcher, 9½" h., footed, clear 35.00
Plate, sherbet, 5½" d., amber
  iridescent 11.50
Plate, sherbet, 5½" d., clear 14.00
Plate, luncheon, 8" d., clear..................95.00
Plate, dinner, 9" d., amber iridescent....38.50
Plate, dinner, 9" d., clear 50.00
Plate, sandwich, 11¾" d., amber
  iridescent 29.00
Plate, sandwich, 11¾" d., clear 33.00
Saucer, amber iridescent......................10.00
Saucer, clear 11.50
Sherbet, footed, amber iridescent,
  2½" h..13.00
Sherbet, footed, clear, 2½" h. 23.50
Sherbet, footed, amber iridescent,
  4" h..13.00
Sherbet, footed, clear, 4" h. 19.50
Sugar bowl, cov., footed, amber
  iridescent or clear 23.00
Sugar bowl, open, footed, amber
  iridescent or clear 9.50
Tumbler, clear, 4" h. 135.00
Tumbler, footed, amber iridescent,
  6" h..16.00
Tumbler, footed, clear, 6" h. 17.50
Tumbler, footed, clear, 6½" h. 31.00
Vase, 9" h., amber iridescent...............23.00
Vase, 9" h., clear 25.00
Vase, 9" h., pink...................................66.00
Water set: pitcher & 7 tumblers; clear,
  in original box, 8 pcs. 225.00

LACE EDGE or Open Lace, Hocking Glass Co., 1935-38 (Press-mold)

Lace Edge Bowls

Bowl, cereal, 6½" d., clear 5.50
Bowl, cereal, 6½" d., pink (ILLUS.
  front) 18.50

Bowl, 7¾" d., ribbed, pink 33.50
Bowl, salad or butter dish bottom,
  7¾" d., pink 18.00
Bowl, 9½" d., plain or ribbed, clear.......12.50
Bowl, 9½" d., plain or ribbed, pink
  (ILLUS. back) 20.00
Butter dish or bonbon, cov., pink..........62.00
Candlesticks, pink, pr. 245.00
Candlesticks, pink frosted, pr. 50.00
Candy jar, cov., ribbed, pink, 4" h........46.50
Compote, cov., 7" d., footed, pink..........44.00
Compote, open, 7" d., footed, pink 19.00
Console bowl, three-footed, pink,
  10½" d...186.00
Cookie jar, cov., pink, 5" h. 65.00
Creamer, pink 21.00
Cup, pink...22.00
Flower bowl w/crystal block, pink 22.50
Flower bowl without crystal block,
  pink 15.00
Plate, salad, 7¼" d., clear......................4.50
Plate, salad, 7¼" d., pink 18.50
Plate, luncheon, 8¾" d., pink 19.00
Plate, dinner, 10½" d., pink...................26.50
Plate, grill, 10½" d., pink 17.50
Plate, 13" d., solid lace, pink................36.50
Platter, 12¾" oval, pink.........................30.00
Platter, 12¾" oval, five-part, clear.........16.50
Platter, 12¾" oval, five-part, pink..........27.50
Relish dish, three-part, deep, pink,
  7½" d..63.00
Relish plate, three-part, pink, 10½" d. ..21.00
Relish plate, four-part, solid lace,
  pink, 13" d. 45.00
Saucer, pink...12.50
Sherbet, footed, pink 79.00
Sugar bowl, open, pink 20.00
Tumbler, pink, 4½" h., 9 oz...................15.50
Tumbler, footed, pink, 5" h., 10½ oz.....63.00
Vase, 7" h., pink frosted........................49.50

LORAIN or Basket or Number 615, Indiana Glass Co., 1929-32 (Process-etched)

Lorain Creamer & Sugar Bowl

Bowl, cereal, 6", green..........................36.50
Bowl, cereal, 6", yellow.........................52.50
Bowl, salad, 7¼", green.........................41.00
Bowl, salad, 7¼", yellow 55.00
Bowl, berry, 8", clear.............................60.00
Bowl, berry, 8", green 97.00
Bowl, berry, 8", yellow 155.00
Bowl, 9¾" oval vegetable, green 45.00

Bowl, 9¾" oval vegetable, yellow 51.00
Creamer, footed, green 12.00
Creamer, footed, yellow (ILLUS. left) ...22.00
Cup, green...9.50
Cup, yellow...14.50
Cup & saucer, clear 14.00
Plate, sherbet, 5½", green.....................6.00
Plate, sherbet, 5½", yellow 10.50
Plate, salad, 7¾", clear..........................9.00
Plate, salad, 7¾" green 11.00
Plate, salad, 7¾", yellow......................14.00
Plate, luncheon, 8⅜", green 10.50
Plate, luncheon, 8⅜", yellow.................25.00
Plate, dinner, 10¼", clear or green.......36.00
Plate, dinner, 10¼", yellow 49.00
Platter, 11½", green..............................23.00
Platter, 11½", yellow 40.00
Relish, four-part, clear, 8" 14.00
Relish, four-part, green, 8".....................16.00
Relish, four-part, yellow, 8"...................29.50
Saucer, green or yellow 5.00
Sherbet, footed, green...........................17.50
Sherbet, footed, yellow 28.00
Sugar bowl, open, footed, green 10.50
Sugar bowl, open, footed, yellow
  (ILLUS. right) 20.00
Tumbler, footed, green, 4¾" h., 9 oz. ...19.50
Tumbler, footed, yellow, 4¾" h., 9 oz. ..26.00

**MADRID, Federal Glass Co., 1932-39
(Process-etched)**

Madrid Sugar Bowl

Ashtray, amber, 6" sq. 221.00
Ashtray, green, 6" sq. 195.00
Bowl, cream soup, 4¾" d., amber........13.50
Bowl, sauce, 5" d., amber or pink..........5.50
Bowl, sauce, 5" d., blue 35.00
Bowl, sauce, 5" d., green........................8.50
Bowl, soup, 7" d., amber......................13.50
Bowl, soup, 7" d., blue 20.00
Bowl, soup, 7" d., clear...........................6.00
Bowl, soup, 7" d., green........................15.50
Bowl, salad, 8" d., amber......................13.50
Bowl, salad, 8" d., blue 46.50
Bowl, salad, 8" d., green.......................15.50
Bowl, large berry, 9⅜" d., amber 22.00
Bowl, salad, 9½" d., deep, amber.........27.50

Bowl, 10" oval vegetable, amber 16.00
Bowl, 10" oval vegetable, blue..............33.50
Bowl, 10" oval vegetable, green 22.00
Butter dish, cov., amber.......................66.00
Butter dish, cov., clear 49.00
Butter dish, cov., green.........................78.00
Cake plate, amber, 11¼" d. 15.00
Cake plate, pink, 11¼" d.......................12.00
Candlesticks, amber, 2¼" h., pr............16.00
Candlesticks, clear or pink, 2¼" h.,
  pr. 14.50
Candlesticks, iridescent, 2¼" h., pr. 21.50
Console bowl, flared, amber or
  iridescent, 11" d. 14.00
Console set: bowl & pair of candlesticks;
  amber, 3 pcs. 37.00
Console set: bowl & pair of candlesticks;
  iridescent, 3 pcs. 32.00
Console set: bowl & pair of candlesticks;
  pink, 3 pcs...36.00
Cookie jar, cov., amber.........................39.50
Cookie jar, cov., clear 32.50
Cookie jar, cov., pink 36.50
Creamer, amber or clear 7.50
Creamer, blue.......................................14.00
Creamer, green 10.50
Cup, amber...6.50
Cup, blue 19.50
Cup, green...9.00
Cup & saucer, clear 8.00
Cup & saucer, pink 9.00
Gelatin mold, amber, 2⅛" h. 11.50
Gravy boat & platter, amber 1,575.00
Gravy boat platter, amber...................500.00
Hot dish coaster, amber, 5" d. 39.50
Hot dish coaster, clear, 5" d.................23.00
Hot dish coaster, green, 5" d. 31.00
Hot dish coaster w/indentation, amber
  or green 35.00
Hot dish coaster w/indentation, clear....26.50
Jam dish, amber, 7" d...........................20.50
Jam dish, blue, 7" d..............................31.50
Jam dish, clear, 7" d. 10.00
Jam dish, green, 7" d............................25.00
Lazy Susan, walnut base w/seven
  clear hot dish coasters 462.50
Pitcher, juice, 5½" h., 36 oz., amber.....38.00
Pitcher, 8" h., 60 oz., square, amber 43.00
Pitcher, 8" h., 60 oz., square, blue
  or green 130.00
Pitcher, 8½" h., 80 oz., jug-type,
  amber...57.50
Pitcher, 8½" h., 80 oz., jug-type,
  green..188.50
Pitcher w/ice lip, 8½" h., 80 oz.,
  amber...55.50
Plate, sherbet, 6" d., amber, clear or
  green...4.50
Plate, sherbet, 6" d., blue 12.00
Plate, sherbet, 6" d., pink......................3.50
Plate, salad, 7½" d., amber, green or
  pink 9.50
Plate, salad, 7½" d., blue.....................17.00

Plate, luncheon, 8⅞" d., amber 7.50
Plate, luncheon, 8⅞" d., blue................18.50
Plate, luncheon, 8⅞" d., clear................5.50
Plate, luncheon, 8⅞" d., green 9.50
Plate, dinner, 10½" d., amber 35.00
Plate, dinner, 10½" d., blue 54.50
Plate, dinner, 10½" d., clear 21.00
Plate, dinner, 10½" d., green 32.50
Plate, grill, 10½" d., amber 10.50
Plate, grill, 10½" d., clear......................9.00
Plate, grill, 10½" d., green 16.00
Platter, 11½" oval, amber 14.00
Platter, 11½" oval, blue.......................29.00
Platter, 11½" oval, green 16.50
Relish plate, amber, 10½" d. 13.50
Relish plate, clear, 10½" d.....................7.00
Relish plate, pink, 10½" d. 12.00
Salt & pepper shakers, amber,
   3½" h., pr. 40.00
Salt & pepper shakers, green,
   3½" h., pr. 56.00
Salt & pepper shakers, footed, amber,
   3½" h., pr. 52.00
Salt & pepper shakers, footed, blue,
   3½" h., pr. 126.00
Salt & pepper shakers, footed, green,
   3½" h., pr. 81.00
Saucer, amber 4.00
Saucer, blue 8.00
Saucer, green 5.00
Sherbet, amber....................................7.50
Sherbet, blue or green.........................10.00
Sherbet, clear 6.50
Sugar bowl, cov., amber (ILLUS.) 40.00
Sugar bowl, cov., clear 32.50
Sugar bowl, cov., green.......................48.00
Sugar bowl, open, amber 7.50
Sugar bowl, open, blue........................15.00
Sugar bowl, open, green 9.00
Tumbler, juice, amber, 3⅞" h., 5 oz......12.50
Tumbler, juice, blue, 3⅞" h., 5 oz. 32.50
Tumbler, juice, green, 3⅞" h., 5 oz.......48.00
Tumbler, footed, amber, 4" h., 5 oz. 21.50
Tumbler, blue, 4½" h., 9 oz..................25.00
Tumbler, green, 4½" h., 9 oz. 23.50
Tumbler, pink, 4½" h., 9 oz. 13.50
Tumblers, amber, 4½" h., 9 oz., set of
   24 w/box 325.00
Tumbler, footed, amber, 5¼" h.,
   10 oz. 21.00
Tumbler, footed, clear, 5¼" h.,
   10 oz. 14.00
Tumbler, footed, green, 5¼" h.,
   10 oz. 33.50
Tumbler, amber, 5½" h., 12 oz. 19.50
Tumbler, blue, 5½" h., 12 oz................39.00
Tumbler, clear, 5½" h., 12 oz...............20.00
Tumbler, green, 5½" h., 12 oz. 32.00

**MANHATTAN or Horizontal Ribbed,
Anchor Hocking Glass Co., 1938-43
(Press-mold)**

Ashtray, clear, 4" d. 9.50

Ashtray, clear, 4½" sq...........................16.50
Bowl, sauce, 4½" d., two-handled,
   clear 8.50
Bowl, berry, 5⅜" d., two-handled,
   clear or pink 17.00
Bowl, cereal, 5½" d., clear 28.50
Bowl, large berry, 7½" d., clear............13.50
Bowl, 8" d., two-handled, clear 17.00
Bowl, salad, 9" d., clear 20.50
Bowl, fruit, 9½" d., clear......................31.50
Bowl, fruit, 9½" d., pink.......................38.00
Candleholders, clear, 4½" sq., pr. 12.00
Candlesticks, double, clear,
   4¼" h., pr. 32.00
Candy dish, cov., clear 31.50
Candy dish, open, three-footed, clear 6.50
Candy dish, open, three-footed, pink....10.50
Coaster, clear, 3½" d 12.50
Coaster, pink, 3½" d 7.00
Compote, 5¾" h., clear 26.50
Compote, 5¾" h., pink 29.00
Creamer, oval, clear 9.50
Creamer, oval, pink 10.00
Cup, clear 15.00
Pitcher, juice, 42 oz., ball tilt-
   type, clear 29.00
Pitcher w/ice lip, 80 oz., ball tilt-
   type, clear 36.00
Pitcher w/ice lip, 80 oz., ball tilt-
   type, pink 57.00
Plate, sherbet or saucer, 6" d., clear 5.50
Plate, sherbet or saucer, 6" d., pink......12.00
Plate, salad, 8½" d., clear....................12.50
Plate, dinner, 10¼" d., clear 17.50
Plate, dinner, 10¼" d., pink..................12.50
Plate, sandwich, 14" d., clear 20.00

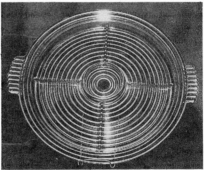

Manhattan Relish Tray

Relish tray, four-part, clear, 14" d.
   (ILLUS.) 16.00
Relish tray, five-part, clear w/clear
   inserts, 14" d. 43.00
Relish tray, five-part, clear w/pink
   inserts, 14" d. 27.00
Relish tray, five-part, clear w/ruby
   inserts, 14" d. 49.00
Relish tray, five-part, pink w/pink
   inserts, 14" d. 47.00

Relish tray insert, clear, pink or ruby 4.50
Salt & pepper shakers, square,
  clear, 2" h., pr. 23.00
Salt & pepper shakers, square,
  pink, 2" h., pr. 55.00
Saucer, clear 5.00
Sherbet, clear 8.00
Sherbet, pink 12.00
Sugar bowl, open, oval, clear or pink 9.50
Tumbler, footed, clear, green or pink,
  10 oz. 17.00
Vase, 8" h., clear 10.50
Water bottle, cov., clear........................15.50
Wine, clear, 3½" h. 5.50

MAYFAIR or Open Rose, Hocking Glass Co., 1931-37 (Process-etched)

Mayfair Plate

Bowl, cream soup, 5", blue 19.00
Bowl, cream soup, 5", pink 42.00
Bowl, cereal, 5½", blue 52.50
Bowl, cereal, 5½", pink 21.00
Bowl, vegetable, 7", blue 43.50
Bowl, vegetable, 7", pink 25.50
Bowl, vegetable, 7", pink frosted 18.00
Bowl, 9" d., 3⅛" h., three-footed
  console, green 7,250.00
Bowl, 9" d., 3⅛" h., three-footed
  console, pink.................................7,000.00
Bowl, 9½" oval vegetable, blue............62.00
Bowl, 9½" oval vegetable, pink............30.00
Bowl, 9½" oval vegetable, yellow 175.00
Bowl, 10", cov. vegetable, blue..........130.00
Bowl, 10", cov. vegetable, pink............97.00
Bowl, 10", open vegetable, blue 62.00
Bowl, 10", open vegetable, pink 25.00
Bowl, 11¾" d., low, blue 63.50
Bowl, 11¾" d., low, green....................32.00
Bowl, 11¾" d., low, pink......................50.00
Bowl, fruit, 12" d., deep, scalloped,
  blue...81.00
Bowl, fruit, 12" d., deep, scalloped,
  green...36.50
Bowl, fruit, 12" d., deep, scalloped,
  pink 53.50
Bowl, fruit, 12" d., deep, scalloped,
  yellow..250.00

Butter dish, cov., blue 282.00
Butter dish, cov., pink 60.00
Candy jar, cov., blue............................271.00
Candy jar, cov., pink..............................50.00
Celery dish, blue, 10" l..........................41.50
Celery dish, pink, 10" l..........................37.50
Celery dish, two-part, blue, 10" l...........51.00
Celery dish, two-part, pink, 10" l........168.00
Cookie jar, cov., blue 275.00
Cookie jar, cov., green........................541.00
Cookie jar, cov., pink 46.50
Creamer, footed, blue...........................70.00
Creamer, footed, pink 24.00
Creamer, footed, pink frosted 15.50
Cup, blue 43.50
Decanter w/stopper, pink, 10" h.,
  32 oz. 146.00
Decanter, no stopper, pink, 10" h.,
  32 oz. 93.00
Goblet, pink, 4" h., 2½ oz. 61.00
Goblet, wine, pink, 4½" h., 3 oz. 71.00
Goblet, cocktail, pink, 4" h., 3½ oz. 72.00
Goblet, claret, pink, 5¼" h., 4½ oz........75.00
Goblet, water, pink, 5¾" h., 9 oz...........58.00
Goblet, water, thin, pink, 7¼" h.,
  9 oz. 121.00
Pitcher, juice, 6" h., 37 oz., blue 142.00
Pitcher, juice, 6" h., 37 oz., clear 14.50
Pitcher, juice, 6" h., 37 oz., pink 48.50
Pitcher, 8" h., 60 oz., jug-type, blue....184.00
Pitcher, 8" h., 60 oz., jug-type, pink......45.50
Pitcher, 8½" h., 80 oz., jug-type,
  blue 189.00
Pitcher, 8½" h., 80 oz., jug-type,
  pink 96.50
Plate, sherbet, 6½" d., pink...................12.00
Plate, sherbet, 6½" d., off-center
  indentation, blue 24.00
Plate, sherbet, 6½" d., off-center
  indentation, pink.................................11.50
Plate, luncheon, 8½", blue....................47.00
Plate, luncheon, 8½", pink 23.50
Plate, dinner, 9½", blue 76.00
Plate, dinner, 9½", pink (ILLUS.) 48.00
Plate, dinner, 9½", yellow 117.50
Plate, grill, 9½", blue...........................48.00
Plate, grill, 9½", pink 36.00
Platter, 12" oval, open handles, blue....62.00
Platter, 12" oval, open handles, clear...14.50
Platter, 12" oval, open handles,
  green or pink 25.50
Platter, 12" oval, open handles,
  yellow..232.00
Platter, 12½" oval, closed handles,
  yellow..200.00
Relish, four-part, blue, 8⅜" 48.50
Relish, four-part, pink, 8⅜" 27.50
Salt & pepper shakers, flat, blue, pr. ..259.00
Salt & pepper shakers, flat, pink, pr......57.00
Salt & pepper shakers, flat, pink
  frosted, pr..39.00
Sandwich server w/center handle,
  blue, 12"...73.00

Sandwich server w/center handle,
   pink, 12" 43.50
Sandwich server w/center handle,
   pink frosted, 12" 20.50
Saucer w/cup ring, blue 20.00
Sherbet, flat, blue, 2¼" h. 127.00
Sherbet, flat, pink, 2¼" h. 153.00
Sherbet, footed, pink, 3" h. 16.00
Sherbet, footed, blue or pink, 4¾" h. 75.00
Sugar bowl, open, footed, blue 75.00
Sugar bowl, open, footed, pink 26.50
Sugar bowl, open, footed, pink
   frosted 16.00
Tumbler, whiskey, pink, 2¼" h.,
   1½ oz. 61.00
Tumbler, juice, footed, pink, 3¼" h.,
   3 oz. 80.00
Tumbler, juice, blue, 3½" h., 5 oz. 100.00
Tumbler, juice, pink, 3½" h., 5 oz. 38.50
Tumbler, water, blue, 4¼" h., 9 oz........88.00
Tumbler, water, pink, 4¼" h., 9 oz........26.50
Tumbler, footed, blue, 5¼" h., 10 oz...123.00
Tumbler, footed, pink, 5¼" h., 10 oz.....34.50
Tumbler, water, blue, 4¾" h., 11 oz....107.00
Tumbler, water, pink, 4¾" h., 11 oz. ...128.50
Tumbler, iced tea, pink, 5¼" h.,
   13½ oz. 46.50
Tumbler, iced tea, footed, blue, 6½" h.,
   15 oz. 183.00
Tumbler, iced tea, footed, pink, 6½" h.,
   15 oz. 37.00
Vase, 5½ x 8½", sweetpea, hat-shaped,
   blue 93.00
Vase, 5½ x 8½", sweetpea, hat-shaped,
   pink 155.00

MISS AMERICA, Hocking Glass Co., 1935-38 (Press-mold)

Miss America Pitcher

Bowl, berry, 4½" d., green 10.00
Bowl, berry, 6¼" d., clear........................9.50
Bowl, fruit, 8" d., curved in at top,
   pink 70.00
Bowl, fruit, 8¾" d., clear........................36.00
Bowl, fruit, 8¾" d., pink 64.00
Bowl, 10" oval vegetable, clear.............14.50
Bowl, 10" oval vegetable, pink..............26.50
Butter dish, cov., clear 198.00

Butter dish, cov., pink 495.00
Cake plate, footed, clear, 12" d. 25.50
Cake plate, footed, pink, 12" d..............41.00
Candy jar, cov., clear, 11½" h...............58.00
Candy jar, cov., pink, 11½" h...............124.00
Celery tray, clear, 10½" oblong 14.50
Compote, 5" d., pink 25.00
Creamer, footed, clear............................8.00
Creamer, footed, pink 15.50
Cup & saucer, pink 26.50
Goblet, wine, clear, 3¾" h., 3 oz...........18.50
Goblet, juice, pink, 4¾" h., 5 oz. 75.00
Goblet, water, clear, 5½" h., 10 oz. 18.00
Goblet, water, green, 5½" h., 10 oz. 14.00
Goblet, water, pink, 5½" h., 10 oz.........39.00
Pitcher, 8" h., 65 oz., clear....................54.00
Pitcher, 8" h., 65 oz., pink...................112.00
Pitcher w/ice lip, 8½" h., 65 oz.,
   clear 55.00
Pitcher w/ice lip, 8½" h., 65 oz., pink
   (ILLUS.) 118.00
Plate, sherbet, 5¾" d., clear 5.50
Plate, sherbet, 5¾" d., pink.....................8.00
Plate, 6¾" d., green 7.50
Plate, salad, 8½" d., clear.......................7.00
Plate, salad, 8½" d., pink 21.50
Plate, dinner, 10¼" d., clear 13.00
Plate, dinner, 10¼" d., pink...................29.00
Plate, grill, 10¼" d., clear.......................9.50
Plate, grill, 10¼" d., pink 22.50
Platter, 12¼" oval, clear........................13.50
Platter, 12¼" oval, pink.........................23.50
Relish, four-part, clear, 8¾" d. 10.00
Salt & pepper shakers, clear, pr. 24.00
Salt & pepper shakers, green, pr........180.00
Salt & pepper shakers, pink, pr. 58.50
Sherbet, clear 7.50
Sherbet, pink 14.00
Sugar bowl, open, footed, clear..............7.00
Sugar bowl, open, footed, pink 17.50
Tumbler, juice, clear, 4" h., 5 oz. 15.50
Tumbler, juice, pink, 4" h., 5 oz. 42.50
Tumbler, water, clear, 4½" h., 10 oz.....15.00
Tumbler, water, green, 4½" h., 10 oz. ..16.50
Tumbler, water, pink, 4½" h., 10 oz. 28.00

MODERNTONE, Hazel Atlas Glass Co., 1934-42, late 1940s and early 1950s (Press-mold)

Ashtray w/match holder, cobalt blue,
   7¾" d...195.00
Ashtray w/match holder, pink,
   7¾" d...42.50
Bowl, cream soup, 4¾" d., amethyst 16.00
Bowl, cream soup, 4¾" d., cobalt
   blue 19.00
Bowl, cream soup, 4¾" d., platonite 6.00
Bowl, berry, 5" d., amethyst or cobalt
   blue 21.00
Bowl, berry, 5" d., platonite....................5.00
Bowl, cream soup w/ruffled rim, 5" d.,
   cobalt blue 53.50

Bowl, cream soup w/ruffled rim, 5" d.,
  platonite 5.00
Bowl, cereal, 6½" d., cobalt blue 70.00
Bowl, cereal, 6½" d., platonite 6.00
Bowl, soup, 7½" d., amethyst 10.00
Bowl, soup, 7½" d., cobalt blue 130.00
Bowl, soup, 7½" d., platonite 12.00
Bowl, large berry, 8¾" d., amethyst......44.00
Bowl, large berry, 8¾" d., cobalt blue ...52.50
Bowl, large berry, 8¾" d., platonite........8.50
Butter dish w/metal lid, cobalt blue 93.50
Cheese dish w/metal lid, cobalt blue,
  7" d...411.00
Creamer, amethyst..................................9.00
Creamer, cobalt blue 11.00
Creamer, platonite 4.50
Cup, amethyst 9.00
Cup, cobalt blue....................................10.50
Cup, platonite 4.00
Custard cup, amethyst...........................11.50
Custard cup, cobalt blue.......................17.50
Plate, sherbet, 5⅞" d., amethyst.............5.00
Plate, sherbet, 5⅞" d., cobalt blue..........6.00
Plate, salad, 6¾" d., amethyst 5.00
Plate, salad, 6¾" d., cobalt blue 10.50
Plate, salad, 6¾" d., platonite 4.00
Plate, luncheon, 7¾" d., amethyst........10.00
Plate, luncheon, 7¾" d., cobalt blue 11.50
Plate, luncheon, 7¾" d., platonite 4.50
Plate, dinner, 8⅞" d., amethyst.............12.00
Plate, dinner, 8⅞" d., cobalt blue..........16.50
Plate, dinner, 8⅞" d., platonite 6.00
Plate, sandwich, 10½" d., amethyst......46.50
Plate, sandwich, 10½" d., cobalt blue...53.00
Plate, sandwich, 10½" d., platonite.......13.50
Platter, 11" oval, cobalt blue 41.50
Platter, 11" oval, platonite......................7.00
Platter, 12" oval, amethyst....................42.50
Platter, 12" oval, cobalt blue 86.00
Platter, 12" oval, platonite....................13.50
Salt & pepper shakers, amethyst, pr. 43.00
Salt & pepper shakers, cobalt blue,
  pr...37.50
Salt & pepper shakers, platonite, pr. 12.50
Saucer, amethyst....................................4.00
Saucer, cobalt blue or platonite 5.00
Sherbet, amethyst 11.00
Sherbet, cobalt blue..............................12.00
Sherbet, platonite 4.00
Sugar bowl, open, amethyst or cobalt
  blue 10.00
Sugar bowl, open, platonite 6.00
Sugar bowl w/metal lid, cobalt blue 40.00
Tumbler, whiskey, clear, 1½ oz. 5.50
Tumbler, whiskey, cobalt blue,
  1½ oz. 39.00
Tumbler, whiskey, platonite, 1½ oz. 11.50
Tumbler, juice, cobalt blue, 5 oz..........43.50
Tumbler, juice, platonite, 5 oz..............10.50
Tumbler, water, cobalt blue, 4" h.,
  9 oz. 33.00
Tumbler, water, platonite, 4" h., 9 oz. 8.00
Tumbler, iced tea, amethyst, 12 oz. 67.00

LITTLE HOSTESS PARTY SET

Creamer, 1¾" h., dark or pastel............11.00
Cup, 1¾" h., pastel 7.00
Cup & saucer, dark................................16.00
Plate, 5¼" d., dark 10.00
Plate, 5¼" d., pastel................................9.50
Saucer, 3⅞" d., pastel 8.50
Sugar bowl, 1¾" h., dark 10.50
Sugar bowl, 1¾" h., pastel....................11.50
Teapot, cov., 3½" h., dark.....................89.00
Teapot, cov., 3½" h., pastel 60.00
Tea set, dark, 14 pcs. 120.00
Tea set, pastel, 14 pcs. 71.00
Tea set, pastel, 16 pcs. 220.00
Tea set, dark, 16 pcs. 210.00

**MOONSTONE, Anchor Hocking Glass
Corp., 1941-46 (Press-mold)**
*(All items clear to opalescent only. Also see
Hobnail.)*

Moonstone Vase

Bonbon, heart-shaped, w/handle,
  6½" w. 11.50
Bowl, berry, 5½" d. 14.00
Bowl, dessert, 5½" d., crimped rim 8.50
Bowl, 6" w., three-part, cloverleaf-
  shaped 11.50
Bowl, 6½" d., two-handled, crimped
  rim 10.00
Bowl, 7¾" d., flat...................................12.00
Bowl, 9½" d., crimped rim.....................18.00
Candleholders, pr. 16.50
Candy dish, cov., two-handled, 6" d. 25.00
Cigarette box, cov., rectangular............20.00
Creamer, footed.....................................8.00
Cup & saucer...13.00
Dinner set, service for four, 23 pcs......275.00
Goblet, 10 oz. 18.50
Plate, sherbet, 6¼" d. 6.00
Plate, luncheon, 8" d..............................13.00
Plate, sandwich, 10" d., crimped rim 23.50
Puff box, cov., 4¾" d..............................20.50
Relish bowl, divided, 7¾" d...................10.00
Sherbet, footed 6.00
Sugar bowl, footed..................................8.00
Vase, bud, 5½" h. (ILLUS.)...................11.00

MOROCCAN AMETHYST, Hazel Ware, Division of Continental Can, 1960's (not true Depression)

Moroccan Amethyst Cup & Saucer

Ashtray, 3¾" triangle 6.50
Ashtray, 6" triangle 10.00
Ashtray, 6⅞" triangle w/metal base 18.00
Ashtray set: round w/silver trim; two
  w/box & label 20.50
Bowl, fruit, 4¾" w. octagon 6.00
Bowl, cereal, 5¾" sq., deep 11.00
Bowl, 6" d...10.50
Bowl, 6" d., w/metal center handle 33.00
Bowl, 6" sq., w/metal center handle......35.00
Bowl, 7¾" oval 16.00
Bowl, 7¾" oval w/center handle...........18.00
Bowl, 7¾" rectangle..............................13.00
Bowl, 9½" oval, low...............................11.50
Bowl, 9½" oval, w/metal center
  handle 42.00
Candy jar, cov., short.............................25.50
Candy jar, cov., tall................................29.00
Celery dish, 9½" l...................................11.50
Chip & dip set, w/metal holder
  (5¾" & 10¾" bowls) 41.50
Cocktail set: cocktail stirrer w/pouring
  lip, stirring rod & two 2½" h. 4 oz.
  tumblers; w/original box, the set 37.00
Cocktail shaker w/chrome lid, 32 oz. 24.00
Cocktail stirrer, w/pouring lip, 6¼" h.,
  16 oz. 23.00
Compote 20.00
Cup (ILLUS.)..6.00
Dinner service for 12 w/serving pieces,
  78 pcs. 425.00
Goblet, wine, 4" h., 4½ oz......................9.50
Goblet, juice, 4⅜" h., 5½ oz..................8.00
Goblet, water, 5½" h., 10 oz. 11.00
Ice bucket 25.50
Plate, 5¾" w. octagon.............................5.50
Plate, salad, 7¼" w. 7.00
Plate, dinner, 9¾" w...............................9.50
Plate, sandwich, 12" w...........................12.50
Punch cup..5.00
Punch set, bowl, base & 9 cups,
  11 pcs. 95.00
Relish, 8" 8.50

Relish, 9½" 10.00
Relish server, two 5¾" sq. bowls in
  metal frame w/handle 28.00
Relish server, two 7¾" l. rectangular
  bowls in metal frame..........................35.00
Sandwich server, w/metal center
  handle, 12"...18.50
Saucer (ILLUS.) 2.00
Sherbet, footed, 4¼" h...........................6.50
Snack set, four seashell-shaped
  plates, w/box......................................50.00
Tidbit server, two-tier 20.00
Tidbit server, three-tier 21.50
Tumbler, juice, 2½" h., 4 oz. 8.50
Tumbler, Old Fashioned, 3¼" h.,
  8 oz. 12.50
Tumbler, water, crinkled bottom,
  4¼" h., 11 oz. 11.00
Tumbler, water, 4⅝" h., 11 oz.............12.50
Tumbler, iced tea, 6½" h., 16 oz...........15.50
Vase, 8½" h., ruffled 35.50

NORMANDIE or Bouquet and Lattice, Federal Glass Co., 1933-40 (Process-etched)

Bowl, berry, 5" d., amber or pink 6.00
Bowl, berry, 5" d., Sunburst iridescent....4.50
Bowl, cereal, 6½" d., amber or pink......18.00
Bowl, cereal, 6½" d., Sunburst
  iridescent 7.50
Bowl, large berry, 8½" d., amber 14.50
Bowl, large berry, 8½" d., pink.............28.00
Bowl, large berry, 8½" d., Sunburst
  iridescent 13.50
Bowl, 10" oval vegetable, amber 15.00
Bowl, 10" oval vegetable, Sunburst
  iridescent 13.00
Creamer, footed, amber, pink or
  Sunburst iridescent 7.50
Cup, amber...7.50
Cup, Sunburst iridescent 5.50
Cup & saucer, pink 11.00
Luncheon set: 4 each 8" d. plates,
  cups & saucers plus creamer &
  sugar bowl; amber, 14 pcs................80.00
Pitcher, 8" h., 80 oz., amber 70.00
Pitcher, 8" h., 80 oz., pink...................100.00
Plate, sherbet, 6" d., amber 4.50
Plate, sherbet, 6" d., pink.......................3.50
Plate, sherbet, 6" d., Sunburst
  iridescent 2.50
Plate, salad, 8" d., amber 8.50
Plate, salad, 8" d., pink or Sunburst
  iridescent 10.50
Plate, luncheon, 9¼" d., amber 8.00
Plate, luncheon, 9¼" d., pink 12.00
Plate, dinner, 11" d., amber 19.50
Plate, dinner, 11" d., pink....................116.00
Plate, dinner, 11" d., Sunburst
  iridescent 13.50
Plate, grill, 11" d., amber 13.50
Plate, grill, 11" d., Sunburst iridescent....7.50
Platter, 11¾" oval, amber 17.00

Platter, 11¾" oval, pink 29.00
Platter, 11¾" oval, Sunburst
  iridescent 12.50
Salt & pepper shakers, amber, pr. 43.00
Salt & pepper shakers, pink, pr. 81.50
Saucer, amber 4.00
Saucer, Sunburst iridescent 3.00
Sherbet, amber, clear or Sunburst
  iridescent 6.00
Sherbet, pink 9.00
Sugar bowl, cov., amber 81.00
Sugar bowl, open, amber 7.00
Sugar bowl, open, Sunburst iridescent...6.00
Tumbler, juice, amber, 4" h., 5 oz. 17.50
Tumbler, juice, pink, 4" h., 5 oz. 35.00
Tumbler, water, amber, 4½" h., 9 oz. ...15.00
Tumbler, water, pink, 4½" h., 9 oz. 41.00
Tumbler, iced tea, amber, 5" h.,
  12 oz. 19.00
Tumbler, iced tea, pink, 5" h., 12 oz. ..104.00

NUMBER 612 or Horseshoe, Indiana Glass Co., 1930-1933 (Process-etched)

Bowl, berry, 4½" d., green 21.00
Bowl, berry, 4½" d., yellow 18.00
Bowl, cereal, 6½" d., green...................22.50
Bowl, cereal, 6½" d., yellow.................19.50
Bowl, salad, 7½" d., green 18.50
Bowl, salad, 7½" d., yellow 19.50
Bowl, vegetable, 8½" d., green.............19.00
Bowl, vegetable, 8½" d., yellow 30.00
Bowl, large berry, 9½" d., green 29.50
Bowl, large berry, 9½" d., yellow 31.50
Bowl, 10½" oval vegetable, green 18.50
Bowl, 10½" oval vegetable, yellow 22.50

Number 612 Butter Dish

Butter dish, cov., green (ILLUS.) 550.00
Creamer, footed, green or yellow 14.00
Cup, green..11.00
Cup, yellow...9.50
Pitcher, 8½" h., 64 oz., green 200.00
Pitcher, 8½" h., 64 oz., yellow 236.00
Plate, sherbet, 6" d., green 5.00
Plate, sherbet, 6" d., yellow 6.00
Plate, salad, 8⅜" d., green or yellow 8.50
Plate, luncheon, 9⅜" d., green 11.50
Plate, luncheon, 9⅜" d., yellow.............13.00
Plate, dinner, 10⅜" d., green 16.50
Plate, grill, 10⅜" d., green 76.00

Plate, sandwich, 11" d., green 14.50
Plate, sandwich, 11" d., yellow 17.00
Platter, 10¾" oval, green 18.00
Platter, 10¾" oval, yellow 21.00
Relish, three-part, footed, green...........15.00
Relish, three-part, footed, yellow 34.50
Saucer, green or yellow...........................4.50
Sherbet, green.......................................14.00
Sherbet, yellow......................................15.50
Sugar bowl, open, footed, green 12.50
Sugar bowl, open, footed, yellow..........14.00
Tumbler, footed, green or yellow,
  9 oz. 20.00
Tumbler, footed, yellow, 12 oz...........102.50

OLD CAFE, Hocking Glass Co., 1936-40 (Press-mold)

Old Cafe Candy Dishes

Bowl, berry, 3¾" d., pink........................7.50
Bowl, nappy, 5" d., handled, clear 3.50
Bowl, nappy, 5" d., handled, pink 7.00
Bowl, cereal, 5½" d., pink or ruby 11.50
Bowl, 9" d., handled, pink 7.50
Bowl, 9" d., handled, ruby.....................12.50
Candy dish, clear, 8" d............................7.50
Candy dish, pink, 8" d.(ILLUS. right) 10.00
Candy dish, ruby, 8" d.(ILLUS. left) 12.00
Cup, ruby 6.50
Cup & saucer, pink 11.00
Cup & saucer, ruby cup, clear saucer ..10.00
Lamp, pink 12.50
Olive dish, clear, 6" oblong 5.00
Olive dish, pink, 6" oblong 6.00
Pitcher, 6" h., 36 oz., clear...................25.00
Pitcher, 6" h., 36 oz., pink....................74.00
Pitcher, 8" h., 80 oz., pink....................84.00
Plate, sherbet, 6" d., clear 4.00
Plate, sherbet, 6" d., pink.....................11.50
Plate, dinner, 10" d., pink......................29.50
Sherbet, low foot, clear...........................3.50
Sherbet, low foot, pink............................8.00
Tumbler, juice, clear or ruby, 3" h..........6.00
Tumbler, juice, pink, 3" h.......................12.50
Tumbler, water, pink, 4" h. 13.00
Tumbler, water, ruby, 4" h. 12.00
Vase, 7¼" h., clear 9.00

OYSTER & PEARL, Anchor Hocking Glass Corp., 1938-40 (Press-mold)

Bowl, 5¼" heart-shaped, w/handle,
  clear or white w/green 7.00

Bowl, 5¼" heart-shaped, w/handle,
  pink 9.50
Bowl, 5¼" heart-shaped, w/handle,
  white w/pink 8.00
Bowl, 5½" d., w/handle, clear 8.50
Bowl, 5½" d., w/handle, ruby 13.00
Bowl, 6½" d., handled, pink 11.50
Bowl, 6½" d., handled, ruby 18.50
Bowl, fruit, 10½" d., clear.....................18.00
Bowl, fruit, 10½" d., pink 23.50
Bowl, fruit, 10½" d., ruby......................44.00
Bowl, fruit, 10½" d., white w/green or
  white w/pink 13.00
Candleholders, clear, 3½" h., pr. 20.50
Candleholders, pink, 3½" h., pr. 17.00
Candleholders, ruby, 3½" h., pr. 41.50
Candleholders, white w/green,
  3½" h., pr. 12.50
Candleholders, white w/pink,
  3½" h., pr. 14.00
Plate, sandwich, 13½" d., clear 12.50
Plate, sandwich, 13½" d., pink..............18.00
Plate, sandwich, 13½" d., ruby 32.00
Relish, divided, clear, 10¼" oval.............8.00
Relish, divided, pink, 10¼" oval............10.00

PARROT or Sylvan, Federal Glass Co., 1931-32 (Process-etched)

Bowl, berry, 5" sq., amber 14.50
Bowl, berry, 5" sq., green 18.50
Bowl, soup, 7" sq., amber.....................29.50
Bowl, soup, 7" sq., green.......................38.50
Bowl, large berry, 8" sq., green 57.50
Bowl, 10" oval vegetable, green 46.50
Butter dish, cov., green.......................315.00
Creamer, footed, green 45.00
Cup & saucer, amber.............................39.00
Cup & saucer, green..............................50.00
Hot plate, green, scalloped edge........775.00
Jam dish, amber, 7" sq. 30.00
Plate, sherbet, 5¾" sq., amber 16.50
Plate, sherbet, 5¾" sq., green 18.00
Plate, salad, 7½" sq., green..................31.50
Plate, dinner, 9" sq., green 43.50
Plate, grill, 10½" sq., amber..................24.00
Plate, grill, 10½" d., green 28.00
Platter, 11¼" oblong, green...................45.50
Salt & pepper shakers, green, pr........205.00
Sherbet, footed, cone-shaped, amber..19.00
Sherbet, footed, cone-shaped, green...22.00
Sugar bowl, cov., green.......................150.00
Sugar bowl, open, green 21.00
Tumbler, green, 4¼" h., 10 oz.....97.50
Tumbler, footed, amber, 5½" h.,
  10 oz. 118.00
Tumbler, footed, cone-shaped, green,
  5¾" h..102.00

PATRICIAN or Spoke, Federal Glass Co., 1933-37 (Process-etched)

Bowl, cream soup, 4¾" d., amber.........13.50
Bowl, cream soup, 4¾" d., clear, green
  or pink 15.00

Bowl, berry, 5" d., amber or green........10.00
Bowl, berry, 5" d., clear.........................9.00
Bowl, berry, 5" d., pink 11.00
Bowl, cereal, 6" d., amber or green 22.00
Bowl, cereal, 6" d., clear or pink 20.00
Bowl, large berry, 8½" d., amber 41.50
Bowl, large berry, 8½" d., clear.............38.00
Bowl, large berry, 8½" d., green 30.00

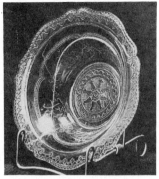

Patrician Berry Bowl

Bowl, large berry, 8½" d., pink
  (ILLUS.) 24.00
Bowl, 10" oval vegetable, amber or
  clear...27.50
Bowl, 10" oval vegetable, green 29.50
Bowl, 10" oval vegetable, pink..............18.00
Butter dish, cov., amber or clear...........81.50
Butter dish, cov., green.........................95.00
Butter dish, cov., pink 227.00
Cookie jar, cov., amber.........................80.00
Cookie jar, cov., clear...........................75.00
Cookie jar, cov., green........................405.00
Creamer, footed, amber 8.00
Creamer, footed, clear or pink 9.00
Creamer, footed, green 11.50
Cup, amber or green 8.00
Cup & saucer, clear 13.00
Cup & saucer, pink 17.00
Jam dish, amber, 6"..............................26.50
Jam dish, green, 6"...............................29.00
Pitcher, 8" h., 75 oz., molded handle,
  amber..102.00
Pitcher, 8" h., 75 oz., molded handle,
  clear...95.00
Pitcher, 8" h., 75 oz., molded handle,
  green...107.00
Pitcher, 8" h., 75 oz., molded handle,
  pink 112.00
Pitcher, 8¼" h., 75 oz., applied handle,
  amber..95.00
Pitcher, 8¼" h., 75 oz., applied handle,
  clear 125.00
Pitcher, 8¼" h., 75 oz., applied handle,
  green..110.00
Plate, sherbet, 6" d., amber or pink 8.50
Plate, sherbet, 6" d., clear 5.50
Plate, sherbet, 6" d., green.....................6.00
Plate, salad, 7½" d., amber or green 13.50
Plate, salad, 7½" d., clear....................12.00

Plate, luncheon, 9" d., amber, clear or
  green...10.00
Plate, luncheon, 9" d., pink...................12.50
Plate, dinner, 10½" d., amber.................6.50
Plate, dinner, 10½" d., green or pink 39.00
Plate, grill, 10½" d., amber or clear 11.50
Plate, grill, 10½" d., green or pink.........10.50
Platter, 11½" oval, amber or clear 27.00
Platter, 11½" oval, green 23.50
Salt & pepper shakers, amber or
  clear, pr...52.50
Salt & pepper shakers, green, pr..........51.00
Salt & pepper shakers, pink, pr. 77.50
Saucer, amber or green..........................9.00
Sherbet, amber or clear........................10.50
Sherbet, green or pink...........................12.50
Sugar bowl, cov., amber......................61.00
Sugar bowl, cov., clear 54.00
Sugar bowl, cov., green.......................43.50
Sugar bowl, cov., pink..........................52.00
Sugar bowl, open, amber or clear 8.00
Sugar bowl, open, green 9.00
Sugar bowl, open, pink 10.50
Tumbler, amber or green, 4" h., 5 oz....27.00
Tumbler, clear, 4" h., 5 oz.....................20.00
Tumbler, footed, amber, 5¼" h.,
  8 oz..44.50
Tumbler, footed, clear, 5¼" h., 8 oz......34.00
Tumbler, footed, green, 5¼" h., 8 oz. ...47.50
Tumbler, amber or green, 4½" h.,
  9 oz..24.00
Tumbler, clear, 4½" h., 9 oz.................26.00
Tumbler, pink, 4½" h., 9 oz..................23.50
Tumbler, iced tea, amber, 5½" h.,
  14 oz. 38.50
Tumbler, iced tea, clear, 5½" h.,
  14 oz. 35.00
Tumbler, iced tea, green, 5½" h.,
  14 oz. 27.00
Tumbler, iced tea, pink, 5½" h.,
  14 oz. 40.00

**PETALWARE, MacBeth-Evans Glass Co.,
1930-40 (Press-mold)**

Bowl, cream soup, 4½" d., clear 5.50
Bowl, cream soup, 4½" d., plain
  Cremax or Monax 10.50
Bowl, cream soup, 4½" d., decorated
  Cremax or Monax 10.50
Bowl, cream soup, 4½" d., Florette.......10.00
Bowl, cream soup, 4½" d., pink 12.50
Bowl, cereal, 5¾" d., clear......................5.00
Bowl, cereal, 5¾" d., plain Cremax
  or Monax...7.00
Bowl, cereal, 5¾" d., decorated
  Cremax or Monax 7.00
Bowl, cereal, 5¾" d., Florette................11.00
Bowl, cereal, 5¾" d., pink 9.50
Bowl, large berry, 9" d., plain Cremax
  or Monax...17.00
Bowl, large berry, 9" d., decorated
  Cremax or Monax 26.00
Bowl, large berry, 9" d., Florette 25.00

Bowl, large berry, 9" d., pink.................17.50
Creamer, footed, clear............................3.50
Creamer, footed, plain Cremax or
  Monax..7.50
Creamer, footed, decorated Cremax
  or Monax..8.50
Creamer, footed, Florette 11.00
Creamer, footed, pink 12.00
Cup, plain Cremax or Monax..................5.00
Cup, decorated Cremax or Monax 6.50
Cup, Florette...9.00
Cup & saucer, clear 4.00
Cup & saucer, clear w/platinum trim.......5.00
Cup & saucer, Red Trim Floral or
  pink 10.00
Lamp shade, Monax, 6" h.......................8.00
Lamp shade, Monax, 11" h...................15.50
Lamp shade, pink, 12" h. 21.00
Mustard jar w/metal cover, cobalt
  blue 15.00
Plate, sherbet, 6" d., clear 1.50
Plate, sherbet, 6" d., plain Cremax or
  Monax..2.50
Plate, sherbet, 6" d., decorated
  Cremax or Monax 4.00
Plate, sherbet, 6" d., pink.......................3.50
Plate, salad, 8" d., clear.........................2.50
Plate, salad, 8" d., plain Cremax or
  Monax..5.00
Plate, salad, 8" d., decorated Cremax
  or Monax..8.50
Plate, salad, 8" d., Florette 8.50
Plate, salad, 8" d., Red Trim Floral or
  pink 6.50
Plate, dinner, 9" d., clear........................6.00
Plate, dinner, 9" d., plain Cremax or
  Monax..7.00
Plate, dinner, 9" d., decorated Cremax
  or Monax..13.00
Plate, dinner, 9" d., pink..........................8.50
Plate, salver, 11" d., clear w/platinum
  trim 5.00
Plate, salver, 11" d., plain Cremax or
  Monax..10.50
Plate, salver, 11" d., decorated
  Cremax or Monax` 19.50
Plate, salver, 11" d., Florette 15.50
Plate, salver, 11" d., Red Trim Floral....18.50
Plate, salver, 11" d., pink 14.00
Plate, salver, 12" d., plain Cremax or
  Monax..10.50
Plate, salver, 12" d., decorated
  Cremax or Monax 10.00
Plate, salver, 12" d., Florette 14.50
Plate, salver, 12" d., Red Trim Floral....40.00
Platter, 13" oval, plain Cremax
  or Monax..19.00
Platter, 13" oval, decorated Cremax
  or Monax..13.50
Platter, 13" oval, pink...........................15.50
Saucer, plain Cremax or Monax 2.00
Saucer, decorated Cremax or Monax.....2.00
Saucer, Florette......................................3.50

Sherbet, low foot, clear, 4½" h...............6.00
Sherbet, low foot, cobalt blue, 4½" h. ...12.00
Sherbet, low foot, plain Cremax or
  Monax, 4½" h.....................................9.00
Sherbet, low foot, decorated Cremax
  or Monax, 4½" h.................................11.00
Sherbet, low foot, Red Trim Floral,
  4½" h...30.00
Sherbet, low foot, pink, 4½" h.................7.50
Sugar bowl, open, footed, clear.............4.50
Sugar bowl, open, footed, plain Cremax
  or Monax...7.00
Sugar bowl, open, footed, decorated
  Cremax or Monax 10.00
Sugar bowl, open, footed, Florette
  or pink..10.00
Tidbit server, plain Cremax or Monax...23.00
Tumbler, juice, pink 5.00
Tumbler, pink, 4¼" h............................29.00
Tumbler, pink, 4¾" h............................27.00

**PINEAPPLE & FLORAL or Number 618 or
Wildflower, Indiana Glass Co., 1932-37
(Press-mold)**

Pineapple & Floral Plate

Ashtray, clear, 4½" l............................13.00
Bowl, berry, 4¾" d., amber 15.00
Bowl, berry, 4¾" d., clear.....................24.50
Bowl, cream soup, 4⅝", amber
  or clear...18.00
Bowl, cereal, 6" d., amber or clear........21.00
Bowl, salad, 7" d., clear 3.50
Bowl, 10" oval vegetable, amber 18.00
Bowl, 10" oval vegetable, clear.............23.50
Compote, diamond-shaped, amber 5.00
Compote, diamond-shaped, clear 3.50
Creamer, diamond-shaped, amber.........9.50
Creamer, diamond-shaped, clear...........5.50
Cup, amber..6.00
Cup, clear..8.00
Plate, sherbet, 6" d., amber (ILLUS.)......4.00
Plate, sherbet, 6" d., clear 3.00
Plate, salad, 8⅜" d., amber or clear 7.00
Plate, dinner, 9⅜" d., amber 12.00
Plate, dinner, 9⅜" d., clear...................13.50
Plate, sandwich, 11½" d., amber..........15.50
Plate, sandwich, 11½" d., clear 12.50
Plate, 11½" d., w/indentation, clear 16.00

Platter, 11", closed handles, amber
  or clear..15.50
Relish, divided, clear, 11½" 14.50
Saucer, amber or clear..........................4.00
Sherbet, footed, amber or clear...........16.00
Sugar bowl, open, diamond-shaped,
  amber..9.00
Sugar bowl, open, diamond-shaped,
  clear...6.00
Tumbler, clear, 4¼" h., 8 oz.................30.50
Tumbler, iced tea, clear, 5" h., 12 oz. ...42.50
Vase, 12½" h., cone-shaped, clear.......42.00
Vase, 12½" h., cone-shaped, clear
  w/holder...60.00

**PRINCESS, Hocking Glass Co., 1931-35
(Process-etched)**

Ashtray, green, 4½"..............................61.00
Ashtray, pink, 4½"................................22.00
Bowl, berry, 4½", green 20.00
Bowl, berry, 4½", pink...........................17.50
Bowl, berry, 4½", yellow 42.00
Bowl, cereal, 5", green or yellow 25.50
Bowl, cereal, 5", pink 22.00
Bowl, salad, 9" octagon, green or
  pink..36.00
Bowl, salad, 9" octagon, yellow 93.00
Bowl, 9½" hat shape, green..................38.00
Bowl, 9½" hat shape, pink 35.00
Bowl, 10" oval vegetable, green 24.00
Bowl, 10" oval vegetable, pink..............25.50
Bowl, 10" oval vegetable, yellow 49.00
Butter dish, cov., green or pink.............81.00
Butter dish, cov., yellow.......................560.00
Cake stand, green, 10" 19.50
Cake stand, pink, 10"............................23.50
Candy jar, cov., green 53.00
Candy jar, cov., pink.............................49.50
Coaster, green, 4"................................31.50
Cookie jar, cov., green..........................51.00
Cookie jar, cov., pink............................48.00
Creamer, oval, green.............................15.50
Creamer, oval, yellow............................12.50
Cup, amber..7.00
Cup, green...9.50
Cup & saucer, pink 17.50
Cup & saucer, yellow............................10.50
Pitcher, 6" h., 37 oz., jug-type, green
  or pink..48.00
Pitcher, 8" h., 60 oz., jug-type, green
  or pink..49.50
Pitcher, 8" h., 60 oz., jug-type, yellow...78.00
Plate, sherbet, 5½", green 8.00
Plate, sherbet, 5½", pink.......................9.00
Plate, sherbet, 5½", yellow 3.50
Plate, salad, 8", amber 8.00
Plate, salad, 8", green 12.50
Plate, salad, 8", pink.............................11.00
Plate, salad, 8", yellow...........................9.50
Plate, dinner, 9", green or pink 21.50
Plate, dinner, 9", yellow 12.00
Plate, grill, 9", green 11.00
Plate, grill, 9", pink 12.50

Plate, grill, 9", yellow.............................5.50
Plate, grill, 10½", closed handles,
    green...11.00
Plate, grill, 10½", closed handles,
    pink 7.00
Plate, grill, 10½", closed handles,
    yellow..5.50
Plate, sandwich, 11¼", handled,
    green...15.00
Plate, sandwich, 11¼", handled, pink...24.00
Platter, 12" oval, closed handles,
    green...21.00
Platter, 12" oval, closed handles, pink..19.00
Relish, green, 7½".................................103.00
Relish, pink, 7½"...................................300.00
Relish, divided, green, 7½"....................24.50
Relish, divided, pink, 7½" 17.00
Salt & pepper shakers, green, 4½" h.,
    pr...46.00
Salt & pepper shakers, pink, 4½" h.,
    pr...42.50
Salt & pepper shakers, yellow, 4½" h.,
    pr...65.00
Salt & pepper (or spice) shakers,
    green, 5½" h., pr. 39.00
Saucer, green...9.00
Sherbet, footed, green or pink 17.50
Sherbet, footed, yellow.........................28.50
Sugar bowl, cov., green.........................27.50
Sugar bowl, cov., pink 44.00
Sugar bowl, cov., yellow.........................23.50
Sugar bowl, open, green 9.00
Sugar bowl, open, pink...........................7.50
Sugar bowl, open, yellow.........................8.50
Tumbler, juice, green, 3" h., 5 oz.........27.50
Tumbler, juice, pink, 3" h., 5 oz. 23.00
Tumbler, juice, yellow, 3" h., 5 oz. 24.50
Tumbler, water, green or pink, 4" h.,
    9 oz. 24.00
Tumbler, water, yellow, 4" h., 9 oz........20.50
Tumbler, footed, green, 5¼" h.,
    10 oz. 28.00
Tumbler, footed, pink, 5¼" h., 10 oz.....24.00
Tumbler, footed, yellow, 5¼" h.,
    10 oz. 20.00
Tumbler, footed, green, 6½" h.,
    12½ oz. 84.00
Tumbler, footed, pink, 6½" h.,
    12½ oz. 67.50
Tumbler, footed, yellow, 6½" h.,
    12½ oz. 22.50
Tumbler, iced tea, green, 5¼" h.,
    13 oz. 35.00
Tumbler, iced tea, pink, 5¼" h.,
    13 oz. 25.50
Tumbler, iced tea, yellow, 5¼" h.,
    13 oz. 22.50
Vase, 8" h., green or pink 29.50
Vase, 8" h., pink frosted.......................20.00

QUEEN MARY or Vertical Ribbed, Hocking Glass Co., 1936-49 (Press-mold)
Ashtray, clear, 2 x 3¾" oval....................3.00

Ashtray, clear, 3½" d. 5.50
Ashtray, ruby, 3½" d. 8.00
Bowl, nappy, 4" d., clear 3.50
Bowl, nappy, 4" d., pink 5.00
Bowl, nappy, 4" d., single handle, clear..4.00
Bowl, nappy, 4" d., single handle, pink ...5.50
Bowl, berry, 5" d., clear or pink..............5.50
Bowl, 5½" d., two-handled, pink 16.00
Bowl, cereal, 6" d., clear 6.00
Bowl, cereal, 6" d., pink 22.00
Bowl, nappy, 7" d., clear 9.50
Bowl, nappy, 7" d., pink 23.50
Bowl, large berry, 8¾" d., clear.............10.00
Butter (or jam) dish, cov., clear.............29.50
Candlesticks, two-light, clear, 4½" h.,
    pr...15.50
Candy dish, cov., clear 23.50
Candy dish, cov., pink 33.00
Celery (or pickle) dish, clear, 5 x 10"
    oval 9.50
Celery (or pickle) dish, pink, 5 x 10"
    oval 17.00
Cigarette jar, clear, 2 x 3" oval...............4.50
Coaster, clear, 3½" d. 2.50
Coaster, pink, 3½" d. 4.00
Coaster-ashtray, clear, 4¼" sq. 3.50
Coaster-ashtray, pink, 4¼" sq. 8.50
Compote, 5¾" d., clear 7.00
Creamer, oval, clear 4.50
Creamer, oval, pink 10.50
Cup, pink 7.50
Cup & saucer, clear.................................8.50
Plate, sherbet, 6" d., clear 3.50
Plate, sherbet, 6" d., pink.......................4.50
Plate, 6⅝" d., clear 4.00
Plate, 6⅝" d., pink..................................10.50
Plate, salad, 8½" d., clear.......................4.50
Plate, dinner, 9¾" d., clear 14.50
Plate, dinner, 9¾" d., pink.....................42.00
Plate, sandwich, 12" d., clear 8.50
Plate, sandwich, 12" d., pink..................15.00
Plate, serving, 14" d., clear.....................9.00
Relish, three-part, clear, 12" d. 10.50
Relish, four-part, clear, 14" d. 10.00
Salt & pepper shakers, clear, pr. 16.50
Saucer, pink...12.00
Sherbet, footed, clear 4.50
Sherbet, footed, pink 7.00
Sugar bowl, open, oval, clear 4.50
Sugar bowl, open, oval, pink 12.50
Tumbler, juice, pink, 3½" h., 5 oz. 9.00
Tumbler, water, clear, 4" h., 9 oz...........6.50
Tumbler, water, pink, 4" h., 9 oz...........10.50
Tumbler, footed, clear, 5" h., 10 oz.......17.50
Tumbler, footed, pink, 5" h., 10 oz.......51.50

RAINDROPS or Optic Design, Federal Glass Co., 1929-33 (Press-mold)
(All items listed are green)

Bowl, cereal, 6" d...................................5.50
Bowl, berry, 7½" d. 28.00
Cup & saucer..6.50
Plate, sherbet, 6" d. 2.00

Plate, luncheon, 8" d..............................5.00
Tumbler, whiskey, 1⅞" h., 1 oz...............5.50
Tumbler, 3" h., 4 oz. 4.00
Tumbler, 3⅞" h., 5 oz. 5.00
Tumbler, 4⅛" h., 9½ oz. 7.50

RIBBON, Hazel Atlas Glass Co., early 1930s (Press-mold)

(While pattern was also made in black, all items listed are green.)
Bowl, berry, 4" d. 12.00
Bowl, 8" d...22.00
Candy dish, cov. 34.00
Creamer, footed.......................................12.00
Cup & saucer...8.00
Plate, sherbet, 6¼" d. 3.50
Plate, luncheon, 8" d................................5.00
Salt & pepper shakers, pr. 23.50
Sherbet, footed...5.00
Sugar bowl, open, footed.......................12.00
Tumbler, 6" h., 10 oz. 24.50

RING or Banded Rings, Hocking Glass Co., 1927-33 (Press-mold)

Bowl, berry, 5" d., clear...........................3.50
Bowl, berry, 5" d., clear w/multicolored
    bands 6.00
Bowl, berry, 5" d., green 5.50
Bowl, soup, 7" d., clear..........................11.50
Bowl, soup, 7" d., clear w/platinum trim ..7.00
Bowl, soup, 7" d., clear w/multicolored
    bands 6.50
Bowl, soup, 7" d., green...........................8.50
Bowl, large berry, 8" d., green 10.50
Butter tub, clear w/multicolored
    bands 23.50
Cocktail shaker, clear 15.50
Cocktail shaker, clear w/multicolored
    bands 23.50
Cocktail shaker, clear w/platinum trim ..14.00
Cocktail shaker, green...........................12.00
Creamer, footed, clear.............................4.00
Creamer, footed, green 8.50
Cup, clear w/platinum trim 4.50
Cup, green...4.50
Cup & saucer, clear w/multicolored
    bands 5.00
Cup & saucer, green w/platinum trim 6.50
Decanter w/stopper, clear.....................19.00
Decanter w/stopper, clear w/multi-
    colored bands 28.00
Dinner set: four each 8" d. plates,
    cups & saucers, low sherbets &
    footed water tumblers plus center
    handled plate; green, 21 pcs. 170.00
Goblet, clear, 7¼" h., 9 oz. 7.00
Goblet, clear w/multicolored bands,
    7¼" h., 9 oz. 10.50
Goblet, clear w/platinum trim, 7¼" h.,
    9 oz. 12.00
Goblet, green, 7¼" h., 9 oz. 10.50
Ice bucket w/tab handles, clear 12.50

Ice bucket w/tab handles, clear
    w/multicolored bands 17.00
Pitcher, 8" h., 60 oz., clear...................14.00
Pitcher, 8" h., 60 oz., clear w/multi-
    colored bands 16.00
Pitcher, 8" h., 60 oz., green 17.00
Pitcher, 8½" h., 80 oz., clear................17.00
Pitcher, 8½" h., 80 oz., clear w/multi-
    colored bands 33.00
Pitcher, 8½" h., 80 oz., green 22.50
Plate, sherbet, 6¼" d., clear 1.50
Plate, sherbet, 6¼" d., clear w/multi-
    colored bands 2.00
Plate, sherbet, 6¼" d., green 2.00
Plate, 6½" d., off-center ring, clear
    w/multicolored bands 5.00
Plate, 6½" d., off-center ring, green........5.00
Plate, luncheon, 8" d., clear...................4.00
Plate, luncheon, 8" d., clear w/multi-
    colored bands 2.50
Plate, luncheon, 8" d., clear
    w/platinum trim 4.50
Plate, luncheon, 8" d., green 4.50
Plate, luncheon, 8" d., green w/platinum
    trim 5.50
Salt & pepper shakers, clear, 3" h.,
    pr..18.00
Salt & pepper shakers, clear w/multi-
    colored bands, 3" h., pr........................24.00
Sandwich server w/center handle,
    clear 14.00
Sandwich server w/center handle,
    clear w/multicolored bands 16.00
Sandwich server w/center handle,
    green...19.50
Saucer, green...2.00
Sherbet, low, clear....................................6.00
Sherbet, low, clear w/multicolored
    bands 16.00
Sherbet, low, green 12.50
Sherbet, footed, clear, 4¾" h. 5.50
Sherbet, footed, clear w/multicolored
    bands, 4¾" h. 6.50
Sherbet, footed, green, 4¾" h.................8.00
Sugar bowl, open, footed, clear..............4.50
Tumbler, whiskey, clear w/multicolored
    bands, 2" h., 1½ oz. 6.50
Tumbler, clear, 3½" h., 5 oz....................3.50
Tumbler, clear w/multicolored bands,
    3½" h., 5 oz. 8.50
Tumbler, green, 3½" h., 5 oz. 12.50
Tumbler, clear, 3¾" h., 8 oz.................10.00
Tumbler, clear w/platinum trim, 3¾" h.,
    8 oz. 7.00
Tumbler, clear, 4¼" h., 9 oz....................5.50
Tumbler, clear w/multicolored bands,
    4¼" h., 9 oz. 8.00
Tumbler, green, 4¼" h., 9 oz. 11.50
Tumbler, green, 4¾" h., 10 oz. 15.50
Tumbler, clear, 5⅛" h., 12 oz..................5.50
Tumbler, clear w/multicolored bands,
    5⅛" h., 12 oz. 8.00
Tumbler, green, 5⅛" h., 12 oz. 13.50
Tumbler, pink, 5⅛" h., 12 oz...................7.00

Tumbler, cocktail, footed, clear, 3½" h. ..4.00
Tumbler, cocktail, footed, clear
    w/multicolored bands, 3½" h. 6.50
Tumbler, cocktail, footed, green,
    3½" h...12.00
Tumbler, water, footed, clear, 5½" h.......4.50
Tumbler, water, footed, clear w/multi-
    colored bands, 5½" h. 6.00
Tumbler, water, footed, green, 5½" h. ...15.50
Tumbler, iced tea, footed, clear, 6½" h...6.50
Tumbler, iced tea, footed, clear
    w/multicolored bands, 6½" h. 8.50
Vase, 8" h., clear 12.50
Vase, 8" h., clear w/multicolored
    bands 25.00

**ROULETTE or Many Windows, Hocking
Glass Co., 1935-39 (Press-mold)**
Bowl, fruit, 9" d., green 14.00
Cup, green...5.50
Pitcher, 8" h., 64 oz., green 30.00
Pitcher, 8" h., 64 oz., pink....................26.50
Plate, sherbet, 6" d., green 3.00
Plate, luncheon, 8½" d., clear................4.00
Plate, luncheon, 8½" d., green 6.00
Plate, sandwich, 12" d., green 15.00
Saucer, green...4.00
Sherbet, green...5.50
Tumbler, whiskey, green, 2½" h.,
    1½ oz. 6.50
Tumbler, whiskey, pink, 2½" h.,
    1½ oz. 11.00
Tumbler, juice, green, 3¼" h., 5 oz.......18.50
Tumbler, juice, pink, 3¼" h., 5 oz. 7.00
Tumbler, Old Fashioned, pink, 3¼" h.,
    7½ oz. 19.00
Tumbler, water, green, 4⅛" h., 9 oz. 19.00
Tumbler, water, pink, 4⅛" h., 9 oz. 15.50
Tumbler, footed, green, 5½" h.,
    10 oz. 22.50
Tumbler, iced tea, green, 5⅛" h.,
    12 oz. 21.50
Tumbler, iced tea, pink, 5⅛" h.,
    12 oz. 14.50

**ROYAL LACE, Hazel Atlas Glass Co.,
1934-41 (Process-etched)**

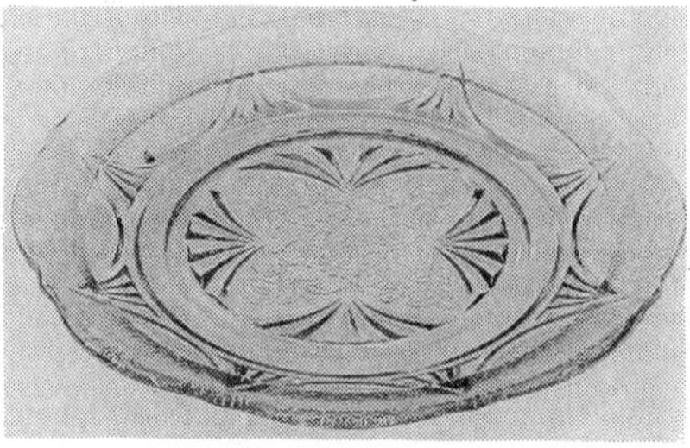

Royal Lace Plate

Bowl, cream soup, 4¾" d., blue............34.50
Bowl, cream soup, 4¾" d., clear...........11.50
Bowl, cream soup, 4¾" d., green or
    pink 28.50

Bowl, berry, 5" d., blue..........................35.00
Bowl, berry, 5" d., clear.........................13.00
Bowl, berry, 5" d., green 28.00
Bowl, berry, 5" d., pink..........................22.50
Bowl, berry, 10" d., green 24.00
Bowl, berry, 10" d., pink.........................30.00
Bowl, 10" d., three-footed, rolled edge,
    blue 250.00
Bowl, 10" d., three-footed, rolled edge,
    clear 29.00
Bowl, 10" d., three-footed, rolled edge,
    pink 47.50
Bowl, 10" d., three-footed, ruffled edge,
    clear 35.00
Bowl, 10" d., three-footed, ruffled edge,
    green...65.00
Bowl, 10" d., three-footed, ruffled edge,
    pink 51.00
Bowl, 10" d., three-footed, straight edge,
    blue 70.00
Bowl, 11" oval vegetable, blue.............43.50
Bowl, 11" oval vegetable, clear............14.00
Bowl, 11" oval vegetable, green 27.50
Bowl, 11" oval vegetable, pink.............29.50
Butter dish, cov., blue 465.00
Butter dish, cov., clear..........................65.00
Butter dish, cov., green.......................250.00
Butter dish, cov., pink 139.00
Candlesticks, rolled edge, blue, pr. 167.50
Candlesticks, rolled edge, clear, pr. 25.00
Candlesticks, rolled edge, pink, pr........42.50
Candlesticks, ruffled edge, blue, pr. ...132.00
Candlesticks, ruffled edge, clear, pr. 28.00
Candlesticks, ruffled edge, green, pr....42.50
Candlesticks, ruffled edge, pink, pr. 45.50
Candlesticks, straight edge, blue, pr. ...90.00
Candlesticks, straight edge, clear, pr. ..32.00
Cookie jar, cov., blue 348.00
Cookie jar, cov., clear 38.00
Cookie jar, cov., green...........................88.00
Cookie jar, cov., pink 44.00
Creamer, footed, blue............................49.00
Creamer, footed, clear...........................12.50
Creamer, footed, green 24.00
Creamer, footed, pink 17.00
Cup, blue 35.50
Cup, clear 6.00
Cup & saucer, green..............................26.50
Cup & saucer, pink 18.50
Nut bowl, green 185.00
Pitcher, 48 oz., straight sides, blue.....146.00
Pitcher, 48 oz., straight sides, clear......37.50
Pitcher, 48 oz., straight sides, green 95.50
Pitcher, 8" h., 64 oz., without ice lip,
    blue 156.00
Pitcher, 8" h., 68 oz., w/ice lip, clear.....40.00
Pitcher, 8" h., 68 oz., w/ice lip, pink 53.50
Pitcher, 8" h., 86 oz., without ice lip,
    pink 70.00
Pitcher, 8½" h., 96 oz., w/ice lip,
    blue 257.00
Pitcher, 8½" h., 96 oz., w/ice lip,
    clear 59.00

Pitcher, 8½" h., 96 oz., w/ice lip,
   green...150.00
Plate, sherbet, 6" d., blue 14.00
Plate, sherbet, 6" d., clear 5.00
Plate, sherbet, 6" d., green or pink 8.00
Plate, luncheon, 8½" d., blue
   (ILLUS.) 31.00
Plate, luncheon, 8½" d., green or pink..15.50
Plate, dinner, 9⅞" d., blue 36.00
Plate, dinner, 9⅞" d., clear 17.00
Plate, dinner, 9⅞" d., green or pink 26.00
Plate, grill, 9⅞" d., blue.........................29.50
Plate, grill, 9⅞" d., pink 17.50
Platter, 13" oval, blue............................46.50
Platter, 13" oval, clear...........................14.00
Platter, 13" oval, green 30.00
Platter, 13" oval, pink...........................32.50
Salt & pepper shakers, blue, pr. 225.00
Salt & pepper shakers, clear, pr. 39.50
Salt & pepper shakers, green, pr........120.00
Salt & pepper shakers, pink, pr. 58.50
Saucer, blue 9.00
Saucer, clear 6.00
Sherbet, footed, blue 34.50
Sherbet, footed, clear or pink 12.50
Sherbet, footed, green 23.00
Sherbet in metal holder, amethyst........34.00
Sherbet in metal holder, blue...............23.50
Sherbet in metal holder, clear................9.00
Sherbet in metal holder, green 5.50
Sugar bowl, cov., blue 198.00
Sugar bowl, cov., clear 23.50
Sugar bowl, cov., green.........................57.00
Sugar bowl, cov., pink...........................38.00
Sugar bowl, open, blue...........................31.00
Sugar bowl, open, clear...........................7.50
Sugar bowl, open, green 21.00
Sugar bowl, open, pink..........................15.50
Toddy or cider set: cookie jar w/metal
   lid & 6 roly-poly tumblers; blue,
   7 pcs. 125.00
Tumbler, blue, 3½" h., 5 oz...................40.00
Tumbler, clear, 3½" h., 5 oz..................12.50
Tumbler, green, 3½" h., 5 oz. 21.50
Tumbler, pink, 3½" h., 5 oz....................18.00
Tumbler, blue, 4⅛" h., 9 oz...................37.00
Tumbler, clear, 4⅛" h., 9 oz..................11.50
Tumbler, green, 4⅛" h., 9 oz. 28.00
Tumbler, pink, 4⅛" h., 9 oz....................18.00
Tumbler, blue, 4⅞" h., 10 oz.................88.00
Tumbler, pink, 4⅞" h., 10 oz.................35.00
Tumbler, blue, 5⅜" h., 12 oz.................66.00
Tumbler, clear, 5⅜" h., 12 oz...............21.00
Tumbler, green, 5⅜" h., 12 oz. 42.00
Tumbler, pink, 5⅜" h., 12 oz.................37.50
Water set: 68 oz. pitcher & six 9 oz.
   tumblers; blue, 7 pcs........................360.00

ROYAL RUBY, Anchor Hocking Glass Co., 1939-60s (Press-mold)
(All items in ruby red.)
Ashtray, 4¼" sq. 4.50

Bowl, berry, 4¼" d. 6.00
Bowl, 4¾" sq..6.50
Bowl, 5¼" d..10.50
Bowl, 6½" d., scalloped 8.50
Bowl, 7⅜" sq.......................................14.00
Bowl, soup, 7½" d................................12.00
Bowl, 8" oval vegetable 35.00
Bowl, berry, 8½" d................................17.50
Bowl, popcorn, 10" d., deep.................45.00
Bowl, salad, 11½" d.............................30.50
Creamer, flat...7.00
Creamer, footed......................................8.00
Cup, round..4.50
Cup, square..6.00
Goblet, ball stem....................................10.00
Juice set, 22 oz. tilted pitcher & six 5 oz.
   tumblers, 7 pcs. 67.50
Pitcher, 22 oz., tilted or upright..............30.50
Pitcher, 3 qt., tilted or upright................41.50
Plate, sherbet, 6½" d. 4.50
Plate, salad, 7" d....................................5.00
Plate, luncheon, 7¾" d...........................6.50
Plate, 8⅜" sq. 7.50
Plate, dinner, 9" d. 10.50
Plate, 13¾" d. 21.50
Playing card or cigarette box, divided,
   clear base 69.00
Popcorn set, 10" d. serving bowl and
   six 5¼" d. bowls, 7 pcs. 125.00
Punch bowl..37.50
Punch bowl & base................................59.00
Punch cup...2.50
Punch set, punch bowl, base & 8 cups,
   10 pcs. 110.00
Saucer, round..2.50
Saucer, square 2.50
Sherbet, footed 7.00
Sugar bowl, flat.......................................7.00
Sugar bowl, footed..................................8.00
Sugar bowl w/slotted lid, footed...........15.50
Tumbler, cocktail, 3½ oz.......................10.50
Tumbler, juice, 5 oz. 5.00
Tumbler, water, 9 oz...............................5.50
Tumbler, water, 10 oz.............................8.50
Tumbler, iced tea, footed, 6" h.,
   12 oz. 11.50
Tumbler, iced tea, 13 oz. 11.00
Vase, 4" h., ball-shaped..........................5.00
Vase, 5" h., ball-shaped........................10.00
Vase, bud, 5½" h., ruffled top 6.50
Vase, 6½" h., bulbous.............................5.00
Vase, various styles, large....................13.00
Wine, footed, 2½ oz..............................11.00

SAILBOATS or Ships or Sportsman Series, Hazel Atlas Glass Co., late 1930s
(All items in cobalt blue with white decoration)
Ashtray 27.50
Cocktail mixer w/stirrer 26.00
Cocktail shaker w/metal lid 48.00
Ice bowl 30.00
Pitcher without ice lip, 82 oz. 62.50
Pitcher w/ice lip, 86 oz..........................72.50

Plate, bread & butter, 5⅞" d. 18.00
Plate, salad, 8" d..................................35.00
Plate, dinner, 9" d. 33.50
Saucer 14.00
Tray, wooden handles (blue boat on
  white) 105.00
Tumbler, juice, 3¾" h., 5 oz. 10.50
Tumbler, roly poly, 6 oz. 9.50
Tumbler, Old Fashioned, 3⅜" h., 8 oz..13.50
Tumbler, water, straight sides, 3¾" h.,
  9 oz..10.50
Tumbler, water, 4⅝" h., 9 oz.................12.50
Tumbler, iced tea, 4⅞" h., 10½ oz.......12.50
Tumbler, iced tea, 12 oz. 21.00

SANDWICH, Anchor Hocking Glass Co., 1939-64 (Press-mold)

Sandwich Pattern

Bowl, 4⁵⁄₁₆" d., clear..................................4.50
Bowl, 4⁵⁄₁₆" d., green................................3.00
Bowl, berry, 4⅞" d., amber 3.00
Bowl, berry, 4⅞" d., clear......................12.50
Bowl, berry, 4⅞" d., pink.........................6.50
Bowl, 5¼" d., scalloped, amber 5.00
Bowl, 5¼" d., scalloped, clear................7.00
Bowl, 5¼" d., ruby.................................17.00
Bowl, cereal, 6½" d., amber..................13.50
Bowl, cereal, 6½" d., clear....................29.00
Bowl, salad, 7" d., clear 7.00
Bowl, salad, 7" d., green.......................52.00
Bowl, 8" d., scalloped, clear...................9.50
Bowl, 8" d., scalloped, green 66.00
Bowl, 8" d., scalloped, pink...................12.00
Bowl, 8" d., scalloped, ruby 45.00
Bowl, 8½" oval vegetable, clear.............6.50
Bowl, salad, 9" d., amber......................23.50
Bowl, salad, 9" d., clear 21.00
Butter dish, cov., clear 40.00
Cookie jar, cov., amber.........................35.00
Cookie jar, cov., clear 34.00
Cookie jar, green (no cover made) 17.00
Creamer, clear 4.50
Creamer, green 23.00
Cup, amber...3.00
Cup, clear 2.50
Cup & saucer, green.............................28.00
Custard cup, clear 4.00
Custard cup, ruffled, clear 12.50
Custard cup, green 3.00
Custard cup liner, clear.........................12.50

Custard cup liner, green 2.00
Pitcher, juice, 6" h., clear.....................53.00
Pitcher w/ice lip, 2 qt., clear.................71.00
Pitcher w/ice lip, 2 qt., green 235.00
Plate, dessert, 7" d., amber 8.00
Plate, dessert, 7" d., clear......................9.00
Plate, 8" d., clear 5.00
Plate, dinner, 9" d., amber 7.00
Plate, dinner, 9" d., clear 15.50
Plate, dinner, 9" d., green.....................74.00
Plate, snack, 9" d., clear 5.00
Plate, sandwich, 12" d., amber 14.00
Plate, sandwich, 12" d., clear 31.50
Punch bowl, clear 18.00
Punch bowl & base, clear (ILLUS.).......38.00
Punch bowl & base, opaque white 22.50
Punch cup, clear (ILLUS.) 2.50
Punch cup, opaque white 2.00
Punch set: punch bowl & 6 cups;
  clear, 7 pcs. 30.50
Punch set: punch bowl, base & 10 cups;
  opaque white, 12 pcs. 45.00
Sherbet, footed, clear 7.50
Sugar bowl, cov., clear 16.00
Sugar bowl, cov., green........................24.00
Sugar bowl, open, clear..........................5.00
Sugar bowl, open, green 22.50
Tumbler, juice, clear, 3 oz. 5.50
Tumbler, juice, green, 3 oz. 3.50
Tumbler, clear, 5 oz...............................6.50
Tumbler, green, 5 oz..............................4.00
Tumbler, water, clear, 9 oz. 8.00
Tumbler, water, green, 9 oz....................4.00
Tumbler, footed, amber, 9 oz. 22.00
Tumbler, footed, clear, 9 oz..................27.00

SHARON or Cabbage Rose, Federal Glass Co., 1935-39 (Chip-mold)

Bowl, berry, 5" d., amber 7.00
Bowl, berry, 5" d., green or pink 11.00
Bowl, cream soup, 5" d., amber............24.50
Bowl, cereal, 6" d., pink........................22.50
Bowl, soup, 7½" d., amber....................42.00
Bowl, soup, 7½" d., pink 39.50
Bowl, berry, 8½" d., amber 5.00
Bowl, berry, 8½" d., green 23.50
Bowl, berry, 8½" d., pink.......................28.50
Bowl, 9½" oval vegetable, amber 17.00
Bowl, fruit, 10½" d., green 31.00
Bowl, fruit, 10½" d., pink.......................36.00
Butter dish, cov., amber........................42.00
Butter dish, cov., green.........................74.50
Butter dish, cov., pink 49.00
Cake plate, footed, amber, 11½" d 22.00
Cake plate, footed, clear, 11½" d 11.00
Cake plate, footed, green, 11½" d 48.50
Cake plate, footed, pink, 11½" d..........36.50
Candy jar, cov., amber..........................42.00
Candy jar, cov., green 177.50
Candy jar, cov., pink 52.00
Cheese dish, cov., amber....................179.00
Cheese dish, cov., pink 805.00
Creamer, amber 12.00

Creamer, green 18.00
Creamer, pink.....................................16.00
Cup, amber..7.50
Cup, pink 13.50
Cup & saucer, green.............................26.00
Jam dish, amber, 7½" d., 1½" h............31.00
Jam dish, green, 7½" d., 1½" h............34.50
Jam dish, pink, 7½" d., 1½" h. 150.00
Pitcher, 9" h., 80 oz., amber 110.00
Pitcher, 9" h., 80 oz., pink.................116.00
Pitcher w/ice lip, 9" h., 80 oz.,
    amber..115.00
Pitcher w/ice lip, 9" h., 80 oz.,
    green...322.00
Pitcher w/ice lip, 9" h., 80 oz.,
    pink 126.50
Plate, bread & butter, 6" d., amber 4.50
Plate, bread & butter, 6" d., green or
    pink 6.50
Plate, salad, 7½" d., amber 15.00
Plate, salad, 7½" d., green 20.50
Plate, salad, 7½" d., pink 25.50
Plate, dinner, 9¼" d., amber 10.00
Plate, dinner, 9¼" d., green or pink 17.00
Platter, 12¼" oval, amber 14.50
Platter, 12¼" oval, green 20.50
Platter, 12¼" oval, pink.......................26.50
Salt & pepper shakers, amber, pr........35.00
Salt & pepper shakers, green, pr..........61.00
Salt & pepper shakers, pink, pr. 48.50
Saucer, amber....................................6.00
Saucer, pink......................................10.00
Sherbet, footed, amber.......................10.50
Sherbet, footed, green........................30.50
Sherbet, footed, pink 14.50
Sugar bowl, cov., amber......................30.50
Sugar bowl, cov., green.......................43.00
Sugar bowl, cov., pink 37.50
Sugar bowl, open, amber 8.00
Sugar bowl, open, green 14.00
Sugar bowl, open, pink 12.00
Tumbler, amber, 4" h., 9 oz. 23.50
Tumbler, green, 4" h., 9 oz. 60.50
Tumbler, pink, 4" h., 9 oz.....................36.00
Tumbler, amber, 5¼" h., 12 oz. 49.00
Tumbler, green, 5¼" h., 12 oz. 87.00
Tumbler, pink, 5¼" h., 12 oz. 41.50
Tumbler, footed, amber, 6½" h.,
    15 oz. 90.00
Tumbler, footed, clear, 6½" h.,
    15 oz. 16.50
Tumbler, footed, pink, 6½" h.,
    15 oz. 44.50

SIERRA or Pinwheel, Jeannette Glass Co., 1931-33 (Press-mold)

Bowl, cereal, 5½" d., green or pink.......12.50
Bowl, berry, 8½" d., green 25.00
Bowl, berry, 8½" d., pink......................27.50
Bowl, 9½" oval vegetable, green 72.50
Bowl, 9½" oval vegetable, pink.............39.50
Butter dish, cov., green.........................65.00
Butter dish, cov., pink 56.50

Creamer, green 19.50
Creamer, pink......................................11.50
Cup, green..13.50
Cup & saucer, pink 16.50
Pitcher, 6½" h., 32 oz., green 115.00
Pitcher, 6½" h., 32 oz., pink.................78.50
Plate, dinner, 9" d., green 18.00
Plate, dinner, 9" d., pink.......................15.50
Platter, 11" oval, green 41.00
Platter, 11" oval, pink...........................37.50
Salt & pepper shakers, green, pr.........35.50
Salt & pepper shakers, pink, pr. 37.00
Saucer, green......................................6.00
Serving tray, two-handled, green or
    pink 17.00
Sugar bowl, cov., green........................30.00
Sugar bowl, cov., pink 16.50
Tumbler, footed, green, 4½" h., 9 oz. ...69.50
Tumbler, footed, pink, 4½" h., 9 oz.......46.50

SPIRAL, Hocking Glass Co., 1928-30 (Press-mold)

Ice or butter tub, green 25.00
Pitcher, 7⅝" h., 58 oz., green 29.50
Plate, sherbet, 6" d., green 2.00
Plate, luncheon, 8" d., green 4.00
Platter, 12" l., oval, green 20.50
Preserve, cov., green 27.50
Sandwich server, w/center handle,
    green..30.00
Sherbet, green.....................................4.50
Sherbet, pink 4.00
Sugar bowl, flat or footed, green 7.00
Tumbler, water, green, 5" h., 9 oz. 12.00

SWANKY SWIGS, early 1930s to early 1940s (Kraft cheese glasses)

Antique No. 1, black, blue, brown,
    green, orange or red 4.00
Band No. 1...3.50
Band No. 2...3.00
Band No. 3...3.00
Band No. 4...1.50
Bustlin' Betsy, blue, brown, green,
    orange, red or yellow 4.00
Carnival, cobalt blue or red...................3.50
Carnival, yellow....................................7.00
Circles & Dot, blue or green 5.50
Daisy (or Bachelor Button), green,
    red or white 2.50
Forget-Me-Not, dark blue, light blue,
    red or yellow 3.00
Kiddy Kup, black, blue, brown, green,
    orange or red 4.50
Posy - Cornflower No. 1, 3½" h. 3.00
Posy - Cornflower No. 1, 4½" h. 15.00
Posy - Cornflower No. 2, dark blue,
    light blue, red or yellow 3.00
Posy - Jonquil......................................4.00
Posy - Tulip...3.50
Posy - Violet 4.00
Sailboat No. 1 (3 boats), blue 13.50
Sailboat No. 2 (4 boats), blue 12.50

Stars No. 1, black, blue, green, red
or yellow..4.50
Texas Centennial, black 7.50
Texas Centennial, red 24.00
Tulip No. 1, black, dark blue, green or
red, 3½" h. 2.50
Tulip No. 1, red or green, 4½" h. 6.00
Tulip No. 2, black, blue, green or red ...16.00
Tulip No. 3, dark blue, light blue or
yellow...3.00

SWIRL or Petal Swirl, Jeannette Glass Co., 1937-38 (Press-mold)

Bowl, cereal, 5¼" d., Delphite...............10.50
Bowl, cereal, 5¼" d., pink 8.50
Bowl, cereal, 5¼" d., ultramarine..........13.50
Bowl, salad, 9" d., Delphite...................25.00
Bowl, salad, 9" d., pink 15.00
Bowl, salad, 9" d., ultramarine 24.00
Bowl, 9" d., rimmed, ultramarine...........22.00
Bowl, fruit, 10" d., closed handles,
footed, ultramarine.............................27.50
Butter dish, cov., pink 153.00
Butter dish, cov., ultramarine..............211.00
Candleholders, double, ultramarine,
pr...35.50
Candy dish, cov., pink 100.00
Candy dish, cov., ultramarine.............139.00
Candy dish, open, three-footed,
pink, 5½" d. 12.00
Candy dish, open, three-footed,
ultramarine, 5½" d..............................14.50
Coaster, pink, 3¼" d., 1" h. 10.00
Coaster, ultramarine, 3¼" d., 1" h........13.50
Console bowl, footed, pink, 10½" d. 16.00
Console bowl, footed, ultramarine,
10½" d...23.50
Creamer, Delphite 9.00
Creamer, pink 7.50
Creamer, ultramarine............................14.00
Cup, ultramarine....................................14.50
Cup & saucer, Delphite.........................11.00
Cup & saucer, pink 7.00
Plate, sherbet, 6½" d., Delphite or
pink 4.50
Plate, sherbet, 6½" d., ultramarine 6.00
Plate, 7¼" d., ultramarine 12.00
Plate, salad, 8" d., Delphite 5.00
Plate, salad, 8" d., pink 6.00
Plate, dinner, 9½" d., Delphite 12.00
Plate, dinner, 9½" d., pink......................8.50
Plate, dinner, 9½" d., ultramarine 15.50
Plate, sandwich, 12½" d., pink..............18.00
Plate, sandwich, 12½" d., ultramarine ..23.00
Platter, 12" oval, Delphite 29.00
Salt & pepper shakers, Delphite, pr......95.00
Salt & pepper shakers, ultramarine,
pr...37.50
Saucer, ultramarine 4.50
Sherbet, pink 10.00
Sherbet, ultramarine.............................16.00
Soup bowl w/lug handles, pink 18.50
Soup bowl w/lug handles, ultramarine..25.00

Sugar bowl, open, Delphite 8.00
Sugar bowl, open, pink 9.00
Sugar bowl, open, ultramarine..............14.00
Tumbler, pink, 4" h., 9 oz......................11.00
Tumbler, ultramarine, 4" h., 9 oz. 16.50
Tumbler, pink, 4⅝" h., 9 oz....................18.50
Tumbler, footed, pink, 9 oz....................14.00
Tumbler, footed, ultramarine, 9 oz........35.50
Tumbler, pink, 5⅛" h., 13 oz.................25.50
Tumbler, ultramarine, 5⅛" h., 13 oz. 80.00
Vase, 6½" h., pink.................................11.00
Vase, 6½" h., ultramarine 17.00
Vase, 8½" h., ultramarine 25.00

TEA ROOM, Indiana Glass Co., 1926-31 (Press-mold)

Tea Room Creamer & Sugar Bowl

Banana split dish, flat, green, 7½" 98.00
Banana split dish, footed, clear, 7½" 46.00
Banana split dish, footed, green, 7½"...81.00
Bowl, salad, 8¾" d., green....................80.00
Bowl, salad, 8¾" d., pink 52.00
Bowl, 9½" oval vegetable, green 69.00
Bowl, 9½" oval vegetable, pink.............62.00
Candlesticks, green or pink, pr.............50.50
Celery or pickle dish, green, 8½".........26.00
Creamer, green, 3¼" h. 14.50
Creamer, green, 4" h. 14.50
Creamer, pink, 4" h...............................11.00
Creamer, footed, green, 4½" h. 22.50
Creamer, rectangular, green 15.50
Creamer & open sugar bowl on
center-handled tray, green.................55.00
Creamer & open sugar bowl on
center-handled tray, pink (ILLUS.) 86.00
Creamer & open sugar bowl on
rectangular tray, green....................108.00
Creamer & open sugar bowl on
rectangular tray, pink 56.00
Cup & saucer, green.............................44.00
Cup & saucer, pink 63.50
Finger bowl, green................................85.00
Finger bowl, pink 48.50
Goblet, green, 9 oz. 77.50
Goblet, pink, 9 oz.................................74.00
Ice bucket, green 70.00
Ice bucket, pink.....................................85.00

Lamp, electric, clear, 9" 95.00
Lamp, electric, green, 9" 61.50
Mustard, cov., clear 72.00
Parfait, clear 65.00
Parfait, green 63.50
Pitcher, 64 oz., green 160.00
Pitcher, 64 oz., pink 150.00
Plate, sherbet, 6½" d., pink...................17.00
Plate, luncheon, 8¼" d., green 32.00
Plate, 10½" d., two-handled, green 50.00
Plate, sandwich, w/center handle,
     green..151.00
Plate, sandwich, w/center handle,
     pink 170.00
Relish, divided, green............................22.50
Relish, divided, pink...............................13.00
Salt & pepper shakers, green, pr..........64.00
Salt & pepper shakers, pink, pr. 53.00
Sherbet, low footed, green 30.00
Sherbet, low footed, pink 23.00
Sherbet, low, flared edge, clear............18.00
Sherbet, low, flared edge, green 27.50
Sherbet, tall footed, clear......................27.50
Sherbet, tall footed, green 37.00
Sherbet, tall footed, pink.......................31.00
Sugar bowl, cov., pink, 3" h. 130.00
Sugar bowl, cov., green, 3" h.............100.00
Sugar bowl, open, green, 4" h. 16.00
Sugar bowl, open, pink, 4" h.................14.00
Sugar bowl, open, footed, green,
     4½" h...17.50
Sugar bowl, open, footed, pink,
     4½" h...14.50
Sugar bowl, open, rectangular, green ..17.50
Sugar bowl, open, rectangular, pink 11.50
Sundae, footed, ruffled, clear 56.00
Sundae, footed, ruffled, green............135.00
Tray, rectangular, for creamer & sugar
     bowl, green 48.00
Tray, rectangular, for creamer & sugar
     bowl, pink...38.00
Tray w/center handle, for creamer &
     sugar bowl, green 209.00
Tray w/center handle, for creamer &
     sugar bowl, pink.................................74.00
Tumbler, footed, clear, 6 oz.................28.00
Tumbler, footed, green, 6 oz. 42.00
Tumbler, footed, pink, 6 oz. 30.00
Tumbler, green, 4³⁄₁₆" h., 8½ oz. 105.00
Tumbler, pink, 4³⁄₁₆" h., 8½ oz.............32.50
Tumbler, footed, green or pink,
     5¼" h., 8 oz. 30.00
Tumbler, footed, green, 11 oz. 62.50
Tumbler, footed, clear, 12 oz...............45.00
Tumbler, footed, green, 12 oz. 82.00
Tumbler, footed, pink, 12 oz. 65.00
Vase, 6½" h., ruffled rim, green 109.00
Vase, 9½" h., ruffled rim, amber 150.00
Vase, 9½" h., ruffled rim, clear 19.00
Vase, 9½" h., ruffled rim, green 127.50
Vase, 11" h., ruffled rim, clear 110.00
Vase, 11" h., straight, green 153.00
Vase, 11" h., straight, pink.................105.00

TWISTED OPTIC, Imperial Glass Co., 1927-30 (Press-mold)

Bowl, cream soup, 4¾" d., pink 8.50
Bowl, cereal, 5" d., amber....................6.50
Candlesticks, yellow, 3", pr.................19.00
Candy jar, cov., green 23.50
Candy jar, cov., yellow........................25.00
Creamer, green 7.00
Creamer, pink 8.00
Plate, sherbet, 6" d., amber 1.50
Plate, sherbet, 6" d., green 3.00
Plate, sherbet, 6" d., pink.......................2.00
Plate, luncheon, 8" d., amber or green...3.00
Plate, luncheon, 8" d., pink 4.50
Preserve jar w/slotted lid, green 22.00
Sandwich server w/center handle,
     amber..17.00
Sandwich server w/center handle,
     green...16.00
Sandwich server w/center handle,
     yellow...29.00
Sherbet, amber, green or yellow 5.50
Sherbet, clear 3.00
Sherbet, pink 6.00
Sugar bowl, open, green 8.00
Sugar bowl, open, pink 6.00

WATERFORD or Waffle, Hocking Glass Co., 1938-44 (Press-mold)

Waterford Pattern

Ashtray, clear, 4" 5.00
Bowl, berry, 4¾" d., clear.......................5.50
Bowl, berry, 4¾" d., pink.......................11.00
Bowl, cereal, 5¼" d., clear 16.50
Bowl, cereal, 5¼" d., pink.....................26.50
Bowl, berry, 8¼" d., clear.....................10.00
Bowl, berry, 8¼" d., pink.......................17.00
Butter dish, cov., clear 24.00
Butter dish, cov., pink 195.00
Cake plate, handled, clear, 10¼" d.........8.00
Cake plate, handled, pink, 10¼" d........12.00
Coaster, clear, 4" d. 3.50
Creamer, oval, clear 4.50
Creamer, oval, pink 12.00
Cup & saucer, clear (ILLUS.)..................9.00
Cup & saucer, pink 20.50

Goblet, amber, 5¼" h............................125.00
Goblet, clear, 5¼" h. 15.50
Goblet, clear, 5½" h. (Miss America
 style) 32.50
Lamp, clear, 4" h....................................29.00
Pitcher, juice, 42 oz., tilt-type, clear......22.50
Pitcher w/ice lip, 80 oz., clear...............29.50
Pitcher w/ice lip, 80 oz., pink 147.50
Plate, sherbet, 6" d., clear 3.00
Plate, sherbet, 6" d., pink.......................7.00
Plate, salad, 7½" d., clear.......................4.50
Plate, salad, 7½" d., pink.......................10.00
Plate, dinner, 9⅝" d., clear......................9.50
Plate, dinner, 9⅝" d., pink......................18.00
Plate, sandwich, 13¾" d., clear 8.50
Plate, sandwich, 13¾" d., pink..............24.50
Relish, five-section, clear, 13¾" d. 14.00
Salt & pepper shakers, clear, short
 or tall, pr. 7.50
Sherbet, footed, clear 3.50
Sherbet, footed, pink 11.50
Sugar bowl, cov., oval, clear...................5.50
Sugar bowl, cov., oval, pink..................27.50
Sugar bowl, open, footed, clear (Miss
 America style) 2.00
Tumbler, footed, clear, 5" h., 10 oz.
 (ILLUS.) 10.50
Tumbler, footed, pink, 5" h., 10 oz........17.50

WINDSOR DIAMOND or Windsor,
Jeannette Glass Co., 1936-46 (Press-mold)
Ashtray, Delphite, 5¾" d. 39.50
Ashtray, green, 5¾" d. 44.50
Ashtray, pink, 5¾" d...............................34.00
Ashtray w/patterned rim, pink 475.00
Bowl, berry, 4¾" d., clear........................5.00
Bowl, berry, 4¾" d., green 7.00
Bowl, berry, 4¾" d., pink..........................8.00
Bowl, 5" d., pointed edge, clear 5.00
Bowl, 5" d., pointed edge, pink 18.00
Bowl, cream soup, 5" d., green or
 pink...23.00
Bowl, cereal, 5⅛" or 5⅜" d., clear...........7.00
Bowl, cereal, 5⅛" or 5⅜" d., green 22.00
Bowl, cereal, 5⅛" or 5⅜" d., pink.........17.00
Bowl, 7" d., three-footed, clear 7.00
Bowl, 7" d., three-footed, pink...............24.00
Bowl, 8" d., pointed edge, clear 11.00
Bowl, 8" d., pointed edge, pink 34.00
Bowl, 8" d., two-handled, clear 5.50
Bowl, 8" d., two-handled, green............21.00
Bowl, 8" d., two-handled, pink 19.50
Bowl, berry, 8½" d., clear.......................10.00
Bowl, berry, 8½" d., green 15.00
Bowl, berry, 8½" d., pink........................17.00
Bowl, 9½" oval vegetable, clear...............8.50
Bowl, 9½" oval vegetable, green 23.00
Bowl, 9½" oval vegetable, pink 19.00
Bowl, 10½" d., pointed edge, clear 25.00
Bowl, 10½" d., pointed edge, pink 107.50
Bowl, 7 x 11¾" boat shape, clear 17.50
Bowl, 7 x 11¾" boat shape, green........30.50
Bowl, 7 x 11¾" boat shape, pink 34.50

Bowl, fruit, 12½" d., clear.......................26.00
Bowl, fruit, 12½" d., pink 96.50
Butter dish, cov., clear...........................24.50
Butter dish, cov., green..........................76.50
Butter dish, cov., pink............................48.50
Cake plate, footed, clear, 10¾" d. 7.50
Cake plate, footed, green or pink,
 10¾" d...19.00
Candlesticks, clear, 3" h., pr. 15.00
Candlesticks, pink, 3" h., pr. 81.00
Candy jar, cov., clear.............................11.00
Coaster, clear, 3¼" d...............................7.00
Coaster, green, 3¼" d............................14.50
Coaster, pink, 3¼" d. 13.00
Creamer, flat, clear..................................4.00
Creamer, flat, green................................12.50
Creamer, flat, pink 10.50
Creamer, footed, clear.............................5.50
Cup, clear 2.50
Cup, green...10.00
Cup, pink...9.50
Pitcher, 4½" h., 16 oz., Amberina
 red...600.00
Pitcher, 4½" h., 16 oz., clear.................19.50
Pitcher, 4½" h., 16 oz., pink.................113.00
Pitcher, 6¾" h., 52 oz., clear.................11.50
Pitcher, 6¾" h., 52 oz., green................48.00
Pitcher, 6¾" h., 52 oz., pink..................25.50
Plate, sherbet, 6" d., clear 2.00
Plate, sherbet, 6" d., green 6.00
Plate, sherbet, 6" d., pink........................4.50
Plate, salad, 7" d., green 17.50
Plate, salad, 7" d., pink 19.50
Plate, dinner, 9" d., clear 5.00
Plate, dinner, 9" d., green or pink 19.00
Plate, sandwich, 10¼", handled, clear....7.00
Plate, sandwich, 10¼", handled,
 green...11.50
Plate, sandwich, 10¼", handled, pink...14.00
Plate, chop, 13⅝" d., clear......................8.50
Plate, chop, 13⅝" d., green or pink 40.00
Platter, 11½" oval, clear...........................7.00
Platter, 11½" oval, green.........................19.50
Platter, 11½" oval, pink...........................18.50
Powder jar, cov., clear............................10.00
Relish, divided, clear, 11½" 9.50
Relish, divided, pink, 11½" 187.50
Salt & pepper shakers, green, pr..........44.50
Salt & pepper shakers, pink, pr. 36.00
Saucer, clear 3.00
Saucer, green 5.00
Saucer, pink..5.00
Sherbet, footed, clear 4.50
Sherbet, footed, green...........................13.00
Sherbet, footed, pink 9.50
Sugar bowl, cov., flat, clear 6.00
Sugar bowl, cov., flat, green 23.00
Sugar bowl, cov., flat, pink.....................24.50
Sugar bowl, cov., footed, clear 6.00
Sugar bowl, cov., no lip, pink..............110.00
Sugar bowl, open, clear...........................3.00
Sugar bowl, open, green 12.00
Sugar bowl, open, pink.............................8.50

Tray, clear, 4" sq., without handles.........5.00
Tray, pink, 4" sq., without handles........37.00
Tray, green or pink, 4⅛ x 9",
   w/handles..12.50
Tray, clear, 4⅛ x 9", without handles....10.00
Tray, pink, 4⅛" x 9", without handles....43.50
Tray, green, 8½ x 9¾", w/handles........29.00
Tray, pink, 8½ x 9¾", w/handles...........22.00
Tray, clear, 8½ x 9¾", without
   handles..12.00
Tray, pink, 8½ x 9¾", without
   handles..75.00
Tumbler, clear, 3¼" h., 5 oz....................7.00
Tumbler, green, 3¼" h., 5 oz. 26.50
Tumbler, pink, 3¼" h., 5 oz.....................22.00
Tumbler, clear, 4" h., 9 oz.......................6.50
Tumbler, green, 4" h., 9 oz. 29.00
Tumbler, pink, 4" h., 9 oz. 17.00
Tumbler, footed, clear, 4" h., 9 oz...........7.00
Tumbler, footed, clear, 5" h., 11 oz.........9.00
Tumbler, clear, 5" h., 12 oz.....................9.00
Tumbler, green, 5" h., 12 oz. 42.50
Tumbler, pink, 5" h., 12 oz.....................26.00
Tumbler, footed, clear, 7¼" h. 12.50
Water set: pitcher & 6 each, 5 oz. tumblers,
   9 oz. tumblers & 12 oz. tumblers; pink,
   in original box, 19 pcs. 400.00

(End of Depression Glass Section)

DUNCAN & MILLER

Duncan & Miller Glass Company, a successor firm to George Duncan & Sons Company, produced a wide range of pressed wares and novelty pieces during the late 19th century and into the early 20th century. During the Depression era and after, they continued making a wide variety of more modern patterns, including mold-blown types and also introduced a number of etched and engraved patterns. Many colors, including opalescent hues, were produced during this era and especially popular today are the graceful swan dishes they produced in the Pall Mall and Sylvan patterns. The numbers after the pattern name indicate the original factory pattern number. The Duncan factory was closed in 1955. Also see ANIMALS and PATTERN GLASS.

Ashtray, Caribbean patt. (No. 112),
   ruby..$20.00
Ashtray, model of a duck, ruby...........110.00
Ashtray, Pall Mall patt. (No. 30), clear
   w/etched duck decoration, rectan-
   gular, 8" l..66.00
Bowl, 4¾" d., Puritan patt., pink..............9.00
Bowl, 6" d., handled, Teardrop patt.
   (No. 301), clear 4.00

Bowl, 7" d., Murano patt. (No. 127),
   pink opalescent.................................28.00
Bowl, 9" oval., Canterbury patt.
   (No. 115), clear 22.00
Bowl, 10" d., Murano patt., milk
   white 145.00
Bowl, 6½ x 11½", model of a Viking
   boat, clear...............150.00 to 175.00
Cake stand, miniature, Teardrop patt.,
   5½" d., 3¼" h. 55.00
Candelabrum, three-light, No. 14,
   w/prisms, clear, 10" h., 8" w..............50.00
Candlesticks, two-light, etched First
   Love patt., clear, pr. 110.00
Candlesticks, Terrace patt. (No. 111),
   amber, pr..115.00
Candy dish, cov., etched First Love
   patt., clear 67.50

Teardrop Champagne

Champagne, saucer-type, Teardrop
   patt., clear (ILLUS.).............................7.50
Cheese stand, Caribbean patt., blue,
   3½" h..35.00
Cigarette box, cov., Caribbean patt.,
   blue 73.00
Cocktail shaker, Caribbean patt.,
   blue 125.00
Cologne bottle w/original stopper,
   Hobnail patt. (No. 118), blue..............58.00
Compote, 5" d., 3" h., Teardrop patt.,
   clear 35.00
Compote, 5½" h., Canterbury patt.,
   ruby w/clear base...............................85.00
Console set: bowl & candlesticks;
   American Way patt. (No. 71), ruby
   red, 3 pcs. 150.00
Cordial, Mardi Gras patt. (No. 42),
   clear 40.00
Cornucopia-vase, etched First Love
   patt., clear, 8" h.................................65.00
Cornucopia-vase, Three Feathers
   patt. (No. 117), clear, 8" h.................45.00
Creamer & open sugar bowl,
   Georgian patt. (No. 103), pink, pr. 30.00
Creamer & open sugar bowl, indivi-
   dual, etched Language of Flowers
   patt., clear, pr. 30.00

Creamer & sugar bowl, large, etched
Language of Flowers patt., clear,
pr. 35.00
Creamer, open sugar bowl &
8" oblong tray, Early American
Sandwich patt. (No. 41), clear,
3 pcs. 35.00
Cruet w/original stopper, Bag
Ware (No. 800), vaseline, large,
ca. 1880s 55.00
Cruet w/original stopper, Early
American Sandwich patt., clear,
3 oz. 35.00
Cruet w/original stopper, Teardrop
patt., clear, 3 oz. 12.00
Cup & saucer, Teardrop patt., clear 35.00
Deviled egg plate, Early American
Sandwich patt., green, 12" d. 35.00
Goblet, Canterbury patt., clear 12.00
Goblet, Early American Sandwich
patt., blue 17.00
Goblet, Early American Sandwich
patt., clear, 9 oz., 6" h. 15.00
Goblet, etched First Love patt., clear....21.00
Goblet, water, Hobnail patt., clear 6.00
Goblet, water, Mardi Gras patt., clear...40.00
Ivy bowl, footed, Hobnail patt., blue
opalescent, 6½" d. 48.00
Marmalade jar, cov., Teardrop patt.,
clear 37.00
Model of a goose, door stop-type,
clear, 4 lb. 395.00
Model of a swan, Pall Mall patt.
(No. 30), ruby, 7" l. 24.00
Model of a swan, Sylvan patt.
(No. 122), blue opalescent, 7" l..........85.00
Model of a swan, Sylvan patt.
(No. 122), milk white w/ruby neck
& head, 7" l. 325.00
Model of a swan, nesting-type,
teakwood, 10½" l...............................60.00
Model of a swan, Sylvan patt.,
blue opalescent, 12" l.......................350.00
Model of a swan, Sylvan patt.,
pink opalescent, 12" l. 350.00
Model of a swan, spread wing-type,
green, 12" w., 11" h............................60.00
Mustard jar, cov., Caribbean patt.,
clear 20.00
Olive dish, Teardrop patt., clear, 7" l. ...15.00
Pitcher, 9½" h., w/ice lip, Canterbury
patt., clear 90.00
Pitcher w/applied amber handle,
Teardrop patt., clear 78.00
Plate, 8" d., Canterbury patt., amber 12.00
Plate, salad, 8" d., Early American
Sandwich patt., clear 10.00
Plate, 8½" d., Spiral Flutes patt.
(No. 40), clear 7.00
Plate, 8½" d., Spiral Flutes patt.,
green..4.00
Plate, 11" d., Teardrop patt., clear........45.00

Plate, 16" d., Early American
Sandwich patt., clear 225.00
Punch set: punch bowl, 18" d.
underplate & twelve cups; Carib-
bean patt., clear, cups clear
w/applied ruby red handles,
14 pcs. 250.00
Relish dish, two-part, Caribbean patt.,
blue, 6" d..22.50
Relish dish, three-part, etched First
Love patt., clear, 10½" l.......................45.00
Relish dish, three-part, Sylvan patt.,
yellow opalescent, 10 x 13" 80.00
Relish dish, four-part, Canterbury
patt., clear, 12" d..................................45.00
Relish dish, five-part, Teardrop patt.,
clear, 12" d..18.00
Relish dish, Sylvan patt., milk white
w/ruby handles, 10" l.........................140.00
Relish dish, Terrace patt. (No. 111),
clear w/gold, 10½" l.............................32.00
Salt & pepper shakers w/original tops,
Mardi Gras patt., clear, pr. 37.50
Salt & pepper shakers w/original tops,
Teardrop patt., clear, pr. 50.00
Seafood sauce cup, Spiral Flutes
patt., clear 20.00
Sherbet, crimped rim, Canterbury
patt., clear, 5½" h. 22.00
Sherbet, Teardrop patt., clear, 3½" h. 4.00
Sugar bowl, cov., Bag Ware
(No. 800), vaseline, ca. 1880s 80.00
Tumbler, Canterbury patt., clear,
5¼" h..9.00
Tumbler, Canterbury patt., yellow
opalescent, 5½" h.................................50.00
Tumbler, old fashioned, Canterbury
patt., clear, 8 oz. 7.50
Tumbler, footed, Caribbean patt.,
blue, 5½" h..35.00
Tumbler, iced tea, Early American
Sandwich patt., clear, 5¼" h. 14.00
Tumbler, juice, footed, cut Eternally
Yours patt., clear, 5 oz. 20.00
Tumbler, water, footed, cut Eternally
Yours patt., clear, 9 oz. 20.00
Tumbler, iced tea footed, cut Eternally
Yours patt., clear, 13 oz. 22.00
Tumbler, bar, Mardi Gras patt., clear....20.00
Tumbler, hi-ball, flat, Teardrop patt.,
clear, 4¾" h..9.00
Tumbler, juice, footed, Teardrop patt.,
clear, 4" h...9.00
Tumbler, iced tea, Teardrop patt.,
clear, 6" h...12.00
Tumbler, whiskey, footed, Teardrop
patt., clear, 3" h....................................16.50
Vase, 2½" h., Chanticleer patt., green
opalescent 55.00
Vase (cigarette holder), 3½" h.,
Grecian Urn line (No. 538), clear 12.50
Vase, 5" h., Canterbury patt., clear.........7.50

Vase, 8" h., ruffled rim, Hobnail patt.,
    blue opalescent..................................62.50
Vase, 8" h., ruffled rim, Caribbean
    patt., blue 140.00
Vase, 10½" h., Teardrop patt., clear.....24.00
Vase, 10½" h., Venetian patt.
    (No. 126), ruby red...........................145.00
Violet bowl, Canterbury patt., clear,
    4½" d..18.00
Wine, Mardi Gras patt...........................25.00

Teadrop Wine

Wine, Teardrop patt., clear, 3 oz.,
    4¾" h. (ILLUS.) 13.50

FENTON

*Fenton Art Glass Company began
producing glass at Williamstown, West
Virginia, in January 1907. Organized by
Frank L. and John W. Fenton, the
company began operations in a newly built
glass factory with an experienced master
glass craftsman, Jacob Rosenthal, as their
factory manager. Fenton has produced a
wide variety of collectible glassware
through the years, including Carnival.
Still in production today, their current
productions may be found at finer gift
shops across the country. William
Heacock's three volumes on Fenton,
published by Antique Publications, are
standard references for collectors.*

Modern Fenton Mark

Barber bottle, Coin Dot patt.,
    cranberry opalescent $225.00

Basket w/wicker handle, Big Cookies
    patt., No. 1681, Mandarin Red,
    10½" d., 5" h. 125.00
Basket, Aqua Crest, 7½" h. 60.00
Basket, Coin Dot patt., French
    Opalescent, No. 1925, 6" h...............85.00
Basket, Coin Dot patt., French
    Opalescent, 13" h. 150.00
Basket, Hobnail patt., blue
    opalescent, 5½" h. 39.00
Basket, Hobnail patt., French
    Opalescent, 6½" h. 24.00
Basket, Hobnail patt., No. 3834, milk
    white, 12" h. 40.00
Basket, Hobnail patt., No. 3839, Plum
    Opalescent, 12" oval........................175.00
Basket, Hobnail patt., crimped rim,
    applied clear handle, Plum
    Opalescent, 12¾" h. 165.00
Basket, No. 203, Blue Overlay,
    ca. 1943, 7¼" d..................................60.00
Basket, Rose Overlay, 8" h...................48.00
Basket, No. 6437, Vasa Murrhina,
    blue & green spatter exterior, white
    interior, 11" h......................................125.00
Bowl, 6" d., low, Ruby Stretch glass ...125.00
Bowl, 7½" d., Peach Crest, ca. 1940....40.00
Bowl, 8" d., footed, Silver Crest............28.00
Bowl, 8½" d., rolled rim, Celeste Blue
    Stretch glass 40.00
Bowl, 8½" d., footed, San Toy patt.,
    clear satin 32.50
Bowl, 8½" d., w/metal handles, Silver
    Crest w/Violets in Snow decoration ...35.00
Bowl, 9½" d., ruffled, No. 682,
    Emerald Crest.....................................55.00
Bowl, 10" d., crimped edge, Black
    Rose...245.00
Bowl, 10" d., Diamond Optic patt.,
    Mulberry...75.00
Bowl, 10" d., double crimped rim,
    Hobnail patt., French Opalescent 60.00
Bowl, 10" d., double crimped edge,
    No. 7224, Silver Crest........................46.00
Bowl, 10" d., flared rim, No. 857, ruby,
    ca. 1933 ....40.00
Bowl, 12" d., Hobnail patt., milk white...20.00
Butter dish, cov., Hobnail patt.,
    No. 3977, milk white 16.00
Cake stand, Silver Crest, 12½" d..........46.00
Candleholders, cornucopia-shaped,
    Rose Crest, 6" h., pr. 75.00
Candleholders, No. 7474, Silver
    Crest, 1968-71, 6" h., pr.....................70.00
Candlestick, Florentine Green Stretch
    glass, 8½" h. 38.00
Candlesticks, Celeste Blue Stretch
    glass, 9½" h., pr. 150.00
Candy dish, cov., footed, Hobnail
    patt., Topaz Opalescent, 7" h. 110.00
Center bowl, three-footed, Pineapple
    patt., No. 2000A, clear w/satin finish,
    12" d..35.00

Center bowl, oval, pedestal base,
dolphin handles under wide flanged
rim, No. 1608, Jade Green 45.00

Cigarette holder, round on dished
base, No. 554, Celeste Blue Stretch
glass 85.00

Compote, open, 6" d., Hobnail patt.,
green opalescent 35.00

Compote, open, 6" d., No. 206,
Emerald Crest...................................25.00

Compote, footed, No. 7228, Silver
Crest, ca. 1963 ....11.00

Console bowl, loop side handles,
footed, No. 1563, Jade Green,
17" l...65.00

Cookie jar, cov., Big Cookies
(No. 1681) patt., Jade Green 125.00

Cookie jar, cov., Big Cookies
(No. 1681) patt., Mandarin Red 130.00

Creamer, Coin Dot patt., No. 1942,
cranberry opalescent, ca. 1944 ....55.00

Cruet, w/original stopper, Fenton's
Drapery, Mulberry 80.00

Cruet, w/original stopper, Hobnail
patt., No. 3863, clear 19.00

Cruet, w/original stopper, Hobnail
patt., No. 3863, milk white 19.00

Cruet, w/original stopper, Spiral Optic
patt., blue 29.00

Cup & saucer, Lincoln Inn patt., Jade
Green...25.00

Dresser bottle w/clear teardrop
stopper, No. 711, bulbous body
w/lady's leg neck, Beaded Melon
patt., Peach Crest, 5½" h. 35.00

Epergne, three-lily, ruffled rim,
No. 1948A, Diamond Lace patt.,
blue opalescent................................120.00

Epergne, three-lily, No. 4808,
Diamond Lace patt., milk white 50.00

Ewer, ruffled rim, applied handle,
No. 192, Rose Overlay,
ca. 1943-48..38.00

Fairy light, Hobnail patt., ruby,
1975-80..15.00

Goblet, Hobnail patt., French
Opalescent...12.00

Goblet, Thumbprint patt., Colonial
Blue, 1960s, 6½" h.............................16.00

Goblet, water, Lincoln Inn patt., Jade
Green...25.00

Hen on Nest cov. dish, basketweave
base, Blue Marble, 1971-73, 9" l.........45.00

Ice bucket w/metal handle, No. 1616,
Ming patt., frosted clear, ca. 1936,
6" h..35.00

Lamp, hurricane-type, No. 170,
Diamond Optic patt., French
Opalescent.......................................125.00

Lamp, hurricane-type, emerald green
Snowcrest w/milk white base,
11" h...110.00

Lamps, Victorian style, Polka Dot
patt., cranberry opalescent, 18" h.,
pr..590.00

Lemonade set: cov. pitcher, six mugs,
six coasters & six clear glass stirring
spoons; Line 220, vaseline, w/ap-
plied cobalt handles, ca. 1926,
19 pcs. 395.00

Model of an egg, pedestal base,
Violets in the Snow decoration,
ca. 1980 ....30.00

Novelty, top hat, Peach Crest,
4½" h...45.00

Novelty, top hat, Rib Optic patt.,
French Opalescent, 6" h. 165.00

Novelty, top hat, Spiral Optic patt.,
green, 4" h. 85.00

Novelty, top hat, crimped rim,
No. 1492, Coin Dot patt., cran-
berry opalescent, ca. 1953 ....65.00

Perfume bottle w/atomizer, ovoid
body w/molded blossoms, private
mold made for Devilbiss, French
Opalescent...65.00

Pitcher, 4" h., Coin Dot patt., green 45.00

Pitcher, 5½" h., squatty, Diamond
Optic patt. 70.00

Pitcher, 6" h., Beaded Melon patt.,
Peach Crest 48.00

Pitcher, 6" h., Spiral Optic patt.,
cranberry opalescent 65.00

Pitcher w/applied black handle, Coin
Dot patt., green opalescent..............175.00

Pitcher, tankard, No. 8964, Hanging Heart patt., turquoise,
70 oz. ....150.00 to 175.00

Pitcher, ball-shaped w/ruffled rim,
applied clear handle, Hobnail patt.,
cranberry opalescent, ca. 1948,
80 oz. 220.00

Pitcher, water, Daisy & Fern patt.,
vaseline opalescent 195.00

Pitcher-vase, No. 3760, Hobnail patt.,
ovoid body tapering to a cylindrical
neck w/a spout pulled into a very
long serrated point, milk white 30.00

Plate, 8½" d., Silver Crest....................30.00

Plate, 11½" d., Ivory Crest...................75.00

Plate, 12" d., Silver Crest.....................40.00

Plate, torte, 16" d., Silver Crest 59.00

Punch set: 10" d. bowl, underplate &
eight punch cups; Hobnail patt., blue
opalescent, 10 pcs............................500.00

Salt & pepper shakers w/original tops,
Lincoln Inn patt., Jade Green, pr. ...125.00

Tidbit tray, three-tier, Ivory Crest, 6",
8½" & 13" d. 45.00

Tumbler, Hobnail patt., French
Opalescent, 15 oz.............................35.00

Vase, 4½" h., No. 3874½, Hobnail
patt., bulbous base, double-crimped
rim, cranberry opalescent 45.00

Vase, 4½" h., crimped rim, Hobnail
patt., blue opalescent.........................20.00
Vase, 5" h., No. 3850, Hobnail patt.,
milk white 10.00
Vase, 5" h., No. 187, triangular-
shaped, Peach Crest ......,...................47.00
Vases, 5½" h., Coin Dot patt.,
cranberry opalescent, pr. 65.00
Vase, 5½" h., Diamond Optic patt.,
Mulberry 125.00
Vase, 6" h., No. 1925, Coin Dot patt.,
French Opalescent 35.00
Vase, 6" h., No. 7551, fan-shaped
w/figural dolphin handles, Jade
Green, ca. 1980 ....35.00
Vase, 6" h., footed, fan-shaped,
Hobnail patt., blue opalescent 28.00
Vase, 7" h., 5" d., ruffled rim, Burmese
decorated w/maple leaves, 1970s 72.00
Vase, 7" h., crimped edge, Diamond
Optic patt., cranberry opalescent.......90.00
Vase, 7¾" h., 6" d., bulbous melon-
ribbed body w/wide horizontal ribbed
neck, double crimped rim, Blue
Overlay 45.00
Vase, 8" h., 9" d., No. 3859, pedestal
base, fan-shaped w/crimped rim,
Hobnail patt., cranberry opalescent ...80.00
Vase, 8" h., pinched rim, Vasa
Murrhina, gold, ruby & green, clear
lining 65.00
Vase, 8½" h., 8¾" d., No. 1458,
corset-shaped w/flared double
crimped rim, cranberry Snow
Crest 150.00
Vase, 10" h., No. 602, trumpet-form,
Mongolian Green, ca. 1930s..............50.00
Vase, 10¾" h., No. 3752, Hobnail
patt., bulbous base, double-crimped
top w/three large ruffles, cranberry
opalescent 135.00
Vase, 11" h., jack-in-the-pulpit form,
Coin Dot patt., cranberry opal-
escent 175.00
Vase, 12" h., swung-type, Hobnail
patt., cranberry opalescent 145.00
Vase, free-blown, wide cushion base
tapering to a swelled body below a
widely flaring rim, No. 3005, Mosaic
Inlaid line, ca. 1926..........................350.00
Water set: pitcher & two tumblers;
Coin Dot patt., cranberry
opalescent, 3 pcs.............................270.00
Water set: 80 oz. pitcher & six 12 oz.
tumblers; Hobnail patt., cranberry
opalescent, 7 pcs.............................525.00
Wine, Lincoln Inn patt., Jade Green 20.00
Wine, Thumbprint patt., Colonial Blue,
1960s, 5" h...8.00
Wine decanter or bottle w/clear
pointed stopper, No. 1667, triple-
lobe form, Rib Optic patt., cranberry,
13½" h..80.00

FOSTORIA

Lido Goblet

Fostoria Glass Company, founded in 1887, produced numerous types of fine glassware over the years. Their factory in Moundsville, West Virginia closed in 1986. Also see ANIMALS.

Fostoria Label

Ashtray, American patt., clear, 2⅞" d. ..$6.00
Ashtray, Coin patt., olive green 55.00
Bonbon, three-toed, American patt.,
clear 17.50
Bouillon cup, Fairfax patt., pink 10.00
Bouillon cup, footed, Versailles
etching, blue 40.00
Bowl, 4" w., tri-cornered, Sylvan patt.,
clear w/gold trim..................................5.00
Bowl, 6¼" d., handled, Raleigh patt.,
Laurel cutting, clear 12.50
Bowl, 6½" d., three-footed, Chintz
etching, clear 20.00
Bowl, 9¼" oval, Pioneer patt., green 22.00
Bowl, 10" d., Romance etching, clear...32.50
Bowl, 10½" d., three-footed, American
patt., clear 22.00
Bowl, 11" d., flared rim, Colony patt.,
clear 32.00
Bowl, 11" d., flared rim, Navarre
etching, clear 55.00
Bowl, 11½" oval, American patt.,
clear 43.00
Bowl, 11½" d., flared rim, Chintz
etching, clear ....
Bowl, fruit, 12" d., footed, American
patt., clear 185.00
Bowl, 12" d., three-footed, Oak Leaf
etching, pink.......................................55.00

Bowl, 12" d., flared rim, Shirley
etching, clear 48.00
Bowl, 12½" oval, 2⅞" h., Flame patt.,
Navarre etching, clear.........................50.00
Bowl, 13" l., oblong, Heirloom cutting,
blue...45.00
Bowl, cream soup, w/underplate,
Fairfax patt., blue 22.50
Bowl, cream soup w/underplate, June
etching, blue 54.00
Bowl, cov., fruit, footed, Coin patt.,
blue...75.00
Butter dish, cov., American patt.,
clear, 1 lb..175.00
Cake plate, two-handled, Baroque
patt., Meadow Rose etching, clear,
10" d...40.00
Cake plate, two-handled, Chintz
etching, clear, 10" d. 40.00
Cake stand (or salver), American
patt., clear, 10" sq., 7¼" h. 75.00
Candelabra w/bobeches & prisms,
two-light, Baroque patt., clear,
pr..145.00
Candlesticks, two-light, bell-shaped
base, American patt., clear, pr. 220.00
Candlesticks, Baroque patt., Navarre
etching, clear, pr. 50.00
Candlesticks, Coin Patt., emerald
green frosted, 4½" h., pr. 80.00
Candlesticks, Coin patt., ruby, 8" h.,
pr..100.00
Candlesticks, Heirloom cutting, green,
2¾" h., pr. 50.00
Candlesticks, two-light, Meadow Rose
etching, clear, pr. 70.00
Candlesticks, Romance etching,
clear, pr. 60.00
Candy box, cov., three-part, Meadow
Rose etching, clear 80.00
Candy dish, cov., three-part, Chintz
etching, clear 65.00
Candy dish, cov., Coin patt., clear........42.00
Candy dish, cov., three-part, Shirley
etching, clear 85.00
Candy jar, cov., urn-shaped, Coin
patt., emerald green, 12½" h. 200.00
Celery dish, Baroque patt., yellow,
11¼" l..25.00
Celery dish, handled, Sunray patt.,
clear, 10" l. 12.00
Celery dish, Trojan etching, yellow,
11½" l..50.00
Celery dish, Wistar patt., clear, 9½"
oval...22.00
Champagne, Chintz etching, clear 20.00
Champagne, Holly cutting, clear...........10.00
Champagne, Navarre etching, blue......24.00
Champagne, tall, Willow etching,
clear..20.00
Cheese & cracker set, Navarre
etching, clear, 2 pcs...........................55.00

Cigarette box, cov., American patt.,
clear..45.00
Claret, Wheat cutting, clear 17.50
Cocktail, American patt., clear,
3½ oz..14.00
Cocktail, Baroque patt., yellow, 3" h. 20.00
Cocktail, Colony patt., clear, 3½" oz.....12.50
Cocktail, Fairfax patt., pink 22.00
Cocktail, Holly cutting, clear, 5¼" h. 16.00
Compote, cov., jelly, 4½" d., 6¼" h.,
American patt., clear...........................25.00
Compote, 4", Sunray patt., clear...........18.00
Compote, 6½", Colony patt., clear........30.00
Compote, 8½", Coin patt., frosted
ruby...75.00
Condiment bottle w/original stopper,
American patt., clear...........................95.00
Console bowl, footed, Versailles
etching, blue 40.00
Console set: bowl & pair of 3½" h.
candlesticks; June etching, blue,
3 pcs...145.00
Cordial, Chintz etching, clear, 1 oz.......55.00
Cordial, Christiana cutting, clear...........20.00
Cordial, Trojan patt., yellow 60.00
Cordial, Wheat cutting, clear 22.50
Creamer, individual size, Baroque
patt., blue 24.00
Creamer, footed, Fairfax patt., pink 10.00
Creamer & open sugar bowl, flared
rim, footed, American patt., clear,
pr..16.00
Creamer & open sugar bowl,
individual size, Baroque patt., blue,
pr..50.00
Creamer & open sugar bowl, Queen
Anne etching, clear, pr. 27.50
Creamer, open sugar bowl &
undertray, Navarre etching, clear,
3 pcs...50.00
Cruet w/original stopper, American
patt., clear, 7 oz. 37.00
Cruet w/original stopper, Chintz
etching, clear 87.00
Cruet w/original stopper, Fairfax patt.,
pink 95.00
Cruet w/original stopper, Raleigh
patt., clear 25.00
Cup & saucer, demitasse, Vernon
etching, green 28.00
Cup & saucer, Baroque patt., clear 9.00
Cup & saucer, Fairfax patt., pink 11.00
Goblet, Acanthus etching, amber 30.00
Goblet, American patt., clear, 5½" h.,
9 oz...14.00
Goblet, Arcady etching, clear, 9 oz.......25.00
Goblet, Buttercup etching, clear,
10 oz. 22.00
Goblet, Colony patt., clear, 5¼" h.,
9 oz. 12.00
Goblet, Corsage etching, clear,
7⅜" h...20.00

Goblet, Florentine etching, clear bowl
w/yellow stem 12.00
Goblet, June etching, pink 55.00
Goblet, June etching, topaz.................33.00
Goblet, Lido etching, clear, 12" h.,
12 oz. (ILLUS.).................................11.00
Goblet, Navarre etching, clear..............28.00
Goblet, Queen Anne patt., clear,
10 oz. 18.00
Goblet, Romance etching, clear,
7⅜" h., 9 oz......................................27.00
Ice bucket w/metal tongs, American
patt., clear 48.00
Ice bucket w/metal tongs, Apple
Blossom cutting, yellow 200.00
Ice bucket, Baroque patt., topaz...........60.00
Ice bucket, Chintz etching, clear.........125.00
Ice bucket, Colony patt., clear 275.00
Ice bucket w/metal handle, Navarre
etching, clear 125.00
Ice bucket, Versailles etching, blue 100.00
Jam jar, cov., Chintz etching, clear,
7½" h...80.00
Ketchup (condiment) bottle w/stopper,
American patt., clear..........................45.00
Marmalade jar, cov., handled,
American patt., clear, 5½".................80.00
Mayonnaise bowl & underplate,
Baroque patt., topaz, 2 pcs. 45.00
Mayonnaise bowl, underplate & ladle,
Chintz etching, clear, 3 pcs...............47.50
Mayonnaise bowl, underplate & ladle,
Romance etching, clear, 3 pcs. 55.00
Nut cup, footed, Fairfax patt., blue 20.00
Oyster cocktail, Beverly etching,
amber 4.00
Oyster cocktails, Willowmere etching,
clear, set of 4 ....24.00
Parfait, Fairfax patt., topaz, 7 oz...........10.00
Pitcher, 5" h., American patt., clear 20.00
Pitcher w/ice lip, 6½" h., footed,
American patt., clear, 3 pt. 50.00
Pitcher w/ice lip, Colony patt., clear,
2 qt. 125.00
Pitcher, water, Queen Anne etching,
clear, 60 oz. 135.00
Plate, bread & butter, 6" d., Lido
etching, clear 5.00
Plate, bread & butter, 6" d., Trojan
etching, pink.......................................6.00
Plate, bread & butter, 6" d., Versailles
etching, green 7.00
Plate, salad, 7" d., American patt.,
clear 10.00
Plate, 7" d., Mayflower etching, clear ...10.00
Plate, salad, 7½" d., Chintz etching,
clear 14.00
Plate, salad, 7½" d., June etching,
topaz 8.00
Plate, salad, 7½" d., Navarre etching,
clear 14.00
Plate, salad, 7½" d., Versailles
etching, blue 10.00

Plate, salad, 7½" d., Wheat cutting,
clear 5.00
Plate, 8" d., Laurel cutting, clear.............9.00
Plate, salad, 8½" d., American patt.,
clear 11.00
Plate, luncheon, 8½" d., Holly cutting,
clear 12.00
Plate, luncheon, 8½" d., Meadow
Rose etching, clear 15.00
Plate, dinner, 9" d., Colony patt.,
clear 17.50
Plate, 9½" d., Baroque patt., clear........12.00
Plate, dinner, 9½" d., Chintz etching,
clear 45.00
Plate, luncheon, 9½" d., Fairfax patt.,
topaz 12.00
Plate, dinner, 9½" d., Navarre etching,
clear 40.00
Plate, dinner, 10" d., Seville patt.,
amber 20.00
Plate, dinner, 10¼" d., Fairfax patt.,
blue 40.00
Plate, torte, 14" d., American patt.,
clear 30.00
Plate, torte, 20" d., American patt.,
clear 125.00
Platter, 12" oval, Pioneer patt., green...22.00
Punch bowl & base, American patt.,
clear, 14" d. bowl, 2 pcs...................235.00
Punch set: punch bowl, base & ten
cups; Coin patt., clear, 12 pcs. 525.00
Relish dish, two-part, Baroque patt.,
blue, 6½" l. 20.00
Relish dish, two-part, Holly cutting,
clear, 8½" l. 25.00
Relish dish, boat-shaped, American
patt., clear, 8½" l. 19.00
Relish dish, divided, oval, Versailles
etching, green, 8½" l. 26.00
Relish dish, three-part, American
patt., clear, 6 x 9½" 37.50
Relish dish, three-part, Baroque patt.,
clear, 10" l. 20.00
Relish, three-part, Romance etching,
clear, 10" l. 40.00
Relish dish, three-part, Fairfax patt.,
amber, 11½" l.....................................12.00
Relish dish, five-part, Navarre etching,
clear, 13¼" l. 85.00
Salt & pepper shakers w/original tops,
Baroque patt., topaz, pr. 90.00
Salt & pepper shakers w/original tops,
Fairfax patt., pink, pr. 50.00
Salt & pepper shakers w/original
tops, footed, Navarre etching, clear,
pr..95.00
Salt & pepper shakers w/original tops,
Versailles etching, blue, pr..............225.00
Sandwich server w/center handle,
Chintz etching, clear, 12" d...............40.00
Sandwich server w/center handle,
Colony patt., clear 29.00

Sauceboat, Beverly etching, green.......55.00
Sauceboat & underplate, American
    patt., clear, 2 pcs. 45.00
Sauceboat & underplate, Fairfax patt.,
    topaz, 2 pcs. 32.00
Sauceboat w/attached underplate,
    Pioneer patt., green 32.00
Sherbet, Coin patt., ruby.......................50.00
Sherbet, low, Cynthia cutting, clear......16.50
Sherbet, Colony patt., clear, 5 oz. 8.00
Sherbet, low, Florentine etching,
    clear, 7 oz. 8.00
Sherbet, Jamestown patt., green,
    7 oz...9.00
Sherbet, low, Laurel cutting, clear 10.00
Sherbet, Lido etching, clear, 6 oz. 7.00
Shrimp bowl, American patt., clear,
    12¼" d...325.00
Syrup pitcher w/original glass top &
    underplate, American patt., clear,
    10 oz., 3 pcs. ....100.00 to 150.00
Toothpick holder, American patt.,
    clear..35.00
Tumbler, whiskey, American patt.,
    clear, 2 oz. 17.50

American Iced Tea Tumbler

Tumbler, iced tea, footed, Amer-
    ican patt., clear, 5½" h., 12 oz.
    (ILLUS.). 15.00
Tumbler, footed, Arcady etching,
    clear, 12 oz. 25.00
Tumbler, cocktail, Baroque patt.,
    yellow, 3" h., 3½ oz............................10.00
Tumbler, footed, Beverly etching,
    amber...5.00
Tumbler, iced tea, footed, Chintz
    etching, clear, 12 oz...........................20.00
Tumbler, old-fashioned, Coin patt.,
    clear..55.00
Tumbler, juice, Colony patt., clear,
    3⅝" h., 5 oz..16.00
Tumbler, footed, Colony patt., clear,
    5¾" h., 12 oz.......................................9.00
Tumbler, water, Cynthia cutting, clear ..21.50
Tumbler, footed, Fairfax patt., blue,
    6" h., 12 oz..20.00

Tumbler, iced tea, Holly cutting, clear,
    12 oz. 16.00
Tumbler, iced tea, Jamestown patt.,
    clear..16.00
Tumbler, juice, Jamestown patt.,
    green...14.00
Tumbler, footed, June etching, clear,
    6" h., 12 oz...22.00
Tumbler, footed, Lido etching, clear,
    9 oz. 10.00
Tumbler, iced tea, footed, Queen
    Anne patt., clear, 13 oz. 20.00
Tumbler, footed, Romance etching,
    clear, 6" h. 25.00
Tumbler, Versailles etching, green,
    5¼" h., 9 oz...25.00
Tumbler, iced tea, Wheat cutting,
    clear..15.00
Urn, cov., Coin patt., frosted emerald
    green, 12" h. 200.00
Vase, 7" h., Baroque patt., blue..........120.00
Vase, bud, 8" h., Coin patt., frosted
    blue 55.00
Vase, 8" h., Vesper etching, green.......70.00
Vase, 10" h., flared rim, American
    patt., clear 48.00
Water set: pitcher & six tumblers;
    Rosby patt., clear, 7 pcs. 180.00
Water set: pitcher & six stemmed
    goblets; Vesper etching, green,
    7 pcs. 375.00
Wine, Acanthus etching, amber...........28.50
Wine, Alexis patt., clear 12.00
Wine, footed, American patt., clear,
    4⅜" h., 2½ oz. 12.00
Wine, Coin patt. clear 55.00
Wine, Corsage etching, clear, 5½" h. ...17.50
Wine, Holly cutting, clear 30.00
Wine, Lido etching, clear, 3 oz. 20.00
Wine, Navarre etching, clear 35.00

FRY

Numerous types of glass were made by the H.C. Fry Company, Rochester, Pennsylvania. One of its art lines was called Foval and was blown in 1926-27. Cheaper was its milky-opalescent ovenware (Pearl Oven Ware) made for utilitarian purposes but also now being collected. The company also made fine cut glass.

Collectors of Fry Glass will be interested in the recent publication of a good reference book, The Collector's Encyclopedia of Fry Glassware, *by The H.C. Fry Glass Society (Collector Books, 1990).*

Bell, Foval bell w/Delft blue handle &
    rim trim, 6½" h...............................$325.00

Bowl, 9¼" d., 5½" h., Foval, deep rounded & gently flaring white opal sides w/a jade green applied rim band & raised on a round applied jade green foot, No. 2504, w/a Fry company catalog No. 12, 2 pcs. 275.00

Bowl, 12" d., footed, Foval, w/applied Delft blue foot..................................285.00

Cake pan, Pearl Oven Ware, 9" d. 18.00

Fry Foval Candlestick

Candlesticks, Foval, bell-form socket above a blue connector to the twisted shaft wrapped w/a thin thread of blue, blue base connector to the round Foval foot, 16" h., pr. (ILLUS. of one) 495.00

Candlesticks, footed, clear & black striped decoration w/clear ball connector, pr..................................500.00

Casserole dish, cov., Pearl Oven Ware, 8" d. 28.00

Coffeepot, cov., Foval w/applied jade green handle & finial on cover, 6½" h...225.00

Compote, open, 6½" d., 9" h., Foval, Quilted patt. bowl, swirl stem w/open ring at the mid-point........................350.00

Compote, open, 9" d., 5" h., Foval bowl w/Delft blue stem....................235.00

Cup & saucer, Foval, applied green handle 59.00

Luncheon set: plate & goblet; Diamond Optic patt., clear w/black trim, 2 pcs. 150.00

Mug, iridescent green w/applied cobalt blue handle............................35.00

Perfume bottle w/original turquoise stopper, Foval bulbous base............295.00

Pitcher, 9½" h., 5½" d., Diamond Optic patt., clear w/applied green handle 125.00

Platter, 9 x 12" oval, Foval, engraved w/flowers & ferns 65.00

Reamer, opaque green, embossed "F4/133/2/4" 30.00

Rose bowl, Foval w/three applied Delft blue feet..................................250.00

Vase, cov., 5" h., 7½" d., footed, Foval, sterling silver cover 299.00

Vase, 7½" h., Diamond Optic patt. (No. 2565), clear w/azure blue trim 150.00

Vase, 23" h., bulbous base tapering to a long pulled neck, clear w/applied black lines decoration 85.00

Wine, royal blue bowl w/clear twisted stem 20.00

GOOFUS

This is a name collectors have given a pressed glass whose colors were sprayed on and then fired. Most pieces have intaglio or convex back designs. Several American glass companies, including Northwood Glass Co., produced this style ware early in the 20th century.

Bowl, 10¾" d., shallow, relief-molded red roses on gold $39.00

Bread tray, relief-molded Last Supper scene 50.00

Plate, 5¾" d., relief-molded rose & lattice decoration in red & gold 17.50

Plate, 7" d., relief-molded red on gold thistle design, advertising, molded into design "Henry Baack" 125.00

Vase, 7½" h., relief-molded red grapes on gold 20.00

Wall pocket, relief-molded bird & grapes decoration, 7¾"......................55.00

GREENTOWN

Greentown glass was made in Greentown Indiana, by the Indiana Tumbler & Goblet Co. from 1894 until 1903. In addition to its famed Chocolate and Holly Amber glass, it produced other types of clear and colored glass. Miscellaneous pieces are listed here. Also see PATTERN GLASS.

Animal covered dish, rabbit, teal blue $185.00

Butter dish, cov., Holly patt., clear ....150.00 to 200.00

Cake stand, Austrian patt., clear 110.00

Compote, open, Austrian patt., clear, 8 x 8"...65.00

Cordial, Austrian patt., clear 75.00
Cordial, Shuttle patt., clear 25.00
Creamer, child size, Austrian patt.,
   canary, 2⅛" d., 3¼" h........................90.00
Cruet w/original stopper, Cord
   Drapery patt., clear 115.00
Mug, Indoor Drinking Scene, clear 45.00
Mug, Outdoor Drinking Scene, Nile
   green...85.00
Mug, Serenade (Troubador), amber,
   4¾" h...95.00
Nappy, cov., handled, Austrian patt.,
   clear 20.00
Novelty, model of a dustpan, amber.....75.00
Novelty, model of a dustpan, blue
   (little roughness) 55.00
Pitcher, water, Fleur-de-lis patt.............35.00
Pitcher, water, Squirrel patt.,
   clear 225.00
Sauce dish, footed, Herringbone
   Buttress patt., emerald green 85.00
Spooner, child's, Austrian patt., clear ...55.00
Toothpick holder, Holly patt., clear 85.00
Tumbler, Brazen Shield patt., cobalt
   blue 55.00
Vase, 6" h., Herringbone Buttress
   patt., emerald green.........................175.00
Vegetable bowl, Cord Drapery patt.,
   clear, 7½" l. 25.00
Wine, No. 11 patt., clear 12.00

HEISEY

Heisey Puritan Pitcher

Numerous types of fine glass were made by A.H. Heisey & Co., Newark, Ohio, from 1895. The company's trade-mark -- an H enclosed within a diamond -- has become known to most glass collectors. The company's name and molds were acquired by Imperial Glass Co., Bellaire, Ohio, in 1958, and some pieces have been reissued. The glass listed below consists of miscellaneous pieces and types. Also see ANIMALS and PATTERN GLASS.

Heisey "Diamond H" Mark

Ashtray, Empress patt., Sahara
   (yellow) $100.00
Banana split dish, footed, Greek
   Key patt., clear.................................33.00
Basket, Lariat patt., clear, 7½" h..........95.00
Bowl, cov., 5½" d., Ridgeleigh patt.,
   clear 45.00
Bowl, 6" d., Pineapple & Fan patt.,
   emerald green, late 1890s 65.00
Butter dish, cov., Lariat patt., clear.......50.00
Cake salver, Plantation patt., clear,
   13"...135.00
Cake stand, Waverly patt., Orchid
   etching, clear, 12" 175.00
Candelabra, Old Williamsburg patt.,
   Sahara, 20½" h., pr. 1,200.00
Candelabra, three-light, Old Williams-
   burg (No. 300) patt., Sahara w/clear
   prisms, pr. 950.00
Candlesticks, Empress patt.
   (No. 135), Alexandrite (orchid),
   pr..895.00
Candlesticks, Oak Leaf patt., pink
   frosted, pr..150.00
Candlesticks, Old Williamsburg patt.,
   Sahara, 12" h., pr. 340.00
Candlesticks, two-light, Waverly patt.,
   Orchid etching, clear, pr...................100.00
Candy dish, cov., w/seahorse
   handles, Waverly patt., Rose
   etching, clear 187.00
Celery tray, oval, Coarse Rib patt.,
   clear, 9" l. 25.00
Champagne, Kohinoor patt., clear........22.00
Champagne, Rose etching, clear 37.50
Champagne, Spanish patt., cobalt
   blue bowl w/clear stem, 5½ oz...........85.00
Champagne, saucer-type, Spanish
   patt., Killarney cutting, clear..............25.00
Champagne, saucer-type, Victorian
   patt., clear 12.50
Chip & dip set, Greek Key patt., clear,
   2 pcs. 195.00
Cigarette box, cov., w/small
   horsehead finial, Puritan patt.,
   No. 1489, clear 65.00
Coasters, Lariat patt., clear, set of 6.....60.00
Cocktail, Gascony patt., Tangerine
   (orange) 100.00
Cocktail, Orchid etching, clear,
   5⅝" h., 4 oz......................................50.00
Cocktail shaker, cov., Orchid etching,
   clear, sterling silver top & base........160.00
Compote, jelly, 6¾" h., Rose etching,
   clear 40.00

Console set: bowl & pair of candle vases w/prisms & inserts; Ipswich patt., clear, bowl 11½" d., 5" h., 3 pcs. 375.00

Cordial, Carcassone patt., Old Colony etching, Sahara 145.00

Cordial, Lariat patt., w/Moonglo cutting, clear 110.00

Creamer & sugar bowl, Crystolite patt., clear, pr. 30.00

Creamer & sugar bowl, Petal patt., Moongleam (green), pr. 65.00

Creamer & sugar bowl, Queen Ann patt., Danish Princess etching, clear, pr. 85.00

Cruet w/original stopper, Empress patt., Sahara 135.00

Cruet w/original stopper, Lariat patt., clear 125.00

Cruet w/original stopper, Pleat & Panel patt., Flamingo 75.00

Crushed fruit jar, cov., Greek Key patt., clear 335.00

Cup & saucer, Orchid etching, clear.....49.50

Decanter w/original stopper, Coronation patt., clear 65.00

Domino sugar tray, Narrow Flute patt., Moongleam 60.00

Goblet, Carcassonne patt., Sahara, 9 oz. 35.00

Goblet, Impromptu patt., clear 22.50

Goblet, Ipswich patt., clear, 8 oz. 18.00

Goblet, Kimberly patt., Belfast cutting, clear 42.50

Goblet, King Arthur patt., Moongleam 42.00

Goblet, Old Dominion patt., Alexandrite 315.00

Ice bucket, Empress patt., clear 52.50

Ice bucket, Empress patt., Orchid etching, clear 225.00

Ice bucket, Minuet etching, clear 150.00

Ice bucket, Waverly Orchid etching (No. 1519), clear 450.00

Ice bucket, cov. w/tongs, Empress patt., Alexandrite 495.00

Ice bucket, cov., Puritan patt. (No. 341), clear, 6" d. 57.50

Lamp, Windsor patt., clear, 9" h. 225.00

Lamps, hurricane-type, Plantation patt., clear, 15" h., pr.....................675.00

Lemon dish, cov., w/dolphin finial, Queen Anne patt., clear, Farberware holder 70.00

Lemon dish, cov., Tudor patt., clear w/cutting...25.00

Luncheon set: four cups & plates & dolphin-footed creamer & sugar bowl; Empress patt., Sahara, 10 pcs. 195.00

Marmalade jar, cov., Crystolite patt., clear, 6" h. 38.00

Marmalade jar, cov., Minuet etching, clear 100.00

Marmalade jar, footed, handled, Pleat & Panel patt., Flamingo 35.00

Matchbox, cov., Banded Flute patt., clear 225.00

Mayonnaise bowl, three-handled, Provincial patt., Zircon 150.00

Mayonnaise bowl & spoon, Minuet etching, No. 1509, clear....................85.00

Mayonnaise bowl & underplate, Lariat patt., clear, 2 pcs. 39.00

Mug, eight-sided w/elephant head & trunk forming handle, amber.........895.00

Mugs, Pineapple & Fan patt., emerald green, set of 3................................135.00

Mustard jar, cov., Crystolite patt., clear 20.00

Mustard jar, cov., Narrow Flute patt., clear 32.00

Mustard jar, cov., Twist patt., Flamingo 60.00

Nappy, Whirlpool (Provincial) patt., clear, 5½" 10.00

Nasturtium bowl, Twist patt., No. 1252, clear, 8" d. 25.00

Nut cup, Empress patt., Flamingo 28.00

Nut dish, individual, footed, Colonial patt., clear 10.00

Nut dishes, Octagon patt., green, set of 7...100.00

Oyster cocktail, Victorian patt. (No. 1425) clear, 5 oz. 11.00

Parfait, Old Glory patt., clear 27.50

Parfait, Plantation patt., clear 35.00

Perfume bottle w/stopper, Ridgeleigh patt., clear 69.00

Pitcher, tankard, Beaded Swag patt., ruby-stained, late 1890s 125.00

Pitcher, water, Charter Oak patt., clear 120.00

Pitcher, Colonial patt., clear, 1½ qt.....135.00

Pitcher, Empress patt., Sahara w/Old Colony etching, 73 oz. 195.00

Pitcher, Minuet etching, No. 4164, ½ gal., clear 295.00

Pitcher, Prince of Wales Plumes patt., clear w/gold trim, early 1900s 250.00

Pitcher, water, Puritan patt., clear, 3 qt. (ILLUS.) 115.00

Plate, 6" d., handled, Crystolite patt., clear 10.00

Plate, 6" d., Tudor patt., clear 7.00

Plate, 7" d., Empress patt., clear 25.00

Plate, 7" d., Minuet etching, clear 12.00

Plate, 7" sq., Empress patt., Tangerine 140.00

Plate, 7½" d., Queen Ann patt., Sahara 25.00

Plate, 8" d., Acorn & Leaves patt., Flamingo 25.00

Plate, 8" d., Orchid etching, clear 18.00

Plate, 8" d., Ipswich patt., Sahara.........26.00

Plate, 8¼" d., Octagon Spiral patt.,
clear 20.00
Plate, 8¼" d., Rose etching, clear 25.00
Plate, 8½" d., Crystolite patt., clear 15.00
Plate, 8½" d., Empress patt.,
Tangerine.......................................125.00
Plate, 8½" sq., Old Sandwich patt.,
Sahara 30.00
Plate, torte, 12" d., rolled rim, Lariat
patt., clear 28.00
Plate, 13" d., Crystolite patt., clear 30.00
Plate, 13" d., Ridgeleigh patt., clear 32.00
Plate, torte, 14" d., Orchid etching,
clear..65.00
Plate, torte, 14" d., Rose patt.,
clear..65.00
Plate, torte, 14" d., Waverly patt.
w/Orchid etching, clear 42.50
Plate, dinner, square, Old Colony
etching, Queen Ann patt., clear 60.00
Plates, 7" d., Pleat & Panel patt.,
Flamingo, set of 2 ....30.00
Plates, 8" d., Crystolite patt., clear,
set of 8..75.00
Platter, 14" oval, Empress patt.,
Sahara 90.00
Platter, 14" l., Rose etching, clear 76.00
Pretzel jar, cov., etched Fisherman
patt...695.00
Puff box, cov., Winged Scroll patt.,
green, late 19th c. 50.00
Punch cup, Pillows patt., clear,
ca. 1900..22.00
Punch cup, Pinwheel & Fan patt., clear..7.50
Punch cup, Prince of Wales patt.,
clear, early 1900s 9.00
Punch cup, Prison Stripe patt.,
No. 357, clear 20.00
Punch cup, Victorian patt., clear...........12.00
Punch bowl & base, Banded Flute
patt., clear, 2 pcs. 225.00
Punch bowl & base, Greek Key patt.,
clear, 2 pcs. ....350.00 to 450.00
Punch set: bowl, ten cups & ladle;
Ridgeleigh patt., clear, 12 pcs. 200.00
Punch set: bowl, base & ten cups;
Beaded Panel & Sunburst patt.,
No. 1235, clear, 12 pcs....................300.00
Punch set: bowl, ten cups & ladle;
Ridgeleigh patt., clear, 12 pcs. 200.00
Punch set: bowl, twelve cups;
Colonial patt., clear, 13 pcs. 225.00
Punch set: bowl, base & eleven cups;
Greek Key patt., clear, 13 pcs. 500.00
Relish dish, Crystolite patt., clear,
6" oval..20.00
Relish dish, two-part, Waverly patt.,
clear, 6"..22.00
Relish dish, three-part, Lariat patt.,
clear, 10" l 35.00
Relish dish, two-part, Ridgeleigh patt.,
clear, 10" d.......................................36.50

Relish dish, four-part, Whirlpool
(Provincial) patt., Limelight (blue
green), 10" l. 240.00
Relish dish, two-part, Fern patt.,
Zircon...275.00
Relish dish, two-part, Orchid etching,
clear 40.00
Relish dish, three-part, Orchid
etching, clear, 11¼" l. 50.00
Relish dish, Empress patt., clear,
13" l...18.00
Relish dish, five-part, Colonial patt.,
clear 35.00
Relish dish, five-part, Williamsburg
patt., clear 42.50
Relish tray, five-part, Crystolite patt.,
clear 25.00
Rose bowl, Fancy Loop patt., clear,
late 1890s, 4" h. 45.00

Heisey Pillows Rose Bowl

Rose bowl, footed, Pillows patt.
(No. 325), clear (ILLUS.)..................225.00
Salt dip, individual size, Ridgeleigh
patt., clear 8.00
Salt shaker w/original top, Beaded
Swag patt., souvenir, milk white,
late 1890s 35.00
Salt shaker w/original top, Winged
Scroll patt., green w/gold trim,
late 1890s 72.50
Salt & pepper shakers w/original
sanitary tops, Banded Flute patt.,
clear, early 20th c., pr. 95.00
Salt & pepper shakers w/original
tops, Beaded Swag patt., clear,
late 1890s, pr. 50.00
Salt & pepper shakers w/original tops,
Empress patt., Sahara, pr. 135.00
Salt & pepper shakers w/original
metal tops, Pineapple & Fan patt.,
clear, late 1890s, pr. 40.00
Salt & pepper shakers w/original
metal tops, Pineapple & Fan patt.,
emerald green w/gold, late 1890s,
pr..195.00

Salt & pepper shakers w/original tops,
Rose etching clear, pr. 85.00
Salt & pepper shakers w/original
sanitary tops, Victorian patt.
(No. 1425), clear, pr. 85.00
Sherbet, Carcassone patt., clear
w/cobalt bowl 55.00
Sherbet, Ipswich patt., Sahara 32.50
Sherbet, Jamestown patt., clear 6.00
Sherbet, low, Rose etching, clear.........22.50
Sherbet, Whirlpool (Provincial) patt.,
clear 8.00
Spooner, Pineapple & Fan patt.,
emerald green w/gold trim, late
1890s 45.00
Spooner w/underplate, Queen Anne
patt. (No. 365), clear, 2 pcs. 40.00
Sugar bowl, open, Minuet etching,
clear 35.00
Sugar bowl, open, individual, Twist
patt., Moongleam 35.00
Syrup pitcher w/original top, Beaded
Swag patt., milk white, late 1890s ...160.00
Table set: creamer, cov. sugar bowl,
cov. butter dish & spooner;
Pineapple & Fan patt., emerald
green w/gold trim, 4 pcs. 360.00
Toothpick holder, Beaded Swag patt.,
milk white w/floral decoration, late
1890s 85.00
Toothpick holder, Beaded Swag patt.,
ruby-stained, late 1890s 55.00
Toothpick holder, Fancy Loop patt.,
clear, late 1890s 60.00
Toothpick holder, Fancy Loop patt.,
emerald green w/gold trim, late
1890s 200.00
Toothpick holder, Fandango patt.,
clear, late 1890s 95.00
Toothpick holder, Pineapple &
Fan patt., emerald green, late
1890s ....200.00 to 225.00
Toothpick holder, Punty Band patt.,
clear, late 1890s 50.00
Tray, Empress patt., Sahara, 13" d. 40.00
Tumbler, Banded Flute patt., clear,
early 20th c. 55.00
Tumbler, footed, Barcelona cutting,
clear, 6½" h. 18.00
Tumbler, old-fashioned, etched
Sportsman scene, clear 55.00
Tumbler, Minuet etching, clear,
12 oz. 40.00
Tumbler, Pineapple & Fan patt., clear
w/gold trim, late 1890s 30.00
Tumbler, iced tea, Plantation patt.,
clear, 12 oz. 47.00
Tumbler, juice, footed, Rose etching,
clear, 5 oz. 35.00
Tumbler, iced tea, footed, Rose
etching, clear, 12 oz...........................40.00
Tumbler, iced tea, footed, Twist patt.
(No. 1252), Marigold, 8 oz. 50.00

Tumbler, water, Victorian patt., clear,
3¾" d., 9 oz.......................................25.00
Tumbler, whiskey, Victorian patt.,
clear 39.00
Vase, 4" h., spherical, Empress patt.
Sahara 145.00
Vase, 7" h., fan-shaped, Pineapple &
Fan patt., emerald green w/gold
trim, late 1890s 30.00
Vase, 8" h., dolphin-footed, Empress
patt., Alexandrite 550.00
Vase, 8" h., Fancy Loop patt., clear,
late 1890s 70.00
Vases, 7½" h., Ipswich patt., No.
1405, w/12 prisms each, clear,
pr...75.00
Water set: pitcher & four tumblers;
Narrow Flute patt., clear, early
20th c., 5 pcs. 270.00
Wine, Gascony patt., Sportsman
etching, clear 95.00
Wine, Minuet etching, clear, 2½ oz. 35.00
Wine, New Era patt., clear....................18.00
Wine, Orchid etching, clear, 3 oz..........65.00
Wine, Spanish patt., cobalt blue 200.00

HISTORICAL & COMMEMORATIVE

Reference numbers are to Bessie M. Lindsey's book, American Historical Glass. *Also see MILK WHITE GLASS.*

Admiral Dewey Covered Dish

Battleship Maine dish, cov., milk
white, 7¼" l., No. 466 ....$95.00
Bryan (William J.) cup, cov., bust
portrait of Bryan, "The People's
Money" above, clear, overall
5" h., No. 336 ....67.00
Bunker Hill platter, "Prescott 1776
Stark-Warren 1876 Putnam," clear,
9 x 13½", No. 44 ....80.00 to 90.00
Civil War liquor glass, shield, flag
w/thirty-five stars, inscribed "A
Bumper to the Flag," 3½" h.,
No. 480 ....115.00
Columbia bread tray, shield-shaped,

Columbia super-imposed against 13
vertical bars, amber, 11½ x 9½",
No. 54 ....165.00
Columbus mugs, bust portraits of
Columbus & George Washington,
inscribed on base, "World's
Columbian Exposition, 1893,"
clear, 2½" d., No. 2 ....80.00
Columbus mug, Columbus in landing
scene front, reverse w/flagship
"Santa Maria," inscribed on base,
"World's Fair 1893," clear, 2½" d. 45.00
Columbus plate, bust portrait of
Columbus center w/dates "1492-
1892," pilot wheel border, clear,
9" d., No. 4 ....57.50
Columbus plate, bust portrait of
Columbus center, openwork club
border, milk white, 9½" d., No. 7........64.00
Dewey (Admiral) dish, cov., ribbed
base, amber, No. 387 ....230.00
Dewey (Admiral) dish, cov., tile base,
milk white, 6¾" l., 4½" h., No. 390
(ILLUS.) 65.00
Emblem butter dish, cov., bullet finial,
clear, No. 64 ....215.00

Emblem Tall Eagle Jar

Emblem Tall Eagle jar, cov., model of
an eagle w/eagle head cover,
American shield at front base under
a banner w/"E Pluribus Unum," milk
white, 6¾" h., No. 55 (ILLUS.) 195.00
Garfield cup plate, flaring rim, clear,
3" d., No. 297 ....100.00 to125.00

Golden Rule plate, "Do Unto Others,
etc.," clear, 11" d., No. 221 ....83.00
Grant Peace plate, bust portrait of
Grant center, maple leaf border,
amber, 10½" d., No. 289......55.00 to 70.00
Grant Peace plate, bust portrait of
Grant center, maple leaf border,
clear, 10½" d., No. 289 ....42.00

Grant Peace plate, bust portrait of
Grant center, maple leaf border,
vaseline, 10½" d., No. 289................90.00
Harrison-Morton tray, bust portraits
w/stippled ivy leaf border, clear,
8½ x 9½", No. 324 ....250.00 to 275.00
Indian match holder, milk white,
2¾" h., No. 12 ....65.00
Indian Chief plate, bust portraitof
Indian center, milk white,7½" d. 60.00
Kaiser Wilhelm I plate, bust portrait of
Kaiser center, laurel & oak leaf
border, clear, 9¾" sq., No. 445..........65.00
Kitchen stove dish, cov., amber,
4½ x 6¾", 4½" h., No. 149 ....300.00
Knights of Labor platter, amber,
11¾" l., No. 512 ....180.00 to 200.00
Liberty Bell plate, closed handles,
scalloped rim w/thirteen original
states & "100 Years Ago," clear,
8" d., No. 37 ....85.00
Louisiana Purchase Exposition plate,
inscribed "World's Fair St. Louis,
1904," forget-me-not & openwork
border, clear, 7¼" d., No. 105............17.50
Louisiana Purchase Exposition plate,
inscribed "World's Fair St. Louis,
1904," and "Festival Hall & Cascade
Gardens," open work & forget-me-
not border, clear w/frosted center
scene, 7¼" d., No. 106 ....30.00
Louisiana Purchase Exposition
tumbler, four features of St. Louis
Exposition in relief, milk white,
5" h., No. 107 ....45.00

Martyr's Mug

Martyr's mug, Lincoln & Garfield bust
portraits & inscription, clear, 2⅝" h.,
No. 272 (ILLUS.) 100.00
McKinley (William B.) cup, cov.,
bust portrait opposite handle,
"Protection & Prosperity," clear,
overall 5" h., No. 335 (ILLUS.
top next column) ....80.00 to 100.00
McKinley Memorial platter, "It's God's
Way" etc., clear, 8 x 10½", No. 356 ...60.00

McKinley "Protection & Prosperity" Cup

Moses in the Bulrushes dish, cov., lid
w/full figure of an infant, base
w/design resembling rushes, milk
white, 4" w., 5½" l., No. 214 ....90.00
Old Abe (eagle) compote, cov., clear,
No. 478 ....130.00
Old Glory plate, Betsy Ross making
first flag pictured in center, clear,
5½" d., No. 52 ....38.00
Old Statehouse tray, shows Inde-
pendence Hall above "Old State-
house, Philadelphia, Erected 1735,"
amber, No. 32 ....55.00
Pickwick (Mr.) bottle, full figure of Mr.
Pickwick (character created by
Charles Dickens), marked "Mr. Pick-
wick," clear, 8¾" h., No. 408 ....22.50
Plymouth Rock paperweight, dated
1620, clear, 3¼" l., No. 17 ....95.00
Railroad train platter, Union Pacific
Engine No. 350, amber, 9 x 12",
No. 134 ....225.00

Rock of Ages Bread Tray

Rock of Ages bread tray, clear,
No. 236 (ILLUS.) 85.00

Rock of Ages bread tray, clear
w/translucent deep blue
center, No. 236 ....165.00
Rock of Ages bread tray, clear w/milk
white center, No. 236 ....155.00

Theodore Roosevelt Platter

Roosevelt (Theodore) platter, frosted
portrait center, Teddy bears, etc.
border, clear, 7¾ x 10¼", No. 357
(ILLUS.) 175.00
Ruth statuette, Ruth shown as
gleaner resting on one knee w/wisps
of grain in each hand, "Gillinder &
Sons, Centennial Exhibition"
inscribed on base, satin finish, clear,
4½" h., No. 216 ....75.00 to 100.00
Sampson pattern pitcher, honoring
Rear Admiral William T. Sampson,
leafy garlands, tassels & drops,
clear w/partly stippled background,
No. 402 ....135.00
Shakespeare statuette, frosted bust of
Shakespeare, marked "Gillinder &
Sons, Centennial Exhibition," 5" h.,
No. 405 ....85.00
Three Presidents platter, bust
portraits of Garfield, Washington &
Lincoln, inscribed "In
Remembrance," clear, 10 x 12½",
No. 249 ....70.00
Three Presidents platter, bust
portraits of Garfield, Washington
& Lincoln, inscribed "In Remem-
brance," clear w/frosted center,
10 x 12½", No. 249 (ILLUS. top
next page) ....75.00 to 100.00
Uncle Sam dish, cov., battleship base,
milk white, 6½" l. 80.00
Washington Centennial patt. platter
w/bear paw handles, frosted center,
"First in War," etc., clear, 8½ x 12",
No. 27 ....130.00

Three Presidents Platter

Washington Bi-Centennial Bottle

Washington Bi-Centennial bottle, oval
  portrait medallion of Washington
  front & American eagle w/olive
  branches & thunderbolts in oval
  medallion reverse, "1732-1932,"
  clear, qt., No. 262 (ILLUS.) 22.50
Washington Bi-Centennial plate, bust
  portrait of Washington center, large
  star border on stippled ground
  w/reserve at bottom w/"G. Washington - 1732-1932," clear, 8" d.,
  No. 258 ....60.00
Washington Monument paperweight,
  milk white, 2¾" sq. base, 5½" h.,
  No. 255 ....175.00
Whisk broom dish, Daisy & Button
  patt. below handle, amber, 5" w.,
  7½" l...65.00

IMPERIAL

*Imperial Glass Company, Bellaire,
Ohio, was organized in 1901 and was in
continuous production, except for very brief
periods, until its closing in June 1984. It*

*had been a major producer of Carnival
Glass (which see) earlier in this century
and also produced other types of glass,
including an Art Glass line called "Free
Hand Ware" during the 1920s and its
"Jewels" about 1916. The company
acquired a number of molds of other
earlier factories, including the Cambridge
and A.H. Heisey companies, and reissued
numerous items through the years. Also see
ANIMALS.*

Imperial Nucut Mark

Early Imperial Cross Mark

Later Imperial Marks

CANDLEWICK PATTERN

Ashtray, heart-shaped, No. 400/172,
  clear, 4½" $10.00
Basket, No. 400/173, clear, 5" h. 250.00
Bonbon dish, heart-shaped, No. 51H,
  clear w/gold trim, 6" w. 15.00
Bonbon dish, heart-shaped, No. 51H,
  clear w/gold trim, 6" w. 15.00
Bowl, cream soup, 5", two-handled,
  No. 400/50, clear w/gold beads 55.00
Bowl, fruit, 5" d., 400/1F, clear...............8.00
Bowl, 5", heart-shaped, No. 400/40H,
  clear 25.00
Bowl, 6" d., baked apple, No. 400/13B,
  clear 33.00
Bowl, 7" d., No. 400/5F, blue 55.00
Bowl, 7" d., two-handled,
  No. 400/62B, red..............................150.00
Bowl, 9" d., four-toed, square
  crimped, No. 400/74SC, black
  amethyst 200.00
Bowl, 9" d., heart-shaped,
  No. 400/49H, clear 140.00
Bowl, fruit, 10" d., footed, pedestal
  base, ruffled rim, No. 400/103C,
  clear 110.00
Bowl, 12" d., bell-shaped,
  No. 400/106B, clear 65.00
Cake plate, birthday, 72 candle holes,
  No. 400/160, clear, 13" d. 310.00
Cake stand, No. 400/103D, clear,
  11" d...73.00

Candleholders, No. 400/80, blue,
3½", pr. 165.00
Candleholders, mushroom,
No. 400/86, clear w/gold beading,
pr...60.00
Candleholders w/applied handle,
No. 400/90, clear, 5", pr. ....75.00 to 100.00
Candleholders, three-light,
No. 400/115, clear, pr. 55.00
Candleholders, footed urn shape,
No. 400/129R, clear, 6" h., pr. 125.00
Candy box, cov., No. 400/59, clear,
5½" d...45.00
Candy box, cov., No. 400/259, clear,
7" d...115.00
Champagne, saucer-type, No. 3400,
clear, 6 oz. 11.50
Cheese & cracker server, No. 400/88,
clear..30.00
Compote, 4½" d., No. 400/63B, clear ...16.00
Compote, 8", No. 400/48F, clear 75.00
Cordial, No. 3400, clear......................35.00
Cream soup bowl w/underplate, two-
handled, No. 400/50, clear, 5" d.
bowl & 6¾" d. underplate, 2 pcs. 53.00
Creamer & open sugar bowl,
No. 400/18, clear, pr. 50.00
Creamer & open sugar bowl, pedestal
base, No. 400/31, clear, pr. 25.00
Cruet w/original stopper, applied
handle, No. 400/279, clear, 6 oz........40.00
Cup & saucer, clear...............................11.50
Goblet, water, No. 3400, clear, 9 oz. 15.00
Mayonnaise bowl & underplate,
No. 40, blue, 2 pcs..............................56.00
Mustard jar, spoon & underplate,
No. 400/156, clear, 3 pcs..................45.00
Pitcher, water, 80 oz., No. 400/24,
clear ....100.00 to 150.00
Pitcher, water, star-cut, No. 400/24,
clear, 80 oz. 190.00
Plate, bread & butter, 6" d.,
No. 400/1D, clear..................................6.50
Plate, salad, 7" d., No. 400/3D, clear......7.00
Plate, luncheon, 8" d., No. 400/5D,
clear..7.00
Plate, 8½" d., handled, crimped rim,
No. 400/62C, clear..............................20.00
Plate, dinner, 10" d., No. 400/10D,
clear 38.00
Plate, 10" d., two-handled,
No. 400/72D, ruby..............................75.00
Plate, 10" d., two-handled,
No. 400/72D, clear..............................25.00
Plate, 14" d., two-handled,
No. 400/113D, clear............................32.50
Platter, 16" oval, No. 400/131D, clear ..75.00
Punch bowl & underplate, 13" d. bowl
No. 400/20B & 17" d. underplate
No. 400/20V, clear, 2 pcs. 95.00
Relish dish, three-part, No. 400/208,
clear, 10" l. 78.00
Relish dish, five-part, No. 400/209,
clear, 13½" d. 65.00

Relish tray, three-part, No. 400/56,
clear, 10½" d. 50.00
Relish tray, four-part, No. 400/55,
clear, 8½" d. 16.50
Salt & pepper shakers, No. 400/96,
clear, pr. 10.00
Sandwich server, center handle,
No. 68D, clear, 11½" d.........................38.00
Seafood cocktails, footed, 400/190,
clear, set of 4 ....320.00
Sherbet, low, floral cutting, No.
400/19, clear, 5 oz. 15.00
Strawberry set: 7" d. plate & sugar dip
bowl; No. 400/83, clear, 2 pcs. 55.00
Sugar bowl, open, No. 400/122, clear 6.50
Teacup & saucer, mallard cutting,
No. 400/35, clear 15.00
Tray, heart-shaped center handle,
No. 400/149D, clear, 9" d...................40.00
Tray, pastry, heart-shaped center
handle, No. 400/68D, clear,11½" d. 30.00
Tumbler, juice, No. 400/19, clear,
5 oz. 12.00
Vase, bud, 5¾" h., No. 400/107, clear..28.00
Vase, 8" h., No. 400/87C, clear 22.00
Vase, 8" h., fan-shaped, etched stars
design, No. 400/87F, clear.................40.00
Vase, 8" h., flip-type, ruffled rim,
No. 400/143C, clear............................66.00
Water set: 80 oz. pitcher No. 400/24 &
six 12 oz. tumblers No. 400/19;
clear, 7 pcs. 250.00

CAPE COD PATTERN

Ashtray, No. 160/134/1, clear, 4" d.......10.00
Bowl, cream soup, 5½", tab-handled,
No. 160/198, clear 38.00
Bowl, fruit, 9" d., footed, No. 160/67F,
clear..60.00
Bowl, 10" d., footed, No. 160/137B,
clear..50.00
Box, cov., handled, clear 32.00
Cake plate, square, four-footed,
No. 160/220, clear, 10" w..................80.00
Cake stand, round, footed,
No. 160/67D, clear, 10½" d...............35.00
Candleholder, Aladdin style, No.
160/90, clear, 4" h............................125.00
Candleholders, two-light, No.
160/100, clear, pr.............................100.00
Coaster w/spoon rest, clear...................7.50
Comport, clear, 4½" d..........................18.00
Compote, 6", cov., footed, No. 160/140,
clear 55.00
Cruet w/original stopper, No. 160/119,
amber, 4 oz,..30.00
Decanter w/original stopper,
No. 160/163, clear, 30 oz.....50.00 to 75.00
Egg cup, No. 160/225, clear.................15.00
Epergne, plain center, No. 160/196,
clear, 2 pcs. 175.00
Goblet, water, stemmed, No. 1600,
clear, 10 oz. 10.00

Parfait, stemmed, No. 1602, clear,
6 oz. 16.00
Pitcher w/ice lip, No. 160/239, clear,
60 oz. 75.00
Plate, dinner, 10" d., No. 160/10D,
clear 33.00
Plate, 16" d., cupped, No. 160/20V,
clear 35.00
Platter, 13½" l. oval, No. 160/124D,
clear 68.00
Punch cup, clear....................................5.00
Punch set: punch bowl, underplate &
twelve cups; clear, 14 pcs................150.00
Salt & pepper shakers w/original tops,
cobalt blue, pr. 90.00
Sherbet, low, No. 1600, clear, 6 oz. 8.00
Tom & Jerry punch bowl, footed, No.
160/200, clear 275.00
Tumbler, flat, No. 160, clear, 10 oz. 8.00
Wine, No. 160/27, clear, 4½" h..............6.00

FREE HAND WARE

Graceful Free Hand Vase

Decanter w/original stopper, ship
decoration, peach blow, w/original
label 115.00
Vase, 7" h., iridescent orange w/dark
threading...165.00
Vase, 7⅜" h., 3½" d., cushion footed
baluster-form w/flared rim, overall
white decoration on butterfly blue
iridescent ground, ca. 1924 ....350.00
Vase, 8½" h., blue iridescent ground,
gold iridescent interior.....................110.00
Vase, 8½" h., cylindrical shape, white
drape design over mustard ground,
orange iridescent interior 150.00
Vase, 9¾" h., iridescent orange over
opaque white 50.00
Vase, 10" h., baluster-form w/flaring
foot & rim, opaque white heart &
vine decoration on a translucent
cobalt blue ground 495.00
Vase, 10" h., iridescent yellow orange
exterior, blue interior 125.00
Vase, 11½" h., footed slender body
w/rounded shoulders & expanded

tooled trefoil rim, dark iridescent
body decorated w/orange hearts
& vines (ILLUS.)...............................660.00

JEWELS LINE

Candlesticks, marigold, 8" h., pr. 38.00
Plate, 7¾" d., Pearl Green lustre 65.00

MISCELLANEOUS PATTERNS & LINES

Animal covered dish, lion on lacy
base, caramel slag...........................135.00
Animal covered dish, rooster on lacy
base, jade green 135.00
Animal covered dish, rooster on lacy
base, purple slag 175.00
Bonbon, dolphin handled, cut florals
on a pink ground, 6" d.........................30.00
Bowl, Cathay line, Phoenix patt., blue
satin 95.00
Bowl, 9" d., Rose patt., red slag 65.00
Compote, cov., Frosted Panels patt.,
Rubigold...60.00
Pitcher, Mt. Vernon patt........................23.00
Tumbler, Grape patt., ruby 12.00
Urn, Snake Dance patt., pink, 8½" h. ...85.00
Vase, 8½" h., model of a dancing
lady, red slag 98.00
Water set: pitcher & four tumblers;
Frosted Panels patt., Rubigold, 5
pcs. 175.00

IOWA CITY GLASS

*This ware, made by the Iowa City Glass
Manufacturing Co., Iowa City, Iowa, from
1880 to about 1883, was produced in many
shapes and patterns. The Frosted Stork
pattern and pieces decorated with mottos
and various animals are probably best
known among collectors.*

Goblet, Deer & Doe patt., clear $200.00
Goblet, Clear Stork patt......................150.00
Pickle castor, cov., Frosted Stork
patt...95.00
Plate, "Elaine," swan border 95.00
Platter, oval, "Be Industrious," clear
beehive center, deer border................50.00
Platter, oval, "Be Industrious," clear
beehive center, 1-0-1 border,
8 x 11½" 125.00
Platter, oval, Frosted Stork patt., 1-0-1
border, 8 x 11½" 58.00

LACY

*Lacy Glass is a general term developed
by collectors many years ago to cover the
earliest type of pressed glass produced in*

this country. "Lacy" refers to the fact that most of these early patterns consisted of scrolls and geometric designs against a finely stippled background which gives the glass the look of fine lace. Formerly this glass was often referred to as "Sandwich" for the Boston & Sandwich Glass Company of Sandwich, Massachusetts which produced a great deal of this ware. Today, however, collectors realize that many other factories on the East Coast and in the Pittsburgh, Pennsylvania and Wheeling, West Virginia areas also made lacy glass from the 1820s into the 1840s. All pieces listed are clear unless otherwise noted. Numbers after salt dips refer to listings in Pressed Glass Salt Dishes of the Lacy Period, 1825-1850, *by Logan W. and Dorothy B. Neal. Also see SANDWICH GLASS.*

Rectangular Lacy Dish

Bowl, 5⅛" d., 1" h., round w/shallow sides and small rim scallops, starburst in center, hairpin border design (several scallops tipped, mold roughness) $33.00

Bowl, 5½" d., Acanthus & Tulip patt. 135.00

Bowl, 5¾" w., Roman Rosette patt., hexagonal finely scalloped rim (four scallops lightly tipped)........................49.50

Bowl, 5⅝" d., Acanthus & Tulip patt., shallow sides w/finely scalloped rim, sapphire blue (three scallops lightly tipped, trace of mold roughness) 550.00

Bowl, 6" w., octagonal w/small rim scallops, American eagle & stars in center, acanthus leaves & shield border 330.00

Bowl, 6⅛" w., octagonal, Eagle patt., Boston & Sandwich (overall scallop roughness, section of jagged roughness on base rim) 330.00

Bowl, 6⅜" d., "Industry" patt., shallow sides, attributed to the New England Glass Co. (overall small spalls & rim flaking) 132.00

Bowl, 6½" d., shallow sides decorated w/grapes & leaves & tulips (eight lightly tipped scallops)......................627.00

Bowl, 7¾" d., Lyre patt., shallow sides w/a finely scalloped rim line w/bull's eyes, Midwestern, ca. 1840 (light stippling, usual mold roughness) 104.50

Bowl, 8" l., 1⅝" h., shallow oblong sides w/triple end lobes, oak leaf scrolls in center & around the sides (several tipped scallops, mold roughness)..88.00

Bowl, 8¼" d., 1⅞" h., Acorn & Rose patt., shallow sides w/finely scalloped rim (mold roughness) 115.50

Bowl, 8⅜" l., 1⅝" h., oval w/scalloped rim, paired S-scrolls in center, tight S-scrolls around border (shallow spalls on two scallops, mold roughness) 77.00

Bowl, 9¼" d., shallow sides w/scalloped rim, Gothic Arch design, fire-polished (mold roughness) 302.50

Bowl, 9¼" d., shallow sides w/scalloped rim, S-scrolls & shells design w/bull's-eyes in rim, Midwestern, ca. 1835 (trace of tipping) 990.00

Bowl, 9½" d., Tulip patt., low sides w/scalloped rim (four scallops lightly tipped)....................................214.50

Bowl, 9½" oval, 2½" h., Crossed Peacock Feather patt., shallow flaring & scalloped sides, Midwestern, ca. 1840 (several shallow rim chips) 121.00

Bowl, cov., 7⅛" d., 5½" h., round flaring sides w/a galleried rim supporting a domed cover w/flora-form finial, a band of Roman arches & thistles around the sides, Boston & Sandwich, ca. 1840 (one scallop slightly disfigured w/chip, two shallow spalls on top of rim) 715.00

Butter dish, cov., Roman Rosette patt., probably Pittsburgh, 6½" d., 4" h. (one rim chip, overall scallop tipping) 495.00

Candlestick, a lacy Peacock Eye socket attached by multiple wafers to a plain square stepped base, 5¹¹⁄₁₆" h. (some corners w/shallow chips, others w/usual roughness) 1,100.00

Compote, cov., 6¼" d., 4¾" h., Peacock Feather patt., deep round bowl w/flared rim supporting the low domed cover w/floral-form finial, on a low domed base, Midwestern (base mold roughness, two points on rim tipped, shallow chips & severe roughness on edge of rim) ...522.50

Compote, open, 4½" d., 4⅜" h., deep conical bowl w/scalloped rim & early

strawberry diamond design, on
applied short pedestal & round foot
(one rim bead w/shallow flake,
mold roughness) 121.00
Compote, open, 4¾" d., 3½" h., round
Heart patt. bowl, on applied knopped stem & round foot, attributed to
Boston & Sandwich, ca. 1830
(shallow rim scallop flake, usual
mold roughness) 660.00
Compote, open 6" d., 3¾" h., round
w/deeply scalloped rim, Pine Tree
& Shield patt., on applied short
pedestal & plain round foot (base
appears to be lightly polished) 357.50
Compote, open, 6½" w., 4" h., Eagle
patt., octagonal bowl on a knopped
stem & round lacy foot (roughness,
chip on base) 880.00
Compote, open, 6½" d., 4¼" h., round
bowl w/Heart & Sheaf of Wheat
patt., small rim, on applied clear
pedestal & plain round foot (mold
roughness) 357.50
Compote, open, 10¾" l., 6⅛" h.,
shallow oblong bowl w/scalloped
flanged rim in the Princess Feather
patt., applied w/a wafer to the flaring
Leaf patt. pedestal base, attributed
to New England area, ca. 1830-40
(one scallop w/small flake)............2,475.00
Dish, miniature, oval, scroll design,
scalloped rim, 2⅞" l. (minor chips) 60.50
Dish, oval w/scalloped rim & paneled
sides, Constitution & Eagle patt.,
Boston & Sandwich Glass Co.,
6¼" l., 1⅜" h. (two scallops
flaked, usual mold roughness) 550.00
Dish, oval, Hairpin patt., attributed to
Boston & Sandwich, 8½" l. (some
roughness, small chips on underside
of rim)...275.00
Dish, oblong w/angled sides,
Pineapple & Gothic Arch patt.,
Boston & Sandwich Glass Co.,
6½ x 9" (minor rim chipping) 192.50
Dish, rectangular w/notched corners,
Peacock Eye patt., probably
Boston & Sandwich, 7½ x 10"
(ILLUS.) 1,430.00
Dish, round w/shallow sides, Princess
Feather & Snail Shell design, attributed to New England, roughness,
9¼" d., (ILLUS. top next column) 385.00
Dish, oval, a band of diamonds,
sheaves of wheat & acanthus leaves
around the sides, 9⅜" l. (two scal-
lops flaked) 495.00
Dish, shell-shaped w/wide loop end
handle, attributed to New England,
ca. 1830-40, 7¾ x 9½" (shallow non-
disfiguring spalls on three scallops,
usual mold roughness) 6,050.00

Large Lacy Dish

Honey dish, round w/scalloped rim,
Roman Rosette patt., cobalt blue,
4" d. (three scallops lightly tipped) ...357.50
Honey dish, Nectarine patt. 40.00
Lamp, whale oil table-type, free-blown
spherical font w/top opening
tapering to a knopped stem applied
w/a wide wafer to a pressed lacy
Hairpin patt. foot, Midwestern,
ca. 1830, 7¼" h...........................1,870.00
Pitcher & bowl set, miniature, each
piece w/tiny flowers against a
stippled ground, ca. 1840, bowl
3¼" d., pitcher 2½" h., 2 pcs.
(chips) 181.50
Plate, 5¼" d., round w/gently scal-
loped rim, Rose & Thistle patt. (light
tipping on several scallops) 77.00
Plate, 5¾" d., Gothic Arch border,
large center square divided into
sixteen small squares, yellowish
green (two scallops tipped) 330.00

Triple-Heart Lacy Plate

Plate, 5¾" d., triple-heart center
design, crescents w/diamonds
border design, medium green, three
scallops tipped (ILLUS.)...................385.00
Plate, 5⅞" d., fan & star design (mold
roughness) 55.00

Plate, 7" d., Waffle patt. center & fans around flanged rim (shallow spall on face)..44.00

Plate, 7½" w., octagonal Eagle patt. (usual mold roughness) 385.00

Plate, 7⅜" d., round w/scalloped rim, four-heart lobed center surrounded by strawberry diamond design, heart & blossom border band (shallow spalls on underside of scallops, mold roughness) 55.00

Plate, 8" d., round w/central flowers & leaves design framed w/concentric bands of intricate diamonds (mold roughness)...99.00

Plate, 10" w., octagonal, Beehive patt. (mold roughness, tipping on the scallops)..110.00

Salt dip, boat-shaped, BT-7 (heat check at stern) 220.00

Salt dip, boat-shaped, "Fayette" on stern, opalescent medium blue, Boston & Sandwich, BT 5 (flake on foot rim, usual mold roughness) ...1,045.00

Salt dip, boat-shaped, marked "Fayette" on stern, probably Boston & Sandwich, BT 4a (flaking, mold roughness) 385.00

Salt dip, flaring casket-form on a flaring base, shell design on sides, reddish amethyst, probably Boston & Sandwich (SL 1) 715.00

Salt dip, cov., sleigh-shaped w/scrolled sides & feet, domed cover w/knob finial, probably Boston & Sandwich, CD 2a (refracting small bubble on rim, some severe mold roughness on base & cover)............412.50

Salt dip, model of a small rowboat, bands of knobs down the sides, New England, cobalt blue (BT 9) 825.00

Salt dip, oblong octagonal, Eagle patt., Providence Flint Glass Co., EE 5 (one scallop tipped)................214.50

Salt dip, oval w/deeply serrated rim & overall heavy raised diamonds, Boston & Sandwich, blue opalescent, OL 15 (minute flake on one point)..412.50

Salt dip, oval bowl w/deeply fluted rim, diamonds around the sides, raised on an oblong footed base, probably Boston & Sandwich (OP 2b) 203.50

Salt dip, oval bowl w/finely scalloped rim, raised on four feet, opalescent, probably Boston & Sandwich, OP 17 (tiny flakes on tips of three feet).......302.50

Salt dip, oval, footed, Peacock Feather patt., probably Boston & Sandwich (PO 5) 88.00

Salt dip, rectangular w/columnar corners, Bird Bath patt., New England Glass Co., opalescent, BB 1 (flake on one corner) 385.00

Salt dip, rectangular w/columnar corners, Bird Bath patt., New England Glass Co., opaque white, BB 1 (annealing lines, one flake on corner, grey striations across interior bottom)..605.00

Salt dip, rectangular w/ringed columns at corners, Bird Bath patt., New England Glass Co., BB 2 (mold roughness on corners & lower rim)..227.50

Salt dip, rectangular w/columnar corners, Eagle patt., Boston & Sandwich, EE 1a (mold roughness) 104.50

Salt dip, rectangular w/slightly flaring sides, Hearts & Gothic Arches patt., Boston & Sandwich, opalescent medium blue w/striations, GA 4a (severe flaking & small chips along rim & sides)......................................275.00

Salt dip, rectangular w/columnar corners, finely waffled sides, New England Glass Co. (OG 2) 66.00

Salt dip, rectangular w/columnar corners, strawberry diamond point in sides, Boston & Sandwich, yellowish green (SD 7) 495.00

Salt dip, rectangular w/columnar corners & strawberry diamond design on the sides, cobalt blue, probably Boston & Sandwich, SD 7 variant (mold roughness) 104.50

Salt dip, rectangular casket-shape w/flared sides, on small knob feet, ornate scroll design around the sides, deep olive green, ca. 1840 (cooling crack on one side)..............231.00

Salt dip, round flaring bowl on a short stem & round scalloped foot, silvery opaque mottled violet blue, probably Boston & Sandwich, RP 3 (unseen base flake, rim chip).........................302.50

Salt dip, round bowl w/flaring paneled sides w/a scalloped rim, on a short round scalloped foot, New England (RP 10) 115.50

Salt dip, scrolled sofa shape w/scrolled rim & legs, Eagle patt., Boston & Sandwich, EE 7 (minor mold roughness) 357.50

Salt dip, sleigh-shaped, Eagle patt., molded eagles at each corner, Boston & Sandwich, EE 3b (mold roughness) 412.50

Salt dip, sleigh-shaped w/scroll feet, Lyre patt., peacock green, probably Boston & Sandwich, LE 3 (mold roughness, refracting annealing line on one scroll) 550.00

Salt dip, sleigh-shaped w/scrolled sides & rope-twist band around

base, Scroll patt., Providence Flint
Glass Co., SC 1 (trace of mold
roughness) 275.00
Salt dip, sleigh-shaped w/scrolled
ends & feet, molded shell design,
probably Boston & Sandwich, SL 15
(mold roughness, flaking on rim &
feet)...88.00
Sauce dish, Oak Leaf patt., 4½" d. 60.00
Sugar bowl, cov., Acanthus patt.,
floral-form finial, 5⅜" h. (small chips
on rims) 132.00

Rare Acanthus Leaf Sugar Bowl

Sugar bowl, cov., octagonal,
Acanthus Leaf patt., Boston &
Sandwich Glass Co., ca. 1830-40,
unique deep emerald green, usual
mold roughness, 5½" h.
(ILLUS.) 17,600.00
Sugar bowl, cov., octagonal,
Acanthus patt., flora-form finial on
domed cover, canary yellow, 5½" h.
(usual cover rim flaking, two shallow
spalls on foot) 1,760.00
Sugar bowl, cov., early California
patt., ca. 1850-60, medium
amethyst, 6" h. (unseen chips on
underside of base, minor mold
roughness) 935.00
Sugar bowl, cov., octagonal, Gothic
Arch patt., Boston & Sandwich
Glass Co., ca. 1840-50, opaque
starch blue, 5⅜" h. (small chips on
rim of base, one on finial attachment
of cover) 1,430.00
Sugar bowl, cov., Gothic Arch patt.,
petal foot, peacock blue, ca. 1840,
5¾" h. (tiny spall on base rim,
multiple flakes on circular disk
under lid finial) 1,045.00
Sugar bowl, cov., Gothic Arch patt.,
purplish blue, 5½" h. (usual flaking
along cover edge) 1,320.00
Sugar bowl, cov., octagonal, footed,
Gothic Arch patt., silvery white
opaque, ca. 1840-60........................750.00

Clear Lacy Sugar Bowl

Sugar bowl, cov., round flaring sides
raised on a short pedestal base, tall
domed cover w/a flora-form finial,
Gothic Arch & Peacock Feather
patt., probably Pittsburgh, 6" h.
(ILLUS.) 880.00
Sugar bowl, cov., 'Ihmsen'-type,
octagonal w/each panel featuring a
relief-molded design of a piece of
glassware produced by C. Ihmsen &
Company of Pittsburgh, ca. 1851,
opaque white, 5⅜" h. (shallow chip
on base rim & four along rim) 4,290.00
Tray, oblong w/scalloped rim, Butterfly
patt., 8¼" l. (one small rim chip) 176.00
Tray, oblong, an overall design of
delicate scrolls w/shell-form fans at
the ends & a curved diamond in the
center all on a finely stippled
ground, attributed to Boston &
Sandwich, 8⅞ x 11⅝" (one scallop
missing, another chipped).............1,100.00
Tray, rectangular, Peacock Eye &
Shield patt., Boston & Sandwich, ca.
1835, 4⅝ x 8¼" (overall scallop
roughness & flaking) 522.50

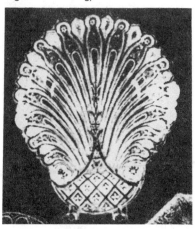

Shell-shaped Tray

Tray, shell-shaped w/Hairpin patt.,
closed tab handle w/diamonds,
attributed to New England area,
ca. 1830, 9½" l. (ILLUS.)...............8,250.00
Tray, oval w/open loop end handles,
open chain border, center diamond
surrounded by scrolls, fans & leaf
scrolls in border, ca. 1830, Boston &
Sandwich Glass Co., 8½ x 11¾"
(chip under one handle, minor rim
roughness) 2,200.00
Tureen, cover & undertray, miniature,
oval, raised scroll designs on a
stippled ground, ca. 1840, 3" l.,
3 pcs. (chips) 126.50
Vegetable dish, cov., Princess
Feather patt., no grape clusters on
flanged rim, domed cover w/loop
handle, 10¾" l., 4¾" h. (mold
roughness, some tipping, one
shallow chip) 2,475.00
Window pane, rectangular, large
diamond w/scrolls in center,
quartered suns & rays at corners,
Pittsburgh, 5 x 6⅞" (edge chips &
roughness) 4,730.00

McKEE

*The McKee name has been associated
with glass production since 1834, first
producing window glass and later bottles.
In the 1850s a new factory was established
in Pittsburgh, Pennsylvania, for
production of flint and pressed glass. The
plant was relocated in Jeannette,
Pennsylvania in 1888 and operated there
as an independent company almost
continuously until 1951 when it sold out to
Thatcher Glass Manufacturing Company.
Many types of collectible glass were
produced by McKee through the years
including Depression, Pattern, Milk White
(which see) and a variety of utility
kitchenwares.*

Early McKee Mark, ca. 1880

PRESCUT

McKee Prescut Mark

Kitchenwares
Bowl, 6" d., Chalaine Blue $45.00
Bowl, 7½" d., Chalaine Blue 50.00

Bowl, 9" d., Skokie Green....................15.00
Canister w/original glass cover, round,
Chalaine Blue, 10 oz..........................50.00
Canister w/original glass cover, round,
Chalaine Blue, 24 oz..........................55.00
Canister w/original glass cover, round,
"Flour," Chalaine Blue.........................55.00
Canister w/original glass cover, round,
French Ivory w/red polka dots,
10 oz..16.00
Canister w/original glass cover, round,
"Sugar," Chalaine Blue 55.00
Measuring cup, Skokie Green, 2 cup ...18.00
Mixing bowls, nesting-type, French
Ivory w/red polka dots, 9" d., 8" d.,
7" d., 6" d., set of 4............................60.00
Refrigerator dish, cov., rectangular,
Chalaine Blue, 5 x 8" 85.00
Refrigerator dish, cov., rectangular,
French Ivory w/blue polka dots,
4 x 5"...33.00
Salt & pepper shakers w/original
metal lids, Chalaine Blue, pr. 100.00
Salt & pepper shakers w/original tops,
French Ivory w/blue polka dots, pr.....32.00
Salt & pepper shakers w/original tops,
Roman Arch patt., black, 4½" h., pr. ...45.00

McKee Water Dispenser

Water dispenser w/glass top, Skokie
Green, 4½ x 5 x 11" (ILLUS.)...........225.00

Pres-Cut Lines
Bowl, 7" d., Rock Crystal patt., clear 15.00
Candlestick, Rock Crystal patt.,
amber, 8" h. 40.00
Champagne, Aztec patt., clear 17.00
Cheese & cracker server, Rock
Crystal patt., ruby.............................175.00
Cocktail, Rock Crystal patt., clear,
3½ oz., 4¼" h.,..................................13.50
Compote, 7" d., 3½" h., Rock Crystal
patt., clear 38.00
Cordial, Rock Crystal patt., clear,
1 oz. 20.00
Cordial, Rock Crystal patt., ruby,
1 oz. 60.00
Cracker jar, cov., Aztec patt., milk
white 60.00

Creamer & open sugar bowl,
Sunbeam patt., blue w/gold trim,
pr. 45.00
Cruet w/original stopper, Rock Crystal
patt., clear 65.00
Goblet, footed, low, Rock Crystal
patt., amber, 8 oz. 50.00
Goblet, footed, Rock Crystal patt.,
ruby, 8 oz. 45.00
Goblet, water, Rock Crystal patt.,
clear, 6½" h. 16.50
Goblet, water, Rock Crystal patt.,
green...20.00
Icer w/liner, Rock Crystal patt., clear....33.00
Mayonnaise bowl & underplate, Rock
Crystal patt., pink, 2 pcs. 25.00
Nut bowl w/center handle, Rock
Crystal patt., ruby, 8½" d. 135.00
Parfait, Rock Crystal patt., clear 25.00
Pitcher, water, cylindrical, Rock
Crystal patt., amber, 2 qt. 150.00
Punch cup, Sunbeam patt., clear 25.00
Relish, five-part, Rock Crystal patt.,
clear, 12¼" d. 25.00
Sandwich server w/center handle,
Rock Crystal patt., ruby 135.00
Sugar bowl, cov., footed, Rock Crystal
patt., clear 36.00
Sundae, Rock Crystal patt., ruby,
6 oz. 33.00
Tumbler, Aztec patt., clear....................10.00
Tumbler, juice, Rock Crystal patt.,
clear 12.00
Tumbler, Rock Crystal patt., clear,
5 oz. 12.50
Tumbler, iced tea, Rock Crystal patt.,
clear, 11 oz., 6½" h. 19.50
Tumbler, iced tea, Rock Crystal patt.,
ruby, 11 oz., 6½" h. 50.00
Tumbler, Rock Crystal patt., clear,
12 oz. 55.00
Vase, 11" h., footed, cylindrical, Rock
Crystal patt., clear............................55.00
Wine, Rock Crystal patt., clear,
4¾" h. 16.00

Miscellaneous Patterns & Pieces

"Bottoms Up" Whiskey Tumbler

Animal covered dish, rabbit on split-
ribbed base, milk white 325.00

Butter dish, cov., Wild Rose w/Bow-
knot patt., green (worn old gold) 100.00
Candlesticks, Laurel patt., French
Ivory, pr. 25.00
Cruet, Wild Rose with Bowknot patt.,
frosted clear w/Goofus decoration 45.00
Egg cup, French Ivory 6.50
Mug, Outdoor Drinking Scene patt.,
green opaque....................................75.00
Mug, Serenade (Troubador) patt.,
blue opaque 55.00
Mug, Serenade (Troubador) patt.,
French Ivory......................................90.00
Mug, Serenade (Troubador) patt.,
green opaque....................................85.00
Pin tray, embossed scrolling patt.,
clear, decorated w/pink & blue trim,
2½ x 5" 10.00
Tom & Jerry set: bowl & twelve
mugs; vaseline, all pieces signed,
13 pcs. 150.00
Tumbler, whiskey, w/coaster base,
"Bottoms Up," French Ivory, 2 pcs.
(ILLUS.) 50.00
Vase, 8" h., footed, triangular w/relief-
molded nude on each side, opaque
black 175.00
Vase, 10½" h., Rainbow patt., French
Ivory 90.00

MILK WHITE

This is opaque white glass that resembles the color of and was used as a substitute for white porcelain. Opacity was obtained by adding oxide of tin to a batch of clear glass. It has been made in numerous forms and shapes in this country and abroad from about the first quarter of the last century. It is still being produced, and there are many reproductions of earlier pieces. Also see HISTORICAL and PATTERN GLASS.

"American Hen" Covered Dish

Animal covered dish, "American Hen,"
eagle w/eggs inscribed "Porto Rico,"
"Cuba," & "Philippines," 6" l., 4" h.
(ILLUS.) $66.00

Animal covered dish, Boar's Head
w/glass eyes ....675.00 to 775.00
Animal covered dish, "The British
Lion" on base, 6¼" l. 110.00
Animal covered dish, Camel resting,
6¼" l. ....100.00 to 125.00
Animal covered dish, Cat on coarse
rib base, 5½" l., 4" h. 95.00
Animal covered dish, Cat on split-
ribbed base, signed "McKee," 5½"
(tiny ear fleck out) 295.00
Animal covered dish, Chick & Eggs on
lacy-edge pedestal base, Atterbury,
1880s ....75.00 to 100.00
Animal covered dish, Chick in Egg
cover on sleigh-shaped base,
5½" l. 70.00
Animal covered dish, Chicks on
Round Basket, 4½" w., 3" h. 65.00
Animal covered dish, Cow on round
paneled base, France, 5¾" l. 180.00
Animal covered dish, Deer on
"fallen tree" base, Flaccus,
6¾" l. ....225.00 to 250.00
Animal covered dish, Dog (Chow) on
wide ribbed base, Westmoreland
Specialty Company, 5½" h.................65.00
Animal covered dish, Duck w/wavy
base, glass eyes, Challinor, Taylor
& Co., 5¼" h.....................................125.00
Animal covered dish, Pintail Duck on
split-rib base, Kemple Glass Co.,
mid-20th c., 5½" l. 55.00
Animal covered dish, Fish, Entwined
Fish (2) on lacy-edge base, shell
finial, Atterbury, 7½" d......150.00 to 175.00
Animal covered dish, Fish on Skiff
base, 7½" l. 32.50
Animal covered dish, Fish w/glass
eyes, Challinor, Taylor & Co.,
8¾" l...75.00
Animal covered dish, Fish, Vallery-
sthal, 7" l. 100.00
Animal covered dish, Flat Fish,
8½" l. 200.00
Animal covered dish, Fox on ribbed
top & lacy-edge base, Atterbury,
7¾" l...160.00
Animal covered dish, Hen on
Basketweave base, Kemple Glass
Co., mid-20th c. 55.00
Animal covered dish, Hen on Basket-
weave base, signed "Vallerysthal,"
7½" l...125.00
Animal covered dish, Hen on Chick
base, Flaccus, 6¼" l.........250.00 to 300.00
Animal covered dish, Hen on flared
Basketweave base, 5⅝" l...................75.00
Animal covered dish, Hen on ribbed
flared base 100.00
Animal covered dish, Hen w/blue
head on lacy base, amber glass
eyes, Atterbury..................................140.00

Animal covered dish, Hen w/straight
head w/glass eyes on lacy base,
Westmoreland Specialty
Company 50.00
Animal covered dish, Kittens (3) on
square base, gold trim, 3½" sq. 40.00
Animal covered dish, Lamb on "Bo
Peep" base, 6" l. base, 4¼" h. 295.00
Animal covered dish, Lion on Picket
base, 5½" l. 65.00
Animal covered dish, Lamb on split-
ribbed base, lamb facing right,
McKee, 5½" l......................75.00 to 100.00

Lion on Scroll Base Dish

Animal covered dish, Lion on scroll
base, 5¾" l. (ILLUS.)...........................75.00
Animal covered dish, Majestic Lion,
molded bird & foliage base,
6¾" h. 2,600.00

Ribbed Lion on Lacy Base

Animal covered dish, Ribbed Lion on
lacy-edge base, patent dated,
Atterbury (ILLUS.) 150.00
Animal covered dish, Ribbed Lion on
ribbed base, Atterbury, 7½" l. 225.00
Animal covered dish, Mule-Eared
Rabbit on ribbed octagonal base,
5½" l., 4½" h.......................80.00 to 100.00
Animal covered dish, Rabbit, original
red glass eyes, patent date
stamped on bottom, Atterbury,
9" l. ....250.00 to 275.00

Animal covered dish, Rabbit on Split
   Rib base, 5½" l....................................65.00

Robin on Nest Dish

Animal covered dish, Robin on Nest,
   6¼" d. (ILLUS.) 150.00
Animal covered dish, Robin
   with Berry, Kemple Glass Co.,
   mid-20th c., 5½" l. 150.00
Animal covered dish, Rooster on wide
   rib base, Westmoreland Specialty
   Co., 5½" l. 60.00
Animal covered dish, Standing
   (Pedestal) Rooster, Westmoreland....55.00
Animal covered dish, Squirrel on
   acorn-shaped dish, Vallerysthal,
   7¼" l...50.00
Animal covered dish, "square block"
   Swan w/glass eyes, Atterbury, 8" l...240.00

Swan with Raised Wings Dish

Animal covered dish, Swan w/raised
   wings & glass eyes on lacy-edge
   base, Atterbury, 9½" l., 6" h.
   (ILLUS.) ....150.00 to 175.00
Animal covered dish, Turkey, Imperial
   Glass Co. 50.00
Animal covered dish, Turkey on split-
   ribbed base, McKee...........................90.00
Animal covered dish, Wooly Lamb on
   Octagon coarse ribbed base, 5¼" l....70.00
Basket, two-handled, chick emerging
   from egg on cover...............................95.00
Bottle, model of an Octopus, tentacles
   winding around a large American
   coin, 4½" h. (no metal cap) 650.00

Bottle, model of a Sitting Bear,
   10¾" h...85.00
Bowl, 7" d., 5" h., Chain & Petal
   Edge patt. 25.00
Bowl, 8" d., 3" h., Open Lattice Edge,
   apple blossom decoration in center,
   Atterbury 40.00
Bowl, 8" d., footed, Wide Weave
   Basket design 30.00
Bowl, 8¾ x 9¼", rectangular w/open
   edge border 40.00
Bowl, 8¾ x 12¾", 2⅞" h., Beaded Rib
   patt. w/interior floral design...............60.00
Bowl, 10" d., 4" h., Daisy patt.,
   unpainted 70.00
Bowl, 10" l., 5¾" h., oblong, Shell
   patt., two ribbed & two petal feet 25.00
Bowl, round, Daisy & Tree of Life
   patt..40.00
Box, cov., heart-shaped, embossed
   floral design highlighted w/touches
   of blue & gold.....................................35.00
Butter dish, cov., w/snowflake-shaped
   insert, Crossed Fern patt. w/Ball &
   Claw base 90.00
Butter dish, cov., Roman Cross patt.....50.00
Butter dish, cov., Versailles patt.
   w/pink decoration..............................45.00
Compote, open, 7¼" h., six-sided,
   Scroll patt...60.00
Compote, open, 7½" h., Jenny Lind
   figural bust pedestal, ribbed bowl 85.00
Compote, open, 8¼" d., 8¼" h., Atlas
   stem, open-edge border, Atterbury..100.00
Covered dish, Admiral Dewey on
   Battleship base, 5½" l. 125.00

Hand & Dove Dish

Covered dish, Hand & Dove on lacy-
   edge base, Atterbury, 8¾" l., 4¾" h.
   (ILLUS.) ....100.00 to 150.00
Covered dish, pear-shaped lid resting
   in petalled leaf bowl, w/original fired
   paint & Westmoreland label under-
   neath...35.00
Covered dish, Santa on Sleigh,
   5½" l...185.00
Covered dish, Snare Drum w/Cannon
   finial, 4½" d., 4" h. ....70.00 to 90.00
Creamer, Owl, miniature, 3½" h. 47.00

Dresser tray, Chrysanthemum patt.,
  7½ x 10" 35.00
Egg cup, cov., model of a Hen on
  Nest, 2½" w., 2½" h. 175.00

Blackberry Goblet

Goblet, Blackberry patt. (ILLUS.)..........38.00
Match holder, model of a bulldog
  head w/striker on back of the head,
  2¼" h...85.00
Model of a cat, sitting, 8" h. 200.00
Model of a tramp's shoe, 2⅛" h. 42.00
Mug, Bleeding Heart patt., 3¼" h..........60.00
Plate, 5½" d., Woof Woof ....50.00 to 75.00
Plate, 6" d., Dog and Cats, open
  leaf border.......................................100.00
Plate, 6" d., Three Puppies, open
  leaf border...85.00
Plate, 6¼" d., Easter Rabbits, old
  paint..35.00
Plate, 6¼" d., Mother Goose w/bun-
  nies in relief.......................................45.00
Plate, 7" w., diamond-shaped, Easter
  Chicks (2), openwork scroll & leaf
  border 38.00
Plate, 7" d., Ancient Castle (Garfield
  Monument)..50.00

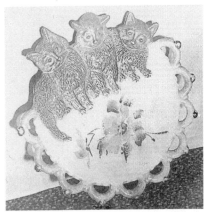

Three Kittens Plate

Plate, 7" d., Three Kittens (ILLUS.) 35.00
Plate, 7" d., Challinor's Forget-Me-Not
  patt. 40.00

Three Owls Plate

Plate, 7" d., Three Owls (ILLUS.) 40.00
Plate, 7¼" d., Easter Bunny & Egg.......60.00
Plate, 7¼" d., Lacy-Edge Indian, good
  paint...55.00
Plate, 7¼" d., Setting Hen & Chicks,
  openwork border.................................55.00
Plate, 7½" d., "Easter" ducks, scroll
  border 40.00

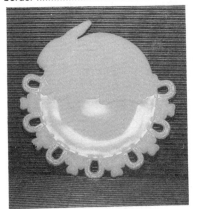

Rabbit & Horseshoe Plate

Plate, 7½" d., Rabbit & Horseshoe
  (ILLUS.) 55.00
Plate, 8" d., Diamond and Shell
  border 40.00
Plate, 8" d., Hearts & Anchor border 30.00
Plate, 8" d., Serenade...........................42.00
Plate, 8¼" d., Wicket border 35.00
Plate, 9" d., Angel Head, openwork
  border 30.00
Plate, 9" d., Gothic edge.........10.00 to 20.00
Plate, 10½" d., Closed Lattice Edge
  border, h.p. autumn leaves &
  grapes, sawtooth under base 35.00
Plate, 10½" d., Open Lattice Edge
  border, game bird in center................75.00

Platter, 9¾ x 13¼", Retriever, lily
pad border 110.00
Platter, 10½ x 13¾", flattened fish
form w/scale details 125.00
Salt dip, figural turtle.............................45.00
Salt dip, model of a basket w/handle....35.00
Salt shaker w/original top, Chain &
Swag patt...35.00
Sugar shaker w/original top, h.p. Apple
Blossom patt. 135.00
Sugar shaker w/original top, Grape
patt., raised bunch of grapes w/leaf
& vine decoration, old screw cap,
4½" h...45.00
Sugar shaker w/original top, Little
Shrimp patt. 75.00
Sugar shaker w/original top, Parian
Swirl patt., enameled floral
decoration, Northwood.....................110.00
Sugar shaker w/original top, Quilted
Phlox patt., Northwood 125.00
Sugar shaker w/original top, Quilted
Phlox patt., decorated w/blue
flowers, Northwood 195.00
Syrup pitcher w/original hinged lid,
Apple Blossom patt. 160.00
Syrup pitcher w/original metal top,
Banded Shell patt., 5½" h. 65.00
Syrup pitcher w/original hinged tin
cover, pressed Blackberry patt.,
applied strap handle, ca. 1860,
7¼" h...137.50
Syrup pitcher w/original top, Catherine
Ann patt. 125.00
Syrup pitcher w/original metal top,
Challinor's Tree of Life patt...............80.00
Syrup pitcher w/original top, Petunia
Swirl patt. 85.00
Table set: creamer, cov. sugar bowl,
cov. butter dish, spooner; Versailles
patt. w/h.p. rose decoration, 4 pcs...125.00
Tile, owl decoration in fired-on paint,
6" sq..55.00
Water set: pitcher & four tumblers;
Apple Blossom patt., 5 pcs. 160.00
Whimsey, Easter Egg with Emerging
Chick, 3¼" l. 40.00
Whimsey, Straw Hat (College Hat),
w/old paint, McKee, 4" d. 40.00

NEW MARTINSVILLE

The New Martinsville Glass Mfg. Co.
opened in New Martinsville, West Virginia
in 1901 and during its first period of
production came out with a number of
colored opaque pressed glass patterns and
also developed an art glass line they
named "Muranese" but which collectors
today refer to as "New Martinsville Peach
Blow." The factory burned in 1907 but

reopened later that year and began
focusing on production of various clear
pressed glass patterns many of which were
then decorated with gold or ruby staining
or enameled decoration. After going
through receivership in 1937 the factory
again changed the focus of its production
to more contemporary glass lines and
figural animals. The firm was purchased
in 1944 by The Viking Glass Company
(now Dalzell-Viking) and some of the long-
popular New Martinsville patterns are now
produced by this still-active firm.

Ashtray, embossed w/"New Martins-
ville Centennial - 1838-1938" & a log
cabin along the Ohio River, green ...$50.00
Book ends, model of an elephant,
clear, pr. 185.00
Book ends, model of a prancing
horse, clear, pr. 175.00
Bowl, 7 x 12" rectangle, Janice patt.
(No. 4500 Line), ruby 40.00
Cordial, Moondrops patt. (No. 37
Line), cobalt blue 30.00
Dresser set: two cologne bottles
w/original stoppers & cov. powder
jar; Queen Ann patt. (No. 18 Line),
clear, 3 pcs. 80.00
Liqueur set: decanter w/stopper &
three liqueur tumblers; Moondrops
patt., green, 4 pcs. 45.00
Pitcher, water, Moondrops patt.,
clear 50.00
Plate, torte, 18" d., Radiance patt.
(No. 4200 Line), Prelude etching,
clear 95.00
Relish dish, divided, Radiance patt.,
blue 24.00
Relish dish, five-part, Prelude etching,
clear, 13" l. 85.00
Tumbler, Moondrops patt., ruby 12.00
Tumbler, water, footed, Prelude
etching, clear 18.00

NORTHWOOD

Harry Northwood (1860-1919) was born
in England, the son of noted glass artist
John Northwood. Brought up in the glass
business, Harry immigrated to the United
States in 1881 and shortly thereafter
became manager of the La Belle Glass
Company, Bridgeport, Ohio. Here he was
responsible for many innovations in
colored and blown glass. After leaving La
Belle in 1887 he opened The Northwood
Glass Company in Martins Ferry, Ohio in
1888. The company moved to Ellwood City,
Pennsylvania in 1892 and Northwood
moved again to take over a glass plant in

Indiana, Pennsylvania in 1896. One of his major lines made at the Indiana, Pennsylvania plant was Custard glass (which he called "ivory"). It was made in several patterns and some pieces were marked on the base with "Northwood" in script.

Harry and his family moved back to England in 1899 but returned to the U.S. in 1902 at which time he opened another glass factory in Wheeling, West Virginia. Here he was able to put his full talents to work and under his guidance the firm manufactured many notable glass lines including opalescent wares, colored and clear pressed tablewares, various novelties and, probably best known of all, Carnival glass. Around 1906 Harry introduced his famous "N" in circle trade-mark which can be found on the base of many, but not all, pieces made at his factory. The factory closed in 1925.

In this listing we are including only the clear and colored tablewares produced at Northwood factories. Also see CARNIVAL, MILK WHITE and, under Pattern Glass, ROYAL IVY and ROYAL OAK.

Northwood Valentine Bowl

Northwood Signature Mark, ca. 1898

Northwood "N" in Circle Mark, ca. 1906

Berry set: master bowl & five sauce
    dishes; Parian Swirl patt., ruby
    w/enameled decoration, 6 pcs. $145.00

Berry set: master bowl & nine sauce
    dishes; Leaf Medallion (Regent)
    patt., purple w/gold trim, 10 pcs. 625.00
Bowl, 9" w., crimped rim, Valentine
    (No. 14) patt., clear (ILLUS.) 49.00
Bowl, 11" d., rolled edge, Jade Blue.....50.00
Bowl, master berry, Leaf Medallion
    (Regent) patt., purple w/gold 120.00
Bowl, master berry, Mikado (Flower &
    Bud) patt., clear w/gold & enameled
    trim 132.00
Butter dish, cov., Cherry & Cable
    (Cherry Thumbprints) patt., clear
    w/ruby & gold trim 100.00
Butter dish, cov., Gold Rose patt.,
    green w/gold 100.00
Butter dish, cov., Panelled Holly patt.,
    blue opalescent w/gold trim 375.00
Butter dish, cov., Peach patt., clear......95.00
Butter dish, cov., Strawberry & Cable
    patt., clear 110.00
Celery vase, Leaf Umbrella patt., ruby
    & white spatter 225.00
Compote, jelly, Leaf Medallion
    (Regent) patt., cobalt blue w/gold
    trim...120.00
Compote, jelly, Leaf Medallion
    (Regent) patt., purple w/gold trim 80.00
Creamer, Cherry & Cable (Cherry
    Thumbprints) patt., clear 45.00
Creamer, Panelled Holly patt., blue
    opalescent 95.00

Panelled Holly Creamer

Creamer, Panelled Holly patt., white
    opalescent w/gold & red (ILLUS.) 85.00
Creamer, Panelled Holly patt., green
    w/gold trim 75.00
Cruet w/original stopper, Parian Swirl
    mold, Daisy & Fern patt., blue
    opalescent 80.00
Cruet w/original stopper, Parian Swirl
    patt., ruby..450.00
Pickle castor, Leaf Mold patt. insert,
    rubina, w/silver plate frame..............265.00

Pickle castor, Leaf Mold patt. insert,
vaseline w/cranberry spatter, satin
finish, ornate silver plate frame,
cover & tongs (resilvered) 375.00
Pitcher, water, Grape & Gothic
Arches patt., green w/gold trim 100.00
Pitcher, water, Leaf Medallion
(Regent) patt., purple w/gold trim 350.00
Pitcher, water, Leaf Mold patt.,
cranberry & white spatter................395.00
Pitcher, water, Leaf Umbrella patt.,
cased blue 550.00
Pitcher, Leaf Umbrella patt., cased
lemon yellow 495.00
Pitcher, water, Memphis patt., clear
w/gold 90.00
Pitcher, water, Panelled Holly patt.,
white opalescent w/red & green.......225.00
Rose bowl, Jewel (Threaded Swirl)
patt., rubina......................................90.00
Salt shaker w/original top, Leaf Mold
patt., cranberry & white spatter 125.00
Salt shaker w/original top, Leaf
Umbrella patt., Rose du Barry
(cased mauve) 125.00
Salt shaker w/original top, Leaf
Umbrella patt., ruby 165.00
Salt & pepper shakers w/original tops,
Leaf Medallion (Regent) patt., cobalt
blue w/gold trim, pr. 200.00
Salt & pepper shakers w/original tops,
Leaf Mold patt., cranberry & white
spatter...125.00
Sauce dish, Leaf Medallion (Regent)
patt., cobalt blue w/gold trim 30.00
Sauce dish, Memphis patt., green
w/gold trim 20.00
Spooner, Cherry & Cable (Cherry
Thumbprints) patt., clear w/ruby &
gold trim 75.00
Spooner, Leaf Mold patt., vaseline
w/cranberry spatter, satin finish 90.00
Spooner, Panelled Holly patt., blue
opalescent 75.00
Sugar bowl, cov., Apple Blossom
patt., milk white 125.00
Sugar bowl, cov., Leaf Medallion
(Regent) patt., green w/gold trim 195.00
Sugar bowl, cov., Leaf Medallion
(Regent) patt., purple w/gold trim 210.00
Sugar bowl, cov., Ribbed Pillar patt.,
pink spatter, satin finish 95.00
Sugar shaker w/original top, Aurora
patt., Ring Neck mold, rubina
(ILLUS. top next column) 265.00
Sugar shaker w/original top, Leaf
Mold patt., blue 350.00
Sugar shaker w/original top, Leaf
Mold patt., red & white spatter
w/mica flecks 315.00
Sugar shaker w/original top, Leaf
Mold patt., lemon yellow 325.00
Sugar shaker w/original top, Leaf
Mold patt., ruby ....400.00 to 425.00

Aurora Rubina Sugar Shaker

Sugar shaker w/original top, Leaf
Umbrella patt., cased blue 220.00
Sugar shaker w/original top, Leaf
Umbrella patt., ruby 355.00
Sugar shaker w/original top, Parian
Swirl patt., ruby 285.00
Sugar shaker w/original top, Quilted
Phlox patt., amethyst 185.00
Sugar shaker w/original top, Ribbed
Pillar patt., pink & white spatter,
satin finish.......................................160.00
Sugar shaker w/original top, Ring
Neck mold, clear w/cranberry &
white spatter, satin finish 269.00
Syrup pitcher w/original top, Leaf
Mold patt., vaseline w/cranberry
spatter..595.00
Syrup pitcher w/original top, Ribbed
Pillar patt., pink & white spatter,
satin finish.......................................250.00
Table set: cov. butter dish, creamer &
sugar bowl; Mikado patt., 3 pcs. 275.00
Table set: cov. butter dish, creamer &
spooner; Leaf Medallion (Regent)
patt., purple w/gold trim, 3 pcs. 500.00

Cherry & Cable Table Set

Table set: creamer, cov. sugar bowl,
spooner & cov. butter dish; Cherry &
Cable (Cherry Thumbprints) patt.,
clear w/ruby & gold trim, 4 pcs.
(ILLUS.) 450.00
Table set: creamer, cov. sugar bowl,
cov. butter dish & spooner; Leaf
Medallion (Regent) patt., cobalt blue
w/gold trim, 4 pcs.............................675.00

Table set, Panelled Holly patt., white opalescent w/purple berries & green leaves decoration, 4 pcs. 475.00

Toothpick holder, Leaf Mold patt., vaseline w/cranberry spatter............225.00

Toothpick holder, Leaf Umbrella patt., Rose du Barry (cased mauve) 225.00

Tumbler, Leaf Medallion (Regent) patt., purple w/gold trim 89.00

Tumbler, Leaf Mold patt., vaseline w/cranberry spatter 95.00

Tumbler, Netted Oak patt., milk white ..60.00

Tumbler, Panelled Holly patt., white opalescent 35.00

Tumbler, Parian Swirl patt., ruby 30.00

Tumbler, Strawberry & Cable patt., clear 35.00

Water set: pitcher & six tumblers; Memphis patt., clear w/gold trim, 7 pcs. ....175.00 to 200.00

Water set: pitcher & ten tumblers; Leaf Medallion (Regent) patt., purple w/gold trim, 11 pcs. 600.00

Cup & saucer, Penny (No. 991) line, red...9.50

Goblet, Aristocrat line, red, 5¾" h. 12.00

Plate, 6" sq., Crow's Foot (No. 412) line, amber 1.25

Plate, 8½" sq., Crow's Foot (No. 412) line, amber 3.50

Platter, 6½ x 8¾" oval, Aristocrat line, red...18.00

Platter, 11¼" l., Crow's Foot (No. 412) line, amber 15.00

Platter, 9¼ x 12½" oval, Aristocrat line, red..30.00

Rose bowl, footed, Gothic Garden etching, yellow 30.00

Salt & pepper shakers w/original tops, Party (No. 191) line, amber, pr. 18.00

Sandwich server w/center handle, Mrs. "B" line, amber 16.00

Sherbet, ball stem, Aristocrat line, ruby, 5 oz. 14.00

Tray w/handles, Crow's Foot (No. 412) line, amber, 10½" sq. 16.00

Vase, 5" h., elliptical-shaped, etched Lela Bird patt., ebony.........................95.00

Vase, 8¼" h., Crow's Foot (No. 412) line, red..62.50

PADEN CITY

The Paden City Glass Manufacturing Company began operations in Paden City, West Virginia in 1916, primarily as a supplier of blanks to other companies. All wares were hand-made, that is, either hand-pressed or mold-blown. The early products were not particularly noteworthy but by the early 1930s the quality had improved considerably and the firm continued to turn out high quality glassware in a variety of beautiful colors until financial difficulties necessitated its closing in 1951. Over the years the firm produced in addition to tablewares, items for hotel and restaurant use, light shades, shaving mugs, perfume bottles and lamps.

Bowl, 9" d., pedestal foot, etched Peacock & Rose patt., pink..............$75.00

Bowl, cream soup, footed Crow's Foot (No. 412) line, red 20.00

Cheese & cracker set, Simplicity (No. 700) line, pink w/heavy silver trim, 13" d., 2 pcs. 45.00

Cheese stand, Crow's Foot (No. 412) line, clear, 5" d., 3" h. 8.00

Console bowl, footed, Triumph (No. 701) line, pink w/floral cutting & gold trim, 12" d...45.00

Creamer, Party (No. 191) line, green 3.50

Cup & saucer, Crow's Foot (No. 412) line, amber 6.50

Cup & saucer, Crow's Foot (No. 412) line, red 10.00

PATTERN GLASS

Though it has never been ascertained whether glass was first pressed in the United States or abroad, the development of the glass pressing machine revolutionized the glass industry in the United States and this country receives the credit for improving the method to make this process feasible. The first wares pressed were probably small flat plates of the type now referred to as "lacy," the intricacy of the design concealing flaws.

In 1827, both the New England Glass Co., Cambridge, Massachusetts and Bakewell & Co., Pittsburgh, took out patents for pressing glass furniture knobs and soon other pieces followed. This early pressed glass contained red lead which made it clear and resonant when tapped (flint). Made primarily in clear, it is rarer in blue, amethyst, olive green and yellow.

By the 1840s, early simple patterns such as Ashburton, Argus and Excelsior appeared. Ribbed Bellflower seems to have been one of the earliest patterns to have had complete sets. By the 1860s, a wide range of patterns was available.

In 1864, William Leighton of Hobbs, Brockunier & Co., Wheeling, West Virginia, developed a formula for "soda lime" glass which did not require the expensive red lead for clarity. Although "soda lime" glass did not have the brilliance of the earlier flint glass, the formula came into widespread use because glass could be produced cheaply.

An asterisk (*) indicates a piece which has been reproduced.

ACTRESS

Bowl, cov. $110.00
Bowl, 6" d., flat......................................45.00
Bowl, 6" d., footed 50.00
Bowl, 7" d., footed 60.00
Bread tray, Miss Neilsen, 12½" l..........87.50
Butter dish, cov., Fanny Davenport &
  Miss Neilson ....100.00 to 125.00
Cake stand, Maude Granger & Annie
  Pixley, 10" d., 7" h. 125.00
Cake stand, frosted stem....145.00 to 165.00
Celery vase, Pinafore scene...............175.00
Cheese dish, cov., "Lone Fisherman"
  on cover, "The Two Dromios" on
  underplate......................225.00 to 235.00
Compote, cov., 6" d., 10" h. 100.00
Compote, cov., 7" d., 8½" h. 145.00
Compote, cov., 8" d.,
  12" h.................................150.00 to 175.00
Compote, open, 7" d., 7" h., Miss
  Neilsen..150.00
Compote, open, 7" d., 7" h., Maggie
  Mitchell & Fanny Davenport.............110.00
Compote, open, 8" d., 5" h....................75.00
Compote, open, 10" d., 6" h..................80.00
Compote, open, 10" d., 9" h................100.00
Creamer, clear.......................................70.00
Creamer, frosted.................................125.00
Goblet, Lotta Crabtree & Kate
  Claxton...............................75.00 to 85.00
Marmalade jar, cov., Maude Granger
  & Annie Pixley...................................110.00
*Pickle dish, Kate Claxton, "Love's
  Request is Pickles," 5¼ x 9¼" 45.00
Platter, 7 x 11½", Pinafore scene 100.00
*Relish, Miss Neilsen, 5 x 8"................40.00
Relish, Maude Granger,
  5 x 9"...................................75.00 to 95.00
Sauce dish, Maggie Mitchell & Fanny
  Davenport, 4½" d., 2½" h..................24.00
Spooner, Mary Anderson & Maude
  Granger...74.00
Sugar bowl, cov., Lotta Crabtree &
  Kate Claxton 97.00

ADONIS (Pleat & Tuck or Washboard)

Celery 27.50
Creamer, blue..35.00
Creamer, clear.......................................25.00
Plate, 10" d., clear 13.50
Plate, 10" d., green...............................35.00
Relish dish...9.50
Salt shaker w/original top 27.50
Sauce dish...7.00
Sugar bowl, cov. 28.00

ALABAMA (Beaded Bull's Eye with Drape)

Butter dish, cov......................................50.00
Cake stand, 8" d. 100.00 to125.00
Castor set, 4-bottle, original silver
  plate stand, green 375.00
Celery tray, clear 38.00
Celery tray, ruby-stained 125.00
Compote, cov., 5" d. 125.00
Creamer...42.00
Creamer & cov. sugar bowl, individ-
  ual size, pr. 100.00
Cruet w/original stopper.........................55.00
Pitcher, water.......................................150.00
Relish, 5 x 8⅛"......................................25.00
Salt shaker w/original top 30.00
Sauce dish..17.50
Spooner..48.00
Sugar bowl, cov. 55.00
Sugar bowl, cov., miniature 48.00
Syrup pitcher w/original top ....85.00 to 95.00
Table set: creamer, cov. sugar bowl,
  spooner & cov. butter dish; 4 pcs. ...200.00
Toothpick holder 65.00
Tray, water, 10½" 125.00

ALASKA (Lion's Leg)

Alaska Butter Dish

Banana boat, blue opales-
  cent ....200.00 to 250.00
Banana boat, emerald
  green................................165.00 to 185.00
Banana boat, vaseline opalescent......200.00
Banana boat, vaseline opalescent
  w/enameling......................................325.00
Berry set: master bowl & 4 sauce
  dishes; emerald green,
  5 pcs. ....250.00 to 275.00
Bowl, 8" sq., blue opales-
  cent ....150.00 to 200.00
Bowl, 8" sq., clear opalescent
  w/enameled florals.............................65.00
Bowl, 8" sq., emerald green..................55.00
Bowl, 8" sq., emerald green
  w/enameled florals...........................125.00
Bowl, 8" sq., emerald green w/gold &
  enameling, w/silver plate stand........145.00

Bowl, 8" sq., vaseline opalescent 140.00
Bowl, 8" sq., vaseline opalescent
  w/enameled florals...........................225.00
Butter dish, cov., blue opalescent
  (ILLUS.) ....350.00 to 375.00
Butter dish, cov., emerald green
  w/enameled florals...........200.00 to 250.00
Butter dish, cov., vaseline opales-
  cent...268.00
Celery (or jewel) tray, blue opales-
  cent...132.00
Celery tray, blue opalescent
  w/enameled florals...........................250.00
Celery tray, emerald green................. 75.00
Celery tray, emerald green w/gold........85.00
Celery tray, vaseline opalescent
  w/enameled florals...........................170.00
Creamer, blue opalescent 75.00
Creamer, clear opalescent .....40.00 to 55.00
Creamer, emerald green 48.00
Creamer, vaseline opalescent..............68.00
Cruet w/original stopper, blue
  opalescent 260.00
Cruet w/original stopper, emerald
  green..275.00
Cruet w/original stopper, vaseline
  opalescent w/enameled
  florals ....200.00 to 250.00
Pitcher, water, blue opalescent 350.00
Pitcher, water, blue opalescent
  w/enameled florals...........................550.00
Pitcher, water, clear opalescent
  w/enameled florals & gold trim.........125.00
Pitcher, water, emerald green
  w/enameled florals...........................285.00
Pitcher, water, vaseline opalescent....350.00
Pitcher, water, vaseline opalescent
  w/enameled florals...........425.00 to 500.00
Salt shaker w/original top, blue
  opalescent 85.00
Salt shaker w/original top, emerald
  green...70.00
Salt shaker w/original top, emerald
  green w/enameling 75.00
Salt shaker w/original top, vaseline
  opalescent 75.00
Sauce dish, blue opalescent................47.00
Sauce dish, clear opalescent...............25.00
Sauce dish, clear opalescent
  w/enameled florals.............................35.00
Sauce dish, emerald green.................. 20.00
Sauce dish, emerald green w/enam-
  eled florals & leaves...........................38.00
Sauce dish, vaseline opalescent..........38.00
Sauce dish, vaseline opalescent
  w/enameled florals.............................48.50
Spooner, blue opalescent.......65.00 to 75.00
Spooner, clear opalescent w/enam-
  eled florals 75.00
Spooner, emerald green.......................34.00
Spooner, emerald green w/enameled
  florals 70.00
Spooner, vaseline opalescent 60.00

Spooner, vaseline opalescent
  w/enameled florals.............................75.00
Sugar bowl, cov., blue opalescent......200.00
Sugar bowl, cov., emerald green
  w/enameled florals.............................73.00
Sugar bowl, cov., vaseline opales-
  cent...210.00
Sugar bowl, cov., vaseline opalescent
  w/enameled florals...........................245.00
Table set, blue opalescent,
  4 pcs. ....650.00 to 700.00
Table set, vaseline opalescent,
  4 pcs. ....550.00 to 600.00
Tumbler, blue opalescent 70.00
Tumbler, emerald green 46.00
Tumbler, vaseline opalescent..............77.00
Tumbler, vaseline opalescent
  w/enameled florals.............................80.00
Water set: pitcher & 6 tumblers;
  vaseline opalescent,
  7 pcs. ....800.00 to 850.00

ALEXIS - See Priscilla Pattern

ALMOND THUMBPRINT (Pointed Thumbprint)
Champagne, non-flint 40.00
Compote, cov., 6½" d., 8" h.,
  flint ....75.00 to 85.00
Goblet..30.00
Salt dip, master size, flint....................20.00
Spooner, fluted, non-flint 20.00
Tumbler, footed, flint...........................39.00
Wine, flint...15.00

AMAZON (Sawtooth Band)
Banana stand 66.00
Bowl, 8" d., scalloped 24.00
Butter dish, cov....................................90.00
Cake stand, 8" to 9½" d. ....35.00 to 45.00
Champagne...30.00
Compote, open, jelly, 4½" d.................25.00
Compote, open, 9½" d., 8" h...45.00 to 55.00
Cordial, ruby-stained 38.00
Creamer...48.00
Cruet w/bar in hand stopper, clear 75.00
Goblet..28.00
Pitcher, water.......................................60.00
Salt shaker w/original top 20.00
Sauce dish, flat or footed.....................12.00
Spooner..30.00
Sugar bowl, cov. 47.50
Tumbler, engraved 35.00
Tumbler 20.00
Vase, double-bud 75.00
Wine 25.00

AMBERETTE - See Klondike Pattern

ANIMALS & BIRDS ON GOBLETS & PITCHERS

GOBLETS:
Bird & roses, acid-etched 30.00

Deer & Doe w/lily-of-the-valley,
  pressed 100.00
Dog w/rabbit in mouth, acid-etched 105.00
Flamingo Habitat, acid-etched..............43.00
Giraffe, acid-etched 75.00
Ibex, acid-etched 86.00
Lion in the Jungle, acid-etched.............90.00
Ostrich Looking at Moon, pressed......125.00
Owl-Possum, pressed 90.00
Stork & Flowers, acid-etched...............65.00

PITCHERS:

Squirrel Pitcher

Bringing Home Cows, pressed 750.00
Flamingo Habitat, acid-etched............125.00
Fox & Crow, pressed..........................150.00
Heron, pressed...................................143.00
Squirrel, pressed, non-Greentown
  (ILLUS.) 150.00 to175.00

APOLLO

Bowl, 8" d..22.50
Cake stand, engraved, 9" d. 47.50
Cake stand, plain, 9" to 10½" d. 50.00
Celery tray 16.00
Compote, cov., 4¾" d., 8¾" h. 45.00
Compote, cov., 6" d. 45.00
Compote, cov., 8" d. 65.00
Compote, open, 5" d..............................25.00
Creamer, engraved................................57.50
Creamer, plain......................................45.00
Goblet, engraved 35.00
Goblet, frosted 48.00
Goblet, plain 32.00
Lamp, kerosene-type, clear, 7" h..........60.00
Lamp, kerosene-type, blue, 9'" h. 265.00
Lamp, kerosene-type, clear, 10" h........72.00
Lamp, kerosene-type, blue base
  w/vaseline font 245.00
Sauce dish, flat or footed......................14.00
Spooner..40.00
Sugar bowl, cov., etched 75.00
Sugar shaker w/original top 37.00
Syrup pitcher w/original top ...90.00 to110.00
Toothpick holder...................................28.00
Tray, water..40.00
Tumbler, frosted 30.00

ARGUS (McKee & Brother, Pittsburgh)

Argus Spillholder

Celery vase, flint...................................70.00
Champagne, flint 75.00
Champagne, flint, cut panels w/gilt
  florals 95.00
Creamer, applied handle, flint.............105.00
Egg cup, flint..........................25.00 to 35.00
Egg cup, handled, flint 80.00
Goblet, flint 72.50
Goblet, Five-Row...................................55.00
Goblet, master size, flint.......................45.00
Mug, applied handle, flint......................60.00
Salt dip, cov., master size, flint.............90.00
Salt dip, open, master size, flint............35.00
Spillholder, flint (ILLUS.).........45.00 to 55.00
Tumbler, footed, flint, 4" h....................40.00
Wine, flint, 4" h......................................45.00
Wine (Hotel Argus), non-flint 18.00

ART (Job's Tears)

Banana stand 100.00
Bowl, 7" d., flared rim, footed...............26.50
Bowl, 8" sq., shallow.............................34.00
Bowl, 8½" d...40.00
Bowl, 9¾" d...38.00
Bowl, rectangular.................................20.00
Butter dish, cov.....................................45.00
Cake stand, 9" to 10½" d. 63.00
Celery vase...46.00
Compote, cov., 6" d., 10" h. 54.00
Compote, cov., 7" d. 65.00
Compote, cov., 8" d., high stand..........99.00
Compote, open, jelly, 5" d....................27.50
Compote, open, 9" d., 7¼" h..................48.00
Compote, open, 10" d., 9" h..................50.00
Cracker jar, cov., 7" d., 8" h., to top
  of finial 5.00
Creamer..42.00
Goblet...54.00
Pitcher, water, 9½" h. 150.00
Relish, 4¼" x 7¾" 18.50
Sauce dish, flat or footed......................14.00
Spooner..27.00
Sugar bowl, cov., engraved.................48.00
Sugar bowl, cov., plain 41.00
Tumbler 30.00

ASHBURTON

Ale glass, flint, 6½" h. 85.00
Bitters bottle w/original pewter lid 65.00
Celery vase, scalloped rim, canary
    yellow, flint ....700.00 to 850.00
Celery vase, scalloped rim, clear,
    flint 135.00
Champagne, barrel-shaped, flint 85.00
Claret, flint, 5¼" h. 68.00
Cordial, flint, 4¼" h. 45.00
Cordial, non-flint 55.00
Creamer, applied handle,
    flint ....275.00 to 325.00
Decanter, bar lip w/patent pewter
    stopper, canary yellow, flint 1,600.00
Decanter, bar lip w/patent pewter
    stopper, clear, flint 155.00
Decanter, bar lip & facet-cut neck,
    canary yellow, flint, qt. 600.00
Decanter, bar lip & facet-cut neck,
    clear, flint, qt. 55.00
Decanter w/original stopper, clear,
    flint, qt. 97.50
Egg cup, clambroth, flint 155.00
Egg cup, clear, flint 31.00
Egg cup, non-flint 15.50
Egg cup, disconnected ovals 35.00
Goblet, short, flint 42.00
Goblet, barrel-shaped, flint 44.00
Goblet, flared, flint, clear......................52.50
Goblet, flared, flint, clear w/gold,
    6" h...100.00
Goblet, non-flint 30.00
Goblet, disconnected ovals 35.00
Honey dish, 3½" d. 9.00
Mug, applied handle, 3" h. 60.00
Pitcher, water, applied hollow
    handle, flint ....400.00 to 450.00
Pomade jar, cov., white opaque, flint..195.00
Sugar bowl, cov., flint 175.00
Tumbler, bar, flint..................................58.00
Tumbler, water, flint...............................59.00
Tumbler, water, footed...........75.00 to 85.00
Tumbler, whiskey, applied
    handle, flint 100.00 to125.00
Vases, 9¼" h., shaped pedestal base,
    flint, pr. 160.00
Wine, clear, flint....................................46.00
Wine, clear, knob stem 85.00
Wine w/cut design, clear w/gold trim ..125.00
Wine, peacock green, flint 650.00
Wine, non-flint..30.00

ATLANTA (Lion or Square Lion's Head)

Bowl, 5 x 8"' oblong, flat 50.00
Butter dish, cov....................................125.00
Celery vase..60.00
Compote, cov., 5" sq., 6" h. 95.00
Compote, cov., 8" sq., 9½" h. 130.00
Compote, open, 4¼" sq., 4" h...............46.00
Compote, open, 6" sq., 7½" h...............75.00

Compote, open, 8" sq., high stand 95.00
Creamer..48.00
Egg cup 95.00
*Goblet...85.00
Marmalade jar, cov., w/lion's head
    finial 100.00
Relish, boat-shaped................................30.00
Salt dip, individual size 35.00
Salt dip, master size, flint......................20.00
Spooner, fluted, non-flint 20.00
Tumbler, footed, flint..............................39.00
Wine, flint..15.00

ATLAS (Crystal Ball or Cannon Ball)

Butter dish, cov......................................50.00
Cake stand, 8" to 10" d. 28.00
Celery vase...39.50
Champagne, 5½" h..................................37.00
Cordial 42.00
Creamer, flat or pedestal base 22.00
Goblet, engraved 30.00
Goblet, plain 30.00
Pitcher, milk, tankard, applied handle...45.00
Pitcher, water, tankard, applied
    handle...50.00
Salt dip, individual size 15.00
Salt dip, master size 20.00
Sauce dish, flat or footed.......................12.50
Spooner 30.00
Toothpick holder 25.00
Tray, water...65.00
Tumbler 28.00
Wine 25.00

AZTEC

Aztec Creamer

Bowl, cov., 8½" d., clear 72.50
Claret..40.00
Creamer (ILLUS.) 26.50
Cruet w/original stopper.........................48.00
Dresser bottle w/original stopper 37.50
Goblet...32.50
Pitcher, water..60.00
Salt & pepper shakers w/original
    tops, pr. 35.00
Sugar bowl, open.................................. 22.50
Toothpick holder 30.00
Wine 16.50

BABY THUMBPRINT - See Dakota Pattern

BALDER - See Pennsylvania Pattern

BALTIMORE PEAR

Baltimore Pear Creamer

Bowl, 4 x 8"...19.00
Bread plate, 12½" l. 48.00
*Butter dish, cov. 53.00
Cake plate, side handles, 10"
    octagon 38.00
*Cake stand, high pedestal................. 55.00
*Creamer (ILLUS.).................25.00 to 35.00
*Goblet..35.00
*Plate, 9" d..28.00
Relish, 8¼" l......................................22.50
*Sauce dish, flat or footed 15.00
Spooner...45.00
*Sugar bowl, cov................................53.00
Tray, water...28.00

**BAMBOO - See Broken Column
Pattern**

BANDED BEADED GRAPE MEDALLION

Creamer...41.00
Dish, open, 5 x 8" oval.........................15.00
Egg cup 25.00
Goblet..32.50
Spooner...30.00
Tumbler, footed 35.00

BANDED BUCKLE

Compote, cov., 6" 50.00
Egg cup 28.50
Goblet..28.00
Spooner...30.00

**BANDED PORTLAND (Portland Maiden
Blush, Portland with Diamond Point Band
or Virginia)**

Berry set: master bowl & 8 sauce
    dishes; pink-stained w/gold trim,
    9 pcs. 295.00
Bowl, berry, 9" d. 30.00
Butter dish, cov., pink-stained 150.00
Candlesticks, pr..................................75.00

Celery tray, pink-stained, 10" oval 75.00
Celery tray, clear, 5 x 12" 25.00
Celery vase, clear................................32.00
Cologne bottle w/original stopper,
    clear 51.00
Compote, cov., 8" d., high stand........110.00
Creamer, individual size, clear 29.00
Cruet w/original stopper.......................60.00
Dresser jar, cov., clear, 3½" d. 36.00
Goblet, clear 35.00
Goblet, pink-stained.............................68.00
Pitcher, water, 9½" h. 95.00
Pitcher, child's, pink-stained 32.50
Pomade jar, cov...................................27.50
Relish, pink-stained, 4 x 6½" 28.00
Relish, 4 x 8½" oval 14.00
Salt & pepper shakers w/original tops,
    clear, pr..55.00
Salt & pepper shakers w/original tops,
    pink-stained, pr. 85.00 to100.00

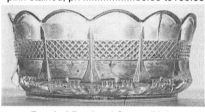

Banded Portland Sauce Dish

Sauce dish, 4½" d. (ILLUS.) 15.00
Spooner, pink-stained..........................75.00
Sugar bowl, cov., pink-stained...........112.00
Sugar shaker w/original top 50.00
Syrup jug w/original top, pink-
    stained 365.00
Toothpick holder, clear 41.00
Toothpick holder, pink-stained.............58.00
Tumbler 35.00
Vase, 6" h., flared, clear 32.00
Vase, 6" h., flared, pink-stained...........35.00
Vase, 9" h. 42.00
Wine, clear..28.00
Wine, gold-stained...............................35.00
Wine, pink-stained 75.00

BARBERRY

Bowl, 6" oval.......................................18.00
Butter dish, cov., shell finial 50.00
Butter dish, cov., pattern on base
    rim 110.00
Cake stand, 9½" d. 48.00
Cake stand, 11" d. 125.00
Celery vase...49.00
Compote, cov., 6" d., high stand, shell
    finial 42.50
Compote, cov., 8" d., high stand, shell
    finial 95.00
Compote, cov., 8" d., low stand, shell
    finial 77.50
Compote, open, 8½" d., 7" h................42.00
Egg cup 20.00
Goblet...26.00

Pitcher, water, 9½" h., applied handle ..84.00
Plate, 6" d., blue ....40.00 to 50.00
Plate, 6" d., clear 19.00
Sauce dish, flat or footed......................11.00
Spooner, footed 32.00
Tumbler, footed 28.00
Wine 35.00

BARLEY

Barley Goblet

Bowl, 6¼ x 8½" oval, scalloped rim 18.50
Bowl, 10" oval 36.00
Butter dish, cov....................................32.50
Cake stand, 8" to 10½" d. 37.50
Celery vase...45.00
Compote, open, 7" d., 8" h...................25.00
Compote, open, 8½" d., 8" h.................33.00
Compote, open, 8¾" d., 6½" h.,
  scalloped rim.....................................31.00
Creamer..23.00
Goblet (ILLUS.).....................................25.00
Marmalade jar, cov. 50.00
Pickle castor w/silver plate frame &
  tongs 80.00
Pitcher, water..46.00
Plate, 6" d. 30.00
Relish, 8" l., 6" w...................................19.00
Relish, handled, 9½" l., 5¼" w. 17.50
Sauce dish, flat or footed......................12.50
Spooner...20.00
Wine, 3¾" h. 31.00

BASKETWEAVE

Bread plate, amber 30.00
Bread plate, blue 29.00
Creamer, amber 35.00
Cup, blue 40.00
Cup & saucer, vaseline.........................37.50
*Goblet, blue...35.00
*Goblet, clear..27.00
*Goblet, vaseline 35.00
Mug, 3" h. 12.00
Pitcher, milk, blue 50.00
*Pitcher, water, amber 55.00
*Pitcher, water, blue 75.00

*Pitcher, water, vaseline 77.00
Plate, 8¾" d., handled, amber 27.50
*Tray, water, scenic center, amber,
  12"...38.00
*Tray, water, scenic center, blue, 12" ...55.00
*Tray, water, scenic center, vaseline,
  12"...50.00
Vase, 8½" h. 12.50
Wine 22.00

BEADED BAND

Butter dish, cov......................................36.00
Goblet 28.00
Pitcher, water...85.00
Relish, 5¼ x 8½"....................................10.00
Sauce dish, flat, 4¼" d...........................12.50
Wine 27.00

BEADED BULL'S EYE WITH DRAPE
- See Alabama Pattern

BEADED DEWDROP - See
Wisconsin Pattern

BEADED GRAPE (California)

Beaded Grape Open Compote

Bowl, 6½" sq., green..............................28.00
Bowl, 7½" sq., green..............................30.00
Bowl, 8" sq..28.00
Bowl, 6¼ x 8½" rectangle, green..........28.00
Bowl, 9" sq., four-footed 15.00
Bread tray, green, 7 x 10".....................60.00
Butter dish, cov., square, clear.............55.00
Butter dish, cov., square,
  green.............................70.00 to 80.00
Cake stand, green, 9" sq.,
  6" h.............................75.00 to 85.00
Celery tray, green 40.00
Celery vase..32.00
Compote, cov., 4⅞" sq., 6" h., green 55.00
*Compote, cov., 8½" sq., high stand ..125.00
Compote, open, 8½" sq., high stand,
  clear (ILLUS.)...................................72.50
Compote, open, 8½" sq., high stand,
  green..85.00
Cordial 15.00
Creamer, clear.......................................35.00
Creamer, green 42.50
Cruet w/original stopper, green 115.00

*Goblet...35.00
Pitcher, water, round, green 78.00
Pitcher, water, square, green 125.00
Pitcher, water, tankard...........................78.00
*Plate, 8" sq., clear 27.50
*Plate, 8" sq., green..............................37.50
Relish, green w/gold, 4 x 7" 35.00
Salt shaker w/original top, clear...........32.50
Salt & pepper shakers w/original
   tops, green, pr.....................................75.00
*Sauce dish, green 15.00
Sauce dish, handled 15.00
Spooner...40.00
Sugar bowl, cov. 54.00
Toothpick holder, clear 23.00
Toothpick holder, green.........................60.00
*Tumbler...27.50
*Wine, clear 35.00
*Wine, green..60.00

BEADED GRAPE MEDALLION

Butter dish, cov......................................50.00
Celery vase............................55.00 to 65.00
Compote, cov., 8¼" d., low stand.........85.00
Compote, open, 8¼" d., low stand........25.00
Creamer, applied handle 58.00
Egg cup 28.00
Goblet..30.00
Honey dish, 3½" d. 8.00
Pitcher, water, applied handle 125.00
Salt dip, individual size 26.00
Salt dip, master size, footed, oval........55.00
Salt shaker w/original top 35.00
Sauce dish...11.00
Spooner...32.00
Wine 47.50

BEADED LOOP (Oregon, U.S. Glass Co.)

Berry set, master bowl & 6 sauce
   dishes, 7 pcs......................................65.00
Butter dish, cov......................................46.50
Cake stand, 9" to 10½" d. 45.00
Celery vase, 7" h. 29.00
Compote, cov., 7" d. 95.00
Compote, open, jelly, clear 38.00
Compote, open, 7" d., clear 25.00
Compote, open, 7½" d., low stand,
   clear 38.00
Creamer...35.00
*Goblet...39.00
Goblet, w/gold trim................................32.50
Mug, footed..38.00
Pickle dish, boat-shaped, 7¼" l. 12.00
Pitcher, milk, 8½" h. 35.00
Pitcher, water, tankard..........................50.00
Relish...18.00
Salt shaker w/original top 25.00
Sauce dish, flat or footed......................10.00
Spooner, clear 26.00
Spooner, ruby-stained 65.00
*Sugar bowl, cov....................................39.00
Toothpick holder 60.00

Tumbler 50.00
Vase, small 37.00
Wine 57.50

BEADED TULIP

Bowl, 6⅝ x 9½" oval 20.00
Goblet..34.00
Pitcher, water...67.50
Tray, wine, 9" d.......................................26.00
Wine, amber 55.00
Wine, clear...31.00

BEARDED HEAD - See Viking Pattern

BEARDED MAN - See Queen Anne Pattern

BELLFLOWER

Bellflower Goblet

Bowl, 7½" d., 2" h. 110.00
Bowl, 8" d., 4½" h., scalloped rim 95.00
Butter dish, cov....................................125.00
Castor bottle w/original stopper 38.00
Celery vase, fine rib, single vine.........130.00
Compote, open, 4½" d., low stand,
   scalloped rim.......................85.00 to100.00
Compote, open, 6" d., low stand...........59.00
Compote, open, 7" d., low stand,
   scalloped rim......................................87.50
Compote, open, 8" d., 5" h., scalloped
   rim, single vine.................................100.00
Compote, open, 8" d., 8" h., dome-
   footed, single vine............................125.00
Compote, open, 8" d., high stand,
   flint 285.00
Compote, open, 9½" d., 8½" h.,
   scalloped rim, single vine................162.00
Cordial, barrel-shaped, knob stem,
   rayed base 95.00
Cordial, fine rib, single vine, knob
   stem 150.00
Cordial, fine rib, single vine, plain
   stem 60.00
Creamer, fine rib, double vine, applied
   handle 160.00
Creamer, fine rib, single vine, applied
   handle 190.00

Decanter w/bar lip, single vine, qt.......130.00
Decanter w/bar lip, patent stopper,
   double vine, qt. 385.00
Egg cup, fine rib, single vine.................50.00
Goblet, barrel-shaped, fine rib, single
   vine, knob stem..................................54.00
*Goblet, barrel-shaped, fine rib, single
   vine, plain stem (ILLUS.) 48.00
Goblet, coarse rib 45.00
Goblet, double vine...............................64.00
Goblet, single vine, fine rib, pale
   green, 5⅞" h. 210.00
Honey dish, rayed center, 3¼" d. 22.50
Honey dish, ringed center, 3½" d. 22.50
Lamp, kerosene-type, 8½" h.................175.00
*Pitcher, milk, double vine 350.00
Pitcher, water, 8¾" h., coarse rib,
   double vine 395.00
Plate, 6" d., fine rib, single vine 115.00
Salt dip, cov., master size, footed,
   beaded rim, fine rib, single vine 72.50
Salt dip, open, master size, footed,
   scalloped rim, single vine...................50.00
Sauce dish, double vine 20.00
Sauce dish, single vine.........................20.00
Spooner, low foot, double vine 60.00
Spooner, scalloped rim, single vine......40.00
Sugar bowl, cov., double vine...............55.00
Syrup pitcher w/original top, applied
   handle, fine rib, single vine,
   clear ....600.00 to 700.00
Syrup pitcher w/original top, applied
   handle, fine rib, single vine, fiery
   opalescent 1,100.00
Tumbler, bar, fine rib, single vine 90.00
Tumbler, coarse rib, double vine 105.00
Tumbler, fine rib, single vine,
   banded..150.00
Tumbler, whiskey................140.00 to 180.00
Wine, barrel-shaped, knob stem,
   fine rib, single vine, rayed
   base ....100.00 to 125.00
Wine, barrel-shaped, fine rib, double
   vine, w/cut bellflowers 325.00
Wine, straight sides, plain stem, rayed
   base 55.00

BIRD & FERN - See Hummingbird Pattern

BIRD & STRAWBERRY (Bluebird)
Berry set: master bowl & 5 sauce
   dishes; w/color, 6 pcs. 525.00
Berry set: master bowl & 6 sauce
   dishes; footed, 7 pcs........150.00 to 200.00
Bowl, 5½" d., clear................................24.00
Bowl, 5½" d., w/color 35.00
Bowl, 7½" d., footed, clear...................62.00
Bowl, 7½" d., footed, w/color 70.00
Bowl, 9" d., flat, w/color 75.00
Bowl, 9½" l., 6" w., oval,
   footed..................................55.00 to 65.00
Bowl, 10" d., flat, clear...........60.00 to 70.00

Bowl, 10" d., flat, w/color & gold trim ..115.00
Butter dish, cov., clear..........................87.50
Butter dish, cov., w/color ....175.00 to 225.00
Cake stand, 9" to 9½" d. 60.00
*Compote, cov., 6½" d., 9½" h............145.00
Compote, cov., jelly 130.00
Creamer, clear......................................47.50
Creamer, w/color 125.00
Dish, heart-shaped 47.50
Pitcher, water.......................................287.50
Plate, 12" d. 75.00
Punch cup..22.00
Sauce dish, flat or footed, clear 26.00
Sauce dish, w/color 34.00
Spooner, clear 49.00
Spooner, w/color...................100.00 to125.00
Sugar bowl, cov. 65.00
Sugar bowl, open...................................32.00
Table set, 4 pcs. 225.00 to250.00
Tumbler, clear..52.50
Tumbler, w/color....................................95.00
Wine 55.00

BLEEDING HEART
Bowl, cov., 7" d., 5" h..........................110.00
Bowl, 8"..33.00
Butter dish, cov......................................55.00
Cake stand, 9½" to 11" d. 115.00
Compote, cov., 8" d., high stand,
   w/Bleeding Heart finial .....150.00 to 175.00
Compote, open, 8½" d., high stand 37.50
Creamer...50.00
Egg cup...44.00
Goblet, knob stem 40.00
Mug, 3" h. 57.50
Salt dip, master size, flat, oval..............92.00
Salt dip, master size, footed 68.00
Sauce dish, flat......................................15.00
Spooner..35.00
Sugar bowl, cov. 78.00
Tumbler, bar 140.00
Tumbler, flat..110.00
Wine, knob stem..................150.00 to175.00

BLOCK & FAN
Bowl, berry, 8" d., footed 27.50
Bowl, 9¾" d...32.00
Butter dish, cov......................................38.00
Cake stand, 9" to 10" d. 50.00
Celery tray 20.00
Celery vase..35.00
Compote, open, 8" d., high stand 45.00
Cracker jar, cov. 75.00
Cruet w/original stopper, small, 6" h......25.00
Cruet w/original stopper, medium.........45.00
Goblet, clear..52.00
Goblet, ruby-stained 110.00
Ice bucket 45.00
Pitcher, water...48.00
Plate, 10" d. 25.00
Relish, 11½" l...45.00
Salt shaker w/original top 20.00
Sauce dish, flat or footed, clear...........12.50

Sauce dish, flat or footed, ruby-
   stained 30.00
Spooner...28.00
Sugar shaker w/original top 40.00
Syrup pitcher w/original top, 7" h. 140.00
Wine, clear..50.00
Wine, ruby-stained................................75.00

**BLOCK & STAR - See Valencia
Waffle Pattern**

**BLUEBIRD - See Bird & Strawberry
Pattern**

BOHEMIAN (Floradora)

Bohemian Cologne Bottle

Berry bowl, boat-shaped, green 47.50
Butter dish, cov., green w/gold trim 110.00
Cologne bottle w/original stopper,
   clear w/gold trim................................100.00
Cologne bottle w/original stopper,
   green w/gold trim 225.00
Cologne bottle w/original stopper,
   rose-stained w/gold trim (ILLUS.) 130.00
Creamer, individual size, green 30.00
Creamer, clear w/rose & goldtrim 75.00
Mug, clear w/rose-stained leaves &
   gold trim 70.00
Spooner, clear w/rose-stained flowers
   & gold trim...55.00
Table set, green w/gold trim, 4 pcs.....350.00
Toothpick holder, green w/gold trim ...225.00
Tumbler, clear w/rose-stained flowers..45.00

BOW TIE
Bowl, 6" d..25.00
Bowl, berry, 8" d. 38.00
Bowl, 10" d., 5" h. 60.00
Butter dish, cov.....................................80.00
Compote, open, 6½" d., low stand........40.00
Compote, open, 8" d., low stand...........45.00
Compote, open, 8¼" d., high stand 55.00
Creamer...35.00
Goblet..62.50
Marmalade jar, cov. 55.00
Pitcher, milk 55.00

Pitcher, water..95.00
Relish, rectangular................................28.00
Salt dip, individual size 22.50
Spooner...34.00
Tumbler 55.00

**BROKEN COLUMN (Irish Column,
Notched Rib or Bamboo)**
Bowl, 7" d..40.00
Butter dish, cov......................................85.00
Cake stand, 9" to 10" d. 90.00
Celery vase..55.00
Compote, cov., 5" d., high stand...........80.00
Compote, open, jelly, w/red notches ..195.00
Compote, open, 5" d., 6" h.....................32.00
Compote, open, 6" d., high stand 35.00
Compote, open, 7" d., low stand...........50.00
Cracker jar, cov. 100.00
*Creamer, clear 38.00
Creamer, w/red notches 245.00
Cruet w/original stopper........................85.00
*Goblet...55.00
Marmalade jar w/original cover...........100.00
Pickle castor, cov., clear, original
   ornate frame 250.00
Pickle castor, w/red notches, w/frame
   & tongs...............................400.00 to425.00
*Pitcher, water, clear 90.00
Pitcher, water, w/red notches 225.00
Plate, 5" d. 32.00
*Plate, 8" d. 40.00
Punch cup, blue.....................................95.00
Punch cup, clear....................................25.00
Relish, w/red notches, 9" l., 5" w. 78.00
Salt shaker w/original top 55.00
*Sauce dish, clear..................................15.00
Sauce dish, w/red notches 32.00
*Spooner, w/red notches 125.00
*Sugar bowl, cov., clear.........................72.00
Sugar bowl, cov., w/red notches.........250.00
Syrup pitcher w/metal top 130.00
Tumbler, clear..45.00
Tumbler, w/red notches 75.00
Vase, 6½" h. 30.00
Water set: pitcher & 5 tumblers; w/red
   notches, 6 pcs...................................650.00
*Wine 85.00

BRYCE - See Ribbon Candy Pattern

BUCKLE
Butter dish, cov......................................81.00
Champagne, flint 75.00
Compote, open, 8" d., low stand, flint...38.50
Compote, open, 8" d., low stand, non-
   flint 17.50
Creamer, applied handle, flint..............95.00
Egg cup, flint...37.00
Egg cup, non-flint..................................25.00
Goblet, flint (ILLUS. top next column)...45.00
Goblet, non-flint 26.00
Lamp, kerosene-type, brass & iron
   base ....125.00 to 150.00

Buckle Goblet

Pitcher, water, bulbous, applied
  handle, flint ....550.00 to 600.00
Salt dip, master size, footed, flint..........35.00
Salt dip, master size, flat, oval, flint 22.50
Spooner, non-flint 30.00
Sugar bowl, cov., w/acorn finial, flint 95.00
Sugar bowl, cov., w/acorn finial, non-
  flint 43.00
Tumbler, bar, flint...................................90.00

BUCKLE WITH STAR
Cake stand, 9" d. 35.00
Celery vase...32.00
Compote, open, 8" d.............................37.50
Creamer..32.50
Goblet...24.00
Sauce dish, flat or footed.......................9.50
Spooner...30.00
Sugar bowl, open....................................24.00
Syrup pitcher w/metal top 70.00
Tumbler, bar 65.00
Wine 24.00

BULL'S EYE
Ale glass...45.00
Celery vase, flint 75.00
Cordial, flint..85.00
Cruet w/original stopper.......................195.00
Decanter w/bar lip, flint, qt. 110.00
Egg cup, clear, flint, 3¾" h.....45.00 to 55.00
Egg cup, jade green 385.00
Goblet, flint...72.00
Salt dip, individual size, rectangular 35.00
Tumbler, flat, flint...................................70.00
Wine, knob stem, flint 58.00

BULL'S EYE VARIANT - See Texas Bull's Eye Pattern

BULL'S EYE WITH DIAMOND POINT
Celery vase...180.00
Champagne 687.50
Compote, cov., 5½" d. 50.00
Compote, open, jelly..............................30.00
Cordial 357.50
Decanter w/bar lip, pt..........................209.00

Goblet..155.00
Honey dish...25.00
Lamp, kerosene-type, applied strap
  handle, original burner & attached
  burner cover, 3" h. 250.00
Sauce dish...22.50
Spillholder..87.50
Spooner..137.00
Sugar bowl, cov. 132.00
Tumbler, bar 135.00
Tumbler, water......................................120.00
Tumbler, whiskey..................................148.00

BULL'S EYE WITH FLEUR DE LIS
Compote, open, 8¼" d., low stand......125.00
Creamer..155.00
Decanter, bar lip, qt. 110.00
Goblet...98.00
Pitcher, water, 9½" h. ....450.00 to 500.00
Sugar bowl, cov. 130.00
Vase, 8½" h., flared rim 145.00

BUTTON ARCHES
Berry set: 8" d. master bowl & 6 sauce
  dishes; ruby-stained, 7 pcs. 158.00
Bowl, 8" d., ruby-stained, souvenir 45.00
Compote, open, jelly, 4½" h., ruby-
  stained 40.00
*Creamer, ruby-stained 37.50
Creamer, ruby-stained, souvenir,
  3½" h..30.00
*Creamer, individual size, ruby-
  stained 28.00
Cruet w/original stopper, ruby-
  stained 175.00
Goblet, clambroth 26.00
Goblet, clear 24.00
Mug, clear..18.00
Mug, ruby-stained..................................30.00
Pitcher, tankard, 8¾" h. 117.00
Pitcher, water, tankard, ruby-stained,
  souvenir of Pan American
  Exposition 150.00
Punch cup, ruby-stained, souvenir 28.50
Salt dip..18.50
Salt shaker w/original top, ruby-
  stained 25.00
Salt & pepper shakers, w/original
  tops, clear, pr. 35.00
Sauce dish, clear 15.00
Sauce dish, ruby-stained 30.00
*Spooner, ruby-stained.........................42.50
Spooner, ruby-stained w/clear band.....62.50
Spooner, ruby-stained & engraved.......44.00
Sugar bowl, cov., clear 45.00
*Sugar bowl, cov., ruby-stained............85.00
Syrup pitcher w/original top, clear 40.00
*Toothpick holder, ruby-stained............28.00
Toothpick holder, ruby-stained,
  souvenir 32.50
Tumbler, clambroth, souvenir 23.00
Tumbler, clear..16.00
Tumbler, clear w/frosted band 22.00
Tumbler, ruby-stained............................42.50

Tumbler, ruby-stained, souvenir 39.50
Wine, clear.....................................26.00
Wine, ruby-stained.............................37.50

CABBAGE ROSE

Cabbage Rose Tumbler

Bitters bottle, 6½" h. 125.00
Butter dish, cov.....................................95.00
Cake stand, 9½" to 12½" d. 58.00
Celery vase...62.00
Compote, cov., 6" d., low stand............95.00
Compote, cov., 6" d., high stand.........110.00
Compote, cov., 7½" d., high stand......115.00
Compote, cov., 8½" d., 7" h. 125.00
Compote, open, 7" d., low stand..........38.00
Compote, open, 7½" d., high stand 60.00
Creamer, applied handle 55.00
Egg cup 33.00
*Goblet...45.00
Pickle or relish, 7½" to 8½" l. 20.00
Salt dip, master size 30.00
Sauce dish...15.00
*Spooner..40.00
Sugar bowl, cov. 70.00
Tumbler, bar 42.00
Tumbler (ILLUS.) 42.00
Wine ....35.00 to 45.00

CABLE

Butter dish, cov......................................90.00
Celery vase..82.00
Champagne 250.00
Compote, open, 7" d., 5" h....................52.50
Compote, open, 8" d., 4¾" h................70.00
Decanter w/stopper, qt. ......300.00 to 325.00
Egg cup, clambroth, flint....................385.00
Egg cup, clear......................................55.00
Goblet...95.00
Honey dish, 3½" d., 1" h. 15.00
Lamp, whale oil, 11" h. 122.50
Plate, 6" d. 90.00
Salt dip, individual size 30.00
Salt dip, master size 36.00
Sauce dish...26.00
Spooner, chartreuse green.............1,200.00
Spooner, clambroth w/gilt trim 850.00

Spooner, clear ....35.00 to 45.00
Spooner, starch blue w/original gilt
  decoration of grape leaves 1,500.00
Tumbler, footed 335.00
Tumbler, whiskey................................230.00

CABLE WITH RING

Creamer, applied handle, flint.............165.00
Lamp, kerosene-type, w/ring handle,
  flint 195.00
Sauce dish, flint 14.00

CALIFORNIA - See Beaded Grape Pattern

CAMEO - See Classic Medallion Pattern

CANADIAN

Bowl, berry, 7" d., 4½" h., footed 63.00
Bowl, 8" d., handled..............................44.00
Bowl, 9½" d..55.00
Bread plate, handled, 10" d. 48.00
Butter dish, cov.....................................80.00
Celery vase..70.00
Compote, cov., 7" d., low stand 125.00
Compote, cov., 7" d., 11" h. 125.00
Compote, cov., 8" d., low stand...........92.00
Compote, cov., 8" d., 11" h. 150.00
Compote, open, 8" d., 5" h...................55.00
Creamer...55.00
Goblet...57.00
Pitcher, milk, 8" h. ....100.00 to 125.00
Pitcher, water..110.00
Plate, 6" d., handled 32.00
Plate, 7" d., handled 45.00
Plate, 8" d., handled 45.00
Sauce dish, flat or footed....................20.00
Spooner...45.00
Sugar bowl, cov. 77.50
Wine ....40.00 to 50.00

CANE

Cane Water Pitcher

Bowl, 9½" oval, amber...........................28.00
Bread platter, amber............................125.00
Cordial 18.00

Creamer, blue.................................42.00
Creamer, clear...............................25.00
Goblet, amber................................34.00
Goblet, blue..................................55.00
Goblet, clear.................................20.00
Goblet, vaseline..............................37.00
Pickle castor w/tongs, amber..............150.00
Pitcher, water, amber 68.00
Pitcher, water, blue..........................72.00
Pitcher, water, clear (ILLUS.) 40.00
Plate, 6" d., amber...........................12.00
Relish, blue...................................50.00
Spooner, amber..............................42.00
Sugar bowl, cov., apple green..............47.50
Toddy plate, amber, 4½" d. 10.00
Tray, water, blue.............................53.00
Waste bowl, amber..........................35.00
Waste bowl, vaseline........................30.00

CANNON BALL - See Atlas Pattern

CAPE COD
Bread platter................................48.00
Compote, cov., 8" d., 12" h. 155.00
Compote, open, 8" d., 5½" h...............45.00
Cruet w/original stopper....................43.00
Goblet.......................................47.00
Marmalade jar, cov. 65.00
Pitcher, water...............................95.00
Plate, 6" d...................................35.00
Plate, 10" d., open handles.................48.00
Sauce dish, flat or footed..................16.00

CARDINAL BIRD
Butter dish, cov............................90.00
Creamer.....................................41.00
*Goblet.....................................34.00
Sauce dish, flat or footed.................16.00
Spooner.....................................37.00
Sugar bowl, cov. 55.00

CATHEDRAL

Cathedral Compote

Bowl, 6" d., crimped rim, blue..............25.00
Bowl, 6" d., clear...........................16.00
Bowl, 7" d., clear...........................20.00
Bowl, berry, 8" d., amber...................48.00
Butter dish, cov............................44.00

Cake stand, amber 55.00
Cake stand, clear, 10" d., 4½" h. 38.00
Cake stand, vaseline 60.00
Compote, cov., 7¼" d., 10½" h. 85.00
Compote, cov., 8" d., high stand,
    blue...................................185.00
Compote, open, 9" d., 5½" h., amber ...65.00
Compote, open, 9" d., 5½" h., blue.......65.00
Compote. open, 10½" d., 8" h.,
    shaped rim, clear (ILLUS.) 55.00
Compote, open, 10½" d., 8" h., ruby-
    stained 125.00
Creamer....................................35.00
Cruet w/original stopper, amber 100.00
Goblet, amber..............................37.00
Goblet, clear...............................38.00
Goblet, ruby-stained 65.00
Relish, fish-shaped, amber..................40.00
Relish, fish-shaped, blue 42.50
Sauce dish, flat or footed, blue 25.00
Sauce dish, flat or footed, ruby-
    stained 22.00
Sauce dish, flat or footed, vaseline.......20.00
Spooner, clear 28.00
Spooner, vaseline..........................48.00
Sugar bowl, cov. 50.00
Tumbler 24.00
Wine, amber 60.00
Wine, blue.................45.00 to 55.00
Wine, clear.................................26.00
Wine, vaseline 65.00

CERES (Goddess of Liberty)
Butter dish, cov., lady's head finial 125.00
Compote, open, 7½" d., low stand,
    woman in beaded oval..................25.00
Creamer....................................42.00
Mug, clear..................................18.00
Mug, opaque-turquoise....................60.00
Mug, purple-black 53.00
Spooner, milk white 22.00

CHAIN WITH STAR
Bread plate, handled 33.00
Cake stand, 8¾" to 10" d. 38.00
Creamer....................................28.00
Goblet......................................24.00
Pitcher, water..............................50.00
Plate, 7" d. 27.50
Relish......................................14.00
Sauce dish.................................12.50
Spooner....................................24.00
Tumbler 18.00
Wine 35.00

CHANDELIER (Crown Jewel)
Butter dish, cov...........................100.00
Cake stand, 10" d. 75.00
Celery vase.................................40.00
Compote, open, 9¼" d., 7¾" h.............57.00
Creamer....................................55.00
Goblet......................................50.00
Goblet, engraved...........................60.00

Inkwell......................................55.00
Pitcher, water, tankard, ½ pt.................65.00
Pitcher, water, tankard, ½ gal.............125.00
Salt dip, footed............................36.00
Sauce dish, flat..........................16.00
Spooner 45.00
Tumbler 40.00
Waste bowl...............................25.00

CHECKERBOARD (Barred Hobstar)

Bowl, 9" d., flat...........................16.00
Celery tray 35.00
Celery vase, footed, 6½" h. 18.00
Compote, open, 8" d.......................15.00
Creamer..................................19.00
Goblet...................................30.00
Honey dish, cov., 5" w. 30.00
Sauce dish, flat..........................15.00
Spooner 21.00
Tumbler 12.50
Wine 17.50

CLASSIC

Classic Goblet

Bowl, open, 8" hexagon, open log
  feet.................................100.00 to 125.00
Butter dish, cov., open log feet...........225.00
Celery vase, collared base 150.00
Celery vase, open log feet.................165.00
Compote, cov., 6½" d., collared
  base..................................200.00
Compote, cov., 7½" d., 8" h., open
  log feet................................220.00
Compote, open, 7¾" d., open log
  feet....................................150.00
Creamer, collared base 125.00
Creamer, open log feet.......150.00 to 175.00
Goblet (ILLUS.)...................275.00 to 300.00
Pitcher, water, collared
  base..................................225.00 to 275.00
Pitcher, water, 9½" h., open log feet...425.00
Plate, 10" d., "Blaine" or "Hendricks,"
  signed Jacobus, each 215.00
Plate, 10" d., "Cleveland".................200.00
Plate, 10" d., "Warrior" ....150.00 to 175.00
Sauce dish, open log feet.................40.00
Spooner, collared base.....................95.00

Spooner, open log feet 135.00
Sugar bowl, cov., open log feet 185.00

CLASSIC MEDALLION (Cameo)

Classic Medallion Spooner

Bowl, 6¾" d., 3½" h., footed 35.00
Bowl, 8" d., footed..........................40.00
Creamer....................................30.00
Sauce dish, footed............................8.00
Spooner (ILLUS.)............................25.00
Sugar bowl, cov. 55.00
Table set, 4 pcs. 130.00

COLLINS - See Crystal Wedding Pattern

COLONIAL (Empire Colonial)

Celery vase, flint...........................95.00
Champagne, flint 75.00
Claret, flint, 5½" h. 70.00
Compote, open, 9" d., 3¾" h., flint........25.00
Egg cup, flint..............................45.00
Goblet, flint 55.00
Plate, 6¼" d., canary yellow, flint........250.00
Sugar bowl, cov., flint 125.00
Toothpick holder, flint 22.00

COLORADO (Lacy Medallion)

Banana bowl, two turned-up sides,
  blue...................................35.00
Banana stand, green 45.00
Berry set: 8" d. master bowl & five
  4" d. sauce dishes; green w/gold,
  6 pcs..................................160.00
Berry set: master bowl & 6 sauce
  dishes; clear w/gold, 7 pcs.............125.00
Bowl, 5" d., ruffled rim, blue...............40.00
Bowl, 7" d., footed..........................25.00
Bowl, 7½" d., footed, turned-up sides,
  blue w/gold...............................50.00
Bowl, 7½" d., footed, turned-up sides,
  green....................................29.00
Bowl, 9" d., green w/gold....................45.00
Bowl, 10" d., footed, flared &
  scalloped rim.............................45.00
Bowl, 10" d., footed, fluted, green.........48.00
Butter dish, cov., blue w/gold.............260.00
Butter dish, cov., clear 85.00
Butter dish, cov., green.....................125.00
Cake stand 65.00

Celery vase, green w/gold 70.00
Cheese dish, cov., blue w/gold.............70.00
Compote, open, 6" d., 4" h., crimped
  rim 22.00
Creamer, blue, souvenir 60.00
Creamer, clear......................................34.00
Creamer, green 42.50
Creamer, ruby-stained..........................54.00
Creamer, individual size, green
  w/gold 40.00
Cup, punch, green 28.00
Cup, punch, green, souvenir 25.00
Cup & saucer, green.............................45.00
Mug, green, souvenir, miniature 22.50
Mug, green 30.00
Mug, green souvenir..............................32.00
Mug, ruby-stained.................................55.00
Nappy, tricornered, blue w/gold............40.00
Nappy, tricornered, green w/gold 29.00
Rose bowl, blue 60.00
Salt shaker w/original top, ruby-
  stained, souvenir 75.00
Sauce dish, blue w/gold........................30.00
Sauce dish, clambroth 20.00
Sauce dish, clear 13.00
Sauce dish, green w/gold 24.00
Sauce dish, green, souvenir 27.50
Sherbet, blue w/gold.............................48.00
Spooner, blue w/gold..............50.00 to 60.00
Spooner, clear 40.00
Spooner, green w/gold 60.00
Sugar bowl, cov., clear, large 53.00
Sugar bowl, cov., green, large..............80.00
Sugar bowl, open, individual size,
  clear 20.00
Sugar bowl, open, individual size,
  green..35.00
Sugar bowl, open, individual size,
  ruby-stained 50.00
Table set, blue, 4 pcs. 525.00
Table set, green w/gold,
  4 pcs. ....325.00 to 350.00
*Toothpick holder, blue w/gold 60.00
*Toothpick holder, clear w/gold 25.00
*Toothpick holder, green w/gold...........35.00
*Toothpick holder, green w/gold
  souvenir 30.00
*Toothpick holder, ruby-stained,
  souvenir 55.00
Tumbler, green w/gold...........................32.00
Tumbler, green w/gold, souvenir 30.00
Vase, 2½" h., green 45.00
Vase, 10½" h., blue 78.00
Water set: pitcher & 6 tumblers;
  green w/gold, 7 pcs...........................450.00
Wine, clear...26.00
Wine, green w/gold................................40.00
Wine, green, souvenir............................35.00
Wine, ruby-stained w/gold 40.00

COLUMBIAN COIN

Bowl, 8½" d., 3" h., frosted coins 75.00
Celery vase, frosted coins 110.00

Compote, cov., 8" d., frosted coins.....157.00
Compote, open, 8" d., clear coins.........68.00
Creamer, gilded coins.........................125.00
Cruet w/original stopper, frosted
  coins 195.00
*Goblet, gilded coins.............................80.00
Lamp, kerosene-type, milk white,
  8" h...400.00
Lamp, kerosene-type, frosted coins,
  12" h...180.00
Mug, frosted coins 120.00
Pitcher, milk, gilded coins 195.00
Relish, frosted coins, 5 x 8" 68.00
Sauce dish, flat or footed, frosted
  coins 42.00
Spooner, gilded coins............................77.50
Syrup pitcher w/original top, frosted
  coins 335.00
*Tumbler, clear coins............................30.00
*Tumbler, gilded coins 55.00
Wine, frosted coins 145.00

COMPACT - See Snail Pattern

CORD & TASSEL

Cord & Tassel Creamer

Cake stand, 9½" d. 65.00
Compote, cov., 8" d. 75.00
Creamer (ILLUS.) 36.00
Goblet..38.00
Lamp, kerosene-type, applied handle ..85.00
Pitcher, water...98.00
Salt shaker w/original top, blue............45.00
Spooner..23.00
Syrup pitcher w/original top, applied
  handle 110.00
Tumbler, water..50.00
Wine 38.00

CORD DRAPERY

Bowl, 6¼" d., footed, amber 175.00
Bowl, 10" d., 3½" h. 42.00
Butter dish, cov., clear 70.00
Butter dish, cov., green 175.00
Cake stand, amber 145.00
Cake stand, clear..................................40.00
Compote, cov., jelly 55.00
Compote, cov., 9" d. 70.00

Creamer, blue 125.00
Creamer, clear 40.00
Cruet w/original stopper..........80.00 to 90.00
Goblet 85.00
Mug..40.00
Pickle dish, amber, 5¼ x 9¼" oval........85.00
Pickle dish, clear, 5¼ x 9¼" oval 37.50
Pitcher, water, amber 185.00
Pitcher, water, clear.............................65.00
Pitcher, water, cobalt blue 225.00
Pitcher, water, green 235.00
Punch cup..15.00
Salt shaker w/original top 55.00
Sauce dish, flat or footed.....................15.00
Sugar bowl, cov., clear 60.00
Sugar bowl, cov., green......................165.00
Toothpick holder 95.00

CORONA - See Sunk Honeycomb Pattern

COTTAGE (Dinner Bell or Finecut Band)
Bowl, master berry, 9¼" l., 6½" w.
  oval 25.00
Butter dish, cov., clear 36.00
Cake stand, amber 50.00
Cake stand, clear..................................35.00
Celery vase, amber 85.00
Celery vase, clear.................................35.00
Champagne 65.00
Compote, open, jelly, 4½" d., 4" h.,
  clear 24.00
Compote, open, jelly, 4½" d., 4" h.,
  green..42.50
Creamer, amber 60.00
Creamer, clear......................................27.00
*Goblet, amber 45.00
*Goblet, blue 48.00
*Goblet, clear..27.00
Pitcher, milk, clear 35.00
Pitcher, water, 2 qt...............................72.50
Plate, 7" d. 22.50
Plate, 10" d. 42.50
Sauce dish..12.50
Tray, water..40.00
Tumbler 19.00
*Wine, amber..53.00
*Wine, blue 45.00

CROESUS
Berry set: master bowl & 6 sauce
  dishes; clear, 7 pcs. 300.00
Berry set: master bowl & 6 sauce
  dishes; green w/gold, 7 pcs. 395.00
Berry set: master bowl & 6 sauce
  dishes; purple, 7 pcs. ....400.00 to 425.00
Bowl, 7" d., 4" h., footed, purple 68.00
Bowl, 7" d., 4" h., footed, purple
  w/gold 225.00
Bowl, 8" d., purple..............................175.00
Bowl, berry or fruit, 9" d., green..........108.00
Bowl, berry or fruit, 9" d., purple 165.00

*Butter dish, cov., clear.........................98.00
*Butter dish, cov., green .....150.00 to 165.00
*Butter dish, cov., purple ....200.00 to 225.00
Celery vase, gree w/gold......................170.00
Celery vase, purple..............................300.00
Compote, open, jelly,
  green................................225.00 to 275.00
Compote, open, jelly, purple...............280.00
Condiment tray, green 62.50
Condiment tray, purple 90.00
*Creamer, green...................80.00 to 100.00
*Creamer, purple 145.00
Creamer, individual size, purple,
  3" h...130.00
Cruet w/original stopper,
  green................................200.00 to 225.00
Cruet w/original stopper, purple..........350.00
Pickle dish, green w/gold.....................35.00
Pitcher, milk, green...............................85.00
Pitcher, water, green 285.00
Pitcher, water, purple..........400.00 to 500.00
Relish, boat-shaped, green 60.00
Salt shaker w/original top, green
  w/gold 100.00
Sauce dish, clear..................................23.00
Sauce dish, green w/gold.....................37.00
Sauce dish, purple w/gold 42.00
*Spooner, green 73.00
*Spooner, green w/gold........90.00 to 100.00
*Spooner, purple...................................80.00
*Spooner, purple w/gold 97.50
*Sugar bowl, cov., clear........................78.00
*Sugar bowl, cov., green 110.00
Sugar bowl, cov., green w/gold 185.00
*Sugar bowl, cov., purple....150.00 to 175.00
*Sugar bowl, cov., purple w/gold 180.00
Table set, purple, 4 pcs. 630.00
*Toothpick holder, green 65.00
*Toothpick holder, green w/gold..........95.00
*Toothpick holder, purple....100.00 to 125.00
Toothpick holder, purple w/gold..........130.00
*Tumbler, green....................................42.00
*Tumbler, green w/gold 54.00
*Tumbler, purple w/gold.......................70.00
Water set: pitcher & 5 tumblers;
  green, 6 pcs. ....450.00 to 500.00
Water set: pitcher & 6 tumblers;
  purple, 7 pcs. ....850.00 to 900.00

CROWFOOT (Turkey Track, Yale)
Bowl, 10" d..30.00
Butter dish, cov.....................................45.00
Cake stand, 9" d. 52.00
Compote, cov., 7" d. 68.00
Creamer...35.00
Goblet 35.00
Pitcher, water..60.00
Spooner 25.00
Sugar bowl, cov.....................................35.00
Tumbler 25.00

CROWN JEWEL - See Chandelier Pattern

CRYSTAL BALL - See Atlas Pattern

CRYSTAL WEDDING (Collins)

Crystal Wedding Sugar Bowl

Banana stand, 10" h. 110.00
Banana stand, low pedestal 108.00
Bowl, cov., 5" sq. 68.00
Bowl, cov., 7" sq. 67.00
Butter dish, cov., clear........................110.00
Butter dish, cov., ruby-stained............130.00
Cake stand, 9" sq., 8" h. 60.00
Cake stand, 10" sq. 65.00
Celery vase...45.00
Compote, cov., 4" sq., 6½" h. 37.50
Compote, cov., 5" sq. 58.00
Compote, cov., 7" sq., low stand 85.00
Compote, cov., 7" sq., high
   stand ....75.00 to 100.00
Compote, open, 5" sq. 45.00
Compote, open, 6" sq. 48.00
Compote, open, 6¼" sq., high stand,
   scalloped rim......................................45.00
Compote, open, 7" sq., high
   stand ....50.00 to 75.00
Compote, open, 8" sq., low stand.........55.00
Creamer, clear..38.00
Creamer, ruby-stained.........................125.00
*Goblet, clear..40.00
Goblet w/fern engraving 85.00
*Goblet, ruby-stained.............................62.50
Honey dish, cov., 6" sq. 90.00
Lamp, kerosene-type, 7" h.................100.00
Lamp, kerosene-type, 9" h., frosted &
   clear..145.00
Lamp base, kerosene-type, square
   font, 10" h...285.00
Lamp, kerosene-type, banquet-style,
   blue base, clear font 195.00
Pitcher, 12" h., tankard, water 85.00
Pitcher, water, square, engraved........195.00
Pitcher, water, square, plain..............175.00
Plate, 9" sq. 45.00
Salt dip...45.00
Salt shaker w/original top 125.00
Sauce dish...12.00
Spooner, clear 35.00

Spooner, ruby-stained 95.00
Sugar bowl, cov., amber-stained........125.00
Sugar bowl, cov., clear 54.00
Sugar bowl, cov., ruby-stained
   (ILLUS.) 100.00
Table set: creamer, cov. sugar bowl &
   spooner; clear, 3 pcs. 185.00
Table set, ruby-stained, 4 pcs. 400.00
Tumbler 45.00
Wine 95.00

CUPID & VENUS (Guardian Angel)

Cupid & Venus Sauce Dish

Bowl, open, 8" d., footed......................28.00
Bowl, 9" oval 50.00
Bread plate, amber, 10½" d. 155.00
Bread plate, clear, 10½" d. 45.00
Bread plate, vaseline, 10½" d. 145.00
Butter dish, cov. 110.00
Cake plate, 11" d. 45.00
Celery vase...55.00
Champagne..110.00
Compote, cov., 7" d., high stand.........110.00
Compote, cov., 7" d., low stand 65.00
Compote, cov., 9" d., low stand 82.00
Compote, open, 7" d., low stand..........30.00
Compote, open, 8½" d., low stand,
   scalloped rim......................................40.00
Cordial 85.00
Creamer...55.00
Goblet..67.00
Honey dish, 3½" d. 15.00
Marmalade jar, cov. 125.00
Mug, 2½" h. 32.00
Mug, 3½" h. 40.00
Pitcher, milk...65.00
Pitcher, water...90.00
Relish, oval, 4½ x 7"..............................30.00
Sauce dish, footed, 3½" to 4½" d.
   (ILLUS.) 14.00
Spooner...35.00
Sugar bowl, cov. 70.00
Wine 85.00

CURRIER & IVES

Bowl, master berry or fruit, 10" oval,
   flat w/collared base 35.00
Compote, cov., 7½" d., high stand........90.00
Compote, cov., 11½" d., amber..........145.00
Compote, open, 7½" d., high stand,
   scalloped rim......................................50.00

Cup & saucer, blue 85.00
Cup & saucer, clear 42.50
Goblet, amber..95.00
Goblet, clear 30.00
Lamp, kerosene-type, 9½" h.................80.00
Pitcher, milk..65.00
Pitcher, water, amber 145.00
Pitcher, water, clear.............................75.00
Salt shaker w/original top, blue.............75.00
Salt & pepper shakers w/original tops,
   pr...65.00
Sauce dish, flat or footed.....................15.00
Spooner...35.00
Sugar bowl, cov. ....35.00 to 45.00
Syrup jug w/original top, amber..........210.00
Syrup jug w/original top, blue 162.00
Syrup jug w/original top, clear 70.00

"Balky Mule" Water Tray

Tray, wine, Balky Mule on Railroad
   Tracks, clear, 9½" d. (ILLUS.)............49.00
Tray, water, Balky Mule on Railroad
   Tracks, blue, 12" d. 150.00
Tray, water, Balky Mule on Railroad
   Tracks, clear, 12" d. 65.00
Tumbler, footed 38.00
Waste bowl 42.00
Wine, clear..25.00
Wine, ruby-stained...............................85.00

CURTAIN

Bowl, cov., 7" d..................100.00 to 125.00
Bowl, open, 7½" d.................................20.00
Cake stand, 9½" d. 47.50
Celery vase...28.00
Compote, open 8" d., 6½" h. 47.50
Creamer...35.00
Goblet..25.00 to 30.00
Mug, amber 65.00
Salt & pepper shakers w/original tops,
   pr...65.00
Spooner...25.00
Sugar bowl, cov. 50.00

CURTAIN TIEBACK

Cake stand, 9" d., 6½" h. 23.00
Creamer...32.00

Curtain Tieback Goblet

Goblet (ILLUS.).....................................25.00
Pitcher, water...52.00
Sauce dish, flat or footed......................12.00

CUT LOG

Cut Log Individual Creamer

Bowl, 7" d..33.00
Bowl, master berry or fruit, 8" d.,
   footed...40.00
Butter dish, cov. 64.00
Cake stand, 9¼" d., high stand.............62.00
Cake stand, 10½" d., high stand...........77.00
Celery tray 45.00
Celery vase..40.00
Compote, cov., jelly, 5½" d., high
   stand..65.00
Compote, cov., 7¼" d., high stand........95.00
Compote, open, jelly, 5" d.....................30.00
Compote, open, 9¾" d., scalloped rim,
   high stand 65.00
Compote, open, 10¾" d., scalloped
   rim, high stand 75.00
Creamer...35.00
Creamer, individual size (ILLUS.).........18.00
Creamer & cov. sugar bowl, pr. 125.00
Cruet w/original stopper, small,
   3¾" h..36.00
Cruet w/original stopper, large, 5" h. 50.00
Goblet..55.00
Mug, small 18.00
Olive dish, handled, 5" d. 25.00
Pitcher, water, tankard, clear................96.00
Pitcher, water, tankard, ruby-stained..240.00

Relish, boat-shaped, 9¼" l.....................23.00
Salt dip, master size 65.00
Salt shaker w/original tin top................60.00
Sauce dish, flat or footed......................20.00
Spooner...40.00
Sugar bowl, cov. 60.00
Sugar bowl, cov., individual size..........30.00
Tumbler, juice......................................40.00
Tumbler, water.....................................40.00
Vase, 16" h. 58.00
Wine 23.00

DAHLIA

Dahlia Water Pitcher

Bread platter, 8 x 12"............................45.00
Butter dish, cov., clear.........................52.00
Cake stand, amber, 9½" d. 75.00
Cake stand, blue, 9½" d. 52.50
Cake stand, clear, 9½" d. 30.00
Cordial...40.00
Creamer...28.00
Goblet..38.00
Mug, amber 45.00
Mug, blue...60.00
Mug, clear..32.00
Mug, child's 20.00
Pickle dish 15.00
Pitcher, milk, applied handle................55.00
Pitcher, water, blue (ILLUS.) 125.00
Pitcher, water, clear.............................50.00
Plate, 7" d. 18.00
Plate, 9" d., w/handles, apple green.....42.50
Plate, 9" d., w/handles, clear...............25.00
Plate, 9" d., w/handles, vaseline..........42.50
Relish, blue, 5 x 9½".............................25.00
Relish, clear, 5 x 9½"............................13.00
Relish, green, 5 x 9½" 25.00
Sauce dish, flat, amber........................22.00
Sauce dish, flat, clear 15.00
Sauce dish, footed...............................7.00
Spooner...35.00
Sugar bowl, cov., vaseline...................60.00
Wine, amber 55.00
Wine, clear...32.00

DAISY & BUTTON

Banana boat, 14" l. 45.00

Basket, silver plate handle, 6" h 125.00
Berry set: triangular master bowl &
    4 sauce dishes; vaseline, 5 pcs. 150.00
Berry set: octagonal master bowl &
    10 sauce dishes; amber, 11 pcs. 140.00
Berry set: master bowl & 12 sauce
    dishes; vaseline, 13 pcs.................225.00
Bowl, 7 x 9½", sapphire blue 30.00
Bowl, 8" w., tricornered.......................45.00
Bowl, berry or fruit, 8½" d. 35.00
Bowl, 9" sq., amber..............................40.00
*Bowl, 10" oval, blue............................65.00
Bowl, 10 x 11" oval, 7 ¾" h., flared,
    vaseline...95.00
Bowl, 11" d., amber 38.00
Bowl, 12" l., 9" w., shell-shaped oval,
    blue...75.00
Bowl, fruit, rectangular, ornate silver
    plate frame....................................250.00
*Bread tray, amber 25.00
*Butter chip, fan-shaped......................9.50
*Butter chip, round..............................6.00
Butter chip, square, amber 15.00
Butter chip, square, Amberina.............75.00
Butter chip, square, clear.....................7.50
Butter chip, square, purple 15.00
Butter chip, square, vaseline 25.00
Butter dish, cov., scalloped base..........65.00
Butter dish, cov., square, clear 45.00
Butter dish, cov., square, green............60.00
Butter dish, cov., triangular, amber.......60.00
*Butter dish, cov., model of Victorian
    stove, green...................................215.00
Cake stand, blue...................................50.00
Cake stand, clear, 9" sq., 6" h. 45.00
Canoe, vaseline, 4" l............................18.00

Daisy & Button Canoe

Canoe, amber, 8" l. (ILLUS.) 35.00
Canoe, blue, 8" l. 46.00
Canoe, vaseline, 8" l.............................100.00
Canoe, amber, 11" l. 60.00
Canoe, blue, 11" l. 60.00
Canoe, amber, 12" l.............................42.50
Canoe, green, 13" l. 48.00
Canoe, vaseline, 14" l. 85.00
Castor set, 4-bottle, blue, in glass
    frame...375.00
Castor set, 5-bottle, amber, blue
    & clear bottles, in original
    frame..............................100.00 to 145.00
Castor set, 5-bottle, vaseline, in
    original frame..................................495.00
Celery tray, flat, boat-shaped,
    4½ x 14"...90.00

Celery vase, square...............................65.00
Celery vase, triangular, amber 65.00
Celery vase, triangular, clear...............45.00
Cheese dish, cov., clear 62.00
Cheese dish, cov., vaseline................165.00
Compote, cov., 8" d., high stand..........55.00
Compote, cov., 8½" d., low stand,
   amber...60.00
Creamer, child's, amber 25.00
*Creamer, blue 40.00
*Creamer, clear 29.00
*Cruet w/original stopper, amber........100.00
*Cruet w/original stopper, blue 95.00
*Cruet w/original stopper, clear 45.00
Cuspidor, blue 38.00
Dish, 2½ x 6 x 9"..................................32.00
*Dish, fan-shaped, 10" w. 35.00
Dresser tray, amber, 8 x 11"................75.00
*Goblet, amber 32.00
*Goblet, blue 25.00
*Goblet, clear.......................................22.50
*Hat shape, amber, 2½" h. 29.00
*Hat shape, blue, 2½" h........................35.00
*Hat shape, vaseline, 2½" h. 38.00
*Hat shape, from tumbler mold,
   4½" widest d. 55.00
*Hat shape, blue, from tumbler mold,
   4¾" widest d. 45.00
Hat shape, clear, 8 x 8", 6" h. 85.00
Ice cream set: 2 x 7 x 9½" ice cream
   tray & two square sauce plates;
   amber, 3 pcs....................................85.00
Ice tub, amber 4¼ x 6¾"......................60.00
Inkwell w/original insert, cat seated on
   cover 245.00
Inkwell, vaseline 175.00
Match holder, wall-hanging scuff,
   blue 75.00
Match holder, wall-hanging scuff,
   clear 65.00
*Pickle castor, sapphire blue insert,
   w/silver plate frame & tongs.............238.00
*Pickle castor, vaseline insert,
   w/silver plate frame & tongs.............185.00
Pitcher, 5⅛" h., applied handle,
   amber...55.00
Pitcher, water, tankard, 9" h., amber ..125.00
Pitcher, water, bulbous, applied
   handle, clear 95.00
Pitcher, water, bulbous, applied
   handle, ruby-stained buttons 325.00
Plate, 9" d., vaseline 40.00
*Plate, 10" d., scalloped rim, amber 28.00
*Plate, 10" d., scalloped rim, blue.........35.00
Powder jar, cov., amber, 3¾" d.,
   2" h...30.00
Powder jar, cov., blue 38.00
Relish, "Sitz bathtub" 145.00
*Rose bowl, vaseline 38.00
*Salt dip, canoe-shaped, vaseline,
   2 x 4"..12.00
*Salt shaker w/original top, corset-
   shaped, blue 25.00

*Salt & pepper shakers w/original
   tops, vaseline, pr................................50.00
Salt & pepper shakers, blue & amber,
   pr., w/clear glass stand 55.00
*Sauce dish, amber, 4" to 5" sq. 15.00
Sauce dish, Amberina, 4" to 5" sq. 115.00
*Sauce dish, blue, 4" to 5" sq. 16.00
*Sauce dish, vaseline, 4" to 5" sq. 20.00
Sauce dish, w/amber-stained buttons ..20.00
Sauce dish, tricornered, clear..............12.50
Sauce dish, tricornered, vaseline 16.00
*Slipper, "1886 patent," amber.............46.00
*Slipper, "1886 patent," blue................47.00
Slipper, ruby-stained buttons...............80.00
•Spooner, amber...................................40.00
Spooner, Amberina, 5" h. 150.00
Spooner, amethyst 30.00
*Spooner, clear.....................................30.00
Syrup pitcher, w/original pewter top,
   blue 175.00
Table set: creamer, open sugar bowl
   & spooner; vaseline, 3 pcs.................65.00
Toothpick holder, fan-shaped, amber ...35.00
Toothpick holder, square, blue 24.00
*Toothpick holder, three-footed,
   amber..30.00
Toothpick holder, three-footed,
   Amberina 170.00
*Toothpick holder, three-footed,
   electric blue.......................................55.00
Toothpick holder, urn-shaped, clear 22.50
Toothpick holder, urn-shaped,
   vaseline...30.00
Tray, clover-shaped, amber..................65.00
Tray, vaseline, 10 x 12" 89.00
Tray, ice cream, handled, blue,
   9¼ x 16½"..30.00
Tray, water, amber, 11" d. 95.00
Tray, water, triangular, vaseline 95.00
Tumbler, water, amber 22.50
Tumbler, water, blue.............................30.00
Tumbler, water, blue, pattern halfway
   up..30.00
Tumbler, water, clear............................20.00
Tumbler, water, vaseline 30.00
Waste bowl, blue 28.00
Waste bowl, vaseline............................30.00
Whimsey, "canoe," wall hanging-type,
   ruby-stained buttons, 11" l. 110.00
Whimsey, "cradle," amber 45.00
*Whimsey, "dustpan," light blue............42.50
*Whimsey, "sleigh," amber,
   4½ x 7¾"..225.00
Whimsey, "wheel barrow," vaseline....125.00
*Whimsey, "whisk broom" dish,
   amber..28.00
*Whimsey, "whisk broom" dish, blue 75.00
*Wine 20.00

DAISY & BUTTON WITH CROSSBARS (Mikado)

Bowl, 5 x 8"...20.00
Bread tray, amber, 9 x 12" (ILLUS.) 25.00

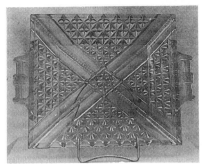

Daisy & Button w/Crossbars Bread Tray

Bread tray, canary yellow, 9 x 12" 52.00
Butter dish, cov., blue 58.00
Butter dish, cov., canary yellow 65.00
Butter dish, cov., clear 45.00
Celery vase, amber 38.00
Celery vase, clear..................................32.00
Compote, open, 7" d., low stand,
  amber...38.00
Compote, open, 7" d., high stand,
  blue 85.00
Compote, open, 7" d., high stand,
  canary yellow 45.00
Compote, open, 8" d., high stand,
  amber...45.00
Creamer, amber 37.00
Creamer, canary yellow.........................40.00
Creamer, clear.......................................30.00
Creamer, individual size, amber 21.00
Creamer, individual size, blue 24.00
Creamer, individual size, canary
  yellow...22.00
Creamer, individual size, clear 14.00
Cruet w/original stopper, amber 115.00
Cruet w/original stopper, clear.............55.00
Goblet, amber..40.00
Goblet, blue 45.00
Goblet, canary yellow 35.00
Goblet, clear 28.00
Mug, amber, 3" h. 25.00
Mug, clear, 3" h.....................................15.00

Daisy & Button w/Crossbars Pitcher

Pitcher, milk, amber (ILLUS.) 55.00

Pitcher, milk, blue 60.00
Pitcher, milk, canary yellow 45.00
Pitcher, water, amber 75.00
Pitcher, water, canary yellow..............85.00
Pitcher, water, clear...............................52.00
Relish, amber, 4½ x 8" 30.00
Salt shaker w/original top, canary
  yellow...35.00
Salt & pepper shakers, blue & amber,
  pr., w/clear glass stand 85.00
Spooner, amber......................................32.00
Spooner, canary yellow 30.00
Sugar bowl, cov., amber......................42.00
Sugar bowl, cov., blue 75.00
Syrup pitcher w/original top, clear 50.00
Tumbler, amber 25.00
Tumbler, canary yellow...........................24.00
Water set: pitcher & 6 tumblers;
  canary yellow, 7 pcs. 250.00
Wine, canary yellow...............................28.00
Wine, clear...25.00

DAISY & BUTTON WITH NARCISSUS

Daisy & Button w/Narcissus Wine

Bowl, 6 x 9½" oval, footed 46.00
Decanter w/original stopper.................52.00
Goblet 20.00
Pitcher, water..60.00
Punch cup..10.00
Sauce dish, flat or three-footed 18.00
Sugar bowl, cov. 35.00
Tumbler 17.00
Water set: pitcher & 5 tumblers;
  cranberry-stained color, 6 pcs. 150.00
*Wine (ILLUS.)......................................22.00

DAISY & BUTTON WITH THUMBPRINT PANELS

Bowl, 7" w., heart-shaped, amber
  panels 42.50
Bowl, 8" sq., amber...............................28.00
Bowl, 9" sq., amber...............................28.00
Cake stand, vaseline, 10½" d.,
  7¼" h...75.00
Celery vase, amber panels.................125.00
Celery vase, clear.................................26.00

Creamer, applied handle, amber
panels 68.00
*Goblet, amber panels...........................45.00
*Goblet, blue panels 55.00
Pitcher, water, vaseline 165.00
Salt shaker w/original top, amber
panels 75.00
Spooner, amber panels 75.00
Tray, water, vaseline 95.00
Tumbler, amber panels........................38.50
Tumbler, clear.......................................25.00
Tumbler, vaseline 30.00

DAISY & BUTTON WITH "V" ORNAMENT
Bowl, 7" d., 2½" h., vaseline 19.00
Bowl, 9" d., blue....................................34.00
Celery vase, amber 40.00
Celery vase, clear.................................38.00
Celery vase, electric blue 70.00
Celery vase, vaseline 85.00
Creamer...30.00
Mug, amber 16.00
Mug, blue...23.00
Mug, miniature, vaseline.......................30.50
Pitcher, water..75.00
Salt & pepper shakers, amber, pr.........55.00
Sauce dish, amber.................................15.00
Toothpick holder, amber........................45.00
Toothpick holder, blue 45.00
Toothpick holder, clear 25.00
Tumbler, amber 26.00

DAISY IN PANEL - See Two Panel Pattern

DAKOTA (Baby Thumbprint)
Butter dish, cov., engraved...................72.00
Butter dish, cov., plain 55.00
Cake stand, 8" d., engraved 50.00
Cake stand, 8" d., plain.........................45.00
Cake stand, 9½" d. 55.00
Cake stand, 10¼" d., engraved 67.00
Cake stand, 10¼" d., plain....................58.00
Cake stand w/high domed cover 295.00

Dakota Engraved Celery Vase

Celery vase, flat base, engraved
(ILLUS.) 42.00
Celery vase, flat base, plain 35.00

Celery vase, pedestal base, en-
graved..50.00
Celery vase, pedestal base, plain.........42.00
Cologne bottle w/original stopper,
7" h..135.00
Compote, cov., jelly, 5" d., 5" h.............45.00
Compote, cov., 6" d., high stand,
engraved..........................75.00 to 100.00
Compote, cov., 6" d., high stand,
plain 58.00
Compote, cov., 8" d., high stand,
engraved..190.00
Compote, open, jelly, 5" d., 5½" h.,
engraved..35.00
Compote, open, jelly, 5" d., 5" h.,
plain 36.00
Compote, open, 6" d. 30.00
Compote, open, 7" d., engraved...........40.00
Compote, open, 7" d., plain 35.00
Compote, open, 8" d., high stand 55.00
Creamer, table, engraved.....................50.00
Creamer, table, plain 45.00
Creamer, hotel....................................110.00
Cruet w/original stopper, engraved.....145.00
Goblet, clear, engraved 35.00
Goblet, clear, plain................................24.00
Goblet, ruby-stained, engraved 95.00
Goblet, ruby-stained, plain....................65.00
Pitcher, milk, jug-type, engraved, pt. ...235.00
Pitcher, milk, tankard, engraved, pt. 145.00
Pitcher, milk, tankard, plain, pt. 90.00
*Pitcher, tankard, water, engraved,
½ gal. 254.00
Plate, 10" d. 63.00
Salt shaker w/original top 50.00
Sauce dish, flat or footed, clear,
engraved..18.00
Sauce dish, flat or footed, clear,
plain 15.00
Sauce dish, flat or footed, cobalt
blue 55.00
Shaker bottle w/original top, 5" h. 68.00
Shaker bottle w/original top, hotel
size, 6½" h. 65.00
Spooner, engraved 35.00
Spooner, plain 40.00
Sugar bowl, cov., engraved 62.50
Sugar bowl, cov., plain 48.00
Tray, water, piecrust rim, engraved,
13" d..125.00
Tray, water, piecrust rim, plain,
13" d..95.00
Tray, wine, 10½" d. 100.00
Tumbler, clear, engraved......................45.00
Tumbler, clear, plain 30.00
Tumbler, ruby-stained...........................45.00
Waste bowl, engraved 75.00
Waste bowl, plain 58.00
Wine, clear, engraved...........................40.00
Wine, clear, plain..................................30.00
Wine, ruby-stained................................50.00

DART
Butter dish, cov. 28.00

Compote, cov., 8½" d., high stand........38.00
Compote, open, jelly............................13.50
Compote, open....................................25.00

Dart Creamer

Creamer (ILLUS.) 31.00
Goblet..25.00
Pitcher, water.....................................30.00
Salt shaker w/original top 22.50
Sauce dish, footed................................7.00
Spooner...25.00
Sugar bowl, cov. 32.00

DEER & DOG

Celery vase...75.00
Compote, cov., 6" d., 8" h., frosted
  dog finial..90.00
Compote, cov., 8" oval, 8¾" h.,
  frosted dog finial 155.00
Compote, cov., 8" d., 13" h., frosted
  dog finial ....225.00 to 250.00
Creamer..90.00
Goblet, straight sides...........................62.50
Goblet, U-shaped.................................75.00
Mug, w/stacked ball handle 50.00
Pitcher, water, applied reeded
  handle ....125.00 to 150.00
Sauce dish, footed...............................16.00
Spooner...92.00
Sugar bowl, cov., frosted dog
  finial ....150.00 to 175.00

DEER & PINE TREE

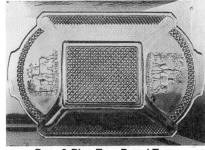

Deer & Pine Tree Bread Tray

Bowl, 5½ x 7¼".....................................45.00
Bowl, 5½ x 8".......................................55.00

Bread tray, amber, 8 x 13"....................75.00
Bread tray, apple green, 8 x 13".........100.00
Bread tray, blue, 8 x 13".....................110.00
Bread tray, canary yellow, 8 x 13"......100.00
Bread tray, clear, 8 x 13" (ILLUS.)........45.00
Butter dish, cov...................................105.00
Cake stand 110.00
Celery vase...80.00
Compote, cov., 8" sq., high stand.......200.00
Creamer..62.50
*Goblet..50.00
Marmalade jar, cov. 110.00
Mug, child's, apple green......................45.00
Mug, child's, blue................................42.00
Mug, large, blue..................................55.00
Mug, large, clear.................................37.50
Pickle dish 18.00
Pitcher, water.....................125.00 to 150.00
Sauce dish, flat or footed.....................18.00
Spooner...45.00
Sugar bowl, cov. 62.50
Tray, water, handled, 9 x 15".............135.00
Vegetable dish, 5¾ x 9".......................50.00

DELAWARE (Four Petal Flower)

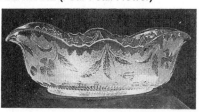

Delaware Banana Boat

Banana boat, green w/gold, 11¾" l.......90.00
Banana boat, rose w/gold, 11¾" l.
  (ILLUS.) 120.00
Berry set: boat-shaped master bowl &
  5 boat-shaped sauce dishes; rose
  w/gold, 6 pcs. ....250.00 to 300.00
Berry set: round master bowl & 4
  sauce dishes; rose w/gold, 5 pcs.....250.00
Bowl, 8" d., clear..................................50.00
Bowl, 8" d., clear w/gold 55.00
Bowl, 8" d., green w/gold 50.00
Bowl, 8" d., rose w/gold 57.50
Bowl, 9" d., scalloped rim, green
  w/gold 70.00
Bride's basket, boat-shaped open
  bowl, green w/gold, in silver plate
  frame, 11½" oval 160.00
Bride's basket, boat-shaped open
  bowl, rose w/gold in silver plate
  frame, 11½" oval ....200.00 to 225.00
Bride's basket, boat-shaped open
  bowl, green w/gold, miniature 175.00
Bride's basket, rose w/gold,
  miniature 85.00
Butter dish, cov., clear........................125.00
*Butter dish, cov., green w/gold..........125.00
Butter dish, cov., rose w/gold 165.00

Celery vase, rose band w/gold 45.00
Celery vase, green w/gold 82.50
Celery vase, purple w/gold 59.00
Celery vase, rose w/gold 88.00
Claret jug, rose w/gold........150.00 to 175.00
*Creamer, clear w/gold 45.00
Creamer, green w/gold 58.00
Creamer, rose w/gold 55.00
Creamer, individual size, clear w/gold ..25.00
Creamer, individual size, green
  w/gold 50.00
Creamer, individual size, rose w/gold...60.00
Cruet w/original stopper, clear...........100.00
Cruet w/original stopper, green
  w/gold 185.00
Cruet w/original stopper, rose
  w/gold 325.00
Marmalade dish w/silver plate holder,
  green w/gold 45.00
Marmalade dish w/silver plate holder,
  rose w/gold 85.00
Pin tray, green w/gold...........................55.00
Pin tray, rose w/gold 90.00
Pitcher, milk, green w/gold 85.00
Pitcher, tankard, green w/gold............150.00
Pitcher, tankard, rose
  w/gold ....200.00 to 225.00
Pitcher, water, clear w/gold ....50.00 to 75.00
Pitcher, water, green
  w/gold ....125.00 to 150.00
Pitcher, water, rose w/gold 175.00
Pomade jar w/jeweled cover, green
  w/gold ....185.00 to 200.00
Pomade jar w/jeweled cover, rose
  w/gold 335.00
Powder jar, cov., green w/gold 225.00
Punch cup, clear...................................16.00
Punch cup, clear w/gold 30.00
Punch cup, green w/gold 35.00
Punch cup, rose w/gold 45.00
Salt shaker w/original top 85.00
Sauce dish, boat-shaped, clear 18.00
Sauce dish, boat-shaped, green
  w/gold 35.00
Sauce dish, boat-shaped, rose
  w/gold 40.00
Sauce dish, round, green w/gold 22.50
Sauce dish, round, rose w/gold 24.00
Shade, gas, rose w/gold 295.00
Spooner, green w/gold 50.00
Spooner, rose 60.00
Spooner, rose w/gold............................75.00
Sugar bowl, cov., clear 62.50
*Sugar bowl, cov., green w/gold 90.00
Sugar bowl, cov., rose w/gold...............90.00
Sugar bowl, individual size, rose
  w/gold 95.00
Table set, green w/gold, 4 pcs............400.00
Table set, rose w/gold, 4 pcs..............450.00
Toothpick holder, clear 45.00
Toothpick holder, green w/gold 101.00
Toothpick holder, rose w/gold.............125.00
Tumbler, green w/gold..........................40.00

Tumbler, rose w/gold 50.00
Vase, 6" h., green w/gold.......................65.00
Vase, 8" h., clear 105.00
Vase, 8" h., green w/gold....................105.00
Vase, 8" h., rose w/gold......................105.00
Vase, 9½" h., amethyst.......................100.00
Vase, 9½" h., green w/gold.................110.00
Vase, 9½" h., rose w/gold...................115.00
Water set: water pitcher & 3 tumblers;
  rose w/gold, 4 pcs..........................295.00
Water set: water pitcher & 4 tumblers;
  green w/gold, 5 pcs.........................550.00

DEW & RAINDROP

Dew & Raindrop Wine

Celery 11.00
Compote, cov., jelly 50.00
*Cordial...30.00
*Goblet..28.00
Pitcher, water..50.00
*Punch cup 12.00
Spooner 35.00
Sugar bowl, cov. 35.00
*Wine (ILLUS.)......................................20.00

DEWDROP
Bread tray..25.00
Compote, cov., 11" d. 60.00
Cordial 40.00
Goblet, amber..25.00
Goblet, clear 25.00
Goblet, vaseline.....................................36.00
Mug, applied handle 26.00
Pitcher, water, collared base 50.00
Tumbler 15.00

DEWDROP WITH STAR
Bread tray, "Give Us This Day Our
  Daily Bread".......................................43.00
Butter dish, cov......................................55.00
Cake stand, 11" d. 45.00
Cheese dish, cov. 130.00
Compote, cov., 7⅛" d., 9½" h. 82.50
Compote, cov., 11" h. 77.00
Honey dish...13.50
*Plate, 7" d...15.00
Plate, 9" d. 13.50
Relish, 9" l..15.00
*Sauce dish, footed 7.00

DEWEY (Flower Flange)

Dewey Cruet

Bowl, 8" d...35.00
*Butter dish, cov., amber 85.00
*Butter dish, cov., clear 55.00
*Butter dish, cov., green 80.00
Butter dish, cov., green, miniature........75.00
Creamer, cov., individual size..............45.00
Creamer, amber 60.00
Creamer & cov. sugar bowl, individual
    size, canary yellow, pr. 150.00
Cruet w/original stopper, amber 125.00
Cruet w/original stopper, canary
    yellow (ILLUS.) 170.00
Cruet w/original stopper,
    green................................150.00 to 200.00
Mug, amber 60.00
Mug, clear..35.00
Mug, green...62.00
Parfait, amber 65.00
Parfait, clear 40.00
Pitcher, water, amber 110.00
Pitcher, water, canary yellow..............145.00
Pitcher, water, clear...............................78.00
Plate, footed, canary yellow..................85.00
Plate, footed, green...............................65.00
Salt shaker w/original top, amber 62.50
Sauce dish, canary yellow....................35.00
Sauce dish, green...................................30.00
Sugar bowl, cov., clear 35.00
Sugar bowl, cov., green..........................75.00
Tray, serpentine shape, amber, small ..45.00
Tray, serpentine shape, clear, small.....28.00
Tray, serpentine shape, amber, large...55.00
Tumbler, amber 55.00
Tumbler, canary yellow...........................55.00
Tumbler, clear...45.00
Water set: pitcher & 6 tumblers; clear,
    7 pcs. ....300.00 to 350.00

DIAGONAL BAND

Celery vase..30.00
Compote, open, 7½" d., high stand 18.00
Creamer..30.00
Goblet...20.00
Marmalade jar w/original lid..................50.00

Pickle castor insert 35.00
Sauce dish, flat or footed..........7.00 to 10.00
Spooner..25.00
Tray, handled, 7¼ x 13"..........................20.00
Wine 22.00

DIAGONAL BAND & FAN

Celery 45.00
Compote, open, 6" d., 5¼" h.................35.00
Creamer...30.00
Creamer & cov. sugar bowl, pr. 75.00
Goblet...25.00
Pitcher, milk..38.00
Plate, 6" d. 15.00
Plate, 7" d. 24.50
Sauce dish, footed.................................12.50
Sauce dishes, set of 6 ....75.00
Spooner..35.00
Sugar bowl, cov. 30.00
Wine 25.00

DIAMOND & BULL'S EYE BAND -
See Reverse Torpedo Pattern

DIAMOND & SUNBURST

Diamond & Sunburst Goblet

Bowl, cov., 8" d. 35.00
Cake stand, 8" d. 28.00
Compote, cov., 7" d., high stand...........48.00
Creamer, applied handle 40.00
Goblet (ILLUS.)......................................25.00
Pitcher w/applied handle, milk..............40.00
Sauce dish, handled, flat, 3¾" d. 10.00
Spooner..22.00
Toothpick holder 40.00
Tumbler 25.00

DIAMOND MEDALLION (Finecut &
Diamond or Grand)

Bread plate, 10" d. 20.00
Cake stand, 9" d. 25.00
Cake stand, 10" d. 30.00
Celery vase...25.00
Compote, cov., 6" d., 9" h. 65.00
Compote, cov., 8" d., low stand............80.00
Creamer, footed.....................................20.00
Goblet...30.00
Pitcher, water..38.00

Relish, 7½" oval 9.00
Salt shaker w/original top 32.50
Spooner 15.00
Wine 25.00

DIAMOND POINT

Diamond Point Creamer

Bar bottle, flint.......................................125.00
Butter dish, cov., flint 82.50
Celery vase, pedestal base w/knob
  stem, flint 90.00
Champagne, flint ....125.00 to 150.00
Claret, flint..100.00
Compote, open, 6" d., high stand,
  flint 75.00
Compote, open, 7" d., low stand, flint ...67.50
Compote, open, 7" d., high stand, milk
  white 175.00
Compote, open, 7½" d., high stand,
  flint 165.00
Compote, open, 8" d., shallow bowl,
  high stand, non-flint 65.00
Compote, open, 10¼" d., high stand,
  milk white 350.00
Cordial, flint...195.00
Creamer, applied handle, flint
  (ILLUS.) 165.00
Cup plate, flint.......................................60.00
Decanter w/original stopper, pt. 100.00
Decanter w/original stopper, qt. 165.00
Decanter w/bar lip, qt............................65.00
Egg cup, cov., powder blue opaque,
  flint ....550.00 to 750.00
Egg cup, canary yellow,
  flint ....300.00 to 350.00
Egg cup, clambroth, flint......................135.00
Egg cup, clear, flint 50.00
Egg cup, translucent sea green..........650.00
Goblet, clear, flint.................................58.00
Goblet, amber, non-flint 25.00
Goblet, blue, non-flint 32.00
Goblet, clear, non-flint 35.00
Honey dish, clear, flint 18.00
Honey dish, milk white, flint 60.00
Honey dish, coarse points, non-flint 12.00
Lamp, whale oil, w/wafer connector,
  flint, 10⅛" h. 295.00

Pitcher, milk, applied handle, milk
  white, flint...550.00
Pitcher, water, bulbous, flint 350.00
Pitcher, water, non-flint.........................75.00
Plate, 8" d., milk white, flint.................125.00
Salt dip, cov., master size, flint..........195.00
Sauce dish, flint, 4¼" d. 20.00
Sauce dish, non-flint, 3½" to 5½" d.......10.00
Spillholder, clear, flint 42.50
Spillholder, clear w/gold rim, flint........165.00
Spooner, non-flint 28.00
Sugar bowl, cov., flint 95.00
Sugar bowl, cov., non-flint 45.00
Toothpick holder, non-flint 35.00
Tumbler, flint...45.00
Tumbler, bar, flint.................................95.00
Tumbler, whiskey, handled, flint,
  3" h..150.00
Wine, flint..100.00
Wine, non-flint.......................................30.00

DIAMOND POINT WITH PANELS -
See Hinoto Pattern

DIAMOND QUILTED

Bowl, 7" d., amber 25.00
Celery vase, blue..................................65.00
Champagne, amethyst 37.50
Champagne, turquoise blue 37.50
Champagne, vaseline............................26.00
Claret, vaseline......................................18.00
Compote, open, 6" d., 6" h..................22.50
Compote, open, 8" d., low stand,
  amethyst 45.00
Compote, open, 9" d., low stand,
  vaseline...38.00
Cordial, amber 40.00
*Goblet, amber 40.00
*Goblet, amethyst 38.00
*Goblet, blue...37.50
*Goblet, vaseline 35.00
Pitcher, water, amber 52.00
Relish, amber, 4½ x 7½" 14.00
Relish, leaf-shaped, turquoise blue,
  5½ x 9"..22.00
Relish, leaf-shaped, vaseline,
  5½ x 9"..20.00
*Salt dip, amethyst, master size,
  rectangular 22.00
Sauce dish, flat or footed, amber..........18.00
Sauce dish, flat or footed, turquoise
  blue 13.00
Sauce dish, flat or footed, vaseline.......12.50
Spooner, amber.....................................28.00
Spooner, turquoise blue 38.00
Spooner, vaseline..................................35.00
Sugar bowl, cov., vaseline...................55.00
Tray, water, cloverleaf-shaped,
  amethyst, 10 x 12" 45.00
*Tumbler, amber...................................30.00
*Tumbler, vaseline................................26.00
Wine, amethyst......................................42.00
Wine, clear...20.00
Wine, vaseline 38.00

DIAMOND THUMBPRINT

Bowl, 7" d., footed, scalloped rim 95.00
Bowl, 8" d., footed, scalloped rim 100.00
*Butter dish, cov. ....150.00 to 200.00
Celery vase.........................175.00 to 200.00
Compote, open, 7" d., low stand,
    extended scalloped rim 125.00
Compote, open, 8" d., high stand 125.00
Compote, open, 8" d., low stand...........75.00
Compote, open, 10½" d., high
    stand ....200.00 to 250.00
Compote, open, 11½" d., high stand ..300.00
Cordial, 4" h....................................295.00
*Creamer, applied handle...................200.00
Decanter w/bar lip, qt., 10½" h. 195.00
Decanter w/original stopper, qt...........225.00
*Goblet...450.00
Honey dish...25.00
Pitcher, water......................400.00 to 600.00
Sauce dish, flat......................................20.00
*Spooner...86.00
*Sugar bowl, cov....................................150.00
Tray, serpentine shape, amber,
    small 45.00
*Tumbler ....50.00 to 90.00
Tumbler, bar, 3¾" h. 150.00
Tumbler, whiskey.................................150.00
Wine 235.00

DINNER BELL - See Cottage Pattern

DORIC - See Feather Pattern

DOUBLE LEAF & DART - See Leaf & Dart Pattern

DOUBLE LOOP - See Ribbon Candy Pattern

DOUBLE RIBBON

Bread plate 24.00
Butter dish, cov.....................................45.00
Creamer...45.00
Goblet..27.50
Lamp, kerosene-type, frosted, dated
    1872..135.00
Relish..12.50

DOUBLE WEDDING RING (Wedding Ring)

*Goblet...70.00
Sauce dish..25.00
Spooner 70.00
Syrup pitcher w/original top, 6" h. 165.00
Tumbler, bar 70.00
Wine 89.00

DRAPERY

Creamer, applied handle 35.00
Goblet..28.00
Plate, 6" d. 23.00
Spooner...35.00
Sugar bowl, cov. 40.00

EGG IN SAND

Egg in Sand Gob

Bread tray, handled ....
Creamer........................
Dish, flat, swan center, 7" d. ......
Goblet, blue ....
Goblet, clear (ILLUS.)................
Pitcher, milk ....
Pitcher, water.....................
Platter, 12½" oblong ....
Relish, 5½ x 9".....................
Spooner, amber.....................
Spooner, blue ....
Spooner, clear ....
Sugar bowl, cov. ....
Tumbler ....

EGYPTIAN

Egyptian Spooner

Bread platter, Cleopatra center,
    9 x 12"...57.00
*Bread platter, Salt Lake Temple
    center...248.00
Butter dish, cov......................................73.00
Celery vase.........................75.00 to 100.00
Compote, cov., 6" d., 6" h., sphinx
    base ....100.00 to 125.00
Compote, cov., 7" d., high stand,
    sphinx base....................................195.00

Compote, cov., 8" d., high stand,
  sphinx base.....................................225.00
Creamer..45.00
Goblet...45.00
Pickle dish 20.00
Pitcher, water.....................200.00 to 225.00
Plate, 10" d. 65.00
Plate, 12" d., handled 85.00
Relish, 5½ x 8½"..................................32.50
Sauce dish, flat....................................18.50
Sauce dish, footed...............................16.50
Spooner (ILLUS.).................................45.00
Table set, 4 pcs. 295.00

EMERALD GREEN HERRINGBONE - See Paneled Herringbone Pattern

EMPIRE COLONIAL - See Colonial Pattern

EMPRESS

Bowl, master, berry, 8½" d. 40.00
Butter dish, cov., green......................130.00
Compote, open, 6" d., high standard,
  emerald green.................................125.00
Creamer & cov. sugar bowl, green
  w/gold, pr.......................................200.00
Cruet w/original stopper, emerald
  green..195.00
Salt & pepper shakers w/original tops,
  emerald green, pr. 195.00
Spoonholder, emerald green................68.00
Table set, 4 pcs. 650.00
Toothpick holder, emerald green
  w/gold 195.00
Tumbler, water, emerald green 69.00

ENGLISH HOBNAIL CROSS - See Klondike Pattern

ESTHER

Esther Sauce Dish

Berry set: master bowl & 5 sauce
  dishes; green, 6 pcs.........................215.00
Bowl, 8" d., clear.................................35.00
Bowl, 8" d., green w/gold.....................72.50
Butter dish, cov., amber-stained.........125.00
Butter dish, cov., clear.........................75.00
Butter dish, cov., green......................145.00
Cake stand, 10½" d., 6" h. 50.00
Celery vase, amber-stained...............125.00
Celery vase, clear................................35.00

Celery vase, green 85.00
Compote, open, jelly, 5" d., amber-
  stained w/enamel decoration 135.00
Compote, open, jelly, 5" d., green 60.00
Creamer, green 90.00
Cruet w/original stopper, clear,
  miniature 30.00
Cruet w/original stopper, green,
  miniature ....200.00 to 275.00
Cruet w/ball-shaped stopper, clear......35.00
Cruet w/ball-shaped stopper,
  green..............................250.00 to 300.00
Goblet, amber-stained w/enamel
  decoration ....125.00 to 150.00
Goblet, clear 60.00
Pitcher, water, amber-
  stained ....200.00 to 250.00
Plate, 10¼" d. 30.00
Relish, clear, 4½ x 8½".........................22.50
Relish, green, 4½ x 8½" 36.00
Relish, green, 5½ x 11" 42.50
Salt & pepper shakers w/original tops,
  clear, pr..65.00
Salt & pepper shakers w/original tops,
  green, pr. 130.00
Sauce dish, clear, engraved (ILLUS.)...15.00
Sauce dish, green................................25.00
Sauce dishes, amber-stained, set
  of 6...150.00
Spooner, clear 35.00
Spooner, green.....................................68.00
Sugar bowl, cov., green......................125.00
Toothpick holder, amber-
  stained ....100.00 to 150.00
Toothpick holder, green......................115.00
Tray, ice cream, clear...........................67.50
Tray, ice cream, green........................145.00
Tumbler, clear......................................32.00
Tumbler, amber-stained 45.00
Tumbler, green.....................................55.00
Tumbler, green w/gold..........................65.00
Water set: pitcher & 6 tumblers; green,
  7 pcs. 545.00
Wine, amber-stained 75.00
Wine, ruby-stained, souvenir 75.00

EUREKA (McKee's)

Butter dish 80.00
Creamer..40.00
Egg cup 30.00
Goblet..28.00
Salt dip, master size 22.00
Spooner..50.00

EXCELSIOR

Bar bottle, flint, qt................................70.00
Cake stand, flint, 9¼" h.......................150.00
Celery vase, flint..................................78.00
Champagne 85.00
Cologne bottle w/faceted stopper.........95.00
Creamer, applied handle 275.00
Egg cup 47.50
Egg cup, double, fiery opalescent,
  flint..295.00

Excelsior Goblet

Goblet, flint (ILLUS.) 68.00
Platter, 9¼" l. 22.00
Spillholder, flint 76.00
Sugar bowl, cov. ....100.00 to 125.00
Tumbler, bar, flint, 3½" h. 60.00
Wine, flint...50.00

EYEWINKER
Banana boat, flat, 8½" 90.00
Banana stand 115.00
Bowl, cov., 9" d. 85.00
Bowl, 6½" d..25.00
Bowl, master berry or fruit, 9" d.,
    4½" h...70.00
*Butter dish, cov. 72.50
Cake stand, 8" d. 58.00
Cake stand, 9½" d. 65.00
Celery vase, 6½" h. 55.00
*Compote, cov., 6" d., high stand 50.00
Compote, open, 4" d., 5" h., scalloped
    rim 32.50
Compote, open, 5½" d., high stand 60.00
Compote, open, 8½" d., high stand 75.00
Compote, open, 9½" d., high stand 82.00
Creamer...45.00
*Goblet..25.00
Pitcher, milk 70.00
*Pitcher, water 80.00
Plate, 7" sq., 1½" h., turned-up sides ...24.00
Salt shaker w/original top 35.00
*Sauce dish, round 34.00
Sauce dish, square................................12.00
*Spooner..45.00
Sugar bowl, cov. 52.00
Syrup pitcher w/silver plate top...........135.00
*Tumbler...28.00

FEATHER (Doric, Indiana Swirl or Finecut & Feather)
Berry set, master bowl & 6 sauce
    dishes, 7 pcs......................................120.00
Bowl, 7 x 9" oval 24.00
Bowl, 8" d...25.00
Bowl, 8½" oval, flat 25.00
Butter dish, cov., clear 60.00
Butter dish, cov., green.........................195.00
Cake stand, 8½" d. 32.50

Cake stand, clear, 9½" h. 47.00
Cake stand, green, 9½" h. ..125.00 to 150.00
Cake stand, 11" d. 60.00
Celery vase...40.00
Compote, open, jelly, 5" d., 4¾" h.,
    amber-stained...................................110.00
Compote, open, jelly, 5" d., 4¾" h.,
    clear 23.00
Compote, open, 8" d., low stand..........45.00
Compote, open, 8" d., high stand 38.00
Cordial 43.00
Creamer, clear......................................38.00
Creamer, green 75.00
Cruet w/original stopper, clear.............37.00
Cruet w/original stopper, green 250.00
Doughnut stand, 8" w., 4½" h. 36.00
Goblet, amber-stained 140.00

Feather Goblet

Goblet, clear (ILLUS.)............................60.00
Pickle dish 15.00
Pitcher, milk 47.50
Pitcher, water, clear..............................60.00
Pitcher, water, green ....175.00 to 200.00
Plate, 10" d. 40.00
Relish, 8¼" oval, amber-stained...........75.00
Relish, 8¼" oval, clear 18.00
Salt & pepper shakers w/original tops,
    green, pr. 225.00
Sauce dish, flat or footed, clear............14.50
Sauce dish, flat or footed, green...........45.00
Spooner...30.00
Sugar bowl, cov., clear 46.00
Sugar bowl, cov., green.......................150.00
Syrup pitcher w/original top, clear 135.00
Syrup pitcher w/original top, green 315.00
Toothpick holder 85.00
Tumbler, clear..45.00
Tumbler, green 85.00
*Wine..37.50

FESTOON
Bowl, berry, 8" rectangle......................23.00
Bowl, berry, 5½ x 9" rectangle..............25.00
Butter dish, cov.....................................42.00
Cake stand, high pedestal,
    9" d.......................................30.00 to 40.00

Compote, open, 9" d., high stand 56.00
Creamer...30.00
Marmalade jar, cov. 32.00
Mug, handled...58.00
Pitcher, water..60.00
Plate, 7" d. 36.00
Plate, 8" d. 42.00
Plate, 9" d. 47.50
Sauce dish...10.00
Spooner...35.00

Festoon Sugar Bowl

Sugar bowl, cov. (ILLUS.).....................55.00
Tray, water, 10" d. 36.00
Tumbler 24.50
Waste bowl 53.00

FINECUT
Bread tray, handled, canary,
    7½ x 14½".......................................55.00
Cake stand, amber, 10" d., 7¼" h.........45.00
Cake stand 35.00
Creamer...28.00
Goblet, canary 35.00
Goblet, clear 22.50
Pickle castor, canary, w/Reed & Barton
    silver plate frame & fork 275.00
Pitcher, water, canary..........................100.00
Plate, 7" d. 15.00
Plate, 10" d., amber..............................42.50
Plate, 10" d., canary 45.00
Relish, boat-shaped, apple green.........35.00
Salt & pepper shakers w/original tops,
    canary, pr...48.00
Salt & pepper shakers w/original tops,
    clear, pr..35.00
Toothpick holder, hat shape on plate,
    blue..25.00
Tray, water, canary, 9¼" d....................48.00

FINECUT & BLOCK
Bowl, round, handled, pink blocks 50.00
Butter dish, cov., two-handled 55.00
Celery tray, clear w/amber blocks,
    11" l..85.00

Champagne, amber...............................70.00
Cordial 35.00
*Creamer, clear 30.00
Creamer, clear w/amber blocks...........70.00
Creamer, clear w/pink blocks 75.00
Egg cup, double.....................................29.00
*Goblet, amber 50.00
*Goblet, clear...40.00
Goblet, clear w/blue blocks...................55.00
Goblet, clear w/yellow blocks 52.00
Pitcher, water, clear w/amber blocks....85.00
Pitcher, water, clear w/blue blocks 125.00
Pitcher, water, clear w/pink blocks 110.00
Punch cup, clear w/yellow blocks 55.00
Salt dip..12.00
Sauce dish, amber.................................15.00
Sauce dish, clear w/amber blocks........13.00
Sauce dish, clear w/blue blocks 22.50
Spooner, clear 40.00
Spooner, clear w/amber blocks 45.00
Tumbler, clear w/blue blocks 40.00
*Wine, amber..58.00
*Wine, blue 58.00
*Wine, clear 24.00
Wine, clear w/amber blocks...................48.00
Wine, clear w/blue blocks 45.00
Wine, clear w/pink blocks 60.00
Wine, clear w/yellow blocks..................35.00

FINECUT & DIAMOND - See Diamond Medallion Pattern

FINECUT & FEATHER - See Feather Pattern

FINECUT & PANEL (Paneled Finecut)

Finecut & Panel Plate

Bread tray, amber, 9 x 13"...................47.50
Bread tray, clear, 9 x 13" 29.00
Cake stand, square, blue......................75.00
Celery vase...25.00
Compote, open, high stand, amber 45.00
Compote, open, high stand, blue..........50.00

Creamer, amber 42.50
Goblet, amber....................................32.00
Goblet, clear 18.00
Goblet, vaseline.................................27.50
Pitcher, water, amber 100.00
Plate, 6" d., amber (ILLUS.)..................25.00
Plate, 6" d., blue 28.00
Plate, 6" d., clear 13.00
Plate, 6" d., vaseline..........................22.50
Relish, blue, 3½ x 7"...........................22.50
Relish, vaseline, 3½ x 7" 21.50
Salt shaker w/original top, amber 37.50
Salt shaker w/original top, clear............35.00
Sauce dish, amber..............................12.00
Sauce dish, clear 8.00
Sauce dish, vaseline...........................14.00
Sugar bowl, cov., vaseline....................60.00
Tray, water, vaseline, 12" w..................95.00
Tumbler, amber 18.00
Waste bowl, vaseline...........................29.50
Wine, amber 30.00
Wine, blue...28.00
Wine, clear..20.00
Wine, vaseline 36.00

FINECUT BAND - See Cottage Pattern

FISHSCALE

Fishscale Compote

Bowl, cov., 7" d. 55.00
Bowl, 6" d..39.00
Butter dish, cov..................................40.00
Cake stand, 9" d. 25.00
Cake stand, 10" d. 35.00
Celery vase..31.00
Compote, cov., 7½" d. 85.00
Compote, open, jelly...........................18.00
Compote, open, 6" d. 20.00
Compote, open, 7" d., high stand
  (ILLUS.) 31.00
Creamer...27.50
Goblet...34.00
Mug...35.00
Pickle dish 18.00
Pitcher, milk......................................35.00
Pitcher, water.....................................50.00

Plate, 7" d. 28.50
Plate, 8" d. 32.50
Plate, 9" sq. 35.00
Relish, 5 x 8½" 22.50
Sauce dish, flat or footed....................10.00
Spooner...21.00
Sugar bowl, cov. 38.00
Tray, water, round 35.00
Tumbler 95.00
Waste bowl..50.00

FLORIDA - See Paneled Herringbone Pattern

FLOWER FLANGE - See Dewey Pattern

FLUTE

Flute Claret

Bar bottle, clear, flint, qt.......................72.00
Bar bottle, pewter closure w/marble
  stopper, emerald green, flint,
  11" h...1,700.00
Claret (ILLUS.)....................................22.00
Compote, open, 8¼" d., 3" h................35.00
Egg cup, single 35.00
Goblet...26.00
Mug, applied handle 135.00
Pitcher, water.....................................75.00
Relish..30.00
Tumbler, whiskey, handled..................55.00
Wine 35.00

FLYING ROBIN - See Hummingbird Pattern

FOUR PETAL FLOWER - See Delaware Pattern

FROSTED CIRCLE

Bowl, 8" d., 3¼" h. 20.00
Butter dish, cov...................................65.00
Cake stand, 9½" d. 47.50
Champagne...48.00
Claret...45.00
Compote, open, 9" d., 6" h...................46.50
Compote, open, 10" d., high stand,
  scalloped rim....................................55.00

Creamer..46.00

Frosted Circle Goblet

*Goblet (ILLUS.) 28.00
Pitcher, water, tankard..........................80.00
Plate, 7" d. 22.50
Plate, 9" d. 37.50
Sauce dish..12.00
Spooner..45.00
Sugar bowl, cov. 60.00
Tumbler 26.00

FROSTED LEAF

Celery vase........................100.00 to 125.00
Champagne..225.00
Egg cup 100.00
Goblet...95.00
Goblet, flint 125.00
Goblet, lady's......................................160.00
Salt dip..50.00
Sauce dish...25.00
Tumbler, footed 120.00
Wine 140.00

FROSTED LION (Rampant Lion)

Frosted Lion Compote

Bowl, cov., 3⅞ x 6⅞" oblong, collared
   base 80.00

Bowl, cov., 4⅝ x 7⁷⁄₁₆" oblong, collared
   base 110.00
*Bread plate, rope edge, closed
   handles,10½" d. 78.00
*Butter dish, cov., frosted lion's head
   finial 90.00
Butter dish, cov., rampant lion finial....140.00
*Celery vase 70.00
Cheese dish, cov., rampant lion
   finial 425.00
Compote, cov., 5" d., 8½" h. 175.00
*Compote, cov., 6¾" oval, 7" h.,
   collared base, rampant lion
   finial ....150.00 to 175.00
Compote, cov., 7" d., 11" h., lion head
   finial 150.00
Compote, cov., 7¾" oval, low collared
   base, rampant lion finial..................128.00
Compote, cov., 8" d., 13" h., rampant
   lion finial...165.00
Compote, cov., 8¼" d., high stand,
   frosted lion head finial (ILLUS.) 145.00
Compote, cov., 5½ x 8¾" oval, 8¼" h.,
   rampant lion finial............................185.00
Compote, open, 5" d., low stand..........62.00
Compote, open, 7" d., 6¼" h...............125.00
Compote, open, 7" oval, 7½" h. 135.00
Compote, open, 8" d.............................175.00
Creamer..75.00
*Egg Cup 90.00
*Goblet...93.00
Marmalade jar, cov., rampant lion
   finial 145.00
*Pitcher, water ....525.00 to 550.00
Platter, 9 x 10½" oval, lion handles 95.00
Salt dip, cov., master size, collared
   base, rectangular 295.00
*Sauce dish, 4" to 5" d. 25.00
*Spooner..54.00
*Sugar bowl, cov., frosted lion's head
   finial 50.00
Sugar bowl, cov., rampant lion finial.....80.00
Table set, cov. sugar bowl, creamer
   & spooner, 3 pcs. 225.00

FROSTED RIBBON (Duncan's No. 150)

Butter dish, cov.....................................60.00
Celery vase..40.00
Compote, cov., 8" d., 11" h. 95.00
Goblet...35.00
Pitcher, water..75.00
Sauce dish...12.00
Spooner..33.00
Sugar bowl, cov. 54.00
Wine 65.00

FROSTED ROMAN KEY - See Roman Key Pattern

FROSTED STORK

Bowl, 9" oval, 1-0-1 border 45.00
*Bread plate, round...............................55.00
Compote, open, 8" d. 45.00

Creamer...45.00
*Goblet..65.00
Jam jar, cov. 350.00
Plate, 9" d., 1-0-1 border 58.00
Platter, 8 x 11½" oval, 1-0-1 border......70.00
Platter, 8 x 11½" oval, deer & dog
    border 81.00
Sauce dish..28.00
Spooner...40.00
Tray, water, 11 x 15½".........................100.00
Waste bowl..50.00

GALLOWAY (Mirror or misnamed Virginia)
Bowl, 9½" d., flat...................................30.00
Butter dish, cov......................................55.00
Cake stand, 9¼" d., 6" h. 52.00
Compote, open, 4¼" d., 6" h.................33.00
Compote, open, 8½" d., 7" h.................60.00
Compote, open, 8¾" d., flared, rose-
    stained 85.00
Creamer, clear..22.00
Creamer, rose-stained...........................75.00
Creamer, individual size, clear 19.00
Goblet..90.00
Mug, 4½" d. 37.50
Olive dish, 4 x 6"...................................19.00
Pitcher, milk...70.00
Pitcher, water...45.00
Punch cup..10.00
Relish, 8¼" l. 14.50
Salt shaker w/original top 20.00
Salt & pepper shakers w/original tops,
    gold trim, 3" h., pr.............................47.50
Sauce dish, flat or footed......................11.00
Spooner, clear.......................................22.50
Spooner, rose-stained 80.00
Sugar bowl, cov., rose-stained 85.00
Sugar shaker w/original top 35.00
Syrup pitcher w/metal spring top 75.00
Table set, 4 pcs. ....225.00 to 275.00
*Toothpick holder, clear.........................22.50
*Toothpick holder, green 50.00
Tumbler..25.00
Vase, 9½" h. 32.00
Waste bowl...38.00
Water set: pitcher & 4 tumblers; rose-
    stained, 5 pcs.....................................495.00
Wine 41.00

GARFIELD DRAPE
Bowl, 6" d...42.50
Bread plate, "We Mourn Our Nation's
    Loss," 11½"8 d..................................58.00
Butter dish, cov......................................78.00
Cake stand, 9½" d. 85.00
Celery vase, pedestal base 50.00
Compote, cov., 8" d., 12½" h..............185.00
Creamer..50.00
Goblet (ILLUS. top next column) 45.00
Pitcher, milk...85.00
Pitcher, water...95.00
Sauce dish, flat or footed......................12.00

Garfield Drape Goblet

Spooner...40.00
Sugar bowl, cov. 80.00

GEORGIA - See Peacock Feather Pattern

GIANT BULL'S EYE
Bottle, brandy, original stopper,
    7½" h..48.00
Butter dish, cov......................................45.00
Goblet..60.00
Pitcher, water...85.00
Toothpick holder 35.00
Tray, round, wine...................................32.00
Wine 25.00

GODDESS OF LIBERTY - See Ceres Pattern

GOOD LUCK - See Horseshoe Pattern

GOOSEBERRY
Cake stand 52.00
Creamer..40.00
*Goblet...30.00
*Mug...45.00
Spooner..25.00
Tumbler, bar 40.00
Tumbler, water.......................................32.00

GOTHIC
Butter dish, cov...................100.00 to 125.00
Castor bottle 29.50
Castor set: mustard, cruet & shaker &
    original wire holder...........................165.00
Celery vase..145.00
Champagne..195.00
Compote, open, 7" d., 3½" h...............62.50
Compote, open, 8" d., 4" h...................62.50
Creamer, applied handle 100.00
Egg cup, 3½" h. (ILLUS. top next
    page)...50.00
Goblet..62.00
Sauce dish...18.00

Gothic Egg Cup

Spooner 56.00
Sugar bowl, cov. 125.00
Wine, 3¾" h. 108.00

GRAND - See Diamond Medallion Pattern

GRAPE & FESTOON
Butter dish, cov., stippled leaf...............40.00
Compote, cov., 8" d., low stand, acorn
   finial, stippled leaf 55.00
Compote, cov., large, high stand,
   w/bird's nest finial 85.00
Creamer, stippled leaf 42.00
Egg cup, stippled leaf 20.00
Goblet, stippled leaf..............................23.00
Goblet, veined leaf................................25.00
Mug...20.00
Pitcher, water, stippled leaf 90.00
Relish, stippled leaf 10.00
Salt dip, footed, stippled leaf 22.00
Sauce dish, flat, stippled leaf, 4" d..........9.00
Spooner, stippled leaf...........................25.00
Spooner, veined leaf..............................25.00
Wine, stippled leaf 50.00

GRAPE & FESTOON WITH SHIELD
Compote, cov., 8¼" d., 10½" h. 140.00
Goblet, w/American shield....................60.00
Mug, 1⅞" h. 35.00
Mug, sapphire blue, 2½" h....................48.00

GRASSHOPPER (Locust)
Bowl, cov., 7" d., footed 50.00
Butter dish, cov., no insect, clear..........45.00
Butter dish, cov., w/insect, clear 70.00
Celery vase, w/insect.............................75.00
Compote, cov., 8¼" d 65.00
Creamer, amber 65.00
Creamer, w/insect 45.00
Pitcher, water, w/insect..........................85.00
Plate, 7½" d., footed 18.00
Plate, 8½" d., footed 18.00
Plate, 10½" d., footed 28.00
Salt dip, master size 38.00
Sauce dish, footed, no insect 14.00

Spooner, no insect, clear.......................60.00
Spooner, w/insect, clear 75.00
Sugar bowl, cov., no insect....................40.00
Sugar bowl, cov., w/insect.....................70.00

**GUARDIAN ANGEL - See Cupid & Venus
Pattern**

HAIRPIN (Sandwich Loop)
Celery vase..60.00
Champagne 80.00
Decanter w/stopper, qt. 90.00
Egg cup, clear..35.00
Goblet..45.00
Salt dip, master size 20.00
Sauce dish, amethyst, 4" d. 85.00
Sauce dish, clear, 4" d...........................15.00
Spooner...50.00
Tumbler 55.00
Wine 55.00

HALLEY'S COMET
Celery vase..42.00
Goblet..32.00
Pitcher, water, tankard...........................92.00
Pitcher, water, tankard, engraved..........95.00
Spooner...50.00
Wine 18.00

HAMILTON

Hamilton Compote

Butter dish, cov......................................75.00
Compote, open, 7" d., low stand..........46.00
Compote, open, 8" d., 5½" h.
   (ILLUS.) 70.00
Compote, open, 8" d., 8" h.................325.00
Creamer...60.00
Egg cup 38.00
Goblet..60.00
Honey dish, 3½" d. 20.00
Sauce dish...14.00
Spooner...40.00
Sugar bowl, cov. ....100.00 to 125.00
Tumbler, whiskey, applied handle 95.00

HAMILTON WITH LEAF
Butter dish, cov., frosted leaf...............85.00

Compote, open, 8" d., 8" h., frosted
  leaf 95.00
Egg cup, clear leaf................................63.00
Goblet, clear leaf 45.00
Sugar bowl, cov., clear leaf 95.00
Tumbler, bar, clear leaf.........................90.00
Tumbler, bar, frosted leaf 135.00
Tumbler, whiskey, handled, clear
  leaf 100.00
Wine 70.00

HAND (Pennsylvania, Early)

Hand Goblet

Bread plate, 8 x 10½" oval....................38.00
Butter dish, cov....................................125.00
Cake stand, 12¼" d., engraved 175.00
Celery vase..42.00
Claret...85.00
Compote, cov., 7" d., high stand..........95.00
Compote, open, 7¾" d., 6¾" h..............40.00
Compote, open, 9" d., low stand...........36.00
Creamer..40.00
Goblet (ILLUS.)......................................55.00
Marmalade jar, cov. 65.00
Mug...95.00
Pitcher, water...68.00
Relish...22.50
Sauce dish, 4½" d 12.50
Spooner..45.00
Sugar bowl, cov. 65.00
Tumbler, water..97.00
Wine 69.00

HARP

Bowl, 6" d...45.00
Goblet, flared sides (ILLUS. top next
  column) 950.00
Lamp, kerosene, hand-type w/applied
  finger grip ....125.00 to 175.00
Lamp, kerosene, hexagonal font,
  shaped base, brass collar, flint,
  9½" h..475.00
Salt dip, master size 70.00
Spillholder...100.00

Harp Goblet

HEARTS OF LOCH LAVEN - See Shuttle Pattern

HEART WITH THUMBPRINT

Heart with Thumbprint Creamer

Banana boat, 6½ x 7½" 115.00
Banana boat, 6½ x 11" 145.00
Barber bottle w/original pewter
  stopper..163.00
Berry set, master bowl & 5 sauce
  dishes,6 pcs. 125.00
Bowl, 7" sq., 3½" h.................................37.50
Bowl, 8" d., 2" h., flared rim 25.00
Bowl, 9" d...35.00
Bowl, 10" d., scalloped rim 45.00
Butter dish, cov......................................125.00
Cake stand, 9" d., 5" h. ....150.00 to 175.00
Card tray, clear 19.00
Card tray, green......................................55.00
Celery vase..53.00
Compote, open, jelly, two handles,
  green..25.00
Compote, open, 7½" d., 7½" h.,
  scalloped rim...................................145.00
Cordial, 3" h. ....200.00 to 250.00
Creamer..39.00
Creamer, individual size, clear
  (ILLUS.) 30.00

Creamer & open sugar bowl, individual
   size, green w/gold, pr.........................65.00
Cruet w/original stopper.........................65.00
Goblet, clear 55.00
Goblet, green w/gold 125.00
Ice bucket 75.00
Lamp, kerosene-type, green,
   9" h............................250.00 to 275.00
Nappy, heart-shaped...............................42.50
Olive dish...19.50
Plate, 6" d. 25.00
Plate, 10" d. 34.00
Plate, 12" d. 65.00
Punch cup, clear......................................22.50
Rose bowl, 3¾" d.....................................55.00
Sauce dish...15.00
Spooner...55.00
Sugar bowl, cov., large 95.00
Sugar bowl, open, individual size, green
   w/gold 45.00
Syrup jug w/original pewter top 108.00
Syrup jug w/original pewter top,
   miniature, 4" h..................100.00 to 125.00
Tray, 4¼ x 8¼" 30.00
Tumbler, water, clear w/gold 45.00
Vase, 6" h., trumpet-shaped, clear 41.00
Vase, 6" h., trumpet-shaped, green......75.00
Vase, 10" h., trumpet-shaped................65.00
Waste bowl 85.00
Wine, clear..48.00
Wine, green w/gold.................................135.00

HEAVY PANELED FINECUT (Paneled Diamond Cross)
Goblet, clear 28.00
Goblet, vaseline.......................................35.00

HERCULES PILLAR (Pillar Variant)
Champagne 135.00
Egg cup, double..65.00
Goblet..55.00
Syrup jug w/pewter top, amber, 8" h...125.00
Syrup jug w/original top, clear 85.00

HERO (*Called Ruby Rosette when ruby-stained*)
Berry set; master bowl & 5 sauce
   dishes; Ruby Rosette, 6 pcs. 165.00
Butter dish, cov., Ruby Rosette 51.00
Creamer, Ruby Rosette...........................40.00
Pitcher, clear, ½ gal................................65.00
Spooner, clear 15.00
Spooner, Ruby Rosette 62.00
Table set, Ruby Rosette, 4 pcs. 265.00
Tumbler, Ruby Rosette............................39.00

HERRINGBONE (Herringbone with Star & Shield Motif)
Berry set, master bowl & 6 sauce
   dishes, 7 pcs......................................125.00
Celery vase...30.00
Creamer...25.00
Goblet..20.00

Mustard jar, cov. 12.00
Pitcher, milk 85.00
Spooner...35.00
Sugar bowl, cov. 32.00

HERRINGBONE BAND
Goblet..20.00
Spooner, pedestal base, scalloped
   rim 22.00
Sugar bowl, open......................................20.00
Wine 22.00

HERRINGBONE WITH STAR & SHIELD MOTIF - See Herringbone Pattern

HICKMAN (Le Clede)

Hickman Creamer

Bowl, 6" d., green 25.00
Bowl, 8" d..25.00
Butter dish, cov..35.00
Cake stand, 8½" to 9½" d. 38.00
Celery dish, boat-shaped, green 22.00
Celery tray 18.00
Compote, cov., 5" d. 42.00
Compote, cov., 7" d., high stand...........82.00
Compote, open, 8½" d., 12" h...............65.00
Compote, open, 9½" d., 8" h..................45.00
Condiment set, miniature, salt &
   pepper shakers & cruet w/original
   stopper on cloverleaf-shaped tray,
   4 pcs. ....75.00 to 100.00
Creamer, clear w/gold 25.00
Creamer, green (ILLUS.) 27.00
Creamer & open sugar bowl,
   individual size, oval, green, pr. 38.00
Cruet w/triple pouring spout & faceted
   stopper..31.00
Goblet, clear 35.00
Goblet, green..85.00
Ice tub, clear 45.00
Ice tub, green..60.00
Pitcher, water..45.00
Plate, 6" d. 11.00
Punch cup, clear..8.00
Punch cup, green 18.50
Relish, green 22.50
Salt dip..22.50
Sauce dish, green.....................................12.50
Sauce dish, ruby-stained 18.50

Sugar bowl, cov. 65.00
Toothpick holder 42.00
Vase, 8" h., trumpet-shaped, green......18.00
Vase, 10" h., green 37.50
Wine, clear...27.00
Wine, green 45.00

HIDALGO (Frosted Waffle)
Bowl, 9" sq., clear & frosted.................24.00
Butter dish, cov......................................50.00
Celery dish, boat-shaped, 13" l............35.00
Celery vase, amber-stained.................49.00
Celery vase, clear................................30.00
Compote, open, 7" sq., high stand 45.00
Creamer..35.00
Goblet, clear 20.00
Goblet, engraved 22.00
Goblet, frosted 35.00
Goblet, ruby-stained 75.00
Pitcher, water, ...43.00
Sauce dish, handled 15.00
Sugar shaker w/original top 45.00
Tray, water..55.00
Tumbler, frosted 35.00
Waste bowl 25.00

HINOTO (Diamond Point with Panels)

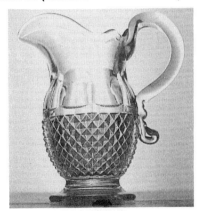

Hinoto Creamer

Champagne 90.00
Creamer, applied handle (ILLUS.)........90.00
Egg cup, handled...................................45.00
Goblet..85.00
Tumbler, footed 47.50

HOBNAIL
*Butter dish, cov., clear..........................85.00
Celery vase, footed, square, clear........20.00
*Cologne bottle, amber, 6½" h..............37.50
*Cologne bottle, clear, 6½" h. 22.00
*Creamer, fluted top, applied handle,
  amber, 2 x 3".....................................25.00
Creamer, three-footed, blue 25.00
*Creamer, individual size, amber..........31.00
*Cruet w/original stopper, 4½" h. 45.00
Egg cup, single 28.50

Egg cup, double....................................15.00
*Goblet...15.00
Mug, amber 30.00
Mug, blue...21.00
Mug, clear..8.00
Pitcher, 7" h., blue 80.00
Pitcher, 8" h., square top, amber 235.00
Pitcher, 8" h., square top, sapphire
  blue...265.00
Pitcher, water, blue..............................125.00
*Punch cup 22.50
*Rose bowl, 6" d., 5½" h. 85.00
Salt shaker w/original top, blue............35.00
Spooner, ruffled rim, amber 35.00
*Spooner, clear......................................30.00
Spooner, frosted 35.00
*Sugar bowl, cov....................................20.00
*Toothpick holder, amber 39.00
*Toothpick holder, blue.........................25.00
Toothpick holder, vaseline...................30.00
Tray, water, amber, 11½" d. 55.00
Tray, water, blue, 11½" d......................55.00
Tumbler, amber 30.00
Tumbler, seven-row, amber..................20.00
*Tumbler, eight-row, amber 22.50
*Tumbler, ten-row, amber.....................30.00
*Tumbler, ten-row, blue 28.00
*Tumbler, clear 15.00
Tumbler, ten-row, ruby-stained...........110.00
Tumbler, vaseline..................................38.00
*Vase, 5½" h., cone-shaped, ruffled rim,
  vaseline..45.00

Hobnail Wine

*Wine, amber..25.00
*Wine, clear (ILLUS.)..............................25.00
Wine, green 22.50

HOBNAIL WITH THUMBPRINT BASE
Butter dish, cov., child's, blue 95.00
Creamer, amber (ILLUS. top next
  page)...29.00
Creamer, blue..35.00
Creamer, child's, amber 20.00
Pitcher, 7" h., clear 30.00
Pitcher, 7" h., ruby-stained rim 65.00
Pitcher, 8" h., blue 80.00
Spooner, blue 35.00

Hobnail w/Thumbprint Base Creamer

Sugar bowl, cov., child's, blue 85.00
Waste bowl, amber................................35.00
Waste bowl, blue 35.00

HONEYCOMB

*Butter dish, cov., non-flint, clear..........45.00
Butter dish, cov., non-flint, clear
  w/gold 75.00
Cake stand, 9" d., 5¾" h., cable
  border 35.00
Celery vase, flint...................................60.00
Celery vase, non-flint.............................22.00
Celery vase w/frosted Roman Key
  etching, flint...75.00
Celery vase, New York Honeycomb,
  flint 45.00
Celery vase, New York Honeycomb,
  non-flint..28.00
Champagne, flint 40.00
*Champagne, non-flint...........................30.00
Claret, flint 50.00
Claret, New York Honeycomb, flint.......45.00
Compote, open, 7" d., 7" h., flint...........55.00
Compote, open, 8" d., 6¼" h., flint......110.00
*Creamer, non-flint................................45.00
Decanter w/bar lip, flint, 10½" h..........110.00
Decanter w/original stopper, flint,
  13" h...110.00
Egg cup, flint..30.00
Egg cup, New York Honeycomb, flint...30.00
Goblet, flint 36.00
Goblet, flint, engraved 65.00
*Goblet, non-flint...................................14.00
Goblet, Laredo Honeycomb...................45.00
Goblet, New York Honeycomb, flint......22.00
Mug, flint..28.00
Mug, child's..35.00
Mustard pot, w/original pewter lid,
  etched, flint 75.00
Pitcher, milk, flint..................................90.00
Pitcher, water, 8½" h., molded handle,
  polished pontil, flint ....150.00 to 175.00
*Salt & pepper shakers w/original tops,
  non-flint, pr. 75.00
Sauce dish, flint 12.50
Spillholder, flint 40.00

Spooner, non-flint 23.00
Tumbler, bar 24.00
Tumbler, Vernon Honeycomb, flint.......65.00
Wine, flint 35.00
*Wine, non-flint 10.00

HORN OF PLENTY (McKee's Comet)

Horn of Plenty Spillholder

Bar bottle w/original stopper, qt. 150.00
Bowl, 7½" d...70.00
Bowl, 8" oval 110.00
Butter dish, cov....................................125.00
Butter pat...16.00
Celery vase..200.00
Champagne...195.00
Compote, cov., 6¼" d., 7½" h. 250.00
Compote, open, 6" d...............................75.00
Compote, open, 7" d., 3" h...................125.00
Compote, open, 7" d., 5½" h................225.00
Compote, open, 7" d., 7½" h., waffle
  base 110.00
Compote, open, 8" d., 6" h...................130.00
Compote, open, 8" d., 8" h...................124.00
Compote, open, 9" d., low stand..........100.00
Compote, open, 9" d., 8½" h................195.00
Compote, open, 10½" d., 9¾" h.........350.00
Creamer, applied handle, 7" h. 158.00
Creamer & cov. sugar bowl, pr. 325.00
Decanter, bar lip, pt. 110.00
Decanter w/original stopper, pt...........150.00
Decanter w/original stopper, qt...........175.00
Dish, 6¾ x 10", 2¼" h. 140.00
Egg cup, 3¾" h. 48.00
*Goblet..73.50
*Hat whimsey.......................................350.00
Honey dish...18.00
*Lamp, w/whale oil burner, all-glass,
  11" h...............................200.00 to 250.00
Peppersauce bottle w/stopper.............168.00
Plate, 6" d., canary yellow 247.50
Plate, 6" d., clear 95.00
Relish, 5 x 7" oval 95.00
Salt dip, master size, oval.....................85.00
Sauce dish, 3½" to 5" d. 17.00
Spillholder, 4½" h. (ILLUS.) 80.00

Sugar bowl, cov. 120.00
*Tumbler, water, 3⅝" h. 85.00
Tumbler, whiskey, 3" h. 130.00
Tumbler, whiskey, handled.................220.00
Wine 175.00

HORSESHOE (Good Luck or Prayer Rug)

Horseshoe Goblet

Bowl, cov., 5 x 8" oval, flat, triple
   horseshoe finial................................295.00
Bowl, open, 7" d., footed......................47.50
Bowl, open, 5 x 8" oval, footed 30.00
Bowl, open, 6 x 9" oval 27.50
*Bread tray, single horseshoe
   handles 50.00
Bread tray, double horseshoe
   handles 87.00
Butter dish, cov...................................115.00
Cake stand, 7" d. 35.00
Cake stand, 8" d., 6½" h. 76.00
Cake stand, 9" d., 6½" h. 69.00
Cake stand, 10" d. 87.00
Cake stand, 10¾" d. 127.00
Celery vase...87.00
Cheese dish, cov., w/woman churning
   butter in base 275.00
Compote, cov., 7" d., high stand...........75.00
Compote, cov., 8" d., low stand..........210.00
Compote, cov., 8" d., high stand.........175.00
Creamer..35.00
Doughnut stand 95.00
Goblet, knob stem 40.00
Goblet, plain stem (ILLUS.) 27.50
Marmalade jar, cov. 225.00
Pitcher, milk 90.00
Pitcher, water.....................................128.00
Plate, 7" d. 45.00
Plate, 8" d. 80.00
Plate, 10" d. 86.00
Relish, 5 x 8"...5.00
Salt dip, individual size 17.50
Salt dip, master size, horseshoe
   shape 100.00
Sauce dish, flat or footed.....................14.00
Spooner...35.00
Wine 295.00

HUBER

Ale glass...45.00
Celery vase..50.00
Champagne, straight sides...................45.00
Egg cup, single 30.00
Egg cup, double, engraved...................90.00
Goblet, barrel-shaped, clear 25.00
Goblet, engraved, clear 42.50
Goblet, straight-sided, clear.................25.00
Spooner...28.50
Sugar bowl, cov. 56.00
Tumbler, bar 22.50
Wine, clear...15.00
Wine, engraved 40.00

HUMMINGBIRD (Flying Robin or Bird & Fern)

Butter dish, cov., blue........................110.00
Butter dish, cov., clear 49.00
Celery vase..32.50
Creamer, amber ....75.00 to 100.00
Creamer, blue.......................................85.00
Creamer, clear......................................45.00
Goblet, amber.......................................65.00
Goblet, blue..65.00
Goblet, clear 50.00
Pitcher, water, amber 150.00
Pitcher, water, clear..............................90.00
Spooner, amber....................................40.00
Spooner, clear......................................30.00
Sugar bowl, cov., blue 110.00
Tray, water, amber 155.00
Tray, water, clear..................................50.00
Tumbler, amber 60.00
Wine 64.00

ILLINOIS

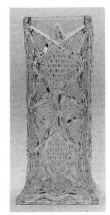

Illinois Straw Jar

Basket, applied handle, 7 x 7" 95.00
Bowl, 6" sq..26.00
*Butter dish, cov., 7" sq. 75.00
Celery tray 35.00
*Celery vase 37.50
Cheese dish, cov., square 60.00
Creamer, small 25.00

Creamer, large 40.00
Cruet w/original stopper 110.00
Doughnut stand, 7½" sq., 4¼" h. 65.00
Pitcher, water, tankard 75.00
Pitcher, water, tankard, w/glass lid 125.00
Pitcher, water, squatty, silver plate
   rim, clear 95.00
Pitcher, water, squatty, silver plate
   rim, green 175.00
Plate, 7" sq. 25.00
Relish, 3 x 8½" 17.50
Sauce dish 14.00
Soda fountain (straw-holder) jar,
   cov., 12½" h. 250.00
Soda fountain (straw-holder) jar,
   no lid, 12½" h. (ILLUS.) 110.00
Sugar shaker w/original pewter top 65.00
Toothpick holder 30.00
Vase, 6" h. 25.00
Vase, 9" h., 4" d. 41.00

INDIANA

Cruet w/original stopper 28.00
Spooner 20.00
Toothpick holder 25.00

INDIANA SWIRL - See Feather Pattern

INVERTED FERN

Inverted Fern Sugar Bowl

Bowl, 7" d. 45.00
Butter dish, cov. 85.00
Creamer, applied handle 150.00
Egg cup 38.00
*Goblet 46.00
Pitcher, water 360.00
Salt dip, master size, footed 40.00
Sauce dish, 4" d. 17.50
Spooner 50.00
Sugar bowl, cov. (ILLUS.) 60.00
Wine 45.00

INVERTED LOOPS & FANS - See Maryland Pattern

IOWA (Paneled Zipper or Zippered Block)

Compote, jelly 24.00
Cruet w/original stopper 50.00
Lamp, kerosene-type 105.00
Olive dish, handled 22.50
Pitcher, water, gold trim 95.00
Punch cup 22.00
Salt & pepper shakers w/original tops,
   clear, pr. 45.00
Salt & pepper shakers w/original tops,
   ruby-stained, pr. 150.00
Sauce dish, flat 15.00
Toothpick holder, clear 21.00
Toothpick holder, ruby-stained 60.00
Wine 30.00
Wine, w/gold trim 35.00

IRISH COLUMN - See Broken Column Pattern

IVY IN SNOW

Ivy in Snow Sauce Dish

Bowl, 7" d. 22.00
*Cake stand, 8" to 10" d. 42.00
*Celery vase, 8" h. 35.00
*Creamer, clear 25.00
Creamer, ruby-stained ivy sprigs 85.00
*Goblet, clear 50.00
Goblet, green & red ivy sprigs & gold
   band at top & base 175.00
Honey dish, cov., amber-stained ivy
   sprigs 87.50
Plate, 10" d. 30.00
*Sauce dish, flat or footed (ILLUS.) 12.00
*Spooner, clear 28.00
Sugar bowl, cov., clear 30.00
Sugar bowl, cov., ruby-stained 135.00
Syrup jug w/original top, clear 70.00
Syrup jug w/original top, ruby-stained
   ivy sprigs 295.00
Tumbler, clear 30.00
Tumbler, ruby-stained 40.00
Wine, clear 38.00

JACOB'S LADDER (Maltese)

Bowl, 7½ x 10¾" oval 25.00
Bowl, 9" d., flat 40.00
Butter dish, cov., Maltese Cross finial .. 55.00
Cake stand, 8" to 12" d. 52.00
Celery vase 38.00

Compote, cov., 8¼" d., high stand......128.00
Compote, open, 7" d., high stand 35.00
Compote, open, 8" d., high stand 42.00
Compote, open, 10" d., 5" h..................42.00
Compote, open, 10" d., high stand 55.00
*Creamer 35.00
Cruet w/original stopper, footed............85.00
Dish, 8" oval.......................................18.00
Goblet..65.00
Honey dish, open...................................9.00
Marmalade jar, cov. ....100.00 to 135.00
Pickle dish, Maltese Cross handle........18.00
Pitcher, water, applied handle 185.00
Plate, 6" d., amber 105.00
Plate, 6" d., clear 35.00
Plate, 6" d., purple 110.00
Relish, Maltese Cross handles,
  5½ x 9½" oval 20.00
Salt dip, master size, footed 25.00
Sauce dish, flat or footed, blue.............20.00
Sauce dish, flat or footed, canary 72.00
Sauce dish, flat or footed, clear.............8.00
Spooner...25.00
Sugar bowl, cov. 65.00
Syrup jug w/metal top.........100.00 to 125.00
Wine 32.00

JEWEL & CRESCENT - See Tennessee Pattern

JEWEL & DEWDROP - See Kansas Pattern

JEWEL & FESTOON (Loop & Jewel)
Butter dish, cov......................................60.00
Compote, 6½" d....................................60.00
Creamer..24.00
Creamer, individual size 35.00
Relish, 4¼ x 8¼" rectangle...................17.00
Table set, creamer, cov. sugar & cov.
  butter dish, 3 pcs. 125.00

JEWEL BAND - See Scalloped Tape Pattern

JEWELED DIAMOND AND FAN - See Tacoma Pattern

JEWELED MOON & STAR (Moon & Star with Waffle)
*Banana boat, w/amber & blue
  staining 225.00
Butter dish, cov., w/amber & blue
  staining 70.00
Cake stand, w/amber & blue staining,
  10" d...235.00
Carafe..38.00
Celery vase, clear.................................25.00
Celery vase, frosted w/amber & blue
  staining 82.50
*Compote, open, 9" d., high stand,
  clear 52.00
*Goblet...38.00

Pitcher, water, bulbous, applied
  handle, w/amber & blue staining......175.00
Salt shaker w/original top, w/amber
  & blue staining 125.00
Spooner, w/amber & blue staining........48.00
Tumbler, clear......................................22.50
Tumbler, w/amber & blue staining 60.00
*Wine...42.50

JOB'S TEARS - See Art Pattern

JUMBO and JUMBO & BARNUM

Jumbo Marmalade Jar

Butter dish & cover w/frosted elephant
  finial, oblong.....................................700.00
Castor holder (no bottles) 100.00
Creamer..185.00
Creamer, w/Barnum head at handle...295.00
Marmalade jar w/Barnum head
  handles & cover w/frosted elephant
  finial (ILLUS.) 450.00
Spoon rack ....600.00 to 750.00
Sugar bowl w/Barnum head handles
  & cover w/frosted elephant
  finial ....350.00 to 450.00

KAMONI - See Pennsylvania Pattern

KANSAS (Jewel & Dewdrop)
Banana bowl...55.00
Bowl, 7½" d..22.00
Bowl, 8½" d..35.00
Bread tray, "Our Daily Bread", 10½"
  oval 42.50
Butter dish, cov....................................65.00
Cake stand, 8" to 10" d. 48.00
Cake tray, "Cake Plate," 10½" oval 78.00
Celery vase...45.00
Compote, cov., 7" d., high stand.........125.00
Compote, open, jelly, 5" d....................42.00
Compote, open, 8" d., high stand 57.50
Creamer..47.00
Goblet..62.50
Mug, small, 3½" h. 30.00

Pitcher, milk 72.00
Pitcher, water 60.00
Relish, 8½" oval 28.00
Sauce dish, 4" d 13.50
Spooner 75.00
Toothpick holder 55.00
Tumbler, water, footed 55.00
Wine 55.00

KENTUCKY

Kentucky Sauce Dish

Celery tray 25.00
Nappy, handled, green 15.00
Punch cup, clear 7.00
Punch cup, green 28.00
Sauce dish, footed, blue w/gold
  (ILLUS.) 32.00
Sauce dish, footed, clear 7.00
Sauce dish, footed, green 14.00
Toothpick holder, clear 30.00
Toothpick holder, green 100.00
Tumbler, green 50.00
Wine, clear 24.00
Wine, green 45.00

KING'S CROWN (Also see Ruby Thumbprint)

Banana stand 130.00
Bowl, berry or fruit, 8¼" d., flared rim ...27.00
Bowl, 9¼" oval, scalloped rim, round
  base 67.50
Butter dish, cov. 65.00
*Cake stand, 9" d. 85.00
Cake stand, 10" d. 85.00
Castor bottle, w/original top 16.50
Castor set, salt & pepper shakers, oil
  bottle w/stopper & cov. mustard jar in
  original frame, 4 pcs. 325.00
Celery vase, engraved 60.00
Celery vase, plain 48.00
*Compote, cov., 5" d., 5½" h.,
  engraved 30.00
Compote, cov., 7" d., 7" h. 95.00
Compote, cov., 8" d., 12" h. 92.00
Compote, cov., 11" d. 145.00
Compote, open, jelly 45.00
Compote, open, 7½" d., high stand 42.00
Compote, open, 8½" d., high stand 85.00
*Cordial 50.00
Creamer, clear 40.00
*Creamer, individual size, clear 16.50

Creamer, individual size, clear w/gold ..29.50
Creamer, individual size, w/green
  thumbprints 35.00
*Cup and saucer 55.00
*Goblet, clear 30.00
Goblet, clear w/engraved moose, doe
  & dog 95.00
Goblet, w/green thumbprints 25.00
Goblet, w/green thumbprints,
  souvenir 18.00
Lamp, kerosene-type, low hand-type
  w/finger hold 120.00
*Lamp, kerosene-type, stem base,
  10" h. 180.00
Mustard jar, cov. 62.00
Pitcher, 5" h., souvenir 40.00
Pitcher, tankard, 8½" h. 110.00
Pitcher, tankard, 13" h., engraved 122.50
Pitcher, tankard, 13" h., plain 195.00
Pitcher, bulbous 125.00
*Plate, 8" sq. 70.00
Punch bowl, footed ....225.00 to 250.00
Punch cup 22.50
Relish, 7" oval 10.00
Salt dip, individual size 37.50
Salt & pepper shakers w/original tops,
  pr. 65.00
Sauce dish, boat-shaped 22.00
*Sauce dish, round 17.00
Spooner 38.00
Toothpick holder, clear 28.00
Toothpick holder, clear, souvenir 50.00
Toothpick holder, rose stain, souvenir ..30.00
Tray, square 29.00
*Tumbler, clear 22.00
Water set, bulbous pitcher & 6 goblets,
  7 pcs. ....250.00 to 300.00
*Wine, clear 25.00
Wine, cobalt blue ....100.00 to 150.00
Wine, cobalt blue, souvenir 165.00
Wine, w/green thumbprints 15.00

KLONDIKE (Amberette or English Hobnail Cross)

Klondike Butter Dish

Bowl, 6" sq., frosted w/amber cross ...200.00
Bowl, 7¼" sq., scalloped top, clear
  w/amber cross 185.00
Bowl, master berry or fruit, 8" sq., clear
  w/amber cross 85.00

Bowl, master berry or fruit, 8" sq., frosted
w/amber cross 250.00
Bowl, 11" sq., frosted w/amber
cross 255.00
Bread plate, clear w/amber cross,
8½ x 11" oval 120.00
Butter dish, cov., clear 150.00
Butter dish, cov., clear w/amber
cross ....225.00 to 250.00
Butter dish, cov., frosted w/amber
cross (ILLUS.) ....450.00 to 475.00
Butter pat, clear w/amber cross............35.00
Celery vase, clear w/amber cross 138.00
Celery vase, frosted w/amber cross ...225.00
Champagne, frosted w/amber cross...700.00
Condiment set: tray, cruet, salt & pepper
shakers; frosted w/amber cross,
4 pcs. 1,350.00
Creamer, clear w/amber cross 90.00
Creamer & open sugar bowl, frosted
w/amber cross, pr. 200.00
Cruet w/original stopper, clear
w/amber cross 425.00
Cruet w/original stopper, frosted w/amber
cross ....700.00 to 750.00
Dish, oval, flat, shallow, clear w/amber
cross 130.00
Goblet, clear 95.00
Goblet, clear w/amber cross...............195.00
Jam dish, frosted w/amber cross,
4¾" sq., 5½" h., in silver plate
holder..125.00
Pitcher, water, clear..............................50.00
Pitcher, water, clear w/amber
cross ....250.00 to 275.00
Punch cup, frosted w/amber cross 85.00
Relish, boat-shaped, clear, 4 x 9".........40.00
Relish, boat-shaped, clear w/amber
cross, 4 x 9" 115.00
Relish, boat-shaped, frosted w/amber
cross, 4 x 9" 146.00
Salt shaker w/original top, clear
w/ambercross 68.00
Salt shaker w/original top, frosted
w/amber cross ....75.00 to 100.00
Salt & pepper shakers w/original tops,
clear 150.00
Salt & pepper shakers w/original tops,
frosted w/amber cross,
pr.....................................200.00 to 250.00
Sauce dish, flat or footed, clear w/amber
cross 22.50
Sauce dish, flat or footed, frosted
w/amber cross 72.00
Spooner, clear 40.00
Spooner, clear w/amber cross..............85.00
Spooner, frosted w/amber
cross ....275.00 to 300.00
Sugar bowl, cov., clear 95.00
Sugar bowl, cov., clear w/amber cross,
6¾" h..165.00
Sugar bowl, open, clear w/amber
cross 75.00

Table set, frosted w/amber cross,
4 pcs. 950.00
Toothpick holder, clear 125.00
Toothpick holder, clear w/amber
cross 375.00
Tray, clear w/amber cross, 11" sq. 45.00
Tumbler, clear.......................................25.00
Tumbler, clear w/amber cross 90.00
Tumbler, frosted w/amber cross 145.00
Vase, 7" h., trumpet-shaped, clear 35.00
Vase, 8" h., trumpet-shaped, clear 50.00
Vase, 8" h., trumpet-shaped, clear
w/amber cross 130.00

LACY MEDALLION - See Colorado Pattern

LEAF - See Maple Leaf Pattern

LEAF & DART (Double Leaf & Dart)

Bowl, 8¼" d., low foot 20.00
Butter dish, cov., pedestal base 90.00
Celery vase, pedestal base 35.00
Creamer, applied handle 45.00
Egg cup 21.00
Goblet..28.00
Honey dish, 3½" d. 5.00
Lamp, kerosene-type, applied handle ..75.00
Pitcher, water, applied handle 95.00
Salt dip, cov., master size......................95.00
Salt dip, open, master size 32.00
Sauce dish...9.00
Spooner 25.00
Sugar bowl, cov. 55.00
Sugar bowl, open...................................25.00
Tumbler, footed 30.00
Wine 36.00

LE CLEDE - See Hickman Pattern

LIBERTY BELL

Liberty Bell Plate

Bowl, berry or fruit, 8" d., footed 95.00
*Bread platter, "Signer's", twig
handles 100.00

Bread platter, w/thirteen original states,
twig handles, 8¼ x 13".......................85.00
Butter dish, cov.................................100.00
Butter dish, cov., miniature.................150.00
Compote, open, 8" d.............................75.00
Creamer, applied handle....................110.00
Creamer, miniature..............................86.00
*Goblet..45.00
Mug, miniature, 2" h...........................125.00
Mug, snake handle.............................300.00
Pickle dish, closed handles,
1776-1876w/thirteen original
states, 5½ x 9¼"oval..........................50.00
Plate, 6" d., closed handles, scalloped
rim, w/thirteen original states.............75.00
Plate, 6" d., no states, dated................62.50
Plate, 8" d., closed handles, scalloped
rim, w/thirteen original states.............60.00
Plate, 10" d., closed handles, scalloped
rim, w/thirteen original states
(ILLUS.)..95.00
Relish, shell handles, 7 x 11¼".............70.00
Salt dip..55.00
Salt shaker w/original pewter top.......110.00
Sauce dish..25.00
Spooner...62.00
Sugar bowl, cov..................................105.00
Table set, 4 pcs..................400.00 to 450.00

LILY-OF-THE-VALLEY

Bowl, 5½ x 8" oval................................32.50
Butter dish, cov..................................115.00
Celery vase...68.00
Champagne...39.00
Compote, cov., 8" d., low stand..........128.00
Compote, cov., 8½" d., high stand......130.00
Compote, open, 7" d., low stand...........47.50
Creamer, three-footed, molded
handle...65.00
Creamer, plain base, applied handle....58.00
Cruet w/original stopper......150.00 to 200.00
Egg cup...43.00
Goblet...75.00
Pitcher, milk, applied handle...............112.00
Pitcher, water, bulbous, applied
handle..120.00
Relish, 4½ x 7"....................................25.00
Relish, 5½ x 8"....................................28.00
Salt dip, open, master size,
three-footed.......................................60.00
Sauce dish..17.50
Spooner, plain base.............................45.00
Spooner, three-footed...........................75.00
Wine...155.00

LINCOLN DRAPE & LINCOLN DRAPE WITH TASSEL

Compote, open, 6¾" d., 5¼" h..............85.00
Compote, open, 7⅛" d., 5" h...............110.00
Compote, open, 7½" d., 3½" h.............50.00
Compote, open, 8" d., medium
stand...110.00
Compote, open, 8¼" d., 5⅛" h.,
domed foot...87.50

Creamer...200.00

Lincoln Drape Egg Cup

Egg cup (ILLUS.)..................................75.00
Goblet.................................125.00 to 150.00
Goblet w/tassel...................225.00 to 275.00
Salt dip, master size.............................55.00
Salt dip, master size, w/tassel.............125.00
Sauce dish, 4" d..................................22.50
Spillholder...54.00
Sugar bowl, cov..................................165.00
Syrup pitcher w/original pewter top,
clear..150.00
Syrup pitcher w/original top, opaque
white...600.00

LION - See Atlanta Pattern

LION, FROSTED - See Frosted Lion Pattern

LION'S LEG - See Alaska Pattern

LOCUST - See Grasshopper Pattern

LOG CABIN

Log Cabin Compote

Butter dish, cov..................................295.00
Compote, cov. (ILLUS.).......................350.00

Compote, cov., "Lutteds Cough
Drops" 325.00
*Creamer, 4¼" h. 132.00
Sauce dish, flat oblong 85.00
*Spooner, clear....................................125.00
Spooner, sapphire blue 395.00
*Sugar bowl, cov., 8" h., clear.............250.00

LOOP (Seneca Loop)

Butter dish, cov., flint 195.00
Celery vase, flint....................................75.00
Celery vase, non-flint............................27.50
Compote, cov., 7" d., 9" h., flint 75.00
Compote, open, 7" d., 5¾" h., flint........94.00
Compote, open, 7⅝" d., 6¾" h., flint.....65.00
Compote, open, lobed rim, 8" d.,
6" h., canary, flint 1,760.00
Compote, open, 8" d., 6" h., non-flint....75.00
Compote, open, 8" d., 8" h., flint...........85.00
Compote, open, 8" d., 8¼" h., milk
white w/fiery opalescence 600.00
Compote, open, 9¼" d., 6½" h., flint.....65.00
Compote, open, 9½" d., 7" h., flint......275.00
Compote, open, 10" d., 8" h.,
flint ....275.00 to 300.00
Compote, open, 12¼" d., 9½" h.,
flint 400.00
Cordial, 2¾ h., non-flint 35.00
Creamer, clear, flint 60.00
Decanter, w/original stopper, flint,
pt. 130.00
Egg cup, flint..22.00
Goblet, flint 25.00
Goblet, non-flint 12.00
Pitcher, water, applied handle, flint.....195.00
Salt dip, master size, flint....................25.00
Spooner, flint..32.00
Sugar bowl, cov., flint 100.00
Tumbler, footed, non-flint.....................35.00
Vase, 9⅝" h., flint................................75.00

LOOP & DART

Loop & Dart Compote

Bowl, 5 x 8" oval, round ornaments 37.50

Butter dish, cov., diamond ornaments,
non-flint 38.00
Butter dish, cov., round ornaments,
flint 80.00
Butter pat, round ornaments.................35.00
Celery vase, diamond ornaments.........32.00
Celery vase, round ornaments, flint......50.00
Celery vase, round ornaments, non-
flint 35.00
Champagne, round ornaments, flint 85.00
Compote, cov., 6½" d., high stand,
round ornaments................................90.00
Compote, cov., 7" d., 10" h., diamond
ornaments 65.00
Compote, cov., 8" d., 10" h., round
ornaments (ILLUS.) 95.00
Compote, cov., 8" d., low stand, round
ornaments 74.00
Creamer, applied handle, round
ornaments 45.00
Egg cup, round ornaments 24.00
Goblet, diamond ornaments.................50.00
Goblet, round ornaments......................30.00
Pitcher, water, round ornaments 125.00
Plate, 6" d., round ornaments 35.00
Salt dip, master size, round
ornaments 45.00
Spooner, diamond ornaments 15.00
Spooner, round ornaments...................32.00
Sugar bowl, cov., diamond
ornaments 45.00
Sugar bowl, cov., round ornaments,
flint 75.00
Tumbler, flat or footed, diamond
ornaments 25.00
Wine, diamond ornaments....................32.00
Wine, round ornaments 45.00

LOOP & JEWEL - See Jewel & Festoon Pattern

LOOP & PILLAR - See Michigan Pattern

LOOP WITH DEWDROPS

Celery vase...30.00
Compote, cov., 9" d. 55.00
Creamer...50.00
Goblet..35.00
Sugar bowl, cov. 25.00
Wine 27.00

LOOP WITH STIPPLED PANELS - See Texas Pattern

LOOPS & DROPS - See New Jersey Pattern

LOOPS & FANS - See Maryland Pattern

LOUISIANA

Bowl, cov., round, 6" d........................125.00
Bowl, open, square, 7" w. 20.00
Cake stand, high stand, 10" d..............68.00

Compote, open, deep bowl, jelly,
5½" d..18.00
Compote, open, deep bowl, 6" d. 19.00

Louisiana Goblet

Goblet (ILLUS.)......................................45.00
Mug..12.00
Spooner...38.00
Tumbler, water.......................................28.00

MAGNET & GRAPE

Magnet & Grape Goblet

Champagne, frosted leaf, flint.............176.00
Champagne, stippled leaf, non-flint......45.00
Cordial, 4" h., frosted leaf, flint.........150.00
Creamer, stippled leaf, non-flint...........35.00
Egg cup, clear leaf, non-flint.................33.00
*Egg cup, frosted leaf, flint...................83.00
Goblet, clear leaf, non-flint...................18.00
*Goblet, frosted leaf, flint (ILLUS.)........77.00
Goblet, frosted leaf & American Shield,
    flint..375.00
Goblet, stippled leaf, non-flint...............30.00
Salt dip, master size, footed, non-flint ..24.00
Sauce dish, frosted leaf, flint 18.50
Spooner, frosted leaf, flint....................68.00
Spooner, stippled leaf, non-flint............28.00
Sugar bowl, cov., frosted leaf &
    American Shield, flint 325.00

*Wine, frosted leaf, flint......................225.00

MAINE (Stippled Flower Panels)
Bowl, 6" d...30.00
Bread plate 26.00
Butter dish, cov.....................................55.00
Cake stand, 8½" d., green....................65.00
Compote, open, jelly, 4¾" d..................28.00
Compote, open, 7" d., clear...................32.00
Compote, open, 7" d., green.................52.00
Compote, open, 8" d., clear...................35.00
Compote, open, 8" d., green.................42.50
Creamer..28.00
Pitcher, water, clear..............................85.00
Pitcher, water, w/red & green stain.....115.00
Platter, oval...38.00
Relish, 7¼" l..14.00
Salt & pepper shakers, w/original
    tops, pr..63.00
Spooner...32.00
Syrup pitcher w/original top 70.00
Table set, 4 pcs. 275.00
Wine, clear...42.50
Wine, green 65.00

MALTESE - See Jacob's Ladder Pattern

MANHATTAN
*Basket, applied handle, 7 x 10",
    11½" h...145.00
*Bowl, 8¼" d. 25.00
Bowl, 9" d..22.00
Bowl, 10½" d..15.00
Bowl, master berry, pink-stained 40.00
Bread plate 20.00
Butter dish, cov.....................................48.00
Cake stand ....35.00 to 40.00
Carafe, water, pink-stained...................65.00
Celery tray 26.00
Compote, open, large 47.50
Cracker jar, cov., pink-stained 55.00
Creamer...27.50
Creamer, individual size 25.00
Creamer & open sugar bowl, pr...........42.00
Cruet w/original stopper........................47.50
*Goblet...25.00
Marmalade jar, cov. 37.50
Pickle castor in silver plate frame,
    w/tongs 110.00
Pitcher, water, pink-stained 100.00
Pitcher, water, w/silver rim....................90.00
Plate, 5" d., pink-stained.......................25.00
*Plate, 10¾" d. 20.00
*Punch cup 20.00
Salt shaker w/original top 24.50
Sauce dish, flat, amber or pink-
    stained 12.50
*Sauce dish, flat, clear..........................12.00
Spooner...20.00
Toothpick holder, blue-stained 55.00
Toothpick holder, clear 32.00
Toothpick holder, purple-stained eyes..30.00
*Tumbler...12.50

Tumbler, clear w/gold trim 25.00
Tumbler, footed 30.00
Tumbler, pink-stained 16.00
Vase, 6" h. 20.00
*Wine...25.00

MAPLE LEAF (Leaf)
Berry set: oval master bowl & 10
   footed sauce dishes; canary yellow,
   11 pcs. 145.00
Bowl, 5½" oval, clear 24.00
Bowl, 9" oval, footed 24.00
Bowl, 6 x 10" oval, footed, blue 60.00
Bowl, 6 x 10" oval, footed, canary
   yellow...55.00
Bowl, 6 x 10" oval, footed, clear 52.00
Bowl, 10" sq., canary yellow 48.00
Bread plate, Grant, "Let Us Have
   Peace," blue, 9½" d. 85.00
Bread tray, canary yellow, 9¼ x 13¼" ..55.00
Bread tray, clear, 9¼ x 13¼" 32.00
Bread tray, clear & frosted,
   9¼ x 13¼" 40.00
Celery vase...36.00
Compote, cov., 8" d., four log feet,
   clear & frosted................................175.00
Compote, cov., 9" d., high stand,
   canary yellow 163.00
Compote, open, 8 x 10½".......................65.00
*Creamer, canary yellow 65.00
Goblet, canary yellow 75.00
*Goblet, clear...38.00
Pitcher, milk, canary yellow 74.00
*Pitcher, water 45.00
Plate, 9" d., canary yellow 37.50
Platter, 10½" oval, blue.........................55.00
Platter, 10½" oval, canary yellow..........39.00
Sauce dish, leaf-shaped, canary
   yellow, 5½" l. 16.00
*Spooner, blue...45.00
Spooner, green..45.00
Sugar bowl, cov., canary yellow 75.00
*Toothpick holder....................................30.00
Tumbler, clear, frosted...........................40.00
Tumbler, clear, plain 35.00
Waste bowl, canary yellow 30.00
Wine 28.00

MARYLAND (Inverted Loops & Fans or Loops & Fans)
Banana bowl, flat, 5 x 11¼" 36.00
Bread platter 25.00
Cake stand, 9" d. 65.00
Celery vase...30.00
Compote, cov., jelly 32.00
Compote, cov., 7" d., high stand..........35.00
Compote, open, medium 28.00
Dish, oval, large.....................................25.00
Goblet (ILLUS. top next column) 33.00
Pickle dish 14.00
Pitcher, milk...42.00
Pitcher, water, clear...............................48.50
Pitcher, water, ruby-stained...............105.00

Maryland Goblet

Plate, 7" d. 22.50
Platter 30.00
Relish..30.00
Sauce dish..18.00
Syrup pitcher 55.00
Toothpick holder 35.00
Tumbler 28.00
Wine 50.00

MASCOTTE
Bowl, cov., 7" d. 90.00
Butter dish, cov., engraved..................85.00
Butter pat...12.50
Cake basket w/handle 70.00
Cake stand, 10" d. 48.00
Celery vase...40.00
Cheese dish, cov. 65.00
Compote, cov., 5" d. 44.00
Compote, cov., 7" d. 45.00
Compote, cov., 8" d., 12" h. 90.00
Compote, open, jelly...............................20.00
Creamer..35.00
Goblet..30.00
Jar, cov., globe-type, embossed patent
   date, milk white 265.00
Pitcher, water...125.00
Salt shaker w/original top 14.00
Sauce dish, flat or footed, each............11.00
Spooner, clear 30.00
Spooner, vaseline....................................135.00
Sugar bowl, cov., engraved 48.00
Sugar bowl, cov., plain 39.00
Tray, water, clear.....................................58.50
Tray, water, engraved..............................75.00
Tumbler, clear...28.00
Tumbler, engraved 34.00
Wine, clear..26.00
Wine, engraved 35.00

MASSACHUSETTS
Banana boat, 6½ x 8½" 55.00
Bar bottle, bar lip, 11" h. 50.00
Bar bottle, green, 11" h. 60.00

Bar bottle w/original pewter top,
11" h. 80.00
Bowl, 6" sq. 18.00
Bowl, 8" l., pointed sides.......................37.50
Bowl, master berry, 9" sq.....................32.00

Massachusetts Butter Dish

*Butter dish, cov., clear (ILLUS.) 55.00
Butter dish, cov., green.........................65.00
Champagne 45.00
Cologne bottle w/stopper......................48.00
Cordial 45.00
Creamer...32.00
Cruet w/original stopper........................42.00
Decanter w/stopper 88.00
Goblet 45.00
Mug, 3½" h., clear.................................20.00
Mug, 3½" h., clear w/gold trim 24.00
Plate, 6" sq., w/advertising 90.00
Plate, 8" sq. 35.00
Punch cup..14.00
Relish, 8½" l..12.50
Rum jug, 5" h..100.00
Sauce dish...15.00
Spooner..20.00
Sugar bowl, cov. 35.00
Toothpick holder 50.00
Tumbler, juice 19.00
Tumbler, water...25.00
Vase, 6½" h., trumpet-shaped, clear 22.00
Vase, 7" h., clear w/gold 24.00
Vase, 9" h., trumpet-shaped, clear 32.50
Vase, 9" h., trumpet-shaped, green......38.00
Vase, 10" h., trumpet-shaped, green....60.00
Whiskey shot glass, clear 16.00
Wine, blue...110.00
Wine, clear..35.00

MEDALLION

Cake stand, high stand, amber,
9¼" d. 40.00
Cake stand, high stand, 9¼" d..............36.00
Creamer, amber 35.00
Creamer, canary yellow.........................42.50
Creamer, clear..18.00
Goblet, amber...34.00
Goblet, green..45.00
Pitcher, water, amber, ½ gal.................65.00
Pitcher, water, blue, ½ gal. 75.00
Pitcher, water, clear, ½ gal. 85.00
Relish tray, amber 20.00

Spooner, green.......................................40.00
Tumbler, water, green 35.00

MEDALLION SPRIG

Butter dish, cov., amethyst/clear 70.00
Cruet..265.00
Pitcher, water, green/clear....................80.00
Syrup pitcher, green 345.00

MELROSE

Cake stand, 8" to 10" d. 29.50
Celery vase, ruby-stained.....................65.00
Compote, open, jelly, 5½" d..................29.00
Compote, open, 7" d., 7" h...................25.00
Goblet..20.00
Pitcher, milk 42.50
Pitcher, water..32.00
Salt shaker w/original top 20.00
Wine 18.00

MICHIGAN (Paneled Jewel or Loop & Pillar)

Michigan Celery Vase

Bowl, 8" d., clear....................................36.00
Bowl, 8" d., pink-stained w/gold trim.....75.00
Bowl, 8¾" d., scalloped & flared rim 28.00
Bowl, 10" d..35.00
Butter dish, cov., blue-stained 175.00
Butter dish, cov., clear 60.00
Butter dish, cov., pink-stained 375.00
Butter dish, cov., yellow-stained,
enameled florals ....150.00 to 175.00
Celery vase (ILLUS.) 45.00
Compote, open, jelly, 4½" d., blue-
stained 125.00
Compote, open, 8½" d., high stand 65.00
Compote, open, 9¼" d...........................85.00
Compote, open, flared, 9¾" d., pink-
stained, enameled florals.................425.00
Creamer, 4" h. 30.00
Creamer, individual size 45.00
Creamer, individual size, yellow-stained,
enameled florals 55.00
Goblet, clear 35.00
Goblet, clear w/blue stain 40.00
Goblet, clear w/gold...............................40.00

Goblet, clear w/green stain,
  w/enamel 49.00
Mug, clear..25.00
Mug, yellow-stained, enameled
  florals 28.00
Pitcher, water, 8" h. 48.00
Pitcher, water, tankard, 12" h., clear.....75.00
Pitcher, water, tankard, 12" h., pink-
  stained 245.00
Plate, tea, 6" d., yellow-stained w/pink
  florals 25.00
Punch cup, clear.................................6.00
Punch cup, enameled decoration.........25.00
Punch cup, pink-stained 30.00
Relish, clear..18.00
Relish, pink-stained 24.00
Salt shaker w/original top 27.50
Salt & pepper shakers w/original tops,
  individual size, pr. 75.00
Sauce dish, clear.................................13.00
Sauce dish, yellow-stained 19.50
Spooner, blue-stained 125.00
Spooner, clear 40.00
Spooner, pink-stained..........................71.00
Sugar bowl, cov., blue-stained 150.00
Sugar bowl, cov., clear........................75.00
Sugar bowl, cov., pink-stained, gold
  trim.....................................100.00 to 125.00
Sugar bowl, cov., child's, 4¾" h...........40.00
Sugar bowl, individual size 22.00
Syrup jug w/pewter top 165.00
Table set, pink-stained,
  4 pcs. ....350.00 to 375.00
Toddy mug, tall 45.00
Toothpick holder, blue-stained on top
  w/yellow enameled dots...100.00 to 125.00
*Toothpick holder, clear.......................37.50
Toothpick holder, clear, enameled
  florals 45.00
Toothpick holder, pink-stained, gold
  trim.....................................275.00 to 300.00
Toothpick holder, yellow-stained 55.00
Toothpick holder, yellow-stained,
  enameled florals 90.00
Tumbler, clear.....................................28.00
Tumbler, pink-stained, gold trim 55.00
Tumbler, yellow-stained, enameled
  florals 35.00
Vase, 6" h., clear 35.00
Vase, 6" h., pink-stained, enameled
  florals 40.00
Vase, 8" h., green-stained, white
  enameled dots 60.00
Vase, 12" h. 24.00
Waste bowl..68.00
Water set: pitcher & 3 tumblers; yellow-
  stained, enameled florals, 4 pcs. 225.00
Wine, blue-stained...............................40.00
Wine, clear...35.00
Wine, yellow-stained............................50.00

**MIKADO - See Daisy & Button with
Crossbars Pattern**

MINERVA

Minerva Compote

Bread tray, 13" l. 60.00
Butter dish, cov....................................80.00
Cake stand, 8" d. 82.50
Cake stand, 9" d. 95.00
Cake stand, 10½" d. 115.00
Compote, cov., 8" d., low stand..........175.00
Compote, cov., 8" d., high
  stand ....150.00 to 175.00
Compote, open, 8" d., 8½" h.
  (ILLUS.) 90.00
Creamer...45.00
Goblet..99.00
Marmalade jar, cov. 150.00
Pickle dish, "Love's Request is
  Pickles," oval....................................28.00
Pitcher, water.......................................200.00
Plate, 8" d., Bates (J.C.) portrait center,
  scalloped rim.....................................75.00
Plate, 9" d., handled, plain center.........56.00
Platter, 13" oval 60.00
Relish, 5 x 8" oblong............................32.00
Relish, 6 x 9" oblong............................59.00
Sauce dish, footed, 4" d.......................20.00
Sauce dish, flat, 5" d............................20.00
Spooner...42.00
Sugar bowl, cov. 70.00
Table set, creamer, cov. butter dish
  & spooner, 3 pcs..............................195.00

MINNESOTA

Basket w/applied reeded handle 75.00
Bowl, 6" sq..32.00
Bowl, 6 x 8¼".......................................38.00
Bowl, 8" sq...32.00
Bowl, 8½" d., clear...............................40.00
Bowl, 8½" d., ruby-stained...................100.00
Bowl, 7½ x 10½"....................................38.00
Butter dish, cov....................................44.00
Carafe..48.00
Celery tray, 13" l. 40.00
Cheese dish, cov. 58.00
Compote, open, 7"................................40.00

Compote, open, 9" sq. 50.00
Cracker jar, cov. 125.00
Creamer, 3½" h. 40.00
Creamer, individual size 15.00
Creamer, individual size, w/gold trim....18.00
Cruet w/original stopper........................50.00
Goblet..30.00

Minnesota Goblet

Goblet, clear w/gold (ILLUS.) 35.00
Mug...25.00
Nappy, 4½" d. 12.00
Pickle dish 12.00
Pitcher, water, tankard............50.00 to 75.00
Plate, 7⅜" d., turned-up rim.................17.00
Relish, 3 x 5".......................................10.00
Relish, 6½ x 8¾" oblong......................26.00
Salt shaker w/original top, ruby-
    stained 50.00
Sauce dish..10.00
Spooner, clear 35.00
Spooner, clear w/gold..........................52.50
Sugar bowl, cov. 45.00
Syrup pitcher w/original top 65.00
Toothpick holder, three-handled,
    clear 32.50
Toothpick holder, three-handled,
    green..125.00
Tumbler 18.00
Wine 23.00

MIRROR - See Galloway Pattern

MISSOURI (Palm & Scroll)
Bowl, 8" d...22.00
Bowl, 8¾" d., green 41.00
Butter dish, cov., green........................85.00
Cake stand, 9" d., 4¾" h. 40.00
Cake stand, 10" d. 62.50
Compote, jelly......................................32.00
Creamer..35.00
Doughnut stand, 6" d. 55.00
Pitcher, milk, clear 45.00
Pitcher, milk, green 125.00
Pitcher, water, clear.............................52.00
Pitcher, water, green 125.00

Sugar bowl, cov. 47.00
Syrup pitcher 68.00
Table set, green, 4 pcs. ....250.00 to 300.00
Tumbler, green 35.00
Wine, clear..36.00
Wine, green 55.00

MONKEY
Butter dish, cov....................................195.00
Mug, amethyst 360.00
Mug, clear..90.00
*Spooner, clear....................................125.00
Spooner, white opalescent 175.00
Sugar bowl, open...................................90.00

MOON & STAR
Bowl, cov., 6" d. 30.00
*Bowl, cov., 7" d....................................38.00
*Bowl, master berry, 8¼" d., 4" h..........35.00
Bowl, fruit, 9" d., footed........................35.00
Bread tray, scalloped rim, 6½ x 10¾"...65.00

Moon & Star Butter Dish

*Butter dish, cov. (ILLUS.) 46.00
*Cake stand, 9" d...................................65.00
Cake stand, 10" d. 95.00
Celery vase..38.00
*Compote, cov., 6" d., high stand 55.00
*Compote, cov., 6" d., low stand...........50.00
Compote, cov., 7" d., 9" h. 45.00
Compote, cov., 7" d., 11" h. 70.00
Compote, cov., 13½" h. 125.00
Compote, open, 7" d., 7½" h.................30.00
Compote, open, 8" d., 8" h....................58.00
Compote, open, 9" d., 6½" h.................35.00
*Creamer 52.00
*Cruet w/original stopper, applied
    handle...125.00
*Egg cup 35.00
*Goblet...45.00
Pickle dish, 8" l. 17.00
*Pitcher, water, 9¼" h., applied rope
    handle 150.00
Relish, oblong..20.00
Salt dip, individual size, footed 32.00
*Salt shaker w/original top 30.00

*Sauce dish, flat or footed, each...........20.00
*Spooner..45.00
*Sugar bowl, cov.....................................60.00
*Syrup pitcher w/original top...............125.00
*Toothpick holder.....................................21.00
*Tumbler, flat 85.00
*Wine..45.00

MOON & STAR WITH WAFFLE - See Jeweled Moon & Star Pattern

MORNING GLORY

Champagne, flint 375.00
Compote, 7¾" d., 5" h., flint 300.00
Compote, 9" d., 8" h., flint 425.00
Egg cup, flint.......................225.00 to 325.00
Honey dish, 3½" d., flint........................60.00
Salt dip, individual size, flint...............130.00
Salt dip, master size, pedestal, flint 225.00
Spooner, flint ....300.00 to 350.00
Sugar bowl, open, flint.........................190.00
*Wine, flint ....75.00 to 100.00

NAIL

Bowl, berry, master, ruby-stained.........85.00
Butter dish, cov.....................................72.50
Cake stand 42.50
Celery tray, flat, 5 x 11" 22.50
Celery vase, engraved...........................50.00
Celery vase, plain..................................26.00
Celery vase, ruby-stained......................65.00
Compote, jelly, 5¼", clear.....................67.50
Compote, jelly, ruby-stained.................85.00
Compote, 7" d., ruby-stained..............155.00
Cordial 55.00
Creamer, clear, engraved......................35.00
Creamer, clear, plain 50.00
Goblet, clear, engraved 65.00
Goblet, clear, plain.................................48.00
Goblet, ruby-stained 95.00
Pitcher, water, clear...............................85.00
Pitcher, water, ruby-
    stained ....200.00 to 225.00
Salt shaker w/original top,
    w/engraving 65.00
Sauce dish, flat or footed......................12.00
Spooner, clear 45.00
Spooner, clear, engraved 35.00
Spooner, ruby-stained 60.00
Sugar bowl, cov., clear 50.00
Sugar bowl, cov., clear w/engraved
    cover 40.00
Sugar bowl, open...................................17.00
Syrup jug w/original top 28.00
Table set, spooner, creamer & cov.
    butter dish, 3 pcs. 175.00
Tumbler, clear..15.00
Tumbler, ruby-stained............................60.00
Tumbler, ruby-stained, souvenir 42.50
Wine, clear, engraved............................55.00
Wine, clear, plain 52.00
Wine, ruby-stained, souvenir 59.00

NAILHEAD

Bowl, 7¾" d., 2⅝" h. 50.00
Butter dish, cov......................................46.50
Cake stand, 9" d. 30.00
Cake stand, 10½" d. 45.00
Celery vase..42.00
Compote, cov., 8½" d., 12" h. 90.00
Compote, cov., 12" d. 65.00
Creamer...26.00
Goblet, plain 38.00
Pitcher, water...40.00
Plate, 6" or 7" d. 18.50
Plate, 7" sq. 15.00
Plate, 9" sq. 22.50
Plate, 9" d. 22.00
Sauce dish, 4"..7.00
Spooner 19.00
Sugar bowl, cov. 45.00
Tumbler, ruby-stained............................35.00
Wine 25.00

NEPTUNE - See Queen Anne Pattern

NESTOR

Nestor Butter Dish

Berry set: master berry bowl &
    4 sauce dishes; purple, 5 pcs. 165.00
Berry set: master berry bowl &
    6 sauce dishes; blue, 7 pcs. 275.00
Bowl, master berry, green w/gold &
    enameling 65.00
Butter dish, cov., blue w/gold &
    enameling (ILLUS.)...........................150.00
Butter dish, cov., blue w/gold trim.......125.00
Butter dish, cov., purple
    w/enameling......................................125.00
Compote, jelly, blue w/enameling.........45.00
Compote, jelly, green w/enameling 35.00
Compote, jelly, purple............................32.50
Creamer, blue w/enameling...................75.00
Creamer, green w/gold & enameling 40.00
Creamer, purple.....................................75.00
Cruet w/original stopper, blue
    w/enameling......................................125.00
Cruet w/original stopper, green 85.00
Cruet w/original stopper, purple............95.00
Salt shaker w/original top, purple 55.00

Sauce dish, blue w/gold trim &
  enameling 35.00
Sauce dish, green w/enameling 35.00
Sauce dish, purple w/gold trim 25.00
Spooner, blue w/gold & white
  enameling 80.00

Spooner, green w/gold & enameling 35.00
Spooner, purple w/gold trim 30.00
Sugar bowl, cov., green w/gold &
  enameling 60.00
Sugar bowl, cov., purple
  w/enameling 125.00
Toothpick holder, blue 100.00
Toothpick holder, blue w/gold &
  enameling 225.00
Toothpick holder, green w/gold &
  enameling 150.00
Toothpick holder, purple w/gold &
  enameling 145.00
Tumbler, green 30.00
Water set: pitcher & 6 tumblers; green
  w/gold & enameled deco-
  ration, 7 pcs. 315.00

NEW ENGLAND PINEAPPLE
Champagne, flint 190.00
Compote, open, 5" d., low stand 85.00
Compote, open, 9" d., flint 145.00
Compote, open, high stand, 10½" d.,
  9⅜" h. (rim chips) 350.00
*Cordial, flint, 4" h. 119.00
Creamer, applied handle, flint 235.00
Decanter w/bar lip, flint, qt. 175.00
Decanter w/original stopper, flint, qt. ..205.00
Egg cup, flint 55.00
*Goblet, flint 72.00
Goblet, lady's, flint 135.00
Honey dish, flint 35.00
Pitcher, water 310.00
Plate, 6" d., flint 195.00
Salt dip, master size, flint 50.00
Sauce dish, flint 30.00
Spillholder, flint 60.00
Sugar bowl, cov., flint 155.00
Tumbler, bar, flint 105.00
Tumbler, water, flint 85.00
*Wine, flint 245.00

NEW HAMPSHIRE (Bent Buckle)
Creamer 25.00
Creamer, individual, 3¼" h. 25.00
Cruet w/original stopper, clear 60.00
Cruet w/original stopper, rose-
  stained 289.00
Goblet, clear 30.00
Goblet, rose-stained 60.00
Mug, medium size 18.50
Olive dish, diamond shaped, 6⅝" w.,
  rose-stained 20.00
Sauce dish, round, 4" d., rose-stained ..14.00
Sugar bowl, cov., breakfast size,
  clear 13.50
Sugar bowl, cov., breakfast size,
  rose-stained 17.00

Sugar bowl, open, individual, double-
  handled, rose-stained 21.00
Toothpick holder, clear 19.50
Toothpick holder, rose-stained 60.00
Tumbler, water 18.00

vase, 6" h., thick stem, rose-stained 22.50
Wine, flared bowl, clear 19.00
Wine, flared bowl, rose-stained 55.00

NEW JERSEY (Loops & Drops)
Berry set, master bowl & 3 sauce
  dishes, 4 pcs. 75.00
Berry set: master bowl & 6 sauce
  dishes, 7 pcs. 175.00
Bowl, 9" d. 28.00
Bread plate 28.00
Butter dish, cov., ruby-
  stained ....150.00 to 200.00
Butter dish, cov., w/gold trim 75.00
Carafe, water 75.00
Celery tray, flat 25.00
Compote, open, jelly 32.00
Compote, open, 7" d., low stand 32.00
Compote, open, 7" d., high stand 60.00
Creamer, clear 36.00
Creamer, ruby-stained 65.00
Creamer, w/gold trim 60.00
Cruet w/original stopper 45.00
Goblet, clear 32.50
Goblet, ruby-stained 195.00
Goblet, w/gold trim 30.00
Pitcher, water, bulbous ....150.00 to 175.00
Plate, 10½" d. 30.00
Relish 12.50
Salt shaker w/original top 35.00
Salt & pepper shakers w/original tops ..40.00
Sauce dish, flat 13.00
Spooner, clear 27.50
Spooner, ruby-stained 65.00
Sugar bowl, cov. 53.00
Syrup pitcher w/original lid 115.00
Table set, 4 pcs. 215.00
Toothpick holder, clear 48.00
Toothpick holder, w/gold trim 65.00
Tumbler, clear 28.00
Vase, 8" h., green 26.00
Vase, 10" h. 20.00
Water set, pitcher & 6 tumblers,
  7 pcs. 175.00
Wine 40.00

NOTCHED RIB - See Broken Column Pattern

OAKEN BUCKET (Wooden Pail)
Butter dish, cov., amber 70.00
Butter dish, cov., blue 85.00
Butter dish, cov., clear 65.00
Creamer, amber 45.00
Creamer, amethyst ....75.00 to 100.00
Creamer, blue 65.00
Creamer, clear 32.00

Creamer, vaseline 45.00
Pitcher, water, amber 80.00

Oaken Bucket Pitcher

Pitcher, water, amethyst
    (ILLUS.) ....125.00 to 150.00
Pitcher, water, blue............................100.00
Pitcher, water, clear............................55.00
Pitcher, water, vaseline 120.00
Spooner, blue 55.00
Spooner, clear 35.00
Spooner, vaseline................................48.00
Sugar bowl, cov. 50.00
Toothpick holder, amber.......................30.00
Toothpick holder, blue 22.50
Toothpick holder, clear 20.00

**OLD MAN OF THE MOUNTAIN - See Viking
Pattern**

**OLD MAN OF THE WOODS - See Queen
Anne Pattern**

ONE-HUNDRED-ONE
Bread plate, 10" d. 75.00
Butter dish, cov....................................55.00
Celery 47.50
Compote, cov., 7" d., high stand...........85.00
Compote, open 25.00
Creamer, 4¾" h. 32.00
*Goblet...42.00
Pitcher, water.......................................125.00
Plate, 7" d. 20.00
Plate, 8" d. 20.00
Relish..16.50
Sauce dish..13.50
Spooner..22.50

OPEN ROSE
Butter dish, cov....................................65.00
Creamer..40.00
Egg cup 22.00
*Goblet..32.00
Goblet, lady's..35.00
Salt dip, master size 24.00
Sauce dish..10.00

Open Rose Spooner
*Spooner (ILLUS.) 30.00
Tumbler 41.00

OREGON No. 1 - See Beaded Loop Pattern

OREGON No. 2 - See Skilton Pattern

OWL IN FAN - See Parrot Pattern

PALM & SCROLL - See Missouri Pattern

PALMETTE

Palmette Goblet
Celery vase...55.00
Compote, open, 8" d., low stand...........24.00
Creamer, applied handle 58.00
Cruet..95.00
Cup plate, 3⅜" d. 45.00
Goblet (ILLUS.).....................................45.00
Lamp, kerosene-type, table model
    w/stem 82.00
Pitcher, water, applied
    handle ....100.00 to 125.00
Relish..17.50
Salt dip, master size, footed 20.00
Sauce dish..10.00

Spooner ....
Tumbler, water, flat 76.00
Tumbler, water, footed 47.50
Wine 50.00

PANELED CANE

Goblet, amber.................................35.00
Goblet, blue 30.00
Goblet, clear 25.00
Spooner 18.00
Tray, water.....................................12.00

PANELED DAISY
Berry set, master bowl & 6 sauce
  dishes, 7 pcs. 85.00
Bowl, 5 x 7" oval 20.00
Butter dish, cov..............................45.00
Cake stand, 8" to 11" d., high stand 44.00
Celery vase....................................35.00
Compote, cov., 8" d., 12½" h. 125.00
*Goblet...25.00
Plate, 9" sq. 28.00
Relish, 5 x 7" oval 17.50
Spooner 30.00
Sugar bowl, cov. 45.00
Tray, water......................................31.00

PANELED DEWDROP
Bread platter, 9½ x 12½" 50.00
Celery vase.....................................38.00
Cordial, 3¼" h. 45.00
Creamer..25.00
Goblet...45.00
Sugar bowl, cov. 40.00
Wine 28.00

PANELED DIAMOND CROSS - See Heavy Paneled Finecut Pattern

PANELED FINECUT - See Finecut & Panel Pattern

PANELED FORGET-ME-NOT

Paneled Forget-Me-Not Compote

Bread platter, 7 x 11" oval 35.00
Butter dish, cov................................40.00

Compote, open, 7" d., high stand 50.00
Compote, open, 8½" d., high stand 40.00
Creamer...32.00
Cruet w/original stopper......................55.00
Goblet, amethyst 750.00
Goblet, clear 35.00
Mustard jar, cov. 40.00
Pitcher, milk 60.00
Pitcher, water, amethyst...................175.00
Pitcher, water, clear..........................65.00
Relish, handled, 4½ x 7¾"...................21.00
Relish, scoop-shaped, 9" l. 19.50
Sauce dish, flat or footed...................11.00
Spooner 30.00
Sugar bowl, cov. 35.00
Wine 125.00

PANELED 44 - See Reverse 44 Pattern

PANELED GRAPE
*Butter dish, cov. 46.00
*Compote, cov., 4" d., high stand 30.00
*Creamer...30.00
Creamer, individual size 25.00
*Goblet..30.00
Parfait 35.00
*Pitcher, water, 8¾" h. 55.00
*Sauce dish 15.00
*Spooner..25.00
Sugar bowl, open..............................28.00
Toothpick holder 38.00
Tumbler 25.00
Water set, cov. pitcher & 6 goblets,
  7 pcs. ....200.00 to 250.00
*Wine 16.00

PANELED HEATHER
Creamer...17.00
Cruet w/original stopper......................30.00
Goblet...28.00
Sauce dish, flat 8.00
Sauce dish, footed.............................17.00
Spooner 20.00
Table set, h.p. florals, gilt trim,
  4 pcs. 158.00
Tumbler 25.00
Vase, 6½" h. 17.50

PANELED HERRINGBONE (Emerald Green Herringbone or Florida)
Bowl, 6" d., ruby & amber-stained 55.00
Bowl, master berry, 9" sq., green 30.00
Butter dish, cov., clear 50.00
Butter dish, cov., green.......................73.00
Compote, open, jelly, 5½" sq., green....35.00
Cruet w/original stopper,
  green................................100.00 to 125.00
*Goblet, clear....................................35.00

*Goblet, green 75.00
Pitcher, milk, green..............................75.00
Pitcher, water, clear.............................42.00
Pitcher, water, green 85.00
*Plate, 9", green...................................35.00
Relish, 4½ x 8" oval, green..................15.00
Sauce dish, green................................12.50
Spooner, green.....................................25.00
Syrup pitcher w/original top,
  green......................150.00 to 200.00
Tumbler, green 21.00
Wine, clear..22.50
Wine, green 48.00

PANELED JEWEL - See Michigan Pattern

PANELED STAR & BUTTON - See Sedan Pattern

PANELED THISTLE
*Bowl, 8" d. 18.50
*Bowl, 8" d., w/bee...............................35.00
Bowl, 9" d., deep, w/bee.......................29.00
*Butter dish, cov., w/bee......................50.00
Cake stand 38.00
Cake stand, w/bee...............................60.00
Candy dish, cov., footed, 5" sq.,
  6¼" h...30.00
Celery vase..45.00
Compote, open, 5" d., low stand...........19.00
*Compote, open, 6" d., high stand........45.00
Cordial 18.00

Paneled Thistle Creamer

*Creamer (ILLUS.)................................45.00
*Creamer, w/bee...................................60.00
Cruet w/stopper 45.00
*Goblet..34.00
*Honey dish, cov., square....................60.00
Honey dish, open.................................10.00
Pitcher, milk 31.00
*Plate, 7" sq. 28.00
*Plate, 7" sq., w/bee 23.00
Plate, 9½" d. 26.00
*Relish, w/bee, 4 x 9½".......................24.00
Rose bowl, 5" d., 2¾" h. 40.00

Salt dip, individual size 17.50
*Salt dip, master size...........................12.50
*Salt & pepper shakers w/original
  tops, pr...65.00
*Sauce dish, flat or footed 14.00
*Spooner, handled................................45.00
*Sugar bowl, cov...................................45.00
*Tumbler 30.00
Vase, 9¼" h., fan-shaped 25.00
Vase, 13½" h., pulled top rim...............35.00
*Wine 24.00
*Wine, w/bee 30.00

PANELED ZIPPER - See Iowa Pattern

PARROT (Owl in Fan)
*Goblet..50.00
Pitcher, water..75.00
Wine 75.00

PAVONIA (Pineapple Stem)

Pavonia Tumbler

Butter dish, cov., clear, engraved.........85.00
Butter dish, cov., clear, plain 72.00
Cake stand, 10" d. 60.00
Celery vase, engraved..........................45.00
Celery vase, plain 40.00
Compote, cov., 6" d., high stand...........55.00
Compote, cov., 7" d., engraved 100.00
Compote, cov., 8" d., engraved 125.00
Compote, open, 7" d.............................48.00
Creamer, engraved...............................41.00
Creamer, plain 38.00
Goblet, engraved 36.00
Goblet, plain 35.00
Pitcher, water, tall tankard, clear,
  engraved..75.00
Pitcher, water, tall tankard, clear,
  plain 60.00
Pitcher, water, tall tankard, ruby-
  stained ....125.00 to 150.00
Salt dip, master size 16.50
Salt shaker w/original top 28.00
Sauce dish, flat or footed......................14.00
Spooner, clear 39.00
Spooner, ruby-stained 45.00

Sugar bowl, cov., clear 50.00
Sugar bowl, cov., green 88.00
Tray, water 74.00
Tumbler, clear, engraved (ILLUS.)....35.00
Tumbler, clear 32.00
Tumbler, ..., stained 40.00
Tumbler, ruby-stained, engraved..........45.00
Waste bowl 58.00
Water set: tankard pitcher & 6 tumblers;
   ruby-stained, 7 pcs. 375.00
Wine, clear, engraved....................32.00
Wine, clear, plain 21.00
Wine, ruby-stained........................39.00

PEACOCK FEATHER (Georgia)
Bonbon dish, footed.......................22.50
Bowl, 6 x 8" oval 27.50
Bowl, 8" d.................................30.00
Butter dish, cov..........................45.00
Cake stand, 8½" d., 5" h. 31.00
Compote, open, 6" d. 18.00
Compote, open, 6¾" d., low stand........25.00
Creamer....................................22.50
Cruet w/original stopper..................40.00
Goblet 25.00
Lamp, kerosene-type, low hand-type
   w/handle, 5½" h. 95.00
Lamp, kerosene-type, table model
   w/handle, 9" h., blue 220.00
Lamp, kerosene-type, table model
   w/handle, 9" h., clear 85.00
Lamp, kerosene-type, table model,
   10" h., amber 275.00
Lamp, kerosene-type, table model,
   12" h., amber 325.00
Mug.......................................40.00
Pitcher, water............................52.00
Relish, 8" oval...........................14.00
Salt & pepper shakers w/original tops,
   pr..85.00
Sauce dish................................12.50
Spooner...................................37.00
Sugar bowl, cov. 38.00
Tumbler 35.00
Water set, pitcher & 6 tumblers,
   7 pcs. ....250.00 to 275.00

PENNSYLVANIA (Balder or Kamoni)
Bowl, berry or fruit, 8½" d., clear w/gold
   trim......................................30.00
Butter dish, cov., clear 58.00
Butter dish, cov., green.................85.00
Cake stand 45.00
Carafe....................................45.00
Celery tray, 4½ x 11" 28.00
Celery vase...............................22.50
Creamer, 3" h., clear w/gold trim,
   small 25.00
Creamer, 3" h., green w/gold trim,
   small 75.00
Cruet w/original stopper..................44.00
Decanter w/original stopper, 10¾" h.....75.00
Goblet, clear 27.00

Punch cup, clear w/gold 20.00
Salt & pepper shakers w/original
   tops, pr................................65.00
Sauce dish, round or square 12.50
*Spooner..................................21.00
Sugar bowl, cov., child's, green w/gold
   trim...................................145.00
Syrup pitcher w/original top 55.00
Table set, child's, 4 pcs. 250.00
Table set, 4 pcs. 225.00
Toothpick holder, clear 38.00
Toothpick holder, clear w/gold............69.00
Toothpick holder, green..................140.00
Tumbler, juice 16.00
Tumbler, water, clear.....................23.00
Tumbler, water, clear w/gold trim 25.00
Tumbler, water, ruby-stained.............49.00
Tumbler, whiskey, clear...................16.50
Tumbler, whiskey, green w/gold trim 25.00
Vase, 5¾" h., green 60.00
Whiskey shot glass, clear 19.50
Whiskey shot glass, green................25.00
Wine, clear...............................16.00
Wine, green 25.00

PENNSYLVANIA, EARLY - See Hand Pattern

PETAL & LOOP
Bowl, 8" d., flat, flint 85.00
Compote, open, 9" d., 6" h., flint..........65.00

PICKET

Picket Sauce Dish

Butter dish, cov..........................60.00
Compote, cov., 6" d., high stand..........80.00
Compote, open, 6" d., high stand 60.00
Creamer...................................36.00
Goblet....................................45.00
Pitcher, water............................72.00
Salt dip, master size 42.50
Sauce dish, flat (ILLUS.).................10.00
Sauce dish, footed, 4½" d.................17.50
Spooner 50.00
Sugar bowl, cov. 50.00

PICKET BAND (Staves With Scalloped Band)
Goblet....................................45.00
Spooner...................................30.00

PILLAR
Bitters bottle............................40.00
Celery vase, 9⅜" h. 90.00

Champagne, flint, 6" h. 60.00
Decanter w/bar lip, pt.......................55.00
Decanter w/bar lip, qt.......................205.00
Goblet...85.00

PILLAR & BULL'S EYE

Pillar & Bull's Eye Goblet

Bar bottle 60.00
Decanter w/bar lip, 10" h. 75.00
Flip glass, 5" d., 7½" h. 175.00
Goblet (ILLUS.)....................................85.00
Wine 75.00

PILLAR VARIANT - See Hercules Pillar Pattern

PILLOW & SUNBURST
Creamer, cov., individual size...............15.00
Creamer & sugar bowl, pr....................42.00
Sugar bowl, cov. 20.00
Toothpick holder, clear w/gold trim.......25.00

PILLOW ENCIRCLED
Bowl, 8" d., ruby-stained........................51.00
Celery vase..35.00
Creamer, clear.......................................25.00
Cruet w/original stopper, clear
   w/enameled floral decoration.............35.00
Lamp, kerosene, finger-type.................75.00
Mug..35.00
Pitcher, water, tankard, clear................42.00
Pitcher, water, tankard, ruby-stained..102.00
Salt shaker w/original top 35.00
Salt & pepper shakers w/original tops,
   ruby-stained, pr................................85.00
Sauce dish, footed................................11.50
Spooner, ruby-stained 62.00
Sugar bowl, cov., clear 35.00
Sugar bowl, cov., ruby-stained 125.00
Tumbler, clear.......................................25.00
Tumbler, ruby-stained...........................42.00

PINEAPPLE & FAN
Bowl, 9" d...45.00
Celery tray 36.00

Creamer..35.00
Cruet, w/original stopper, green 235.00
Rose bowl...30.00
Salt dip, individual...................................8.00
Salt & pepper shakers, w/original metal
   tops, pr..40.00
Sugar bowl, cov. 45.00
Sugar shaker 43.00
Toothpick holder, clear 75.00
Toothpick holder, green w/gold 125.00
Tumbler, green w/gold...........................25.00
Wine 12.50

PINEAPPLE STEM - See Pavonia Pattern

PLEAT & PANEL (Darby)

Pleat & Panel Goblet

Bowl, 5 x 8"...32.00
Bowl, 6" sq., flat....................................28.00
Bowl, 7" d., 4½" h., footed 21.50
Bowl, 8" sq., flat....................................45.00
Bowl, cov., 8" rectangle, flat 90.00
Bowl, 8" rectangle, footed....................35.00
Bread tray, closed handles, 8½ x 13"...45.00
Bread tray, pierced handles.................35.00
Butter dish, cov., footed, tab
   handles ....75.00 to 100.00
Cake stand, 8" sq. 40.00
Cake stand, 9" to 10" sq. 75.00
Celery vase, footed...............................38.00
Compote, cov., 7" sq., high stand.........85.00
Compote, cov., 8" d., high stand...........98.00
Compote, open, 8" d., high stand 35.00
Creamer...25.00
*Goblet (ILLUS.) 28.00
Lamp, kerosene-type, stem 125.00
Marmalade jar, cov. 100.00
Pitcher, milk 180.00
Pitcher, water..125.00
Plate, 5" sq. 22.00
Plate, 6" sq. 22.50
Plate, 7" sq., canary.............................48.00
Plate, 7" sq., clear................................19.00
Plate, 8" sq. 32.00
Relish, cov., oblong, handled 65.00

...., rooted..............................22.50
Spooner...35.00
Sugar bowl, cov. 85.00
Sugar bowl, open...............................20.00
Tray, water, 9½ x 14"...........................45.00

PLEAT & TUCK - See Adonis Pattern

PLUME

Plume Compote

Berry set, 8½" sq. master bowl & five
    4½" sq. sauce dishes, 6 pcs. 95.00
Bowl, cov., 8" d. 42.50
Bowl, open, 6" d....................................24.00
Bowl, open, 8½" sq. master berry.........35.00
Bowl, open, 9" d....................................30.00
Butter dish, cov....................................48.00
Cake stand, 9" d., high stand...............50.00
Celery vase...38.00
Compote, open, 6" d., collared base 36.00
Compote, open, 7" d., collared base
    (ILLUS.) 40.00
Compote, open, 8" d., high stand 40.00
Creamer, applied handle, clear 28.00
Creamer, ruby-stained.........................60.00
Cruet w/original stopper.......................38.00
*Goblet, clear......................................32.50
Goblet, engraved 45.00
Goblet, ruby-stained & engraved..........75.00
Pitcher, water, bulbous, clear,
    engraved...75.00
Pitcher, water, bulbous, clear, plain......65.00
Pitcher, water, bulbous, ruby-
    stained ....200.00 to 250.00
Relish..22.00
Sauce dish, flat or footed.....................10.00
Spooner, clear 31.00
Spooner, ruby-stained 60.00
Tumbler, clear......................................35.00
Tumbler, ruby-stained, souvenir...........40.00

Thumbprint Pattern

POLAR BEAR

Polar Bear Waste Bowl

*Goblet, clear......................................125.00
Goblet, clear & frosted.......................175.00
Pitcher, water, clear............................525.00
Tray, water, clear, 16" l......................165.00
Tray, water, frosted, 16" l...................250.00
Waste bowl (ILLUS.)............................90.00

POPCORN

Popcorn Cake Stand

Cake stand, 11" d. (ILLUS.)..................70.00
Creamer...20.00
Goblet..40.00
Goblet w/raised ears of corn................41.00
Wine 35.00

PORTLAND
Bowl, 8" d..25.00
Bowl, 10" d., flared..............................25.00
Butter dish, cov....................................48.00
Cake stand, 10½" 55.00
*Candlestick.......................................110.00
*Celery tray...25.00
Celery vase...42.50
Compote, cov., 6½" d., high stand......125.00
Compote, cov., 7" d., high stand.........100.00
Compote, cov., 8" d., high stand...........40.00
Compote, open, 7" d., high stand 45.00

Cordial 25.00
Creamer...40.00
*Creamer, individual size.....................18.00
Cruet w/original stopper.......................45.00
Goblet...39.00
Pitcher, water..52.50
Pitcher, water, miniature......................26.00
Punch bowl, 15" d., 8½" h...150.00 to 175.00
Punch cup..18.00
Salt shaker w/original top 16.00
Sauce dish, 4½" d................................10.00
Spooner..25.00
Sugar bowl, cov. 55.00
Sugar shaker w/original top 50.00
Table set, clear w/gold trim, 4 pcs. 350.00
Toothpick holder 27.00
Tumbler 25.00
Vase, 6" h., scalloped rim....................28.00
Wine 29.00

PORTLAND MAIDEN BLUSH - See Banded Portland Pattern

PORTLAND WITH DIAMOND POINT BAND - See Banded Portland Pattern

POST (Square Panes)
Berry set, 7½" d. master bowl & 3 sauce
   dishes, 4 pcs. 47.50
Butter dish, cov....................................67.50
Cake stand, 9½" d. 55.00
Celery vase...32.00
Compote, cov., 5" sq., 10" h. 68.00
Compote, cov., 8" d. 85.00
Creamer...35.00
Goblet, engraved 55.00
Goblet, plain 35.00
Lamp, kerosene-type, collared,
   3½" h...125.00
Lamp, kerosene-type, collared, 5" h. ...125.00
Lamp, kerosene-type, collared,
   engraved, 5" h.................................125.00
Lamp, kerosene-type, 7½" h...............110.00
Lamp, kerosene-type, 8½" h...............125.00
Pitcher, milk 75.00
Pitcher, water..90.00
Salt dips, individual size, set of 6..........37.50
Spooner...30.00
Sugar bowl, cov. 40.00

POWDER & SHOT
Compote, open, 7⅞" d., low stand........95.00
Creamer, applied handle, flint...............95.00
Egg cup, flint...45.00
Goblet, flint (ILLUS. top next column)...62.00
Honey dish, flint....................................10.00
Salt dip, master size 44.00
Sauce dish...15.00
Spooner...40.00
Sugar bowl, cov. 95.00
Sugar bowl, open...................................50.00

Powder & Shot Goblet

Wine, flint, 3½" h...................................55.00

PRAYER RUG - See Horseshoe Pattern

PRESSED DIAMOND
Butter dish, cov., amber........................45.00
Butter dish, cov., blue 95.00
Creamer, amber, 4¾" h. 38.00
Creamer, canary, 4¾" h........................40.00
Goblet, blue 30.00
Salt shaker w/original top, tall, blue......47.50
Sauce dish, flat, round, blue 24.50
Sauce dish, flat, round, canary 22.50
Spooner, flat, amber 40.00
Spooner, flat, canary 35.00
Spooner, flat, clear 30.00
Tumbler, water, flat, blue 28.00

PRESSED LEAF
Butter dish, cov.....................................60.00
Champagne..45.00
Compote, cov., acorn finial, low stand..45.00
Egg cup 30.00
Goblet..45.00
Pitcher, water, applied handle 95.00
Salt dip, master size 31.00
Spooner...30.00
Sugar bowl, cov. 45.00
Wine 48.00

PRIMROSE
Bread plate 30.00
Cake stand, clear, 10" d. 48.00
Creamer...30.00
Goblet..30.00
Pickle dish 13.00
Pitcher, milk, blue 65.00
Pitcher, milk, clear 42.00
Pitcher, water..45.00
Plate, 4½" d., amber or blue................15.00
Plate, 4½" d., clear 13.00
Plate, 6" d., amber 16.50
Plate, 7" d., amber 22.50
Plate, 7" d., blue 16.00

Relish, amber, 5 x 9¼" 22.50
Relish, clear 12.50
Sugar bowl, cov. 40.00
Tray, water, 11" d. 34.00
Wine, blue..45.00

Primrose Wine

Wine, clear (ILLUS.) 25.00

PRINCESS FEATHER (Rochelle)
Bowl, cov., 8" d. 85.00
Bowl, 5 x 7" oval 25.00
Butter dish, cov.....................................50.00
Celery vase...40.00
Compote, cov., 8" d., low stand 100.00
Creamer..60.00
Goblet, flint 32.00
Lamp, kerosene-type, 12" h.................75.00
Lamp, kerosene, hand-type w/finger
　grip handle 120.00
Plate, 6" d., non-flint 29.00
Plate, 7" d., amber, flint 225.00
Plate, 7" d., clear, non-flint...................22.00
Plate, 8" d., non-flint 24.00
Plate, 9" d., non-flint 32.50
Spooner, clear, non-flint.......................26.00
Spooner, milk white, flint.......................48.00
Sugar bowl, cov., clear, non-flint 60.00
Sugar bowl, cov., milk white, flint........135.00

PRISCILLA (Alexis)
Banana stand 95.00
Bowl, 8" d., 3½" h., straight sides, flat ..38.00
Bowl, 8" d., 3½" h., w/pattern on base..45.00
*Bowl, 10¼" to 10½" d. 35.00
Butter dish, cov.....................................95.00
Cake stand, 9" to 10" d., high stand 65.00
Compote, cov., jelly 55.00
*Compote, cov., 8" d. 100.00
Compote, cov., 12" d. 145.00
*Compote, open, 8" d., 8" h. 55.00
*Creamer 45.00
Creamer, individual size 28.00
Cup & saucer...32.00
*Goblet...38.00
Pitcher, water, bulbous 120.00
Plate, 10½" d., turned-up rim................25.00
Relish...23.00

*Sauce dish, flat, 4½" to 5" d. 25.00
Spooner...35.00
Sugar bowl, cov. 45.00
Sugar bowl, cov., individual size..........31.00
Syrup pitcher w/original pewter top,
　clear 115.00
Syrup pitcher w/original pewter top,
　green w/gold 450.00
Table set, 4 pcs. ....200.00 to 225.00
Toothpick holder 32.00
Tumbler 45.00
*Wine...40.00

PSYCHE & CUPID

Psyche & Cupid Goblet

Celery vase...38.00
Creamer..40.00
Goblet (ILLUS.).....................................50.00
Pitcher, water...85.00
Table set, spooner, cov. sugar bowl
　& creamer, 3 pcs.............................185.00

PYGMY - See Torpedo Pattern

QUEEN (Daisy & Button with Pointed Panels)

Queen Goblet

Bowl, 8" d., footed, amber 25.00
Butter dish, domed cover, blue.............75.00
Dish, flat, 7" oval, amber.......................22.50
Goblet, amber.......................................33.00
Goblet, apple green (ILLUS.)................25.00
Sauce dish, flat, 4" d., amber...............12.50
Spooner, amber....................................25.00
Spooner, blue 45.00
Toothpick holder...................................25.00
Tumbler, water, flat, amber...................32.50
Wine 21.00

QUEEN ANNE (Bearded Man, Neptune, Old Man of the Woods)
Butter dish, cov.....................................65.00
Celery vase, amber 65.00
Celery vase, clear.................................40.00
Creamer..47.50
Pitcher, water, 2 qt...............................70.00
Spooner..40.00
Sugar bowl, open..................................50.00
Syrup pitcher 95.00

QUEEN'S NECKLACE
Cologne bottle, w/stopper, 3½" h..........75.00
Condiment set w/toothpick center,
    pepper & cruet w/stopper.................145.00
Goblet...70.00
Spooner..33.00
Toothpick holder 60.00

RAMPANT LION - See Frosted Lion Pattern

RED BLOCK
Bowl, berry or fruit, 8" d. 85.00
Butter dish, cov.....................................95.00
Celery vase, 6½" h. 135.00
Creamer, large......................................80.00
Creamer, small, applied handle............35.00
Cruet w/original stopper......................150.00
Decanter, whiskey, w/original
    stopper, 12" h..................................175.00
Dish, rectangular, 5 x 7½" 55.00
*Goblet..40.00
Mug, plain, 3" h.....................................26.00
Mug, souvenir, 3" h...............................42.00
Pitcher, 8" h., bulbous.........................225.00
Pitcher, tankard, 8" h. ....175.00 to 200.00
Salt shaker w/original top 49.00
Sauce dish, 4½".....................................35.00
Spooner..35.00
Sugar bowl, cov. 70.00
Tumbler, souvenir.................................32.00
Tumbler 35.00
*Wine 35.00

REVERSE 44 (Paneled 44, U.S. Glass "Athenia")
Berry set: master bowl & 6 sauce
    dishes; clear w/gold or platinum
    stain, 7 pcs.....................................225.00
Bowl, 8" d., shallow sides, clear
    w/gold or platinum stain 75.00

Butter dish, cov., clear w/gold or
    platinum stain..................................135.00
Champagne, clear w/platinum stain 75.00
Compote, jelly, clear w/gold or
    platinum stain....................................80.00
Compote, open, 5½" d., high
    standard, clear 32.00
Creamer, after dinner, clear.................45.00
Creamer, berry, clear w/gold or
    platinum stain....................................95.00
Creamer, table size, clear w/gold or
    platinum stain....................................30.00
Creamer, tankard, clear w/gold or
    platinum stain....................................30.00
Cruet w/original stopper, clear.............58.00
Goblet, clear 30.00
Goblet, clear w/gold or platinum stain ..60.00
Pitcher, tankard-type, footed, clear.....105.00
Pitcher, tankard-type, footed, clear
    w/gold or platinum stain 150.00
Sauce dish, 4" d., straight sides, clear
    w/gold or platinum stain 20.00
Spoonholder, handled, clear w/gold
    or platinum stain 55.00
Sugar bowl, open, after dinner, clear....45.00
Table set: creamer, cov. sugar bowl
    & spooner; clear w/platinum stain,
    3 pcs. 295.00
Toothpick holder, footed, handled,
    clear 35.00
Toothpick holder, footed, handled,
    clear w/gold or platinum stain 85.00

REVERSE TORPEDO (Diamond & Bull's Eye Band)
Banana stand 135.00
Basket, high stand 160.00
Bowl, 7" d., ruby-stained.......................22.50
Bowl, 7½" d...48.00
Bowl, 9" d., piecrust rim 75.00
Bowl, 10¼" d., piecrust rim 65.00
Butter dish, cov.....................................75.00
Cake stand 95.00
Celery vase...55.00
Compote, cov., 6" d., high stand..........85.00
Compote, open, jelly.............................40.00
Compote, open, 5" d., flared rim,
    high stand 50.00
Compote, open, 7" d., smooth rim,
    high stand 55.00
Compote, open, 8" d., piecrust rim,
    high stand 100.00
Compote, open, 10" d., piecrust rim,
    high stand 125.00
Creamer..67.50
Goblet...85.00
Goblet, w/engraved flower...................100.00
Lamp, kerosene-type, 9" h..................145.00
Pitcher, water......................125.00 to 150.00
Pitcher, water, tankard w/engraved
    flowers 225.00
Salt shaker w/original top 40.00
Sauce dish..22.00

Spooner..52.00
Sugar bowl, cov.......................................72.50
Tumbler..50.00

RIBBED FORGET-ME-NOT

Creamer..35.00
Creamer, individual size 25.00
Mug..20.00

RIBBED GRAPE

Ribbed Grape Plate

Compote, open, 8" d., 5" h....................85.00
Goblet...60.00
Plate, 6" d. (ILLUS.).............................36.00
Sauce dish, 4" d...................................20.00
Spooner...45.00

RIBBED PALM

Bowl, 8" d., footed...............................65.00
Butter dish. cov.....................................88.00
Celery vase..75.00
Champagne..125.00
Compote, open, 7¼" d., 4¼" h..............45.00
Creamer.............................125.00 to 150.00
Egg cup 45.00
*Goblet...45.00
Pitcher, water, 9" h., applied
    handle ....250.00 to 300.00
Salt dip, master size 35.00
Salt dip, master size, footed 50.00
Sauce dish..14.00
Spillholder..50.00
Tumbler 120.00
*Wine..65.00

RIBBED IVY

Butter dish, cov......................................95.00
Champagne ....150.00 to 200.00
Compote, cov., 6" d., high stand.........250.00
Compote, open, 7½" d., high stand,
    rope edge rim....................................100.00
Compote, open, 8" d., 5" h....................75.00
Compote, open, 8½" d., 7½" h., high
    stand..95.00
Creamer, applied handle 145.00
Egg cup 40.00

Ribbed Ivy Goblet

Goblet (ILLUS.).....................................55.00
Spooner...50.00
Sugar bowl, cov. 110.00
Sweetmeat, cov. 325.00
Tumbler, water......................................100.00
Tumbler, whiskey....................................85.00
Wine 80.00

RIBBON (Early Ribbon)

Ribbon Waste Bowl

Bread tray 35.00
Butter dish, cov.....................................72.50
Celery vase..38.00
Compote, cov., 8" d. 96.00
Compote, open, 8" d., low stand..........40.00
Compote, open, 8" d., 8" h., frosted
    dolphin stem on dome base.............295.00
*Compote, open, 5½ x 8" rectangular
    bowl, 7" h., frosted dolphin stem on
    dome base 295.00
Compote, open, 8½" d., 4½" h..............50.00
Compote, open, 10½" d., frosted
    dolphin stem on dome base.............395.00
Creamer..34.00
Dresser bottle w/stopper....................125.00
*Goblet...35.00
Pitcher, water.......................................120.00
Plate, 7" d. 34.00
Platter, 9 x 13" 60.00

Sauce dish, flat or footed......................12.50
Spooner 30.00
Sugar bowl, cov., 4¼" d., 7¾" h............72.00
Table set, 4 pcs. ....200.00 to 225.00
Waste bowl (ILLUS.).............................42.50

RIBBON CANDY (Bryce or Double Loop)
Butter dish, cov., flat.............................48.00
Butter dish, cov., footed........................50.00
Cake stand, child's, 6½" d., 3" h. 125.00
Cake stand, 8" to 10½" d. 38.00
Celery vase...45.00
Compote, cov., 7" d. 95.00
Creamer..32.00
Doughnut stand 32.00
Goblet.................................50.00 to 75.00
Pitcher, milk...42.00
Plate, 8½" d. 30.00
Relish, 8½" l...14.00
Sauce dish, flat, 3½" d..........................10.00
Sauce dish, footed, 4" d........................12.00
Spooner..24.00
Sugar bowl, cov. 48.00
Wine 95.00

RISING SUN

Rising Sun Wine

Butter dish, cov., green suns 85.00
Butter dish, cov., pink suns...................50.00
Celery vase, gold suns 55.00
Compote, open, jelly, pink suns............18.00
Compote, open, 7" d., 6" h.....................18.00
Cruet w/stopper 65.00
Goblet, clear..35.00
Goblet, gold suns...................................25.00
Goblet, green suns 21.00
Goblet, pink suns...................................25.00
Goblet, purple suns 25.00
Pitcher, water, clear...............................50.00
Pitcher, water, gold suns 44.00
Sugar bowl, open, three-handled,
    pink suns w/gold trim 25.00
Sugar dispenser, mechanical, in silver
    plate frame (worn)..............................65.00
Toothpick holder, three-handled,
    clear 28.00

Toothpick holder, three-handled,
    green suns 32.50
Toothpick holder, three-handled,
    pink suns..38.00
Toothpick holder, three-handled,
    red suns 45.00
Tumbler, red suns...................................25.00
Vase, 6½" h., 4½" d., gold suns............25.00
Vase, 6½" h., 4½" d., pink suns.............35.00
Water set: pitcher & 4 tumblers; clear,
    5 pcs. 120.00
Water set: pitcher & 4 tumblers; green
    suns, 5 pcs. 154.00
Wine, clear...25.00
Wine, gold suns 23.50
Wine, green suns....................................28.00
Wine, pink suns (ILLUS.)   29.00

ROCHELLE - See Princess Feather Pattern

ROMAN KEY (Roman Key with Flutes or Ribs)
Frosted unless otherwise noted

Roman Key Goblet

Celery vase..70.00
Champagne 120.00
Compote, open, 7¾" sq., 7¼" h...........65.00
Compote, open, 8" d., 6" h....................60.00
Decanter w/stopper, qt. 252.00
Egg cup 30.00
Goblet (ILLUS.).....................................45.00
Salt dip, master size 35.00
Sauce dish...13.00
Spooner...32.00
*Sugar bowl, cov....................................125.00
Tumbler, bar 98.00
Tumbler, footed 63.00
Wine 50.00

ROMAN ROSETTE
Bowl, 8" d...24.00
Bread platter, 9 x 11" 28.00
Butter dish, cov......................................55.00
Cake stand, 9" to 10" d. 58.00

Celery vase, ruby-stained.....................95.00
Compote, cov., 6" d., high stand...........70.00
Compote, open, jelly, 5" d.....................22.50
Cordial 47.50
Creamer...35.00
*Goblet..42.50
Marmalade dish, footed, clear 24.00
Mug, 3" h. 20.00
Pitcher, milk.......................................60.00
Pitcher, water.....................................78.00
Plate, 7" d. 33.00
Relish, 3½ x 8½"................................10.00
Sauce dish..20.00
Spooner..21.00
Sugar bowl, cov. 40.00
Wine, clear..48.00
Wine, ruby-stained..............................65.00

ROMAN ROSETTE, EARLY

Cup plate, opalescent, flint, 3½" d. 77.00
Honey dish, clear, 4⅛" d., flint.............20.00
Honey dish, cobalt blue, flint, 4⅛" d. 55.00
Honey dish, purple, flint, 4⅛" d...........200.00
Plate, 5" d., cobalt blue, flint 375.00
Plate, 6" d., deep amethyst, flint.........400.00
Sauce dish, cobalt blue, 4" d. 55.00
Sauce dish, reddish amber,
   5⅜" d...............................100.00 to 150.00
Toddy plate, purple, flint, 5½" d. 325.00

ROSE IN SNOW

Bitters bottle w/original stopper 100.00
Bowl, 7" d., footed, canary...................38.00
Butter dish, cov., round........................55.00
Butter dish, cov., square......................50.00
Cake plate, handled, amber, 10" d. 45.00
Cake plate, handled, blue, 10" d...........35.00
Cake plate, handled, clear, 10" d.........22.50
Cake stand, 9" d. ....100.00 to 150.00
Cologne bottle w/original stopper 95.00
Compote, cov., 6" d., 8" h. 85.00
Compote, cov., 7" d., 8" h. 95.00
Compote, cov., 7" d., low stand 125.00
Compote, cov., 8" d., 10" h., canary ...155.00
Compote, open, 5" d., blue 110.00
Compote, open, 6" d., canary 42.00
Compote, open, 6" d., low stand...........50.00
Compote, open, 8" sq., low stand.......110.00
Compote, open, 8" d., high stand 70.00
Creamer, round 35.00
Creamer, square..................................39.00
Dish, 8½ x 11" oval, 1½" h.................130.00
*Goblet, amber 45.00
*Goblet, blue.......................................85.00
*Goblet, clear......................................70.00
*Goblet, vaseline 32.00
Mug, blue, large.................................110.00
Mug, clear, 3½" h................................40.00
*Mug, applied handle, "In Fond
   Remembrance," yellow 35.00
Pitcher, water, applied handle 132.00
Plate, 5" d. 32.00
Plate, 6" d. 30.00

*Plate, 9" d., amber..............................40.00
*Plate, 9" d., clear................................30.00
*Relish, 5½ x 8" oval, blue....................65.00
*Relish, 5½ x 8" oval, clear...................23.00
Relish, 6¼ x 9¼".................................19.00
Sauce dish, flat or footed.....................10.00
Spooner, round....................................25.00
Spooner, square...................................28.00
Sugar bowl, cov., round.......................37.50
*Sugar bowl, cov., square.....................51.00
Tumbler 38.00

ROSE SPRIG

Rose Sprig Goblet

Bowl, 6 x 9" oblong 27.50
Bread tray, two-handled, canary...........40.00
Bread tray, two-handled, clear..............32.00
Cake stand, amber, 9" octagon,
   6½" h..68.00
Cake stand, blue, 9" octagon,
   6½" h..125.00
Cake stand, clear, 9" octagon,
   6½" h..70.00
Cake stand, 10" octagonal....................72.00
Celery vase..39.00
Compote, open, 7" oval, amber............58.00
Compote, open, 7" d., 5" h., canary......47.50
Compote, open, 8" oval 50.00
Compote, open, 9" oval, high stand,
   blue 22.00
*Goblet, amber 50.00
*Goblet, blue..55.00
*Goblet, canary....................................60.00
*Goblet, clear (ILLUS.) 40.00
Pitcher, milk, amber.............................80.00
Pitcher, milk, blue 95.00
Pitcher, milk, canary 75.00
Pitcher, milk, clear 45.00
Pitcher, water, amber 50.00
Pitcher, water, clear.............................48.00
Plate, 6" sq., blue................................45.00
Plate, 6" sq., clear...............................27.50
Relish, boat-shaped, amber, 8" l. 35.00
Relish, boat-shaped, blue, 8" l..............45.00
Relish, boat-shaped, canary, 8" l.........40.00
Relish, boat-shaped, clear, 8" l............32.50

Sauce dish, flat......................................13.00
Sauce dish, footed, amber....................18.50
Sauce dish, footed, canary....................20.00
Sauce dish, footed, clear.....................17.50
Tumbler 39.00
Whimsey, sitz bath-shaped bowl,
   blue, 7 x 10".....................................85.00
Whimsey, sitz bath-shaped bowl,
   canary, 7 x 10"..................................47.50
*Whimsey, sleigh (salt dip), amber,
   4 x 4 x 6"..47.00
Wine 36.00

ROSETTE

Bowl, 7½" d..16.00
Butter dish, cov......................................40.00
Cake stand, 8½" to 11" d......................28.00
Celery vase...28.00
Compote, cov., 11½" h..........................50.00
Compote, open, jelly, 4½" d., 5" h. 17.50
Compote, open, 7¼" d., 6" h.................30.00
Creamer...32.00
Goblet..32.50
Pitcher, milk...50.00
Pitcher, water, tankard..........................55.00
Plate, 7" d. 20.00
Plate, 9" d., two-handled.......................21.00
Relish, fish-shaped 12.00
Sauce dish...7.50
Spooner...31.00
Sugar bowl, cov. 32.00
Tumbler 16.00
Wine 25.00

ROYAL CRYSTAL

Royal Crystal Pitcher

Bowl, round, flat, 8" d., flared sides 12.00
Bread plate..25.00
Cake stand, high standard, 9" d. 25.00
Creamer, 5¼" h., ruby-stained..............59.00
Cruet w/original stopper, 5 oz...............35.00
Pitcher, bulbous, milk, 1 qt., ruby-
   stained (ILLUS.)..............................250.00
Salt shaker w/original top, ruby-
   stained 65.00

ROYAL IVY (Northwood)

Royal Ivy Sugar Shaker

Berry set: master bowl & 3 sauce
   dishes; craquelle, (cranberry &
   vaseline spatter), 4 pcs.....................175.00
Berry set: master bowl & 6 sauce
   dishes; frosted rubina crystal,
   7 pcs. 310.00
Bowl, 8" d., frosted rubina
   crystal ....150.00 to 200.00
Bowl, fruit, 9" d., craquelle (cranberry
   & vaseline spatter)...........................235.00
Bowl, fruit, 9" d., frosted craquelle 150.00
Butter dish, cov., rubina
   crystal ....150.00 to 175.00
Creamer, clear & frosted 45.00
Creamer, rubina crystal 165.00
Creamer, frosted rubina crystal 185.00
Cruet w/original stopper, clear &
   frosted..135.00
Cruet w/original stopper, craquelle
   (cranberry & vaseline spatter)..........495.00
Cruet w/original stopper, rubina
   crystal 295.00
Cruet w/original stopper, frosted rubina
   crystal ....350.00 to 375.00
Marmalade jar, w/original silver plate
   lid, clear & frosted 100.00
Pickle castor, frosted rubina crystal
   insert,complete w/silver plate
   frame................................350.00 to 375.00
Pickle castor, cased spatter
   (cranberry & vaseline w/white lining)
   insert, complete w/silver plate frame
   & tongs.............................300.00 to 350.00
Pitcher, water, cased spatter (cranberry
   & vaseline w/white lining).................325.00
Pitcher, water, clear & frosted 90.00
Pitcher, water, craquelle (cranberry &
   vaseline spatter)...............................350.00
Pitcher, water, rubina crystal 250.00
Pitcher, water, frosted rubina crystal ..300.00
Rose bowl, clear & frosted....................60.00
Rose bowl, rubina crystal 78.00
Rose bowl, frosted rubina crystal 95.00
Rose bowl, craquelle (cranberry &
   vaseline spatter) 180.00

Salt shaker w/original top, cased spatter
(cranberry & vaseline w/white
lining) 125.00
Salt shaker w/original top, rubina
crystal 48.00
Salt shaker w/original top, frosted
rubina crystal 78.00
Salt & pepper shakers w/original tops,
cased spatter (cranberry & vaseline
w/white lining), pr. 225.00
Sauce dish, craquelle (cranberry &
vaseline spatter) 50.00
Spooner, clear & frosted......................50.00
Spooner, craquelle (cranberry &
vaseline spatter) 150.00
Spooner, rubina crystal.........................65.00
Spooner, frosted rubina crystal............80.00
Sugar bowl, cov., frosted rubina
crystal 200.00
Sugar shaker w/original top, cased
spatter (cranberry & vaseline w/white
lining) 300.00
Sugar shaker w/original top, rubina
crystal 130.00
Sugar shaker w/original top, frosted
rubina crystal (ILLUS.) .....200.00 to 250.00
Syrup pitcher w/original top, cased
spatter (cranberry & vaseline w/white
lining) 490.00
Syrup pitcher w/original top, clear &
frosted...............................100.00 to 150.00
Syrup pitcher w/original top, frosted
rubina crystal ....500.00 to 525.00
Toothpick holder, cased spatter
(cranberry & vaseline w/white
lining) 145.00
Toothpick holder, clear & frosted..........47.50
Toothpick holder, craquelle (cranberry
& vaseline spatter) 235.00
Toothpick holder, rubina crystal............85.00
Toothpick holder, frosted rubina
crystal 125.00
Tumbler, cased spatter (cranberry &
vaseline w/white lining) 85.00
Tumbler, clear & frosted 52.50
Tumbler, craquelle (cranberry & vaseline
spatter)..76.00
Tumbler, rubina crystal.........................66.00
Tumbler, frosted rubina crystal.............70.00
Water set: pitcher & 5 tumblers; rubina
crystal, 6 pcs. 595.00
Water set: pitcher & 6 tumblers; cased
spatter (cranberry & vaseline w/white
lining), 7 pcs....................................955.00

ROYAL OAK (Northwood)
Berry set: master bowl & 4 sauce
dishes; rubina crystal, 5 pcs. 290.00
Bowl, berry, 7½" d., frosted crystal.......65.00
Butter dish, cov., frosted crystal 55.00
Butter dish, cov., frosted rubina
crystal 250.00
Creamer, frosted crystal 75.00

Creamer, rubina crystal ......150.00 to 175.00
Creamer, frosted rubina
crystal ....200.00 to 225.00
Cruet w/original stopper, frosted rubina
crystal 250.00
Pickle castor, rubina crystal insert,
w/resilvered frame & tongs 450.00
Pitcher, 8½" h., frosted crystal.............82.00
Pitcher, water, rubina
crystal ....300.00 to 350.00
Salt shaker w/original top, rubina
crystal 100.00
Sauce dish, rubina crystal 50.00
Spooner, frosted crystal.......................48.00
Spooner, frosted rubina crystal............95.00
Sugar bowl, cov., frosted rubina
crystal 180.00
Sugar shaker w/original top, frosted
crystal 95.00
Sugar shaker w/original top, rubina
crystal 138.00
Sugar shaker w/original top, frosted
rubina crystal ....145.00 to 165.00
Table set, frosted rubina crystal,
4 pcs. 595.00
Toothpick holder, frosted crystal...........60.00
Toothpick holder, rubina crystal..........150.00
Tumbler, frosted rubina crystal 90.00

RUBY ROSETTE - See Hero Pattern

RUBY THUMBPRINT
*Bowl, 8½" d. 90.00
Bowl, master berry or fruit, 10" l., boat
shaped 125.00
Butter dish, cov., engraved.................225.00
Celery vase..100.00
Champagne, souvenir 45.00
*Claret..65.00
Compote, open, jelly, 5¼" h..................49.00
Compote, open, 7" d., engraved.........150.00
Compote, open, 7" d., plain 145.00
Compote, open, 8½" d., 7½" h.,
scalloped rim...................200.00 to 225.00
Cordial, engraved 40.00
Creamer, engraved................................85.00
*Creamer, plain.....................................60.00
Creamer, individual size 30.00
Cup, engraved 35.00
*Cup, plain...30.00
Cup & saucer, engraved.......................65.00
*Cup & saucer, plain.............................60.00
*Goblet, plain 40.00
Goblet, souvenir 42.00
Pitcher, milk, 7½" h., bulbous 100.00
Pitcher, milk, tankard, 8⅜" h..............125.00
*Pitcher, water, tankard, 11" h. 132.00
Pitcher, water, tankard, 11" h.,
w/engraved leaf band 190.00
*Plate, 8¼" d. 22.00
Sauce dish, boat-shaped......................28.00
*Sauce dish, round 20.00
*Sherbet..20.00

Spooner 65.00
Toothpick holder, engraved 47.50
Toothpick holder, plain 38.00
Tumbler, engraved 55.00
*Tumbler, plain 36.00
Water set, bulbous pitcher & 6 tumb-
   lers,w/engraved family names &
   dated 1897, 7 pcs. 595.00
*Wine..40.00

SANDWICH LOOP - See Hairpin Pattern

SANDWICH STAR

Compote, open, 9¾" d., 8½" h.,
   scalloped rim....................................220.00
Decanter w/patented stopper, pt. 135.00
Decanter w/bar lip, pt............................75.00
Decanter w/bar lip, qt..........................125.00
Spillholder, canary yellow 275.00
Spillholder, clambroth 300.00
Spillholder, clear 65.00
Spillholder, electric blue...................1,200.00
Spillholder, sapphire blue 770.00
Toddy plate..25.00

SAWTOOTH

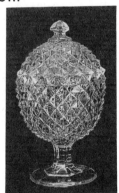

Sawtooth Covered Egg Cup

Butter dish, cov., clear, flint 78.00
*Butter dish, cov., clear, non-flint..........50.00
Butter dish, cov., sapphire blue, non-
   flint 230.00
Cake stand, non-flint, 7½" d., 6" h. 30.00
*Cake stand, non-flint, 9½" d., 4½" h....75.00
Celery vase, knob stem, flint.................45.00
Celery vase, knob stem, non-flint 42.50
Celery vase, stepped pedestal base,
   notched rim, flint 125.00
Champagne, knob stem, flint.................85.00
Champagne, non-flint.............................35.00
Compote, open, 7½" d., 5½" h...............38.00
Compote, open, 7½" d., 7½" h., flint.....55.00
Compote, open, 8" d., low stand,
   blue, flint 250.00
Compote, open, 8" d., low stand,
   canary, flint 200.00
Compote, open, 9½" d., 10" h., flint....100.00

Creamer, applied handle, clear,
   flint 75.00
Creamer, applied handle, cobalt blue,
   flint 230.00
Creamer, miniature, non-flint................29.00
Decanter w/original stopper, flint,
   14" h...145.00
Egg cup, cov., canary, flint 192.50
Egg cup, cov., clear, flint (ILLUS.) 100.00
Goblet, knob stem, flint.........................35.00
Goblet, knob stem, non-flint..................25.00
Goblet, plain stem, non-flint..................18.00
Lamp, whale oil, w/marble base 150.00
Pitcher, water, applied handle, flint.....215.00
Pomade jar, cov.....................................60.00
Salt dip, cov., master size, footed,
   flint 100.00
Salt dip, cov., master size, footed,
   milk white, flint 75.00
Salt dip, cov., master size, footed,
   non-flint...35.00
Salt dip, master size, flint.....................45.00
Salt dip, master size, non-flint 22.00
Spillholder, flint.....................................48.00
Spillholder, jagged sawtooth rim,
   sapphire blue, flint, 5½" h. 700.00
Spooner, clear, non-flint 50.00
Spooner, cobalt blue, non-flint..............85.00
Spooner, milk white, flint.......................75.00
Tumbler, bar, flint, 4½" h. 58.00
Tumbler, bar, non-flint 32.50
Wine, flint..45.00
Wine, non-flint.......................................18.00

SAWTOOTH BAND - See Amazon Pattern

SCALLOPED TAPE (Jewel Band)

Scalloped Tape Creamer

Bread platter ....35.00 to 45.00
Cake stand, 9½" d. 32.00
Celery vase, 8" h. 28.00
Compote, cov., 8¼" d., 12" h. 55.00
Creamer (ILLUS.) 25.00
Egg cup 25.00
Goblet..16.00

Pitcher, water, 9¼" h. 55.00
Sugar bowl, cov. 35.00
Wine, blue..55.00
Wine, clear...15.00

SEDAN (Paneled Star & Button)

Sedan Sauce Dish

Creamer...27.00
Goblet...22.00
Mug, miniature.......................................15.00
Sauce dish, flat, 4½" d. (ILLUS.) 4.00
Wine, clear...23.00
Wine, blue..85.00

SENECA LOOP - See Loop Pattern

SHELL & JEWEL (Victor)

Shell & Jewel Pitcher

Bowl, 10" d..25.00
Compote, open, 7" d., 7½" h.................55.00
Creamer...22.50
Pitcher, milk...32.00
Pitcher, water, blue................................82.00
Pitcher, water, clear (ILLUS.) 45.00
Pitcher, water, green 90.00
Sauce dish...8.00
Spooner...30.00

Tumbler, amber 32.00
Tumbler, blue...40.00
Tumbler, clear..18.00
Tumbler, green 44.00
Water set, pitcher & 6 tumblers,
 7 pcs. ....170.00 to 190.00

SHELL & TASSEL
Bowl, 7½" l., shell-shaped, three applied
 shell-shaped feet 55.00
Bowl, 9" oval, clear 50.00
Bowl, 9" oval, vaseline........................175.00
Bowl, 10" oval, amber...........................90.00
Bowl, 10" oval, clear 55.00
Bowl, 6½ x 11½" oval, amber 90.00
Bowl, 6½ x 11½" oval, blue 125.00
Bowl, 6½ x 11½" oval, clear 50.00
Bread tray, 9 x 13" 55.00
Bride's basket, 8" oval bowl in silver
 plate frame.......................................150.00
Bride's basket, 5 x 10" oval amber bowl
 in silver plate frame..........250.00 to 275.00
Bride's basket, 8" oval blue bowl in
 silver plate frame 350.00
Butter dish, cov., round, dog
 finial ....150.00 to 175.00
Butter pat, shell-shaped.......................16.00
Cake stand, shell corners, 8" sq. 42.50
Cake stand, shell corners, 9" sq. 62.00
Cake stand, shell corners,
 10" sq. ....100.00 to 150.00
Celery vase, round, handled.................85.00
Compote, cov., 4¼" sq., 8" h. 45.00
Compote, cov., 5¼" sq. 60.00
Compote, open, jelly.............................85.00
Compote, open, 6½" sq., 6½" h...........45.00
Compote, open, 7½" sq., 7½" h...........95.00
Compote, open, 8" sq., 7½" h..............56.00
Compote, open, 9½" d., 9" h.................90.00
Compote, open, 10" sq., 8" h................70.00
Creamer, round 45.00
Creamer, square....................................50.00
Dish, 7 x 10" rectangle..........................35.00
Doughnut stand, 8" sq., signed..........225.00
*Goblet, round, knob stem....................65.00
Mug, miniature, blue ....100.00 to 125.00
Oyster plate, 9½" d. ....225.00 to 250.00
Pickle jar, cov. ....150.00 to 175.00
Pitcher, water, round 225.00
Pitcher, water, square..........................125.00
Plate, shell-shaped w/three shell-
 shaped feet, large 70.00
Platter, 8 x 11" oblong 52.00
Platter, 9 x 13" oval..............................56.00
Salt dip, shell-shaped 16.00
Salt & pepper shakers w/original
 tops, pr..260.00
Sauce dish, flat or footed, 4" to 5" d. 20.00
Sauce dish, footed, w/shell handle 15.00
Spooner, round......................................51.00
Spooner, square 50.00
Sugar bowl, cov., round, dog finial 110.00
Table set, 4 pcs. 495.00

Tray, ice cream.................................125.00
Vase ....175.00 to 200.00

SHERATON
Bread platter, amber, 8 x 10".............40.00
Bread platter, blue, 8 x 10" 55.00
Bread platter, clear, 8 x 10" 30.00
Butter dish, cov............................40.00
Cake stand, 10½" d. 42.00
Celery vase....................................28.00
Compote, open, 8" d., high stand 32.50
Creamer, amber 35.00
Creamer, blue................................42.00
Goblet, amber....................................35.00
Goblet, clear 25.00
Pitcher, milk....................................32.50
Pitcher, water, blue.............................85.00
Pitcher, water, clear...........................42.50
Plate, 7" sq., amber 20.00
Plate, 8½" sq, ...20.00
Relish, handled, blue..........................22.50
Relish, handled, clear 16.00

SHOSHONE

Shoshone Jelly Compote

Banana bowl, clear, 8¼ x 10½" 45.00
Bowl, 8" d., ruffled, green 30.00
Butter dish, cov., clear w/gold trim........70.00
Cake stand, clear..............................45.00
Cake stand, green 48.00
Carafe...38.00
Celery vase, ruby-stained....................95.00
Compote, jelly (ILLUS.) 30.00
Compote, open, 7 x 9", scalloped rim...38.00
Creamer, clear w/gold trim 35.00
Cruet w/original stopper, clear..............55.00
Cruet w/original stopper, green 135.00
Cruet w/original stopper, ruby-
    stained 195.00
Pitcher, tankard-type 50.00
Plate, 7½" d., green 28.00
Relish, 7½" l...................................30.00
Salt & pepper shakers w/original tops,
    ruby-stained, pr..............................125.00
Salt dip, individual size 20.00
Sauce dish, ruby-stained....................23.00
Spooner, amber-stained......................45.00
Spooner, clear 35.00

Sugar bowl, cov., clear w/gold trim.......58.00
Table set, clear w/gold trim, 4 pcs. 200.00
Toothpick holder, clear w/gold trim.......40.00
Toothpick holder, ruby-stained 95.00
Wine, clear.....................................45.00
Wine, ruby-stained.............................55.00

SHRINE
Butter dish, cov..................................75.00
Compote, open, jelly...........................22.50
Goblet..50.00
Pickle dish 19.50
Pitcher, beer, 1 gal. 200.00
Pitcher, water...................................75.00
Tumbler, 4" h. 40.00

SHUTTLE (Hearts of Loch Laven)
Butter dish, cov.................................110.00
Cake stand 125.00
Celery vase......................................46.00
Cordial, small...................................32.00
Creamer, tall tankard..........................30.00
Goblet..60.00
Mug, amber 300.00
Mug, clear..28.00
Pitcher, water...................................140.00
Salt shaker w/original top 60.00
Spooner, scalloped rim........................50.00
Tumbler 50.00
Wine 18.00

SKILTON (Early Oregon)
Bowl, 8" d., 2½" h., ruby-stained...........30.00
Bread tray 32.00
Butter dish, cov., ruby-stained..............97.50
Cale stand, 9" d. 43.00
Compote, open, 7" d...........................55.00
Compote, open, 8½" d., low stand,
    ruby-stained 67.50
Creamer, ruby-stained.........................40.00
Goblet..33.00
Pitcher, water, tankard, ruby-stained..115.00
Sauce dish......................................11.00
Spooner, clear 28.00
Spooner, ruby-stained 44.50
Sugar bowl, cov., ruby-stained 82.50
Syrup pitcher w/original top 65.00
Tumbler, ruby-stained..........................38.00

SNAIL (Compact)
Banana stand, 10" d., 7" h..125.00 to 150.00
Bowl, 7" d., low 35.00
Bowl, 5¼ x 8", oval 35.00
Bowl, 9" d., 2" h. 50.00
Butter dish, cov..................................95.00
Cake stand, 10" d. 100.00
Celery vase.......................................45.00
Cheese dish, cov. 125.00
Compote, cov., 7" d., 8" h.,
    engraved..185.00
Compote, cov., 7" d., 11½" h. 145.00
Compote, open, 8" d., 6" h....................85.00

Compote, open, 10" d., 7" h.................145.00
Cracker jar, cov., 8" d., 9" h. 295.00
Creamer, clear.....................................58.00
Creamer, ruby-stained.........................70.00
Cruet w/original stopper......................125.00
Goblet..100.00
Pitcher, water, tankard.......................110.00
Pitcher, wine, tankard.........................295.00
Plate, 7" d. 46.00
Punch cup...32.50
Relish, 7" oval......................................22.50
Relish, 9" oval......................................31.50
Rose bowl, miniature, 3" h....................36.00
Rose bowl, 4½" h..................................43.00
Rose bowl, double, miniature 35.00
Rose bowl, medium..............................55.00
Rose bowl, large...................................85.00
Salt dip, individual size 25.00
Salt dip, master size, 3" d. 40.00
Salt shaker w/original top, clear............40.00
Salt shaker w/original top, ruby-
  stained 65.00
Sauce dish..18.00
Spooner, clear 42.00
Spooner, ruby-stained 75.00
Sugar bowl, cov., individual size...........75.00

Snail Sugar Bowl

Sugar bowl, cov., plain (ILLUS.) 68.00
Sugar bowl, cov., ruby-stained 95.00
Sugar shaker w/original top 115.00
Syrup jug w/original brass top 110.00
Tumbler 45.00
Vase, 12½" h., scalloped rim 75.00

SPIKED ARGUS - See Argus Pattern

SPIREA BAND
Berry set: master bowl & 6 footed sauce
dishes; blue, 7 pcs..............................150.00
Bowl, 8" oval, flat, amber 20.00
Butter dish, cov.....................................45.00
Cake stand, amber, 8½" d. 45.00
Cake stand, blue, 10½" d. 80.00
Celery vase...25.00
Compote, cov., 7" d., low stand,
  amber..55.00

Creamer, amber 32.00
Creamer, blue.......................................35.00
Creamer, clear......................................32.00
Goblet, amber.......................................34.00
Goblet, blue 33.00

Spirea Band Goblet

Goblet, clear (ILLUS.)...........................20.00
Pitcher, water..45.00
Platter, 8½ x 10½", amber 24.00
Platter, 8½ x 10½", blue 35.00
Relish, blue, 4½ x 7"............................32.50
Salt shaker w/original top, blue.............54.00
Spooner, amber....................................24.00
Spooner, vaseline.................................30.00
Sugar bowl, cov., blue 50.00
Sugar bowl, cov., clear 28.00
Wine, amber 23.00
Wine, blue...28.00
Wine, clear..15.50

SPRIG
Bowl, 7" oval...25.00
Bowl, 8" oval, footed.............................35.00
Bread platter, 11" oval 35.00
Butter dish, cov.....................................65.00
Cake stand 44.00
Celery vase...42.50
Compote, cov., 6" d., low stand............50.00
Compote, cov., 6" d., high stand...........90.00
Compote, cov., 8" d., low stand............76.00
Compote, cov., 8" d., high stand...........95.00
Compote, open, 6" d.............................32.50
Compote, open, 7" d., low stand...........38.00
Compote, open, 8" d., high stand 39.00
Creamer..37.00
Goblet...31.00
Pickle castor, resilvered frame &
  tongs...85.00
Pitcher, water..55.00
Relish, 6¾" oval....................................14.00
Relish, 7¾" oval....................................18.00
Relish, 8¾" oval....................................22.00
Sauce dish, flat or footed......................12.00
Spooner...25.00
Sugar bowl, cov. 55.00

Sugar bowl, open..................................20.00
Wine 45.00

SQUARE LION'S HEAD - See Atlanta Pattern

SQUARE PANES - See Post Pattern

SQUIRREL - See "Animals & Birds on Goblets & Pitchers"

S-REPEAT
Berry set, apple green 85.00
Butter dish, cov., amethyst w/gold......125.00
Butter dish, cov., clear 125.00
Butter dish, cov., sapphire blue
   w/gold 150.00
Compote, jelly 40.00
Condiment set, apple
   green...............................200.00 to 250.00
Condiment set, clear...........................190.00
Condiment set, sapphire
   blue ....200.00 to 250.00
Condiment tray, amethyst.....................37.50
Condiment tray, apple green 35.00
Cruet, amethyst 195.00
*Cruet, apple green 95.00
Decanter w/stopper, wine, amethyst ..175.00
Decanter w/stopper, wine, apple
   green w/gold 125.00
Decanter w/stopper, wine, sapphire
   blue w/gold..195.00
Pitcher, green 85.00
Punch cup, clear...................................16.00
Salt shaker w/original top, sapphire
   blue 40.00
Salt & pepper shakers, apple green,
   pr...70.00
Salt & pepper shakers, clear, pr. 38.00
Sauce dish, amethyst w/gold...............30.00
Sauce dish, apple green w/gold 27.50
Syrup pitcher w/original top 70.00
*Toothpick holder, amethyst................62.00
*Toothpick holder, apple green............50.00
*Toothpick holder, sapphire blue..........55.00
Tumbler, amethyst.................................40.00
Tumbler, sapphire blue........................38.00
*Wine, apple green 40.00
*Wine, sapphire blue 57.50

STAR ROSETTED
Butter dish, cov....................................55.00
Cake (or bread) plate, "A Good
   Mother Makes A Happy Home" 45.00
Compote, open, 6½" d..........................16.00
Compote, open, 7½" d..........................18.00
Creamer..30.00
Goblet...30.00
Plate, 7" d., amber 45.00
Plate, 7" d., apple green 35.00
Plate, 7" d., blue 12.00
Plate, 7" d., clear 10.00
Sauce dish, flat or footed......................5.00
Sugar bowl, cov. 42.00

Sugar bowl, open..................................12.00

STATES (THE)
Bowl, 7" d., three-handled 50.00
Bowl, 7½" d..22.50
Bowl, 9" d..35.00
Butter dish, cov.....................................56.00
Cocktail, flared......................................22.00
Compote, open, 5 x 5½" 34.00
Creamer...27.00
Creamer, individual size 30.00
Creamer & sugar bowl, pr....................65.00
Cruet w/stopper 55.00
Goblet..35.00
Punch bowl, 13" d., 5½" h.....................95.00
Punch cup..15.00
Salt & pepper shakers w/original
   tops, pr. 60.00
Sauce dish...10.00
Spooner 23.00
Sugar bowl, cov. 46.00
Tumbler 25.00
Wine, clear..27.00
Wine, clear w/gold trim 29.00
Wine, green 60.00

STAVES WITH SCALLOPED BAND - See Picket Band Pattern

STIPPLED CHAIN
Butter dish, cov.....................................30.00
Creamer...30.00
Goblet..22.00
Relish, 6⅛ x 8¼"...................................10.00
Spooner 22.50
Sugar bowl, cov. 29.50

STIPPLED CHERRY
Bread platter...26.00
Butter dish, cov.....................................62.00
Celery 35.00
Pitcher, water..44.00
Plate, 6" d. 25.00

STIPPLED FLOWER PANELS - See Maine Pattern

STIPPLED FORGET-ME-NOT
Cake stand, 8" to 9" d. 90.00
Celery vase..31.00
Compote, open, 6" d., 6½" h.................32.50
Cup & saucer...35.00
Goblet..45.00
Pitcher, milk...37.00
Pitcher, water..42.00
Plate, 7" d. 22.50
Plate, 7" d., w/baby in tub reaching
   for ball on floor center 65.00
Plate, 9" d., w/kitten center, handled 65.00
Plate, 9" d., w/star center, handled.......55.00
Plate, 11" d., w/stork center..................85.00
Relish...13.00
Tray, water...88.00

Stippled Forget-Me-Not Wine

Wine (ILLUS.) 35.00

STIPPLED GRAPE & FESTOON
Butter dish, cov., w/clear leaf................65.00
Celery vase...39.50
Compote, 8" d., low stand, w/clear
leaf...110.00
Creamer...32.00
Goblet..30.00
Pitcher, water...95.00
Spooner..30.00
Spooner, w/clear leaf.............................28.00
Sugar bowl, cov., w/clear leaf...............70.00

STIPPLED IVY
Goblet..25.00
Salt dip, master size..............................30.00
Spooner..29.00
Sugar bowl, open...................................25.00
Tumbler, water.......................................24.00

STRIGIL
Bowl, flared, 9" d...................................24.50
Celery 24.00
Plate, 5¼" d. 6.50
Plate, 8" d. 22.50
Plate, 11" d. 26.50
Sauce dish, 4" to 4¼" (plain or flared) 6.50
Spooner 15.00
Tumbler 32.50
Wine, clear...14.50
Wine, gilt trim..30.00

SUNK HONEYCOMB (Corona)
Bowl, 8¼" d., ruby-stained w/h.p. floral
decoration 75.00
Cake stand, ruby-stained.....................125.00
Celery, ruby-stained 72.50
Cheese dish, cov., ruby-stained 170.00
Compote, cov., 7" d., 11" h. 165.00
Creamer, ruby-stained, 4½" h..............52.50
Creamer, ruby-stained, souvenir 45.00
Cruet w/original stopper, clear.............30.00
Cruet w/original stopper, ruby-
stained 110.00

Cruet w/original stopper, ruby-stained,
souvenir "Mother, World's Fair,
1893"...95.00
Cup & saucer, ruby-stained.................35.00
Goblet, clear 39.00
Goblet, ruby-stained 45.00
Mug, clear, souvenir 25.00
Mug, ruby-stained, 3" h........................34.00
Pitcher, tankard, 8¼" h. 150.00
Pitcher, water, bulbous, ruby-
stained 95.00
Punch cup..22.00
Salt dip, individual size 17.50
Salt shaker w/original top, ruby-
stained 37.50
Sugar bowl, cov., hotel size, ruby-
stained, engraved 195.00
Syrup pitcher w/original top, clear 135.00
Syrup pitcher w/original top, ruby-
stained 175.00
Table set: cov. butter dish, cov. sugar
bowl, creamer & spooner; ruby-
stained, 4 pcs....................................350.00
Toothpick holder, ruby-stained,
souvenir 42.50
Tumbler, clear, engraved.......................24.00
Tumbler, ruby-stained............................50.00
Water set, pitcher & 6 goblets,
7 pcs. 350.00
Wine, clear..14.00
Wine, clear, engraved.............................22.00
Wine, ruby-stained.................................35.00
Wine, ruby-stained, engraved..............40.00

SWAN

Swan Creamer

Celery vase, etched................................38.00
Compote, cov., w/swan finial, 8" d......365.00
Compote, open, 8½" h...........................85.00
Creamer, amber 55.00
Creamer, clear (ILLUS.) 42.50
*Creamer, milk white 38.00
Cup, handled 35.00
Marmalade jar, cov. 110.00
Pitcher, water....................200.00 to 250.00

Sauce dish, flat or footed......................20.00
Spooner..42.00
Sugar bowl, cov. 185.00

TACOMA (Jeweled Diamond and Fan)

Banana dish, flat...................................35.00
Butter dish, cov., amber-stained...........95.00
Celery vase...22.50
Creamer...60.00
Pitcher, water, ruby-stained...............120.00
Punch cup..22.00
Sauce dish, ruby-stained.....................24.00
Toothpick holder..................................20.00

TEARDROP & TASSEL

Teardrop & Tassel Salt Shaker

Berry set: master bowl & 6 sauce
  dishes; teal blue, 7 pcs. 395.00
Bowl, 7½" d...38.00
Bowl, 8¼" d...55.00
Butter dish, cov., clear..........................65.00
Butter dish, cov., cobalt blue 150.00
Butter dish, cov., emerald green.........200.00
Compote, cov., 5" d., 7½" h. 85.00
Compote, cov., 7" d., 11½" h. 95.00
Compote, cov., 9½" d. 95.00
Compote, open, 5" d..............................25.00
Compote, open, 6" d..............................35.00
Compote, open, 8½" d...........................42.00
Creamer, amber 175.00
Creamer, clear......................................45.00
Creamer, cobalt blue 125.00
Creamer, Nile green ....150.00 to 200.00
Creamer, white opaque.........................75.00
Creamer & cov. sugar bowl, emerald
  green, pr. 325.00
Creamer & cov. sugar bowl, white
  opaque, pr..175.00
Goblet, clear 150.00
Goblet, emerald green.........................225.00
Pickle dish, amber 90.00
Pickle dish, clear..................................29.00
Pitcher, water, clear..............................70.00
Pitcher, water, cobalt blue 225.00
Pitcher, water, emerald
  green...............................250.00 to 275.00

Relish, clear...35.00
Relish, emerald green 100.00
Relish, Nile green 175.00
Relish, teal blue..................................175.00
Salt shaker w/original top, clear
  (ILLUS.) 125.00
Salt & pepper shakers w/original
  tops, Nile green, pr. 350.00
Sauce dish, clear..................................13.50
Sauce dish, cobalt blue 30.00
Sauce dish, emerald green...................75.00
Spooner, clear 50.00
Spooner, cobalt blue............................90.00
Spooner, Nile green............................175.00
Spooner, white opaque.........................65.00
Sugar bowl, cov., clear 60.00
Sugar bowl, cov., cobalt blue..............135.00
Sugar bowl, cov., Nile green...............300.00
Tumbler, clear.......................................37.00
Tumbler, cobalt blue.............................58.00
Tumbler, emerald green 165.00
Water set, pitcher & 6 tumblers,
  7 pcs. 285.00

TENNESSEE

Butter dish, cov. 90.00
Cake stand, 8½" d., high stand.............32.00
Compote, open, 8" d., flared rim,
  shallow round bowl, high stand..........48.00
Pitcher, milk, 1 qt. 125.00
Relish tray...20.00
Sauce dish, flat, round..........................12.00
Toothpick holder.................................200.00
Wine 125.00

TEXAS (Loop with Stippled Panels)

Texas Toothpick Holder

Cake stand, 9½" to 10¾" d. 62.50
Celery vase...75.00
Compote, open, jelly............................100.00
Compote, cov., 6" d., 11" h. 165.00
Creamer..26.00
*Creamer, individual size......................18.00
Goblet, clear 38.00
Goblet, ruby-stained 110.00
Relish, handled, 8½" l..........................20.00
Salt dip, master size, footed, 3" d.,
  2¾" h...22.00
Sauce dish, flat or footed......................25.00

Spooner, ruby-stained 95.00
Toothpick holder, clear (ILLUS.)...........35.00
Toothpick holder, clear w/gold..............55.00
Vase, 7½" h., trumpet-shaped,
    pink-stained 95.00
Vase, bud, 8" h. 30.00
Vase, 9" h. 35.00
Vase, 10" h. 30.00
*Wine 115.00
Wine, ruby-stained..............................125.00

TEXAS BULL'S EYE (Bull's Eye Variant)

Butter dish, cov.....................................40.00
Celery vase..50.00
Cordial 25.00
Goblet..30.00
Pitcher, water, ½ gal.............................55.00
Sugar bowl, open...................................32.00
Tumbler 25.00
Wine 24.00

THISTLE, PANELED - See Paneled Thistle Pattern

THOUSAND EYE

Thousand Eye Butter Dish

Bowl, 8" d., 4½" h., footed, amber 35.00
Bowl, 11" rectangle, shallow, amber.....32.00
Bread tray, amber.................................32.00
Bread tray, apple green 52.00
Bread tray, blue 40.00
Bread tray, clear 28.00
Butter dish, cov., amber......................115.00
Butter dish, cov., blue 145.00
Butter dish, cov., clear (ILLUS.)............50.00
Cake stand, blue, 8½" to 10" d. 88.00
Cake stand, blue, 12½" d. 60.00
Celery vase, three-knob stem, amber ..48.00
Celery vase, three-knob stem,
    apple green.......................................55.00
Celery vase, three-knob stem, clear.....40.00
Celery vase, three-knob stem, clear
    to opalescent w/purple tint 130.00
Celery vase, plain stem, amber............45.00
Compote, cov., 12" h. 115.00
*Compote, open, 6" d., low stand,
    amber..22.00

*Compote, open, 6" d., low stand,
    blue 38.00
Compote, open, 6½" d., three-knob
    stem, blue 30.00
Compote, open, 7½" d., 5" h................35.00
Compote, open, 8" d., 3¾" h., apple
    green..40.00
Compote, open, 8" d., 6" h., three-
    knob stem, amber 38.00
Compote, open, 8" d., 6" h., three-
    knob stem, apple green 65.00
Compote, open, 8" d., 6" h., three-
    knob stem, blue 65.00
Compote, open, 8" d., high stand,
    three-knob stem, vaseline..................58.00
Compote, open, 8" sq., low stand,
    apple green...65.00
Compote, open, 9½" d., low stand,
    amber...27.00
Compote, open, 10" d., 6½" h., three-
    knob stem, blue 85.00
Creamer, amber 42.00
*Creamer, clear 35.00
Creamer, clear opalescent 95.00
Creamer & cov. sugar bowl, amber,
    pr...100.00
Cruet w/original three-knob stopper,
    amber...135.00
Cruet w/original three-knob stopper,
    apple green.......................................135.00
Cruet w/original three-knob stopper,
    blue ....125.00 to 150.00
Cruet w/original three-knob stopper,
    clear 32.00
Cruet w/original three-knob stopper,
    vaseline...........................100.00 to 125.00
Egg cup, blue...65.00
Egg cup, clear..25.00
*Goblet, amber 30.00
*Goblet, apple green..............................40.00
*Goblet, blue..32.00
*Goblet, clear...28.00
*Goblet, vaseline 32.00
Lamp, kerosene-type, pedestal base,
    amber, 14" h. to collar.......................225.00
Lamp, kerosene-type, pedestal base,
    blue font, amber base, 12" h. 195.00
Lamp, kerosene-type, pedestal base,
    blue, 12" h...155.00
Lamp, kerosene-type, flat base, ring
    handle, amber....................................325.00
Lamp, kerosene type, flat base, ring
    handle, clear 110.00
*Mug, amber, 3½" h...............................28.00
*Mug, blue, 3½" h. 28.00
*Mug, clear, 3½" h. 20.00
*Mug, vaseline, 3½" h............................32.00
Mug, miniature, amber...........................30.00
Pickle dish, apple green 25.00
Pitcher, water, three-knob stem, blue...95.00
*Pitcher, water, clear 75.00
Pitcher, water, vaseline 60.00
Plate, 6" d., amber 22.50

Plate, 6" d., apple green 17.00
Plate, 6" d., blue 18.00
*Plate, 6" d., clear 14.50
Plate, 8" d., amber 26.00
Plate, 8" d., apple green 25.00
*Plate, 8" d., clear 28.00
Plate, 8" d., vaseline 32.00
Plate, 10" sq., w/folded corners, blue ...28.00
Plate, 10" sq., w/folded corners, clear ..28.00
Platter, 8 x 11" 30.00
Salt & pepper shakers w/original tops,
    blue, pr. 75.00
*Salt & pepper shakers w/original tops,
    clear, pr. 65.00
Sauce dish, flat or footed, amber..........12.50
Sauce dish, flat or footed, blue 16.00
*Sauce dish, flat or footed, clear...........10.00
Spooner, three-knob stem, amber 52.00
Spooner, three-knob stem, clear 38.00
Spooner, three-knob stem, vaseline 42.00
Sugar bowl, cov., three-knob stem,
    amber...55.00
Sugar bowl, cov. 37.50
*Sugar bowl, open, three-knob stem 25.00
Syrup pitcher w/original top, amber 100.00
*Toothpick holder, amber 38.00
*Toothpick holder, blue.........................40.00
*Toothpick holder, clear........................24.00
*Toothpick holder, vaseline 38.00
Tray, water, amber, 12½" d. 65.00
Tray, water, blue, 12½" d....................120.00
Tray, apple green, 14" oval...................60.00
*Tumbler, apple green 39.00
*Tumbler, blue 30.00
*Tumbler, clear 18.00
*Wine, amber.......................................20.00
*Wine, apple green 42.50
*Wine, blue 42.50
*Wine, clear 20.00
*Wine, vaseline....................................38.00

*Champagne.......................................165.00
Claret..152.00
Claret, engraved 265.00
Compote, cov., 4½" d., 6½" h. 100.00
*Compote, cov., 6" d. 125.00
Compote, cov., 7" d. 285.00
Compote, cov., 8" d., 13" h. 315.00
Compote, open, 6" d., high stand 80.00
Compote, open, 7" d., high stand 90.00
Compote, open, 8½" d., high stand 125.00
Compote, open, 9½" d., high stand 160.00
*Cracker jar, cov. 1,250.00
Creamer (ILLUS.) 90.00
*Creamer w/mask spout 150.00
Goblet, engraved 150.00
*Goblet, plain 82.00
*Lamp, kerosene-type, pedestal
    base, 8" h..165.00
Marmalade jar, cov. 350.00
Pitcher, water.......................................450.00
*Salt dip 44.00
*Salt shaker w/original top 65.00
*Sauce dish 30.00
*Spooner...60.00
Spooner, engraved 100.00
*Sugar bowl, cov...................................155.00
*Sugar shaker, w/original top..............155.00
*Wine...85.00

THREE PANEL

Three Panel Creamer

Bowl, 7" d., footed, blue.......................30.00
Bowl, 7" d., footed, vaseline 31.50
Bowl, 9" d., footed, blue.......................25.00
Bowl, 10" d., amber 49.00
Bowl, 10" d., blue.................................65.00
Bowl, 10" d., clear................................20.00
Bowl, 10" d., vaseline 45.00
Butter dish, cov., vaseline....................50.00
Celery vase, amber 47.50
Celery vase, clear.................................35.00
Celery vase, vaseline 55.00
Compote, open, 7" d., low stand,
    amber..32.00
Compote, open, 7" d., low stand,
    vaseline...27.50

THREE FACE

Three Face Creamer

Butter dish, cov.,
    engraved........................200.00 to 225.00
Butter dish, cov., plain 185.00
*Cake stand, 8" to 10½" d..................150.00
Celery vase.........................100.00 to 125.00

Compote, open, 8½" d., low stand,
blue 40.00
Compote, open, 9" d., 4¼" h., amber ...40.00
Compote, open, 9" d., vaseline.............45.00
Compote, open, 10" d., low stand,
blue 65.00
Creamer, amber 35.00
Creamer, blue (ILLUS.) 45.00
Creamer, clear..20.00
Creamer, vaseline 38.00
Cruet w/original stopper.......................155.00
*Goblet, amber 32.00
*Goblet, blue...42.00
*Goblet, clear..25.00
*Goblet, vaseline 40.00
Lamp, kerosene-type, amber.............145.00
Mug, amber 35.00
Mug, clear..30.00
Pitcher, milk, 7" h....................................44.50
Pitcher, water, vaseline 110.00
Sauce dish, footed, amber.....................17.00
Sauce dish, footed, blue 19.50
Sauce dish, footed, clear.......................11.50
Sauce dish, footed, vaseline.................15.00
Spooner, amber.......................................32.00
Spooner, blue 38.00
Spooner, clear 15.00
Spooner, vaseline....................................35.00
Sugar bowl, cov., blue 75.00
Sugar bowl, cov., clear 55.00
Sugar bowl, cov., vaseline.....................65.00
Sugar bowl, open.....................................25.00
Table set, blue, 4 pcs. 245.00
Table set, clear, 4 pcs. 175.00
Tumbler, amber 35.00
Tumbler, blue...40.00
Tumbler, clear..12.00

THUMBPRINT, EARLY (Bakewell, Pears & Co.'s "Argus")

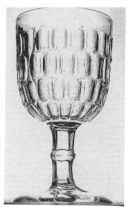

Early Thumbprint Goblet

*Butter dish, cov. 115.00
*Cake stand, 8" to 9½" d.....................275.00
*Celery vase, plain base.......................110.00
Celery vase, scalloped rim, pattern
in base 155.00

*Compote, open, 6" d., low stand,
scalloped rim.......................................35.00
Compote, open, 7½" d., low stand........55.00
*Compote, open, 8" d., high stand......100.00
Compote, open, 8½" d., high stand,
scalloped rim, flint ....125.00 to 150.00
Compote, open, 14" d., 12" h..............600.00
*Creamer 90.00
Goblet, plain stem (ILLUS.) 38.00
Inkwell...350.00
Pickle dish 40.00
Pitcher, milk..90.00
*Pitcher, water, 8¼" h. ....300.00 to 400.00
*Sauce dish, clear....................................8.00
Sauce dish, milk white 75.00
Spillholder...48.00
*Sugar bowl, cov......................................60.00
Sweetmeat bowl, 6½" d., 7" h. 190.00
*Wine, baluster stem 60.00

TONG
Celery vase...95.00
Sugar bowl, cov. 100.00

TORPEDO (Pygmy)
Bowl, 7" d., flat, clear 15.00
Bowl, 8" d...32.50
Bowl, 9" d...32.00
Bowl, 9½" d..42.50
Butter dish, cov.......................................75.00
Celery vase..40.00
Compote, cov., jelly 43.00
Compote, cov., 6" d. 78.00
Compote, cov., 7" d., 7¼" h....................65.00
Compote, cov., 8" d., 14" h. 135.00
Compote, open, jelly, 5" d., 5" h. 47.50
Compote, open, 7" d., high stand 52.00
Compote, open, 8" d., high stand,
flared rim..110.00
Compote, open, 8 x 10½", 8" h.,
ruffled rim 145.00
Creamer, collared base 55.00
Creamer, footed......................................37.50
Cruet w/original faceted stopper...........75.00
Cup & saucer..65.00
Goblet, clear 50.00
Goblet, ruby-stained 80.00
Lamp, kerosene, hand-type w/finger
grip, w/burner & chimney 125.00
Lamp, kerosene-type, 10" h.................185.00
Pickle castor, silver plate cover &
tongs 250.00
Pitcher, milk, 8½" h.................................95.00
Pitcher, water, tankard, 12" h. 75.00
Salt dip, individual size, 1½" d. 26.00
Salt dip, master size 45.00
Salt & pepper shakers w/original
tops, pr...95.00
Sauce dish...17.50
Spooner..40.00
Sugar bowl, cov. 95.00
Syrup jug w/original top,
clear ....100.00 to 125.00

Syrup jug w/original top, ruby-
  stained 250.00
Tumbler, clear..38.00
Tumbler, clear, engraved.....................55.00
Tumbler, ruby-stained...........................48.00
Wine, clear..90.00
Wine, ruby-stained.................................95.00

TREE OF LIFE - PORTLAND

Butter dish, cov...................................110.00
Butter pat, green...................................20.00
Celery vase..100.00
Celery vase, in silver plate holder.......135.00
Champagne...75.00
Compote, open, 7" d., high stand,
  w/applied red serpent on stem.........245.00
Compote, open, 7½" d., scalloped
  rim..45.00
Compote, open, 7¾" d., 11" h., Infant
  Samuel stand, signed "Davis"..........125.00
Compote, open, 8½" d., 5" h., signed
  "Davis" 60.00
Compote, open, 8¾" d., in two-handled
  Meriden silver plate holder, bowl
  signed "Davis"...................................185.00
Compote, open, 10" d., 6" h., signed
  "Davis" ....100.00 to 125.00
Creamer, signed "Davis"......................55.00
Creamer, blue, in silver plate
  holder..............................175.00 to 200.00
Creamer, clear, in silver plate holder....85.00
Creamer, cranberry in silver plate
  holder...190.00
Epergne, single lily, red snake around
  stem, 18" h.......................................450.00
*Goblet...50.00
Goblet, signed "Davis".........................90.00
Ice cream set, tray & 6 leaf-shaped
  desserts, 7 pcs.................................150.00
Mug, applied handle, 3½" h. 45.00
Pitcher, water, applied handle, clear ...78.00
Plate, 7¼" d. 50.00
Powder jar, cov., red coiled snake
  finial on cover...................................350.00
Salt dip, individual size, footed,
  amber...65.00
Salt dip, footed, "Salt" embossed in
  bowl, clear...135.00
Sauce dish, leaf-shaped, blue 18.00
Sauce dish, leaf-shaped, clear 15.00
Spooner..30.00
Spooner, in handled silver plate holder
  w/two Griffin heads 110.00
Sugar bowl, cov., blue, in silver plate
  holder..............................175.00 to 200.00
Sugar bowl, cov., clear, in silver plate
  holder...88.00
Sugar bowl, cov., clear 63.00
Syrup pitcher w/original metal top,
  blue opaque 100.00
Table set: cov. sugar bowl, creamer
  & spooner; in ornate silver plate
  holders, the set 180.00

Toothpick holder, apple green............125.00
Tray, ice cream, 14" rectangle.............48.00
Waste bowl, amber................................50.00
Waste bowl, blue 52.00
Waste bowl, blue, in ornate silver
  plate holder 175.00
Waste bowl, clear 30.00
Waste bowl, green.................................45.00

TREE OF LIFE WITH HAND (Tree of Life-Wheeling)

Tree of Life with Hand Creamer

Butter dish, cov...................................125.00
Cake stand, frosted base, 11½" d. 85.00
Celery vase...47.00
Compote, open, 5½" d., 5½" h., clear
  hand & ball stem 48.00
Compote, open, 5½" d., 5½" h., frosted
  hand & ball stem 65.00
Compote, open, 8" d., clear hand & ball
  stem 55.00
Compote, open, 9" d., frosted hand &
  ball stem 80.00
Compote, open, 10" d., 10" h., frosted
  hand & ball stem 95.00
Creamer, w/hand & ball handle
  (ILLUS.) 75.00
Mug, applied handle, 3" h. 125.00
Pitcher, water, 9" h. 68.00
Sauce dish, flat or footed.....................19.00
Spooner..42.00

TRIPLE TRIANGLE

Butter dish, cov., handled, ruby-
  stained 85.00
*Goblet, clear...50.00
*Goblet, ruby-stained............................40.00
Mug, ruby-stained..................................25.00
Tumbler, water, ruby-stained................25.00
*Wine, clear 60.00
*Wine, ruby-stained 35.00

TULIP WITH SAWTOOTH

Celery vase, flint....................................85.00
Celery vase, non-flint............................45.00

Champagne, non-flint 75.00
Compote, cov., 6" d., low stand, flint 75.00

Tulip with Sawtooth Compote

Compote, cov., 7" d., 12½" h.
(ILLUS.) 247.50
Compote, open, 8" d., low stand,
flint 75.00
Compote, open, 9" d., 7⅜" h., flint........78.00
Compote, open, 9" d., 10" h., flint.......135.00
Cruet w/original stopper, flint, 8⅝" h...165.00
Egg cup, flint...35.00
*Goblet, flint 50.00
Goblet, non-flint 25.00
Pitcher, 9¾" h., flint..............................250.00
Salt dip, cov., flint, 5½" h. 285.00
Salt dip, master size, scalloped rim,
flint 35.00
Salt dip, open, non-flint..........................15.00
Spooner, flint 65.00
Spooner, non-flint 28.00
Sugar bowl, open, non-flint.....................32.50
Toothpick holder 39.00
Tumbler, bar, flint...................................80.00
Tumbler, flint...45.00
Wine, flint..45.00
*Wine, non-flint 25.00

TURKEY TRACK - See Crowfoot Pattern

TWO PANEL (Daisy in Panel)
Bowl, cov., 7" oval, vaseline 75.00
Bowl, 6 x 8" oval, blue 38.50
Bowl, 7½ x 9" oval, apple green 36.00
Butter dish, cov., blue 85.00
Butter dish, cov., vaseline.....................50.00
Celery vase, clear..................................30.00
Celery vase, vaseline 45.00
Compote, cov., 6½ x 8", 11" h.,
vaseline..85.00
Compote, cov., high stand, apple
green..135.00
Compote, cov., high stand, blue 85.00
Compote, open, 9" oval, 4" h., apple
green..60.00

Compote, open, 9" oval, 4" h.,
vaseline..45.00
Creamer, amber 45.00
Creamer, apple green............................45.00
Creamer, blue..45.00

Two Panel Goblet

*Goblet, amber (ILLUS.) 35.00
*Goblet, apple green 35.00
*Goblet, blue..42.00
*Goblet, clear...20.00
*Goblet, vaseline 32.00
Lamp, kerosene-type, pedestal base,
blue, 7¾" h., No. 1 burner...............145.00
Pitcher, water, blue................................90.00
Pitcher, water, clear...............................36.00
Relish, blue 30.00
Salt dip, master size, apple green 28.00
Salt dip, individual size, apple
green..24.00
Sauce dish, flat or footed, amber..........10.00
Sauce dish, flat or footed, apple
green..13.50
Sauce dish, flat or footed, clear 9.50
Spooner, amber......................................38.00
Spooner, blue 35.00
Spooner, vaseline...................................35.00
Sugar bowl, cov., amber........................50.00
Sugar bowl, cov., apple green 55.00
Sugar bowl, cov., vaseline.....................54.00
Tray, water, blue.....................................60.00
Tumbler, vaseline....................................40.00
Waste bowl, amber.................................36.00
*Wine, amber..35.00
*Wine, apple green 40.00
*Wine, blue 35.00
*Wine, clear 29.00
*Wine, vaseline.......................................35.00

U.S. COIN
*Bowl, berry, 6" d., frosted coins, plate
rim 400.00
Bowl, berry, 7" d., frosted quarters,
plain rim ....300.00 to 350.00
Bowl, berry, 8" d., frosted half dollars,
plain rim 400.00

Bowl, berry, 9" d., frosted dollars,
  plain rim 800.00
Bowl, berry, 6" d., frosted coins,
  scalloped rim....................................800.00
Bowl, berry, 7" d., frosted quarters,
  scalloped rim....................................800.00
Bowl, berry, 8" d., clear half dollars,
  scalloped rim....................................320.00
Bowl, berry, 8" d., frosted half dollars,
  scalloped rim....................................900.00
Bowl, berry, 9" d., frosted dollars,
  scalloped rim.................................1,200.00
Bread tray, frosted quarters & half
  dollars 230.00

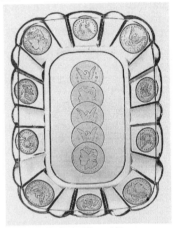

U.S. Coin Bread Tray

*Bread tray, frosted dollars & half
  dollars (ILLUS.)................350.00 to 395.00
Butter dish, cov., clear dollars & half
  dollars 490.00
Butter dish, cov., frosted dollars & half
  dollars ....400.00 to 500.00
Cake plate, frosted dollars & quarters,
  7" d....................................400.00 to 450.00
Cake stand, clear dollars, 10" d..........375.00
Cake stand, frosted dollars,
  10" d....................................425.00 to 450.00
Celery tray, clear quarters 195.00
Celery tray, frosted quarters 300.00
Celery vase, clear quarters.................245.00
Celery vase, frosted
  quarters.............................350.00 to 375.00
Champagne, flared rim, frosted half
  dimes 800.00
Claret, flared rim, frosted half dimes...600.00
Claret, straight rim, frosted half
  dimes 600.00
Compote, cov., 6" d., high stand,
  quarters on lid, twenty cent pieces
  on base 495.00
*Compote, cov., 6" d., high stand,
  frosted dimes & quarters..350.00 to 400.00
Compote, cov., 7" d., high stand,
  clear dimes & quarters....................300.00
Compote, cov., 7" d., high stand,
  frosted dimes & quarters..500.00 to 550.00

Compote, cov., 8" d., high stand, frosted
  quarters & half dollars......475.00 to 500.00
Compote, cov., 9" d., high stand,
  frosted dollars 600.00
Compote, cov., 9" d., high stand, frosted
  dollars & quarters........................1,500.00
Compote, cov., 6" d., low stand, clear
  twenty cent pieces & quarters..........350.00
Compote, open, 7¼" d., high stand, straight
  rim, frosted quarters......................495.00
Compote, open, 7½" d., high stand, straight
  rim, frosted dimes & quarters..........300.00
Compote, open, 7½" d., high stand, straight
  rim, frosted quarters......................495.00
Compote, open, 8¼" d., high stand, straight
  rim, frosted quarters......................522.50
Compote, open, 8½" d., high stand,
  straightrim, frosted dimes &
  quarters..........................350.00 to 400.00
Compote, open, 8½" d., high stand, straight
  rim, frosted quarters......................522.50
Compote, open, 9¾" d., high stand,
  straightrim, frosted quarters & half
  dollars ....350.00 to 400.00
Compote, open, 10½" d., straight rim,
  frosted quarters & half dollars..........500.00
Compote, open, 7" d., high stand,
  flared rim, frosted dimes &
  quarters.............................300.00 to 350.00
Compote, open, 8¼" d., high stand,
  flared rim, frosted dimes &
  quarters.............................350.00 to 400.00
Compote, open, 9½" d., high stand,
  flared rim, frosted quarters & half
  dollars 600.00
Compote, open, 10½" d., high stand,
  flared rim, frosted quarters & half
  dollars 700.00
Compote, open, 7¼" d., high stand,
  flared & scalloped rim, frosted
  dimes & quarters..............................750.00
Compote, open, 6" d., low stand,
  flared & scalloped rim, frosted
  twenty cent pieces 800.00
Compote, open, 7" d., low stand,
  straight top w/scalloped rim, frosted
  twenty cent pieces 450.00
Compote, open, 7" d., low stand,
  flared & scalloped rim, frosted
  twenty cent pieces 600.00
*Creamer, frosted quarters 450.00
Cruet w/original stopper, frosted
  quarters, 5½" h. ....625.00 to 650.00
Epergne, clear quarters & dollars 632.00
Epergne, frosted quarters & dollars....800.00
Finger bowl, straight rim, frosted
  coins 500.00
Finger bowl, flared rim, frosted
  coins 500.00
Goblet, straight top, frosted dimes,
  6½" h...............................250.00 to 300.00
Goblet, straight top, frosted half
  dollar, 7" h. 400.00

Goblet, flared top, frosted half dollars,
7" h. 450.00
Lamp, kerosene-type, square font,
frosted quarters & half dollars,
8½" h. ....300.00 to 350.00
Lamp, kerosene-type, square font,
frosted dollars & quarters,
9½" h. ....400.00 to 450.00
Lamp, kerosene-type, square font,
frosted half dollars & dollars,
10¼" h. 500.00
Lamp, kerosene-type, square font,
frosted half dollars & dollars,
11" h. 550.00
Lamp, kerosene-type, square font,
frosted half dollars & dollars,
11½" h. 675.00
Lamp, kerosene-type, round font,
frosted quarters, 8" h. ......300.00 to 400.00
Lamp, kerosene-type, round font,
frosted quarters, 8½" h. 350.00
Lamp, kerosene-type, round font,
frosted quarters, 9" h. 400.00
Lamp, kerosene-type, round font,
frosted half dollars, 9½" h. 400.00
Lamp, kerosene-type, round
font, frosted half dollars,
10" h. ....400.00 to 450.00
Lamp, kerosene-type, round
font, frosted half dollars,
10" h. ....400.00 to 450.00
Lamp, kerosene-type, round font,
frosted half dollars, 11½" h. 450.00
Lamp, kerosene-type, round font,
frosted dollars, 11½" h. ....750.00 to 800.00
Lamp, kerosene-type, flaring font,
frosted quarters, 8½" h. 600.00
Lamp, kerosene-type, flaring font,
frosted quarters, 9" h. 600.00
Lamp, kerosene-type, flaring font,
frosted quarters, 9½" h. 600.00
Lamp, kerosene-type, flaring font,
frosted quarters, 10" h. 600.00
Lamp, kerosene-type, handled,
frosted twenty cent pieces, 5" h. 500.00
Lamp, kerosene-type, handled,
clear quarters, 5" h. ....450.00 to 500.00
Lamp, kerosene-type, handled,
frosted quarters, 5" h. 350.00
Mug, frosted dollars 350.00
Pickle dish, frosted half dollars,
3¾ x 7½" ....200.00 to 225.00
Pitcher, milk, frosted half
dollars ....600.00 to 650.00
Pitcher, water, frosted
dollars ....600.00 to 700.00
Preserve dish, clear half dollars in rim,
dollars in base, 5 x 8" ....300.00 to 350.00
Preserve dish, frosted half dollars
in rim, dollars in base,
5 x 8" ....300.00 to 350.00
Salt & pepper shakers w/original tops,
frosted coins, pr. 300.00

Sauce dish, flat, plain rim, frosted
quarters, 3¾" d. ....125.00 to 150.00
Sauce dish, flat, plain rim, clear
quarters, 4¼" d. 110.00
Sauce dish, flat, plain rim, frosted
quarters, 4¼" d. 150.00
Sauce dish, flat, scalloped rim, frosted
quarters, 4" d. 350.00
Sauce dish, flat, scalloped rim, frosted
quarters, 4½" d. 400.00
Sauce dish, footed, plain top, frosted
quarters...........................150.00 to 195.00
Sauce dish, footed, scalloped rim,
frosted quarters.................................350.00
Spooner, clear quarters ......225.00 to 250.00
*Spooner, frosted
quarters............................275.00 to 300.00
*Sugar bowl, cov., frosted quarters &
half dollars.......................350.00 to 400.00
Syrup jug w/original dated pewter top,
frosted coins ....500.00 to 550.00
Toothpick holder, clear
dollars ....150.00 to 175.00
*Toothpick holder, frosted
dollars ....150.00 to 175.00
Tumbler, frosted dime on
side ....150.00 to 200.00
Tumbler, dollar in base, clear sides
w/clear 1879 coin.............200.00 to 225.00
Tumbler, dollar in base, clear sides
w/frosted 1882 coin...........................250.00
Tumbler, dollar in base, paneled sides
w/clear 1878 coin.............150.00 to 200.00
Waste bowl -- See FINGER BOWL
Water tray, frosted coins....................500.00
Wine, frosted half dimes 600.00

VALENCIA WAFFLE (Block & Star)
Bread platter...30.00
Butter dish, cov., apple green...............55.00
Celery vase, clear.................................30.00
Compote, cov., 7" sq., low stand,
amber...64.00
Compote, cov., 7" sq., low stand,
blue ....50.00 to 75.00
Compote, cov., 7" sq., low stand,
clear 40.00
Compote, cov., 8" sq., low stand,
clear 125.00
Compote, cov., 8" sq., 9" h., amber......90.00
Compote, open, 7" sq., low stand,
amber...32.50
Compote, open, 7" sq., light blue..........55.00
Compote, open, 8" d., 8" h., amber 60.00
Goblet, amber.......................................35.00
Goblet, blue 45.00
Goblet, clear 25.00
Pitcher, water, 7½" h., amber 60.00
Pitcher, water, blue...............................72.00
Relish, amber, 5⅜ x 9" 22.50
Salt dip, master size, blue 45.00
Salt shaker w/original top, apple
green...30.00

Spooner, amber.....................................38.00
Spooner, yellow.....................................35.00
Tray, water..25.00
Tumbler, ruby-stained...........................30.00

VICTOR - See Shell & Jewel Pattern

VICTORIA
Compote, cov., 6½" d. 67.50
Compote, cov., 8" d., high stand.........200.00
Tumbler 25.00
Wine 27.50

VIKING (Bearded Head or Old Man of the Mountain)

Viking Sugar Bowl

Apothecary jar w/original stopper 75.00
Bowl, cov., 8" oval 100.00
Bowl, 8" sq...45.00
Butter dish, cov., clear..........................75.00
Butter dish, cov., frosted......................85.00
Celery vase..55.00
Compote, cov., 7" d., low stand 82.00
Compote, cov., 9" d., low stand 110.00
Creamer..60.00
Egg cup 65.00
Marmalade jar, cov., footed 75.00
Mug, applied handle 62.50
Pickle jar w/cover.................................95.00
Pitcher, water, 8¾" h., clear...............115.00
Pitcher, water, 8¾" h., clear &
    frosted...310.00
Relish..25.00
Salt dip, master size 35.00
Sauce dish, footed...............................18.00
Spooner...30.00
Sugar bowl, cov. (ILLUS.)......................65.00

VIRGINIA - See Banded Portland Pattern

WAFFLE
Celery vase..85.00
Champagne 135.00
Creamer, applied handle 125.00
Egg cup 45.00

Goblet...95.00
Sugar bowl, cov. 125.00
Syrup pitcher, applied handle 85.00
Tumbler, bar 80.00
Wine 110.00

WAFFLE AND THUMBPRINT

Waffle & Thumbprint Spillholder

Bowl, 6 x 8¼", flint 45.00
Compote, open, 6" d., 6" h., flint.........195.00
Compote, open, 7" d., high stand,
    non-flint..55.00
Decanter w/bar lip, flint, pt. 100.00
Decanter w/matching stopper, pt........325.00
Decanter w/matching stopper, qt........375.00
Decanter w/bar lip, qt............................75.00
Egg cup, flint..30.00
Goblet, flint 100.00
Lamp, w/original whale oil burner,
    flint, 11" h...153.00
Pitcher, 9½" h., tapering body
    w/arched wide spout, applied strap
    handle, made from decanter mold,
    flint 460.00
Salt dip, master size, flint.....................29.00
Spillholder, flint (ILLUS.) 100.00
Sugar bowl, cov., flint 195.00
Tray, 8¼" l. 66.00
Tumbler, bar, flint.................................70.00
Tumbler, whiskey, handled, flint,
    3" h...275.00
Wine, flint...95.00

WASHBOARD - See Adonis Pattern

WASHINGTON CENTENNIAL
Bread platter, Carpenter's Hall
    center...100.00
Bread platter, George Washington
    center..84.00
Bread platter, George Washington
    center, frosted 130.00
Bread platter, Independence Hall
    center, frosted 95.00
Cake stand, 8½" to 11½" d. 75.00
Celery vase..52.00

Champagne 68.00
Compote, open, 7" d., low stand..........45.00
Egg cup 39.00
Goblet..50.00
Pickle dish 34.00
Pitcher, water...................................110.00
Relish, bear paw handles, dated
    1876...35.00
Salt dip, master size 60.00
Sauce dish, flat or footed.....................11.00
Spooner..35.00
Sugar bowl, cov. 72.50
Sugar bowl, open.................................20.00
Syrup pitcher, w/dated pewter top
    w/tiny figural finial 165.00
Tumbler 58.00
Wine 48.00

WASHINGTON, EARLY

Early Washington Celery Vase

Butter dish, cov., flint 55.00
Celery vase, flint (ILLUS.)...................125.00
Egg cup, flint......................................55.00
Salt dip, individual size, flint.................20.00
Spooner, flint 29.00

WASHINGTON (State)

Creamer w/colored enameling..............45.00
Pitcher, milk, ruby-stained 95.00
Toothpick holder, clear w/enamel
    decoration 49.00

WEDDING BELLS

Creamer, four-footed, pink-stained.......65.00
Pitcher, water.....................................47.00
Sauce dish, clear w/gold trim...............18.00
*Sugar bowl, cov., clear.......................55.00
Toothpick holder, pink-stained..............90.00
Wine, amethyst-stained 55.00

WEDDING RING - See Double Wedding Ring Pattern

WESTMORELAND (Gillinder's)

Celery tray 37.50
Celery vase..37.50

Cologne bottles, original stoppers,
    pr. 85.00
Compote, cov., low footed 27.50
Compote, jelly......................................25.00
Creamer..25.00
Cruet, 5" h...35.00
Lamp, finger, one-handle, 3½" h. (no
    shade) 115.00
Lamp, 7½" h. 255.00
Lamp, 8½" h. 125.00
Pitcher, tall, scalloped rim....................65.00
Water bottle, 8¼" h. 45.00

WESTWARD HO

Westward Ho Compote

Bowl, 8"..125.00
Bowl, 9" oval 95.00
Bread platter 115.00
*Butter dish, cov. ....125.00 to 150.00
*Celery vase 135.00
*Compote, cov., 4" d., low stand.........100.00
Compote, cov., 5" d., high stand..........95.00
*Compote, cov., 6" d., low stand........120.00
Compote, cov., 6" d., high stand.........325.00
*Compote, cov., 4 x 6¾" oval, low
    stand 150.00
Compote, cov., 5 x 7¾" oval, high
    stand ....200.00 to 225.00
Compote, cov., 8" d., low stand
    (ILLUS.) 325.00
Compote, cov., 8" d., high
    stand ....275.00 to 325.00
Compote, cov., 5½ x 8" oval, high
    stand 440.00
Compote, cov., 8" d., 14" h. 350.00
Compote, cov., 6½ x 10" oval, low
    stand ....225.00 to 250.00
Compote, open, 7" d., low stand..........175.00
Compote, open, 9" oval, high stand....100.00
*Creamer ....125.00 to 150.00
*Goblet..75.00
Marmalade jar, cov. 295.00
Mug, child's, clear, 2½" h....................250.00
Mug, child's, milk white, 2½" h...........175.00
Pickle dish, oval..................................65.00

Pitcher, milk, 8" h. 495.00
Pitcher, water 405.00
Platter, 9 x 13" 170.00
Relish, deer handles 100.00
Sauce dish, footed ....35.00 to 40.00
Spooner ....75.00 to 100.00
*Sugar bowl, cov. ....125.00 to 150.00
*Wine 225.00

Spooner, amber 45.00
Spooner, clear 30.00
Sugar bowl, cov., blue 65.00
Sugar bowl, cov., clear 40.00
Tumbler, amber 32.00
Tumbler, clear (ILLUS.) 20.00

WILDFLOWER

Wildflower Sauce Dish

Basket, cake, oblong w/metal
  handle 145.00
Bowl, 6½" sq., blue 35.00
Bowl, 7" sq. 17.50
Bowl, 8" sq., 5" h., footed, amber 22.50
Bowl, 8" sq., 5" h., footed, apple
  green...32.50
Bowl, 8" sq., 5" h., footed, vaseline 20.00
Butter dish, cov., flat, blue 50.00
Cake stand, apple green, 9½" to 11" 66.00
Cake stand, clear, 9½" to 11" 46.00
Cake stand, blue, w/bail handle..........225.00
Celery vase, amber 50.00
Celery vase, apple green......................65.00
Celery vase, blue..................................75.00
Celery vase, clear.................................35.00
*Champagne, amber 50.00
*Champagne, blue.................................50.00
*Champagne, clear................................30.00
Compote, cov., 6" d., amber 40.00
Compote, cov., 6" d., clear 49.00
Compote, cov., 8" d., amber 90.00
Compote, cov., 8" d., clear ...75.00 to 100.00
Compote, open, 10½" d., 7½" h.,
  blue 125.00
Compote, open, 10½" d., 8¼" h.,
  amber...78.00
*Creamer, amber 35.00
*Creamer, blue 45.00
*Creamer, clear 35.00
*Creamer, vaseline 42.00
*Goblet, amber 36.00
*Goblet, apple green.............................40.00
*Goblet, blue 37.00
*Goblet, clear.......................................30.00
*Goblet, vaseline 30.00
Pitcher, water, amber 65.00
Pitcher, water, apple green...................95.00
Pitcher, water, blue 85.00
Pitcher, water, clear..............................42.50
Pitcher, water, vaseline 76.00

WHEAT & BARLEY

Wheat & Barley Tumbler

Bowl, cov., 7" d. 42.50
Bowl, open, 7" d....................................16.50
Bread plate, amber 30.00
Bread plate, clear 35.00
Butter dish, cov.....................................35.00
Cake stand, amber, 8" to 10" d. 40.00
Cake stand, blue, 8" d. 55.00
Cake stand, clear, 8" to 10" d. 38.00
Cake stand, 11½" d. 40.00
Compote, open, jelly, amber 20.00
Compote, open, jelly, blue 40.00
Compote, open, jelly, clear 25.00
Compote, open, 8¼" d., amber..............65.00
Creamer, amber 45.00
Creamer, blue..55.00
Creamer, clear.......................................25.00
*Goblet, amber 45.00
*Goblet, blue...75.00
*Goblet, clear..40.00
Mug, amber 45.00
Mug, clear..19.00
Pitcher, milk, amber..............................60.00
Pitcher, milk, clear 45.00
Pitcher, water, amber 125.00
Pitcher, water...53.00
Plate, 6" d. 30.00
Plate, 7" d. 21.00
Plate, 9" d., closed handles, amber 45.00
Plate, 9" d., closed handles, vaseline ...35.00
Salt shaker w/original top, blue.............38.00
Salt & pepper shakers w/original
  tops, pr. 38.00
Sauce dish, flat, handled, amber 13.00
Sauce dish, flat, handled, clear 10.00
Sauce dish, footed, amber....................14.00
Sauce dish, footed, clear 11.50

Plate, 10" sq., blue.................................45.00
Plate, 10" sq., clear................................21.00
Plate, 10" sq., vaseline 28.00
Platter, 8 x 11", apple green 47.50
Platter, 8 x 11", blue 45.00
Platter, 8 x 11", vaseline 47.50
Relish, vaseline 27.50
*Salt dip, turtle-shaped, amber.............45.00
*Salt shaker w/original top, amber........35.00
Salt shaker w/original top, apple
    green..30.00
Salt shaker w/original top, blue.............55.00
Salt shaker w/original top, vaseline 55.00
Salt & pepper shakers w/original tops,
    vaseline, pr. 110.00
*Sauce dish, flat or footed, amber 13.50
*Sauce dish, flat or footed, apple
    green..22.50
*Sauce dish, flat or footed, blue............17.00
*Sauce dish, flat or footed, clear
    (ILLUS.) 12.00
*Sauce dish, flat or footed, vaseline 14.50
Spooner, amber.....................................30.00
Spooner, blue 35.00
Spooner, clear 22.00
Spooner, vaseline..................................34.00
*Sugar bowl, cov., vaseline 45.00
Sugar bowl, open, amber 25.00
Sugar bowl, open, blue..........................30.00
Syrup pitcher w/original top,
    amber....................140.00 to 160.00
Syrup pitcher w/original top, blue 350.00
Tray, dresser, blue, 4 x 9"......................45.00
Tray, dresser, vaseline, 4 x 9" 28.50
Tray, water, amber, 11 x 13" 45.00
Tray, water, blue, 11 x 13"....75.00 to 100.00
Tray, water, vaseline, 11 x 13" 50.00
Tumbler, amber 38.00
Tumbler, apple green 40.00
Tumbler, blue...45.00
Tumbler, clear..22.00
Tumbler, vaseline 35.00
Vase, 10½" h. 58.00
Waste bowl, amber................................48.00
Waste bowl, clear 28.00
Water set: pitcher, tray & 5 tumblers;
    apple green, 7 pcs. 318.00
*Wine, clear 50.00

WILLOW OAK

Bowl, cov., 7" d., flat 42.50
Bowl, 7" d., amber 14.00
Bowl, 7" d., blue.....................................47.50
Bowl, 7" d., clear (ILLUS. top next
    column) 35.00
Bread plate, clear, 9" d. 40.00
Bread plate, amber, 11" d......................42.00
Bread plate, clear, 11" d. 32.00
Butter dish, cov., amber.........................65.00
Butter dish, cov., clear 55.00
Cake stand, amber, 8" to 10" d.............57.00
Cake stand, blue, 8" to 10" d. 65.00
Cake stand, clear, 8" to 10" d. 35.00

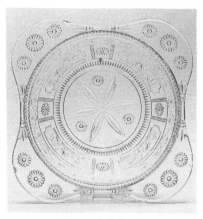

Willow Oak Bowl

Celery vase, amber 45.00
Celery vase, blue...................................125.00
Celery vase, clear..................................48.00
Compote, cov., 6" h. 75.00
Compote, cov., 8" d. 65.00
Compote, open, 6" d., scalloped top.....40.00
Compote, open, 8" d., low stand,
    amber..65.00
Creamer, amber 35.00
Creamer, blue...65.00
Creamer, clear 32.00
Creamer, vaseline 45.00
Goblet, amber...42.50
Goblet, blue 36.00
Goblet, clear 32.00
Pitcher, milk, amber................................95.00
Pitcher, milk, clear 40.00
Pitcher, water, amber 80.00
Pitcher, water, blue.................................75.00
Pitcher, water, clear................................48.00
Plate, 7" d., clear 26.00
Plate, 9" d., handled, amber 38.00
Plate, 9" d., handled, blue......................47.50
Plate, 9" d., handled, clear.....................45.00
Salt shaker w/original top, amber 40.00
Salt shaker w/original top, blue.............66.00
Salt shaker w/original top, clear............28.00
Sauce dish, flat or footed.......................15.00
Spooner, amber......................................35.00
Spooner, blue 50.00
Spooner, clear 28.00
Sugar bowl, cov. 41.00
Table set, amber, 4 pcs. .....350.00 to 375.00
Table set, clear, 4 pcs. 300.00
Tray, water, clear, 10½" d.......................32.00
Tumbler, amber 32.00
Tumbler, blue..65.00
Waste bowl, amber.................................48.00
Waste bowl, clear 29.00

WINDFLOWER

Butter dish, cov......................................45.00
Compote, cov., 8½" d., low stand.........70.00
Compote, open, 8" d................................30.00

Creamer..32.00
Egg cup 32.50
Pitcher, water.......................................65.00
Salt dip, master size 20.00
Sauce dish...12.50
Spooner 34.00
Sugar bowl, cov. 39.00

WISCONSIN (Beaded Dewdrop)

Wisconsin Wine

Banana stand, turned-up sides,
  7½" w., 4" h. 72.00
Bonbon, handled, 4" 24.00
Bowl, 6½" d..35.00
Bowl, 8" d..42.00
Butter dish, cov.....................................90.00
Cake stand, 8¼" d., 4¾" h. 42.50
Cake stand, 9¾" d. 45.00
Celery tray, flat, 5 x 10" 42.50
Celery vase...47.00
Compote, cov., 10½" d. 64.00
Compote, open, 6½" d., 3½" h...............30.00
Compote, open, 6½" d., 6½" h...............26.00
Compote, open, 7½" d., 5½" h...............42.00
Compote, open, 7" d., 4" h.,
  tricornered, medium...........................25.00
Creamer, individual size 35.00
Cruet w/original stopper.......................40.00
Cup & saucer..55.00
Dish, cov., oval 26.50
Doughnut stand, 6" d. 40.00
Marmalade jar, cov. 125.00
Mug, 3½" h. 34.00
Nappy, handled, 4" d. 20.00
Pitcher, milk..75.00
Pitcher, water, 8" h. 65.00
Plate, 5" sq. 24.00
Plate, 6½" sq. 26.00
Punch cup...16.50
Relish, 4 x 8½".......................................20.00
Salt shaker w/original top 55.00
Sauce dish..14.00
Spooner 38.00
Sugar bowl, cov., 5" h. 95.00
Sugar shaker w/original top 63.00
Syrup pitcher w/original top, 6½" h. 75.00
*Toothpick holder...................................41.00

Tumbler 45.00
Vase, 6" h. 58.00
Wine (ILLUS.) 95.00

WOODEN PAIL - See Oaken Bucket Pattern

WYOMING

Bowl, 7" d., footed................................42.50
Cake stand, 9" d., high stand................57.00
Cake stand, 10" d., high stand..............55.00
Compote, open, 8" d., shallow bowl 40.00
Creamer, open, individual, tankard
  shape 30.00
Mug..65.00
Pitcher, water, pressed handle, 3 pt. 55.00
Relish tray...28.00
Sauce dish, flat, round, 4" d.................18.00

X-RAY

Berry set: 8" d. master bowl & 6 sauce
  dishes; emerald green, 7 pcs...........155.00
Berry set: 8" d. master bowl & 8 sauce
  dishes; amethyst, 9 pcs. 295.00
Butter dish, cov., emerald green
  w/gold ....100.00 to 150.00
Carafe, large, emerald green w/gold ..135.00
Celery vase, emerald green 50.00
Compote, cov., high stand, emerald
  green...65.00
Compote, jelly, clear 42.00
Compote, jelly, emerald green.............47.00
Creamer, breakfast size, emerald
  green w/gold 55.00
Cruet w/original stopper, emerald
  green w/gold 100.00
Pitcher, water, 9½" h., emerald green
  ½ gal. 65.00
Rose bowl, emerald green w/gold 68.00
Salt shaker w/original top, amethyst.....50.00
Salt shaker w/original top, clear...........18.50
Sauce dish, clear, 4½" d......................12.00
Sauce dish, emerald green, 4½" d. 22.50
Spooner, emerald green w/gold 45.00
Sugar bowl, cov., emerald green
  w/gold 54.00
Sugar bowl, cov., breakfast size,
  emerald green w/gold 65.00
Syrup pitcher, clear w/gold 225.00
Table set, emerald green, 4 pcs.........300.00
Toothpick holder, emerald green..........60.00
Tray, condiment....................................37.50
Tumbler, amethyst.................................42.50
Tumbler, emerald green 25.00
Water set: pitcher & 4 tumblers;
  emerald green w/gold, 5 pcs............225.00

YALE - See Crowfoot Pattern

ZIPPER

Butter dish, cov.....................................39.00
Butter dish, cov., ruby-stained 100.00
Cheese dish, cov. 45.00

Creamer..35.00
Cruet w/original stopper........................36.00
Goblet...25.00
Pitcher, milk......................................55.00
Relish, 6 x 9½".....................................45.00
Sauce dish, flat or footed............6.00 to 8.00
Sugar bowl, cov. 35.00
Sugar bowl, cov., ruby-stained 65.00
Toothpick holder, green w/gold 45.00
Wine, clear...30.00
Wine, ruby-stained..............................37.50

ZIPPERED BLOCK - See Iowa Pattern

(End Of Pattern Glass Section)

PHOENIX

Phoenix Bluebell Vase

This ware was made by the Phoenix Glass Co. of Beaver County, Pennsylvania, which produced various types of glass from the 1880s. One special type that attracts collectors now is a molded ware with a vague resemblance to cameo in its "sculptured" decoration. Similar pieces with relief-molded designs were produced by the Consolidated Lamp & Glass Co. (which see) and care must be taken to differentiate between the two companies' wares. Some Consolidated molds were moved to the Phoenix plant in the mid-1930s but later returned and used again at Consolidated. These pieces we will list under "Consolidated."

Candy dish, cov., Phlox patt., tan on
milk white ground..........................$125.00
Compote, cov., Lacy Dewdrop patt.,
blue decoration on a milk white
ground...125.00

Platter, 14" d., Jonquil patt., pearlized
white on white satin ground 190.00
Vase, 6" h., 5" d., bulbous base
w/short flaring neck, Aster patt.,
green on milk white ground.............125.00
Vase, 6" h., 5" d., bulbous base
w/short flaring neck, Aster patt., tan
on milk white ground.........................95.00
Vase, 7" h., bulbous base w/trumpet-
form sides, Bluebell patt., brown on
milk white ground............................115.00
Vase, 7" h., bulbous base w/trumpet-
form sides, Bluebell patt., pearlized
finish 63.00
Vase, 7" h., bulbous base w/trumpet-
form sides, Bluebell patt., pink
pearlized finish (ILLUS.) 75.00
Vase, 8¾" h., footed, tapering
cylindrical body w/flaring rim,
Primrose patt., green background
w/frosted design..............................125.00

Wild Geese Vase

Vase, 9¼" h., pillow-shaped, Wild
Geese patt., white birds on a blue
ground (ILLUS.) 185.00
Vase, 9½" h., baluster-form, Wild
Rose patt., burgundy ground
w/pearlized design 300.00
Vase, 10½" h., ovoid body, Wild Rose
patt., pearlized flowers on a rose
ground..225.00
Vase, 10½" h., ovoid body, Wild Rose
patt., white pearlized finish 160.00
Vase, 11½" h., baluster-form, Dancing
Girls line, brown shadow figures on
brown ground...................................495.00
Vase, 11½" h., Dancing Girls line,
clear w/frosted nudes.......................195.00
Vase, 11½" h., baluster-shaped,
Philodendron patt., sky blue ground
w/pearlized white leaves..................200.00
Vase, 18" h., tall ovoid body, Thistle
patt., pearlized white thistles on
white ground 400.00
Vase, 18" h., tall ovoid body, Thistle
patt., white thistles on a pale blue
ground, w/original paper label..........550.00

PILLAR-MOLDED

This heavily ribbed glassware was produced by blowing glass into full-sized ribbed molds and then finishing it by hand. The technique evolved from earlier "pattern moulding" used on glass since ancient times but in pillar-molded glass the ribs are very heavy and prominent. Most examples found in this country were produced in the Pittsburgh, Pennsylvania area from around 1850 to 1870, but similar English-made wares made before and after this period are also available. Most American pieces were made from clear flint glass and colored examples or pieces with colored strands in the ribs are rare and highly prized. Some collectors refer to this as "steamboat" glass believing that it was made to be used on American riverboats but most likely it was used anywhere that a sturdy, relatively inexpensive glassware was needed, such as taverns and hotels.

Decanter w/bar lip, eight-rib, clear, tapering conical form w/applied neck rings, 9¾" h. $82.50
Decanters w/matching ribbed pear-shaped stoppers, eight-rib, clear, bell-shaped body w/notched ribs tapering to ringed cylindrical neck, cut panels between the ribs on the shoulder, pr. 14" h............................412.50
Decanter w/original blown stopper w/airtrap, eight-rib, clear, 12⅝" h. 200.00
Pitcher, 5⅝" h., eight-rib, clear, rounded conical body tapering to a flaring rim w/pinched spout, applied strap handle w/curl end....................550.00
Pitcher, 7¼" h., eight-rib, deep amethyst, slightly tapering cylindrical body w/neck ring & wide slightly flaring rim, applied strap handle, tiny broken blister inside, wear, scratches 8,800.00
Pitcher, 8⅝" h., eight-rib, clear, bulbous base w/deeply waisted sides to a flared rim w/a wide spout, applied strap handle 330.00
Pitcher, tankard, 9½" h., eleven-rib, clear, applied handle........................385.00
Pitcher, 10½" h., eight-rib, clear, bulbous base tapering in at mid-section & out at top, applied foot & handle 605.00
Sugar bowl, cov., eight-rib, clear, deep rounded bowl w/galleried rim, tall slender pyramidal cover w/button finial, on slender waisted applied stem & round foot, 10⅝" h. (small

flake on top of finial at pontil) 1,870.00
Syrup jug w/original metal neck & cover, eight-rib, clear, ovoid footed base tapering to a cylindrical neck fitted w/hinged metal rim & spouted cover, applied strap handle, 11¼" h..247.50

Pillar-Molded Syrup Pitcher

Syrup pitcher w/original hinged metal lid, twelve-rib, amber, footed pear-shaped body w/applied strap handle, Pittsburgh, mid-19th c., 7" h. (ILLUS.) 2,640.00
Vase, 8" h., eight-rib, clear, tall flaring tulip-form bowl w/swirled ribs at the top, applied knopped stem & disc foot (shallow chip on one rib) 440.00
Vase, 9¾" h., 5½" d., eight-rib, clear, deep tulip-form bowl w/the ribs swirled at the top, on an applied pedestal w/knob at base above the disc foot 214.50
Vase, 11½" h., 5" d., eight-rib, tall flaring tulip-form bowl applied w/a wafer to a knopped octagonal pressed pedestal base, soft bluish opalescence at the rim, probably New England Glass Company.........550.00

RUBY-STAINED

This name derives from the color of the glass - a deep red. The red staining was thinly painted on clear pressed glass patterns and .refired at a low temperature. Many pieces were further engraved as souvenir items and were very popular from the 1890s into the 1920s. This technique should not be confused with "flashed" glass where a clear glass piece is actually dipped in molten glass of a contrasting color. Also see PATTERN GLASS.

Berry set: master bowl & four sauce
  dishes; Bar & Flute patt., 5 pcs......$160.00
Berry set: master bowl & six sauce
  dishes; Riverside's Victoria patt.,
  7 pcs. 265.00
Berry set: master bowl & six sauce
  dishes; Spearpoint Band patt.,
  7 pcs. 175.00
Bowl, berry, individual, Bar & Flute
  patt..20.00
Bowl, master berry, Bar & Flute patt.....80.00
Butter dish, cov., Duncan's Empire
  patt., 5¼" h.....................................110.00
Butter dish, cov., Heavy Gothic patt. ...155.00
Butter dish, cov., Lenore patt................95.00

Majestic Ruby-Stained Butter

Butter dish, cov., Majestic patt.,
  7½" d., 6" h. (ILLUS.) 110.00
Butter dish, cov., Tacoma patt..............80.00
Butter dish, cov., Tarentum's Atlanta
  patt..90.00
Butter dish, cov., Triple Triangle patt....90.00

Melrose Celery Vase

Celery vase, Melrose patt., engraved
  blossom & leaf band, 6¼" h.
  (ILLUS.) 110.00
Compote, 8¼" x 8½", open, Scroll with
  Cane Band patt................................220.00
Creamer, Almond Thumbprint patt.,
  4½" h..20.00
Creamer, Arched Ovals patt. 45.00

Majestic Creamer

Creamer, Majestic patt., 4½" h.
  (ILLUS.) 75.00
Creamer, Prize patt. 85.00
Creamer, Puritan patt. 39.00
Creamer, individual, Truncated Cube
  patt..30.00
Cruet w/original stopper, Button Panel
  patt...369.00
Cruet w/original stopper, National's
  Eureka patt. 250.00
Cruet w/original stopper, The Prize
  patt...350.00
Cruet w/original stopper, Zippered
  Swirl & Diamond patt. 85.00
Cup, Arched Ovals patt., souvenir........27.50
Goblet, Beaded Dart Band patt. 25.00
Goblet, Diamond Band w/Panels patt...25.00
Goblet, Swag Block patt. 50.00
Pitcher, tankard, Hexagon Block
  patt...110.00
Pitcher, water, Carnation patt., w/gold
  trim 265.00
Pitcher, water, Foster Block patt.........225.00
Pitcher, water, Ladder with Diamond
  patt...250.00
Pitcher, water, Leaf & Star patt.,
  w/gold trim 300.00
Pitcher, water, Triple Triangle patt........75.00
Sauce dish, Millard patt. 25.00

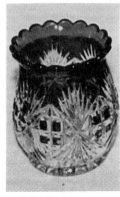

Majestic Spooner

Spooner, Majestic patt., 4⅛" h.
(ILLUS.) 65.00
Spooner, Triple Triangle patt. 55.00
Straw holder, The Prize patt. 95.00
Sugar bowl, cov., Heavy Gothic
patt. 125.00
Sugar shaker w/original top, Late
Block patt. 295.00
Syrup pitcher w/original top, Beauty
patt. 395.00
Syrup pitcher w/original top, Millard
patt. 275.00
Syrup pitcher w/original top, Zippered
Corner patt. 395.00
Table set: cov. butter dish, creamer,
cov. sugar bowl & spooner; Dia-
mond Band with Panel patt.,
4 pcs. 190.00
Toothpick holder, Box-In-Box patt.,
w/enameled floral decoration...........145.00
Toothpick holder, National's Eureka
patt. 95.00
Toothpick holder, Summit patt.,
souvenir 50.00
Toothpick holder, Tarentum
Thumbprint patt., dated "1914" 24.00
Tumbler, Arched Ovals patt.,
souvenir 45.00
Tumbler, Diamond & Sunburst Variant
patt. 29.00
Tumbler, Late Block patt.......................15.00

Blocked Thumbprint Water Set

Water set: 10½" h., 5½" d. pitcher,
four 3" d., 4" h. tumblers;
Blocked Thumbprint patt., ruby
& clear frosted bands, 5 pcs.
(ILLUS.) 225.00
Water set: pitcher & six tumblers;
Diamond Band with Panel patt.,
7 pcs. 145.00
Wine, Block Band patt. 24.00
Wine, Riverside's Esther patt. 28.00
Wine, Rustic Rose patt. 25.00
Wine, Teardrop & Thumbprint patt. 30.00
Wine, Triple Triangle patt. 25.00

SANDWICH

Sandwich Columnar Candlestick

*Numerous types of glass were produced
at The Boston & Sandwich Glass Works in
Sandwich, Massachusetts, on Cape Cod,
from 1826 to 1888. Those listed here
represent a sampling. Also see PATTERN
GLASS and LACY.*

*All pieces are pressed glass unless
otherwise noted.*

Bowl, 6" d., lacy, Rayed Peacock Eye
patt., clear $135.00
Candlestick, the hexagonal tulip-
shaped socket above a ring-and-
knob shaft applied w/a wafer to the
flaring hexagonal base, medium
green, ca. 1840, 7" h. (minute flake
in side of socket) 1,210.00
Candlestick, Dolphin patt., the petal-
form dark blue socket on a short
knob stem applied w/a wafer to the
milky clambroth figural dolphin
pedestal on a double-step square
foot, ca. 1850, 9¾" h. 715.00
Candlesticks, dark blue petal socket
atop a milky clambroth columnar
standard w/stepped, square base,
ca. 1850, minor base chips, heat
check in one socket, 9¼" h.,
pr. (ILLUS. of one) 1,320.00
Candlesticks, Acanthus Leaf patt.,
opaque blue hexagonal leaf-molded
socket applied w/a wafer to the
baluster-form acanthus leaf-molded
milky clambroth pedestal & domed,
leaf-molded hexagonal foot,
10⅞" h., pr. (very minor flakes
under foot.....................................1,870.00
Candlesticks, Petal & Loop patt.,
clear, pr. 120.00
Celery tray, footed, Diamond Point
patt., applied gold on rim & feet 125.00
Cologne bottle w/original lily-shaped
stopper, urn-shaped body raised on

a pedestal base, black amethyst
body decorated w/a h.p. stork in a
circle of flowers, base & stopper
w/matching numbers, 7½" h. 250.00
Cologne bottle w/original steeple-
shaped stopper w/air trap, ring-
necked bottle, dark green 250.00
Compote, open, 8¼" h., 8" d., Ribbon
patt., upright reticulated sides on the
bowl, thick wafer joining bowl to
large flaring hexagonal base, clear ..770.00
Compote, open, 9½" d., 6¾" h.,
Petal & Loop patt., moonstone 1,650.00
Egg cup, Diamonds in Oval patt.,
starch blue, ca. 1840-50 ....385.00
Lamp, kerosene table-type, cut
overlay, the inverted pear-shaped
font in blue cut to white cut to clear
w/a band of oblong cartouches
above a band of thumbprints, on a
reeded brass pedestal & a stepped
white marble foot w/brass trim,
ca. 1860-75, 12" h. 977.50

Rare Sandwich Lamp

Lamp, kerosene table-type, lavender
blown-molded ribbed onion-form
font w/a metal connector ring to the
ribbed matching pedestal base,
attributed to Sandwich, ca. 1865-80,
12¼" h. (ILLUS.) 6,900.00
Salt shaker, "Christmas" salt w/dated
metal top w/agitator, amber, lid
signed "Dana K. Alden, Boston" 65.00
Salt shakers, "Christmas" salt w/dated
metal top w/agitator, in original box
labeled "Dana K. Alden's World
Renowned Table Salt Bottles," two
amethyst, one each cobalt blue,
pale aqua blue, vaseline & amber,
set of 6 (one top & agitator badly
corroded) 715.00
Salt & pepper shakers, "Christmas"
salt w/dated metal top w/agitator,
amber, 2⅝" h., pr. 247.50

Salt & pepper shakers, "Christmas"
salt w/dated metal top w/agitator,
deep cobalt blue, 2⅝" h., pr. 275.00
Spill holder, Sandwich Star patt.,
clear 75.00
String holder, domical, overlay, cut
thumbprint design w/cobalt blue cut
to clear 275.00
Sugar bowl, cov., lacy, octagonal
Acanthus Leaf patt., deep emerald
green, 5½" h. (usual mold rough-
ness) 17,600.00
Sugar bowl, cov., lacy, Gothic Arch
patt., opaque blue w/lightly 'sanded'
surface, 5¼" h. (small chips).........1,375.00
Sugar bowl, cov., lacy, octagonal
Gothic Arch patt., opaque starch
blue, 5⅜" h. (three shallow chips on
upper rim of base & finial).............1,430.00
Sugar bowl, cov., lacy, Gothic Arch
patt., octagonal flaring sides
w/arches on a low foot, matching
domed cover w/button finial, canary
yellow, ca. 1840 (minor roughness
inside cover) 1,100.00
Vase, 9¼" h., ovoid opaque
moonstone Sawtooth patt. body
raised on a blown jade green
pedestal foot & w/a tall blown jade
green slender trumpet neck
w/flattened ruffled rim, ca. 1860....1,980.00
Vase, 10" h., "Trevaise" art glass,
baluster-form body tapering to a flat
mouth, opaque green w/gold
iridescent heart-shaped leaf & vine
decoration, recessed button pontil,
Alton Manufacturing Co. of
Sandwich, late 19th c......................920.00
Vases, 10½" h., tulip-type, flaring
paneled bowl above a knopped
stem & flaring octagonal base,
canary yellow, ca. 1850, pr. (traces
of mold roughness) 1,430.00

STIEGEL & STIEGEL-TYPE

*This glass was made at the American
Flint Glass works of "Baron" Henry W.
Stiegel at Manheim, Pennsylvania, from
1765 until the 1770's. It is difficult to
attribute pieces positively to Stiegel.*

Bottle, half post-type, blown, clear
w/polychrome floral enameling on
one side & barrel, compass & tools
on the other, pewter cap, 6⅜" h.....$132.00
Bottle, pocket-type, blown, molded
Daisy & Diamond design above
thirty vertical ribs, sheared & fire
polished lip, amethyst, 4¾" h.
(ILLUS.) 126.50

Stiegel-Type Bottle

Bottle, pocket-type, blown, Ogival
  pattern, sheared & fire polished lip,
  amethyst, 5½" h. (slight roughness
  on bottom edge)..........................3,850.00
Creamer, ovoid body tapering to a
  short cylindrical neck w/flared rim &
  pinched shoulder, applied strap
  handle, overall diamond quilted
  patt., brilliant sapphire blue,
  3⅜" h..1,430.00
Mug, blown w/applied handle, clear
  w/polychrome floral enameling one
  side & deer on the other, 5⁵⁄₁₆" h.
  (check at handle) 412.50
Salt dip, mold-blown in the expanded
  diamond design, bell-shaped bowl
  w/incurved rim on a short round
  base, cobalt blue.............................132.00
Sugar bowl, cov., circular footed body,
  the domed cover w/flanged rim &
  acorn finial, blue, possibly Manheim,
  Pennsylvania, late 18th c., 7" h.....1,265.00

STRETCH

Collectors have given this name to a
glassware related to Carnival Glass which
features a lightly iridized finish somewhat
resembling the skin of an onion. It is most
often found on pastel-colored wares in light
blue, green, amethyst, amber and pink.
Stretch wares, popular in the 1920s, were
produced by many American glass firms
including Fenton, Northwood and
Imperial.

Bowl, 10½" d., blue............................$25.00
Candleholders, blue, 7½" h.,
  pr...65.00 to 75.00
Candy dish, cov., blue 60.00
Candy dish, cov., dolphin-shaped
  base, blue 75.00

Northwood Stretch Compote

Compote, open, deep flaring bowl
  raised on a tall paneled stem
  w/double knobs above a round foot,
  blue, Northwood Glass Co.
  (ILLUS.) 55.00
Plate, 9" d., amethyst...........................14.00
Plate, luncheon, pearl iridescent
  w/green trim 45.00
Powder jar, cov., vaseline....................40.00
Vase, 8" h., fan-shaped, No. 857,
  Celeste Blue, Fenton Art Glass Co....50.00
Vase, 8" h., fan-shaped, No. 857,
  Tangerine, Fenton Art Glass Co. 90.00
Whipped cream bowl w/matching
  ladle, footed, green, 6¾" d., 2 pcs. 68.00

TIFFIN

Tiffin Glass Label

A wide variety of fine glasswares were
produced by the Tiffin Glass Company of
Tiffin, Ohio. Beginning as a part of the
large U.S. Glass Company early in this
century, the Tiffin factory continued
making a wide range of wares until its
final closing in 1984. One popular line is
now called "Black Satin" and included
various vases with raised floral designs.
Many other acid-etched and hand-cut
patterns were also produced over the years
and are very collectible today. The three
"Tiffin Glassmasters" books by Fred
Bickenheuser are the standard references
for Tiffin collectors.

Basket, flower, No. 6553, clear...........$85.00

Candlesticks, Black Satin, No. 82,
8½" h., pr. 45.00

Candy dish, cov., coralene florals
decoration on Black Satin ground......88.00

Candy dish, cov., heart-shaped,
decorated w/pink flowers, green 58.00

Carafe, etched Roses patt., clear.........72.00

Champagne, etched Flanders patt.,
pink 36.00

Champagne, etched June Night patt.,
clear, 6 oz. 18.00

Cocktail, etched Cordelia patt...............10.00

Compote, 7½", twist stem, No. 315,
vaseline satin 55.00

Console set: 13" d. bowl w/deep
everted rim & pair of candleholders;
Fontaine etching, bowl No. 8153,
candleholders No. 9758, twilite,
3 pcs. 385.00

Creamer & sugar bowl, etched
Fuchsia patt., clear, pr. 50.00

Creamer & sugar bowl, etched June
Night patt., clear, pr. 40.00

Flower bowl, cut Twilight patt.,
No. 9153-108, clear, 10" d. 165.00

Goblet, etched Cherokee Rose patt.,
clear, 8" h. 18.00

Goblet, etched Classic patt., clear........28.00

Goblet, Diamond Optic patt., All Rose-
Pink, 10 oz. 30.00

Goblet, etched Flanders patt., pink.......42.00

Goblet, Franciscan patt., citron.............10.00

Goblet, water, etched Fuchsia patt.,
clear, 7⅝" h. 24.00

Goblet, etched Persian Pheasant
patt., clear 35.00

Parfait, etched Byzantine patt., clear....22.00

Plate, 8" d., etched Flanders patt.,
yellow..11.50

Plate, 8⅛" d., etched Fuchsia patt.,
clear 22.00

Rose bowl w/three ball feet, Copen
blue, medium 45.00

Sherbet, etched Classic patt., clear......22.00

Sherbet, etched Fuchsia patt., clear.....25.00

Tumbler, iced tea, footed, Fuchsia
patt., clear 30.00

Tumbler, footed, etched June Night
patt., clear, 10½ oz. 30.00

Tumbler, juice, footed, etched Persian
Pheasant patt., clear, 5 oz. 15.00

Vase, 5" h., etched Poppy patt., black
amethyst 85.00

Vase, 6" h., four-footed, cut Twilight
patt., clear 85.00

Vase, 6½" h., Black Satin ground
w/alternating glossy stripes................55.00

Vase, bud, 10" h., etched Cherokee
Rose patt., clear.................................45.00

Vase, 11" h., footed, etched June
Night patt., clear.................................75.00

Vase, 19" h., free-form, No. 17424,
Desert Red..75.00

Wine, etched June Night patt., clear.....35.00

VASELINE

Vaseline Cologne Bottle

Vaseline is a term used to describe a wide range of pressed, free-blown and mold-blown glasswares popular since the mid-19th century. It refers to the yellowish green color of such wares which resembles the hue of petroleum jelly. The color was obtained by adding uranium salts to the glass batch and the term is fairly modern. Originally the yellow color was called "canary" by glass manufacturers.

Popular in Victorian pressed glass and early 20th century decorative glasswares, the color was not widely produced after the 1930s.

For additional background see Yellow-Green Vaseline! A Guide to The Magic Glass *by Jay L. Glickman (Antique Publications, 1991).*

Cologne bottle w/original facet-cut
vaseline stopper, cylindrical body
w/embossed oval ring pattern on
sides, 19th c., 2" d., 4¾" h.
(ILLUS.) $110.00

Compote, open, 8" d., footed, three-
panel design 65.00

Cruet w/original stopper, Big Button
patt..85.00

Cruet w/original stopper, Ranson
patt..175.00

Dish, opalescent, oval w/scalloped
rim, pressed paneled cane design,
England, ca. 1900, 6½ x 8½" 75.00

Salt dip, master-size, opalescent, in
silver plate frame w/spoon, 2⅛" d.,
4½" h...75.00

Salt dip, master-size, opalescent,
scalloped edge, vaseline shell trim
applied around sides, in silver plate
footed frame, 3¼" d., overall 2" h.....125.00

Toothpick holder, petticoat style,
Radiant patt., gold trim....................110.00

VICTORIAN COLORED GLASS

There are, of course, many types of colored glassware of the Victorian era and we cover a great variety of these in our various glass categories. However, there are some pieces of pressed, mold-blown and free-blown Victorian colored glass which don't fit well into other specific listings, so we have chosen to include a selection of them here.

Inverted Thumbprint Pitcher

Animal covered dish, Cow on oval
  paneled base, black opaque..........$500.00
Animal covered dish, Lion on picket
  base, opaque blue w/white head,
  5½" l...85.00
Box w/hinged cover, free-blown,
  cobalt blue, lacy-style, decoration
  w/enameled dainty white leaves &
  gold flowers around sides w/gold
  dots, scallops w/dainty white leaves
  in reserves, 2" d., 1¼" h...................145.00
Box w/hinged lid, free-blown, cobalt
  blue, decorated w/white enameled
  daisies & leaves on cover, 2" d.,
  1¼" h...135.00
Cracker jar, cov., free-blown, barrel-
  shaped, lime green enameled
  w/overall decoration of dainty blue
  forget-me-nots, green leaves &
  lavender foliage, resilvered cover,
  rim & bail handle, 4¾" d., 6½" h.......225.00
Cracker jar, cov., free-blown, barrel-
  shaped, lime green decorated
  overall w/sprays of dainty pink &
  blue flowers & green leaves,
  resilvered rim, handle & cover,
  5" d., 6¾" h. 225.00
Cracker jar, cov., pressed, rectangular
  shape, Water Lilies & Cattails patt.,
  opaque chartreuse, silver plate lid,
  rim & bail handle, 6" d., 9" h.............150.00

Creamer, mold-blown, bulbous body
  w/squared mouth, Inverted
  Thumbprint patt., amber body &
  applied amber handle, ca. 1880s,
  5" h..30.00
Decanter w/original spear-shaped
  amethyst cut to clear bubble
  stopper, bulbous amethyst cut to
  clear body w/eight-cut panels, short
  cylindrical neck, pattern cut under
  scalloped foot, 3⅞" d., 11" h. 145.00
Pitcher, 8" h., 5½" d., mold-blown
  Inverted Thumbprint patt., footed
  ovoid body tapering to a short
  cylindrical neck, applied angular
  handle, aqua blue decorated w/large
  white & yellow blossoms & green
  leaves & branch (ILLUS.)................165.00
Salt dip, master-size, chartreuse
  green w/green threaded decoration,
  clear applied snail feet, 1¾" d.,
  1¼" h..65.00
Salt shaker w/original top, Challinor's
  Forget-Me-Not patt., Nile green.........40.00
Salt & pepper shakers w/original tops,
  Inverted Thumbprint patt., blue, pr...120.00
Sugar shaker w/original top, Argus
  Swirl patt., peach bloom 250.00
Syrup pitcher w/original top, Inverted
  Thumbprint patt., blue, Hobbs,
  Brockunier & Co..............................140.00
Toothpick holder, Jefferson Optic
  patt., blue 65.00
Tumble-up (water carafe w/tumbler
  lid), free-blown, footed spherical
  body w/cylindrical neck fitted w/a
  tumbler, sapphire blue enameled
  w/large white flowers & leaves,
  4⅞" d., 7¾" h., 2 pcs.......................195.00
Vase, 6⅞" h., 6½" d., ovoid melon-
  ribbed body w/widely flaring rolled &
  crimped rim w/applied clear edging,
  clear applied feet w/gold trim,
  sapphire blue, decorated overall
  w/dainty pink & white flowers & tan
  leaves 325.00

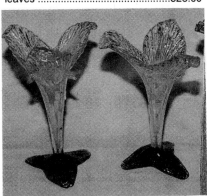

Flower-Form Vases

Vase, 8" h., 4" d., trumpet-form
w/vaseline petals applied around the
rim, body sharply tapering to four
applied vaseline petal-shaped feet,
cased creamy body w/chartreuse
lining 95.00

Vases, 4¼" h., 2¾" d., squatty bulbous bases tapering to a trumpet-
form neck w/slightly flaring &
scalloped rim, cobalt blue decorated
w/white daisies w/yellow centers,
pink buds & green leaves, pr. 125.00

Vases, 8⅛" h., 5⅜" w., flower-form
w/large flaring triple-petal rim w/pink
opalescent tips spattered w/pink
specks then shading to yellow &
clear, green three-leaf applied
foot, pr. (ILLUS. bottom of previous
page)..185.00

WESTMORELAND

Westmoreland Cat on Lacy Base Dish

*The Westmoreland Specialty Company
was founded in East Liverpool, Ohio in
1889 and relocated in 1890 to Grapeville,
Pennsylvania where it remained until its
closing in 1985.*

*During its early years Westmoreland
specialized in glass food containers and
novelties but by the turn of the century they
had a large line of milk white items and
clear tableware patterns. In 1925 the
company name was shortened to The Westmoreland Glass Company and it was
during that decade that more colored
glasswares entered their line-up. When
Victorian-style milk glass again became
popular in the 1940s and 1950s, Westmoreland produced extensive amounts in
several patterns which closely resemble late
19th century wares. These and their figural animal dishes in milk white and
colors are widely collected today but buyers
should not confuse them for the antique
originals. Watch for Westmoreland's "WG"*

*mark on some pieces. A majority of our
listings are products from the 1940s
through the 1970s. Earlier pieces will be
indicated.*

Early Westmoreland Label & Mark

Animal covered dish, Cat on a lacy
base, glass eyes, opaque blue,
copied from the Atterbury original
(ILLUS.) $55.00

Animal covered dish, Cat on a lacy
base, glass eyes, purple slag,
copied from the Atterbury original......70.00

Animal covered dish, Chick and Eggs,
milk white, copied from the Atterbury
original 95.00

Animal covered dish, Duck on a wavy
base, purple slag, copied from the
Challinor, Taylor & Co. original 110.00

Animal covered dish, Hen on nest,
chocolate brown w/iridizing, gold
yellow & green trim, copied from
antique original 125.00

Animal covered dish, Hen on nest, red
& yellow slag, copied from antique
original 75.00

Animal covered dish, Lamb on picket
base, Green Marble, copied from
antique original, 5½" l. 65.00

Animal covered dish, Rabbit on picket
base, chocolate, copied from
antique original, 5½" l. 40.00

Animal covered dish, Robin on Twig
Nest, light blue, copied from antique
original 75.00

Animal covered dish, Rooster on
ribbed base, milk white w/blue head,
copied from antique original, 5½" l.....95.00

Animal covered dish, Rooster on
ribbed base, purple slag, copied
from antique original, 5½" l. 118.00

Ashtray, Beaded Grape (No. 1884)
patt., milk white, 6½" l. 9.00

Banana stand, Doric (No. 3) patt., milk
white 30.00

Banana stand, Paneled Grape
(No. 1881) patt., milk white 90.00

Banana stand, Ring & Petal
(No. 1885) patt., clear 38.00

Basket, oval w/open handle, Paneled
Grape (No. 1881) patt., milk white 28.00

Batter pitcher, Old Quilt (No. 500)
patt., milk white 35.00

Bowl, cov., 9" d., Beaded Grape
(No. 1884) patt., milk white 55.00

Bowl, 13" d., Thousand Eye
(No. 1000) patt., clear 35.00

Butter dish, cov., Old Quilt (No. 500)
 patt., milk white, ¼ lb. 34.00
Candleholders, Old Quilt patt., milk
 white, pr. 20.00
Candlesticks, model of a dolphin
 w/hexagon base, milk white,
 9" h., pr. 125.00
Candy dish, cov., English Hobnail
 (No. 555) patt., clear 28.00
Candy dish, cov., Old Quilt patt.,
 clear 22.50
Celery tray, Old Quilt patt., milk white,
 10" l..30.00
Celery vase, Old Quilt patt., milk
 white, 6½" h. 35.00
Cheese dish, cov., Old Quilt patt., milk
 white 60.00
Compote, 8", ball stem, Della Robia
 (No. 1058) patt., colored trim 85.00
Compote, 8" h., shell-shaped bowl
 w/dolphin base, Mother of Pearl
 Dolphin & Shell line, milk white
 w/mother of pearl finish......................77.00
Compote, 11" d., 6½" h., Lattice Edge
 (No. 1890) patt., milk white 75.00
Console set: 9½ x 12" oval, footed
 bowl w/flared rim & two 4" h. candle-
 sticks; Paneled Grape patt., milk
 white, 3 pcs. 85.00
Creamer, Old Quilt patt., milk white......14.00
Creamer & open sugar bowl, Della
 Robbia patt., milk white, pr. 24.00
Cruet w/original stopper, Della Robbia
 patt., milk white 18.00
Cup & saucer, English Hobnail patt.,
 milk white 15.00
Cup & saucer, Old Quilt patt., milk
 white 30.00
Cup & saucer, Paneled Grape patt.,
 milk white 16.50
Decanter w/original stopper, Paneled
 Grape patt., milk white 125.00
Dresser set: two cologne bottles
 w/original stoppers, cov. puff box &
 oval tray; Paneled Grape patt.,
 clear, 4 pcs. 215.00
Goblet, water, American Hobnail
 (No. 77) patt., milk white 14.00
Goblet, water, Della Robbia patt.,
 colored trim, 6" h., 8 oz. 37.50
Goblet, water, Della Robbia patt.,
 milk white 16.00
Goblet, Paneled Grape patt., Honey
 Amber Carnival 12.00
Goblet, water, Paneled Grape patt.,
 milk white 13.00
Goblet, brandy or wine, Princess
 Feather (No. 201) patt., blue..............17.00
Gravy boat & underplate, Paneled
 Grape patt., milk white, 2 pcs. 52.50
Honey dish, cov., Beaded Grape patt.,
 milk white 14.00
Honey dish, cov., Old Quilt patt., milk
 white 20.00

Pitcher, water, 12" h., Paneled Grape
 patt., milk white, 1 qt. 50.00
Planter, Paneled Grape patt., milk
 white, 4½" sq. 30.00
Plate, 7" d., Beaded Edge patt., clear...12.00
Plate, dinner, 10½" d., Beaded Edge
 patt., clear 20.00
Plate, dinner, 10½" d., Paneled Grape
 patt., milk white 25.00
Punch cup, Old Quilt patt., milk white.....8.00
Punch cup, Paneled Grape patt.,
 Brandywine blue 10.00
Punch cup, Paneled Grape patt.,
 milk white 9.00
Punch set: 5 qt. punch bowl, 18" d.
 underplate, twelve cups & ladle;
 Paneled Grape patt., milk white,
 15 pcs. 550.00
Salt & pepper shakers w/original tops,
 Old Quilt patt., milk white, pr. 14.00
Salt & pepper shakers w/original tops,
 footed, Paneled Grape patt., milk
 white, pr. 18.00
Sherbet, American Hobnail patt., milk
 white 15.00
Sherbet, Della Robbia patt., milk
 white 12.00
Spooner, Paneled Grape patt., milk
 white 20.00
Sugar bowl, cov., Old Quilt patt., milk
 white 9.00
Syrup pitcher w/original top, Old Quilt
 patt., milk white 30.00
Table set: cov. butter dish, cov. sugar
 bowl, creamer & spooner; Ring &
 Petal (No. 1875) patt., cobalt blue,
 4 pcs. 600.00
Tumbler, pilsner-type, American
 Hobnail (No. 77) patt., clear 18.00
Tumbler, iced tea, footed, Della
 Robbia patt., milk white.......................18.00
Tumbler, Old Quilt patt., clear, 9 oz......10.00
Tumbler, iced tea, Paneled Grape
 patt., milk white, 12 oz. 18.00
Tumbler, water, Paneled Grape patt.,
 clear 15.00
Vase, 6" h., Paneled Grape patt., milk
 white 10.00
Vase, 9" h., fan-shaped w/octagonal
 foot, Old Quilt patt., milk white 20.00
Vase, 9" h., flared rim, Paneled Grape
 patt., milk white 29.00
Vase, bud, 11" h., Paneled Grape
 patt., milk white 25.00
Vase, 12" h., Paneled Grape patt.,
 milk white 50.00
Vase, 16" h., "swung"-type, Paneled
 Grape patt., milk white 30.00
Water set: 9" h. pitcher & six 6" h.
 tumblers; Paneled Grape patt.,
 clear, 7 pcs. 200.00
Wine set: decanter w/original stopper
 & eight 2 oz. wines; Paneled Grape
 patt., milk white, 9 pcs. 185.00

GLOSSARY OF SELECTED
GLASS TERMS

Applied - A handle or other portion of a vessel which consists of a separate piece of molten glass attached by hand to the object. Most often used with free-blown or mold-blown pieces but also used with early pressed glass.

Banana stand - A dish, usually round, with two sides turned-up to form a valley and resting atop a pedestal base. A *banana bowl* is usually an oblong or boat-shaped bowl with deep sides. Popular form in late Victorian pattern glass.

Bar lip - A style of lip used on early pressed and mold-blown decanters where a thick ring of applied glass forms the rim of the piece.

Berry bowl - A small dish, most often round, used to serve individual helpings of ripe berries but also used for ice cream or other desserts. It was usually part of a set which included a large (master) berry bowl and several small ones. A popular form in pressed glass.

Celery vase - A tall vase-form vessel, often with a pedestal base, used to serve celery in the Victorian era. It was a common pressed glass piece used in most homes.

Crimping - A method of decorating the rims of bowls and vases. The glassworker used a special hand tool to manipulate the nearly-molten pressed or blown glass and form a ribbon-like design.

Crystal - A generic term generally used today when referring to thin, fine quality glass stemware produced since the early 20th century. Derived from the Italian term *cristallo* referring to delicate, clear Venetian blown glass produced since the 14th century.

Egg cup - A small footed cup, sometimes with a cover, that was meant to hold a soft-boiled egg at breakfast. Most commonly found in early pressed flint glass patterns of the 1840-70 era.

Elegant glass - A modern collector's term used when referring to the better quality 20th century glasswares of such companies as Heisey, Cambridge or Fostoria. Meant to differentiate these wares from the less expensive Depression glass of the same era.

Epergne - A French term used to describe a special decorative vessel popular in the 19th century. It generally consists of one or more tall, slender trumpet-form vases centering a wide, shallow bowl base. The bowl base could also be raised on a pedestal foot. It sometimes refers to a piece with a figural pedestal base supporting several small bowls or suspending several small baskets. Also made from silver or other metals.

Etching - A method of decorating a piece of glass. The two main types are *acid etching* and *needle etching*. In acid etching a piece is covered with an acid-resistant protective layer and then scratched with a design which is then exposed to hydrofluoric acid or acid fumes, thus leaving a frosted design when the protective layer is removed. Needle etching is a 20th century technique where a hand-held or mechanized needle is used to draw a fine-lined design on a piece. Ornate repetative designs were possible with the mechanized needle.

Fire-polishing - A process used to finish early American mold-blown and pressed glass where a piece is reheated just enough to smooth out the mold seams without distorting the overall pattern.

Flint glass - The term used to refer to early 19th century glass which was produced using *lead oxide* in the batch, thus producing a heavy and brilliant glass with a belltone resonance when tapped. When first developed, powdered flints were used instead of lead oxide, hence the name. Nineteenth century American glassmakers used "flint" to describe any quality glass, whether or not it was made with lead.

Galleried rim - A form of rim most often used in early free-blown or mold-blown glass objects, usually sugar bowls. The rim is turned-up around the edge to form a low shelf or gallery which will support the cover.

Knop - Another term for 'knob,' usually referring to a finial on a lid or a bulbous section on the stem of a goblet or wine glass.

Marigold - The most common color used in Carnival glass, generally a bright iridescent orange.

Milk white glass - Also known as *milk glass*; an opaque solid white color popular in the late 19th century for some glass patterns, novelties and animal covered dishes. Glassmen referred to it as *opal* (o-pál).

Mold-blown - A method of glass production where a blob of molten glass (called a "gather") is blown into a patterned mold and then removed and further blown and manipulated to form an object such as a bottle.

Novelty - A pressed glass object generally made in the form of some larger item like a hatchet, boat or animal. They were extremely popular in the late 19th century and many were meant to be used as match holders, toothpick holders and small dresser boxes.

Opal - Pronounced o-pál, this was the term used by 19th century glassmen to describe the solid white glass today known as milk glass.

Pattern glass - A term generally referring to the popular pressed glass tablewares produced from the mid-19th century into the early 20th century.

Pontil mark - The scar left on the base of a free-blown, mold-blown and some early pressed glass by the pontil or punty rod. The hot glass object was attached at the base to the pontil rod so the glassworker could more easily handle it during the final shaping and finishing. When snapped off the pontil a round scar remained which, on finer quality pieces, was polished smooth.

Pressed glass - Any glass produced by a pressing machine. First widely produced in the 1820s in a limited range of pieces, by the turn of the century it was possible to produce dozens of different objects by mechanical means.

Rose bowl - A decorative small spherical or egg-shaped bowl, generally with a scalloped or crimped incurved rim, which was designed to hold rose petal potpourri. It was widely popular in the late 19th century and was produced in many pressed glass patterns as well as more expensive art glass wares such as satin glass.

Scalloping - A decorative treatment used on the rims of plates, bowls, vases and similar objects. It was generally produced during the molding of the object and gave the rim a wavy or ruffled form.

Sheared lip - A type of lip sometimes used on early American free-blown or mold-blown pieces, especially bottles and flasks. It refers to the fact that the neck of the piece is snipped or sheared off the blow pipe.

Sickness - A term referring to cloudy staining found in pressed or blown glass pieces, especially bottles, decanters and vases. It is caused when a liquid is allowed to stand in a piece for a long period of time causing a chemical deterioration of the interior surface. Generally it is nearly impossible to remove completely.

Spall - A shallow rounded flake on a

glass object, generally near the rim of a piece.

Spill holder - Also called a 'spill,' is a small vase-form glass holder used in the 19th century to hold *spills*. The spill was a rolled up thin tube of paper which had been placed under an oil lamp during filling to catch any drips or 'spills' of oil. Once rolled up it could be used as a punk to light lamps. What collectors today call spill holders were produced mainly in flint glass in the 1850s and 1860s, however, research shows that the manufacturers listed them as *spoon holders,* not spills, a term that doesn't appear until the 1870s.

Spooner - A vase or goblet-form glass piece which was meant to hold a bunch of spoons at the center of a table. It was part of the table set common in Victorian pattern glass.

Stemware - A general term for any form of drinking vessel raised on a slender pedestal or stemmed base.

Strap handle - An early form of applied handle on glass objects. It is a fairly thick ribbon of glass generally terminating at the base with a decorative squiggle or curlique. It is flattened where later applied handles are round.

Table set - A matching set of four pieces commonly produced in late 19th century pressed pattern glass. The set included a spooner (spoon holder), creamer, covered sugar bowl and covered butter dish.

Vaseline - A greenish yellow color of glass which was popular in Victorian pressed and blown glass. It was named by collectors for its resemblance to vaseline petroleum jelly. In original glass company catalogs or advertisements this color was simply called "canary" (canary yellow).

Waste bowl - A small, deep bowl commonly part of a ceramic tea set, but also produced in glass. It was made to hold the dregs from the bottoms of tea cups or the teapot.

Whimsey - A glass or ceramic novelty item. Generally in Victorian glass it is a free-blown or mold-blown object, often made by a glassworker as a special present and not part of regular glass production. Glass shoes, pipes and canes are examples of whimseys.

APPENDIX I

GLASS COLLECTORS' CLUBS

Types of Glass

Akro Agate
  Akro Agate Art Association
  Joseph Bourque
  Box 758
  Salem, NH 03079

  Akro Agate Collector's Club, Inc.
  Roger Hardy
  10 Bailey St.
  Clarksburg, WV 26301-2524

Cambridge
  National Cambridge Collectors
  P.O. Box 416
  Cambridge, OH 43725-0416

Candlewick
  National Candlewick Collector's Club
  c/o Virginia R. Scott
  275 Milledge Terrace
  Athens, GA 30606

Carnival
  American Carnival Glass Association
  c/o Dennis Runk
  P.O. Box 235
  Littlestown, PA 17340

  Collectible Carnival Glass Association
  c/o Wilma Thurston
  2360 N. Old S.R. 9
  Columbus, IN 47203

  Heart of America Carnival Glass
    Association
  c/o C. Lucile Britt
  3048 Tamarak Dr.
  Manhattan, KS 66502

  International Carnival Glass Association
  c/o Lee Markley, Secretary
  R.R. 1, Box 14
  Mentone, IN 46539

  New England Carnival Glass Club
  c/o Eva Backer, Membership
  12 Sherwood Rd.
  West Hartford, CT 06117

Depression
  National Depression Glass Association
  P.O. Box 69843
  Odessa, TX 79769

  20-30-40 Society, Inc.
  P.O. Box 856
  LaGrange, IL 60525

  Western Reserve Depression Glass Club
  c/o Ruth Gullis, Membership
  8669 Courtland Dr.
  Strongville, OH 44136

Duncan
  National Duncan Glass Society
  P.O. Box 965
  Washington, PA 15301

Fenton
  Fenton Art Glass Collectors of America
  P.O. Box 384
  Williamstown, WV 26187

  National Fenton Glass Society
  P.O. Box 4008
  Marietta, OH 45750

Findlay
  Collectors of Findlay Glass
  P.O. Box 256
  Findlay, OH 45839-0256

Fostoria
  The Fostoria Glass Society of America
  P.O. Box 826
  Moundsville, WV 26041

Fry
  H.C. Fry Glass Society
  P.O. Box 41
  Beaver, PA 15009

Greentown
  National Greentown Glass Association
  LeAnne Milliser, PR.
  19596 Glendale Ave.
  South Bend, IN 46637

Heisey
  Heisey Collectors of America
  P.O. Box 4367
  Newark, OH 43055

Imperial
  National Imperial Glass Collector's Society
  P.O. Box 534
  Bellaire, OH 43906

Milk Glass
  National Milk Glass Collectors Society
  c/o Helen Storey
  46 Almond Dr.
  Hershey, PA 17033

Morgantown
  Old Morgantown Glass Collectors' Guild
  P.O. Box 894
  Morgantown, WV 26507

  Morgantown Collectors of America, Inc.
  c/o Jerry Gallagher
  420 1st Ave. N.W.
  Plainview, MN 55964

Phoenix & Consolidated Glass Collectors
  c/o Jack D. Wilson
  P.O. Box 81974
  Chicago, IL 60681-0974

Stretch Glass
  Stretch Glass Society
  c/o Joanne Rodgers
  P.O. Box 770643
  Lakewood, OH 44107

Tiffin
  Tiffin Glass Collectors' Club
  P.O. Box 554
  Tiffin, OH 44883

Westmoreland
  National Westmoreland Glass
    Collectors' Club
  P.O. Box 372
  Westmoreland City, PA 15692

Westmoreland Glass Collectors Club
  c/o Harold Mayes
  2712 Glenwood
  Independence, MO 64052

Special Glass Clubs

Antique and Art Glass Salt Shaker
  Collectors' Society
2832 Rapidan Trail
Maitland, FL 32751

Glass Knife Collectors' Club
P.O. Box 342
Los Alamitos, CA 90720

Marble Collectors' Society
P.O. Box 222
Trumbull, CT 06611

National Reamer Collectors
c/o Larry Branstad
Rt. 1, Box 200
Grantsburg, WI 54840

National Toothpick Holder
  Collectors' Society
c/o Joyce Ender, Membership
Red Arrow Hwy., P.O. Box 246
Sawyer, MI 49125

Pairpoint Cup Plate Collectors
P.O. Box 52D
East Weymouth, MA 02189

Paperweight Collectors Association
P.O. Box 468
Garden City Park, NY 11010

Perfume and Scent Bottle Collectors
c/o Jeanne Parris
2022 E. Charleston Blvd.
Las Vegas, NV 89104

General Glass Clubs

Glass Collectors Club of Toledo
2727 Middlesex Dr.
Toledo, OH 43606

Glass Museum Foundation
1157 N. Orange, Box 921
Redlands, CA 92373

Glass Research Society of New Jersey
Wheaton Village
Millville, NJ 08332

National Early American Glass Club
P.O. Box 8489
Silver Spring, MD 20907

APPENDIX II

Museum Collections of American Glass

Many local and regional museums around the country have displays with some pressed glass included. The following are especially noteworthy.

New England

Connecticut: Wadsworth Atheneum, Hartford.

Maine: Jones Gallery of Glass and Ceramics (June - October), Sebago; Portland Museum of Art, Portland.

Massachusetts: Old Sturbridge Village, Sturbridge; Sandwich Glass Museum (April-November), Sandwich.

New Hampshire: The Currier Gallery of Art, Manchester.

Vermont: Bennington Museum (March-November), Bennington.

Mid-Atlantic

Delaware: Henry Francis du Pont Winterthur Museum, Winterthur.

New Jersey: Museum of American Glass, Wheaton Village, Millville.

New York: Corning Museum of Glass, Corning; Cooper-Hewitt Museum, the Smithsonian Institution's National Museum of Design (by appointment), New York; Metropolitan Museum of Art, New York; New-York Historical Society, New York.

Pennsylvania: Historical Society of Western Pennsylvania, Pittsburgh; Philadelphia Museum of Art, Philadelphia; Westmoreland Glass Museum, Port Vue.

Southeast

Florida: Lightner Museum, Saint Augustine; Morse Gallery of Art (Tiffany glass), Winter Park.

Louisiana: New Orleans Museum of Art, New Orleans.

Tennessee: Houston Antique Museum, Chattanooga.

Virginia: Chrysler Museum of Norfolk, Norfolk.

Washington, D.C.: National Museum of American History, Smithsonian Institution.

West Virginia: The Huntington Galleries, Inc., Huntington; Oglebay Institute - Mansion Museum, Wheeling.

Midwest

Indiana: Greentown Glass Museum, Greentown; Indiana Glass Museum, Dunkirk.

Michigan: Henry Ford Museum, Dearborn.

Minnesota: A.M. Chisholm Museum, Duluth.

Ohio: Cambridge Glass Museum, Cambridge; Milan Historical Museum, Milan; National Heisey Glass Museum, Newark; Toledo Museum of Art, Toledo.

Wisconsin: John Nelson Bergstrom Art Center and Mahler Glass Museum, Neenah.

Southwest and West

California: Los Angles County Museum of Art, Los Angeles; Wine Museum of San Francisco and M.H. de Young Museum, San Francisco.

Texas: Mills Collection, Texas Christian University, Fort Worth.

AMERICAN PRESSED GLASS & BOTTLES

INDEX

Acanthus, 35; Acorn, 35; Acorn Burrs, 35; Advertising & Souvenir Items, 36; Amaryllis (Dugan), 37; Apple Blossoms, 37; Apple Blossom Twigs, 37; Apple Tree, 37; April Showers (Fenton), 37; Australian, 37; Banded Drape, 38; Basket (Fenton's Open Edge), 38; Basket (Northwood) or Bushel Basket, 38; Beaded Bull's Eye (Imperial), 38; Beaded Cable (Northwood), 38; Beaded Shell (Dugan or Diamond Glass Co.), 39; Beauty Bud Vase, 39; Big Fish Bowl (Millersburg), 39; Bird with Grapes, 39; Blackberry (Fenton), 39; Blackberry Bramble, 40; Blackberry Miniature Compote, 40; Blackberry Spray, 40; Blackberry Wreath (Millersburg), 40; Bouquet, 40; Broken Arches (Imperial), 40; Bushel Basket, 38; Butterfly (Northwood), 40; Butterfly & Berry (Fenton), 41; Butterfly & Fern (Fenton), 41; Buzz.Saw, 47; Captive Rose, 41; Carnival Holly, 63; Caroline, 42; Cattails & Water Lily, 100; Chatelaine, 42; Cherry (Dugan), 42; Cherry or Cherry Circles (Fenton), 42; Cherry or Hanging Cherries (Millersburg), 42; Cherry Circles, 42; Christmas Compote, 43; Chrysanthe-mum or Windmill & Mums, 43; Cobble-stones Bowl (Imperial), 43; Coin Dot, 43; Coin Spot (Dugan), 44; Comet or Ribbon

Tie (Fenton), 44; Concave Diamond, 46; Constellation (Dugan), 44; Coral (Fenton), 44; Corn Bottle, 44; Corn Vase (Northwood), 44; Cornucopia, 44; Cosmos, 44; Crab Claw (Imperial), 44; Crackle, 45; Crucifix, 45; Cut Cosmos, 45; Daisy & Plume, 45; Daisy Cut Bell, 45; Daisy Squares, 45; Daisy Wreath (Westmoreland), 45; Dandelion (Northwood), 45; Dandelion Paneled (Fenton), 46; Diamond & Rib Vase (Fenton), 46; Diamond Concave or Concave Diamond (Dugan), 46; Diamond Lace (Imperial), 46; Diamond Point Columns, 46; Diamond Ring (Imperial), 47; Diamonds (Millersburg), 47; Diving Dolphins Footed Bowl (Sowerby), 47; Dogwood Sprays, 47; Double Dutch Bowl, 47; Double Star or Buzz Saw (Cambridge), 47; Double Stem Rose, 48; Dragon & Lotus (Fenton), 48; Dragon & Strawberry Bowl or Dragon & Berry (Fenton), 48; Drapery (Northwood), 48; Embroidered Mums (Northwood), 49; Estate (Westmoreland), 49; Fan (Dugan), 49; Fanciful (Dugan), 49; Fantail, 49; Farmyard (Dugan), 49; Fashion (Imperial), 49; Feather & Heart, 50; Feather Stitch Bowl, 50; Feathered Serpent, 50; Fentonia, 50; Fenton's Flowers Rose Bowl, 75; Fern, 50; Field Flower (Imperial), 50; Field Thistle (English), 50; File (Imperial), 50; File & Fan, 51; Finecut & Roses (Northwood), 51; Finecut Flowers, 51; Fine Rib (Northwood & Fenton), 51; Fisherman's Mug, 51; Fishscale & Beads, 51; Fleur De Lis (Millersburg), 51; Floral & Grape (Dugan or Diamond Glass Co.), 52; Floral & Wheat Compote (Dugan), 52; Flowers & Beads, 52; Flowers & Frames, 52; Flute (Imperial), 52; Flute (Northwood), 53; Flute & Cane, 53; Fluted Scroll, 53; Formal, 53; Four Flowers, 83; Four Seventy Four (Imperial), 53; Frolicking Bears (U.S. Glass), 53; Frosted Block, 53; Fruit Salad, 53; Fruits & Flowers (Northwood), 53; Garden Path, 54; Garland Rose Bowl (Fenton), 54; God & Home, 54; Goddess of Harvest (Fenton), 55; Golden Harvest or Harvest Time (U.S. Glass), 55; Good Luck, 55; Grape & Cable,